T0326335

CONSERVATION, MARKETS, AND THE ENVIRONMENT IN SOUTHERN AND EASTERN AFRICA

FUTURE RURAL AFRICA

Series Editors
Michael Bollig and Detlef Müller-Mahn

In recent years, there has been a social-ecological transformation in land use in Africa, brought about by climate change and the globalisation of natural resource management and rural landscapes, such that rural Africa has become a laboratory of global future-making. This new series offers a rich and valuable perspective on the processes and practices that produce and critically reflect upon visions of the future on the continent. Volumes within the series will address social-ecological, cultural, and economic development in sub-Saharan Africa, and their relation to climate change, sustainability, and migration.

Showcasing cutting-edge research into societal change and the reverberations of global dynamics playing out in sub-Saharan Africa, the series will provide an essential resource for an interdisciplinary scholarly audience in areas such as geography, anthropology, history, political science, natural science, and African studies as well as political planners, governmental and non-governmental organisations.

Published in association with the University of Bonn and Cologne's Collaborative Research Centre 'Future Rural Africa', funded by the German Research Council (DFG), the series will be mainly monographs, but we also welcome occasional edited volumes that enable a continent-wide, multi-disciplinary approach – see https://boydellandbrewer.com/future-rural-africa.

Please contact the Series Editors with an outline or download the proposal form at www.jamescurrey.com:

Prof. Dr Michael Bollig, University of Cologne:
michael.bollig@uni-koeln.de

Prof. Dr Detlef Müller-Mahn, University of Bonn:
mueller-mahn@uni-bonn.de

Previously published titles in the series are listed at the back of this volume.

CONSERVATION, MARKETS, AND THE ENVIRONMENT IN SOUTHERN AND EASTERN AFRICA

COMMODIFYING THE 'WILD'

Edited by
Michael Bollig, Selma Lendelvo,
Alfons Mosimane, Romie Nghitevelekwa

JAMES CURREY

Published in association with
Future Rural Africa

First published 2023
James Currey

ISBN 978 1 84701 340 8 (paperback)

James Currey is an imprint of Boydell & Brewer Ltd
PO Box 9, Woodbridge, Suffolk IP12 3DF, UK
and of Boydell & Brewer Inc.
668 Mt Hope Avenue, Rochester, NY 14620-2731 (US)
website: www.boydellandbrewer.com

The workshop on which this edited volume is based as well as the Open Access
License was financed through the CRC Grant "Future Rural Africa" (SFB TR 228).
The final editing process has been supported by the ERC Advanced Grant to M.
Bollig "Rewilding the Anthropocene" (Project Nr. 101020976). Views and opinions
expressed are however those of the authors only and do not reflect those of the
German Research Council or the European Research Council.

European Research Council
Established by the European Commission

Funded by

DFG Deutsche
Forschungsgemeinschaft
German Research Foundation

Future Rural Africa

A CIP catalogue record for this book is available
from the British Library

The publisher has no responsibility for the continued existence or accuracy
of URLs for external or third-party internet websites referred to in this book,
and does not guarantee that any content on such websites is, or will remain,
accurate or appropriate

This publication is printed on acid-free paper

CONTENTS

PART 3: PLANTS FROM THE WILDERNESS FOR A GLOBAL
MARKET: THE COMMODIFICATION OF NON-DOMESTICATED
(WILD) PLANTS

PART 4: COMMODIFYING WILDLIFE

ILLUSTRATIONS

MAPS

FIGURES

TABLES

Full credit details are provided in the captions to the images in the text. The editors, contributors, and publisher are grateful to all the institutions and persons for permission to reproduce the materials in which they hold copyright. Every effort has been made to trace the copyright holders; apologies are offered for any omission, and the publisher will be pleased to add any necessary acknowledgement in subsequent editions.

CONTRIBUTORS

Michael Bollig is Professor of Social and Cultural Anthropology at the University of Cologne where his key interests lie in the environmental anthropology of sub-Saharan Africa. His current research projects focus on the social-ecological dynamics connected to large-scale conservation projects, the commodification of nature and the political ecology of pastoralism. He is the author of *Shaping the African Savannah: From Capitalist Frontier to Arid Eden in Namibia* (2020), *Risk Management in a Hazardous Environment* (2006), co-author of *African Landscapes* (2009) with O. Bubenzer, *Pastoralism in Africa* (2013) with M. Schnegg and H. P. Wotzka, and *Resilience and Collapse in African Savannahs* (2017) with D. Anderson.

Johannes Dittmann is a PhD candidate at the University of Bonn (Department of Geography) and associated member of the Collaborative Research Centre (CRC-TRR 228) Future Rural Africa – Future-Making and Socio-Ecological Transformation. His key interests lie in development geography and political ecology of eastern and southern Africa. His current research focuses on social-ecological transformations in context of large-scale conservation and agricultural schemes in Kenya, Tanzania, and Namibia.

Ezequiel Fabiano is a Senior Lecturer at the University of Namibia where his key interest lies on ecosystem dynamics. His current research projects focus on wildlife population demography, conservation genetics, and impact of wildlife management on biodiversity. He is a co-author of 'Cheetahs: Biology and Conservation', in *Biodiversity of the World: Conservation from Genes to Landscapes*, a volume in the Biodiversity of World: Conservation from Genes to Landscapes series with C. Sutherland, A. Fuller, L. Boast, *et al.* (2018) and several scientific manuscripts.

Clemens Greiner is the academic coordinator of the Global South Studies Center (GSSC). He was trained in Social and Cultural Anthropology and Geography at the University of Hamburg, where he received his PhD in Anthropology on the basis of a multi-sited ethnography of rural–urban migration in Namibia. In his current research, Greiner focuses on rural change, political ecology, translocality, and (energy) infrastructures. His regional specialisation is on eastern and southern Africa, where he has conducted extensive fieldwork.

Lee Hewitson's research interests include the political ecology of (neoliberal) nature conservation and natural resource governance approaches, particularly in Africa. With an empirical focus on African elephant (*Loxodonta africana*) conservation, his PhD explored the production and transformation of values and knowledge in the context of Namibia's Community-Based Natural Resource Management (CBNRM) programme. He has written popular publications on issues including trophy hunting and the commodification of indigenous natural products in Namibia.

Carolin Hulke is a research associate at the University of Cologne, Institute of Geography and associate to the multidisciplinary research project 'Future Rural Africa' (CRC-TRR228/1). She is conducting her PhD research on southern African agricultural regional value chains, livelihood strategies and rural development.

Linus Kalvelage is a postdoctoral researcher and lecturer at the Institute of Geography, University of Cologne, Germany, and a member of the inter-disciplinary Global South Studies Center. With a focus on environmental economic geography, Linus works at the interface of economy, nature and space, analysing regional development trajectories through nature conservation and energy transition in peripheral regions. His doctoral research within the Collaborative Research Centre (CRC 228) 'Future Rural Africa' looked at the intersection of growth corridors, tourism value chains and protected areas in Southern Africa. His postdoctoral research is concerned with sustainable energy transitions, in particular green hydrogen projects in the European and African periphery.

Michael Mugo Kinyanjui is an administrator working with the Ministry of Interior and Coordination of National Government in Kenya. Currently he is serving in the Ministry Headquarters and is engaged in policy development. His interests and duties revolve around peace initiatives, conflict management, food security, and environmental management. He is the author of 'Factors Influencing Urban Agriculture Performance in Mathare Sub-county, Nairobi City County, Kenya' (2018).

Eric M. Kioko is a lecturer at Kenyatta University, Nairobi in the Department of Environmental Studies and Community Development where his research and teaching focuses on the dynamics of human-environment relations. His key interests lie in the areas of environmental conflicts and peacebuilding, dynamics of ethnic relations, community conservation, environmental crimes, and social-ecological implications of mega projects. He is the author of 'Cooperation in the Midst of Conflict' with M. Gravesen (2019), 'Appeasing the Land' with W. Okumu (2018), 'Conflict Resolution and Crime Surveillance'

(2017), 'Turning Conflict into Coexistence' (2016), and 'Crosscutting Ties and Coexistence' with M. Bollig (2015).

Selma Kosmas is a lecturer at the University of Namibia's Department for Wildlife Management and Tourism Studies. She is currently doing her PhD, with her research focused on using non-invasive DNA for ecological inferences particularly of large carnivores, using Angola as the study area.

Léa Lacan is a postdoctoral researcher at the Department of Social and Cultural Anthropology, University of Cologne. After completing her PhD on forest conservation and human-forest relations in Kenya under the Collaborative Research Center (CRC 228) 'Future Rural Africa', she is currently working as a member of the European Research Council Grant Project 'Rewilding the Anthropocene', in Zambia. Her research focuses on social-ecological transformations and changing human-environment relations in the context of conservation projects at the local level, at the intersection of political ecology and multi-species approaches.

Jessica-Jane Lavelle is a post-doctoral researcher with the Bio-economy Research Chair at the University of Cape Town. Her research focuses on social and environmental dimensions of the bio-economy including the political ecology of natural resource governance and transformative ways of accessing, using and researching biodiversity and indigenous and local knowledge. As an engaged scholar she seeks to promote social and environmental justice through research, activism and contributions to policy design and implementation.

Selma Lendelvo is the Director for Grants Management and Resource Mobilisation at the University of Namibia (UNAM). She has been extensively involved in research with UNAM since 2001, mainly focusing in the field of environmental management and sustainable natural resource management across Namibia and abroad. She is interested in natural resource management and land reform including wildlife management, community-based tourism, conservancy management, environmental management, rural development, and gender.

Lioba Lenhart is Associate Professor at the Institute of Peace and Strategic Studies (IPSS), Gulu University, Uganda. She has conducted extensive ethnographic field research in Indonesia and Uganda and has worked as a trainer and consultant in the field of crisis prevention, conflict transformation, and peace building in Germany, Indonesia, and Uganda. Her current research interests are conflicts over land and natural resources with a focus on conservation conflicts, environmental justice, migration and forced displacement, transitional justice, and mental health in post-conflict situations.

Kenneth Matengu is the Vice Chancellor of the University of Namibia. He holds a PhD in Human Geography from the University of Eastern Finland. He holds an academic post of Research Professor at the Multidisciplinary Research Centre, Social Sciences Division at the University of Namibia. His research interests include access and equity in education, higher education governance, and management. His more than sixty publications to date include articles, books, and book chapters on tourism, community-based management, decentralisation of rural water supply and local government, higher education coordination and governance, and innovation. Prof. Matengu has interest in indigenous knowledge and specialty in innovation diffusion and technology transfer, and the knowledge-based economy, as well as community resource management, poverty, and the social aspects of HIV and AIDS. He is a member of several international academic bodies including serving as a Commissioner of the International Geographical Union, and serving as an Executive to the IGU Commission on African Studies and the International AIDS Society. He was recently appointed by the President of the Republic of Namibia as a Member of the High Level Panel on the Namibian Economy.

Joseph Mbaiwa is the Director of the Okavango Research Institute (ORI), University of Botswana. He holds a PhD in Parks, Recreation and Tourism Sciences from Texas A&M University. He is also a Professor of Tourism Studies. He is widely published in areas of tourism development, community-based natural resource management, rural livelihoods, and biodiversity conservation. Prof. Mbaiwa is on the editorial boards of academic journals such as the *South African Geographical Journal*, the *Journal of Sustainable Tourism*, the *Journal of Ecotourism*, etc. He was a taskforce member appointed by the Ministry of Environmental, Natural Resource Conservation and Tourism to prepare a proposal dossier that resulted in the Okavango Delta being listed as the 1,000th UNESCO World Heritage Site. Prof. Mbaiwa is a Board Member of the Botswana Tourism Organisation. He is also a member of the 2019–2021 Ramsar Scientific and Technical Review Panel for the 2019–2021 triennium.

Alfons Mosimane is the Executive Dean for the Faculty of Education and Human Sciences at the University of Namibia. Dr Mosimane is a geographer with keen interests in the interaction between society and environment. His research interests are on social-ecological systems, collective action, common-pool resource management, development of local institutions, benefit sharing, and sustaining collective identity. He is a Senior Researcher at the University of Namibia and has completed more than twenty consultancies and research projects. Dr Mosimane is knowledgeable about community-based natural resource management (CBNRM) in Namibia and southern Africa, as well as other community-based approaches in the forestry, land, and water sectors. For the past twenty years Dr Mosimane researched institutional development and governance systems in community-based natural resource management (CBNRM) in Namibia. Dr Mosimane has conducted more than thirty socio-economic baseline studies and several qualitative studies in Namibia, since 1996. He has published more than fifteen peer-reviewed papers and book chapters. Dr Mosimane has collaborated with universities in the United Kingdom, Germany and the United States of America on various research programmes.

Detlef Müller-Mahn is Professor of Development Geography at the University of Bonn. He served as the spokesperson of the Collaborative Research Center (CRC-TRR 228) 'Future Rural Africa' during the first funding phase 2018–2021. His research focuses on the political ecology of land-use change and rural development in East Africa and the Middle East. Recent publications include 'Envisioning African Futures: Development corridors as dreamscapes of modernity' in *Geoforum* (2020), 'Rethinking African futures after Covid-19' in *Africa Spectrum* (2021, with Eric Kioko), and 'Megaprojects – Mega Failures? The politics of aspiration and the transformation of rural Kenya' in *The European Journal of Development Research* (2021, with Kennedy Mkutu and Eric Kioko).

Sthembile Ndwandwe is a doctoral candidate in the Department of Environmental and Geographical Science at the University of Cape Town. Her candidature is associated with the Bio-Economy Research Chair which responds to the social and environmental dimensions of the bio-economy. She is a Charles R. Wall African Policy Fellow, a fellowship run by the African Wildlife Foundation and the United Nations Environmental Programme. She is a member of the National Steering Committee for the UNDP Global Environment Facility (GEF) Small Grants Programme (SGP) which focuses on community projects located in the Vhembe Biosphere Reserve in Limpopo, as well as wildlife economy projects across South Africa.

Romie Vonkie Nghitevelekwa is a Senior Lecturer in the Department of Social Sciences at the University of Namibia, where she focuses on sociology of development, sociology of the environment, and rural sociology. Her research interests lie in communal land reform, land rights, security of tenure, changing land uses in the communal areas, commodification of land, gender, and natural resource use. She is the author of *Securing Land Rights: Communal Land Reform in Namibia* (2020).

Javier Revilla Diez holds a Chair in Human Geography at the Institute of Geography and is associated with the Global South Study Center at the University of Cologne. He has research interests in the regional outcomes of participating in global production networks, regional impacts of transformation processes induced by political and structural change, and impacts of natural risks on people, firms, and regions. He participates in the collaborative research center 'Future Rural Africa: Future-making and social-ecological transformation' and concentrates on the desired and undesirable regional socio-economic effects of growth corridors and value-chain integration in Namibia and Tanzania.

Martin Shapi is a Senior Researcher in the Social Sciences Division (SSD) of the Multidisciplinary Research Center (MRC) at the University of Namibia (UNAM). He has been extensively involved in Research with UNAM since 2002 primarily focusing on conservation of natural resources, especially community-based natural resource management (CBNRM) in Namibia, and the trade-off between property rights (often called tenure security in communal areas) and resettlement farmers, and their impact on enhanced investment incentives, agricultural productivity, and livelihood improvement. Mr Shapi also has interest in the efficiency and profitability of smallholder farmers in the communal areas of Namibia.

Sian Sullivan is Professor of Environment and Culture at Bath Spa University. She is interested in discourses and practices of difference and exclusion in relation to ecology and conservation. She has carried out long-term research on conservation, colonialism, and culture in Namibia (www.futurepasts.net and www.etosha-kunene-histories.net), and also engages critically with the financialisation of nature (see www.the-natural-capital-myth.net). She has co-edited *Political Ecology: Science, Myth and Power* (2000), *Contributions to Law, Philosophy and Ecology: Exploring Re-embodiments* (2016), *Valuing Development, Environment and Conservation: Creating Values that Matter* (2018), and *Negotiating Climate Change in Crisis* (2021).

Hauke-Peter Vehrs is a post-doctoral researcher in the German Research Council (DFG)-funded Collaborative Research Centre 228 'Future Rural Africa: Future-making and social-ecological transformation' at the University of Cologne. He has undertaken research in Nigeria, Kenya, and Namibia, and currently he is engaged in research activities in Namibia's Zambezi Region with a focus on human–animal relations, environmental history, and the perceptions of the future against the background of extensive conservation efforts in the region. He previously completed his PhD in cultural anthropology on the historical ecology and pastoral livelihood transformations in East Pokot, Kenya.

Ibrahim Maina Waziri is Professor of Social and Economic History at the University of Maiduguri. His research interests lie in the history of Africa, particularly sub-Saharan/Chad Basin in pre-colonial, colonial, and post-colonial periods. His current research projects focus on the social and economic history of north-eastern Nigeria, examining colonial urbanisation and the growth of the cash economy under British colonial rule. He is also involved with the Consortium of Research Centres for Northern States of Nigeria (CRCNN), Mambayya House, Bayero University Kano, the Bonn Centre for Dependency and Slavery Studies, University of Bonn, and is the Director of the Manuscript Conservation Laboratory of the Centre for Trans-Saharan Studies, University of Maiduguri.

Rachel Wynberg is a Professor in the Department of Environmental and Geographical Science at the University of Cape Town in South Africa where she holds a national Research Chair focused on Environmental and Social Dimensions of the Bio-economy. With a background in both the natural and social sciences, her interdisciplinary research spans topics relating to bio-politics and the biodiversity-based economy, social and environmental justice, agroecology, and sustainable agricultural futures. She has been involved in research and policy making relating to access and benefit sharing since the inception of the Convention on Biological Diversity in 1992, advising governments, civil society organisations, and international agencies. Her publications include over 220 scientific papers, technical reports, and popular articles, and five co-edited books and monographs.

ACKNOWLEDGEMENTS

This volume originated in the workshop, Commodifying the 'Wild': Conservation, Markets and the Environment in Southern and Eastern Africa, that the University of Namibia's (UNAM) Multidisciplinary Research Center and the Collaborative Research Center 228 Future Rural Africa (hosted by the German universities Cologne and Bonn) co-organised in north-eastern Namibia's Zambezi Region. The Zambezi Region's capital, Katima Mulilo, seemed a most appropriate place for such a gathering. The town is surrounded by protected areas of different types, and conservation is the characterising feature of the development projects of the wider region. The workshop took place at UNAM's wonderful Katima Mulilo Campus, close to the Zambezi River. We were very grateful to UNAM's leadership at the Campus for hosting us cordially and arranging an excellent meeting space for us. Special thanks go to Dr Bennet Kangumu, who as the head of the Katima Mulilo Campus was instrumental in facilitating the organisation of the workshop. Dr Ekkehard Klingelhöfer, at that time head of the Department of Wildlife Management and Tourism Studies at the Katima Mulilo Campus, contributed to the swift organisation of the workshop and facilitated evenings out at the Zambezi.

The event profited throughout from the close and cordial working relationship between the three universities. For many years, memoranda of understanding have paved the way for a very productive partnership. Joint workshops, joint teaching, and the joint supervision of MA and PhD theses evidence the cooperative spirit of the collaboration. Prof. Kenneth Matengu, Vice Chancellor of the University of Namibia, has supported our project and has contributed as a co-author to this volume.

We, the editors of this volume, thank all participants who enriched the discussions. We acknowledge specifically the contributions of those who were not able to contribute to this volume or who did not plan to contribute from the beginning. Karine Nuulimba facilitated discussions of workshop participants with practitioners from the region. These were experts from different ministries, from development projects, and from community-based organisations. Their input was essential to focus discussions and raise questions on the practical use of research efforts.

The volume is based on empirical research in many different rural settings in Namibia, South Africa, Botswana, Kenya, Uganda, and Nigeria. Acknowledgements leave too little space to thank all those people in particular who have contributed to the fieldwork of the authors, who were able to present their results at the workshop. Hundreds of rural citizens, dozens of field assistants, officers in different governmental departments, employees of non-governmental organisations and of numerous development projects, and many more people contributed significantly and decisively to the data analysed and discussed in this volume. We dearly hope that the results presented here will instigate discussions and finally lay the ground for future policies that will make their lives easier, their livelihoods more resilient, and the distribution of benefits accruing from the commodification of the 'wild' more just.

The volume profited greatly from the critical feedback from three anonymous reviewers. Their input was essential and we hope that we have taken account of many of their hints and advices.

The workshop was made possible through the grant the Collaborative Research Center Future Rural Africa received from the German Research Council. During the phase of finalisation of this volume one of the editors benefited additionally from the ERC Advanced Grant Rewilding the Anthropocene.

Throughout the review process Ms Sarah Mund, researcher at the University of Cologne, has accompanied the becoming and finalisation of the volume. Painstakingly she worked on references and facilitated the production of maps, most of which were drawn by Ms Monika Feinen, cartographer at the Institute of African Studies of the University of Cologne. Sarah Mund took also account of James Currey's style sheet, applied it to all contributions to the volume and communicated many times with all contributors. Sarah's talent for organisation, order, and communication facilitated the finalisation of the volume greatly.

The editorial team:
Michael Bollig
Selma Lendelvo
Alfons Mosimane
Romie Nghitevelekwa

ABBREVIATIONS

ABS	Access and benefit sharing
ACTC	Acholi Culture and Tourism Centre
AICc	Akaike Information Criteria corrected for small samples
ARC	Agricultural Research Council
BABS	Bioprospecting access and benefit sharing
BBBEE	Broad-Based Black Economic Empowerment
BioPANZA	Bio Products Advancement Network South Africa
CAMPFIRE	Communal Areas Management Programme for Indigenous Resources
CBD	Convention on Biological Diversity
CBNRM	Community-based natural resource management
CFAs	Community forest associations
CHAs	Controlled Hunting Area
CI	Confidence interval
CITES	Convention on International Trade in Endangered Species of Wild Fauna and Flora
CKGR	Central Kalahari Game Reserve
CPR	Common-pool resource
CRIAA SA-DC	Centre for Research Information in Africa – Southern Africa Development and Consulting
CSIR	Council for Scientific and Industrial Research
CWA	Community wildlife association
DFFE	Department of Forestry, Fisheries and the Environment
DWNP	Department of Wildlife and National Parks, Botswana
EPWP	Expanded Public Works Programme
EU-TRACES	European Union Trade Control and Expert System
EWB	Elephants Without Borders
FAO	Food and Agriculture Organization of the United Nations
GCC	Global commodity chain

GDP	Gross domestic product
GIZ	German international development agency
GLM	George Local Municipality
GLTP	Great Limpopo Transfrontier Park
GoB	Government of Botswana
GPN	Global production network
GTV	Geographical transfer of value
GVC	Global value chains
HCOP	Honeybush Community of Practice
HWC	Human–wildlife conflict
IDP	(National) integrated development plans
INP	Indigenous natural products
INTERPOL	International Criminal Police Organization
IRDNC	Integrated Rural Development and Nature Conservation (NGO)
IUCN	International Union for the Conservation of Nature
JTHS	Jamy Traut Hunting Safaris
KAZA	Kavango-Zambezi Transfrontier Conservation
KFS	Kenya Forest Service
KfW	Kreditanstalt für Wiederaufbau / German Bank for Reconstruction and Development
KLM	Kou-Kamma Local Municipality
LRA	Lord's Resistance Army
LToV	Labour theory of value
MCA-N	Millennium Challenge Account–Namibia
MEFT	Ministry of Environment, Forestry and Tourism, Namibia
MET	Ministry of Environment and Tourism, Namibia
MNEs	Multinational enterprises
MoU	Memorandum of understanding
NACSO	Namibian Association of CBNRM Support Organisations
NBES	National Biodiversity Economy Strategy
NDP	National Development Plan
NILALEG	Namibia Integrated Landscape Approach for the Enhancing Livelihoods and Environmental Governance to Eradicate Poverty
NEMA	National Environment Management Authority (Uganda)
NGO	Non-governmental organisation
NRT	Northern Rangeland Trust
OLS	Ordered logistic regression

PPF	Peace Parks Foundation
PTO	Permission to occupy (Namibia and South Africa)
REDD	Reducing Emissions from Deforestation and Forest Degradation in Developing Countries
RSF	Revenue Sharing Fund of the Uganda Wildlife Authority
SADC	Southern African Development Community
SANBI	South African National Biodiversity Institute
SHDC	Sustainably Harvested Devil's Claw
TA	Traditional authority
TFCA	Transfrontier conservation area
TK	Traditional knowledge
UAC	United African Company
UNAM	University of Namibia
UNDP	United Nations Development Programme
UNEP	United Nations Environment Programme
UNIDO	United Nations Industrial Development Organization
UNODC	United Nations Office on Drugs and Crime
US	United States
USAID	United States Agency for International Development
UWA	Uganda Wildlife Authority
WIMSA	Working Group of Indigenous Minorities in Southern Africa
WMA	Wildlife management area
WWF	World Wide Fund for Nature

PART 1

INTRODUCTION

Introduction: Practices, Discourses, and Materialities Surrounding the Commodification of the 'Wild'

MICHAEL BOLLIG, LINUS KALVELAGE, LÉA LACAN,
SELMA LENDELVO, ALFONS MOSIMANE, AND
ROMIE NGHITEVELEKWA

'Commodities are made not born'. Prudham (2009: 137)

Introduction

This volume is concerned with the practices, discourses, and materialities surrounding the commodification of the 'wild' – a topic which has found considerable academic attention in the past decade (Smessaert *et al.* 2020). The 'wild' is commonly conceived of as a conceptual opposite to the destructive tendencies of commodification. The volume's core concern is with the – always laborious and often tense and conflictive, but frequently also synergetic, or co-constitutive – relationships between commodification and wilderness, especially against the backdrop of novel forms of commodification, such as wildlife-park tourism, or trophy hunting, or trade in herbal medicines, perfumes, and luxury exotic food items in which the 'wild' is tightly interwoven with human management. Currently, neoliberal approaches that aim at the commodification and marketisation of nature are dominant in addressing global environmental challenges. The hope is that by valorising nature and attaching a price label to single items or functions and establishing a market for them, biodiversity can be safeguarded and 'wild' landscapes can be protected from human interference (Heynen & Robbins 2005). While so-called 'wild' resources have long sustained livelihoods and been shaped by local management patterns in southern and eastern Africa (Sullivan & Homewood 2004), the commodification of the 'wild' and its integration in wider markets is deemed to have an immense future perspective and, indeed, it is thought to open up a new frontier of capitalist expansion and establish new avenues to wealth: it is apparently sustainable, non-exploitative, participatory, and in addition to that, creates new livelihood options at different societal levels. In this projection, the commodification of the 'wild' will invigorate rural livelihoods, reduce poverty, and add important assets to otherwise vulnerable rural economies. The neoliberal logic dominant since the 1990s followed upon state-led approaches that allowed only for windows of commodification under tight control of governmental agencies, but in general distrusted markets and greatly relied on a clear-cut separation of the wild on the one hand and humans on the other, of nature and culture. It was the state's privilege to protect wildernesses and wildlife, and protected areas were carved out of cultural landscapes in many instances. Generally, market-led approaches and the ensuing commodification of wildlife were thought to be environmentally destructive and easily captured by dominant groups at the cost of the wider rural population. Certainly, it was not only a market-pessimistic stand towards the development of Africa's rural areas adopted by colonial states, but also widespread rules of reciprocity and control of individualistic economic strategising that hampered swift market integration. Social norms and values in many rural societies control social dynamics essential for commodification: privatisation is hindered by e.g., kin-group ownership of land, and the individuation of prospective commodities is hampered by religious and moral frameworks. It is these social institutions and morality which inform actors in the present and often lead to intra-societal conflicts about the morals of the economy (or the status quo and future of a moral economy).

The first part of this introductory chapter touches upon different trajectories of theorising the commodification of the 'wild'. A rich and varied literature results from a critique of neoliberal approaches to the commodification of nature in general and the commodification of the 'wild' in particular. The concept of 'green grabbing' has been a critical escalation of this approach and the argument that green grabbing is a new form of accumulation by dispossession has motivated a number of follow-up studies. A second approach adopts the concepts of 'resource frontier', 'conservation frontier', and 'salvage accumulation'. Anna Tsing and others thought that conservation offers new opportunities to accumulate capital by drawing resources previously untapped into the global market. A third paradigm that is progressively receiving more attention applies a multispecies approach and takes off from the observation that commodities are co-produced by humans and non-human actors. A fourth approach looks at value chains and the consequences for actors engaged in (or denied access to) them. More than the other three approaches, the global value-chain approach links dynamics in remote regions in the Global South to the metropolises in the Global North.

All contributions to this volume refer to cases and policies that relate to the neoliberal environmental governance of nature in general (McCarthy &

Prudham 2004; Heynen & Robbins 2005) and neoliberal conservation in particular (Sullivan 2006; Brockington & Duffy 2010; Sullivan 2012a; Büscher *et al.* 2012; Dunlap & Sullivan 2019). Many cases reported upon here are placed along conservation and/or resource frontiers (Tsing 2003; Högselius 2020) e.g. in northern Namibia, in northern Kenya, and in Uganda. Chapters examine how commodities are being made from the 'wild', by looking at the discourses, practices, and institutions from which their economic value is being created and developed (in line with Bracking *et al.* 2018). Contributions focus on how commodification processes emerge, how they are financed, brought about by political decisions, managed and monitored, fitted with legal terms and references, and how they are linked to the outside world (outside markets, stakeholders, and financiers). Other chapters deal with the impact of these commodification processes on society, on rural livelihoods, on gender relations, and on political hierarchies. Contributions to this volume focus on all stages involved in transforming the 'wild' into commodities, including extraction, grading, transportation, storage, and distribution, or the establishment of an environmental infrastructure that lays the foundation for the marketisation of the 'wild' to the tourism industry. Yet other chapters analyse discourses and practices of marketing the 'wild' as central to creating desire and longing for wild things, spaces, and experiences.

This edited volume resulted from a conference in Katima Mulilo, north-eastern Namibia, in September 2019. The conference was jointly organised by the University of Namibia (UNAM) Katima Mulilo Campus' conservation focus, the UNAM Multidisciplinary Research Centre at Windhoek Campus and the Collaborative Research Centre 228 Future Rural Africa of the Universities of Cologne and Bonn. Part of the event was dedicated to an exchange of analyses and ideas between experienced scientists and junior researchers. A day with practitioners in conservation was embedded in the conference and gave wide room for a critical reflection on the relation between critical social sciences and development practitioners.

Katima Mulilo is situated at the heart of the Kavango-Zambezi Transfrontier Conservation Area (KAZA), one of the world's largest nature conservation projects, almost equal to the size of Spain. The Conservation Area and its lush riverine wilderness sites are at the centre of a number of commodification agendas. Pushed by an international alliance of donors and conservationists, KAZA is envisioned as an umbrella for existing conservation efforts and thus a cornerstone of biodiversity conservation but also as a motor of regional economic development. Wilderness tourism projects based on a steadily growing tourism infrastructure but also on increasing game numbers, big-game trophy hunting for leisure, and the hunt for medically useful wild plants are nowadays key commodification agendas. In many quarters, it is taken for granted that this approach will bring more sustainability and at the same time ensure economic progress. A number of contributions to this volume directly address commodification in this region (Lavelle; Hewitson & Sullivan; Fabiano *et al.*; Kalvelage; Nghitevelekwa *et al.*; Mosimane *et al.*; Dittmann & Müller-Mahn).

Theoretical approaches

There has been a rapid and sustained interest in the commodification of nature in the last two or three decades (Castree 2003: 274). Smessaert *et al.* demonstrate that literature is fragmented and 'that no comprehensive state-of-the art exists on debates on the commodification of nature' (Smessaert *et al.* 2020: 2). They surmise that in contrast to some overtly positive statements from governmental bodies, conservation sciences, and economics, most contributions originating with social science authors critically engage with the commodification of nature, particularly highlighting its problematic social impacts. Despite considerable differences in the social science literature on the commodification of the 'wild', there are some common denominators (Smessaert *et al.* 2020): (1) the literature mainly deals with the process and effects of privatisation, marketisation, and monetary valuation and seeks theoretical impetus in theories with a post-Marxist-cum-political-economy basis; (2) it originates predominantly out of critical geography, political ecology, ecological economics, and anthropology; and (3) most of the critical literature is produced in the Global North and comments upon case studies in the Global South. We delineate some pertinent trajectories of the social sciences' engagement with recent trends in conservation and the commodification of nature here, but without any claim to completeness or an attempt to discuss these approaches in depth.

The neoliberalisation of nature and green grabbing

A number of scholars have focused on neoliberal conservation approaches (McCarthy & Prudham 2004; Heynen & Robbins 2005; Sullivan 2006; Brockington *et al.* 2008; Brockington & Duffy 2010; Büscher *et al.* 2012; Büscher & Fletcher 2020) and explored how natures are used, transformed, and purportedly 'saved' in and through the expansion of 'green capitalism'. Neoliberalisation is analysed as the latest and perhaps most comprehensive form of capitalism: it succeeds 19th century trade-company-based mercantilism, state-controlled colonial capitalism, and developmentalist fringe capitalism, which have all informed and shaped the recent neoliberal version of capitalism. While all these stages of capitalism involved commodification, neoliberal approaches intensify the impacts and have their peculiar governance patterns, ways of privatisation, methods of producing enclosures, and approaches to valuation. Scholars adopting this approach comprehensively study how the inclusion in a capitalist set-up transforms rural economies. Close to the topic of conservation and global environmental governance, they argue that nature framed as natural capital, an assemblage of ecosystem services and market-to-come becomes fetishised and charged with power via a diverse set of practices. Some also put forward the commodification of nature through state-supported re-regulation, thereby often dismantling common-pool resources (Heynen & Robbins 2005), and territorialisation as preconditions for neoliberalisation (Igoe & Brockington 2007).

Literature on green grabbing escalates the critique-of-neoliberal-conservation literature and focuses on its most dramatic effect: accumulation by dispossession. In a much cited contribution, Fairhead *et al.* (2012: 238) describe green grabbing – 'the appropriation of land and resources for environmental ends' – as a novel form of valuation and commodification entailing the 'transfer of ownership, use rights and control over resources that were once publicly or privately owned ... From the poor (or everyone including the poor) into the hands of the powerful'. Green grabbing then is a sub-type of land grabbing (Borras 2012). It is market-driven, and reorganises society-nature relations through commodification (Green & Adams 2015). What makes green grabbing special is that dispossession and transfer of rights to economically powerful actors come with the narrative that this move is furthering ecological sustainability and productive use in the long run.

Green grabbing is a characteristic feature of neoliberal nature management. Landscapes, wildlife, forests, etc. are developed into commodities. In order to do so, green grabbing transfers vast tracts of land to users who are deemed to use it (or resources connected to it) in an economically efficient yet sustainable manner. The theoretical contribution of Fairhead *et al.* (2012), itself the entrée piece into a special issue in the *Journal of Peasant Studies* with a number of interesting contributions of the green-grabbing concept all over the Global South (e.g. Gardner 2012), sparked off a number of further studies that sought to research the discursive and material articulation of neoliberal forms of conservation. A good number of contributions problematised processes of dispossession in a neoliberal framework (Benjaminson & Bryceson 2012; Ojeda 2012). Dispossession for conservation purposes by colonial powers had been a regular occurrence in much of eastern and southern Africa, though this was not regularly tied to accumulation but rather to an expansion of state control. Neoliberal dispossession though has directly led to accumulation (Harvey 2006), as common-pool resources or publicly accessible resources are enclosed for the profit of a few. Environments thereby become partitioned and compartmentalised, and their commodifiable parts are differentiated from non-commodifiable ones. Habitually, enclosure directly precedes commodification and marketisation: in many ways, it constitutes a necessary precondition for entering an entity into value chains and/or to promote it on emerging markets.

Fairhead *et al.* (2012) and others have highlighted that green grabbing is promoted and legitimated by an evocation of ecological crisis. For instance, to support climate-change mitigation, forests are valorised for their important role as carbon sinks, and their value is measured in money (Ehrenstein & Muniesa 2013; Nel 2017). The forests' services become buyable by clients who need to offset environmental sins somewhere else on the globe. Such cases link up with literature on the financialisation of nature (Bracking 2012; Sullivan 2012b) and payments for ecosystem services as market-based instruments leading to the commodification of nature (Karsenty 2013). While a price is put on nature for its protection, ecologies and livelihoods are impacted materially, but also symbolically (as argued by Fairhead *et al.* 2012). Although this volume does not focus specifically on cases of financialisation of nature or payments for ecosystem services, contributions illustrate how the creation of commercial value from ecosystems and their products is intertwined with conservation interests and discuss the social and political impacts of putting a price on nature.

Literature on green grabbing has excelled in deciphering vast global networks of involved actors and it has done well to describe different motivations and strategies. Intermediary actors such as NGOs and traditional authorities have been researched as much as international companies engaged in grabbing (e.g. Green & Adams 2015). Green-grabbing literature also showed how local elites enrich themselves in the process of dispossession. In addition, a number of contributions attended to the resistance to green-grabbing schemes (McAfee 1999; Green & Adams 2015). It has also contributed significantly to our understanding of the role of the state in this set-up. Green grabbing is a project of global environmental governance in which the state has the role of a facilitator, making international investment possible and profitable, cushioning negative social repercussions. Green and Adams (2015) show how the Tanzanian state arranged for the financial engagement of international tourism companies in community-run wildlife-management areas in Tanzania. Green-grabbing literature in general was less interested in the perspectives of local actors and their ontologies of nature. It has also not dealt in depth with the ways in which nature is transformed and perhaps, at times, also has resisted its transformation.

This volume has a number of case studies on green grabbing. Lacan describes how Kenyan forests could become resources only as they were emptied and/ or protected from their inhabitants and placed under state control. Hewitson and Sullivan report on the partial dispossession of small-scale farmers in north-eastern Namibia in projects of conservation. There, dispossession is not a simple removal of people from an area by the state, but results from the decision by community-owned conservation projects to spare lands from agricultural production in order to create space for conservation. Also, Lenhart discusses, referring to her Ugandan case, how local smallholders are dispossessed along the buffer zones of national parks and examines how projects intended to compensate for such losses fail.

Resource frontier

In her seminal monograph *Friction* (2005: 28) Anna Tsing described a frontier as 'an edge of space and time: a zone of not yet, not yet mapped, not yet regulated. It is a zone of unmapping'. She described resource frontiers as interstitial spaces between territories of stricter control in which frontiersmen, a term she applies to entrepreneurs active in this zone, 'disengage nature from local ecologies and livelihoods, 'freeing up' natural resources that bureaucrats and generals could offer as corporate raw materials'. In her book, Tsing explores an expanding resource frontier in South Kalimantan in the 1990s, where logging and mining companies invaded and transformed landscapes that were previously used by Dayak swidden agriculturalists. Anna Tsing's resource frontier is a type of land grab, perhaps also a green grab in a perverse sense. Frontiers, for Tsing, 'create wildness so that some – and not others – may reap its rewards' (Tsing 2005: 28). That is, at the frontier, landscapes are emptied of their inhabitants and users, transformed into 'wild', uninhabited resources, and therefore made available to be appropriated by others. She describes how biodiverse cultural forest landscapes are expropriated from their earlier owners in Kalimantan, to be then transformed into monotonous palm oil plantations exploited by logging companies. According to Tsing, at the frontier, making the nature 'wild' is the precondition into its transformation into commodities. While privatisation and the replacement of earlier institutions by an alien ownership structure is the hallmark of green grabbing, deregulation, and predatory open-access systems are the hallmark of resource frontiers.

Anna Tsing's use of the concept of the frontier – an age-old concept that famously originated from US American historiography in the 1920s (Turner 1920), proved to be highly productive and sparked off an entire new field of research. In a recent contribution Rasmussen and Lund (2018: 2) describe frontier situations as typical of the expansion of capitalism into remote zones of the Global South. They mark frontiers as discursive, political, and physical operations that 'classify space as "vacant", "free", "ungoverned"'. Rasmussen and Lund allege that frontiers emerge whenever a resource is newly 'identified, defined, and becomes subject to extraction and commodification'. Frontiers are not spaces in themselves, but something happening in space. Rasmussen and Lund (2018: 2) see the concepts of 'frontier' and 'territorialization' as complementary. While frontiers 'dissolve existing social orders – property systems, political jurisdictions, rights, and social contracts ... territorialization is a shorthand for all the dynamics that establish them and re-order space anew'. Harking back to conceptual work by Tsing (2005) and Geiger (2008), Acciaioli and Sabharwal (2017) argue that conservation frontiers are a new type of frontier, to be added to settlement frontiers, resource frontiers, and techno frontiers. They build on Tsing's notion of 'salvage frontier' where the lines between conservation and exploitation of resources blur, where resources are made, saved, and destroyed at the same time (see Tsing 2003). They argue that conservation creates new boundaries and intermediary zones around protected areas. Thereby they generate conditions for the emergence of new resources and new types of exploitation (Acciaioli & Sabharwal 2017: 34). Tsing's concept of salvage accumulation (Tsing 2015b) refers to the amassment of wealth within a capitalist regime without regulating or directly investing in the conditions under which such commodities are produced.

Social and economic dynamics in Kenya's and Namibia's conservancies show that territorialisation and frontierisation can relate to the same space and happen at the same time. The sandalwood trees illegally harvested in Kenya's conservancies, smuggled via illicit networks across the border into Uganda and from there transported legally to India (as shown by Kioko & Kinyanjui, this volume) signal a frontier situation. The fact that much of the illegal harvesting of trees takes place in northern Kenyan conservancies, i.e. in areas purportedly managed by local communities for conservation, hints at the fact that two competing forces, reterritorialisation via community-based conservation and frontierisation, co-exist and compete for the power to control space. In north-east Namibian conservancies, the harvesting of rosewood trees shows characteristics of a frontier situation but also attempts at regulation and territorialisation. While for some time quotas on rosewood tree harvesting were given to conservancies (i.e. fixed territorial and institutionalised entities), there were numerous allegations that much more rosewood harvesting was conducted illegally, with wood being transported into Zambia and from there legally reimported into Namibia, and from Namibia's Walvis Bay harbour shipped to East Asia, disregarding all rules and regulations.

Trophy hunting is also entrenched with characteristics of a frontier, perhaps in a rather theatrical sense, often motivated by the romantic evocation of an imagined past when frontiersmen penetrated and subjugated what today is framed as wilderness (see Kalvelage, this volume). While the establishment, transfer, and sale of trophy game is highly regulated, trophy hunts are arranged in a manner that sells a frontier experience: tents, guns, and off-road vehicles – the habitus of the frontier is staged in a spectacular way. The thrill of being very close to an unremitting nature is played out.

However, conservancies both in Kenya and (perhaps to a lesser extent) in Namibia are also frontiers in a very factual sense. When during the drought of 2019 thousands of pastoral nomadic herders invaded conservation areas in Kenya's Laikipia county, conservancies became frontiers between open rangelands and enclosed farmlands (Gravesen 2020). In north-eastern Namibia the herding of large herds of cattle along the boundaries of e.g. Mudumu National Park also bears characteristics of a frontier situation. Shepherds dwelling in mobile and rudimentary camps vie for opportunities to sneak into the park and make use of the remaining tufts of grass there (Bollig & Vehrs 2021). Life along this moving frontier is tough, and spectacular in a very concrete sense. Human–wildlife conflict is a daily issue, and thirst as much as carnivores threatens herders and herd.

More-than-human approaches to the commodification of the 'wild'

Whereas ecology did not feature as important in the previously reported two approaches here, recent more-than-human approaches highlight and historicise the role of ecology and biology of species in commodification processes (see also LeCain 2017).

The innovative online platform *Feral Atlas* edited by Tsing and colleagues (2020) is dedicated to scientific research on the ecological effects of human infrastructure entangled with non-human entities. It includes diverse 'field reports', drawn from various scientific disciplines, through which authors discuss the role of capitalism and the commodification of living and non-living entities, human and non-human work, in environmental destruction. For example, Marissa Weiss's contribution documents the unexpected ecological impacts of wooden pallets. She shows that this transformed timber designed to facilitate global cargo conveyed wood-boring beetles now infesting forests around the world. In another contribution, Heather Swanson shows how industrial salmon farming disturbed salmon–lice relationships and led to a proliferation of sea lice that threatens oceanic ecosystems. These cases highlight the complex relations that bind species and organisms together and show how they are unsettled by commodification processes, shedding a new light on their vast and unexpected ecological impacts. In this way an approach that took its inspirations both from science and technology studies and anthropology's ontological turn becomes re-ecologised, and a powerful instrument to analyse the dynamics of human–more-than-human relations in a capitalist set-up.

More-than-human approaches address the question of how humans and other species co-produce commodities. Collard and Dempsey have argued that 'vital qualities' of commodities are key aspects of valorisation and produce value as long as 'they remain alive and/or promise future life' (Collard & Dempsey 2013: 2684). Donna Haraway's ideas on the foundations of encounter value have been instigating a number of studies on commodified wildlife. In Haraway's diction, encounter value is constituted within a 'trans-species relation' where 'subjects of different biological species' interact (Haraway 2008: 46). Value generation rests upon non-human labour, metabolism, and reproduction enacted within material and social relations that define and/or transact a species or members of that species as commodities. More-than-human approaches to the commodification of the 'wild' take off from the assumption that value is generated in the encounter between humans and the wild – 'encounter value': 'encounter value is a process of value-generation, where bodies, ethologies, and liveliness of an animal makes a difference to, and is constitutive of, those historical and material relations that render or transact it as a commodity' (Barua 2017: 279). Encounters across species are often spectacularly enacted by those driving commodification in order to increase its value. Yet, as with the unwaged (re)productive labour of humans, this animal 'work' is hidden behind the fetishised and often intangible commodity – for example a 'wilderness experience' or a 'carbon credit' – only coming to light when actual practices of value creation are explored (Haraway 2008; Barua 2019). Whether the concept of animal labour is apt and productive in this context remains a matter of vivid discussions (see Greiner & Bollig this volume; also Büscher 2022).

Multispecies approaches have also served to follow species in the process of their commodification, as Anna Tsing has prominently done with the matsutake mushroom. In *The Mushroom at the End of the World*, Tsing describes how the matsutake moves in and out of the status of a capitalist commodity from its picking in the Oregon forests to its commercialisation on the Japanese market. Through her focus on the mushroom, Tsing defines commodification in capitalism as a process through which things and beings are 'torn from their lifeworlds to become objects of exchange' (Tsing 2015a: 121). Her multi-species approach allows her to shed light on the entanglements being made and unmade as the mushroom becomes a commodity. She also highlights the more-than-human assemblages the matsutake mushroom depends on and that serve its integration into capitalist channels. Matsutake flourish through multispecies encounters that humans cannot control. In echo with Barua's hidden non-human labour, Tsing points out the 'latent commons, human and not human' (2015a: 271), i.e. the unpredictable and often unnoticed entanglements between multiple species – human disturbance, forest, and fungi – that produce the mushroom.

While Tsing puts forward the commodification of a mushroom through human and non-human assemblages, Maan Barua has impressively shown how lion behaviour and different approaches to the commodification of these carnivores in India's Gir Forest of Gujarat interpenetrate each other. Barua tells us that 'lions' ethologies began to change as a consequence of their commodity life' (Barua 2017: 278). Hewitson & Sullivan (this volume) study how trophy elephants as commodities are 'co-produced with and extracted from the biophysical world ... emphasizing the co-constitution of the economic and the ecological whilst focusing on the inequalities generated by capital accumulation' (Hewitson & Sullivan 2021: 7/8). Hewitson & Sullivan show how elephant behaviour changes with systematic trophy hunting. The elimination of elderly male elephants by trophy hunts leads to more conflict among younger male elephants and is apparently connected to more devastation of human fields. Also, the mobility of elephant herds that are confronted with occasional hunts changes. Changing lion or elephant behaviour in both instances directly impacts the choreography of encounters (Haraway 2008). Obviously, a more-than-human approach is not only applicable to spectacular wildlife but to all species that are discussed in this volume. Of course, the metabolism and reproduction of e.g. Devil's Claw and Honeybush is constitutive for their becoming commodities and, in turn, commodification changes these properties as much as their entanglement with other living and non-living species. Lacan, in her contribution on forests in Kenya's Tugen highlands, touches upon the co-constitution of trees as commodities: indigenous as much as alien species afford certain ecologies with which capitalist modes of transaction may interact. It shows how much the ecological transformations of Kenyan forests are intertwined with economic and political projects of state making and development. Vehrs & Waziri (this volume) reflect upon the interrelationship between *Acacia senegal* (domesticated and non-domisticated), the gum arabic resin harvested from them in northern Nigeria, and the age-old trade in this commodity.

Commodification in global value chain and global production network approaches

Generally concerned with uneven development across space, economic geographers have developed the global value chain (GVC) and global production network (GPN) approaches. These frameworks are useful for understanding linkages between commodified natures and the global capital, and increasingly, scholars encourage a dialogue with concepts concerning the valorisation and commodification of nature to understand the production process at the very beginning of the value chain.

Rooted in world-systems theory (Hopkins & Wallerstein 1977), the chain heuristic allows us to understand how global production is organised by examining the linkages between firms, workers, and consumers in different places (Gereffi *et al.* 2005). By following the material product from the production site to the consumer, GVC research aims to describe the full range of tangible and intangible activities that are needed in the life cycle of a commodity (compare also Revilla Diez, Hulke, & Kalvelage, this volume).

Based on a critique of earlier GVC research, the more recent GPN framework claims to grasp the multitude of actors that affect regional development by applying a network heuristic (Henderson *et al.* 2002). In a quest for '*explicit* causal links between industrial-organizational change at the level of global production networks and the variegated geographical outcomes in labour, technology, capital formation, and social change in different localities and regions' (Yeung 2021: 430, italics original), analysis is guided by three conceptual categories: embeddedness, power, and value (see Kalvelage, this volume, for an application). It is the latter category that has particular potential when looking at the commodification of the 'wild'.

Research relating to GVC/GPN has a pragmatic stance towards the complexities of the value concept, since its blurry definition allows for different ideological perspectives to meet under one conceptual umbrella (Havice & Pickles 2019). Value is understood 'as more than a price-based calculation to denote residual economic surpluses from material and intangible transformations in the complex process of value creation, enhancement, and capture'. It does not just entail profit but also 'surpluses in skills, technologies, and livelihoods embedded in ongoing social relations of production that are explicitly associated with economic activities organised through global production networks' (Yeung 2021: 432). Some authors argue that this pluralistic theorisation of value causes frictions (McGrath 2018) and call for an objective theory of value that allows the circulation of rents and surplus value across space to be tracked.

Notwithstanding these debates, the strength of the GPN methodology lies in the capacity to analyse the interrelatedness of seemingly unrelated processes in different places. The approach is currently undergoing a critical reconsideration of its weaker points, e.g. the production sphere of a commodity. In this way, GPN research has the potential to examine actors and patterned behaviour involved in the valorisation of nature and the commodification of the 'wild', as well as the related development outcomes across space.

By coining the term value capture, the GPN approach has put emphasis on the degree to which surplus is retained locally. Value capture is an important measure for regional development outcomes and occurs when local institutions are capable of retaining resources and invest these to reinforce regional economic growth (Murphy & Schindler 2011). A sole focus on value capture may be misleading, though, since a region can capture value at an aggregate level, but gains are distributed unevenly among households (Fold 2014). Therefore, the concept of value distribution looks more carefully at the practices and institutions that lead to distribution patterns. This is linked to the debate on negative outcomes when regions integrate into GPNs, since the arrival of new economic sectors in a region creates winners and losers (Revilla Diez, Hulke, & Kalvelage, this volume).

More recently, commodification of nature as a form of value creation has gained attention in GPN research. In nature-based industries such as tuna production (Havice & Campling 2017), acoustic guitar woods (Gibson & Warren 2016), or fur (Kleibert *et al.* 2020), the production sphere of the commodity is crucial for development outcomes at a local level. The same is true for hunting tourism, which serves as a research object in this volume (Revilla Diez, Hulke, & Kalvelage this volume; Kalvelage this volume). A promising approach to explore value creation from nature is the integration of the GPN approach with the notion of resource making (Gargallo & Kalvelage 2020; Irarrázaval 2020). By exploring the social-ecological relations, the (non) human work and social practices are regarded that together produce commodities, and thus construct value (Hewitson & Sullivan 2021).

At its core, GVC/GPN research is interested in uneven development outcomes of globalised production. It is surprising that GPN research on the commodification of nature has only recently gained pace. Yet the concept is a powerful tool to analyse structures and actors involved in 'green grabbing' and to reveal emerging global linkages in frontier dynamics. It has the potential to show how commodities co-produced by humans and other species are circulated globally.

There are some obvious overlaps between these approaches, and also controversies. The enormous amount of recent literature produced on the topic (especially in the 2010s), makes it difficult to describe the state of the art in an adequate manner. The matter is even more complicated as the range of topics (water, forests, plants, wildlife, ecosystem services, landscapes, etc.) varies immensely, as do the specific topics researched (privatisation, financialisation, encounter value, etc.). Because a major part of the literature has been theoretically oriented and utterly critical of commodification, there has been (as yet) little policy effect of this research on e.g. projects in conservation and or governance of forests and water resources. Quite to the contrary, the world seems to produce even more examples of commodified 'wilderness' and marketed landscapes, plants, and animals. The commodification of bio-knowledge, genomes, and ecosystem services is rapidly developing, particularly so in countries of the Global South (see Wynberg this volume). This will motivate all four theoretical trajectories described here.

This volume adds to the debate in several other ways. First, because the literature on commodification of nature is fragmented, there is ample space for collaboration across the theoretical frameworks described above. By bringing in and sometimes combining different theoretical angles, contributions in this volume add to their dialogue. Hewitson and Sullivan for instance try to combine a more-than-human approach with a critique of neoliberal conservation frameworks. Kalvelage joins a GPN perspective with political economy concepts. Also, while most research on commodification is conducted by scholars from the Global North on the Global South, this volume presents notable contributions from scholars from southern and eastern Africa looking at the commodification of specific plants (Lavelle on Devil's Claw, Ndwandwe on Honeybush, Vehrs and Waziri on *Acacia senegal*), on commodification within a bio-economy framework (Wynburg), on the impact of commodification processes on social relations and political power (Nghitevelekwa *et al.*; Mosimane *et al.*), on human–wildlife interaction (Fabiano *et al.*) and on the smuggling of tropical timber (Kioko & Kinyanjui).

Second, this volume contributes to addressing the dearth of knowledge on the social consequences of commodification of the 'wild'. How does commodification impact gender structures, for example? Anthropological literature on the historical fur trade in Canada's 19th-century history suggests that commodification tends to increase gender imbalances (Leacock 1978). The examples discussed in this volume (see Nghitevelekwa *et al.*) seem to contradict this knowledge: commodification here opens up new venues for women to earn income independently from their husbands. How does commodification contribute to or go against established authority structures? Mosimane *et al.* (this volume) show that traditional authorities profit from the commodification of the 'wild' – in an abstract sense, as most decision making pertaining to these resources goes via them, but also in a very pecuniary sense. The quest for commodification of wilderness settings in a global market of sceneries and attractions contributes to a redefinition of community–state relations. The communities dealt with, former dwellers of remote marginalised areas, suddenly have something with which they can bargain: they are the stewards of new wealth for the 21st century – untrammelled nature, ecosystem functions of some relevance to mitigating climate change, and repositories of biodiversity (see contributions by Greiner & Bollig and Dittmann & Müller-Mahn, this volume).

Finally, and perhaps most importantly, this volume contributes to the debate on commodification through its specific focus on the 'wild'. The wide range of case studies it covers touches upon the ways in which 'non-domesticated' species and non-humans seemingly resistant to their commodification are being integrated into market logics. They document sophisticated methods that make their integration into the global markets feasible (e.g. quota-setting procedures for trophy hunting, or the creation of forest reserves and plantations within them) and their impacts on livelihoods and ecologies. However, contributions also question how the 'wild' is constructed into a new resource, still untapped, and made ready for commercialisation. In this volume, studies examine the 'wild' as a particular discursive, symbolic, and material category that allows the commodification of nature to go a step further: they document not only how (non-domesticated) plants, animals or landscapes are being commodified but also how their 'wildness' is being marketed. Thus, this volume strives to interrogate the 'wild' that is being increasingly commodified, considering its role as a tool serving the commodification of nature – nature is made wild to be better commercialised – and as a commodified good itself.

The sections of the book

In Part 2, the section following, four contributions are assembled that theorise processes of commodification. Clemens Greiner and Michael Bollig apply Noel Castree's conceptual differentiation (Castree 2003) of commodification and ask what it takes to commodify non-domesticated animals, plants, and landscapes. In reference to Marx's theorisation of the nature of commodities, commodification is taken as a process in which several steps are constitutive and perhaps mandatory to transfer a being or a spatial unit into a commodity that can then be exchanged and can be transferred into money equivalents. The contribution emphasises that social labour and conflict are constitutive for the reification and commodification of the 'wild'.

Javier Revilla Diez, Carolin Hulke, and Linus Kalvelage take another point of departure. They sketch pertinent support for the expansion of GVCs from major global organisations such as the World Trade Organization and the World Bank. The commodification of the 'wild' is lauded by these institutions as an effort to green rural economies and to make them resilient in the era of climate change and biodiversity loss. Revilla Diez *et al.* study the regional economic consequences when non-domesticated animals, plants, and landscapes are 'plugged into' global production networks (GPNs). While a liberalised market is expected by many economists and conservationists to safeguard the environment, the authors here critically question to what extent the commodification of the 'wild' has lived up to these glaring promises.

Rachel Wynberg discusses green economics in a South African (and often also a southern African) perspective. Perhaps no other African country has invested so much energy and has evoked so many expectations pertaining to the ecological, economic, and political prospects of commodification of the 'wild'. Wynberg critically asks to what extent the commodification of non-domesticated plants can contribute to a transformation of a more sustainable future and more social justice. The key concept of 'benefit sharing' has been propagated as the key to restorative and redistributive justice. Wynberg explores the genesis of the concept, its framing in legislative efforts and analyses, and its programmatic embedding in neoliberal approaches to nature, and studies applications of the concept in the South African context. Taking examples of the commodification of plants like *Hoodia parviflora*, Devil's Claw, *Myrothamnus*, *Commiphora*, and rooibos, Wynberg's analysis points towards options for a more sustainable and just use of South Africa's rich biodiversity.

Johannes Dittmann and Detlef Müller-Mahn link the commodification of wilderness landscapes to international politics. They analyse the dominant 'transfrontier conservation' approach as an expression of a joint interest of southern African states in the marketisation of natural resources within a global context. Southern African politics thereby respond to the quest on the part of international institutions for an expansion of protected areas on the one hand and a liberalisation of tourism and natural markets on the other hand. The idea that biodiversity protection offers a giant future market, an idea that Wynberg also explores, is informing the policies of ministries and large international NGOs alike. Dittmann and Müller-Mahn systematically zoom in on the role of the state and the integration of transfrontier conservation into national policies and programmes that outline a path of sustainability and economic development into the 21st century.

Part 3 focuses on the commodification of plants. Jessica-Jane Lavelle presents an in-depth analysis of the progressively flourishing trade in Devil's Claw (*Harpagophythum* spp) in Namibia's north-eastern Zambezi Region. Devil's Claw has been traded on the international pharmaceutical market for a number of decades. However, the growing interest in bio-pharmaceutics brought about an explosive interest in this plant. Lavelle analyses the implications and socio-economic consequences of a US-funded project that laid the basis for a rapid expansion of Devil's Claw harvesting in the region, necessitating changes of regulatory frameworks and the recreation of institutions procedures. Lavelle's study situates the commodification of Devil's Claw within the broader 'natural resource governance framework' of Namibia and asks to what extent the marketisation of this plant can contribute to pro-poor rural development.

Sthembile Ndwandwe acquaints us with the commodification of a plant that has a yet longer history of commodification. Honeybush (*Cyclopia* spp.), a plant endemic to the South Africa's Eastern and Western Cape Provinces, has witnessed a number of attempts at its commodification. In 2015, honeybush finally came to be identified as a key species for biodiversity economy development in South Africa. Ndwandwe presents data from an in-depth study of honeybush commodification in one South African community that has witnessed profound processes of marginalisation during the past century. Will the commodification of honeybush help to address societal cleavages, or reify them? Analysing the changing biodiversity legislative framework Ndwandwe also gets close to the marginalised honeybush harvesters and studies the impact of changing regulatory regimes on their livelihoods during the past century. Ndwandwe stresses that the absence of sovereignty and stable access regimes hinder the transformative capacity of honeybush harvesting and trade.

Lacan, and Kioko and Kinyanjui, focus on the use of forests and timber in Kenya. Léa Lacan takes a comprehensive look at the construction of Kenyan forests into a national resource, which already started early in the 20th century. The British colonial administration identified the rich and 'untouched' forests of the Kenyan Highlands as a peculiar resource for the colony's need for timber, and developed institutions for forest management accordingly. Lacan shows that conservation contributed to and justified the declaration of forests as state property, which was seen as an essential step to safeguard forests from destruction and at the same time to make them commercially more productive. In the process, forest landscapes transformed materially. The colonial state commissioned some highly productive forests to logging companies, who rented stretches of forest for long periods of time. After these areas were cut down, they were to be replanted and, in commercially used forests, such reforestation was often done with exotic, rapidly growing tree species. While Kenyan forests were progressively put under central state control and partly transformed into productive plantations, forest dwellers were partially or completely resettled from the forest and relocated to other sites. Léa Lacan focuses on two forests, the Katimok Forest and the Lembus Forest. While Lembus Forest was earmarked for commercial timber production early on, Katimok Forest was identified as a forest to be preserved in its original state. Lacan explores how human–forest relations changed in both instances and how locals differentially related to the forest, including in the claims they are still putting forward linked to their evictions. Lacan tells the story of a resource in the making, from 'untouched' forests to national assets, and explores the implications for the material forest landscapes and local residents' lives.

Against Lacan's historical analysis of the emergence of Kenya's forest resources, Eric Kioko's and Michael Kinyanjui's account of illegal timber trade highlights the vagaries of forest politics and the dangers of unfettered commodification. Kioko and Kinyanjui accompany smugglers of sandalwood (*Osyris lanceolata*) across Kenya. East African sandalwood only became prominent in international trade networks after commercial sandalwood production in India and Australia collapsed. The sandalwood harvested in Kenya's Samburu, Laikipia, and Baringo counties goes almost entirely to India, but it goes there in twisted ways. Transported illicitly through Kenya and smuggled across the international Kenya/Uganda border, it is sold to timber merchants. From Uganda it is exported legally to India, often crossing again through Kenya (as Ugandan sandalwood) and leaving for India via Kenya's Mombasa port. Kioko and Kinyanjui show how Kenya's community-based natural resource management units, the conservancies, become prone to illegal sandalwood harvesting. It is mainly community members who cut sandalwood in remote areas and transport it to town, on donkey back or carrying it on their own backs. Smugglers buy the timber in the off-the-way shopping centres of Kenya's north, paying smaller sums of money to the illicit timber harvesters and make some down payment to local elders and authorities. Kioko and Kinyanjui show how a number of officials partake in the illicit business and facilitate sandalwood smuggling for their own benefit. Such networks are hard to break as so many profit from the illegal activity. Are domestication and privatisation then the only answers?

Hauke-Peter Vehrs and Ibrahim Waziri look at the history of gum arabic harvesting and a recent move towards respective Acacia trees in north-eastern Nigeria. Gum arabic is a tree resin that is harvested from a limited number of Acacia species endemic to the Sahel. The best-paid gum arabic, however, is harvested only from *Acacia senegal*. Gum arabic is used as an emulsifier or as coating for a number of products. At the local level gum arabic is also used for medicinal treatment and ink. While gum arabic was and still is harvested predominantly from the wild by small-scale farmers, a system of *Acacia senegal* plantations for gum arabic production is gaining ground. While the harvesting of gum arabic from the wild is sporadic and seasonal, *Acacia senegal* plantations require high labour and capital input, because pest control, continuous pruning and weeding, and seed collection are necessary. Did domestication in this instance lead the way to a more sustainable production and equitable access, or did domestication deepen unequal access?

Part 4 deals with the commodification of non-domesticated animals. The section addresses the field from three directions. While Lee Hewitson and Sian Sullivan focus on the topic by drawing attention to elephants as trophy animals, Ezequiel Fabiano and colleagues focus on human–wildlife conflicts in north-eastern Namibia, and Linus Kalvelage deals with the consumption of wildlife by tourists and trophy hunters. These contributions, like many others on the commodification of wildlife and on contemporary conservation in the African context, zoom in on elephants. Carnivores, buffaloes, gazelles, and antelopes, let alone birds and fish, are largely absent from the social science debates on conservation. Also Lenhart's contribution (in Part 5) deals with elephants in and around the Ugandan National Park Murchison Falls. She explores how the protection of this one species shapes state-community relations in a profound way. It is revealing that in this section elephants feature most importantly. Lee Hewitson and Sian Sullivan's contribution makes perfectly clear why a focus on a particular species does make sense, and furthers the debate. Hewitson and Sullivan adopt a more-than-human approach to the subject matter. They supply ample knowledge on elephant ecology, and species-specific patterns of demography and mobility. How these different aspects of being elephant are entangled by trophy hunting is of key significance. Hewitson followed elephants in north-eastern Namibia's Zambezi Region. He did so physically by teaming up with local game guards and accompanying them on their long bush walks. On these walks he partook of their profound knowledge of animal behaviour and shared in their considerations of trophy hunting. Hewitson and Sullivan also followed elephants as a commodity by looking at their local production. Starting with an in-depth analysis on how trophy-elephant quotas are being determined in a co-management effort by local conservancies, NGO staff, and ministerial employees, they describe the political act of their final gazettement by ministerial decree. Trophy elephants are then traded between conservancies and commercial trophy-hunting companies worldwide. Based on Maan Barua's idea of non-human labour (Barua 2017, 2019) Hewitson and Sullivan look at practices of elephants that co-construct their commodity value. Hewitson and Sullivan also follow trophy-elephant commodities post hunt, demonstrating how value transforms spatially by involving taxidermists and finally airlines shipping parts of the trophy animal out of the country. Ezequiel Fabiano and colleagues focus on the topic of human–wildlife co-existence in north-eastern Namibia's conservation areas. Increasing wildlife numbers are good for tourism but habitually challenge smallholder farmers. Human–wildlife conflict has been a salient topic of community-based conservation narratives.

Fabiano, Lendelvo, Mosimane, and Kosmas, in their contribution, are not so much interested in what factually happens on the ground, e.g. how many cows are attacked by carnivores or how many maize fields are destroyed by elephants, but rather in local perceptions of human–wildlife co-existence. Based on structured interviews the authors find a clearly ranked perception of crop raiding and livestock depredation. Not surprisingly, elephants and lions were perceived as the most problematic animals. While elephant damage to fields is indeed significant across the region, lion damage to livestock herds is a rather peculiar issue in the conservancy where Fabiano *et al.* did their study. Interestingly they find evidence that the local perception sees wildlife numbers as shrinking rather than expanding on the whole, but that human–wildlife conflict is concentrated on a limited number of villages. This suggests that settled areas and wilderness areas progressively fall apart and that humans and also wildlife adapt to a situation of co-existence. Further research may well explore to what extent these results document early stages of conviviality in a working landscape.

A question that is already pertinent in Fabiano *et al.*'s contribution, the issue of how justice can be provided for in landscapes in which wildlife and humans have to co-exist due to governmental decree, is taken up in an East African context. Again, crop raiding by elephant herds is a key issue, but, more than in the Namibian case, humans are also directly affected in Uganda's conservation areas. Furthermore, the situation is complicated by frequent poaching activities. While there is some evidence that in the Namibian context too poaching is still of some significance (Lubilo & Hebinck 2019), it is of less significance than it is in Uganda (see Lenhart's later contribution). Here the state summarily suspects locals of being involved in poaching activities or of being attracted by the sizeable profits offered by this business. Linus Kalvelage looks at trophy hunting as part of a tourism global production network. Through trophy hunting, 'wild' (as an amalgam of wilderness and wildlife) nature is turned into commodities. It needs the cooperation of a number of actors at various spatial scales to make commodification work. Institutions, as rule-makers in the game, with sanctions and specification of responsibility, reduce transaction costs when commodities are exchanged between very different kinds of actors. Linus Kalvelage contrasts two different production systems of the trophy hunt in Namibia, private game farms and communal conservancies. By portraying the emergence of trophy hunting in Namibia, light is shed on the colonial legacy of land tenure that continues to play an important role when nature is commodified. In this way, he shows that labour input and investments are relevant for commodification – and the organisation of commodity production largely determines the development outcomes at a local level. This adds to previous research in which Kalvelage shows that there are considerable gains made from the marketisation of the 'wild' as a commodity for the global tourism industry (Kalvelage *et al.* 2022): about one-fifth of the total value gained remains in the region. However, mainly those directly employed in the tourism industry and those few wealthy individuals who can offer services to the tourism sector share these benefits.

Part 5, the concluding main section of the book, discusses the societal impact of commodification of the 'wild' on society, economy, and on political organisation. In the first contribution by Nghitevelekwa, Lendelvo, and Shapi, the effects of commodification on gender relations are explored. Indeed, many plants from the wild are collected and also sold by women. Romie

Nghitevelekwa and colleagues explore changing modes of access to success-fully commodified plants, and identify marketing venues. They highlight that it is especially the local knowledge of women that is a precondition for the incipient commodification of a non-domesticated plant, be it *Commiphora* resins that are used for perfumes, or fruits that are part of traditional relishes. A certain degree of autonomy in subsistence activities allows local women to explore emergent value chains. Additionally, NGOs that function on donor money are likely to respond positively to these women-driven activities as they score highly in the market for long-term donations: projects focusing on the commodification of plants from the wild not only come with the promise of biodiversity protection but have the additional attraction of supporting local women and providing for more gender equity. The contribution adopts a comparative approach and cites experiences from all over northern Namibia.

Alfons Mosimane and colleagues tackle another pertinent linkage between commodification and social dynamics: how the commodification of wilderness landscapes and of wildlife impacts local authority structures. Namibia's rural communities are characterised by a continued dominance of traditional author-ities. These are addressed as chiefs and occasionally as kings. They dominate the management of land, wildlife, and forests to a significant degree and are nowadays part and parcel of nearly all conservationist approaches to biodi-versity protection. Mosimane and colleagues trace the history of engagement of Namibia's traditional authorities with land governance in general and conservation in particular. They outline how the South African colonial admin-istration built up traditional authorities as intermediaries of power, leaving much of the administration of agricultural lands to them. Wildlife though was relegated to the authority of the administration and was taken away from the authority of chiefs. Often, the gazettement of protected areas was also then shifting the authority over land to the state. Recent approaches to community-based conservation try to bring communities, land, and wildlife together again. Traditional authorities gain new power as the stewards of landscapes and as guardians of biodiversity. The contribution shows that conservation is factually invigorating traditional authority, first in a very pecuniary sense, but also in a political sense, relegating decision making regarding access to and exclusion from natural resources to traditional authorities once again.

Joseph Mbaiwa explores in his contribution how wildlife tourism contributes to the economic development of Botswana. He outlines the fundamentals of a sustainable tourism framework as envisioned by the Botswanan government. Joseph Mbaiwa argues that an increasingly specialised and segmented global tourism market sets the framework for Botswana's sustainable green-tourism strategy. Botswana's policy heavily relies on large national parks and game parks, comprising most of the Okavango Delta and the northern Kalahari

Desert. The human population is concentrated in a number of settlements along the buffer zones of these protected areas. Many of them are also working in the tourism industry and/or maintaining the tourism infrastructure, as mostly low-salaried labourers often maintain farmsteads there in such buffer zones. Joseph Mbaiwa outlines perspectives for these mixed tourism-farming economies at the fringe of large protected areas. He argues that de-agrarisation will open venues for more biodiversity protection by lessening the dependence on natural resources, but that a progressively diversified rural economy also comes with new uncertainties – such as those experienced by the southern African ecotourism industry during the Coronavirus crisis.

Lioba Lenhart takes this section of the book to East Africa. Her chapter analyses local people's and conservationists' ways of imagining and practising relations between humans, wildlife, and land in Uganda. Matters of ownership, compensation, and justice are aroused on both widely disparate sides, and biodiversity protection is directly pitched against environmental justice. Lenhart's contribution shows that by and large the Ugandan state has successfully (and often relentlessly) pressed for its end, ensuring the expansion of protected areas. While generally community-led approaches like those portrayed by Fabiano *et al.* offer more space for finding compromises between environmental justice and wildlife protection, Lenhart's contribution also ends on a positive note with the description of some hopeful attempts to find more promising venues for human–wildlife co-existence in the buffer zones around national parks.

The volume ends with a conclusion that tries to highlight perspectives for further research. How wilderness-based economies interact with other segments of the rural economy, whether a diversification of rural livelihoods actually takes place, how increasing inequalities are entangled with the commodification of nature – are obvious topics for further interdisciplinary research. Beyond pinpointing salient topics for meaningful interdisciplinary research, the conclusion tries to outline some pertinent results of studies presented here for practitioners. We argue that attempts to discuss scientific results with communities and practitioners organising conservation and rural development are rare. However, in-depth scientific studies obviously provide knowledge that can be translated into political action. The conclusion singles out some thematic fields where such translation seems conducive and add to concrete action.

Bibliography

Acciaioli, G. & Sabharwal, A. (2017). 'Frontierization and defrontierization', in: J. M. Tejada & B. Tatar (eds), *Transnational Frontiers of Asia and Latin America since 1800* (Abingdon: Routledge), 31–45

Benjaminson, T. & Bryceson, D. (2012). 'Conservation, green/blue grabbing and accumulation by dispossession in Tanzania', *Journal of Peasant Studies*, 335–355.

Barua, M. (2017). 'Nonhuman labour, encounter value, spectacular accumulation: the geographies of a lively commodity', *Transactions of the Institute of British Geographers*, 42, 274–288.

Barua M. (2019). 'Animating capital: Work, commodities, circulation', *Progress in Human Geography*, 43(4), 650–669.

Bollig, M. & Vehrs, H.-P. (2021). 'The making of a conservation landscape: The emergence of a conservationist environmental infrastructure along the Kwando River in Namibia's Zambezi Region', *Africa*, 91(2), 1–26.

Borras, J. (2012). 'The new enclosures: critical perspectives on corporate land deals', *Journal of Peasant Studies*, 39(3–4), 619–647.

Bracking, S. (2012). 'How do investors value environmental harm/care? Private equity funds, development finance institutions and the partial financialization of nature-based industries', *Development and Change*, 43(1), 271–293.

Bracking, S., Fredriksen, A., Sullivan, S., & Woodhouse, P. (eds) (2018). *Valuing Development, Environment and Conservation: Creating Values that Matter* (Abingdon; New York: Routledge).

Brockington, D. & Duffy, R. (2010). 'Capitalism and conservation: the production and reproduction of biodiversity conservation', *Antipode*, 42(3), 469–484.

Brockington, D. & Duffy, R. & Igoe, J. (2008). *Nature Unbound: Conservation, Capitalism and the Future of Protected Areas* (London: Earthscan).

Büscher B. (2022). 'The nonhuman turn: Critical reflections on alienation, entanglement and nature under capitalism', *Dialogues in Human Geography*, 12(1), 54–73.

Büscher, B., & Fletcher, R. (2020). *The Conservation Revolution: Radical Ideas for Saving Nature Beyond the Anthropocene* (La Vergne TN: Verso).

Büscher, B., Sullivan, S., Neves, K., Igoe, J., & Brockington, D. (2012). 'Towards a synthesized critique of neoliberal biodiversity conservation', *Capitalism Nature Socialism*, 23(2), 4–30.

Castree, N. (2003). 'Commodifying what nature?' *Progress in Human Geography*, 27(3), 273–297.

Collard R.-C. & Dempsey J. (2013). 'Life for sale? The politics of lively commodities', *Environment and Planning A: Economy and Space*, 45(11), 2682–2699.

Dunlap, A. & Sullivan, S. (2019). 'A faultline in neoliberal environmental governance scholarship? Or, why accumulation-by-alienation matters', *Environment and Planning E: Nature and Space*, 3(2), 1–28.

Ehrenstein, V. & Muniesa, F. (2013). 'The conditional sink: Counterfactual display in the valuation of a carbon offsetting restoration project', *Valuation Studies*, 1(2), 161–188,

Fairhead, J., Leach, M. & Scoones, I. (2012). 'Green grabbing: A new appropriation of nature?' *Journal of Peasant Studies*, 39, 237–261.

Fold, N. (2014). 'Value chain dynamics, settlement trajectories and regional development', *Regional Studies*, 48(5), 778–790.

Gardner, B. (2012). 'Tourism and the politics of the global land grab in Tanzania: Markets, appropriation and recognition', *Journal of Peasant Studies*, 39(2), 377–402.

Gargallo, E., & Kalvelage, L. (2020). 'Integrating social-ecological systems and global production networks: Local effects of trophy hunting in Namibian conservancies', *Development Southern Africa*, 38(1), 87–103.

Geiger, D. (2008). *Frontier Encounters – Indigenous Communities and Settlers in Asia and Latin America* (Copenhagen: IWGIA).

Gereffi, G., Humphrey, J., & Sturgeon, T. (2005). 'The governance of global value chains', *Review of International Political Economy*, 12(1), 78–104.

Gibson, C., & Warren, A. (2016). 'Resource-sensitive global production networks: Reconfigured geographies of timber and acoustic guitar manufacturing', *Economic Geography*, 92(4), 430–454.

Gravesen, M. (2020). *The Contested Lands of Laikipia: Histories of Claims and Conflict in a Kenyan Landscape* (Leiden: Brill).

Green, K. & Adams, W. (2015). 'Green grabbing and the dynamics of local-level engagement with neoliberalization in Tanzania's wildlife management areas', *Journal of Peasant Studies*, 42, 97–117.

Haraway, D. (2008). *When Species Meet* (Minneapolis: University of Minnesota Press).

Harvey, D. (2006). *Spaces of Global Capitalism: A Theory of Uneven Geographical Development* (London: Verso).

Havice, E. & Campling, L. (2017). 'Where chain governance and environmental governance meet: Interfirm strategies in the canned tuna global value chain', *Economic Geography*, 93(3), 292–313.

Havice, E., & Pickles, J. (2019). 'On value in value chains', in: S. Ponte, G. Gereffi, & G. Raj-Reichert (eds), *Handbook on Global Value Chains* (Cheltenham; Northampton, MA: Edward Elgar Publishing), 169–182.

Henderson, J., Dicken, P., Hess, M., Coe, N. M., & Yeung, H. W. C. (2002). 'Global production networks and the analysis of economic development', *Review of International Political Economy*, 9(3), 436–464.

Hewitson, L. & Sullivan, S. (2021). 'Producing elephant commodities for conservation hunting in Namibian communal area conservancies', *Journal of Political Ecology*, 28(1), 1–24.

Heynen N. & Robbins P. (2005). 'The neoliberalization of nature: Governance, privatization, enclosure and valuation', *Capitalism Nature Socialism*, 16(1), 1–4.

Högselius, P. (2020). 'The historical dynamics of resource frontiers', NTM Zeitschrift für Geschichte der Wissenschaften, Technik und Medizin, 28, 253–266.

Hopkins, T. K., & Wallerstein, I. (1977). 'Patterns of development of the modern world-system', *Review (Fernand Braudel Center)*, 1(2), 111–145.

Igoe, J. & Brockington, D. (2007). 'Neoliberal conservation: A brief introduction', *Conservation & Society*, 5, 432–449.

Irarrázaval, F. (2020). 'Natural gas production networks: Resource making and interfirm dynamics in Peru and Bolivia', *Annals of the American Association of Geographers*, 111(2), 1–19.

Kalvelage, L., Revilla Diez, J., & Bollig, M. (2020) 'How much remains? Local value capture from tourism in Zambezi, Namibia', *Tourism Geographies*, 24(4–5), 759–780.

Karsenty, A. (2013). 'De la nature des "paiements pour services environnementaux"', *Revue du MAUSS*, 2(42), 261–270.

Kleibert, J. M., Hess, M., & Müller, F. C. (2020). 'Sites of contestation in global fur networks', *Geoforum*, 108, 39–48.

LeCain, T. (2017). *The Matter of History – How Things Create the Past* (Cambridge: Cambridge University Press).

Leacock, E. (1978). 'Women's Status in Egalitarian Society: Implications for Social Evolution', *Current Anthropology*, 19, 247–275.

Lubilo, R. & Hebinck, P. (2019). '"Local hunting" and community-based natural resource management in Namibia: Contestations and livelihoods', *Geoforum*, 101, 62–75.

McAfee, K. (1999). 'Selling nature to save it? Biodiversity and the rise of green developmentalism', *Environment and Planning D: Society and Space*, 17(2), 133–154.

McCarthy, J. & Prudham, S. (2004). 'Neoliberal nature and the nature of neoliberalism', *Geoforum*, 35, 275–283.

McGrath, S. (2018). 'Dis/articulations and the interrogation of development in GPN research', *Progress in Human Geography*, 42(4), 509–528.

Murphy, J. T. & Schindler, S. (2011). 'Globalizing development in Bolivia? Alternative networks and value-capture challenges in the wood products industry', *Journal of Economic Geography*, 11(1), 61–85.

Nel, A. (2017). 'Contested carbon: Carbon forestry as a speculatively virtual, falteringly material and disputed territorial assemblage', *Geoforum*, 81, 144–152.

Ojeda, D. (2012). 'Green pretexts: Ecotourism, neoliberal conservation and land grabbing in Tayrona National Natural Park, Colombia', *Journal of Peasant Studies*, 39, 357–375.

Prudham, S. (2009). 'Commodification', in: N. Castree, D. Demeritt, D. Liverman, & B. Rhoads (eds), *A Companion to Environmental Geography* (Malden MA: John Wiley & Sons), 123–142.

Rasmussen, M. B. & Lund, C. (2018) 'Reconfiguring frontier spaces: The territorialization of resource control', *World Development*, 101, 388–399.

Smessaert, J., Missemer, A., & Levrel, H. (2020). 'The Commodification of nature, a review in social sciences', *Ecological Economics*, 172, 106624.

Sullivan, S. (2006). 'Elephant in the room? Problematising 'new' (neoliberal) biodiversity conservation', *Forum for Development Studies*, 33(1), 105–135,

Sullivan, S. (2012a). 'Banking nature? The spectacular financialisation of environmental conservation', *Antipode*, 45(1), 198–217.

Sullivan, S. (2012b). 'Financialisation, biodiversity conservation and equity: Some currents and concerns', Environment and Development Series 16 (Penang: Third World Network). Available at: http://twn.my/title/end/pdf/end16.pdf [Accessed 11 February 2022].

Sullivan, S. & Homewood, K. (2004). 'Natural resources: Use, access, tenure and management', in: T. Bowyer-Bower & D. Potts (eds), *Eastern and Southern Africa* (London: Routledge), 118–166.

Tsing, A. (2003). 'Natural resources and capitalist frontiers', *Economic and Political Weekly*, 38(48), 5100–5106.

Tsing, A. (2005). *Friction: An Ethnography of Global Connection* (Princeton NJ: Princeton University Press).

Tsing, A. (2015a). *The Mushroom at the End of the World: On the Possibility of Life in Capitalist Ruins* (Princeton NJ: Princeton University Press).

Tsing, A. (2015b). 'Salvage accumulation, or the structural effects of capitalist generativity', *Cultural Anthropology*, March. Available at: https://culanth.org/fieldsights/salvage-accumulation-or-the-structural-effects-of-capitalist-generativity [Accessed February 2022].

Tsing, A. L., Deger, J., Keleman Saxena, A., & Zhou, F. (2020). *Feral Atlas: The More-than-human Anthropocene* (Redwood CA: Stanford University Press).

Turner, F. J. (1920). *The Frontier in American History* (New York: H. Holt and Company).

Yeung, H. W. C. (2021). 'The trouble with global production networks', *Environment and Planning A: Economy and Space*, 53(2), 428–438.

PART 2

THEORETICAL PERSPECTIVES

2

Fetishising the 'Wild': Conservation, commodities, and capitalism

CLEMENS GREINER AND MICHAEL BOLLIG

Our starting point: How can we understand the commodification of the 'wild'?

Recent scholarship highlights 'selling out on nature' as a hallmark of contemporary biodiversity conservation (McCauley 2006). Conservation, it is argued, is intimately linked with neoliberal capitalism (Büscher & Fletcher 2020; Igoe *et al.* 2010, Brooks *et al.* 2011). Neoliberal conservation (Fletcher 2020; Apostolopoulou *et al.* 2021) assumes that only the market-based valorisation of nature will motivate actors to conserve it in order to secure long-term profits. This commodification trend includes wildlife, wild products based on non-domesticated plants, animals, landscapes, or wilderness experiences: in short, entities or phenomena related to 'wilderness'.

In Western thought, wilderness is often understood as the opposite of civilisation. This understanding can be traced to the Industrial Revolution, when wilderness emerged as a site of 'civilisational longing' for the pristine, as a last resort and as source of physical health and moral value, distant from the misery of industrialised urban centres (Cronon 1996). Yet wildernesses, as many scholars argue, are hardly remnants of a pre-colonial past, ostensibly characterised by more sustainable lifestyles beyond the maelstrom of capitalism. Rather, the notion of wilderness is socially constructed (Cronon 1996; Callicott & Nelson 1998). Since the late 19th century, wildernesses have increasingly been perceived as survivals from pre-industrial times that need to be protected from the destructive forces of capitalist exploitation.

Since the 1960s, a growing and international environmental movement commented with alarm on such destruction (Bollig & Vehrs forthcoming). The International Union for the Conservation of Nature (IUCN) and the World Wildlife Fund (WWF), both founded in the mid-20th century, initially fostered imaginaries of wilderness as spaces that lay beyond capitalism's final frontier. Large-scale media campaigns and other efforts undertaken by these organisations helped to establish a common-sense understanding of wilderness as a higher good, a landscape valorised due to the absence of human impacts, worthy of protection at all costs, in much of the West and beyond. While by then conservation and business were organised in strictly separate, at times oppositional worlds, the boundaries between the two have since become blurred. As MacDonald (2010) and others have pointed out, IUCN and WWF have increasingly embraced market mechanisms and business-oriented approaches to conservation.

The ideological shift that has accompanied the progressive rise of neoliberalism since the 1980s was thus transferred to nature conservation. Strategies to conserve wilderness have shifted from protection *from* commodification to protection *through* commodification (Igoe & Brockington 2007). Associated new 'green' accumulation opportunities include the sinking of capital into ecosystem restoration and conservation (Clay 2019), the fixing of extraction through rewilding and refaunation (Enns *et al.* 2019), biodiversity offsetting (Neimark & Wilson 2015), and the creation of carbon sinks in the Global South (Bryant *et al.* 2015).

Contemporary wilderness is thus created by or at least deeply enmeshed with processes of commodification. In order to diagnose the status of the wild in the Anthropocene, then, we must deal with commodification in greater theoretical depth. In what follows, we explore whether Marx's analyses of labour, value, and commodity fetishism can be fruitfully adapted to explain (and possibly unmask) these dynamics. The remainder of our contribution proceeds as follows: we begin by laying out the theoretical basis for the commodification concept and its application to nature. Beginning with foundational Marxist analyses, we trace more recent attempts to reinvigorate the commodification concept and to operationalise it for research on contemporary social-ecological dynamics. In a further step, we dissect the notion of the 'wild' into three categories, ranging from wild plants and wildlife to more complex wilderness landscapes, which we then relate to Noel Castree's (2003) seminal discussion of the commodification of nature.

What is commodification and what are (wild) commodities?

Following Bernstein (2010: 102), we define commodification as 'the process through which the elements of production and social reproduction are produced for, and obtained from, market exchange and subjected to its disciplines and compulsions'. From a Marxist perspective, commodification is a process inherent and exclusive to capitalism, since only in capitalism is everything – including human labour – potentially commodifiable. According to Castree

(2003), capitalist commodification is closely linked to six different yet inter-connected processes, which can occur in different combinations: privatisation, alienability, individuation, abstraction, valuation, and displacement (which denotes fetishisation). We will return to these distinctions later in the chapter.

What, then, is a commodity? In the famous first section of *Das Kapital: Kritik der Politischen Ökonomie*, Marx (2002 [1872]) explains the nature of the commodity. In a nutshell, the argument goes as follows: commodities have exchange value as well as use value. While use value refers to the individual or social utility attributed to a good, exchange value refers to the ratio of value for which a commodity can be exchanged against another commodity. In any case, commodities are produced by human labour. What counts here is not individual labour (which is highly variable, such as according to skill and technology, and produces use value only), but what Marx describes as *gesells-chaftlich notwendige Arbeitszeit* (socially necessary labour time, ibid.: 53). This is abstract, average labour that makes commodities comparable and ultimately exchangeable on the market. In market exchange, the exchange value of a commodity becomes independent of its use value, and only in this context is the value of individually spent labour revealed fully. Commodities, therefore, appear to lead a life on the market, apparently independent of their producers.

Turning to natural commodities, such as wildlife products, it is important to understand that, according to Marx, nature itself does not produce exchange value, but only use value (Foster 1999). While nature is extraordinarily productive, it does not produce for a market. Only human labour turns natural products into commodities to be sold on a (socially constructed) market. For Marx, human labour and nature are inseparably interwoven in what is conceived of as the metabolism between humans and nature. According to some Marxist scholars (notably Smith 1984), nature is therefore socially produced.[1]

Many political ecologists have embraced this perspective to point out that 'wild' nature is obviously the result of social labour and political decisions (Robbins 2012). However, more recent approaches ranging from multispecies analyses to neo-materialist theorising have pointed to the high degree of self-organisation or resistance in the non-human world, pointing to the agency of nature (but see Hornborg 2016). Suffice it to say here that natural – or in our case wild – commodities display varying degrees of complexity, as they have undergone different degrees of capitalist subsumption (Smith 2007). They range from relatively simple, singular products – such as Devils Claw, Honey Bush, or resin from *Commiphora* trees that are merely extracted – to

---

[1] Note that this perspective is disputed by scholars who insist that Marx had a more dialectical understanding of nature and society (Napoletano *et al.* 2019; Saito 2016).

highly complex assemblages that we call wilderness landscapes, which are constituted by a multitude of different entities and agents ranging from wildlife to tourist infrastructure to tour operators seeking clients.

Wilderness as commodity: Scarcity, value, and labour

Wilderness, as scholars have pointed out, is a consequence of scarcity (Prudham, 2005). The scarcity of allegedly untouched, uncommodified, or 'pure' nature, aka wilderness, is thus a key marker of capitalist commodification of nature. It implies and reinforces an artificial division between 'ordinary' nature as a commodity and remnant nature 'reified and fetishized, abstracted from the circumstances of its own production' (Prudham 2005: 185).

This point is made forcefully by Garland (2008), who argues that the value of (African) wildlife hinges on the (colonially produced) image of a nature that remains outside human influence, but under constant threat by human interference. Brockington and Duffy (2010: 472) similarly argue that 'consumers thrive on scarcity, anxiety, fear (all help create demand), so perhaps the flourishing of capitalism in conservation, which deals in similar currency, should not be such a surprise'. Indeed, the maintenance of Red Lists for threatened and endangered species (Tomasini 2018), media reports on endangered African wildlife ('t Sas-Rolfes 2017), and the general threat of mass extinction (Ceballos *et al.* 2017) all underline contemporary perceptions of an endangered nature with quantifiable data, visuals, and causalities.

Scarcity is certainly a necessary feature of wilderness, but is neither unique to it nor sufficient to explain its value as a commodity. To understand the commodification of the wild, we must explain how narratives of uniqueness and scarcity – or how 'regimes of value', to adopt Appadurai's (1986: 15) phrase – are produced. Along these lines, we argue that notions of authenticity and 'exclusivity' are central to the conspicuous consumption of wilderness experiences and even wildlife products (Duffy 2016). Wilderness very often has its price, and the creation of exclusive markets for wilderness consumption, such as ecotourism, appears – at least at first blush – to be qualitatively different from what Moore (2017: 249) describes as Capital's rush for 'Cheap Natures', or the appropriation of new biophysical inputs to forestall the rising costs of (re)production. Rather, value is created both by scarcity and through labour directed at managing that scarcity. Thus, scarcity is sometimes actively created in ways that are analogous to the 'planned obsolescence' built into other kinds of consumer goods, i.e. goods becoming antiquated, out of fashion or even obsolete after defined periods of consumption. For example, this can be seen through various 'sumptuary laws' (see Appadurai 1986: 25), such as in the case of hunting rights that were exclusively reserved for elites in pre-industrial Europe (Simon 2017), or with contemporary trophy hunters who pay US$50,000 or more to bag a single elephant (Kalvelage *et al.* 2020; Kalvelage this volume; Hewitson & Sullivan 2021). In Bourdieu's sense (1984), the exclusive consumption of the wild serves as a means for constituting distinction among global elites who inhabit an increasingly unequal world.

The value of wilderness thus cannot be accounted for according to a labour theory of value alone, as Marx might have it, but is also constituted through *scarcity* in a more neo-classical sense, even if such scarcity is merely perceived subjectively, construed through social discourses, or instituted by means of sumptuary laws. Appadurai (1986) similarly identifies this dimension of value in Georg Simmel's (2004 [1907]) *Philosophy of Money*, in which he argues that value is not intrinsic to objects, but is rather a subjective ascription. Scarcity, as Simmel notes, results from an object eluding our urge to possess it, since '[w]e desire objects only if they are not immediately given to us for our use and enjoyment; that is to the extent that they resist our desire' (Simmel 2004 [1907]: 66). Perhaps it is not only the tendency for the rate of profit to fall that pushes capitalism to ever more distant frontiers of the globe, but also the need for exclusive, conspicuous consumption (Veblen 2009 [1899])?

The inclusion of consumption as an act of decommodification certainly offers intriguing lines of thought (Bakker 2005; Sayer 2003). Büscher and Igoe (2013), for example, argue that neoliberal conservation increasingly builds on 'prosumption'. This neologism hints at the blurring of boundaries between production and consumption in late capitalism, as consumers co-create value together with producers. In the prosumption of protected areas, unpleasant and harmful aspects of conservation are often concealed, and 'prosumers engage in new forms of entertainment and self-making that are putatively connected to solving the very kinds of problems they seek to escape through their prosumption' (Büscher & Igoe 2013: 302).

In the following section, we trace the commodification process following Castree's (2003) classification. We discuss privatisation, alienability, and individuation, before turning to abstraction and valuation, as necessary and at times overlapping steps towards commodification. After briefly introducing each step, we illustrate them with examples of wild flora, fauna, and wilderness landscapes. Finally, we consider fetishisation, thereby dwelling on and expanding what Castree offered as displacement.

Privatisation

Castree sees privatisation as the initial step of commodification, suggesting that privatisation involves the 'assignation of legal title to a named individual, group or institution' (Castree 2003: 279). Based on such title, others are excluded from disposing of the property object designated in the title. Privatisation always comes with the proviso that something that has been accessible for all or for defined groups is subsequently owned, managed, and exchanged by a more narrowly defined group of actors. Commodification processes targeting non-domesticated, 'wild' resources often have very different characteristics in respect of privatisation. In fact, many objects stubbornly seem to resist privatisation, which is ambiguous and shrouded in intense negotiations. This implies that constant efforts are needed to come to grips with these resilient and self-organised commodities-in-the-making.

Privatisation in the commodification of 'wild' plants

Let us start with the example of the commodification of Devil's Claw in north-eastern Namibia (see Lavelle this volume). There is no individual and no group that can claim ownership of Devil's Claw as long as it remains in the ground, so anybody can harvest the tuber. Yet harvesters cannot just go anywhere they wish, as they must remain in the territory of the traditional authority with whom they are associated. Nowadays, the right to declare a moratorium on harvesting may be issued by a traditional authority as well as by a conservancy committee, while ownership remains formally vested in the state, as Lavelle explains. However, once Devil's Claw has been harvested, the person who dug it from the ground effectively privatises the tuber through expenditure of labour. Thus, human labour renders an otherwise publicly accessible resource into a commodity that can then be freely traded and exchanged. The same arrangements hold for numerous other resources discussed in this volume, such as the 'bird' plum (*Berchemia discolour*) harvested elsewhere in Namibia (see Nghitevelekwa *et al.* this volume) or the gum arabic in northern Nigeria (Vehrs & Waziri this volume).

There are, however, increasing attempts to privatise what are otherwise openly accessible natural resources. These attempts may involve the plants themselves, but also increasingly their genetic information. The latter is a more complex process involving numerous agencies and widespread public debates, as in the case of *Hoodia parviflora*. Whereas San communities in southern Africa had long used this plant to suppress hunger, major pharmaceutical companies more recently 'discovered' the plant's properties as a possible remedy for obesity. Wynberg (this volume) traces legislation on this issue in

South Africa, which stipulates that once a genetic code is commercially used, benefits must also be distributed to the 'owners' of the knowledge that led to the discovery of the plant's medicinal value. However, this move entails a shift in the status of traditional ecological knowledge from the status of 'common heritage of humankind' to a privatised status attributable to a country or a social group.

Privatisation in the commodification of wildlife

More than wild plants, wild animals have often been more thoroughly privatised, and poaching, i.e. the illegal appropriation of transfer rights, has often been considered a serious crime in many parts of the world. For example, private rights to wildlife dwelling on commercial farmlands were granted to freehold farmers in the 1960s, both in South Africa and in Namibia (Bollig 2020). Today, many game farms trade wildlife, and the privatisation of game animals has contributed positively to their numbers, as Carruthers (2008) argues for South Africa.

Privatisation of wildlife dwelling within communal areas is more difficult. Here the state continues to hold ownership rights to wildlife. Where communities are organised in conservancies like in Namibia, or in game management units like in Zimbabwe, the ministry in charge of wildlife management may allot communities rights or quotas to some animals. The conservancy can exchange such wildlife entitlements with trophy hunters, who often pay high prices to hunt on unfenced stretches of land. In such cases, property rights are assigned by the original owner (the state). The quota is the way a conservancy can claim property rights to wildlife: it cannot attain such rights directly but has to trade in such property rights from the state by establishing specific community-based land-management formats.

Hewitson & Sullivan (this volume) show in great detail the amount of social labour necessary to reach at a quota: careful on-the-ground monitoring, bookkeeping, reporting, comparing different and at times diverging datasets, mapping animal mobility, and negotiating between stakeholders. In their analysis of elephant trophy hunting in north-eastern Namibia, they show how reaching an understanding about sustainable harvesting requires profound institutional infrastructure and sizeable technology input. Nevertheless, the process of defining sustainable-hunting quotas is controversial and accompanied by intense conflict. Animal protectionists as well as conservationists argue that there should be no such quotas, while local stakeholders, for example, argue for higher quotas on elephants, as their gardens are increasingly endangered by growing herds.

Privatisation of wilderness landscapes

Space can be excised from the commons, or from open-access resources, and declared private property on the basis of specific legal frameworks. The privatisation of land involves a great deal of labour input: political decisions on conditions of privatisation, surveying technology, and data management, as with governmental cadastres. In northern Namibia, for example, where arid landscapes are often portrayed as archaic and prototypically wild, the privatisation of land in communal areas has historically been inhibited by colonial legislation. To date, it remains difficult (in fact impossible) to obtain freehold land titles there. However, recent legislation has created space for hybrids. Long-term leaseholds legally defined by Namibia's Communal Land Reform Act of 2002 provide leaseholders with a number of rights that are otherwise typical for landowners. Leasehold applications undergo a process of intense scrutiny by a land board and traditional authorities before they are formalised. And still, the outcomes are often hotly debated and also legally contested.

The excision of protected areas (such as national parks, core conservation areas, or wildlife corridors) from communal lands in southern and eastern Africa proceeds according to another process of privatisation. Vast tracts of land were assigned for wilderness protection, as true wilderness areas, whereas the majority of protected area lands were targeted for use by tourists, while the state was to earn revenue through entrance fees and state-owned lodges within parks (Brockington 2002). Efforts by conservancies, trusts, and community game management areas to define core wilderness areas in the commons can be regarded as an effort to extend this process. Sometimes, this leads to the expropriation or exclusion of people, a process reminiscent of what Marx described as primitive accumulation (Kelly 2011; Sullivan 2013), i.e., the privatisation of land as a means of production by expropriating its previous users (and eventually creating a class of landless proletariat). This process is thus intensely conflictual and leads to a number of drawn-out cases negotiated by local traditional courts as well as formal legal courts (Harring & Odendaal 2012).

Alienability and individuation

Alienability and individuation are more complex characteristics of commodification. Castree (2003) presents them as closely related, whereby alienability refers to the 'capacity of a given commodity ... to be physically and morally separated from their sellers' (2003: 279f). Privatisation does not automatically result in the alienability and individuation of a resource. Castree defines individuation as 'the representational and physical act of separating a specific thing or entity from its supporting context. This involves putting legal and material boundaries around phenomena so that they can be bought, sold and used by equally 'bounded' individuals, groups or institutions' (Castree 2003: 280).[2] Hence, while alienability is a quality of the prospective commodity itself, individuation is a human practice of putting legal and material boundaries around living things so that they can be exchanged.

Alienability and individuation in the commodification of 'wild' plants

At first sight, alienability and individuation in the process of commodifying plants seem to be easy tasks. Plants or plant parts can be dug up (tubers) or collected (resin, fruits, nuts) – processes that always involve considerable time and labour. Let us consider Devil's Claw tubers, which expand rhizomatically underground (Lavelle this volume). Harvesters are discouraged by NGO staff active in sustainable resource management from harvesting the entire plant in order to guarantee plant rejuvenation and future harvests. Thus, plant parts rather than whole plants may be individuated. Similarly, the individuation process for Honey Bush (Ndwandwe, this volume) and *Commiphora* resin (Nghitevelekwa this volume) entails specifying what plant parts, and what quantities of those parts, ought to be harvested. Considerable labour is involved to outline conditions for individuation by scientists and administrative staff working for environmental NGOs and government offices.

The problem of alienability specifically holds true for trees. The much sought-after rosewood tree may serve as an example. Rosewood (*Pterocarpus tinctorius*) is of immense value on Eastern Asian markets. A recent study claims that in Namibia, nearly 60,000 trees were felled in the years leading to 2019, most of them illegally.[3] Consequently, the Ministry of Environment declared the illegality of rosewood logging. While the loss of the rare tree is clearly lamentable, the greater problem comes with the fact that a number of other trees and plants are destroyed in the process of harvesting each tree. Cerutti (2020) reports on the ruinous results of intense rosewood logging for Zambia. Even if conditions for sustainable harvest are specified, trees growing in a natural environment are hardly alienable without causing damage to the wider forest as their supporting context.

---

[2] Note that commodification can also occur without physical or representational individuation. While labour power cannot be physically separated from the body of a labouring person, the *products* of that labour are alienated and individuated. Nonetheless, labour power remains commodified. We thank Jonathan DeVore for this and other astute observations on this contribution (see also DeVore 2017).

[3] *The Namibian Sun*, 'Rosewood harvesting unsustainable. Hardwood trees should be left alone', 12 July 2019.

Alienability and individuation in the commodification of wildlife

On game farms, the alienability and individuation of wildlife are not difficult to accomplish, as a game farmer may easily offer wildlife to trophy hunters. At least with respect to most animals on offer as trophies, the alienability of a trophy animal at first sight does not impact other animals (unlike e.g., the rosewood trees mentioned above). Recent reports about elephant behaviour, however, complicate this picture regarding the alienability of trophy elephants (see Hewitson & Sullivan this volume). When an elephant is shot, the remaining herd mourns the dead elephant for some time. The death of a senior male, in particular, may lead to grave consequences for the sociality of the herd, often resulting in intense conflicts among younger males.

There are also further restrictions regarding the alienability and individuation of wildlife. Wildlife may be shot by a trophy hunter, but there might be severe restrictions on the export of the trophy or its meat. For example, while there is little concern regarding the production and export of biltong from the meat of gazelles or antelopes, the use of lion bones is highly controversial. With so many lions in captivity, many breeders have simply resorted to killing them for the escalating lion-bone trade. Euthanising captive-bred lions for their bones is legal in South Africa with a permit, and the sale of lion bones to Asia for use in traditional medicines has become an important and even lucrative side business for South African lion farmers. However, animal rights proponents allege that this industry poses a serious threat to wild lion populations (Schroeder 2018). Ivory is another example in that direction. While some countries may allow import and export of ivory, other countries do not. Namibia's fight to move their resident herd of elephants from the Convention on International Trade in Endangered Species (CITES) Appendix I to Appendix II (Hewitson & Sullivan this volume), which would allow restricted trade in ivory, is a case in point. This suggests that the individuation of wildlife may often be particularly difficult to achieve due to legal restrictions.

Alienability and individuation in the commodification of wilderness landscapes

Landscapes are not as easily alienated. In the contexts with which we are concerned, the moral and physical separation of a landscape from its seller is difficult to achieve. Only derivates, such as images or postcards, can be alienated, as Büscher and Fletcher (2016) observe. Yet there are ways to legally individuate landscapes by means of easements, i.e. in the form of non-possessory and limited use rights to land or property. In conservation easements, as Kay (2015: 504) explains, landowners agree to sell parts of their property rights in land, e.g. the right to extract a resource from it, while retaining private ownership. In a similar way, a local community constituted as a legal body framed as 'conservancy', may lease a wilderness area to a tour operator or to a prospective lodge owner through a public-private partnership (see Mosimane *et al.* this volume). This requires immense labour, such as by politicians, lawyers, and administrators. Agreement must also be reached on the exact spatial ramifications of wilderness, its boundaries, and where human settlement is permitted.

Landscapes can also be individuated through discursive labour. Bollig & Vehrs (2021), for example, show how the wetlands of the Kwando Basin, which is situated in Namibia's part of the Kavango-Zambezi Transfrontier Conservation Area, are represented as authentic wilderness landscape. The individuation landscape entails the muting and erasure of past human impacts on the landscape and the elevation of its 'wild' part. Alienability here thus rests as a property in the landscape, but results from a semiotic individuation: a landscape is only alienable as a wilderness area once it has been emptied of human pasts. When the wilderness status of the area is established, it can then be commodified by tour operators and by installing lodges. Scholars have provided rich and detailed narratives of the process of individuation, including the representational act of separating out 'wilderness' landscapes from those adjoining landscapes that remain under human use (Brockington 2002; Neumann 1998).

Abstraction

Abstraction is an essential step in the process of commodification, defined as a 'process whereby the qualitative specificity of any individualized thing is ... assimilated to the qualitative homogeneity of a broader type or process' (Castree 2003: 281). Only when commodities are made commensurable can one item of a commodity category be replaced by another thing of that category. Abstraction is thus a necessary precondition in assigning economic value to 'ecosystem services', such as carbon credits, and allow immaterial nature to circulate as capital (Robertson 2012). Yet it is also important to recall Appadurai's (1986) distinction between homogeneous versus singular classes of commodities. Not all commodification requires homogenisation, though. Rather, culturally mediated uniqueness and singularity, such as in the case of artwork, can contribute to ascriptions of something's value. This observation is relevant to understanding the production and marketing of wilderness, as scarcity, authenticity, and uniqueness may constitute part of the value of wilderness experiences (Vidon 2019).

According to Castree (2003: 281), abstraction involves two processes. Functional abstraction implies 'severing the characteristic being measured from the messy uniqueness of the physical site', which involves the identification of 'classifiable similarities between otherwise distinct entities'. This is followed by spatial abstraction, which implies that everything is replaceable by another thing of that category. Abstraction requires ordering and standardisation. A number of agencies contribute to this process, which in many ways is a scientific one involving botany, agricultural, or wildlife sciences. The international division of labour involved in this is highly uneven (Neimark & Wilson 2015).

Abstraction in the commodification of 'wild' plants

When commodifying non-domesticated plants, functional abstraction is a pertinent challenge. Bollig (2020: 305–306) describes how the resin of *Commiphora wildii* became a commodity harvested by local women in north-western Namibia and marketed through an NGO. The resin had been used by local Himba women as an ingredient for perfumes. Since 2004 the NGO Integrated Rural Development and Nature Conservation (IRDNC) explored how Himba people used *Commiphora wildii* (*omumbiri*) with the intention of exploiting such plants commercially. The NGO gazetted a number of prestudies that ascertained that the harvest of the resin was sustainable and that about 50 tons of resin are produced naturally every year in the five conservancies where this investigation was conducted. This step required abstraction: of course, resin from *Commiphora wildii* in different places, resin of different quality and resin harvested and stored in different ways was finely differentiated by locals and also by those conducting the studies. In order to form a commodity, however, it was necessary to homogenise the product and stipulate that any resin from the tree gathered and stored in a particular quality-ensuring manner was acceptable. IRDNC negotiated an access and benefit-sharing contract (ABS, see Wynberg this volume) between the five *Commiphora* resin-producing conservancies and established a company that agrees to annually buy a guaranteed amount of the resin. Therefore, the company defines quality requirements and gives advice on how to collect and how to store the resin. The resin is brought by individual buyers to collection points where it is packaged, stored intermittently and then transported to an oil refinery run in the region's capital Opuwo by the NGO. In its first steps along the commodity chain the resin from individual places and individual gatherers becomes more and more a homogenised commodity.

Spatial abstraction proceeds further along the value chain. Lavelle (this volume) describes how dried Devil's Claw tubers from several north-eastern Namibian sites are mixed together (just like the resin mentioned before), and tubers from the region may be mixed with tubers from north-western or eastern Namibia. The dried tubers are treated further and packaged, and the moment they leave Namibia, the characteristics of single tubers, including their specific harvesting sites in Namibia, are no longer traceable.

Abstraction in the commodification of wildlife

Functional and spatial abstraction are also significant in the commodification of wildlife. When a conservancy includes wildlife on a quota list, both kinds of abstraction processes have already been concluded. Hewitson & Sullivan (this volume) describe how the process of abstraction occurs with trophy animals in north-eastern Namibia. First, the definition of a quota elephant involves a long process of monitoring, negotiating, and decision making. The standard quota elephant is first defined abstractly (old male over the age of 30) and then related to the resident herd (how many animals of that type are around). When a trophy hunter wants to shoot a trophy elephant, they are typically guided to a specific animal, which has been previously targeted by guides and community game rangers. Photography taken from the hunt signals such abstraction. Photographs of the hunter, their hunting guides, and the hunted animals are strikingly standardised. The hunting experience, however, is represented as a unique act. Another point that supports the notion of abstraction is the frequent translocation of large mammals into specific conservation areas. Hausmann *et al.* (2017) found that many tourists are not able to identify (and are not necessarily interested in identifying) the species' natural habitat. Rather, they prefer accessible locations and 'were particularly interested in spotting charismatic species in open habitats (e.g. the succulent-karoo biome), where these species are not naturally distributed' (ibid.: 98).

Abstraction in the commodification of wilderness landscapes

The making of commoditised units of 'wilderness landscapes' for the tourist industry involves functional abstraction by necessitating borders that define where wilderness begins and where it ends. Such boundary-making, read as functional abstraction, involves labour, including the intellectual labour of conservationists who define what areas should be included and excluded, the work of local politicians and administrative staff who institute boundaries, and, finally, the work of labourers who build fences and otherwise materialise functional abstraction. Spatial abstraction also matters. Although the tourism industry frequently seeks to convey the idea to consumers that such landscapes are unique, tourism practice suggests that they are not at all unique. For example, a number of nature conservancies line the Namibian side of the Kwando River. All of them devote space to tourist lodges, and there are currently about fourteen such establishments along a nearly seventy-kilometre stretch of the river. The wilderness experience in these places displays striking similarities. All have wide open verandas that open westward towards the river, where one can readily imagine sundowner cocktails sipped on these verandas while overlooking vistas teeming with wildlife as the sun sets. More broadly, this kind of spatial abstraction suggests that – as a commodity – savannah landscapes are interchangeable to some extent, despite each being marketed as unique. Igoe (2013: 38) takes the abstraction of landscapes a step further by arguing that the abstraction of nature into spectacle, such as movies and images for advertising, can 'move consumers to buy products, take vacations, and to give money to worthy conservation causes'.

Valuation

Valuation may change in relation to use value, functional value, and existence value (from Leopold 1925 to Chardonnet *et al.* 2002) and may have various economic, aesthetic, and moral components. Capitalist commodification, however, permeates and alters all other forms of valuation. Expressions of value are typically communicated through the medium of money, and the pursuit of profit is the ultimate driver of valuation (Castree 2003).

To suit these profitability requirements, some 'wild' entities, however, have to be modified for easier access or higher productivity (Castree 2003). This process of optimising nature bears similarities to what Marx has described as formal and real subsumption. Marx distinguishes between formal and real subsumption to develop his argument about the creation of surplus value, but also to mark the historical transition in which surplus value is created through improving productivity rather than by extending the working day (Boyd *et al.* 2001). While formal subsumption denotes the inclusion of an already existing labour process (or, in our case, of a natural resource) into the capitalist economy, real subsumption refers to the active transformation of the labour process itself in order to gain more profit. Real subsumption of nature, in turn, marks a process where enterprises 'are able to take hold of and transform natural production, and use this as a source of productivity increase' (ibid.: 556).

Valuation in the commodification of 'wild' plants

The example of sandalwood may serve to describe different aspects of valuation. East Indian Sandalwood (*Santalum album*) is counted among the most expensive and sought-after timber products in the world (Arun Kumar *et al.* 2012). Its essential oil is highly valued for its scent in the cosmetics industry, and the wood is sacred to Hinduism as it is burnt in religious ceremonies. Today, supplies of sandalwood have fallen short of global demand, as the tree is close to extinction. Shortages and escalating prices have led to different reactions, which can be understood as exemplifying formal and real subsumption. The search for natural ('wild') substitutes and functional equivalents denotes formal subsumption, where 'capital is forced to work around nature' (Boyd *et al.* 2001: 563). This notably concerns African Sandalwood (*Osyris lanceolata*). In Kenya, the African Sandalwood tree has been under the protection of a presidential ban since 2007, but the tree remains overexploited through illegal logging, mainly for export to Asia (Kioko, this volume). Real subsumption takes place in two different forms. For one, firms mainly based in Australia have invested in attempts to domesticate Sandalwood by growing it on plantations (Keenan & Parija 2017). Furthermore, biotech companies reproduce relevant sandalwood compounds in labs, for example, by infusing its DNA into yeast cultures (Luedi 2017). In both cases, 'capital circulates *through* nature' in order to systematically improve its productivity (Boyd *et al.* 2001: 565, emphasis in original).

The valuation of wildlife

According to capitalist logic, the value attributed to a commodity is determined by its ability to provide returns on investment. Against this background, it is understandable that spectacular megafauna, such as the 'big five', are prime tourist attractions that feature prominently in public culture and media aimed at promoting pro-conservation behaviour (Skibins *et al.* 2013). This focus often comes at the expense of areas of equally high conservation value, but which lack such flagship animals (Hausmann *et al.* 2017). Lions certainly represent such a flagship animal, and are taken to epitomise 'African' wilderness. Consequently, lions feature prominently in southern African hunting value chains as well as in photo tourism, and it has become apparent that local communities must benefit from the protection of lions and other forms of wildlife (Dickman *et al.* 2018). To make more out of the lion, however, the tourism and safari industry has gone a step further. Today, lions are bred in captivity for trade. Schroeder (2018) even reports on farmers' attempts to breed lions with larger manes, or lighter in colour, in order to secure higher prices from trophy hunters. Such lions bred in captivity are used in a form of trophy hunting known as 'canned hunting', which allows wealthy hunters from overseas to be offered easy prey in the form of lions bred solely for the purpose of being hunted and killed. With canned hunting, these typically captive-bred lions are fenced into areas with no chance of escape. Today, there are an estimated 8,000 to 12,000 captive lions in South Africa bred on over 300 farms, which far exceeds the estimated 3,000 wild lions that live in South Africa's nature reserves and national parks (Four Paws in US 2021). The international outcry over such breeding and hunting practices underlines that transitions from 'the wild' to 'the domesticated' are highly contested and full of normative debates.

The valuation of wilderness landscapes

'This is how Africa *should* look!' is the opening quote in Neumann's *Imposing Wilderness* (Neumann 1998: 1). The quote is from Neumann's travel companion, a British ecologist living abroad, who is describing the scenery that opens up to him inside a renowned Tanzanian national park, 'leaving behind the Maasai curios shops, the herds of scrawny cattle, and the desiccated maize fields' (ibid.). This vignette tellingly points to the fact that there are human decisions (and, in fact, human labour) involved in creating 'true wilderness', in making the Serengeti and other national parks look as they *should*. It is above all these colonially influenced postcard views of African nature that generate value, as Garland (2008) notes. She suggests that wildlife conservation in Africa, and thus the creation of parks and conservancies, is 'foremost a productive process, a means of appropriating the value of African nature, and of transforming it into capital with the capacity to circulate and generate further value at the global level' (Garland 2008: 52). Indeed, high hopes are pinned on the economic benefits of wildlife tourism and trophy hunting in open savannah landscapes. However, it remains unclear how much of the actual value generated remains within such regions. Kalvelage *et al.* (2020) suggest that, for the case of the Zambezi in Namibia, only about 20% of revenues remain in the local economy. Whether or not this is a fair share can certainly be questioned.

Discussion: Displacement, or the (double) fetishism of wilderness

We have come to understand that privatisation, individuation, alienability, abstraction, and valuation are closely interlinked processes in the commodification of wild plants, animals, and wilderness landscapes. In fact, these interlinked commodification processes are sometimes difficult to separate analytically. What they all have in common, however, is that the social processes involved in each step is usually rendered invisible or faded out of view when wilderness is talked about by those presenting it on a market and those consuming it as tourists. Castree (2003) describes this as displacement. Displacement, he writes, 'is about something appearing, phenomenally, as something other than itself' (ibid.: 282). In the following, we relate displacement to Marx's notion of commodity fetishism. We hold that fetishisation runs throughout all the aforementioned processes, from privatisation to valuation, and is a constant component of the commodification of 'wilderness'. We therefore do not dissect this complex into plants, animals, and landscapes, but rather use it to advance the discussion of the processes of concealment presented here.

Marx developed the fetish character of the commodity against the background of religious fetishism (Marx 2002 [1872]: 83f). Just as a religious fetish, such as a totem, for example, a fetish is said to have divine powers (which, according to Marx's logic, are merely attributed to what is, in fact, an inanimate thing), commodities also seem to have properties that they do not possess. In this way, Marx superficially refers to the fact that the exchange of commodities on the market, against the universal equivalent of money, obscures the social relations deeply involved in the production of these commodities. Consequently, people begin to treat commodities as if value actually inheres in them. The disclosure of social relations that enter into the production of commodities is precisely what Harvey (1990: 423) points to in writing that '[w]e have to penetrate the veil of fetishisms with which we are necessarily surrounded by virtue of the system of commodity production and exchange and discover what lies behind it'. However, the reading that commodity fetishism is merely 'false consciousness', or involves a claim that humans do not recognise social relations of production involved in producing commodities, is dismissed by some scholars as a truncated interpretation (Heinrich 2005; Iorio 2012).[4] Yet it is precisely this reading that can be more broadly adapted to the constructivist perspective of wilderness, as something produced by humans. For lack of a better word, we call this approach 'deep fetishisation', a phrase to which we will return below.

For Marx, as we have seen, market exchange takes on a peculiar – and particularly coercive – form in capitalism, and entails the abstraction of human labour. The notion of commodity fetishism thus refers to the fact that, in market exchange under capitalism, what are otherwise diverse forms of human labour are equated in the commodity form of mere 'labour-power', the value of which is only revealed in exchange on the labour market. According to Marx, value is always based on the expropriation of human labour, or, more precisely, on the abstraction of 'socially necessary labour time'. Undomesticated 'wilderness' products or wilderness landscapes, however, only partly mature into commodities through human labour. They exemplify what Marx describes

---

[4] Marx, above all, uses the concept of the commodity fetish to refer to the fact that the value of the product of labour is only revealed in the commodity form and in exchange – independently of its material form and use value (Marx, 2002 [1872]: 87). The formation of value is thus subject to the discipline of abstract powers invoked by Adam Smith in his famous description of the market's 'invisible hand' (Harvey 2011). Marx argues that bourgeois economics has not understood the 'sociality' of market relations, but has wrongly assumed that people act consciously and calculatingly in the market (as exemplified in Adam Smith's butcher, brewer, or baker).

as '*Gratisnaturkraft*' (Saito 2016: 150), i.e., the generative activities of nature which are provided without human intervention. As Barua (2017) reminds us, such non-human forces are closely intertwined with encounter value and spectacular accumulation on the conservation frontier. Can we thus apply Marx's understanding of commodity fetishism? If 'wilderness' is not – or is only partially – created by human labour, can it be understood as a commodity at all? For Polanyi (2001 [1944]), after all, nature (or land as a proxy for nature) is not a real but only a fictitious commodity. Here we follow Castree (2003: 277), who writes that what matters is not what a commodity is, but rather what properties things take on in commodification processes.

The key, we argue, rests in the process of wilderness commodification: 'wilderness', as we have demonstrated, is produced. It is produced, for example, through the work of abstraction (Prudham 2009), which includes, among other things, standardisation, systematic representation, 'making legible' through expertise, and, above all, the (never complete) overcoming of considerable moral concerns regarding and resistance to commodification – in the sense of Polanyi's 'double movement'. The production of wilderness also involves highly unequal labour relations among (African) workers who fence, clean, maintain, and protect wilderness objects and areas (Garland 2008). It thus seems that the relatively high exchange value that can be realised from 'wild' commodities in Africa is also linked to the depressed prices paid for African labour in colonial and post-colonial contexts. The profound inequalities of labour relations involved in the process of producing or marketing wilderness are concealed. In our view, this aligns closely with a concise reading of Marx's idea of a commodity fetish. In a broader sense, this also involves what Igoe *et al.* (2010: 493) call the spectacular productions of conservation organisa-tions, which masks 'the inequities and conflicts associated with particular conservation interventions, as well as the costs of global consumerism and the social and environmental contradictions it entails'.

There is, however, also a process of 'deep fetishisation' at work, especially when dealing with notions of wilderness, which approximates what Kopytoff (1986: 83) describes as 'the missing non-economic side of what Marx called commodity fetishization'. Like the objects discussed by Kopytoff, wilderness is sacralised and singularised at the same time as it is commodified. This (Western) notion of wilderness is profoundly enshrined in the Cartesian nature-society dualisms of (popular) Western cultures. It relates to our differentiated understanding of nature and culture. Like precious pieces of art, wilderness is conserved in special places, and national parks indeed bear similarities to the 'public institutions of singularization' described by Kopytoff (1986: 81). In this way wilderness is constituted and branded as something rare, and in many cases also as a scarce good.[5] Conversely, this means that the fetishisation of 'wilderness' ultimately results in a devaluation of the 'ordinary' nature, the one 'that continually surrounds us in our homes and communities' (Petersen & Hultgren 2020: 6). This is why scholars and activists alike increasingly advocate the concept of 'convivial conservation' in a 'post-wild' world (Büscher & Fletcher 2020; Marris 2013).

Against this background, we might therefore also ask if the very notion of wilderness does not involve a 'double fetish'. The notion of the double fetish has been explored in moral economies of organic food and fair-trade consumption (Cook & Crang 1996; Goodman 2004). The concept suggests a fetishisation that obscures the socio-economic and ecological relations of production, which simultaneously inscribes highly aestheticised 'cultural and economic surpluses for consumers' (Hughes 2000: 179). In the case of wilderness, a double fetish conceals relations of production (as with any other commodity produced for the capitalist market), but the 'deep fetishisation' of wilderness – at least in the constructivist version – makes wilderness appear as something spectacularly different from 'ordinary' nature. Deep fetishisation suggests that there is a difference between high-value nature (wilderness) and zones of abjection (e.g., for waste disposal). To understand nature-cultures in the Anthropocene, and to plan for biodiversity conservation in the 21st century, both fetishes must be unmasked.

Conclusion

The 'wilderness' of national parks, as Robbins (2012) notes, is a product of numerous regulations and interventions, some of them directly aiming at commodification. The parallels between, for example, Yellowstone National Park in the USA and Arusha National Park in Tanzania are striking, both of which involved histories of being first successfully marketed as 'natural wonders' and then experiencing the excision of 'native' populations from the terrain. What today is conceived of as 'wilderness', whether plants, animals, or landscapes, as we have demonstrated, is often the product of extensive commodification processes. Put differently, conservation aimed at wilderness or wildlife already presupposes that the object of protection is embedded within a capitalist system, and value from it is not only extracted

---

[5] It seems to us a worthwhile task to analyse when and at what times and under what conditions wilderness in Kopytoff's sense moves within and outside the commodity status, and what consequences this has for the perception of and dealings with 'ordinary' nature in the corresponding periods. See also Malm's (2018) contribution on subaltern wilderness practices.

by (concealed) humans, but also by scarcity (which again, of course, is also to some extent produced by labour).

Our analysis thus suggests that 'wilderness' is a social attribution, rather than the property of a plant, an animal, or a landscape. In this sense, one might argue that Devil's Claw is not much 'wilder' than, say, a sugar snap pea. What makes the Devil's Claw 'wild' is the fact that it is not domesticated,[6] and that it is subject to a double fetishisation. When we buy sugar snap peas in the supermarket, we are usually unaware of the farmers who produced it in, say, Kenya. We do not think about mechanisms of price formation on the market, and we have no clue how the harvester, farmer, or plantation worker makes ends meet. The same holds true for Devil's Claw, as the toils of collection are well hidden. Additionally, however, we are made to believe that the dried tubers are a special remedy, because it can only be found in the allegedly pristine, almost sacred, wilderness of the Kalahari Desert.

When Cronon (1996) published his seminal essay, 'The Trouble with Wilderness', suggesting that the notion of wilderness is a merely historically contingent social construction, he was criticised by numerous observers who accused him of 'undermining progress in environmentalism' (Petersen & Hultgren 2020; Robbins 2012: 130). We suggest that such criticism is misplaced, as it does not touch the root of the problem, namely the profound commodification of nature. Resistance to complete commodification can be simultaneously moral (in the sense of Polanyi's double movement), physical (in the sense of nature's 'agency'), or even figurative (in the sense of Simmel's argument about value as resisting desire).

Moving forward, we suggest that an overemphasis on 'pristine' wilderness misses the target of the much needed push towards convivial conservation that is adequate to face climate change, biodiversity loss, and growing inequality. Indeed, we need to recognise, value, reclaim, and even create 'wilderness' within our domesticated environments. Our environmental concerns should thus go well beyond charismatic wildlife and 'pristine' landscapes.

Bibliography

Apostolopoulou, E., Chatzimentor, A., Maestre-Andrés, S., Requena-i-Mora, M., Pizarro, A., & Bormpoudakis, D. (2021). 'Reviewing 15 years of research on neoliberal conservation: Towards a decolonial, interdisciplinary, intersectional and community-engaged research agenda', *Geoforum*, 124, 236–256.

Appadurai, A. (1986). 'Introduction: Commodities and the politics of value', in: A. Appadurai (ed.), *The Social Life of Things. Commodities in Cultural Perspective* (Cambridge: Cambridge University Press), 3–63.

---

[6] For a critical perspective on the notion of domestication see Tsing (2018).

Arun Kumar, A. N., Joshi, G., & Mohan Ram, H. Y. (2012). 'Sandalwood: History, uses, present status and the future', *Current Science*, 103(12), 1408–1416.

Bakker, K. (2005). 'Neoliberalizing nature? Market environmentalism in water supply in England and Wales', *Annals of the Association of American Geographers*, 95(3), 542–565.

Barua, M. (2017). 'Nonhuman labour, encounter value, spectacular accumulation: the geographies of a lively commodity', *Transactions of the Institute of British Geographers*, 42, 274–288.

Bernstein, H. (2010). *Class Dynamics of Agrarian Change* (Halifax: Fernwood Publishers).

Bollig, M. (2020). *Shaping the African savannah: From capitalist frontier to arid Eden in Namibia* (Cambridge: Cambridge University Press).

Bollig, M. & Vehrs, H.-P. (2021). 'The making of a conservation landscape: The emergence of a conservationist environmental infrastructure along the Kwando River in Namibia's Zambezi Region', *Africa*, 91(2), 1–26.

Bollig, M. & Vehrs, H.-P. (forthcoming). 'Africa, the conservation continent: Future-making and the globalisation of wildlife protection', in: D. Müller-Mahn & M. Bollig (eds), *Future Rural Africa* (Woodbridge: James Currey).

Bourdieu, Pierre (1984). *Distinction: A Social Critique of the Judgement of Taste* (Cambridge MA: Harvard University Press).

Boyd, W., Prudham, S. & Schurman, R. A. (2001). 'Industrial dynamics and the problem of nature', *Society & Natural Resources*, 14(7), 555–570.

Brockington, D. (2002). *Fortress Conservation: The Preservation of the Mkomazi Game Reserve, Tanzania* (Oxford: James Currey).

Brockington, D. & Duffy, R. (2010). 'Capitalism and conservation: The production and reproduction of biodiversity conservation', *Antipode*, 42(3), 469–484.

Brooks, S., Spierenburg, M., Van Brakel, L. O. T., Kolk, A., & Lukhozi, K. B. (2011). 'Creating a commodified wilderness: Tourism, private game farming, and 'third nature' landscapes in KwaZulu-Natal', *Tijdschrift voor Economische en Sociale Geografie*, 102(3), 260–274.

Bryant, G., Dabhi, S., & Böhm, S. (2015). '"Fixing" the climate crisis: Capital, states, and carbon offsetting in India', *Environment and Planning A: Economy and Space*, 47(10), 2047–2063.

Büscher, B. & Fletcher, R. (2016). 'Destructive creation: Capital accumulation and the structural violence of tourism', *Journal of Sustainable Tourism*, 25(5), 651–667.

Büscher, B. & Fletcher, R. (2020). *The Conservation Revolution: Radical Ideas for Saving Nature Beyond the Anthropocene* (La Vergne TN: Verso).

Büscher, B. & Igoe, J. (2013). '"Prosuming" conservation? Web 2.0, nature and the intensification of value-producing labour in late capitalism', *Journal of Consumer Culture*, 13(3), 283–305.

Callicott, J. B. & Nelson, M. P. (1998). *The Great New Wilderness Debate* (Athens GA: University of Georgia Press).

Carruthers, J. (2008). '"Wilding the farm or farming the wild"? The evolution of scientific game ranching in South Africa from the 1960s to the present', *Transactions of the Royal Society of South Africa*, 63, 160–181.

Castree, N. (2003). 'Commodifying what nature?' *Progress in Human Geography*, 27(3), 273–297.

Ceballos, G., Ehrlich, P. R., & Dirzo, R. (2017). 'Biological annihilation via the ongoing sixth mass extinction signalled by vertebrate population losses and declines', *Proceedings of the National Academy of Sciences of the United States of America*, 114(30), E6089–E6096.

Cerutti, O. P. (2020). 'A traded tree: What rosewood means for Africa', *Trade for Development News*, 14 April 2020. Available at: http://trade4devnews. enhancedif.org/en/op-ed/traded-tree-what-rosewood-means-africa [Accessed 24 January 2022].

Chardonnet, P, des Clers, B., Fischer, J., Gerhold, R., Jori, F., & Lamarque, F. (2002). 'The value of wildlife', *Revue scientifique et technique (International Office of Epizootics)*, 21, 15–51.

Clay, N. (2019). 'Fixing the ecosystem: Conservation, crisis and capital in Rwanda's Gishwati Forest', *Environment and Planning E: Nature and Space*, 2(1), 23–46.

Cook, I., & Crang, P. (1996). 'The world on a plate: Culinary culture, displacement and geographical knowledges', *Journal of Material Culture*, 1(2), 131–153.

Cronon, W. (1996). 'The trouble with wilderness: Or, getting back to the wrong nature', *Environmental History*, 1(1), 7–28.

DeVore, J. (2017). 'Trees and springs as social property: A perspective on degrowth and redistributive democracy from a Brazilian squatter community', *Journal of Political Ecology* 24(1), 644–666.

Dickman, A., Packer, C., Johnson, P. J., & Macdonald, D. W. (2018). 'A sideways look at conservation and consistency in tourism policy', *Conservation Biology*, 32(3), 744–746.

Duffy, R. (2016). 'The illegal wildlife trade in global perspective', in: L. Elliot & W. H. Schaedla (eds), *Handbook of Transnational Environmental Crime* (Cheltenham; Northampton, MA: Edward Elgar Publishing), 109–128.

Enns, C., Bersaglio, B., & Sneyd, A. (2019). 'Fixing extraction through conservation: On crises, fixes and the production of shared value and threat', *Environment and Planning E: Nature and Space*, 2(4), 967–988.

Fletcher, R. (2020). 'Neoliberal conservation', in: M. Aldenerfer (ed.) *Oxford Research Encyclopedia of Anthropology*. Available at: https://oxfordre.com/ anthropology/view/10.1093/acrefore/9780190854584.001.0001/acrefore-9780190854584-e-300 [Accessed 24 January 2022].

Foster, J. B. (1999). 'Marx's theory of metabolic rift: Classical foundations for environmental sociology', *American Journal of Sociology*, 105(2), 366–405.

Four Paws in US (2021). 'Canned lion hunting. Born to be killed: lion hunting in South Africa', 23 March. Available at: www.fourpawsusa.org/campaigns-topics/ topics/help-for-big-cats/canned-lion-hunting [Accessed 24 January 2022].

Garland, E. (2008). 'The elephant in the room: Confronting the colonial character of wildlife conservation in Africa', *African Studies Review*, 51(3), 51–74.

Goodman, M. K. (2004). 'Reading fair trade: Political ecological imaginary and the moral economy of fair trade foods', *Political Geography*, 23(7), 891–915.

Harring, S. & Odendaal, W. (2012). '"God Stopped Making Land!"': Land Rights,

Conflict and Law in Namibia's Caprivi Region', Land, Environment and Development Project (Windhoek: Legal Assistance Centre).

Harvey, D. (1990). 'Between space and time: Reflections on the geographical imagination', *Annals of the Association of American Geographers*, 80(3), 418–434.

Harvey, D. (2011). *Marx' Kapital lesen: Ein Begleiter für Fortgeschrittene und Einsteiger*, trans. C. Frings (Hamburg: VSA Verlag).

Hausmann, A., Slotow, R., Fraser, I., & Di Minin, E. (2017). 'Ecotourism marketing alternative to charismatic megafauna can also support biodiversity conservation', *Animal Conservation*, 20(1), 91–100.

Heinrich, M. (2005). *Kritik der politischen Ökonomie* (Stuttgart: Schmetterling Verlag).

Hewitson, L., & Sullivan, S. (2021). 'Producing elephant commodities for "conservation hunting" in Namibian communal-area conservancies', *Journal of Political Ecology*, 28, 1–24.

Hornborg, A. (2016). 'Artifacts have consequences, not agency', *European Journal of Social Theory*, 20(1), 95–110.

Hughes, A. (2000). 'Retailers, knowledges and changing commodity networks: The case of the cut flower trade', *Geoforum*, 31(2), 175–190.

Igoe, J. (2010). 'The spectacle of nature in the global economy of appearances: Anthropological engagements with the spectacular mediations of transnational conservation', *Critique of Anthropology*, 30(4), 375–397.

Igoe, J. (2013). 'Nature on the move II: Contemplation becomes speculation', *New Proposals: Journal of Marxism and Interdisciplinary Inquiry*, 6(1–2), 37–49.

Igoe, J., & Brockington, D. (2007). 'Neoliberal conservation: A brief introduction', *Conservation & Society*, 5(4), 432–449.

Igoe, J., Neves, K., & Brockington, D. (2010). 'A spectacular eco-tour around the historic bloc: Theorising the convergence of biodiversity conservation and capitalist expansion', *Antipode*, 42(3), 486–512.

Iorio, M. (2012). *Einführung in die Theorien von Karl Marx* (Berlin: de Gruyter).

Kalvelage, L., Revilla Diez, J., & Bollig, M. (2020). 'How much remains? Local value capture from tourism in Zambezi, Namibia', *Tourism Geographies*, 24(4–5), 759–780.

Kay, K. (2015). 'Breaking the bundle of rights: Conservation easements and the legal geographies of individuating nature', *Environment and Planning A: Economy and Space*, 48(3), 504–522.

Keenan, R. & Parija, P. (2017). 'This sandalwood plantation is about to make its owners a lot of money: Australia is challenging India's dominance in exports of the aromatic wood', *Bloomberg*, 21 February. Available at: www.bloomberg.com/news/features/2017-02-21/australian-sandalwood-plantation-is-about-to-make-its-owners-a-lot-of-money [Accessed 24 January 2022].

Kelly, A. B. (2011). 'Conservation practice as primitive accumulation', *Journal of Peasant Studies*, 38(4), 683–701.

Kopytoff, I. (1986). 'The cultural biography of things. Commoditization as a process', in: A. Appadurai (ed.), *The Social Life of Things. Commodities in Cultural Perspective* (Cambridge: Cambridge University Press), 64–91.

Leopold, A. (1925). 'Wilderness as a form of land use', *The Journal of Land & Public Utility Economics*, 1(4), 398–404.

Luedi, J. (2017). 'Under the radar: How sandalwood is transforming crime and commerce in Asia', *Global Risk Insights*, 24 February. Available at: https://globalriskinsights.com/2017/02/radar-sandalwood-transforming-crime-commerce-asia/ [Accessed 21 January 2022].

MacDonald, K. I. (2010). 'The devil is in the (bio)diversity: Private sector "engagement" and the restructuring of biodiversity conservation', *Antipode*, 42(3), 513–550.

McCauley, D. J. (2006). 'Selling out on nature', *Nature*, 443(7107), 27–28.

Malm, A. (2018). 'In wildness is the liberation of the world: On maroon ecology and partisan nature', *Historical Materialism*, 3, 3–37.

Marris, E. (2013). *Rambunctious Garden: Saving Nature in a Post-wild World* (New York: Bloomsbury).

Marx, K. (2002 [1872]). *Das Kapital: Kritik der politischen Ökonomie – Der Produktionsprozeß des Kapitals* (Cologne: Parkland).

Moore, J. W. (2017). 'The Capitalocene Part II: Accumulation by appropriation and the centrality of unpaid work/energy', *The Journal of Peasant Studies*, 45(2), 237–279.

Napoletano, B. M., Foster, J. B., Clark, B., Urquijo, P. S., McCall, M. K., & Paneque-Gálvez, J. (2019). 'Making space in critical environmental geography for the metabolic rift', *Annals of the American Association of Geographers*, 109(6), 1811–1828.

Neimark, B. D. & Wilson, B. (2015). 'Re-mining the collections: From bioprospecting to biodiversity offsetting in Madagascar', *Geoforum*, 66, 1–10.

Neumann, R. (1998). *Imposing Wilderness: Struggles Over Livelihood and Nature Preservation in Africa* (Berkeley: University of California Press).

Petersen, B., & Hultgren, J. (2020). 'The case for a 21st century wilderness ethic', *Ethics, Policy & Environment*, online, 1–18. DOI: 10.1080/21550085.2020.1848183.

Polanyi, K. (2001 [1944]). *The Great Transformation: The Political and Economic Origins of Our Time* (Boston MA: Beacon Press).

Prudham, S. (2005). *Knock on Wood: Nature as Commodity in Douglas-Fir Country* (New York: Routledge).

Prudham, S. (2009). 'Commodification', in: N. Castree, D. Demeritt, D. Liverman, & B. Rhoads (eds), *A Companion to Environmental Geography* (Malden MA: Blackwell), 123–142.

Robbins, P. (2012). *Political Ecology: A Critical Introduction*. Second edn (Malden MA: Wiley-Blackwell).

Robertson, M. (2012). 'Measurement and alienation: Making a world of ecosystem services', *Transactions of the Institute of British Geographers*, 37(3), 386–401.

Saito, K. (2016). *Natur gegen Kapital: Marx' Ökologie in seiner unvollendeten Kritik des Kapitalismus* (Campus: Frankfurt/Main).

Sayer, A. (2003). '(De)commodification, consumer culture, and moral economy', *Environment and Planning D: Society and Space*, 21(3), 341–357.

Schroeder, R. A. (2018). 'Moving targets: The 'canned' hunting of captive-bred lions in South Africa', *African Studies Review*, 61(1), 8–32.

Simmel, G. (2004) [1907]. *The Philosophy of Money*. Third Enlarged Edition, ed. D. Frisby (London: Routledge).

Simon, A. (2017). 'The competitive consumption and fetishism of wildlife trophies', *Journal of Consumer Culture*, 19(2), 151–168.

Skibins, J. C., Powell, R. B. & Hallo, J. C. (2013). 'Charisma and conservation: Charismatic megafauna's influence on safari and zoo tourists' pro-conservation behaviors', *Biodiversity and Conservation*, 22(4), 959–982.

Smith, N. (1984). *Uneven Development: Nature, Capital and the Production of Space* (Oxford: Blackwell).

Smith, N. (2007). 'Nature as accumulation strategy', *Socialist Register*, 43, 16–36.

Sullivan, S. (2013). 'Banking Nature? The spectacular financialisation of environmental conservation', *Antipode*, 45(1), 198–217.

't Sas-Rolfes, M. (2017). 'African wildlife conservation and the evolution of hunting institutions', *Environmental Research Letters*, 12(11), 115007.

Tomasini, S. (2018). 'Unpacking the red list: Use (and misuse?) of expertise, knowledge, and power', *Conservation & Society*, 16(4), 505–517.

Tsing, A. L. (2018). 'Nine provocations for the study of domestication', in: H. A. Swanson, M. E. Lien, & G. B. Ween (eds), *Domestication Gone Wild: Politics and Practices of Multispecies Relations* (Durham NC: Duke University Press), 231–251.

Veblen, T. (2009) [1899]. *The Theory of the Leisure Class* (Waiheke Island: The Floating Press).

Vidon, E. S. (2019). 'Why wilderness? Alienation, authenticity, and nature', *Tourist Studies*, 19(1), 3–22.

3

Value Chains and Global Production Networks: Conceptual considerations and economic development in the 'wild'

JAVIER REVILLA DIEZ, CAROLIN HULKE,
AND LINUS KALVELAGE

Introduction

Many national governments in countries of the Global South with 'attractive' flora and fauna are implementing a utilitarian approach to nature conservation. Advocates of the 'wise' use of nature claim that under conditions of global capitalism, the commodification of species is needed to ensure their survival. By creating a so-called 'wildlife economy', wildlife are interpreted as assets rather than as inputs to the economy. The hope is that, by means of the commodification of wildlife through hunting and safari tourism for instance, growth in peripheral areas can be stimulated while at the same time achieving nature conservation goals. Multinational bodies like the World Trade Organization, the United Nations, and the World Bank support the integration of resource-holding regions into global value chains (GVCs). For these organisations, commodifying the 'wild' through photo-safari and hunting tourism offers many opportunities for the creation of jobs, for income, and for poverty reduction.

However, in the social and natural sciences, a polarised debate has emerged on whether or not global commodities of the 'wild' can generate positive socio-economic and ecological effects in countries with a rich wildlife (Koot *et al.* 2020; Prudham 2009). Besides positive outcomes, also negative aspects of a utilitarian approach to nature conservation are stressed. Detrimental side effects regarding other livelihood sources in areas of increasing wildlife include the displacement of small-scale farmers to less usable areas, and damage caused by wildlife. This results in a decrease of harvest and income, and often the precarisation of farmers' livelihoods (Breul *et al.* 2021; Hulke *et al.* 2020). These negative outcomes tie into an increasing number of studies in GVC research showing that the outcomes are not always as positive as expected (e.g. McGrath 2018; Phelps *et al.* 2017). A growing literature is addressing increasing inequalities through GVC integration, collectively referred to as its 'dark side'. At the local level of resource-holding regions, processes of dispossession and exclusion can be observed, reproducing and enforcing social and regional disparities and enhancing environmental degradation (Bolwig *et al.* 2010).

Against this background, this chapter aims to discuss more recent conceptual considerations to provide a more holistic picture of potential benefits and shortcomings of integrating the 'wild' into GVCs. We propose to use the term global production network (GPN) instead of global value chain (GVC) as the GPN approach reflects better the complexities of global capitalism (see further explanations in the third section of this chapter). It allows us to stress the role of uneven power relations that result from the territoriality of GPNs, which can be captured by including the concept of geographical transfer of value (GTV) by focusing on indirectly affected livelihoods – which are addressed in the dis/articulation perspective and by the interactions of GPNs with non-human nature.

After summarising in the second section the optimistic perspective in two reports from multinational organisations in favour of GVC integration, the third section provides an overview of the conceptual foundation and advancements of the GVC and GPN approach. The fourth section suggests considering three further dimensions when the GPN approach is used as a development tool: territoriality and power, wider livelihoods impacts, and environmental concerns. The last section summarises the conceptual considerations and provides an outlook on the impact of commodifying nature.

Expected benefits through global value chain integration – World Development Report 2020 and UNIDO 2015

The integration into GVC (the term used in the World Bank and UNIDO reports reviewed here) has become a very popular instrument of development policy. In its current World Development Report 2020 'Trading for Development in the Age of Global Value Chains', the World Bank concludes that integration into GVCs 'can continue to boost growth, create better jobs, and reduce poverty, provided that developing countries undertake deeper reforms and industrial countries pursue open, predictable policies' (2020: 1). Also the United Nations Industrial Development Organization (UNIDO) 2015 report 'Global Value Chains and development: UNIDO's Support towards Inclusive and Sustainable Industrial Development' assesses GVCs very positively: 'As a window of opportunity to access international markets, to absorb new technologies and to follow international standards of production, GVCs have tremendous implications for UNIDO's vision of inclusive and sustainable industrial development' (UNIDO 2015: 7). Again, integrating into the global division of labour, this time along value chains, is seen as a panacea for development and poverty reduction. It seems that the critical perspective of the proponents of the value-chains concept in explaining global inequalities has been forgotten by multinational development agencies (Ouma *et al.* 2013) (see third section).

For firms in the Global South, as advocated by international organisations like the World Bank and UNIDO, GPN integration offers two advantages: first, a long-term firm-to-firm relationship providing income, growth, and also knowledge and technology transfer from lead firms; second, as a consequence of this it allows firms in the Global South to specialise in specific tasks along the GVC that are conducive to productivity gains (World Bank 2020). Lead firms are willing to share know-how and technology with suppliers in order to become more successful. The interdependence among the firms along the value chain strengthens shared interests and enhances catching-up processes. These gains in productivity and income generate employment opportunities. The productivity gains generated by specialisation, and the use of modern technology needed to fulfil the quality requirements of the lead firm, allow large-scale production and higher export volumes. All in all, the World Bank (2020) proclaims that this stronger integration into the global division of labour will reduce poverty by creating jobs and providing higher and more stable incomes. The expected benefits will be even larger when countries are able to step up from agriculture to manufacturing and services. For instance, African regions that integrate with tourism value chains are expected to benefit from direct and indirect employment caused by increased business activity due to GVC linkages or infrastructure development, thus reducing poverty (Spenceley & Snyman 2016).

However, the World Development Report 2020 acknowledges that GVC integration might 'cause some challenges' (World Bank 2020: 68) and refers to three problems: first, gains from GVC integration can be distributed unevenly between and among countries. Lead firms often originating from the Global North or selected Asian countries like Japan, South Korea, and China are able to appropriate more of the gains due to better market access and financial as well as technological superiority. Within countries, GVC integration can increase regional disparities (as GVC activities tend to concentrate in urban agglomerations) as well as social disparities within the workforce favouring skilled employees. Second, firms connected to lead firms might not be able to upgrade and climb up the value ladder. Due to the skill mix of the workforce, the governance regime along the GVC and the specificity of certain GVCs with limited learning and innovation potential, countries in the Global South might be caught at lower value-added stages. Third, tax-avoidance strategies lead to substantial tax revenue losses including in countries of the Global South. The fragmentation of production has increased intra-firm trade and allows lead firms to decide where profits are declared, often in so-called tax havens (World Bank 2020).

Despite the possible negative impacts described above, the dominant development strategy of GVC integration contested by multilateral development organisations and its application by many national governments of the Global South has demonstrated a rather uncritical use of the concepts. The critical issue is more about how the integration into GVCs is carried out (Altenburg 2007). The policy recipe recommended by the World Bank seems to be straightforward. The five concrete policy measures to enhance GVC integration are very much in line with the Washington Consensus reform agenda, emphasising trade-based specialisation (World Bank 2020). According to the report, countries should

1   remove restrictions for accessing factor markets in order to fully exploit their comparative advantages (e.g. offering a friendly business climate, attracting foreign direct investment, avoiding restrictive labour regulations);

2   enhance trade liberalisation through the reduction of tariffs (e.g. custom levy) and non-tariff barriers (e.g. import quotas, subsidies, onerous regulations, red tape) and sign trade agreements and thus provide a better access to markets and inputs;

3   invest in infrastructure to improve connectivity, and also governance at borders, ports, and in logistics, to reduce trade costs;

4   improve the institutional quality by strengthening law enforcement, protecting intellectual property, and introducing standards and thus creating a sound business environment for foreign and domestic investment;

5   proactively enhance capabilities of small and medium-sized enterprises (SMEs) to link up with lead firms through education and skill formation.

These factors provoke the question of how state interference with the economy may lead to better developmental results. The World Development Report warns against an excessively interventionist policy approach. The report states that 'many of the traditional approaches in industrial policy, including tax incentives, subsidies, and local content policies, are more likely to distort than help in today's GVC context' (World Bank 2020: 161). Nevertheless, state action is not only needed to imply the mentioned reform agenda; as explained later in this chapter, the state is also of the utmost importance in tackling the 'dark side' of GVC integration (see fourth section).

Conceptual foundations – from global value chains to global production networks

In the last several decades the world economy has altered its shape significantly. This shift is dominantly characterised by an increasing globalisation of production and trade as well as the tendency towards vertical disintegration (Gereffi *et al.* 2005). Instead of organising production within its own hierarchical boundaries, multinational enterprises (MNEs) are turning into lead firms integrating strategic partners, suppliers, and customers into a complex network of collaboration and interdependence. This new pattern of industrial organisation started with the shifting of production from mostly multinational enterprises originating from the Global North to low-cost countries. Meanwhile, MNEs from formerly developing countries like South Korea and China are also organising their production in a fragmented and spatially dispersed manner. Today more than 60% of world trade consists of intermediary products (components) and services – embedded in worldwide value chains, which have become the arteries of globalisation.

In order to understand the increasingly fragmented nature of global economy and its consequences, diverse concepts have evolved over the last decades encompassing global commodity chains (GCCs), global value chains (GVCs), and global production networks (GPNs). Their common central concerns are 'globally coordinated interorganizational relationships that underpin the production of goods and services, and the power and value dynamics therein' (Coe 2012: 390). Since their initial key contribution, chain approaches have experienced an enormous popularity among a broad range of disciplines due to their ability to analyse economic globalisation in the everyday practices of diverse target groups like firms, households, workers, and states (Bair & Werner 2011) as well as their ability to sight different kinds of flows between buyers and suppliers, such as material resources, knowledge, information, and finance (Bolwig *et al.* 2010).

The chain heuristic finds its origin in world-systems theory. In an attempt to understand today's capitalist world economy, Hopkins and Wallerstein (1977) analysed global production processes from the 16th century onwards. Concretely, they traced back final goods to their origins as raw materials. Through this commodity-chain analysis Wallerstein was able to unfold the unequal division of labour leading to uneven development (Ouma *et al.* 2013). In 1994, Gereffi adopted the theory's product-specific focus and its chain perspective, though it breaks with the state-centred analysis and rigid distinction between core, periphery, and semi-periphery (Bair 2005). The GCC traces a given line of economic activity from its initial inputs up to the final consumption, revealing the functional and geographical division of value-adding activities cutting across nation-state boundaries and trying to understand the structure of rewards between participants along the chain. The approach puts forward four dimensions that constitute a GCC: input-output structure, territoriality, governance structure, and institutional context (Gereffi 1994). Input-output structure and the territorial dimension are primarily descriptive and illustrate the chain configuration. The institutional dimension enfolds the regulatory mechanisms affecting the several chain segments. Nonetheless, the main emphasis lies on the governance dimension, distinguishing dichotomously between buyer- and producer-driven chains.

In answer to critiques of the simplistic representation of governance types (Dicken *et al.* 2001) the GVC emerged (Gereffi *et al.* 2005), providing a revised version of the GCC. The new wording emphasises more concrete economic concepts such as value-addition, thus shifting away from the neo-Marxian reading in Wallerstein's work towards a more comprehensive understanding of the global division of labour (Ponte *et al.* 2019). Furthermore, it enlarges the simplified governance classification between market and hierarchy by three additional types in between (modular, relational, and captive) as well as explaining its underlying determinants (complexity and codifiability of the transaction, capability of the supplier) (Gereffi *et al.* 2005). Moreover, the notion of value chain 'is thought to better capture a wider variety of products, some of which lack commodity features' (Gibbon & Ponte 2005: 77).

A dominating issue within GVC research is how and under what conditions upgrading takes place, bridging global studies with developmental concerns (Gereffi 2014). The concept of upgrading is used to identify the opportunities for suppliers to 'move up the value chain', classically by distinguishing different types of upgrading (Humphrey & Schmitz 2002). Within the upgrading debate, the role of lead firms providing or blocking upgrading strategies of suppliers experienced most attention (Dolan & Humphrey 2004; Lee *et al.* 2012; Schmitz 2006). Recent attempts try to broaden the concept and claim a more complex and nuanced understanding (Navas-Alemán 2011; Ponte & Ewert 2009; Riisgaard *et al.* 2010). Ponte and Ewert (2009: 1637), for instance, approach upgrading as 'reaching a better deal' considering risks in addition to the rewards gained. Moreover, there are efforts to integrate a social dimension of upgrading by zooming in from the firm level to that of the worker (Barrientos *et al.* 2011; Gereffi & Lee 2014). Another strand in value chain research aims to examine 'environmental upgrading', which is understood as reducing negative impacts of value-chain activities on the environment (De Marchi *et al.* 2013a; Poulsen *et al.* 2018).

Despite its popularity with international development agencies, the GCC/GVC received considerable criticism. A major point of critique results from the fact that 'the institutional dimensions of the GCC/GVC analysis seem to be hijacked by its privileging of governance structures' (Hess & Yeung 2006: 1196). Moreover, it neglects the territorial embeddedness of value chains. Although a territorial dimension is included in the concept that maps the spatial distribution of chain segments, it does not consider the interaction between chains and place. The issue of embeddedness is mostly neglected by GCC/GVC, and reviewers have stated a need to reinsert place and institutions (Bair 2005; Fold 2014; Henderson *et al.* 2002; Neilson *et al.* 2014).

Most prominent objections come from the Manchester School (Coe *et al.* 2008; Henderson *et al.* 2002), which responded to the critique by providing an alternative model: the GPN. This approach combines the vertical perspective of GVC and the horizontal perspective of the 'new regionalism' (Fold 2014). By using a network heuristic, the GPN not only examines vertical chain participants, but also the whole range of actors that exert influence on the global production surrounding the vertical production line (Henderson *et al.* 2002). In short, with its stronger emphasis on developmental outcomes in locations and regions connected through production networks, GPN 1.0 extended the GVC approach by (1) acknowledging the importance of extra-firm actors (e.g. state agencies, non-governmental organisations); (2) stressing a multi-spatial dimension in firm–territory interactions reaching from the local and sub-national to the macro-regional and global level; (3) incorporating inter-firm relations in production systems in addition to the classical vertical integration; and (4) recognising the role of regulatory and institutional factors influencing GVC governance.

These additional perspectives lead to the understanding of regional economic development as a consequence of strategic coupling between lead firms and regional assets and institutions (Coe *et al.* 2004; Yeung 2009; Yeung 2015). The concept of strategic coupling describes 'the coupling process between regional economies and global production networks that is mediated through specific action and practices of key actors and institutions' (Coe *et al.* 2004: 482). However, integration into GPNs does not occur automatically, but only when regional assets promoted by local, regional, or national governments meet the strategic needs of lead firms (Coe *et al.* 2004; Coe & Hess 2011).

In a recent contribution – Global Production Networks 2.0 – Yeung and Coe (2015) offer an additional theoretical framework for explaining the evolutionary dynamics of production networks. They theorise competitive dynamics (optimising cost–capability ratios, sustaining market development, working with financial discipline) and show how these account for changes in network configurations. As a consequence, key actors are adopting strategies resulting in complex configurations of intra-, inter-, and extra-firm network relationships with divergent strategic aims and dynamism resulting in (re) configurations of their GPNs and thus impacting value-capture trajectories and developmental outcomes (Kano *et al.* 2020). Despite these conceptual contributions, criticism has arisen that challenges the increasingly popular framework. An examination of negative effects of GPN integration is needed to contrast the predominantly positive portrayal in the World Development Report. In the following section, light will be shed on 'darker' aspects (Phelps *et al.* 2017) of GPN-driven development and the resulting missing links in its scientific conceptualisation.

The negative aspects and missing links of global production networks

It is an established and proclaimed aim of GPN studies to unpack processes of uneven development that are connected to the global division of labour. McGrath (2018: 516) recently stated that the GPN approach is not acknowledging the contested nature of development and ignores debates within development geography, development studies and development policy. In line with such critical voices on the understanding and disregard of development in GPNs (e.g. Phelps *et al.* 2017; Werner 2016), scholars have asked: what kind of development, and for whom? (Pike *et al.* 2007).

A growing body of literature hence addresses inequalities in GPNs and participation possibilities for people living in regions where GPNs 'touch down' (e.g. Bolwig *et al.* 2010; Kelly 2013; McGrath 2018). They have raised the concern that more light needs to be shed on (unintended) side effects of GPN integration. The aim is to examine the impacts of GPN integration on a variety of actors in a region. These impacts can be categorised into three crucial dimensions: uneven power relations that result from the territoriality of GPNs, which can be captured by including the concept of geographical transfer of value (GTV); indirectly affected livelihoods – which are addressed in the dis/articulation perspective; and lastly the interactions of GPNs with non-human nature. We address the gap in the GPN literature by combining these perspectives: specifically, the exclusion of actors from benefits that result from the appropriation and commodification of nature. Especially regions with people depending largely on environmental resources are often affected by these 'dark' aspects, which we will show in the following.

Territoriality, power, and the geographical transfer of value

So far, the conceptual advancement of GVCs to GPNs emphasises how processes of value creation are geographically spread and bounded and thus yield uneven economic development within and between territories. In this regard, value refers to different forms of economic rents, which can be realised through the market and through non-market transactions. Lead firms are able to generate economic rents when they outcompete other firms due to their having access to scarce resources, key product and process technologies, talents, or established brand names (Coe & Yeung 2015).

The distribution of these rents among actors along the value chain depends at least partly on power relations between four sets of actors: the corporate sector, civil society organisations, the nation-state, and supranational institutions (Davis *et al.* 2018). Gavin Bridge (2008) has shown how the value capture in the oil sector depends on the power balance between the producer and the resource holder. Furthermore, specific network configurations lead to a reduced bargaining power for suppliers and hence limited value capture (Blažek 2016). Based on power relations and governance modes, different categories of GVCs/GCCs have emerged with varying spatial implications for value-creating processes (Gereffi 1994; Gereffi 1999; Gereffi *et al.* 2005). For example, lead firms in producer- and buyer-driven GVCs are originally rooted in the USA, Europe, or Japan, which ensures that the largest portions of revenues are concentrated in their home countries (Gereffi 1999). Nevertheless, GPN researchers have continuously pointed out that regional actors in developing countries/emerging economies can embed processes of value creation in their territories if they successfully align place-specific assets with the global strategies of lead firms, and if local actors are ultimately able to capture the value (Coe *et al.* 2004; Coe & Yeung 2015; Henderson *et al.* 2002).

From a GPN perspective, strategic coupling of regions with GPNs does not necessarily occur directly from the locations of the global headquarters of the lead firms and their strategic partners, but may take place indirectly via other locations acting as intermediaries. In principle, GPNs connect different nodes along the value chain with different functions and capacities impacting the appropriation of value and causing different developmental outcomes. Breul *et al.* (2019) suggest integrating spatial configurations in the GPN framework, using the case study of Singapore in the oil and gas sector as an example. Singapore is able to filter value at the expense of resource-holding regions. As this example shows, the role of territorial intermediaries in GPNs is vital to 'enhance the ability of GPN thinking to contribute to explanations of patterns of uneven territorial development in the global economy' (Coe & Yeung 2015: 22). A few case studies have demonstrated how value is created from commodifying the 'wild' in different places, and have shown which actors are involved. Hassler and Franz (2013) take the example of organic pepper production to demonstrate that intermediary organisations located in Western countries take advantage of their knowledge of consumer preferences, and thus capture the most value, whereas local farmers in India benefit from certification programmes to a lesser extent. In a similar vein, trophy-hunting tourist companies studied in Zambia keep half of the revenues, whereas local communities have only received up to 12% (Lewis & Alpert 1997).

As stated above, GPN studies often fail to depict territorial aspects of regional development directly and indirectly caused by coupling regions to GPNs. The concept of global transfer of value (GTV) provides conceptual underpinnings to integrate the territoriality of GPN/GVC integration and thus currently experiences renewed interest from geographers (Hadjimichalis 1987; Parnreiter 2017). Whereas GPN research focused on the configuration and governance forms of globally fragmented production, crucial questions about how value is transferred across space or restricted to certain places and which actors and place-specific determinants can hamper or support these processes remained unexplored (Parnreiter 2017). Global transfer of value describes a 'process through which value produced at one location is transferred to and realized in another' (Parnreiter 2017: 4), which can increase or reduce socio-economic disparities between these two places. Hence, a discussion of power and value in a globalised economy needs to emphasise the effects of its spatial configurations.

Livelihoods between articulation and disarticulation

Within scholarship on GPN, a lot is known about the governance and value creation caused by global lead firms and related institutions, especially in the Global North. However, 'much less is known about territorial development in places excluded from these [processes]' (Carmody 2020: 2), especially on the African continent, as Carmody has critically highlighted. He states that 'Africa offers potential for us to rethink the nature, constitution and operation-alization of globalisation and its likely future impacts. Whether this happens or not depends on reversing uneven development of theory and empirical focus within economic geography' (ibid: 3). This discrepancy is addressed through the disarticulation perspective (Bair & Werner 2011; Murphy 2019) and related concepts such as dissociation (Ibert *et al.* 2019).

The conceptual and analytical contribution of the disarticulation perspective lies in the change of perspective from looking at actors and processes directly related to the chain/network to explicitly integrating those who are not. The 'inclusionary bias' in most GPN studies stems from their focus on lead firms, their relations, and capital and trade flows (Bair *et al.* 2013; Bair & Werner 2011). Picked up by Ibert *et al.* 2019 with the notion of 'dissociations', such disarticulations are 'practices of weakening or obscuring negative links between a branded commodity and other entities in order to let desired associations overrule undesired ones' (Havice & Pickles 2019a: 74). To overcome the inclusionary bias in regional development studies and thus integrate undesired associations, recent studies include the livelihoods perspective (e.g. Scoones 2009) in GPN studies (Fold 2014; Vicol *et al.* 2019). A prominent example is that of agriculture-based households in the Global South (ibid.: 982).

Livelihood strategies that result from indirect connections to GPNs that enter a region and a changing environment can vary, from diversifying within the existing economic activities, to entering newly emerging economic activities related to the GPN, to remaining locked into the existing activities (Hulke *et al.* 2020). The latter includes the possibility that non-participants fully excluded from newly emerging economic activities might see their livelihoods downgraded as (environmental) resources become scarce and competitive.

More prominently, scholars discuss social downgrading in regard to changing labour conditions and the role of workers in the production segment of GPNs (Barrientos 2013; Barrientos *et al.* 2016a; Cumbers *et al.* 2008). 'Much GPN employment is insecure and unprotected, and ensuring decent work for more vulnerable workers poses significant problems' (Barrientos *et al.* 2011: 320). Especially for small-scale, home-based informal work and low-skilled industrial work in GPNs, unpaid family labour, child labour, insufficient negotiation power, and damage to health can result in social downgrading, as the authors argue. Using the example of horticulture producers for supermarket chains in southern and eastern Africa, Barrientos *et al.* (2016b: 1266) state that '[s]trategic diversification provides opportunities for economic and social upgrading by more capable suppliers and skilled workers, but economic downgrading pressures persist and some are excluded from both global and regional value chains'. Hence, the social risks and opportunities arising from the presence of a GPN in a region only become visible when one explicitly includes non-participants and the 'black box' of households and their livelihoods in GPN studies (Kelly 2013).

These examples portray the importance of engaging with livelihoods through the examination of social up- and downgrading caused by indirect effects of GPNs. Bolwig *et al.* (2010: 185) define these – from a GPN perspective – non-participating actors as 'those who never participated in the value chain, by choice or for lack of capability'. Even though actors are excluded from such internationalised networks and are engaged in an 'alternative' local or regional value chain for local consumption and production, an indirect connection to and influence from GPN-related activities and actors in that region exists (Bolwig *et al.* 2010). Furthermore, as economic activities for the global market and for the local/regional market not only co-exist but could also be interlinked, participation and non-participation forms can fluently merge and dynamically change (Krishnan 2018). An active choice not to participate ('strategic downgrading', as referred to by Barrientos *et al.* 2016a) can indicate a high risk associated with integration into a GPN, or that an alternative income source or a local network integration is more secure and effective for the households' well-being (Hulke *et al.* 2020). Integration into local/regional value chains could hence potentially be a more successful livelihood strategy compared to GPN integration, and deserves more scholarly attention.

To sum up, the disarticulation and livelihood perspectives are necessary to take the negative aspects of GPN integration into account and to actually examine development in a region. In this way one can better derive how regions can be promoted and how the well-being of the people, i.e. their livelihoods, can be improved. Therefore, in the future it will also be necessary to ask normative questions such as: what do we actually want to achieve with regional development and GPN integration? Should a 'good' regional development strategy not also take into account the environment and the people outside a production network? The coupling of a region and its nature with GPNs that make use of wilderness (environment/forest products or wildlife) changes human–nature relations drastically and always results in the exclusion of certain people from the commodification of such products. Environment-dependent livelihoods such as smallholder subsistence farming hence need to be included to the analysis in order to capture which dissociations and disarticulations a commodification process – as beneficial as it may be for the development of a new industrial path – triggers.

The concepts of nature and value in global production networks

GPNs shape and are shaped by nature. On the one hand, studies have shown how the configuration of production networks affects the natural environment; on the other hand, biological processes and the spatial distribution and the materiality of natural resources determine the configuration of GPNs. The production of both physical and intangible commodities depends on natural resources: they either provide the means of production, the conditions of production, or the conditions of reproduction (Baglioni & Campling 2017). However, appropriation of nature in GPN research to date 'remains marginal theoretically and empirically' (ibid.:2427). The underlying problem is how to appropriately account for or 'frame' the value of the environment to current and future economic systems (Coe & Yeung 2019)'. *Value* is one of the key analytical concepts in GPN research, and yet authors have stated that within these frameworks, *value* remains vaguely conceptualised (Havice & Pickles 2019). Critics argue that in GPN research, only 'two very different types of value are referenced: the Marxian concept of surplus value, and the 'more orthodox' one of economic rent' (McGrath 2018 3). Both concepts aim to achieve commensurability, while the former expresses value as dependent on the social labour necessary for the production of a commodity, the latter equates value with the price that is constructed through the dynamics of supply and demand. Marx was well aware that commodity production is a result of human labour with the spontaneous produce of nature, and his theory of value was designed to criticise the exploitation of labour and the environment (Huber 2017). According to Marx, value inadequately represents natural conditions, an issue that is often referred to as the *contradiction of capitalism* (Burkett 1999). While both human labour and nature contribute to the creation of *use value*, nature's contribution to commodity production does not reflect in the exchange value, i.e. the monetary price for a use value, ibid.). This leads to a dynamic in which goods that require the consumption of natural resources are less valuable than those that require high labour inputs, in other words: 'the greater the free gift of nature, the less necessary labour time and hence, less value produced' (Baglioni & Campling 2017: 6). This has led to difficulties in explaining value-creating processes, especially in GPNs based on the extraction of natural resources (Huber 2018; Kenney-Lazar & Kay 2017).

Largely disconnected from GPN literature, alternative approaches exist that draw on anthropological writings (e.g. Graeber 2001) to emphasise how value is made, thus 'making visible some of the practices of assemblage that bring together multiple actors, materials, organisations, institutions, calculative devices, etc., that otherwise are mystified in the appearance and exchange of the commodity as an economically valued entity' (Bracking *et al.* 2018: 6). This approach is promising to GPN research, since it provides the opportunity to expand the Marxian labour theory of value and integrate more-than-human labour into the concept (see Hewitson & Sullivan, this volume). In economic geography, the concept of resource making builds on a similar thought of socially constructed resources being composed partly by forces of nature, and partly by human appraisal (Kama 2020; Allen & Barney 2019). First attempts have been made to blend this concept with GPN research and apply it to the commodification of wildlife (Gargallo & Kalvelage 2021).

Global production network research dealing with nature has mainly focused on three topics: environmental degradation, environmental upgrading, and the role of nature for the configuration of global production. Studies have shown examples of environmental degradation in a variety of value chains such as cotton production in Uzbekistan (Rudenko *et al.* 2008), the iron and steel industry in the United Kingdom (Dahlström & Ekins 2006), or shrimp farming in Bangladesh (Paul & Røskaft 2013). Value-chain activities affect the environment in many ways: through their interaction with the local resource base and the emissions of nutrients, toxic substances, and gases (Bolwig *et al.* 2010). In the case of hunting tourism for instance, the absence of hunting can lead to elephant populations exceeding the local carrying capacity (Gressier 2014) or to an increase in poaching activities (Mbaiwa 2018). Trophy hunts on the other hand can lead to changes in the male-to-female ratio in moose populations (Naevdal *et al.* 2012), to a decrease in horn size in antelope, and a general population decimation in infanticidal carnivores (Packer *et al.* 2009).

Responding to the call of Bolwig *et al.* (2010) to include social and environmental layers in the analysis of global production, researchers have contributed to the debate on *environmental upgrading* in value chains. For example, Khattak *et al.* (2015) analyse drivers of environmental upgrading at the firm level, De Marchi *et al.* (2013b) examine firms' greening strategies, and Poulsen *et al.* (2016) look at ports' potential to reduce air pollutants (for a systematic review, see Khattak & Pinto 2018).

Attention is also drawn by the interrelationship of the resource and the GPN. By examining the seafood industry, Mansfield (2003) exemplifies how the quality of the product shapes the coordination of the industry. In the case of extractive industries, Bridge (2008) has done substantial work on how the spatiality of resources affects the structure and development outcomes of the production network (Bridge & Bradshaw 2017). Havice and Campling (2017) study the intersection of chain governance and environmental governance exploring inter-firm strategies in the canned tuna GPN. While proposing an alternative terminology, Klooster and Mercado-Celis (2016) consider the sustainability of the production process in furniture production in Mexico. More recent studies focus on the spatial organisation of nature-based GPNs (Irarrázaval & Bustos-Gallardo 2018) and the cultural contestations that surround the fur GPN (Kleibert *et al.* 2020). Franz *et al.* (2018) combine the GPN approach with a water-energy-food nexus to explore society-environment relations of a regional agri-food production cluster.

Other researchers have applied the GPN concept to new commodity frontiers, such as ecosystem services (Urzedo *et al.* 2020), recycling trade flows (Crang *et al.* 2013), and the biofuels and carbon market (Neimark *et al.* 2016). Büscher (2014) lays out how conservation and development projects are entangled in a value chain in which the traded commodity is the idea of the 'success' of such projects. All these studies explore new horizons in regard to the concept of value in GVCs/GPNs. From the above it becomes clear that value-chain analysis has been applied to study the intersections of economy and nature, including environmental degradation, environmental upgrading, and the role of natural resources for value-chain configurations. What is also visible, however, is the fact that the GPN concept of value has explanatory limitations when being confronted with the commodification of nature.

Critical remarks and outlook for commodifying nature

With this contribution, we aim to outline discrepancies and shortcomings in established scientific concepts on regional development embedded in a globalised world. There is a need to rethink the implementation of global value chain and global production network approaches in development policies promoted by the World Bank and other influential international organisations. Their dominant narrative of global economic integration as a panacea for regional development falls short in acknowledging the contextual specifics of regions where GPNs 'touch down' as well as their potential negative aspects and risks. To overcome practitioners' misuses of the concepts and thus contribute to more fitting regional development strategies (Rodríguez-Pose 2013), the more critical notions of value, power, territoriality, and disarticulation need to be translated from their scientific uses into actual development strategies. The disarticulation perspective, highlighting the integration of non-participants, the livelihoods concept, and the geographical transfer of value provide helpful and necessary conceptual extensions, as we have outlined.

Especially for sectors that depend on the commodification of nature, the way nature is interpreted and used by GPNs may clash with the local social-ecological system. At such resource frontiers, the negative aspects of coupling with GPNs are often very visible, and the competing notions of *value* associated with nature differ significantly. For a value chain to arise, first of all there must be value. The examination of the very beginning of a value chain inevitably leads to the question of the value of nature. However, 'to take nature seriously, we need to recognise the complementarity between the spheres of circulation and production because the ability of lead firms to govern GVCs cannot be disjoined from the appropriation of nature, strategies to control the labour process and firms' associated ability to capture surplus value' (Baglioni & Campling 2017: 4).

Our literature review reveals that the question of value creation has received by far less attention in GPN research compared to issues like upgrading, value distribution, and capture. Accordingly, the conceptualisation of commodi-fication processes within the GPN framework remains weak. This may be surprising given the prominence of the key concepts *commodity* and *value*. Yet in GPN research, nature has long been regarded as an externality, either as an environment which is impacted by GPN activities, or as inputs to the production. More recently, however, resource geography is increasingly engaged with GPN studies, contributing a different perspective. According to the prevalent view, nature only becomes a resource when humans interact with it (compare Zimmermann 1933). Thus, a resource has a dual quality as a material entity and a social category. Accordingly, Bridge (2009: 1238) proposes to ask why something is regarded as a resource, who benefits from prevailing patterns of resource production and consumption and who pays the price, the valuations of nature that facilitate these patterns and the valuations which can prove more resistive, and to query physical augmentation of supply as the default strategy for dealing with scarcity.

The chapter by Linus Kalvelage in this volume demonstrates that these questions can be worked on using the rich GPN toolbox for analysing the circulation sphere of a commodity, since the actor-centric perspective reveals the mechanics behind the construction of value from wildlife that have an impact on ecological and economic outcomes on a local level. In Namibian hunting tourism, a variety of firm and non-firm actors are involved in the commodification of wildlife, its packaging and marketing, to transform a living creature that initially has only a direct use value for humans into a commodity that can be exchanged on a global market, as part of the hunting experience. The governance of this commodification process has effects on value-capture patterns among participants in the global production network, and is associated with a specific territorial notion, as some places benefit more from the commodification than others (compare Kalvelage *et al.* 2022).

From the above it has become clear that to unleash the framework's potential, it is necessary to look at both sides of the coin of global market integration: the shining light of economic upgrading, and the dark side – including exclusion, power imbalances, and social and environmental downgrading. The commodification of nature is a process that is triggered, negotiated, and practised by people and organisations who follow certain agendas, goals, and strategies. Processes of commodification are embedded not only in a territory, but also in its institutional context. Therefore, the understanding of commodi-fication processes accounts for an appreciation of multiple institutions. We acknowledge recent trends in GPN literature, which highlight the institutional power of the state for regional economic processes (Breul & Revilla Diez 2018; Horner 2017; Smith 2015). In addition to the GPN literature, actor-centred approaches in institutional economic geography have indeed proven that MNEs, political leaders, or a group of actors can trigger institutional changes (Faulconbridge & Muzio 2015; Sotarauta & Mustikkamäki 2015). Hence, the interplay of actors and institutions matters for examining GPNs related to regional development.

Derived from that, a more fit translation of the GPN concept to policy making and regional development strategies should differentiate carefully between *direct* GPN-related institutions and *indirect* space-specific institutions. The former refers to targeted governmental regulations of market activities (the state as regulator, according to Horner 2017) which the World Bank for instance views critically. The latter includes regional measures that enhance the business environment and innovation capacities through, for instance, investment in advanced education, health, or infrastructure (roads, railways airports, ports) (Rodríguez-Pose 2013). Supporting *indirect* institutions could improve regional assets and potentially more inclusive regional development, looking at it from a holistic perspective of not only firms, but also disarticulated livelihoods and nature in places where global production networks touch down.

Bibliography

Allen, M. G. & Barney, K. (2019). 'Resource-making, materiality and the disruptive geographies of the extractive industries in the Asia-Pacific', *The Extractive Industries and Society*, 6(3), 733–736.

Altenburg, T. (2007). 'Donor approaches to supporting pro-poor value chains' (German Development Institute). Report prepared for the Donor Committee for Enterprise Development Working Group on Linkages and Value Chain). Available at: http://value-chains.org/dyn/bds/docs/568/DonorApproachestoPro-PoorValueChains.pdf [Accessed 31 January 2022].

Baglioni, E. & Campling, L. (2017). 'Natural resource industries as global value chains: Frontiers, fetishism, labour and the state', *Environment and Planning A: Economy and Space*, 49(11), 2437–2456.

Bair, J. (2005). 'Global capitalism and commodity chains: Looking back, going forward', *Competition & Change*, 9(2), 153–180.

Bair, J. & Werner, M. (2011). 'Commodity chains and the uneven geographies of global capitalism: A disarticulations perspective', *Environment and Planning A: Economy and Space*, 43(5), 988–997.

Bair, J., Berndt, C., Boeckler, M., & Werner, M. (2013). Guest Editorial. 'Dis/articulating producers, markets, and regions: New directions in critical studies of commodity chain', *Environment and Planning A: Economy and Space*, 45(11), 2544–2552.

Barrientos, S. W. (2013). '"Labour chains": Analysing the role of labour contractors in global production networks', *The Journal of Development Studies*, 49(8), 1058–1071.

Barrientos, S. W., Gereffi, G. & Rossi, A. (2011). 'Economic and social upgrading in global production networks: A new paradigm for a changing world', *International Labour Review*, 150(3–4), 319–340.

Barrientos, S., Gereffi, G. & Pickles, J. (2016a). 'New dynamics of upgrading in global value chains: Shifting terrain for suppliers and workers in the Global South', *Environment and Planning A: Economy and Space*, 48(7), 1214–1219.

Barrientos, S., Knorringa, P., Evers, B., Visser, M. & Opondo, M. (2016b). 'Shifting regional dynamics of global value chains: Implications for economic and social upgrading in African horticulture', *Environment and Planning A: Economy and Space*, 48(7), 1266–1283.

Blažek, J. (2016). 'Towards a typology of repositioning strategies of GVC/GPN suppliers: The case of functional upgrading and downgrading', *Journal of Economic Geography*, 16(4), 849–869.

Bolwig, S., Ponte, S., Du Toit, A., Riisgaard, L., & Halberg, N. (2010). 'Integrating poverty and environmental concerns into value-chain analysis: A conceptual framework', *Development Policy Review*, 28(2), 173–194.

Bracking, S., Fredriksen, A., Sullivan, S., & Woodhouse, P. (2018). 'Introducing values that matter', in: S. Bracking, A. Fredriksen, S. Sullivan, & P. Woodhouse (eds), *Valuing Development, Environment and Conservation* (London: Routledge), 1–17.

Breul, M. & Revilla Diez, J. (2018). 'An intermediate step to resource peripheries: The strategic coupling of gateway cities in the upstream oil and gas GPN', *Geoforum*, 92, 9–17.

Breul, M., Revilla Diez, J. & Sambodo, M. T. (2019). 'Filtering strategic coupling: Territorial intermediaries in oil and gas global production networks in Southeast Asia', *Journal of Economic Geography*, 19(4), 829–851.

Breul, M., Hulke, C. & Kalvelage, L. (2021). 'Path formation and reformation: Studying the variegated consequences of path creation for regional development', *Economic Geography*, 97(3), 213–234.

Bridge, G. (2008). 'Global production networks and the extractive sector: Governing resource-based development', *Journal of Economic Geography*, 8(3), 389–419.

Bridge, G. (2009). 'Material worlds: Natural resources, resource geography and the material economy', *Geography Compass*, 3(3), 1217–1244.

Bridge, G. & Bradshaw, M. (2017). 'Making a global gas market: Territoriality and production networks in liquefied natural gas', *Economic Geography*, 93(3), 215–240.

Burkett, P. (1999). 'Nature's "free gifts" and the ecological significance of value', *Capital & Class*, 23(2), 89–110.

Büscher, B. (2014). 'Selling success: Constructing value in conservation and development', *World Development*, 57, 79–90.

Carmody, P. (2020). 'Economic-geographic theory from the South: African experience and future in the global economy', *Geoforum*, 115(5), 160–163.

Coe, N. (2012). 'Geographies of production II: A global production network A-Z', *Progress in Human Geography*, 36(3), 389–402.

Coe, N. & Hess, M. (2011). 'Local and regional development', in: A. Pike, A. Rodríguez-Pose, & J. Tomaney (eds), *Handbook of Local and Regional Development* (London; New York: Routledge), 128–138.

Coe, N. & Yeung, H. W.-c. (2015). *Global Production Networks: Theorizing Economic Development in an Interconnected World* (Oxford: Oxford University Press).

Coe, N. & Yeung, H. W.-c. (2019). 'Global production networks: Mapping recent conceptual developments', *Journal of Economic Geography*, 19(4), 775–801.

Coe, N., Hess, M., Yeung, H. W.-c., Dicken, P., & Henderson, J. (2004). '"Globalizing" regional development: A global production networks perspective', *Transactions of the Institute of British Geographers*, 29(4), 468–484.

Coe, N., Dicken, P., & Hess, M. (2008). 'Global production networks: Realizing the potential', *Journal of Economic Geography*, 8(3), 271–295.

Crang, M., Hughes, A., Gregson, N., Norris, L., & Ahamed, F. (2013). 'Rethinking governance and value in commodity chains through global recycling networks', *Transactions of the Institute of British Geographers*, 38(1), 12–24.

Cumbers, A., Nativel, C. & Routledge, P. (2008). 'Labour agency and union positionalities in global production networks', *Journal of Economic Geography*, 8(3), 369–387.

Dahlström, K. & Ekins, P. (2006). 'Combining economic and environmental dimensions: Value chain analysis of UK iron and steel flows', *Ecological Economics*, 58(3), 507–519.

Davis, D., Kaplinsky, R. & Morris, M. (2018). 'Rents, power and governance in global value chains', *Journal of World-Systems Research*, 24(1), 43–71.

De Marchi, V., Di Maria, E., & Micelli, S. (2013a). 'Environmental strategies, upgrading and competitive advantage in global value chains', *Business Strategy and the Environment*, 22(1), 62–72.

De Marchi, V., Di Maria, E., & Ponte, S. (2013b). 'The greening of global value chains: Insights from the furniture industry', *Competition and Change*, 17(4), 299–318.

Dicken, P., Kelly, P. F., Olds, K., & Yeung, H. W.-c. (2001). 'Chains and networks, territories and scales: Towards a relational framework for analysing the global economy', *Global Networks*, 1(2), 89–112.

Dolan, C. & Humphrey, J. (2004). 'Changing governance patterns in the trade in fresh vegetables between Africa and the United Kingdom', *Environment and Planning A: Economy and Space*, 36(3), 491–509.

Faulconbridge, J. R. & Muzio, D. (2015). 'Transnational corporations shaping institutional change: The case of English law firms in Germany', *Journal of Economic Geography*, 15(6), 1195–1226.

Fold, N. (2014). 'Value chain dynamics, settlement trajectories and regional development', *Regional Studies*, 48(5), 778–790.

Franz, M., Schlitz, N., & Schumacher, K. P. (2018). 'Globalization and the water-energy-food nexus – Using the global production networks approach to analyze society-environment relations', *Environmental Science and Policy*, 90(November), 201–212.

Gargallo, E. & Kalvelage, L. (2021). 'Integrating social-ecological systems and global production networks: Local effects of trophy hunting in Namibian conservancies', *Development Southern Africa*, 38(1), 87–103.

Gereffi, G. (1994). 'The organization of buyer-driven global commodity chains: How U.S. retailers shape overseas production networks', in: G. Gereffi & M. Korzeniewicz (eds), *Commodity Chains and Global Capitalism* (Westport CT: Greenwood Press), 95–122.

Gereffi, G. (1999). 'International trade and industrial upgrading in the apparel commodity chain', *Journal of International Economics*, 48(1), 37–70.

Gereffi, G. (2014). 'Global value chains in a post-Washington Consensus world', *Review of International Political Economy*, 21(1), 9–37.

Gereffi, G. & Lee, J. (2014). 'Economic and social upgrading in global value chains and industrial clusters: Why governance matters', *Journal of Business Ethics*, 133, 25–38.

Gereffi, G., Humphrey, J., & Sturgeon, T. (2005). 'The governance of global value chains', *Review of International Political Economy*, 12(1), 78–104.

Gibbon, P. & Ponte, S. (2005). *Trading Down: Africa, Value Chains, and the Global Economy* (Philadelphia PA: Temple University Press).

Graeber, D. (2001). *Toward an Anthropological Theory of Value: The False Coin of Our Own Dreams* (New York: Palgrave).

Gressier, C. (2014). 'An elephant in the room: Okavango safari hunting as ecotourism?' *Ethnos*, 79(2), 193–214.

Hadjimichalis, C. (1987). *Uneven Development and Regionalism. State, Territory, and Class in Southern Europe* (London: Croom Helm).

Hassler, M. & Franz, M. (2013). 'The bridging role of intermediaries in food production networks: Indian organic pepper in Germany', *Tijdschrift voor economische en sociale geografie*, 104(1), 29–40.

Havice, E. & Campling, L. (2017). 'Where chain governance and environmental governance meet: Interfirm strategies in the canned tuna global value chain', *Economic Geography*, 93(3), 292–313.

Havice, E. & Pickles, J. (2019a). 'Articulating value and missing links in "Geographies of Dissociation"'. *Dialogues in Human Geography*, 9(1), 73–77.

Havice, E. & Pickles, J. (2019b). 'On value in value chains', in: S. Ponte, G. Gereffi, & G. Raj-Reichert (eds), *Handbook on Global Value Chains* (Cheltenham; Northampton MA: Edward Elgar Publishing), 169–182.

Henderson, J., Dicken, P., Hess, M., Coe, N. M., & Yeung, H. W.-c. (2002). 'Global production networks and the analysis of economic development', *Review of International Political Economy*, 9(3), 436–464.

Hess, M. & Yeung, H. W.-c. (2006). 'Whither global production networks in economic geography? Past, present, and future', *Environment and Planning A: Economy and Space*, 38(7), 1193–1204.

Hopkins, T. K. & Wallerstein, I. (1977). 'Patterns of Development of the Modern World-System', *Review (Fernand Braudel Center)*, 1(2), 111–145.

Horner, R. (2017). 'Beyond facilitator? State roles in global value chains and global production networks', *Geography Compass*, 11(2), e12307.

Huber, M. (2017). 'Value, nature, and labor: A defense of Marx', *Capitalism, Nature, Socialism*, 28(1), 39–52.

Huber, M. (2018). 'Resource geographies I: Valuing nature (or not)', *Progress in Human Geography*, 42(1), 148–159.

Hulke, C., Kairu, J., & Revilla Diez, J. (2020). 'Global visions, local realities – How conservation shapes agricultural value chains in Zambezi Region, Namibia', *Development Southern Africa*, 38(1), 104–121.

Humphrey, J. & Schmitz, H. (2002). 'Developing country firms in the world economy: Governance and upgrading in global value chains' (Duisburg: Institut für Entwicklung und Frieden der Gerhard-Mercator-Universität Duisburg, Heft 61/2002). Available at https://duepublico2.uni-due.de/receive/duepublico_mods_00027102 [Accessed 17 January 2022].

Ibert, O., Hess, M., Kleibert, J., Müller, F., & Power, D. (2019). 'Positioning and "doing" geographies of dissociation', *Dialogues in Human Geography*, 9(1), 88–93.

Irarrázaval, F. & Bustos-Gallardo, B. (2018). 'Global salmon networks: Unpacking ecological contradictions at the production stage', *Economic Geography*, 95(2), 159–178.

Kalvelage, L., Revilla Diez, J., & Bollig, M. (2022). 'How much remains? Local value capture from tourism in Zambezi, Namibia', *Tourism Geographies*, 24(4–5), 759–780.

Kama, K. (2020). 'Resource-making controversies: Knowledge, anticipatory politics and economization of unconventional fossil fuels', *Progress in Human Geography*, 44(2), 333–356.

Kano, L., Tsang, E. W. K., & Yeung, H. W.-c. (2020). 'Global value chains: A review of the multi-disciplinary literature', *Journal of International Business Studies*, 51(4), 577–622.

Kelly, P. F. (2013). 'Production networks, place and development: Thinking through global production networks in Cavite, Philippines', *Geoforum*, 44, 82–92.

Kenney-Lazar, M. & Kay, K. (2017). 'Value in capitalist natures', *Capitalism, Nature, Socialism*, 28(1), 33–38.

Khattak, A. & Pinto, L. (2018). 'A systematic literature review of the environmental upgrading in global value chains and future research agenda', *Journal of Distribution Science*, 16(11), 11–19.

Khattak, A., Stringer, C., Benson-Rea, M., & Haworth, N. (2015). 'Environmental upgrading of apparel firms in global value chains: Evidence from Sri Lanka', *Competition and Change*, 19(4), 317–335.

Kleibert, J. M., Hess, M., & Müller, F. C. (2020). 'Sites of contestation in global fur networks', *Geoforum*, 108(June), 39–48.

Klooster, D. & Mercado-Celis, A. (2016). 'Sustainable production networks: Capturing value for labour and nature in a furniture production network in Oaxaca, Mexico', *Regional Studies*, 50(11), 1889–1902.

Koot, S., Hebinck, P. & Sullivan, S. (2020). 'Science for success – a conflict of interest? Researcher position and reflexivity in socio-ecological research for CBNRM in Namibia', *Society & Natural Resources*. Available at: https://doi.org/10.1080/08941920.2020.1762953 [Accessed 31 January 2022].

Krishnan, A. (2018): 'The origin and expansion of regional value chains: The case of Kenyan horticulture', *Global Networks*, 18(2), 238–263.

Lee, J., Gereffi, G., & Beauvais, J. (2012). 'Global value chains and agrifood standards: Challenges and possibilities for smallholders in developing countries', *Proceedings of the National Academy of Sciences of the United States of America*, 109(31), 12326–12331.

Lewis, D. & Alpert, P. (1997). 'Trophy hunting and wildlife conservation in Zambia', *Conservation Biology*, 11(1), 59–68.

Mansfield, B. (2003). 'Spatializing globalization: A "geography of quality" in the seafood industry', *Economic Geography*, 79(1), 1–16.

Mbaiwa, J. E. (2018). 'Effects of the safari hunting tourism ban on rural livelihoods and wildlife conservation in Northern Botswana', *South African Geographical Journal*, 100(1), 41–61.

McGrath, S. (2018). 'Dis/articulations and the interrogation of development in GPN research', *Progress in Human Geography*, 29(4), 509–528.

Murphy, J. T. (2019). 'Global production network dis/articulations in Zanzibar: Practices and conjunctures of exclusionary development in the tourism industry', *Journal of Economic Geography*, 19(4), 943–971.

Naevdal, E., Olaussen, J. O. & Skonhoft, A. (2012). 'A bioeconomic model of trophy hunting', *Ecological Economics*, 73, 194–205.

Navas-Alemán, L. (2011). 'The impact of operating in multiple value chains for upgrading: The case of the Brazilian furniture and footwear industries', *World Development*, 39(8), 1386–1397.

Neilson, J., Pritchard, B. & Yeung, H. W.-c. (2014). 'Global value chains and global production networks in the changing international political economy: An introduction', *Review of International Political Economy*, 21(1), 1–8.

Neimark, B., Mahanty, S., & Dressler, W. (2016). 'Mapping value in a 'green' commodity frontier: Revisiting commodity chain analysis', *Development and Change*, 47(2), 240–265.

Ouma, S., Boeckler, M., & Lindner, P. (2013). 'Extending the margins of marketization', *Geoforum*, 48, 225–235.

Packer, C., Kosmala, M., Cooley, H. S., Brink, H., Pintea, L., Garshelis, D., *et al.* (2009). 'Sport hunting, predator control and conservation of large carnivores', *PLoS ONE*, 4(6), e5941.

Parnreiter, C. (2017). 'Global cities and the geographical transfer of value', *Urban Studies*, 56(1), 81–96.

Paul, A. K. & Røskaft, E. (2013). 'Environmental degradation and loss of traditional agriculture as two causes of conflicts in shrimp farming in the southwestern coastal Bangladesh: Present status and probable solutions', *Ocean and Coastal Management*, 85, 19–28.

Phelps, N. A., Atienza, M., & Arias, M. (2017). 'An invitation to the dark side of economic geography', *Environment and Planning A: Economy and Space*, 50(1), 236–244.

Pike, A., Rodríguez-Pose, A., & Tomaney, J. (2007). 'What kind of local and regional development and for whom?' *Regional Studies*, 41(9), 1253–1269.

Ponte, S. & Ewert, J. (2009). 'Which way is 'up' in upgrading? Trajectories of change in the value chain for South African wine', *World Development*, 37(10), 1637–1650.

Ponte, S.,Gereffi, G., & Raj-Reichert, G. (eds) (2019), *Handbook on Global Value Chains* (Cheltenham; Northampton MA: Edward Elgar Publishing).

Poulsen, R. T., Ponte, S., & Lister, J. (2016). 'Buyer-driven greening? Cargo-owners and environmental upgrading in maritime shipping', *Geoforum*, 68, 57–68.

Poulsen, R. T., Ponte, S., & Sornn-Friese, H. (2018). 'Environmental upgrading in global value chains: The potential and limitations of ports in the greening of maritime transport', *Geoforum*, 89, 83–95.

Prudham, S. (2009). 'Commodification', in: N. Castree, D. Demeritt, D. Liverman & B. Rhoads (eds), *A Companion to Environmental Geography* (Malden MA: Blackwell), 123–142.

Riisgaard, L., Bolwig, S., Ponte, S., Du Toit, A., Halberg, N., & Matose, F. (2010). 'Integrating poverty and environmental concerns into value-chain analysis: A strategic framework and practical guide', *Development Policy Review*, 28(2), 195–216.

Rodríguez-Pose, A. (2013). 'Do institutions matter for regional development?' *Regional Studies*, 47(7), 1034–1047.

Rudenko, I., Grote, U., & Lamers, J. (2008). 'Using a value chain approach for economic and environmental impact assessment of cotton production in Uzbekistan', in: J. Qi & K. T. Evered (eds), *Environmental Problems of Central Asia and their Economic, Social and Security Impacts.* NATO Science for Peace and Security Series C: Environmental Security (Dordrecht: Springer), 361–380.

Schmitz, H. (2006). 'Learning and earning in global garment and footwear chains', *The European Journal of Development Research*, 18(4), 546–571.

Scoones, I. (2009). 'Livelihoods perspectives and rural development', *The Journal of Peasant Studies*, 36(1), 171–196.

Smith, A. (2015). 'The state, institutional frameworks and the dynamics of capital in global production networks', *Progress in Human Geography*, 39(3), 290–315.

Sotarauta, M. & Mustikkamäki, N. (2015). 'Institutional entrepreneurship, power, and knowledge in innovation systems: Institutionalization of regenerative medicine in Tampere, Finland', *Environment and Planning C: Government and Policy*, 33(2), 342–357.

Spenceley, A. & Snyman, S. (2016). 'Can a wildlife tourism company influence conservation and the development of tourism in a specific destination?' *Tourism and Hospitality Research*, 17(1), 52–67.

United Nations Industrial Development Organization (UNIDO) (2015). 'Global Value Chains and Development: UNIDO's Support towards Inclusive and Sustainable Industrial Development' (UNIDO, December 2015). Available at: www.unido.org/sites/default/files/2016-03/GVC_REPORT_FINAL_0.PDF [Accessed 15 May 2020].

Urzedo, D. I., Neilson, J., Fisher, R., & Junqueira, R. G. P. (2020). 'A global production network for ecosystem services: The emergent governance of landscape restoration in the Brazilian Amazon', *Global Environmental Change*, 61(March), 102059.

Vicol, M., Fold, N., Pritchard, B., & Neilson, J. (2019). 'Global production networks, regional development trajectories and smallholder livelihoods in the Global South', *Journal of Economic Geography*, 19, 973–993.

Werner, M. (2016). 'Global production networks and uneven development: Exploring geographies of devaluation, disinvestment, and exclusion', *Geography Compass*, 10(11), 457–469.

World Bank (2020). 'Trading for Development in the Age of Global Value Chains: World Development Report 2020' (Washington DC: World Bank). Available at: www.worldbank.org/en/publication/wdr2020 [Accessed 18 January 2022].

Yeung, H. W.-c. (2009). 'Regional development and the competitive dynamics of global production networks: An East Asian perspective', *Regional Studies*, 43(3), 325–351.

Yeung, H. W.-c. (2015). 'Regional development in the global economy: A dynamic perspective of strategic coupling in global production networks', *Regional Science Policy & Practice*, 7(1), 1–23.

Yeung, H. W.-c. & Coe, N. M. (2015). 'Toward a dynamic theory of global production networks', *Economic Geography*, 91(1), 29–58.

Zimmermann, E. W. (1933). *World Resources and Industries* (New York: Harper & Brothers).

4

Benefit Sharing and Biodiversity Commodification in Southern Africa: A failed approach for social justice, equity, and conservation?

RACHEL WYNBERG

Introduction

Benefit sharing has emerged as an underlying approach to support the commodification of biodiversity in southern Africa. As a development concept, it is not new, first seeing expression in the 1990s with a range of approaches towards people-based conservation such as community-based natural resource management (CBNRM), revenue sharing, co-management, and recognition of the need for wildlife management to deliver concrete benefits to people to survive as a strategy (Nelson 2010; Wynberg & Hauck 2014).

Benefit sharing was first articulated as a legal expression by the Convention on Biological Diversity (CBD) in 1992, a time that coincided with escalating global concern about biodiversity loss, a growing movement to assert the cultural and environmental rights of indigenous peoples and local communities, as well as changes in science and technology that were opening up commercial opportunities for the use of biodiversity in lucrative pharmaceutical, biotechnology, and agricultural and food industries. This pertained to the use of genetic resources in novel applications, and in particular those arising from the use of non-domesticated plants, fungi and micro-organisms.

Using their leverage as the main repositories of biodiversity, biologically rich countries of the Global South argued that in order to allow companies to access their genetic resources and associated traditional knowledge, the technologically rich industrialised countries should transfer technology and share benefits from biodiversity commercialisation (Macilwain 1998). Through linking the three objectives of the CBD – conservation, sustainable use and equitable benefit sharing – it was argued that incentives would be created for sustainable use and local stewardship (Swanson 1998; Pavoni 2013). By embedding benefits for biodiversity conservation within so-called access and benefit-sharing (ABS) approaches, it was intended that affected species, habitats or ecosystems could receive financial support to ensure their conservation; much needed research could be done with that money on threatened biodiversity; community conservation and custodianship would strengthen; and through such conservation, sustainable use could be assured.

Importantly, the 1990s also ushered in a new era of privatising knowledge. The Trade-Related Aspects of Intellectual Property Rights Agreement (TRIPs) of the World Trade Organization fostered a global intellectual property rights system for agriculture, food, and healthcare. In this neoliberal context, companies' claims to ownership over innovations related to biodiversity expanded (Dutfield 2000). International policies set in place a market-driven framework for biodiversity use, conservation, and social justice, characterised by the idea of 'selling nature to save it' (McAfee 1999). In other words, the commercial use of biodiversity would lead to economic incentives that would ostensibly conserve biodiversity through its valorisation and use (Heynen & Robbins 2005). Access and benefit sharing, with its focus on 'rights' over resources and technologies, formed part of the suite of neoliberal approaches to commodify and marketise nature. State-driven approaches to conservation were replaced by these new frontiers of capitalist expansion (Sullivan 2006; Bollig *et al.* this volume), that espoused a 'win-win' discourse of achieving conservation benefits, supporting rural livelihoods, developing new medicines and other products, and realising profits for industry (Svarstad 2004).

In what has been described as the 'Grand Bargain' (Gollin 1993), the CBD and, its 2010 Nagoya Protocol, laid down a new and unique way of treating trade in genetic resources and regulating bioprospecting. To access genetic resources, users needed to provide 'fair and equitable benefits' to the provider country, including technology transfer; and to receive such benefits, a provider country needed to facilitate access to genetic resources to companies or researchers (hence 'access and benefit sharing') (CBD 1992; Secretariat of the Convention on Biological Diversity 2011). Similarly, bilateral contracts and benefit-sharing agreements were designed to compensate the traditional knowledge holders associated with these resources. In practice, this meant that companies and signatory countries now had an obligation to get permission before collecting resources and knowledge (prior informed consent), mutually agree on the terms of exchange, and share benefits fairly with local providers and countries. This highly transactional approach was thus entirely reliant on contracts being negotiated between the so-called 'provider' and 'user' of genetic resources and traditional knowledge. It formed part of the stable of market-based commodification approaches that have developed since the 1990s, aiming to create 'win-win' solutions for economic development and conservation, including Payment for Ecosystem Services, REDD+, CBNRM and certification among others.

In this way, the CBD represented a fundamental change in the way in which genetic resources were exchanged and viewed. No longer were they the 'common heritage' of humankind; instead, countries now increasingly asserted sovereign rights over their biological resources and control over their access. Moreover, the contributions made by traditional knowledge holders towards the development of new medicines, foods and personal care products was to be recognised and equitably rewarded.

Benefit sharing was interpreted widely to go beyond the sharing of revenue to mean the 'fair and equitable' division and distribution of both monetary and non-monetary benefits but without specifying how these subjective and almost unmeasurable objectives could be assessed. Monetary benefits were expected to reflect the market value of products commercialised based on genetic resources and biodiversity. Non-monetary benefits were anticipated to include a range of options, including stronger research collaborations and technology transfer between the Global North and South, support for conservation, capacity development and skills development. Overall, the intention was to achieve a greater degree of social, environmental, and economic justice in the commercial use of biodiversity, and to contribute towards strengthened rights of indigenous and local communities and reducing inequalities (Reid *et al.* 1993; Wynberg & Laird 2007).

So-called access and benefit sharing (ABS) has had profound impacts on trade and research in natural products and on the range of actors and institutions involved in regulating its use and complying with associated laws (Laird *et al.* 2020). With 196 states members of the CBD and 138 party to its Nagoya Protocol, including 48 African countries, hundreds of laws and policies are now in place to give effect to these international norms. For example, based on Regulation 511/2014, the European Union now requires member states to comply with measures for the use of genetic resources and associated traditional knowledge in research and development. As a result, it is common-place for European companies to insist on an ABS permit before trade in botanical products or other biological resources can proceed. In a similar fashion, governments are closing down industries that do not comply with ABS laws.

A central requirement of these laws is for benefit-sharing agreements to be in place before permits are issued. Over the past 30 years, a range of agreements have been negotiated between different actors including governments, research institutions, companies, and communities, many involving African resources and communities (see e.g. Greene 2004; Gamez 2007; Laird & Wynberg 2008; Robinson 2010; UNDP 2018; Chinsembu & Chinsembu

2020). While the intention is to use these mechanisms to leverage greater social and economic justice, to create incentives for biodiversity conservation and sustainable use, and to strengthen the rights of indigenous and local communities, emerging evidence suggests otherwise (Laird *et al.* 2020).

Through review of a selection of four cases of biodiversity commercialisation in South Africa, and their adoption of different benefit-sharing approaches, this chapter aims to explain this apparent contradiction through posing the following questions:

> First, have historical injustices of biopiracy been addressed through benefit-sharing agreements and, if so, to what extent has restorative justice been achieved?
>
> Second, has the process to develop benefit-sharing agreements been procedurally fair and inclusive?
>
> Third, have the agreements led to an equitable outcome?
>
> And lastly, what positive impacts, if any, have materialised for the conservation and sustainable use of biodiversity?

The chapter argues that ABS has been designed as a universalised instrument of compliance, disconnected from local, cultural and historical contexts, and that its implementation threatens to increase conflict among communities, and entrench or even enlarge existing power imbalances between corporate interests and resource custodians. Solutions are proposed that offer a more place-based, informed and inclusive approach for supporting biodiversity-based livelihoods, recognising that while ABS may have stimulated better business practices, it does not offer a solution for the transformative shift required to address social inequalities or the biodiversity crisis.

Political and legal contexts

Bioprospecting and the biodiversity-based economy[1] have become firmly embedded in economic strategies across southern Africa. South Africa's President Cyril Ramaphosa, launching 'Operation Phakisa'[2] for the Biodiversity

---

[1]   The biodiversity-based economy forms part of wider conceptualisations of the bio-economy and is typically centred on the commercial use of biodiversity for economic development and social upliftment (DEA 2016). Definitions of the bio-economy are commonly associated with modern biotechnology, but also include bio-resources, based on the processing and upgrading of biological raw materials and the establishment of new value chains centred on producing biofuels and managing waste (Bugge *et al.* 2016).

[2]   Operation Phakisa, meaning 'hurry up' in Sesotho, is an initiative of the South African government designed to accelerate the delivery of development priorities.

Economy in 2018, projected the creation of 162,000 jobs and the generation of R47 billion (US$2.6 billion) by 2030, based on a public investment of around R1,18 billion (Government of South Africa 2018). Namibian President Hifikepunye Pohamba has likewise placed biodiversity 'at the centre of our development efforts to achieve sustainable economic growth and poverty allevi-ation in our country, especially in rural areas' (Government of Namibia 2014), while other countries across the region have made similar pronouncements.

These strategies are not new, based to a large extent on the region's long-standing promotion of wildlife-based tourism and hunting as an approach to attract foreign revenue and enable community benefits. At the same time, many of the region's plant species have a long history of commercialisation, often riding on the back of traditional knowledge. For example, the lucrative Devil's Claw (*Harpagophytum procumbens*) industry has its roots in knowledge of '*otjihangatene*' (*Harpagophytum*) passed on in the early 1900s by the Herero Samuel Kariko, to Hellwig, a medical officer of the imperial protection forces in the then German South-West Africa (Brendler 2021). Combined with knowledge published by the botanist Lübbert in 1901, this was later used by German scientists to initiate chemical investigations into the medicinal properties of the plant (Volk 1964), with trade commencing to Germany in the early 1950s (Brendler 2021; Lavelle this volume).

Rooibos, the popular herbal tea indigenous to mountainous regions of the Cape and long used by local people in these areas, was introduced to European markets at the turn of the 20th century and quickly established itself as the health tea of choice in South Africa and abroad (Wynberg 2017). Leaves of *Cyclopia* species (honeybush), similarly have a long history of use as an herbal tea by local people in the southern Cape regions of South Africa, and today form part of a growing industry (Ndwandwe this volume). The fragrant leaves of the buchu shrub (*Agathosma betulina* and *A. crenulata*) were first used medicinally by indigenous peoples of southern Africa and have been traded commercially on global markets for more than 200 years (Low 2007);

Today, a thriving industry exists based on use of the plant as a flavourant and medicine. The commercial use of *Aloe ferox* similarly spans centuries and is grounded on traditional knowledge – both of the plant's medicinal uses and the ways in which it is harvested (Chen *et al.* 2012).

Many ornamental species, such as the geraniums that adorn the streets of cities across the world (mostly cultivars of *Pelargonium zonale* and *P. peltatum*) had their origins in colonial –particularly Dutch – explorations of the botanical treasures of southern Africa for economic gain, and today comprise an industry worth many millions of Euros per annum (Reinten *et al.* 2011). These among many other examples bear testimony to the long-established trade and exploitation of southern African species for commercial gain in pharmaceutical, agricultural, botanical, cosmetics, and food and beverage industries, and to the way in which almost all of these industries drew directly from traditional knowledge.

In recent years, however, commercialisation has taken a turn, with renewed vigour given both to the potential economic value of indigenous southern African resources – and plants in particular, and to the benefits these could create for local livelihoods and conservation. Spurred by new technologies and growing markets for natural products, alongside an increased interest in ethical trade and the marketing opportunities associated with the stories of plants and people among socially conscious consumers, a new currency has materialised for biodiversity. At the same time, there has been a growing trend towards formalisation of the sector, driven in part by concerns over the sustainability of harvesting, as well as those relating to the inequity of exploitative supply chains (Wynberg *et al.* 2015). Fears of biopiracy (see below), and the concentration of intellectual property and capital in the hands of large biotechnology and pharmaceutical corporations in the Global North (Robinson 2010) have provided the backdrop for responses from southern Africa.

Formalisation has seen expression through a raft of international and national laws, as well as social and ecological labelling and certification systems (Raynolds & Long 2007). Two main approaches have evolved in the embracement of commercialisation as a development strategy. The first is biotrade, meaning the commercial collection, processing and sale of products derived from biodiversity, usually for the cosmetic, food, botanical medicine and other sectors relying on the sourcing of raw materials. These non-timber forest products are the backbone of many rural economies throughout the region (Shackleton & Shackleton 2004) and their commercialisation has long been promoted as a way to conserve biodiversity and improve livelihoods for indigenous and local communities (see e.g. Neumann & Hirsch 2000; Arnold & Ruiz-Pérez 2001; Belcher & Schreckenberg 2007).

Over the past three decades a second strategy has emerged, centred on biodiscovery, which is the collection of and research on samples of biological resources in order to discover genetic information or biochemicals of value. Biodiscovery usually takes place in high technology and research intensive sectors, such as pharmaceutical and biotechnology industries, but is also a strategy for crop protection, food and beverage, cosmetics and other industries. Biodiscovery uses what the CBD refers to as genetic resources – genetic material of actual or potential value, with any material of plant, animal, microbial or other origin containing functional units of heredity. Researchers in biodiscovery seek physical access to genetic resources, but increasingly in the form of genetic sequence data accessed through databases. The CBD and accompanying ABS agreements were originally linked to biodiscovery, but implementation of the

Nagoya Protocol has led to increasing use of ABS agreements in biotrade as a tool to strengthen equity and fairness in trade relations.

Southern African countries have increasingly adopted ABS in national laws and regulations, led largely by South Africa which initiated an ABS policy process as early as 1996 (Crouch *et al.* 2008; Wynberg 2018). In 2017 Namibia followed suit with its Access to Biological and Genetic Resources and Associated Traditional Knowledge Act (2), with regulations effective from November 2021. Zimbabwe and Botswana similarly have legal instruments in place relating to ABS but none have been fully adopted in practice (Nott 2019).

South Africa by far has the most developed, complex and wide-ranging ABS regulatory architecture and, with dozens of benefit-sharing agreements brokered to date and more than 130 permits issued to date by the national government, the most experience in ABS implementation. Importantly, and in contrast to the narrow definition of genetic resources embraced by the CBD and Nagoya Protocol, South African law also includes *both* biotrade and biodiscovery within its ambit, essentially setting up a permit system for any and all activities associated with the use and development of biodiversity – from the harvesting of resources through to its research, trade, and processing, requiring benefit-sharing agreements to be negotiated as a condition of the permit approval.

While the legal and political intent of these requirements is clear, there has been surprisingly little analysis of how ABS is located within the broader framing of commodification, nor how ABS has surreptitiously emerged as the dominant discourse for addressing inequalities and injustices in the natural product sector in South Africa. Table 4.1 provides an overview of a selected number of cases from South Africa, characterised by approaches to embed and formalise benefit-sharing in commercial agreements through the inclusion of traditional knowledge holders, harvesters and/or resource custodians as signatories and beneficiaries. A further analysis of these cases is included in the next section.

ABS in practice

Addressing biopiracy and achieving restorative justice

Biopiracy is a term that describes the way that corporations or researchers (usually from the Global North) misappropriate the genetic resources and traditional knowledge of countries and communities (usually from the Global South) without their consent, and, typically, patent this information to enable

Table 4.1 Overview of key features characterising the commodification of *Hoodia gordonii*, *Aspalathus linearis* (rooibos), *Sceletium tortuosum* (kougoed) and *Pelargonium sidoides*.

Plant Species	Origin	Commercial Use	Traditional Use & Knowledge	Benefit-Sharing Agreements (Bsa)
Hoodia GORDONII [now discontinued]	Southern Africa	Food supplements to suppress appetite	Used traditionally by San to quench thirst (and hunger)	BSA between state-based CSIR and the SASC.
ASPALATHUS LINEARIS (ROOIBOS)	Western Cape, South Africa	Food and beverage, Supplements	Used traditionally for various purposes. Many harvesting practices are traditionally based	BSA between the Rooibos Council, SASC and NKC. BSA between Nestlé South Africa, SASC, and NKC.
Sceletium TORTUOSUM (KOUGOED, KANNA)	Western and Northern Cape, South Africa	Medicinal products for depression and anxiety	Long used among San and Khoi as a mild narcotic or intoxicant and to treat pain and other ailments	BSA between HGH Pharmaceuticals and the SASC; SASC receives 5% of net proceeds and a 1% exclusivity payment; 50% of SASC revenues are directed towards Nama-speaking communities where knowledge was first obtained by the researcher
Pelargonium SIDOIDES	Eastern parts of South Africa, Lesotho	Medicinal remedies to treat bronchitis	Widely used as a traditional medicine	BSA between German pharmaceutical company Schwabe, SA company Parceval and two traditional councils.

Plant Species	Governance	Patents	Custodianship & Use	Conservation
Hoodia GORDONII [now discontinued]	Trust set up to distribute benefits. Now discontinued.	Multiple patents linked to appetite suppressant properties, products and processes, and propagation.	Almost all cultivated on private lands.	Over-harvesting in early years led to CITES Appendix II listing; no wider conservation measures exist.
ASPALATHUS LINEARIS (ROOIBOS)	The Andries Steenkamp Trust administers benefits for the SASC. An ABS Trust administers benefits for the NKC.	Over 150 patents for food supplements, medicinal and cosmetic applications.	Mostly cultivated on private farms with a limited amount of wild harvesting and cultivation in communal or church-owned areas.	Significant biodiversity impacts from rooibos industry. BSA does not mention conservation.
Sceletium TORTUOSUM (KOUGOED, KANNA)	SASC receives benefits via the state Biodiversity Fund. A Trust is set up to distribute benefits to Nama communities.	Multiple patents linked to depression and anxiety treatments.	All cultivated on private farms.	No mention in BSA.
Pelargonium SIDOIDES	Funds transferred to traditional leaders through two Trusts. Unclear how community receives funds.	Five patents revoked by Schwabe due to biopiracy claims and lack of novelty. Over 100 patents held by Schwabe and other companies for the processing and preparation of products containing Pelargonium.	Cultivated on private lands in and out of southern Africa. Wild harvesting also occurs on communal lands in the Eastern Cape and Lesotho.	Biodiversity management plan centres on sustainable use of the plant but not wider conservation measures. Industry projects linked largely to social benefits.

(Sources: Wynberg & Chennells 2009; Chennells 2013; Morris 2016; Van Niekerk & Wynberg 2012; Wynberg 2017; Modise 2018; National Khoisan Council 2019).

knowledge to be enclosed and further commodified for the purpose of profit (Dutfield 2009; Robinson 2010). Biopiracy is not new, and has characterised many of the colonial and imperialist patterns of accumulation, but the emergence of global intellectual property rules, alongside growing awareness of the exploitation and rights of indigenous peoples and local communities, has placed it in the spotlight over the past three decades.

As Robinson (2010) observes, it has also moved beyond 'activist' agendas to become a firm part of government positions. 'We must rid the country of the scourge of biopiracy' remarked one high-level government official in the South Africa Ministry of Science and Innovation (personal communication 2020), while another senior official from the Department of Environmental Affairs emphasised the need to curb the 'rampant biopiracy' in the country when introducing South Africa's National Biodiversity Economy Strategy in 2016. While the extent to which this rhetoric is rooted in reality lies beyond the scope of this chapter, its shaping of policies in southern Africa is indisputable.

One of the most iconic biopiracy cases of all – both in southern Africa and globally – is that of *Hoodia gordonii*, a succulent plant first researched in the 1960s for its appetite and thirst-quenching properties by the South African state-funded Council for Scientific and Industrial Research (Wynberg & Chennells 2009). The involvement of the indigenous San, the oldest human inhabitants of Africa, and the intrigue of a plant promising to simultaneously tackle the Western affliction of obesity and the development challenges of the San people triggered the public's imagination, offering hope for resolving the crises of inequality. Initial research and development led to a patent being granted for these properties, and commercial agreements developed with the UK-based company Phytopharm and pharmaceutical giant Pfizer to develop an anti-obesity drug. However, this was without the consent, knowledge, or involvement of the indigenous San, despite their knowledge being the basis for the research. Astonishingly, the Council for Scientific and Industrial Research (CSIR) had told Phytopharm that the hundred-thousand-strong San 'no longer existed' – a statement later defended by the CSIR as a response on their part to avoid raising expectations. In response to NGO intervention and a public outcry, the first-ever benefit-sharing agreement in South Africa was finalised in 2003 – between the CSIR and the South African San Council[3] – which represents the three indigenous San communities of South Africa – ≠Khomani, !Xun and Khwe.

---

3   The South African San Council was established in 2001 as part of the Working Group of Indigenous Minorities in Southern Africa (WIMSA), which is charged with uniting and representing San communities from Botswana, Namibia, and South Africa. As Chennells *et al.* (2009) explain, the South African San Council represents the

While *Hoodia* was later abandoned as a commercial product due to safety and efficacy concerns (Blom *et al.* 2011), the case has been precedent-setting. Although relatively insignificant monetary benefits were generated for the San Council (about US$50,000), the case demonstrated a 'workable' model for benefit sharing with indigenous peoples – a feat long considered unachievable by industry sceptics. At the same time, capacity was built within the South African San Council to negotiate with industry and leverage benefits. Claiming to be primary traditional knowledge holders of all southern African biodiversity, representatives of indigenous San and, more recently Khoi, are now at the frontline of many deals proposed to commercialise the region's biological resources. This has paid rich dividends and a suite of new benefit-sharing agreements has since been negotiated. *Sceletium tortuosum* for example, also known as kougoed or kanna, is a succulent plant well known for its mood-enhancing properties and long used among indigenous San and Khoi as a mild narcotic or intoxicant and to treat pain and other ailments (Gericke & Viljoen 2008). Using knowledge from Nama-speaking traditional healers from two villages in the Northern Cape, Nourivier and Paulshoek, a researcher was guided towards the plant's use and patented an extract that is now incorporated into medication to improve cognitive function and treat anxiety and depression (Chennells 2013; Modise 2018). Initial research did not obtain the prior informed consent of knowledge holders but a later benefit-sharing agreement between the South African San Council and HG&H Pharmaceuticals recognises both the original contribution of Nama communities and those of indigenous San (HG&H and the South African San Council 2011).

The most recent case is that of rooibos tea, *Aspalathus linearis*, South Africa's most successful and oldest indigenous natural product industry, and the array of new products that incorporate the plant, such as cosmetics, slimming preparations, novel foods, extracts, and flavourants. First commercialised at the turn of the 20th century, this is today a US$31 million local industry, employing some 5,000 people and trading amounts of up to 15,000 tons per annum (Barends-Jones 2020). Like many other historical enterprises in South Africa, however, these economic feats have been mirrored by a history of dispossession and marginalisation (Coombe *et al.* 2014; Ives 2017). Beginning with massacres of San and Khoi in rooibos-growing landscapes centuries ago (Penn 2006) and continuing with the relocation of coloured and black people in the area through the 1913 Natives Land Act and the ongoing

---

modern form of San leadership, aiming to represent different San communities in South Africa democratically. Although the council is not the only body that claims to represent San communities, it has been a central actor in negotiating benefit-sharing agreements based on traditional knowledge claims.

marginalisation of such groups through apartheid policies, the geographical and political backdrop to the rooibos industry is one of dispossession and adversity.

Over the past decade, a new set of controversies has arisen about equity and justice in the rooibos industry, centred both on the biological resource and on the traditional knowledge that fostered the growth of this lucrative trade (Wynberg 2017; Wynberg *et al.* 2023). Accusations of biopiracy have taken centre stage, leading to a reassessment of the conditions under which rooibos is traded (Berne Declaration and Natural Justice 2010). At the same time, the South African San Council and National Khoisan Council[4] have launched demands for a stake in rooibos benefits based on traditional knowledge claims, with a benefit-sharing agreement concluded in 2019 between these organisations and the rooibos industry.

Between 2007 and 2010, biopiracy accusations also underpinned a formal patent challenge by two NGOs and traditional healers from the Masakhane community in the Eastern Cape province of South Africa (ACB 2008), linked to the use of *Pelargonium sidoides*, a plant occurring in South Africa as well as much of Lesotho. Widely used locally as a traditional medicine, the red tubers of the plant are used in *Umckaloabo*, a successful cold-care remedy manufactured by the German pharmaceutical company Schwabe and its South African counterpart Parceval Pharmaceuticals (van Niekerk & Wynberg 2012). Largely as a result of negative publicity, and a fear of being labelled 'bio-buccaneers', Schwabe renounced four of its patents in 2010, with a fifth revoked for lack of an inventive step. Shortly thereafter, a benefit-sharing agreement was developed between Parceval and the King Sandile Development Trust, the Imingcangathelo Community Development Trust and other traditional councils, partnerships which Morris (2016) describes as 'entrenching and in some instances expanding, apartheid-associated boundaries and configurations of power'.

Despite both apparent and real victories, all these cases are indisputably rooted in histories of exploitation, oppression, and marginalisation, with cries of biopiracy often echoing the wider injustices that have occurred, especially to indigenous San and Khoi. Here, ABS is offered as the remedy, a chance to make good and to bring about redress through financial redistribution despite acknowledged flaws of representation and conflicting paradigms. Patenting, for

---

4   Although absent from *Hoodia* negotiations, the National Khoisan Council, established by former President Nelson Mandela in 1999 to accommodate Khoisan historical leadership within South Africa's constitutional framework, has increasingly become a partner to various benefit-sharing agreements, in collaboration with the South African San Council. The Khoisan historically comprise five main groupings, namely San, Griqua, Nama, Koranna, and Cape Khoi.

example, and the idea of 'owning' life is abhorrent to many indigenous world-views, yet according to the lawyer representing San in *Hoodia* negotiations, the principle of 'no patents on life' was considered 'too expensive' (Wynberg 2004). As the next sections reveal, ABS and the resources and promises it offers have also led to a clamour for representation, within a political climate where identity is continuously shape-shifting (Mellet 2020). The remedies for biopiracy emerge as modes of accumulation in an extractive economy, arguably entrenching inequalities and a form of 'biodiversity apartheid', rather than achieving restorative justice.

Procedural fairness and representation

Equity is concerned as much with the outcome of negotiations as it is with the process developed to get there. Wynberg and Hauck (2014) emphasise the importance of process in shaping actor involvement in benefit-sharing interventions and their outcomes, and describe how procedural fairness is an integral part of benefit sharing. McDermott *et al.* (2013) articulate the concept of procedural equity, referring to decision making and the inter-linking dimension of contextual equity, relating to the pre-existing conditions that limit or facilitate people's access to decision-making procedures, resources, and, thereby, benefits. As the examples in this chapter illustrate, procedural fairness is very much the beleaguered step-child in the ABS process.

As currently conceptualised, ABS obliges governments – in this case South Africa (but the argument could be made more widely) – to adopt an approach whereby those seeking permits must negotiate with an organised legal entity and agree on a benefit-sharing outcome that is 'mutually acceptable'. In doing so the assumption is made that communities are sufficiently organised and capacitated to develop a legal standing and that those represented are the legitimate claimants. Although recognising that communities will seldom be on an equal footing to those using the resources or knowledge, government assumes that its facilitating role in negotiations will enable this hurdle to be overcome.

Unfolding experiences from South Africa cast doubts on these assumptions and suggest that the ABS legal architecture is pre-destined to prefer groupings that are already organised as legal entities, to favour certain groups over others, and to entrench existing marginalities. Faced with the difficulties of identi-fying traditional knowledge holders and finding representative and legally constituted communities with whom to negotiate benefit-sharing agreements, industry has negotiated either with traditional authorities, who may not be the knowledge holders, or with groups who may not necessarily represent all knowledge holders, but who are sufficiently organised and authorised to engage and negotiate. The concern, as reported by van Niekerk and Wynberg

(2012), Morris (2016) and others, is that this can lead to elite capture by groups who are more organised than others, or by traditional authorities who in some contexts may not be democratically elected or widely accepted. Remarked one industry representative: 'The system of giving money to chiefs is a disaster waiting to happen; now that DEA [Department of Environmental Affairs] have begun to roll out this approach it will be impossible to go back' (personal communication 2016).

In the case of *Pelargonium sidoides*, Morris (2016: 536) similarly describes how ABS has facilitated business partnerships between South African traditional leaders and multinational pharmaceutical companies and has led to a situation where 'ABS rights are currently instruments of tribal subjectification and thus an important mode of accumulation for traditional leaders'. Industry is partly to blame for this situation due to their tendency to look for 'easy' groups with whom to partner and sign benefit-sharing agreements but who may not necessarily be representative of knowledge or resource owners. Government, however, has also been complicit, tending towards 'pragmatic' but naïve solutions, accepting the legitimacy of traditional authorities and other groups without asking deeper questions about what is at stake. This has been bolstered by recent adoption of the Traditional and Khoi-San Leadership Act (3 of 2019), widely criticised as giving new oppressive powers to unelected chiefs in the same way the apartheid government did by giving chiefs the power to take decisions on communal land without consent from those whose rights are directly affected (Pikoli 2019). While the historical role of traditional authorities as collaborators of the colonial and later apartheid governments has left a deep-seated legacy (Mamdani 1996), local contexts will clearly vary. Lavelle (this volume), for example, explains the centrality of traditional authorities in the organised harvesting and trade of Devil's Claw in the Zambezi Region of Namibia, and how, indirectly, they support communities to claim access to land and resources through CBNRM.

The question of priority – or 'who was first' – has been especially controversial, due largely to claims by representatives of indigenous San and Khoi groups over traditional knowledge of all Southern African biodiversity (Chennells Albertyn 2010). In the case of rooibos tea, the South African San Council and the National Khoisan Council initiated demands in 2010 that industry recognise their role as 'primary knowledge holders'. A government-commissioned report concluded there was 'no evidence to dispute this claim' and required the rooibos industry to negotiate a benefit-sharing agreement with participating San and Khoi organisations (DEA 2015). Driven by concerns that they would not receive a licence to operate without this agreement, the rooibos industry entered a series of protracted negotiations with the South African San Council and the National Khoisan Council (and their legal representatives), facilitated by the Department of Environmental Affairs (Wynberg 2017; Schroeder *et al.* 2020; Wynberg *et al.*, 2023). Nine years later, in March 2019, a benefit-sharing agreement was finally signed.

The negotiations were fraught, divisive and, due to the signing of non-disclosure agreements, untransparent. The way in which small-scale rooibos farmers and contemporary custodians of the plant were to be recognised was contentious. Colonial persecution in the region and apartheid policies, led to the relocation, disenfranchisement, and ongoing marginalisation of local coloured and black people, with knowledge of rooibos largely lost by San and Khoi who were moved thousands of kilometres away. The knowledge was retained by the small-scale rooibos farmers and farmworkers who remained but these mixed-race descendants of European settlers, former slaves, and Khoi and San do not readily identify as 'indigenous' and were largely left out of the negotiating process for compensation and eventually included only through the National Khoisan Council (Wynberg 2019; Ives *et al.* 2020; Wynberg *et al.*, 2023). In a similar way, the custodians of *Sceletium* in the Northern Cape had no say in the lodging of a patent based on their knowledge, nor did they participate in negotiating an agreement on the back of this knowledge. Equally, non-San groups with traditional knowledge of *Hoodia* species, such as Nama, Damara, and Topnaar, were excluded from benefit-sharing negotiations, likely due to the sheer impossibility of including representation for multiple groups, located in remote areas across three countries (Wynberg & Chennells 2009).

The requirement for legally constituted entities with which to negotiate has further entrenched these marginalities. A commonality across all cases points to the lack of legal organisation among local resource custodians and knowledge holders – whether they be healers in Paulshoek harvesting *Sceletium*, farmers or farmworkers in the Cederberg tending rooibos fields, or Nama and Damara in Namibia. Benefits from ABS can only be leveraged if these knowledge holders and custodians are constituted as an organised legal entity. The benefits of doing so are palpable. For example, both the South African San Council and the National Khoisan Council were legally constituted prior to the Bioprospecting, Access and Benefit-Sharing (BABS) regulations, and developed capacity to negotiate with industry, and leverage benefits. They also both had significant support from external organisations, with the San Council represented by lawyer Roger Chennells who supported all preceding benefit-sharing agreements, and the National Khoisan Council represented by the legal NGO Natural Justice. Important lessons emerge from these cases, affirming the importance of history, experience and legal support, but also suggesting this could lead to new forms of exclusion.

While recognising and rewarding traditional knowledge is clearly critical and necessary, these experiences suggest that more visible, better organised and resourced, or politically well-connected communities, groups or representative organisations that hold traditional knowledge or genetic resources, may be in a better position to 'prove' origin – perhaps to the exclusion of others with equally legitimate claims who are less organised and advantaged (Dutfield *et al.* 2020).

Equitable benefit sharing?

Those involved in supporting and negotiating the agreements described have largely acknowledged that pragmatism guided their decisions and deliberations, with the justification that a more inclusive process would stall business opportunities and limit benefits for communities (Chennells 2013; Wynberg & Chennells 2009; Wynberg 2018). Once benefits are channelled to representative groups, it is argued, their distribution can be channelled via appropriate governance structures and with suitable oversight (Chennells 2013; Schroeder *et al.* 2020). Two questions emerge from these assumptions: first, what is the nature of the benefits that are agreed upon (and how are decisions reached about them); and second, what does governance look like on the ground.

Table 4.1 summarises the benefits articulated by the agreements. Arising from the *Hoodia* agreement (see Wynberg 2004; Wynberg & Chennells 2009 for comprehensive analyses), the South African San Council was to receive 6% of all royalties received by the CSIR from Phytopharm as a result of the successful exploitation of *Hoodia* products. The South African San Council would also receive 8% of the milestone income received by the CSIR from Phytopharm when certain performance targets were met. In the event of successful commercialisation, these monies would be payable into a trust set up jointly by the CSIR and the South African San Council to 'uplift the standard of living and well-being of the San peoples of southern Africa'. Any intellectual property arising from traditional indigenous knowledge of use of *Hoodia* and related to the CSIR patents remained vested exclusively with the CSIR, and the San Council had no right to claim any co-ownership of the patents or products derived from the patents. San were also prohibited from assisting or entering into an agreement with any third party for the development, research, and exploitation of any competing products or patents. Recognising that knowledge of *Hoodia* was held widely among San across southern Africa, principles were developed collaboratively to guide the sharing of benefits. There was unanimous agreement that 75% of all Trust income would be equally distributed to the constituted San Councils of Namibia, Botswana, and South Africa; that 10% would be retained by the Trust for internal and administration purposes; that 10% would be allocated to the Working Group of Indigenous Minorities in Southern Africa (WIMSA) as an emergency reserve fund; and that 5% would be allocated to WIMSA to cover administration of the San networks. Priorities within the region such as education, leadership empowerment, and land security were agreed upon as non-binding recommendations to the respective San Councils. Although commercialisation was later abandoned due to health concerns arising from clinical trials, a total of about R569,000 (US$690,000) was received by the Trust that was established based on the agreement.

In the case of *Sceletium*, the San Council receives 5% of net proceeds received by HG&H and an annual exclusivity payment of 1% on sales (HG&H Pharmaceuticals and the South African San Council, Benefit-Sharing Agreement 2011). An 'exclusivity' payment is made in respect of product endorsement, marketing and branding assistance and the use of the San logo. The San undertakes to place 50% of all royalties into a trust account for onward payment to the Paulshoek and Nourivier communities. As at 2018, approximately R10 million (US$580,000) had been secured by the San Council arising from the agreement (Modise 2018).

The rooibos benefit-sharing agreement between the Rooibos Council, the South African San Council and the National Khoisan Council requires a form of annual 'tax' for all processed rooibos. The levy of 1.5% of farm-gate price is split equally between the San Council and the National Khoisan Council, with the Andries Steenkamp Trust administering benefits on behalf of the SA San Council and the Khoikhoi Peoples Rooibos ABS Trust doing so for the National Khoisan Council. Of the 50% received by the Khoi Trust, 65% is intended to be equally distributed between Griqua, Nama, Koranna, Cape Khoi, and 'rooibos indigenous farming communities'; the other 15% is allocated to the National Khoisan Council, with 20% for administration (National Khoisan Council, Cederberg Belt Indigenous Farmers Representatives 2019).

Information about the *Pelargonium* benefit-sharing agreement remains confidential but involves undisclosed monetary benefits to two traditional councils based on an agreed additional percentage of the price per kilogram paid to the harvesters. Outside of the formal agreements, an industry-sponsored private trust supports a range of social projects (Feiter 2019). In 2022, a payment of ZAR12,2 million was made to the two Trusts (DFFE, 2022).

At face value these amounts are significant, undeniably creating economic opportunities and providing important recognition of historical injustices. However, given that the scales are tipped from the outset to favour those with economic power, resources, and capacity, the question as to whether they are 'fair and equitable' remains more equivocal. Benefits received by San organisations from *Hoodia*, for example, amount to only a tiny percentage – between 0.03% and 1.2% – of net sales of the product (Wynberg 2004). The terms of the agreement – although now obsolete – are also questionable, leaving profits received by Phytopharm and its partners unchanged and preventing the San Council from using knowledge of *Hoodia* in any other commercial applications.

In the case of rooibos, the 1.5% levy must be paid not only by the large white commercial rooibos farmers who own 93% of the land and dominate the industry, but also by about 200 small-scale 'coloured' rooibos farmers comprising mixed-race descendants of European settlers, former slaves, and Khoi and San, who continue to farm rooibos, but own or manage only 7% of rooibos tea lands and remain economically marginalised. These farmers are included in the benefit-sharing agreement only nominally, as part of the National Khoisan Council, and receive less than 5% of the total value of the levy. *Pelargonium* harvesters may benefit from better pricing, a more secure trade relationship through the ABS agreement, and social responsibility programmes but continue to be suppliers of raw material at low prices.

Combined, these cases suggest that while agreements have led to some financial benefits, a 'business as usual' approach prevails that neither transfers power nor enables a community-based or -owned approach to commercialisation. Control remains vested in two key assets: the land, with ownership remaining highly skewed towards industry partners and the monopolisation of markets through cultivation; and intellectual property which, as Table 4.1 illustrates, demonstrates a rapid increase in the number of patents that remain disassociated from knowledge holders, resource owners, and benefit sharing.

Conservation impacts

The ABS agreements described have largely centred on benefits arising from the use of traditional knowledge, but what of the resource and its conservation? As described earlier, conservation was one of the three pillars of the CBD, intended to serve as an incentive and funding mechanism for biodiversity conservation, while addressing historical inequities around the use of genetic and biological resources. There are multiple ways this can happen. Biodiscovery may contribute to conservation through support for biodiversity research and through fostering equitable collaborations and technology transfer with high biodiversity but income poor countries, while biotrade may involve sustainable harvesting and cultivation of threatened and high-demand species or agroforestry and reforestation schemes for degraded lands (Laird & Wynberg 2020; Wynberg & Laird 2023).

While some exceptions exist, in practice there is little evidence of ABS leading to the leverage of significant conservation benefits, either globally or in its 15 years of implementation in South Africa (Laird & Wynberg 2020; Wynberg & Laird 2023). A common reason is that economic development and restorative justice are seen to 'trump' conservation, especially in developing economies such as South Africa where basic needs are pressing. In contrast to approaches such as CBNRM, where some land and resource rights may be devolved by the state to conservancies or community forests, who manage resources based on agreed management practices (Sullivan 2002), ABS agreements are often disconnected from geographical, historical, and cultural contexts, and the relationship to conservation is perceived as antagonistic rather than mutually supportive or reinforcing. This has been aggravated by regulatory approaches such as those articulated in South Africa's Biodiversity Act, which set up different processes for accessing resources and traditional knowledge, and therefore different negotiating platforms and different benefit-sharing agreements.

Such decouplings are incongruous given that a strong relationship exists between traditional knowledge and conservation. Indigenous peoples and local communities are custodians of about 80% of the world's biodiversity and their ways of life, cultures, customary governance, and knowledge of nature are integrally connected to the conservation and sustainable use of biodiversity in their territories (Forest Peoples Programme *et al.* 2020). Yet, as the South African experience reveals, the picture is inordinately more complex than it seems. Part of the reason for this disconnect is because traditional knowledge holders are not always the same as resource custodians and through land and resource dispossession resulting from colonial and, in the case of South Africa and Namibia, apartheid policies, have been geographically dislocated from resources over which their ancestors held knowledge.

The cases described in this chapter are illustrative of the small role that conservation has played in ABS agreements to date. In the case of *Hoodia*, commercialisation was halted due to health concerns, but it is still noteworthy that the agreement, despite recognising San 'interrelatedness with nature in all its forms, over the ages', includes no mention of conservation aside from a disclaimer that legal 'best practices' will be applied 'with the collection of any plant species for observation, and by ensuring that no negative environmental impacts flow from the proposed bioprospecting collaboration' (CSIR and South African San Council Benefit-sharing agreement 2004). Unsurprisingly, the rooibos benefit-sharing agreement focuses only on traditional knowledge, mostly as a proxy for restorative justice, with no mention of conservation and sustainable use. Similarly, the *Sceletium* agreement, a value chain that is based almost entirely on cultivated material, is centred on traditional knowledge with no attention given to the wild resource or habitat from which it was originally drawn. The reliance of the *Pelargonium* industry on both wild-harvested and cultivated material means that greater emphasis is given to sustainable use, including two large-scale resource assessments and a post-harvest recovery study, but these have been done outside of the formal benefit-sharing agreement and are exclusively species-focused, rather than considering wider conservation measures linked to the habitat or ecosystems in which *Pelargonium sidoides* occurs. 'I have never been asked [by government] to change an agreement to deal with conservation', remarked one of the permit applicants for *Pelargonium* (personal communication 2020).

Despite the small role conservation plays in ABS arrangements, in all these cases the conservation challenges are significant. In the case of *Hoodia*, initial commercial interest led to over-harvesting of the resource, culminating in its inclusion as a CITES (Convention on International Trade in Endangered Species of Wild Fauna and Flora) Appendix II species (Wynberg & Chennells 2009). As noted by Raimondo and Von Staden (2009), substantial environmental impacts arise from the cultivation and, to a lesser extent, wild harvesting of rooibos, while the over-harvesting of *Pelargonium* has been a long-held cause for concern. As Ndwandwe explains (this volume), the strategy of the South African government has been to pursue cultivation as a strategy to achieve both magnitudes of production and to reduce pressures on wild species. However, in the 'Operation Phakisa' rush to roll out a plan, this has been done without giving adequate recognition to the environmental and social implications. Multiple studies reveal how cultivation induces shifts in benefits away from resource-poor wild harvesters towards those who have capital and land, while intensification may also be associated with land clearing, and the use of external inputs such as fertilisers and chemicals (see e.g., Dove 1995; Sunderland *et al.* 2004). Cultivation may also lead to a further disjuncture between resource custodians and knowledge holders, reducing incentives for conservation.

Policies and strategies currently pursued by the South African government for biodiversity commercialisation more generally, and ABS in particular, have clearly not been successful in creating incentives for conservation and sustainable use, despite this being a raison d'etre for these market-based approaches. This is due in part to the lack of legal recognition of indigenous peoples and local communities as custodians of biodiversity, a separation of traditional knowledge and resources in laws and agreements, and a tendency to prioritise economic development over conservation. While ABS agreements and approaches could in theory support customary practices and laws relating to conservation and sustainable use, alongside strengthened land tenure and resource rights, this has rarely occurred.

Conclusion

This chapter set out to review the increasing adoption of benefit sharing as a development model for the commodification of biodiversity and traditional knowledge. Through review of four cases of biodiversity commercialisation in South Africa – *Hoodia gordonii*, *Aspalathus linearis* (rooibos), *Sceletium tortuosum* and *Pelargonium sidoides* – it explored the extent to which historical injustices of biopiracy have been addressed; critiqued the fairness of processes implemented to develop benefit-sharing agreements; analysed their outcomes; and unravelled the relationship between benefit sharing and the conservation and sustainable use of biodiversity.

Through financial redistribution and other means, ABS approaches have been offered as a chance to bring about redress to those whose knowledge or biodiversity has been used commercially, often without consent, and who typically represent some of the most marginalised communities across southern Africa. Unquestionably, the cases described demonstrate that ABS has succeeded in establishing ground-breaking precedents that give recognition to the holders of traditional knowledge, while acknowledging the inherent inequities of trade in natural products and to some extent modifying business practices. They thus represent a small but important step forward towards restorative justice.

However, the cases also suggest that ABS may have created more problems than it seeks to solve. The processes to develop benefit-sharing agreements have tended towards expedience rather than inclusivity, often comprising a hand-wave towards adequate representation. Already, the resources and promises offered are leading to a combined clamour for representation, a rejection of the agreements being negotiated, and a favouring of those more visible, better organised and resourced, or politically well-connected. These issues are emerging across a range of sectors, from mining through to fisheries, urban development and biodiversity commercialisation, and across a range of institutions, including competing Khoisan organisations, and those representing traditional authorities and civic structures. Short-term solutions are unlikely given historical and contemporary entanglements with identity, land, and a convoluted and cumbersome legal framework, but resetting priorities to be contextually embedded and centred on restorative justice is an important first step.

The cases also demonstrate that ABS approaches have not challenged the *modus operandi* of current practices. Instead, ABS continues to remain disconnected from, and indeed ignorant of, the wider political and economic struggles faced by communities, instead serving as a legal compliance mechanism to justify a 'business as usual' approach but without fundamentally shifting power relations or economic disparities. Unlike neighbouring Namibia, Botswana, and Zimbabwe, community-based or -owned approaches to biodiversity commercialisation remain surprisingly absent from South Africa landscapes. Instead, control is vested in the land, markets, and intellectual property. Indeed, as West (2012) concludes, the prominence of ABS structures can be attributed to their ability to incorporate traditional knowledge and genetic resources into dominant structures to protect intellectual property 'without challenging the inherently unequal legal treatment of industrially and traditionally produced knowledge'. Such structures can thus be seen as a 'natural corollary of IPR' (intellectual property rights) (West 2012), with benefit sharing introducing '(previously alien) concepts of "property, exclusivity and exclusion" to local communities' (Brush 2007).

Finally, there is little evidence that ABS has led to conservation, despite this 'use it or lose it' argument being the cornerstone of the CBD. This has been due in part to inadequate recognition of the critical role played by communities as biodiversity custodians and key decision makers in conservation planning and management, but also to the blinkered way that governments have pursued ABS as a silver bullet for economic development. As work commences by CBD parties to implement a post-2020 Biodiversity Framework to stem biodiversity loss, it may well be opportune to think about how to broaden the suite of practical, meaningful, and effective options that are available to support conservation within ABS. This should be done in conjunction with the new thinking that is required to reconceptualise ABS in the context of the Fourth Industrial Revolution, where technological change is increasingly blurring the lines between the physical, digital, and biological spheres, raising questions about broader societal benefits and social justice (Laird *et al.* 2020).

Placed under overwhelming pressure to create jobs, stimulate economic growth, transform a historically white-owned sector to one more representative of the country's population, issue permits quickly, and implement legislation, the South African government has an unenviable task. Operation Phakisa is all about 'hurrying up' the biodiversity-based economy to deliver development priorities but it could well be that a slowing down of the process is what is needed right now – to enable genuine inclusion, to bring in a diversity of voices, to set in place appropriate governance mechanisms, to identify local development and conservation priorities, and, importantly, to challenge current trade and intellectual property models – and thus to bring about the transformative shift required to address the dual crises of social inequality and biodiversity loss. The principled nature of these actions makes them applicable not only to the South African context, but to all countries faced with implementing ABS requirements, and revisioning them to be fit for purpose.

Bibliography

ACB – African Centre for Biodiversity (2008). 'Knowledge not for sale – Umckaloabo and the Pelargonium patent challenges' (Johannesburg: ACB). Available at: www.publiceye.ch/fileadmin/doc/Biopiraterie/Briefing_Paper_Pelargonium_knowledge_not_for_sale_EN.pdf [Accessed 21 January 2022].

Arnold, J. E. M. & Ruiz-Pérez, M. (2001). 'Can non-timber forest products match tropical forest conservation and development objectives?' *Ecological Economics*, 39, 437–447.

Barends-Jones, V. (2020). 'Rooibos tea: The story of the Overberg' (Elsenburg: Western Cape Department of Agriculture, Division for Macro and Resource Economics).

Belcher, B. & Schreckenberg, K. (2007). 'Commercialisation of non-timber forest products: A reality check', *Development Policy Review*, 25(3), 355–377.

Berne Declaration and Natural Justice (2010). 'Dirty business for clean skin: Nestlé's rooibos robbery in South Africa', Briefing Paper. (Zurich; Cape Town: Berne Declaration; Natural Justice). Available at: www.cbd.int/abs/side-events/resumed-abs-9/id2114-berne-policy-brief.pdf [21 January 2022].

Brendler, T. (2021). 'From bush medicine to modern phytopharmaceutical: A bibliographic review of Devil's Claw (*Harpagophytum* spp.)', *Pharmaceuticals*, 14(8), 726. Available at: https://doi.org/10.3390/ph14080726 [Accessed 21 January 2022].

Blom, W. A. M., Abrahamse, S. L., Bradford, R., Duchateau, G. S. M. J. E., Theis, W., & Orsi, A. (2011). 'Effects of 15-d repeated consumption of *Hoodia gordonii* purified extract on safety, ad libitum energy intake, and body weight in healthy, overweight women: a randomized controlled trial', *American Journal of Clinical Nutrition*, 94(5), 1171–1181.

Brush, S. (2007). 'Farmers' rights and protection of traditional agricultural knowledge', *World Development*, 35(9), 1499–1514.

Bugge, M., Hansen, T., & Klitkou, A. (2016). 'What is the bioeconomy? A review of the literature', *Sustainability*, 8, 691.

CBD – Convention on Biological Diversity. (1992). *Convention on Biological Diversity* (Rio De Janeiro: CBD), Available at: www.cbd.int/convention/text [Accessed 21 January 2022].

Chen, W., Van Wyk, B.-E., Vermaak, I., & Viljoen, A.M. (2012). 'Cape aloes – A review of the phytochemistry, pharmacology and commercialisation of *Aloe ferox*', *Phytochemistry Letters* 5, 1–12.

Chennells Albertyn (2010). 'Letter to the Director General, Department Water and Environmental Affairs' 11 October 2010.

Chennells, R. (2013). 'Traditional knowledge and benefit sharing after the Nagoya Protocol: Three cases from South Africa', *Law, Environment and Development Journal*, 9(1), 163–184.

Chennells, R., Haraseb, V., & Ngakaeaja, M. (2009). 'Speaking for the San: Challenges for representative institutions', in: R. Wynberg, R. Chennells, & D. Schroeder (eds), *Indigenous Peoples, Consent and Benefit-Sharing: Learning from the San–Hoodia Case* (Berlin: Springer), 165–192.

Chinsembu W. W. & Chinsembu, K. C. (2020). '"Poisoned chalice": Law on access to biological and genetic resources and associated traditional knowledge in Namibia', *Resources*, 9(7), 83. Available at: https://doi.org/10.3390/resources9070083 [Accessed 21 January 2022].

Coombe, R. J., Ives, S., & Huizenga, D. (2014). 'The social imaginary of geographical indicators in contested environments: The politicized heritage and racialized landscapes of South African rooibos tea', in: M. David & D.

Rachel Wynberg

Halbert (eds), *SAGE Handbook on Intellectual Property* (Thousand Oaks CA: SAGE), 224–237.

Crouch, N. R., Douwes, E., Wolfson, M. M., Smith, G. F. & Edwards, T. J. (2008). 'South Africa's bioprospecting, access and benefit-sharing legislation: Current realities, future complications, and a proposed alternative', *South African Journal of Science*, 104(9–10), 355–366.

CSIR – Council for Scientific and Industrial Research and South African San Council (2004). Benefit-sharing agreement.

DEA – Department of Environmental Affairs (2015). 'Traditional knowledge associated with rooibos and honeybush Species in South Africa' (Pretoria: Siyanda Samahlubi Consulting for Department of Environmental Affairs). Available at: www.dffe.gov.za/sites/default/files/reports/traditionalknowledge_rooibosandhoneybushspecies_report.pdf [Accessed 4 December 2021].

DEA – Department of Environmental Affairs (2016). 'National Biodiversity Economy Strategy' (DEA, Republic of South Africa, March 2016). Available at: www.dffe.gov.za/sites/default/files/reports/nationalbiodiversityecono-mystrategy.pdf [Accessed 21 January 2022].

DFFE, 2022. Payment of benefits from rooibos to San and Khoi communities a milestone for industrywide collaboration, 14 July 2022. https://www.dffe.gov.za/mediareleas e/san.khoi.communitites_rooibosbenefits.

Dove, M. R. (1995). 'Political versus techno-economic factors in the development of nontimber forest products: Lessons from a comparison of natural and cultivated rubbers in Southeast Asia (and South America)', *Society and Natural Resources* 8, 193–208.

Dutfield, G. (2000). *Intellectual Property Rights, Trade and Biodiversity* (London: IUCN and Earthscan).

Dutfield, G. (2009). 'Protecting the rights of indigenous peoples: Can prior informed consent help?' in: R. Wynberg, R. Chennells and D. Schroeder (eds), *Indigenous Peoples, Consent and Benefit-Sharing: Learning from the San–Hoodia Case* (Berlin: Springer), 53–67.

Dutfield, G., Wynberg, R., Laird, S., & Ives, S. (2020). 'Benefit sharing and traditional knowledge: Unsolved dilemmas for implementation – The challenge of attribution and origin: Traditional knowledge and access and benefit sharing', Voices for BioJustice, Policy Brief (Rondebosch: Voices for BioJustice) Available at: www.voices4biojustice.org/wp-content/uploads/2017/12/Traditional-Knowledge-Policy-Brief-1.pdf [Accessed 9 December 2021].

Feiter, U. (2019). 'The development of a treatment for bronchitis based on a plant from South Africa' (Unpublished).

Gamez, R. (2007). 'The link between biodiversity and sustainable development: Lessons from INBIO's bioprospecting programme in Costa Rica', in: C. McManis (ed.), *Biodiversity and the Law: Intellectual Property, Biotechnology and Traditional Knowledge* (London: Earthscan), 77–90.

Gericke, N. & Viljoen, A. (2008). '*Sceletium* – A review update', *Journal of Ethnopharmacology*, 119, 653–663.

Gollin, M. A. (1993). 'An intellectual property rights framework for biodiversity prospecting', in: W. V. Reid, S. A. Laird, C. A. Meyer, R. Gámez, A. Sittenfeld, D. H. Janzen, M. A. Gollin, & C. Juma (eds), *Biodiversity Prospecting: Using*

Genetic Resources for Sustainable Development (Washington DC: World Resources Institute, Instituto Nacional de Biodiversidada. Rainforest Alliance, and African Centre for Technology Studies), 159–197.

Government of Namibia (2014). 'Namibia's Second National Biodiversity strategy and action plan, 2013–2022' (Ministry of Environment and Tourism). Available at: www.met.gov.na/files/files/Namibia's%20Second%20National%20Biodiversity%20Strategy%20and%20Action%20Plan%20(NBSAP%202)%20%20 2013%20-%202022.pdf [Accessed 21 January 2022].

Government of South Africa (2018). 'Address by President Cyril Ramaphosa at the launch of the Biodiversity Economy Operation Phakisa, Kalahari Waterfront, Thohoyandou, Limpopo' (The Presidency, Republic of South Africa). Available at: www.thepresidency.gov.za/speeches/address-president-cyril-ramaphosa-launch-biodiversity-economy-operation-phakisa%2C-kalahari [Accessed 9 December 2021].

Greene, S. (2004). 'Culture as politics, culture as property in pharmaceutical bioprospecting (Indigenous People Incorporated?)', *Current Anthropology*, 45(2), 2111–2138.

Heynen, N. & Robbins, P. (2005). 'The neoliberalization of nature: Governance, privatization, enclosure and valuation', *Capitalism Nature Socialism*, 16(1), 5–8.

HG&H and the South African San Council (2011). 'Review of the Benefit Sharing Agreement between HG&H Pharmaceuticals (Pty) Ltd, Niche Botanicals (Pty) Limited, H. L. Hall and Sons Limited. A Benefit Sharing Agreement as Contemplated by the South African Biodiversity Act 10 of 2004 and the Regulations Promulgated Thereunder'.

Ives, S. F. (2017). *Steeped in Heritage: The Racial Politics of South African Rooibos Tea* (Durham NC, Duke University Press).

Ives, S., Wynberg, R., & Dutfield, G. (2020). 'Rooibos settlement omits other marginalized people', *Nature*, Correspondence, 577(7790), 318.

Laird, S. & Wynberg, R. (2008). 'Access and benefit sharing in practice: Trends in partnerships across sectors'. Technical Series No. 38 (Montreal: CBD Secretariat).

Laird, S., Wynberg, R., Rourke, M., Humphries, F., Ruiz Muller, M., & Lawson, C. (2020). 'Rethink the expansion of access and benefit sharing', *Science*, 367(6483), 1200–1202.

Laird, S. & Wynberg, R. (2020). 'Connecting the dots … biodiversity conservation, sustainable use and access and benefit sharing: With a focus on Cameroon, Madagascar, Namibia, and South Africa' (BioInnovation Africa, GIZ, People and Plants International, University of Cape Town, Voices for Biojustice, February 2020). Available at: https://bio-economy.org.za/wp-content/uploads/2021/08/Laird-and-Wynberg-2021-Connecting-the-Dots.pdf [Accessed 20 January 2022].

Forest Peoples Programme, International Indigenous Forum on Biodiversity, Indigenous Women's Biodiversity Network, Centres of Distinction on Indigenous and Local Knowledge, & Secretariat of the Convention on Biological Diversity (2020). *Local Biodiversity Outlooks 2: The contributions of indigenous peoples and local communities to the implementation of the Strategic Plan for Biodiversity 2011–2020 and to renewing nature and cultures*. A complement to the fifth edition of Global Biodiversity Outlook (Moreton-in-Marsh, UK: Forest Peoples Programme). Available at: https://lbo2.localbiodiversityoutlooks.net [Accessed 18 January 2022].

Low C. (2007). 'Different histories of buchu: Euro-American appropriation of San and Khoekhoe knowledge of buchu plants', *Environment and History*, 13(3), 333–361.

McAfee, K. (1999). 'Selling nature to save it? Biodiversity and green developmentalism', *Environment and Planning D: Society and Space*, 17(2), 133–154.

Macilwain, C. (1998). 'When rhetoric hits reality in debate on bioprospecting', *Nature* 392, 535–540.

Mamdani, M. (1996). *Citizen and Subject: Contemporary Africa and the Legacy of Late*
Colonialism (Princeton NJ: Princeton University Press).

McDermott, M., Mahanty, S., & Schreckenberg, K. (2013). 'Examining equity: A multidimensional framework for assessing equity in payments for ecosystem services', *Environmental Science & Policy*, 33, 416–427.

Mellet, P. T. (2020). *The Lie of 1652: A Decolonised History of Land* (Cape Town: Tafelberg).

Modise, A. (2018). 'Strengthening indigenous governance, benefit sharing and capacity building for traditional phytomedicines', in: UNDP GEF Global ABS Project, *ABS is Genetic Resources for Sustainable Development* (New York: UNDP).

Morris, C. (2016). 'Royal pharmaceuticals: Bioprospecting, rights and traditional authority in South Africa', *American Ethnologist*, 43(3), 525–539.

Secretariat of the Convention on Biological Diversity (2011). 'Nagoya Protocol on Access to Genetic Resources and the Fair and Equitable Sharing of Benefits Arising from their Utilization to the Convention on Biological Diversity' (Montreal: Secretariat of the Convention on Biological Diversity). Available at: www.cbd.int/abs/text [Accessed 9 December 2021].

National Khoisan Council, Cederberg Belt Indigenous Farmers Representatives / Nasionale Khoi en San Raad, Verteenwoordigers van die Sederberg Strook se Inheemse Boere (2019). *The Khoihoi People's Rooibos Biocultural Community Protocol*. Available at: https://naturaljustice.org/wp-content/uploads/2020/04/NJ-Rooibos-BCP-Web.pdf [Accessed 19 January 2022].

Nelson, F. (2010). *Community Rights, Conservation and Contested Land. The Politics of Natural Resource Governance in Africa* (New York: Earthscan).

Neumann, R. P. & Hirsch, E. (2000). *Commercialisation of Non-Timber Forest Products: Review and Analysis of Research* (Bogor: CIFOR).

Nott, M. (2019). 'Benefit Sharing and Environmental Sustainability in Policy and Practice: The Commercialisation of the Resurrection Bush (*Myrothamnus flabellifolia*) in Southern Africa'. Unpublished Master's thesis, University of Cape Town, Cape Town, South Africa.

Pavoni, R. (2013). 'Channelling investment into biodiversity conservation: ABS and PES schemes', in: P. M. Dupuy and J. E. Viñuales (eds), *Harnessing Foreign Investment to Promote Environmental Protection: Incentives and Safeguards* (Cambridge: Cambridge University Press).

Penn, N. (2006). *The Forgotten Frontier: Colonist and Khoisan on the Cape's Northern Frontier in the 18th Century* (Athens OH: Ohio University Press).

Pikoli, Z. (2019). 'Traditional and Khoi-San Leadership Act "brings back apartheid Bantustans", say activists', *Daily Maverick*, 8 December. Available at: www. dailymaverick.co.za/article/2019-12-08-traditional-and-khoi-san-leadership-act-brings-back-apartheid-bantustans-say-activists_[Accessed 18 January 2022].

Raimondo, D. & Von Staden, L. (2009). 'Patterns and trends in the Red List of South African plants', in: D. Raimondo, L. Von Staden, W. Foden, J. E. Victor, N. A. Helme, R. C. Turner, D. A. Kamundi & P. A. Manyama (eds), *Red List of South African Plants 2009, Strelitzia 25*. (Pretoria: South African National Biodiversity Institute).

Raynolds, L. T. & Long, M. A. (2007). 'Fair/alternative trade', in: L. T. Raynolds, D. Murray, and J. Wilkinson (eds), *Fair trade: The challenges of transforming globalization* (Abingdon: Routledge), 15–33.

Reid, W. V., Laird, S. A., Meyer, C. A., Gámez, R., Sittenfeld, A., Janzen, D. H., Gollin, M. A. & Juma, C. (eds) (1993). *Biodiversity Prospecting: Using Genetic Resources for Sustainable Development* (Washington DC: World Resources Institute, Instituto Nacional de Biodiversidada; Rainforest Alliance, African Centre for Technology Studies), 159–197.

Reinten, E. Y., Coetzee, J. H., & van Wyk, B.-E. (2011). 'The potential of South African indigenous plants for the international cut flower trade', *South African Journal of Botany*, 77, 934–946.

Reid, W. V., Laird, S. A., Meyer, C. A., Gámez, R., Sittenfeld, A., Janzen, D. H., Gollin, M. A., & Juma, C. (eds) (1993), *Biodiversity Prospecting: Using Genetic Resources for Sustainable Development* (Washington DC: World Resources Institute; Instituto Nacional de Biodiversidada; Rainforest Alliance; African Centre for Technology Studies).

Robinson, D. F. (2010). *Confronting Biopiracy. Challenges, Cases and International Debates* (London; New York: Earthscan).

Schroeder, D., Chennells, R., Louw, C., Snyders, L., & Hodges, T. (2020). 'The rooibos benefit-sharing agreement – Breaking new ground with respect, honesty, fairness and care', *Cambridge Quarterly of Healthcare Ethics*, 29, 285–301.

Shackleton, C. & Shackleton, S. (2004). 'The importance of non-timber forest products in rural livelihood security and as safety nets: A review of evidence from South Africa', *South African Journal of Science*, 100, 658–664.

Sullivan, S. (2002). 'How sustainable is the communalising discourse of "new" conservation?' in: D. Chatty & M. Colchester (eds), *Conservation and Mobile Indigenous People* (Oxford: Berghahn Press), 158–187.

Sullivan, S. (2006). 'Elephant in the room? Problematising "new" (neoliberal) biodiversity conservation', *Forum for Development Studies*, 33(1), 105–135.

Sunderland, T. C. H., Harrison, S. T., & Ndoye, O. (2004). 'Commercialisation of nontimber forest products in Africa: History, context and prospects', in: T. Sunderland & O. Ndoye (eds), *Forest Products, Livelihoods and Conservation. Case Studies of Non-Timber Forest Product Systems* (Bogor: Centre for International Forestry Research), 1–24.

Svarstad, H. (2004). 'A global political ecology of bioprospecting', in: S. Paulson and L. L. Gezon (eds), *Political Ecology Across Spaces, Scales, and Social Groups* (Ithaca, NY: Rutgers University Press), 239–256.

Swanson, T. (1998). *Intellectual Property Rights and Biodiversity Conservation.*

An Interdisciplinary Analysis of the Values of Medicinal Plants (Cambridge: Cambridge University Press).

UNDP – United Nations Development Programme (2018). 'ABS is Genetic Resources for Sustainable Development' (New York: UNDP GEF Global ABS Project). Available at: https://abs-sustainabledevelopment.net/resource/abs-is-genetic-resources-for-sustainable-development [Accessed 20 January 2022].

Van Niekerk, J. & Wynberg, R. (2012). 'The trade in *Pelargonium sidoides*: Rural livelihood relief or bounty for the bio-buccaneers?' *Development Southern Africa*, 29(4), 530–547.

Volk, O. H. (1964). 'Zur Kenntnis von Harpagophytum procumbens DC', *Deutsch Apotheker-Zeitung*, 104, 573–576.

West, S. (2012). 'Institutionalised exclusion: The political economy of benefit sharing and intellectual property', *Law, Environment and Development Journal*, 8(1), 19–42.

Wynberg, R. (2004). 'Rhetoric, realism and benefit-sharing – Use of traditional knowledge of *Hoodia* species in the development of an appetite suppressant', *World Journal of Intellectual Property*, 6(7), 851–876.

Wynberg, R. (2017). 'Making sense of access and benefit sharing in the rooibos industry: Towards a holistic, just and sustainable framing', *South African Journal of Botany*, 110, 39–51.

Wynberg, R. (2018). 'One step forward, two steps back? Implementing access and benefit-sharing legislation in South Africa', in: C. R. McManis & B. Ong (eds), *Routledge Handbook of Biodiversity and the Law* (Oxford: Routledge), 198–218.

Wynberg, R. (2019). 'San and Khoi claim benefits from rooibos', *Mail & Guardian*, 1 November 2019. Available at: https://mg.co.za/article/2019-11-01-00-san-and-khoi-claim-benefits-from-rooibos [Accessed 9 December 2021].

Wynberg, R. & Chennells, R. (2009). 'Green diamonds of the south: A review of the San–Hoodia case', in: R. Wynberg, R. Chennells, & D. Schroeder (eds), *Indigenous Peoples, Consent and Benefit-Sharing: Learning from the San–Hoodia Case* (Berlin: Springer), 89–126.

Wynberg, R. & Hauck, M. (2014). 'People, power and the coast: A conceptual framework for understanding and implementing benefit sharing', *Ecology and Society*, 19(1), 27.

Wynberg, R., Ives, S. & Bam-Hutchison, J. Access and benefit sharing as a failed development paradigm. The case of Rooibos. *Journal of Southern African Studies*. Currently in press, expected publication 2023.

Wynberg, R. & Laird, S. (2007). 'Bioprospecting: Tracking the policy debate', *Environment*, 49(10), 20–32.

Wynberg, R. & Laird, S. (2023). Access and benefit sharing and biodiversity conservation: the unrealized connection. In: *Access and Benefit Sharing of Genetic Resources, Information and Traditional Knowledge*. Edited by Lawson, C., Rourke, M., and Humphries, F. Routledge, pp 50–70.

Wynberg, R., Laird, S., van Niekerk, J., & Kozanayi, W. (2015). 'Formalization of the natural product trade in Southern Africa: Unintended consequences and policy blurring in biotrade and bioprospecting', *Society & Natural Resources: An International Journal*, 28, 559–574.

5

Transfrontier Conservation Governance, Commodification of Nature, and the New Dynamics of Sovereignty in Namibia

JOHANNES DITTMANN AND DETLEF MÜLLER-MAHN

Introduction

Elephants know no national boundaries. This truism is frequently heard when conservationists explain the establishment of the Kavango-Zambezi Transfrontier Conservation Area (KAZA), the largest in all of Africa. Whenever people talk about KAZA, elephants seem to take centre stage. The trivial fact that these large mammals do not stop their migrations at borders is used to justify an unprecedented international cooperation across southern Africa. Yet the implementation of transfrontier conservation areas (TFCA) does not only concern wildlife ecology. To tell the whole story, one also has to address more complex questions regarding political authority, environmental governance, economic interests, and the marketisation of natural resources. This chapter explores the relationship between emerging new dynamics of political power, the struggle for national sovereignty, and the commodification of nature in north-eastern Namibia.

All over sub-Saharan Africa, the transfrontier conservation paradigm is currently finding its way into environmental policies. It emanated originally from the engagement of the Peace Parks Foundation (PPF), which is based in South Africa. Today it is applied in numerous border regions, most of them in the south of the continent. As part of currently ongoing conservation initiatives, transfrontier conservation areas (TFCAs), dubbed 'peace parks', promise a triple-win situation for nature conservation, economic growth, and peace building (Ramutsindela 2007). Cross-border conservation initiatives are driven by a complex interplay of governmental and non-governmental actors. The main protagonists in the field of conservation comprise international organisations like the PPF, the World Wide Fund for Nature (WWF), and the International Union for the Conservation of Nature (IUCN), together with national governments and regional bodies like the Southern African Development Community (SADC). These actors jointly point at the ecological connectivity paradigm, presenting it as the new goal of conservation in Africa (Goldman 2009).

The overarching goal of cross-border conservation is widely accepted as a common and unifying new mission among countries in the wider region, which can be attributed to two reasons. First, there is the ecological argument. Connecting the growing number of previously more or less fragmented conservation areas is generally seen as a prerequisite for a landscape approach to protect biodiversity. Second, and less obviously, there is a mixture of political and economic interests which also play an important role in decision making. The transfrontier conservation paradigm is widely supported by national elites, heads of state, and development agencies, because it promises economic growth by linking natural resources in border regions to international tourism. As a consequence of these two reasons, the implementation of TFCAs gained an enormous momentum in regard to ecology and politics, transforming the physical landscape as well as regional governance systems. However, the implementation and performance of large-scale cross-border conservation is a multifaceted process with controversial effects. While international consultants and development agencies support the technical implementation of TFCAs, local government agencies are often absorbed by ceaseless negotiations, agreements, implementation plans, and concomitant funds. Under these conditions, national governments may perceive foreign interference in TFCA development not only as a support, but also as a challenge to their sovereignty (van Amerom 2002).

Against this backdrop, the chapter takes the case of KAZA and Namibia to investigate the relationship between the commodification of nature and the transformation of political authority. It focuses on the following questions: how are ecological needs and economic potentials of transfrontier conservation framed? How are they used *to legitimise* international interference in the domestic affairs of states? To what extent does the implementation of KAZA go along with new forms of environmental governance and the emergence of new forms of sovereignty?

The emergence of transfrontier conservation must be seen in light of the changing political economy after the end of the apartheid regime when SADC promoted TFCAs as catalysts of regional integration (Ramutsindela 2007). The first TFCAs in southern Africa were established in the 1990s, with the Kgalagadi Transfrontier Park (Botswana, South Africa), Great Limpopo Transfrontier Park (Mozambique, Zimbabwe, South Africa), and Ais-Ais/ Richtersveld Transfrontier Park (Namibia, South Africa). Later the idea was transferred to regions beyond the borders of South Africa. In 2012, the governments of Angola, Zambia, Zimbabwe, Botswana, and Namibia launched KAZA as the largest TFCA (520,000 km²) in the world. From the beginning, Namibia played a key role in the establishment of KAZA and continues to be a forerunner of conservation initiatives in the region, together with Botswana. Namibia's communal conservancies and its national parks in the north-east of the country are considered important building blocks for the greater transboundary landscape approach. In that context, KAZA plays an essential role as a top-level initiative that is expected to promote the idea further. During fieldwork, different conservation actors repeatedly highlighted the significant role of north-eastern Namibia as it lies 'at the heart of KAZA', by which they allude to the geographically central position of Namibia's administrative regions, Zambezi and Kavango East, in the transfrontier conservation area. Most of KAZA wildlife corridors are supposed to be implemented across north-eastern Namibia to facilitate migration of wildlife from Botswana to Zambia and Angola and back. Considering that Namibia also played a decisive role in the inception and official opening of the initiative, the Namibian case provides an important point of departure for analysing new dynamics of political authority in the context of transfrontier conservation.

TFCAs have witnessed a remarkable increase of scholarly attention in recent years (Ali 2007; Ramutsindela 2007; Andersson *et al.* 2013). Studies address a wide range of topics, including ecological and economic potentials and impacts of transboundary conservation initiatives (Hanks 2003; Suich *et al.* 2005; Naidoo *et al.* 2018), their historical evolution and political background (Ramutsindela 2007; Spierenburg & Wels 2010) and critical implications in regard to local communities and social inequalities (Andersson *et al.* 2013; Spierenburg 2013; Duffy 2016; Büscher & Ramutsindela 2016). Focusing on the relationship between conservation and commodification, Büscher (2013) views TFCAs as neoliberal development interventions that primarily aim at linking peripheral borderlands to global markets, thus 'unlocking' the hidden potentials of previously underutilised natural resources through international tourism and a commodification of nature. From this perspective, he criticises the triple-win promise of peace parks as a political strategy to legitimise TFCAs as apolitical interventions (Büscher 2010). We agree with this position, which also holds true for KAZA, and suggest conceiving of TFCAs in general and KAZA in particular as tools to commodify 'wild' objects, landscapes, and imaginations of Africa. Against this backdrop, new questions arise concerning the relationship between transboundary initiatives, the commodification of nature, and issues of national governance and policy.

In this chapter, we follow the arguments of the above-mentioned authors who have highlighted the neoliberal dynamics in the transformation of conservation areas. Yet, we believe that the 'commodifying the wild' focus needs to

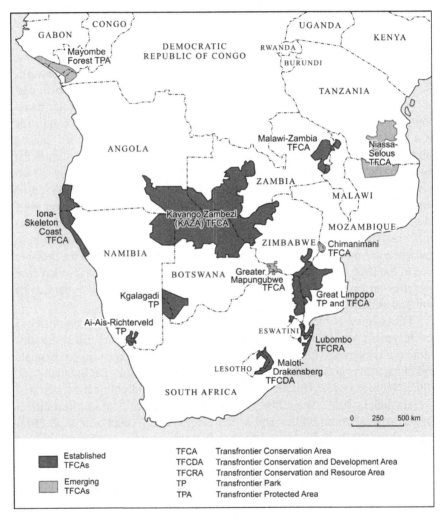

Map 5.1 Transfrontier conservation areas in southern Africa (Source: Editing: Johannes Dittmann; Cartography: Irene Johannsen, Monika Feinen).

be augmented by political geography perspectives on territorial control, state sovereignty, and institutionalised authority in the context of transboundary conservation. Hence, studies that point to the different dimensions of how transboundary conservation reshapes spaces of political authority are particularly vital for our case (van Amerom 2002; Wolmer 2003; Dhliwayo *et al.* 2009; Rusinga & Mapira 2012; Noe 2015; Lunstrum 2013; Ramutsindela 2017). So far, only Lunstrum (2013) has explicitly addressed the question of how transfrontier conservation and the establishment of a new border regime affect territorial control, political authority, and state sovereignty. We propose to expand the argument by linking up to recent debates in political geography on new dynamics of spatiality, territoriality, and sovereignty in the 21st century (Agnew 2005; Kuus & Agnew 2008; Elden 2010; Painter 2010; Agnew 2015).

The chapter will first revisit current theoretical debates on state sovereignty and transboundary environmental governance. In its empirical section, the chapter relates these debates to a case study of KAZA TFCA, describing how the implementation of transfrontier conservation changes the patterns of political authority in Namibia. The chapter illuminates the political conditions of the emergence of KAZA and shows that in the initial phase the Namibian motivation to push the project was largely determined by interests in extending the external and internal sovereignty of the state. It continues to show how the Namibian state re-asserts its sovereignty and legitimises the commodification of ivory in KAZA area by joining a transnational conservation agreement. The final section focuses on the limits to these re-assertions and the contestations of Namibian state sovereignty in the context of KAZA. Therefore, this chapter is less concerned with emphasising that TFCAs have either erosive or enhancing effects on state sovereignty; rather, it intends to illustrate the ambiguity in these effects, showing that sovereignty in TFCAs must be understood as a trans-nationally negotiated, challenged, and graduated phenomenon. The chapter concludes by encouraging further research on transboundary conservation from a post-colonial perspective, asking for alternative views of sovereignty and environmental governance in Africa.

New dynamics of political authority

In political science and geography, sovereignty has long been conceived of as the capacity of a state to exert authority and control over its territory (Biersteker 2013: 246). This understanding implies an idea of the state which is firmly embedded in the political order of the Peace of Westphalia of 1648, i.e. an order in which the state is conceived as a spatially defined phenomenon (ibid.). In this view, the power of the state relies on its territoriality, i.e. its ability to occupy and control a particular geographical space (Allen 2003, Painter 2010). Agnew (2005: 437) defines territoriality as 'the use of territory for political, social, and economic ends ... implied by state sovereignty'. In conventional political theory, the concepts of state, sovereignty, and territory are inherently connected. However, this Western ideal of the nation-state stems from a particular historical setting, which was globally mainstreamed only in the middle of the 20th century as a 'universal form of territorial political organization' (Biersteker 2013: 248).

Agnew (1994) calls the definition of sovereignty in terms of spatial containers a 'territorial trap', which should be overcome by disconnecting it from demarcated boundaries of state territories. In that regard he is supported by other authors who point at the new dynamics of sovereignty and territoriality in the context of globalisation and neoliberalisation (Brenner *et al.* 2003; Painter 2010; Mountz 2013). According to Brenner *et al.* (2003: 4) these political geography perspectives have to be distinguished from closely related but analytically distinct research perspectives that deal with the theorisation of state space. These include among others, globalisation debates that generally challenge the Cartesian image of space as a static, bounded block and call for relational perspectives, as well as debates on new localisms and regionalisms that criticise the national scale as an adequate ordering category in the 21st century (ibid.). Political geography perspectives do not focus on what the role of the state in contemporary world politics is or whether the state loses its significance in the face of globalisation. Following Kuus and Agnew (2008), political geography perspectives theorising the state are concerned with the ways political authority is being reconfigured and spatially articulated. These critical voices agree that there is a threefold flaw in conventional approaches of state theory: first, that state sovereignty is bound to a demarcated territory; second, that foreign and domestic affairs contradict each other; and third, that states can only act within spatial containers (Elden 2010: 801). However, in political practice one still observes the persistence of space-bound concepts of sovereignty as stated by Agnew (2005): 'this standard conception is a poor guide to political analysis. It is a 'truth' that has always hidden more than it reveals. In a globalizing world, this obfuscation is particularly problematic' (ibid.: 456). The state and its boundaries, sovereignty, and territory should not be considered as given facts predetermined by natural boundaries. Instead, sovereignty is contingent and socially constructed (Biersteker 2013). With the rise of *new forms of governance* at levels above or below nation-states, relational perspectives are becoming more appropriate to understand the emergence of new forms of sovereignty and territorial figurations (Brenner *et al.* 2003; Agnew 2005; Painter 2010; Biersteker 2013). This applies especially to newly emerging governing patterns in cross-border regions. Agnew suggests the concept of *graduated sovereignty*, which comes closer to how sovereignty is practised, contested, and negotiated in quotidian politics (Agnew 2005: 442; Mountz 2013; Boeckler *et al.* 2018). Understanding the hybridity of sovereignty means that political authority is not necessarily exercised by the state and through absolute territoriality, but rather as a *continuous contestation of practices through inter-scalar networks* (Kuus & Agnew 2008; Berg & Kuusk 2010).

There are many forms, degrees, and different ways of being sovereign which not only hold true for nation-states, but also for other spatial configurations (Berg & Kuusk 2010: 40) such as regional bodies, transnational networks, and cross-border regions. Conventional conceptualisations of state, territory, and sovereignty are often too narrow and culturally biased, as they are mostly seen in relation to the Western ideal, hence they tend to describe state governance in Africa in terms of deprivation, deficiency, and failure (Sidaway 2003). Ramutsindela (2019) urges us to decolonise concepts of political geography and to identify alternative forms of sovereignty without simply framing them as deviations from Western norms. 'It would appear no region of the world has a wide-range classification of states like Africa' (ibid.: 285). Sovereignty in Africa has been and still is contested, and not only as an effect of colonial border-drawing. What we can see across the continent is not the result of failed nation-building, but the emergence of fragmented forms of political authority (Mbembe 2000), 'where pre-colonial, colonial, modern and trans-national modes of sovereignty compete for their appropriate spatial manifes-tation' (Boeckler *et al.* 2018: 7). Following Sidaway, 'the supposed 'weakness' of certain African states might be interpreted as arising less from a lack or absence of authority and connection (including the presence of the West), but rather as an excess of certain forms of them' (2003: 157). Sovereignty in Africa today is exercised by a number of actors, not only by national governments. Complex transnational private–public partnerships are rapidly expanding all over Africa. This process is driven by several factors, including the 'African land rush', the new role of China as a hegemonic power, and the creation of new networks by international, national, and non-governmental organisations for development and conservation. 'Africa has once again become a living laboratory, this time for the experimentation with new dis/orders and novel kinds of sovereignties' that result in changing transnational relations (Boeckler *et al.* 2018: 3).

Some of these newly emerging forms of political authority can also be observed in the context of cross-border conservation areas, which are to a large extent determined by markets in environmental services. Commodification of nature implies massive transformations of the political economy of states, regions, and landscapes (Liverman 2004: 734–735). This includes new trends of territorialisation and the emergence of transnational spaces where state and non-state actors on different scales intervene in localities under overlapping political authorities (Igoe & Brockington 2007). Mbembe (2000) points out that the exploitation of natural resources in Africa is again becoming a field of contestation where sovereignty is renegotiated. He argues that international policies of conservation put whole territories into a *de facto* extraterritorial status, thereby placing them outside of immediate state authority (ibid.: 283). Observations concerning the increasing neoliberalisation of transnational conservation 'refer to an emerging system where sovereignty has become highly decentralised and fragmented – controlled by different state actors, in different contexts and for different purposes' (Igoe & Brockington 2007: 439).

Transfrontier conservation areas can be conceived of as instruments to commodify nature in international contexts (Ramutsindela 2007). Wolmer clarifies that the implications of transboundary approaches in natural resource management go far beyond biodiversity protection as they are 'bound up with regional debates on national sovereignty, land reform and poverty alleviation' (2003: 261). In a study of the Selous-Niassa Wildlife Corridor, Noe shows that the establishment of TFCAs and wildlife corridors involves the alienation of land, going along with 'complex and highly localised circumstances of power struggles that reflect broader issues of territoriality' (2015: 121). Under these conditions, land management becomes upscaled to the international level, leading to the emergence of new types of border regimes. According to Ramutsindela (2017), the rise of transfrontier conservation in southern Africa caused a new hegemony of space through the denationalisation of conservation and the insertion of green capitalism. Conventional conservation models such as national parks and community-based conservation are challenged by TFCAs, as these imply re-conceptualisations of border and territory, and transcend common ways to frame conservation governance. By 'greening borderlands as a national and regional imperative' Ramutsindela argues (2017: 106), peace parks create transnational spaces that are shaped by processes of commodification of nature.

Only a few studies explicitly address the implications of transfrontier conservation for state sovereignty. For this present chapter, Lunstrum's (2013) study on the Great Limpopo Transfrontier Park (GLTP) is particularly relevant, since it argues 'that the same partnerships that seem to threaten sovereignty in some respects in fact shore up the power of the Mozambican state in other respects' (ibid.: 1). The study shows how the Mozambican state expands its power base in the GLTP. This point is critical for this case study about Namibia in the context of KAZA. Drawing on insights from multi-sited ethnographic fieldwork in Namibia, the following sections deal with the question of how new forms of sovereignty emerge in the processes of re-asserting, negotiating, and challenging political authority in KAZA.

Transfrontier conservation and sovereignty in Namibia

KAZA – design and establishment of a TFCA

The setting up of conservation interventions unfolds along particular pathways that must be considered to illuminate the practices and institutional frameworks of environmental governance. Actors at different scales cooperate, negotiate, and compete on these pathways and thereby reconstitute political authority and state sovereignty (Müller-Mahn *et al.* 2018: 26–27). The KAZA Conservation Area has been configured in a spatially ambitious way by the responsible ministries of five different African countries, together with various donor organisations in the context of development cooperation, and a number of international and national NGOs. The actors driving this process include national governments, experts from the North and the South, government officials at all levels of the administrative hierarchy, and the people living in the area.

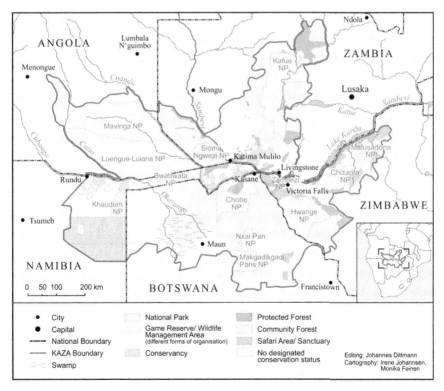

Map 5.2 The Kavango-Zambezi Transfrontier Conservation Area (Source: Editing: Johannes Dittmann; Cartography: Irene Johannsen, Monika Feinen).

Today, the KAZA area is home to a population of 2.67 million people, with an annual growth rate of approximately 2%. The Conservation Area comprises more than 20 national parks, 85 forest reserves, 22 communal conservancies, 11 game sanctuaries, and 103 wildlife management areas. In total, around 371,000 km² of the KAZA area are under conservation management, while 149,000 km² are under agricultural use. This huge conservation initiative aims at making the region a world-class premier transfrontier conservation area and tourism destination (Mosimane *et al.* 2014; KAZA TFCA 2015). In official words the goal is defined as 'to sustainably manage the Kavango Zambezi ecosystem, its heritage and cultural resources based on best conservation and tourism models for the socio-economic well-being of the communities and other stake-holders in the region' (KAZA TFCA 2015: II). The project's main concern is to facilitate the establishment of transboundary wildlife corridors to enable cross-border wildlife movement and ensure connectivity of ecosystems. By promoting transboundary conservation the KAZA initiative aims to increase the potential for international tourism in the area and thereby intends to stimulate new markets for wildlife economy. New sources for revenue are supposed to benefit mainly local communities through joint ventures.

The Conservation Area is mainly financed through the German Bank for Reconstruction and Development (KfW), which so far has contributed €40 million (US$35.7 million) in grants in three funding phases since 2010 (KAZA TFCA 2018). The KfW funds are administered by the KAZA Secretariat with assistance of the PPF and channelled to the five responsible ministries who implement directly or contract NGOs and consultancies for implementation. The funds are mainly spent on operational costs of the KAZA Secretariat, joint cross-border initiatives and the countries' individual conservation programmes. Investments are committed to the aims and vision of the KAZA initiative, which are adopted by the partner countries and KfW as well as to the bilateral conditions of development cooperation between the German government and the five recipient governments. While the first two funding phases (€20 million – US$17.86 million) mainly focused on institutional capacity building, the third phase is more concerned with the implementation of wildlife corridors across the countries. Furthermore, KAZA receives funds through the TFCA programme of SADC, which is also largely funded by German development cooperation, as well as through a number of govern-mental and non-governmental organisations such as the United States Agency for International Development (USAID), World Wildlife Fund for Nature (WWF), Food and Agriculture Organization of the United Nations (FAO) and the Dutch postcode lottery. The KAZA Secretariat acts as a mediator between the five governments, coordinating activities in the KAZA region in regular meetings of a Ministerial Committee, a Committee of Senior Officials, and a

Joint Management Committee. Within the five countries, the KAZA initiative is coordinated by national steering committees under the lead of the respective ministries. Apart from this, there are several working groups that focus on specific tasks like tourism development or wildlife corridor implementation. They consist of technical staff from different governmental and private institutions. Compared to other TFCAs in the wider region, KAZA is not only by far the biggest and most differentiated project area, but it also has a particularly complex governance structure with numerous national and transnational actors collaborating at different levels (Linell *et al.* 2018: 58).

The origins of KAZA date back further than its official opening in 2003. They build on two previous transboundary conservation initiatives, which were not successful. The first one, the Okavango Upper Zambezi International Tourism Initiative (OUZIT), was initiated in 1993 by the Development Bank of South Africa and the Regional Tourism Organisation of Southern Africa, facilitated by the SADC tourism sector. The Initiative grew out of the Spatial Development Initiatives (SDI) programme that was part of the vision to restructure the inherited apartheid space economy of South Africa (Rogerson 2003). It is interesting to note that, from the beginning of the OUZIT project, the establishment of a transboundary conservation area was legitimised by ecological arguments, while the process itself was mainly driven by economic and political interests (see also Goldman 2009). With a focus on international tourism, the project aimed at development and national growth through regional integration. However, OUZIT as well as the following Four Corners Transboundary Natural Resource Management initiative were dropped again by the participating governments. The failure of these two transboundary conservation initiatives preceding KAZA may be explained by the lack of ownership on the side of the participating governments (Mogende 2016). The South African Government largely dominated OUZIT, and the African Wildlife Fund and USAID dominated the Four Corners initiative. From the point of view of the participating governments, these projects were too donor-driven and insufficiently aligned with their own interests, which finally led the Botswanan and Namibian governments to drop out.

However, it is remarkable to note that even failed projects may leave a legacy. The prematurely terminated conservation projects produced a heritage of infrastructures, maps, reports, and memories, leading to the resurgence of past aspirations and instigating a continuation of activities in a new guise and under a new title (Bluwstein & Lund 2018: 454). In 2003 the first Namibian president Sam Nujoma gathered the ministers of environment and tourism of the five neighbouring countries in Katima Mulilo, the regional capital of the Caprivi Region, as north-eastern Namibia was then called, to revitalise the idea of a transboundary conservation area and seize the golden opportunity to take complete ownership ... to sharpen its focus so that it can complement the socio-economic development efforts of ... respective countries.' (Hon. S. Nujoma, President of Namibia 2003 cited in Suich *et al.* 2005: 4). Nujoma wanted the governments to be able to account for their citizens in the KAZA area by taking the complete responsibility and ownership of the initiative (Suich *et al.* 2005). Due to this, KAZA became a project with a strong buy-in among the participating countries that enhanced sovereignty as being founded in distinction to previous projects with stronger foreign influence. Namibia played a key role in drafting the KAZA Memorandum of Understanding, which was signed in 2006. It continued to take the lead in the implementation of the KAZA treaty, which laid the foundation for the official opening of the TFCA in 2012. The process was greatly supported by the Namibian minister of environment and tourism Netumbo Nandi-Ndaitwah, who later also served as minister of international relations. From the beginning, KAZA was envisioned to become an initiative to enhance transboundary collaboration at different scales, and not only in ecological terms, and promote regional integration as a flagship programme of SADC.

During the early years of the KAZA in the early 2000s, the area was still ridden by the consequences of civil war and secession. The Angolan component in Cuando Cubango Province was the scene of the fiercest military conflicts, which also affected parts of Namibia and Zambia. Since independence, Zambia's Western Province has been the scene of a separatist movement building on the identity of the old Lozi kingdom that also reached into today's Namibia (Zeller & Melber 2018). The Namibian component of KAZA, especially the Caprivi, was exposed to different conflicts shortly after the country's independence. The spill-over from the Angolan civil war, disputes between various traditional authorities, and the Caprivi secessionist movement threatened peace and the sovereignty of the young state (Lenggenhager 2018; Kangumu 2011). Soon after the Namibian Defence Force quelled the secession movement that was driven by the Caprivi Liberation Army in 2002 (Melber 2015), the Namibian president gathered representatives of the other KAZA countries in Katima Mulilo to kick off the transnational initiative. As a conservation consultant who was actively involved in the inception of KAZA from the beginning put it in September 2018:

> The war had come to an end. It had caused a lot of unrest in the Zambezi and there was the secessionist movement. That generated some momentum for reaching out from a Namibian perspective. And why not use the existing platform that was already there ... Let us take control over OUZIT and let's put our stamp on it ... this was driven by the desire to have stability in the area where in the previous five years there was not stability ... That is why this government, specifically the president, saw an opportunity.

The emergence of KAZA must be seen in the context of the historical conditions of the emergence of conservation initiatives in north-eastern Namibia. These are often linked to past development pathways, established spatial knowledge, and military and security interventions in pre- and post-independence periods. Nature conservation narratives and institutions had already been used for securing spaces before independence. As Bollig and Vehrs (2021) show, Namibia's Zambezi Region has been constructed as a wilderness by the colonial governments through the reordering of human-environment relations and decoupling humans from wildlife spatially. Already at that time, a path was taken to create a pristine conservation landscape serving visions of economically productive conservation programmes which was later translated into a natural potential for being part of a transfrontier conservation area (ibid.). After 1990, community-based and transfrontier conservation approaches in the region followed in that line (Lenggenhager 2018), although not necessarily in a linear continuity of mind-sets and practices. With the emergence of OUZIT and later KAZA the notion of the Caprivi Strip as a territorial anomaly of colonialism was translated into an image of the region as 'the key to' or 'the heart of' the largest conservation area of Africa.

After the Cold War, new narratives of security emerged in southern Africa to which peace parks were presented as silver-bullet solutions (Ramutsindela 2007). Keeping in mind the aspired multiple-win situation of TFCAs, the institution of KAZA was a means to establish state sovereignty in areas where regional movements opposed it. Political authority strengthened through the initiation of KAZA should be understood not so much as effective but as *symbolic* sovereignty, which is a strategy deployed by states to 'uphold the imagination that the state in question is indeed sovereign' (Müller-Mahn *et al.* 2018: 26). Furthermore, as Ramutsindela argues, narratives of community development and nature conservation that are key within the scope of TFCAs can be seen as depoliticising strategies on the sub-regional level employed by governments to silence local resistance (2007: 109). Linell *et al.* argue that KAZA can be understood as an instrument to demobilise opposition and boost the legitimacy and power of national leaders by introducing international agencies to the national level (2018: 66).

To summarise, the evidence presented above questions the official reading that the KAZA project was launched primarily for conservation purposes and a better commodification of natural resources. We find this explanation insufficient, not least because similar initiatives had already existed before. The Conservation Area makes promises of economic growth and livelihood enhancement through tourism, but these have not become realised yet, as different actors of the regional tourism sector told us. Instead, we assert that the main purpose of the project should rather be seen in relation to its political function. In contrast to its predecessors, KAZA gives the five participating governments full ownership, thereby allowing them a more comprehensive eco-governmental control over peripheral regions, and strengthening their sovereignty.

Transfrontier conservation and the re-asserting of political authority

The KAZA Conservation Area remains politically important, because it allows the Namibian state to establish a particular regime of environmental governance and exert sovereignty not just within its borders, but also in international contexts. This move became possible due to newly emerging global environmental issues, which instigated some sort of environmental solidarity among African states, and strengthened their position in international environmental negotiations (Ramutsindela & Büscher 2019). In this context, the establishment of the TFCAs in its border regions helps the Namibian state not only to gain better control over its periphery, but also to win international recognition, and access to new forms of funding. Following Death (2016), KAZA can be seen as an instrument of the African green state, which mainly has symbolic and representational functions to generate sovereignty, both in terms of internal control over peripheral border areas, and externally in terms of a joint bargaining power of the five participating countries.

This observation is also supported by an analysis of how KAZA is publicly represented. Transfrontier conservation interventions require the constitution of a positively connoted and apolitical discourse that legitimises their existence because of their inherently political implications and contradictions (Büscher 2010). The Conservation Area is glorified as a flagship programme on a pathway to a bright future of African conservation and wildlife economy that coincides with the recent rise of green development visions across sub-Saharan Africa. Connectivity of ecosystems seems to be the leading paradigm that legitimises the establishment of wildlife corridors and other cross-border interventions under KAZA. This goal is based on aspirations of restoring an imagined 'pristine African wilderness' that are still very present in the mindsets of conservation institutions and are broadly mainstreamed to drive the commodification of nature. Further, TFCA initiatives are seen as drivers for regional integration, economic development, and independence from global spatialities of economic power inherited from the colonial period (Ramutsindela 2007; Gibb 2009). In popular debates about borders, the African national border as imposed by colonial powers has primarily negative connotations as being disruptive to natural and social connectivity. Lifting borders and breaking down fences as imperatives of peace parks is instrumentalised to legitimise TFCAs as development interventions in line with Pan-African visions (Ramutsindela 2017). Hence, KAZA represents political visions of regional bodies such as SADC, New Partnership for Africa's Development (NEPAD), and the African Union

(AU) that contribute to Pan-Africanism and African Renaissance. Especially on high political levels, KAZA has a positive reputation as an 'African solution to African challenges' that aims to overcome the curse of colonial border-drawing. Visually and rhetorically the proponents of KAZA, especially PPF, apply sophisticated techniques to uphold a glorifying discourse that is used to attract funding and advance international standing among conservation lobbies. The current Namibian president, who is an honorary patron of the Peace Parks Foundation, shows a strong commitment to KAZA.

How KAZA is presented in this idealising narrative was clearly demonstrated at the Elephant Summit and the Wildlife Economy Summit at Victoria Falls in 2019. The presidents of Namibia, Botswana, Zambia, and Zimbabwe and a state representative of Angola appeared at the venue as one community of interests that directed their arguments against the restrictions imposed by Western-dominated nature conservation institutions, such as the Convention on International Trade in Endangered Species of Wild Fauna and Flora (CITES), which, as they proclaimed, impaired the sovereignty of African environmental policy through international conventions. Particularly the KAZA vision as a joint leitmotif was used here by the presidents themselves to articulate their claims:

> I support KAZA efforts on elephants. We should not be victims of our success in conservation ... The West must humble itself and learn conservation from us, instead of lecturing us on what we ought to do (President of Namibia Hage Geingob. *Namibia Daily News*, 2019)

> [S]ome communities from Europe prefer animal rights sometimes more than human rights. You will see that they are so concerned about elephants, lions and cheetahs ... And these animals are sometimes many because of our good governance, because of our good conservancy policies ... We have a crisis now in Namibia as you know. There is a human–animal conflict ... Now people whose fields are destroyed by elephants want compensation. What do you compensate them from? If you could sell some of this ivory in a controlled way ... It would be easier for the national party to address that issue. (President of Namibia Hage Geingob, *ZimParksTV*, 2019)

The efforts regarding African elephants in KAZA – a project which, as its advocates recurrently emphasise, is not driven by Western institutions but by African governments and their aspirations – serves as an instrument at international conservation summits to assert sovereignty against international restraints and to legitimise claims for the commodification of ivory. This is done by referring to the successes and experiences of conservation policy in southern Africa (e.g. increase in wildlife populations in Namibia) and through criticising the paternalism of Western conservation organisations. During the Wildlife Economy Summit 2019, visions of a paradigm shift towards institutional and economic emancipation from international conservation legislation and a stronger emphasis on conservation as a form of economy were perceivable. The KAZA Conservation Area is considered to be an initiative to drive this shift and thereby enhance the external sovereignty of African states. Compared to its early phase, today the economic motives of the initiative in terms of ecotourism, hunting, and recently ivory trade are emphasised more strongly. For the heads of state of the five participating countries, KAZA today is a platform for strengthening symbolic sovereignty and gaining international acceptance for the commodification of natural resources according to African environmental policy. This trend shows that the presidents promote KAZA as a catalyst of the commodification of natural resources of southern Africa, and that transfrontier conservation is in line with recent neoliberalising developments in many African countries (Büscher 2013).

Furthermore, the KAZA initiative is used to expand conservation efforts on the national level. By using the transfrontier conservation paradigm as a way to support the national community-based and parks programmes in its individual KAZA component, the Namibian government manages to maintain the sovereignty of its domestic conservation initiatives, although entering into an international agreement for joint transboundary efforts. The initial successes of the Namibian conservancy programme confirmed older development visions for north-eastern Namibia, which defined its future as lying in conservation and tourism development (Lenggenhager 2018). The initiative therefore fitted into the path taken as a complementary project on a meta level. However, a new project does not necessarily mean a break with conventional thinking. In the implementation of KAZA in Namibia it is evident that the organisational memory of the prevailing community-based natural resource management (CBNRM) model is still very present.

On the national level, Namibia translates the transfrontier conservation idea into the national conservation agenda, as conservancies and national parks are being promoted with KAZA funds, because they are considered as important building blocks for the transboundary vision. So far, less effort has been put into the establishment of transboundary conservation interventions such as corridors. Most of the individuals who are involved in the national implementation of KAZA have a strong CBNRM background and continue to think through the lens of Namibia's conservation success story. They are confident that the proven concept is the way to go for Namibia under the transboundary paradigm. By saying, 'you cannot work transboundary if you don't solve your own issues first', a government official argued that there are many internal challenges regarding conservation that take priority before working on joint initiatives. Especially among the interviewed NGO representatives, KAZA is considered to be a good idea, but the main reason for promoting it and highlighting its importance is to get additional funding and legitimacy for their usual activities by terming them as contributing to transboundary efforts under KAZA. When asked about why his organisation has an interest in promoting KAZA, a member of a local NGO (September 2018) said

> it is an opportunity to get money. Zambia wanted support in helping communities so we got money through KAZA to work on cross-border CBNRM … it is an opportunity for people to support other activities they are already doing or would like continue to do. CBNRM money had been sharply reduced for various reasons. People get tired of the same programme so you have to rebrand it, come up with a new name.

The Namibian government also uses KAZA funds for infrastructure development in its north-eastern national parks. This shows that despite entering into an international agreement and the entanglement of international processes and actors, the Namibian conservation sector understands that it can maintain its sovereignty, gain international recognition and access new funding opportunities by translating the transfrontier conservation idea into the national programmes that focus on community-based conservation and parks.

The integration of transfrontier conservation into national policy also has implications for regional environmental governance of north-eastern Namibia. Through coordinating KAZA at the national level the Namibian ministry of environment and tourism increases its power of control over natural resources in north-eastern Namibia, where different claims of land use overlap and are continuously contested between state authorities, traditional authorities, NGOs and private investors. As the whole area of north-eastern Namibia is part of KAZA, the conservation sector can stabilise its territorial claims and oppose land uses that run against the KAZA vision. This can currently be observed in context of prospecting activities by the Canadian oil company ReconAfrica in the Kavango regions of Namibia. These activities in north-eastern Namibia are attracting the attention and opposition of a number of different Namibian and international conservation organisations, which accuse the company of veiling its real intention which is allegedly fracking. As the areas in question are within KAZA, environmentalists can argue with the aims and narratives of transboundary conservation in the debate, contributing to at least delaying, if not interfering with, ReconAfrica's activities (NCE 2021). The example shows that transfrontier conservation has territorialising effects with direct consequences for land governance on national level favouring conservation interests.

In this section we emphasised two points. First, that the transfrontier conservation paradigm in the context of KAZA is used on the international level to enhance the sovereignty of African regional and national environmental governance. In KAZA, sovereignty is constituted by a conglomerate of transnational governmental and non-governmental influences and therefore cannot be understood as a capacity of individual states. Second, that today the economic motives related to KAZA have become stronger compared to its initial phase. Against this backdrop, the following section illuminates contestations of political authority, a grasp of which is crucial for an understanding of graduated sovereignty in KAZA.

Nested and contested sovereignties in transfrontier conservation

Although entering a transfrontier conservation initiative serves to re-assert sovereignty, there are also limits to it, because its regulations summon governments to reconfigure regional land-use policies and engage in joint cross-border activities with other governments and transnational actors. The extent to which the KAZA TFCA can challenge political authority is defined in Article 3 of its treaty:

> (1) KAZA TFCA shall be an international organisation, and shall have legal personality with capacity and power to enter into contracts, acquire, or dispose of, movable, inter alia intellectual property, and immovable property and to sue and be sued.
>
> (2) In the territory of a Partner State, the KAZA TFCA shall, pursuant to paragraph 1 of this Article, have such legal capacity as is necessary for the proper exercise of its functions. (KAZA TFCA Treaty, KAZA TFCA 2012, Article 3: 8–9)

Signing a treaty for the establishment of a TFCA results in the rearrangement of authority and space through the deinstitutionalisation of the border and the emergence of post-national borders (Ramutsindela 2017). According to Ramutsindela (2017), TFCA Memoranda of Understandings (MoUs) are instruments to limit the authority of individual states by creating what he calls a 21st century *terra nullius*. Through treaties, new obligations of the state are introducing a transnational space where governmentality is renegotiated to create a transnational conservation territory with green capitalism at its core (ibid.: 108).

Accordingly, our fieldwork revealed that, among national agents, KAZA is not always seen as an opportunity to enhance sovereignty, but also as a threat to it. In general, environmental challenges and the opportunities that come along with environmental solutions create conditions for competition among African states (Ramutsindela & Büscher 2019). This is reflected in issues concerning the perceived ownership of KAZA, which is clearly defined in the treaty as being distributed equally among the five governments. Several interviews and minutes of KAZA meetings show that the ownership is contested and seems to be unclear. This does not mean that KAZA TFCA lacks agreements that define the roles of all involved actors. Issues of contested ownership were mentioned in terms of how the project is managed *de facto* and how certain actors within the initiative think of themselves and their respective roles in KAZA. A Namibian government official confirmed the instrumental role of president Nujoma in the setting up of KAZA and thus claimed it to be a Namibian project: 'I keep telling the KAZA people that this was Nujoma's idea. He wanted to see the area connected and it was Nujoma who brought all the presidents and ministers together to agree on KAZA' (Government of the Republic of Namibia official July 2019). Several representatives of different government levels and funding and advisory agencies confirmed that there is confusion about the coordination of KAZA, referring to assertions and claims of ownership. The Namibian claim shows that ownership is debated, although officially determined in the KAZA regulations.

Among the different stakeholders there are several claims that some actors are more important for KAZA and hence should have more authority, as well as many accusations that some actors fail to meet commitments and hence ought to have less. An interviewed conservation consultant (September 2019) stated: 'Every organization is trying to claim to be the founder, godfather, main actor or whatever in KAZA because it is the place to be!' Angola is often accused of a lack of commitment to KAZA because it does not appear in meetings in a representative manner, and joint decision-making processes are thus slowed down. Angola, on the other hand, replies to these accusations that decision-making processes are often carried out without its consent and thus it has a right to prevent decisions from coming into force. Zimbabwe and Zambia argue that they deserve more financial support from the KAZA funds, as their nature conservation initiatives are not yet as far advanced as those in Namibia and Botswana. Botswana expresses doubts about the benefits it stands to gain from its participation in KAZA, as even without the initiative it has established a successful conservation and tourism model for the region, while Namibia insists on the essential position of its Zambezi Region, as being located 'right at the heart of KAZA'. The partner states are struggling for recognition of their respective political authorities in the project, which has implications for joint cross-border initiatives such as the implementation of the KAZA visa, which is meant to ease border crossings for international tourists throughout the whole area. While Zambia and Zimbabwe have launched the visa pilot project, other countries remain sceptical about potential risks, like illegal wildlife-product trafficking that could be aggravated through eased border crossings. Although the visa is only meant to be issued to international tourists and not to citizens of the five countries, it still is perceived as a threat to national sovereignty and security, which prevents government officials, especially those from the ministries of home affairs and from the ministries of international relations, to adopt the visa programme. The fear of losing sovereignty is a major constraint inhibiting states from fully participating in transboundary conservation initiatives (van Amerom 2002: 269). Dhliwayo *et al.* (2009) argue that the insistence on the inviolability of state sovereignty among the SADC countries is at the expense of community participation in transfrontier conservation. This point should also be considered concerning KAZA, as the majority of our respondents confirmed that community involvement remains low.

Another example of how potential threats to national sovereignty challenge transboundary conservation efforts under KAZA are joint wildlife-security services. Funded through USAID, the KAZA secretariat coordinates trainings for national prosecutors in the partner countries that aim at harmonisation of wildlife-security policies and practices including enabling joint wildlife patrols across boundaries. As came out in several attended KAZA workshops, transboundary wildlife-security efforts are perceived as a major interference to national sovereignty, as security forces of one state trained by transnational institutions operate on the territory of another. Considering political outcries as more than thirty Namibian citizens were shot dead as alleged poachers by the Botswanan Defence Force since the 1990s (Mongudhi *et al.* 2016; *The Namibian Sun* 2019), cross-border patrols remain a politically highly sensitive issue. Currently, different USAID-funded wildlife-security trainings on transnational and national levels run parallel, which causes confusion among national prosecutors and fuels accusations of foreign interference.[1]

Concerns regarding ownership and state sovereignty interference are not only significant in inter-state communication but were also raised in terms of external non-state organisations like the PPF: 'I don't think that the advice from the PPF always helps. Because I think they see KAZA pretty much as theirs, they think it is peace parks. And I think they like the control and they exert the control' (conservation consultant, August 2018). A challenge of the external influence of the PPF that was mentioned by conservationists is that the guidelines for the implementation of KAZA in terms of their general outline followed the blueprints of documents designed for other TFCAs such as the Kgalagadi Transfrontier Park. That means that the logic of projects designed for a transfrontier conservation park between two countries is transferred into the management of a transfrontier conservation area with a variety of different land uses that is coordinated by five different governments. Concerns about the appropriateness of plans that are not derived from local or even national

[1] Interview with conservation expert in Namibia, Windhoek, September 2018.

perspectives but from the views of external agents are significant with regard to the national integrated development plans (IDP) for the individual countries. A Namibian government official commented on the first KAZA IDP for the Namibian component as follows: 'I would have never written such a thing. It was done by a consultant and consultants tend to produce thick documents with a lot of background information but usually they don't really know the local context' (GRN official, 19 June 2019). As the official explained in the discussion, the IDP was written by a PPF consultant funded by KfW who barely knew the Namibian KAZA component. By outsourcing policy making, transfrontier conservation reconfigures political authority over the regions targeted, as foreign expertise is integrated into the national implementation plans of Namibia. According to Noe (2019), in transboundary conservation projects the power of the state is contested through the continuous influence of international conservation agents who incorporate different values, ideologies, and aspirations, and this has direct effects on project implementation.

This section has shown that there are limits to the re-assertions of sovereignty through KAZA that are set by the same partnerships that constitute them. Hence, we argue that a rigid conception of sovereignty as being exclusively bound to state power is insufficient under conditions of the commodification of nature. Sovereignty is a dynamic effect of continually contested practices across inter-scalar actor networks. What we can see in KAZA are various overlapping authorities transcending state borders and scales that lead to re-conceptualisations of political authority and graduated forms of sovereignty.

Conclusion

This chapter took the example of KAZA to scrutinise how transfrontier conservation goes along with a commodification of nature, new forms of regional governance, and a transformation of political authority. It argued, first, that the establishment of TFCAs cannot be sufficiently explained by focusing only on the intended improvements of conservation, or on the commodification of natural resources. Instead, we suggest that the purpose of KAZA should primarily be understood in relation to its political functions. The KAZA initiative makes promises of economic growth and livelihood enhancement through tourism, but these have not yet been realised, as involved politicians prefer to use KAZA as a means to extend their authority. In the early 2000s KAZA served to gain complete ownership of the transboundary conservation idea among the participating governments and to consolidate their state sovereignty over peripheral regions.

Second, our study has shown that the commodification of nature in the crossborder setting of TFCAs does have immediate consequences for environmental governance at national and international scales through a reconfiguration of territoriality and state sovereignty. To understand these new dynamics, the concept of sovereignty has to be disentangled from its previous fixed, spatial association. Sovereignty in KAZA emerges from participating in a transnational conservation initiative in which various governmental actors, funding organisations, and consulting agencies are involved who continuously enhance and contest sovereignty at different scales, making it a nested or *graduated* phenomenon (Agnew 2005). This was exemplified in the way the partner governments use the idealised depiction of KAZA to call for more funding and claim to emancipate African environmental policy from the paternalism of Western nature conservation agencies. At the same time sovereignty becomes an object of contestation through disagreements about ownership, risks to national security, and the interference of non-state actors such as consulting agencies. In this case, graduated sovereignty is the result of contested types of differential governmentalities in a highly complex transboundary conservation mega-project.

Third, the chapter illustrates how the commodification of nature and the establishment of political authority in peripheral border areas mutually reinforce each other in a transboundary conservation regime. Transfrontier conservation is a neoliberal paradigm (Büscher 2013) that commodifies wildlife, plants, and whole landscapes attributed to imaginaries of 'wild' Africa by employing narratives of ecological protection and development. By conceiving TFCAs as instruments of the market, the commodification of nature instigates new dynamics for political authority through the transnationalisation of sovereignty and territory. These new dynamics result in an extension of eco-governmental control, and they contribute to the reinforcement of the commodification of nature. They do so because the internationally recognised KAZA allows the partner governments to legitimise the extension of ecotourism and hunting as well as to claim the legalisation of ivory trade. Therefore, we assert that commodification and the restructuring of political authority are mutually dependent in KAZA.

In conclusion, we want to encourage a post-colonial perspective on transboundary conservation and ask for alternative views of sovereignty and environmental governance in Africa. The newly emerging authoritative and territorial dynamics faced by the KAZA partner states also leave their traces in the implementation process, which makes progress rather slow, at least in the eyes of donor organisations. However, as we would argue in conclusion to the above analysis, this view may reflect a Western perspective that implicitly compares the performance of KAZA with European models of statehood, interstate cooperation, and regional integration. From this Western view, progress is linked to specific paradigms of modernity, economic growth, and development.

In this regard, we would follow Sidaway (2003), who argues that such a notion of failed governance is based on the Hegelian notion of Africa as lacking in civilisational spirit. An understanding of graduated sovereignty in Africa urges us to decolonise concepts at political geography and think of alternative forms of governance that are not framed through a comparison with Western norms (Ramutsindela 2019). A perceived slowness in the implementation of KAZA does not mean that the project generally fails. European ideas of regional integration 'are out of touch with the reality of the economy and polity of sub-Saharan Africa, and in particular with the nature of the African state' (Gibb 2009: 702). As shown, KAZA has different political functions beyond economic growth and ecological protection. The fact that KAZA has symbolic functions should not be interpreted as an indication of a lack of perseverance or 'weak governance'. Using KAZA for representational means is a strategy which effectuates politics by enhancing international recognition and symbolic sovereignty. From this view the partner states reconstitute parts of their sovereignty in KAZA by outsourcing policy making to international consultants to position themselves strategically in today's development economy. Hence, it would be insufficient to explain the slowness of implementation through the weakness or *absence* of political authority, but rather through an *excess* (Sidaway 2003) of various inter-scalar state and non-state forms of nested sovereignties imposed on one transnational space.

Bibliography

Agnew, J. (1994). 'The territorial trap: The geographical assumptions of international relations theory', *Review of International Political Economy*, 1, 53–80.

Agnew, J. (2005). 'Sovereignty regimes: Territoriality, and state authority in contemporary world politics', *Annals of the Association of American Geographers*, 95(2), 437–461.

Agnew, J. (2015). 'Revisiting the territorial trap', *Nordia Geographical Publications*, 44(4), 43–48.

Allen, J. (2003). *Lost Geographies of Power* (Oxford: Blackwell).

Ali, S. H. (2007). *Peace Parks: Conservation and Conflict Resolution* (Cambridge MA: MIT Press).

Andersson, J. A., de Garine-Wichatitsky, M., Cumming, D., Dzingirai, V., & Giller, K. (2013). *Transfrontier Conservation Areas: People Living on the Edge* (London: Routledge).

Berg, E. & Kuusk, E. (2010). 'What makes sovereignty a relative concept? Empirical approaches to international society', *Political Geography*, 29, 40–49.

Biersteker, T. J. (2013). 'State, sovereignty, and territory', in: W. Carlsnaes, T. Rises, & B. A. Simmons (eds), *Handbook of International Relations* (London: SAGE), 245–272.

Bluwstein, J. & Lund, J. F. (2018). 'Territoriality by conservation in the Selous-Niassa Corridor in Tanzania', *World Development*, 101, 453–465.

Boeckler, M., Engel, U., & Müller-Mahn, D. (2018). 'Regimes of territorialization: Territory, border and infrastructure in Africa', in: M. Boeckler, U. Engel, & D. Müller-Mahn (eds), *Spatial Practices: Territory, Border and Infrastructure in Africa* (Leiden and Boston MA: Brill Academic Publishers), 1–20.

Bollig, M. & Vehrs, H. (2021). 'The making of a conservation landscape: The emergence of a conservationist environmental infrastructure along the Kwando River in Namibia's Zambezi Region', *Africa*, 91(2), 270–295.

Brenner, N., Jessop, B., Jones, M., & MacLeod, G. (2003). 'Introduction: State space in question', in: N. Brenner, B. Jessop, M. Jones, & G. MacLeod (eds), *State/Space: A Reader* (Oxford: Blackwell), 1–26.

Büscher, B. (2010). 'Anti-Politics as political strategy: Neoliberalism and trans-frontier conservation in southern Africa', *Development and Change*, 41(1), 29–51.

Büscher, B. (2013). *Transforming the Frontier: Peace Parks and the Politics of Neoliberal Conservation in Southern Africa* (Durham NC: Duke University Press).

Büscher, B. & Ramutsindela, M. (2016). 'Green violence: Rhino poaching and the war to save southern Africa's peace parks', *African Affairs*, 115(458), 1–22.

Death, C. (2016). 'Green states in Africa: Beyond the usual suspects', *Environmental Politics*, 25(1), 116–135.

Dhliwayo, M., Breen, C., & Nyambe, N. (2009). 'Legal, policy, and institutional provisions for community participation and empowerment in transfrontier conservation in southern Africa', *Journal of International Wildlife Law & Policy*, 12, 60–107.

Duffy, R. (2016). 'War, by conservation', *Geoforum*, 69, 238–248.

Elden, S. (2010). 'Land, terrain, territory', *Progress in Human Geography*, 34(6), 799–817.

Gibb, R. (2009). 'Regional integration and Africa's development trajectory: Meta-theories, expectations and reality', *Third World Quarterly*, 30(4), 701–721.

Goldman, M. (2009). 'Constructing connectivity: Conservation corridors and conservation politics in East African rangelands', *Annals of the Association of American Geographers*, 99(2), 335–359.

Hanks, J. (2003). 'Transfrontier conservation areas (TFCAs) in southern Africa: Their role in conserving biodiversity, socio-economic development and promoting a culture of peace', *Journal of Sustainable Forestry*, 17, 163–187.

Igoe, J. & Brockington, D. (2007). 'Neoliberal conservation: A brief introduction', *Conservation & Society*, 5(4), 432–449.

Kangumu, B. (2011). *Contesting Caprivi: A History of Colonial Isolation and Regional Nationalism in Namibia* (Basel: Basler Afrika Bibliographien).

KAZA TFCA (2012). 'Treaty between The Government of the Republic of Angola, The Government of the Republic of Botswana, The Government of the Republic of Namibia, The Government of the Republic of Zambia, And the Government of the Republic of Zimbabwe on the establishment of the Kavango Zambezi Transfrontier Conservation Area'. Available at: https://tfcaportal.org/system/files/resources/KAZA%20TFCA%20Treaty_SIGNED.pdf [Accessed 2 January 2023].

KAZA TFCA (2015). 'Kavango-Zambezi Transfrontier Conservation Area Master

Integrated Development Plan'. Available at: https://kavangozambezi.org/en/publications-2019?start=9 [Accessed 16 November 2020].

KAZA TFCA (2018). 'Collaborative Partnerships Boost Conservation Efforts in KAZA'. Available at: www.kavangozambezi.org/pt/events-public/item/24-collaborative-partnerships-boosts-conservation [Accessed 28 February 2019].

Kuus, M. & Agnew, J. (2008). 'Theorizing the state geographically: Sovereignty, subjectivity, territoriality', in: K. Cox, M. Low, & J. Robinson (eds), *The SAGE Handbook of Political Geography* (London: SAGE), 95–106.

Legal Assistance Centre (LAC) (2021). 'The Law and Oil exploration in Namibia'. Available at: www.lac.org.na/index.php/projects/land-environment-development-lead/oil-exploration [Accessed 18 January 2022].

Lenggenhager, L. (2018). *Ruling Nature, Controlling People: Nature Conservation, Development and War in North-Eastern Namibia since the 1920s* (Basel: Basler Afrika Bibliographien).

Linell, A., Sjöstedt, M., & Sundström, A. (2018). 'Governing transboundary commons in Africa: The emergence and challenges of the Kavango-Zambezi Treaty', *International Environmental Agreements: Politics, Law and Economics*, 19(1), 53–68.

Liverman, D. (2004). 'Who governs, at what scale and at what price? Geography, environmental governance, and the commodification of nature', *Annals of the Association of American Geographers*, 94(4), 734–738.

Lunstrum, E. (2013). 'Articulated sovereignty: Extending Mozambican state power through the Great Limpopo Transfrontier Parl', *Political Geography*, 36, 1–11.

Mbembe, A. (2000). 'At the edge of the world: Boundaries, territoriality, and sovereignty in Africa', *Public Culture*, 12(1), 259–284.

Melber, H. (2015). *Understanding Namibia* (London: Hurst & Company).

Mogende, E. (2016). 'The Politics of the Kavango-Zambezi (KAZA) TFCA in Botswana', MPhil Thesis, Department of Environmental and Geographical Science University of Cape Town. Available at: https://open.uct.ac.za/bitstream/handle/11427/23761/thesis_sci_2016_mogende_emmanuel.pdf [Accessed 28 February 2019].

Mosimane, A., Lendelvo, S., Glatz-Jorde, S., Kirchmeir, H., & Huber, M. (2014). 'Livelihood baseline survey report for the Kavango Zambezi Transfrontier Conservation Area (KAZA TFCA)', Available at: https://kavangozambezi.org/en/publications-2019 [Accessed 16 November 2020].

Mountz, A. (2013). 'Political geography I: Reconfiguring geographies of sovereignty', *Progress in Human Geography*, 37(6), 829–841.

Müller-Mahn, D., Weisser, F., & Willers, J. (2018). 'Struggling for sovereignty: Political authority and the governance of climate change in Ethiopia', in: M. Boeckler, U. Engel, & D. Müller-Mahn (eds), *Spatial Practices: Territory, Border and Infrastructure in Africa* (Leiden and Boston: Brill Academic Publishers), 21–40.

Naidoo, R., Kilian, J. W., Du Preez, P., Beytell, P., Aschenborn, O., Taylor, R. D. & Stuart-Hill, G. (2018). 'Evaluating the effectiveness of local- and regional-scale wildlife corridors using quantitative metrics of functional connectivity', *Biological Conservation*, 2017, 96–103.

Namibia Daily News (2019). 'Four Southern African countries agree on "integrated" elephant management approach', 7 May, via *XINHUA*. Available at: http:// namibiadailynews.info/four-southern-african-countries-agree-on-integrated-elephant-management-approach [Accessed 28 February 2020].

NCE – Namibian Chamber of Environment (2021). 'Recon Africa's Seismic "Thumper" Survey Levels Wilderness and Damages Homes in Kavango East' (Windhoek: Frack Free Namibia, 5 October). Available at: https://n-c-e.org/ sites/default/files/2021-10/FFN_press%20release_seismic%20surveying_5%20 October%202021.pdf [Accessed 12 October 2021].

Noe, C. (2015). 'Washoroba and the proliferation of borders in the Selous-Niassa Wildlife Corridor', in: M. Ramutsindela (ed.), *Cartographies of Nature: How Nature Conservation Animates Borders* (Newcastle upon Tyne: Cambridge Scholars Publishing), 113–139.

Painter, J. (2010). 'Rethinking territory', *Antipode*, 42(5), 1090–1118.

Ramutsindela, M. (2007). *Transfrontier Conservation Areas: At the Confluence of Capital, Politics and Nature* (Boston MA: CABI).

Ramutsindela, M. (2017). 'Greening Africa's borderlands: The symbiotic politics of land and borders in peace parks', *Political Geography*, 56, 106–113.

Ramutsindela, M. (2019). 'Governing territory, scalecraft and intrapreneurialism', *Territory, Politics, Governance*, 7(3), 285–288.

Ramutsindela, M. & Büscher, B. (2019). 'Environmental governance and the (re-)making of the African state', *Oxford Research Encyclopedia of Politics*. Available at: https://oxfordre.com/politics/view/10.1093/ acrefore/9780190228637.001.0001/acrefore-9780190228637-e-903 [Accessed 16 November 2020].

Rogerson, C. (2003). 'The OUZIT initiative: Re-positioning southern Africa in global tourism', *Africa Insight*, 33(1–2), 33–35.

Rusinga, O. & Mapira, J. (2012). 'Challenges of transfrontier conservation areas: Natural resources nationalism, security and regionalism in the Southern African Development Community', *International Journal of Development and Sustainability*, 1(3), 675–687.

Sidaway, J. D. (2003). 'Sovereign excesses? Portraying postcolonial sovereigntyscapes', *Political Geography*, 22, 157–178.

Spierenburg, M. (2013). '"We agreed to move but we did not do so freely": Resettlement from the Limpopo National Park, Mozambique', in: B. Dermann, A. Hellum, and K. B. Sandvik (eds), *Worlds of Human Rights: The Ambiguities of Rights Claiming in Africa* (Leiden: Brill), 101–128.

Spierenburg, M. & Wels, H. (2010). 'Conservative philanthropists, royalty and business elites in nature conservation in southern Africa', *Antipode*, 42(3), 647–670.

Suich, H., Busch, J., & Barbancho, N. (2005). 'Economic impacts of transfrontier conservation areas: Baseline of tourism in the Kavango-Zambezi TFCA'. Conservation International South Africa, Paper no. 4. Available at: www.cbd. int/financial/values/southafrica-valuation1.pdf [Accessed 21 January 2019].

Mongudhi, T, Konopo, J. & Ntibinyane, N. (2016). 'Deadly borders ... 30 Namibians killed through Botswana's shoot-to-kill-policy', *The Namibian*, 9 March. Available at: www.namibian.com.na/148318/archive-read/

Deadly-borders--30-Namibians-killed-through-Botswana&ampamp39s-shoot-to-kill-policy [Accessed 28 February 2020].

The Namibian Sun (2019). 'Two poachers shot dead', 29 August 2019. Available at: www.namibiansun.com/news/two-poachers-shot-dead2019-08-28 [Accessed 28 February 2020].

van Amerom, M. (2002). 'National sovereignty & transboundary protected areas in southern Africa', *GeoJournal*, 58, 265–273.

Wolmer, W. (2003). 'Transboundary conservation: The politics of ecological integrity in the Great Limpopo Transfrontier Park', *Journal of Southern African Studies*, 29(1), 261–278.

Zeller, W. & Melber, H. (2018). 'United in separation? Lozi secessionism in Namibia and Zambia', in: L. de Vries, P. Englebert, & M. Schomerus (eds), *Secessionism in African Politics: Aspiration, Grievance, Performance, Disenchantment* (New York: Palgrave Macmillan), 293–328.

ZimparksTV (2019). 'AU-UN Environment Wildlife Economy Summit 2019'. 24 June 2019. Available at: www.youtube.com/watch?v=ZvHcwqhz0Yc, 1:38:20-1:41:01 [Accessed 28 February 2019].

PART 3

PLANTS FROM THE WILDERNESS FOR A GLOBAL MARKET: THE COMMODIFICATION OF NON-DOMESTICATED (WILD) PLANTS

6

Towards Pro-poor or Pro-profit? The governance framework for harvesting and trade of devil's claw (*Harpagophytum* spp.) in the Zambezi Region, Namibia

JESSICA-JANE LAVELLE

Introduction

Devil's claw (*Harpagophytum* spp.) presents a contextually complex case study of indigenous natural-product commoditisation in southern Africa that is steeped in exploitative history and continues to raise concerns about social justice. Indigenous communities of southern Africa, mainly San and Khoi, were the original knowledge holders of the use of devil's claw for medicinal purposes. The tubers are used primarily in the form of infusions, decoctions, and ointments for the treatment of digestive disorders, pain, diabetes, urinary tract infections, fever, sores, ulcers, boils, and as a general health tonic and analgesic, especially during pregnancy (Van Wyk *et al.* 2002).

According to Brendler (2021), the first colonial descriptions of devil's claw (as grapple plant – *Uncaria procumbens*) were by J. G. Wood and M. C. Cooke in 1870 and 1882, respectively (Wood 1870; Cooke 1882). In 1901, its medicinal properties were noted by A. Lübbert who provided an account of the use of '*KuriKhamiknollen*' in wound healing, the name derived from the Nama for devil's claw '*||khuri||kham*' (Lübbert 1901). A few years later, in 1907, a report was compiled by a medical officer of the German colonial forces in then German South West Africa (Namibia) on medicinal plant uses of the Herero and Nama people. Included was an account of the Herero Samuel Kariko of the use of '*otjihangatene*' to treat cough, diarrhoea, constipation, and venereal diseases (Hellwig 1907). Despite this historical record explicitly noting the source of the traditional knowledge for the medicinal use of devil's claw, it is a German colonial soldier and latterly farmer, G. H. Mehnert, that is widely attributed with the 'discovery' of this knowledge during the Herero and Nama genocide of 1904 to 1908 (Brendler 2021). During the Second World War, Mehnert shared the knowledge of the plant's medicinal properties with a German scientist, O. H. Volk. On Volk's return to Germany he then shared the knowledge with B. Zorn, a chemist at the University of Jena who initiated pharmacological research following which several more chemical analyses and toxicological studies were conducted in the late 1950s and 1960s (see Brendler 2021 for more detail). In the meantime, Mehnert registered his company Harpago (Pty) Ltd, trademarked 'Harpago' and initiated exports to Germany. Erwin Hagen followed suit and trademarked 'Harpago' in Germany in the early 1960s, marketing a devil's claw infusion and later homeopathic preparations through his company Erwin Hagen Naturheilmittel GmbH. In 1977, 'Harpagosan' was registered as a botanical drug in Germany.

Devil's claw has since gained popularity as a natural medicine for rheumatism, arthritis and tendonitis, with increasing amounts exported from southern Africa to Europe, Asia, and the United States (US). Germany is by far the largest market, followed by France. In southern Africa, Namibia is the primary exporter of devil's claw, with exports averaging 700 tonnes with a peak of close to 1,000 tonnes in 2019 (Lavelle 2019; Brendler 2021). The plant is predominantly exported in raw form as dried slices, then it is either milled or packaged for sale as a tea or herbal supplement or undergoes a greater degree of processing. This includes the extraction of active ingredients through water- or alcohol-based extraction methods. Extracts are then manufactured into diverse products, often with patented formulations, before being sold in pharmacies, supermarkets, or health food shops. Between harvester and final shelf destination the material may pass through a number of agents, wholesalers, manufacturers, packagers, and extractors (Wynberg *et al.* 2009).

Based on the average size of the annual world devil's claw market, at 700 tonnes, and an approximate retail value of US$300 per kilogram, the industry is worth an estimated US$210 million per annum. The difference between in-country earnings and overseas trade value is vast with less than 2% captured in-country. Namibian exporters capture 0.7% of trade value (~US$1.47 million), traders 0.45% ($945,000) and harvesters 0.45% ($945,000), equivalent to US$150 to $500 per harvester per year (Wynberg *et al.* 2009; Lavelle 2019). While the domestic price gap may not at first glance seem significant, five or fewer exporters handle all export volumes while up to 5,000 harvesters contribute to the total export volume (Wynberg 2006; MCA-N 2014). Of the approximately 100–200 traders in Namibia, most act as middlemen between the harvesters in the remote rural areas and the exporters close to Windhoek (Natural Resources Institute, henceforth NRI

2011b). Multi-stage trading greatly reduces the price paid to harvesters, and up to 80% of trade between harvesters, middlemen, and exporters is ad hoc and characterised by exploitative harvester prices, minimal value-adding, and few binding contracts.

This inequitable and unjust value chain is a product of many factors. The traditional knowledge of the medicinal properties and applications of devil's claw was first commoditised by European colonialists long before the concept of access and benefit sharing (ABS) was popularised. Traditional knowledge was the basis for initiating German interest in the plant, and failure to recognise the source of this traditional knowledge marked one of the first and most significant incidents of 'biopiracy' in Namibia, with Mehnert laying claim to the 'original recipe' for its processing and subsequent commercialisation (Wynberg 2004; Brendler 2021). The 2014 Nagoya Protocol on Access to Genetic Resources and the Fair and Equitable Sharing of Benefits Arising from their Utilisation seeks to address such historical injustices and mitigate the inequitable distribution of benefits from the use of indigenous biological and genetic resources and associated traditional knowledge through bilateral ABS agreements. It follows that the European Union, including Germany, now regulates compliance measures for the use of genetic resources and associated traditional knowledge in research and development. Namibia is a signatory to the Nagoya Protocol and has enacted the Access to Biological and Genetic Resources and Associated Traditional Knowledge Act No. 2 of 27 June 2017. However, with regulations only gazetted in August 2021 it has yet to be operationalised with functional structures and processes and, as such, no ABS measures are in place for harvesting and trade of devil's claw.

Since the early 1980s, devil's claw has been characterised by high levels of patent activity with over 56 patents granted in Germany, France, the United Kingdom, the US, Japan, Republic of Korea, Russia, Romania, China, and Europe (see Brendler 2021 for list). The majority of patents refer to extraction methods and compositions for known uses. Patents have also been granted for compositions for allegedly new uses. Early patents enabled predominantly German companies to develop multiple standardised extracts and products that now limit Namibia to capture less than 2% of the value chain. While legal restrictions do not preclude Namibian companies from utilising existing patents, market access is a crucial factor that impedes local value-addition, with European trade dominated by a few companies. In particular, German Martin Bauer GmbH & Co. and its subsidiaries that are estimated to control 75% of world trade in devil's claw. In-country primary processing has been met with resistance from European companies and an extraction facility for a single resource carries major risks and is unlikely to be economically feasible in

Namibia without sufficient quantities of other marketable botanicals. Further, the existence of patents acts as a perceptual barrier of risk for many local firms who lack knowledge of the scope of patent protection and the differences between granted patents and published patent applications (Wynberg *et al.* 2009).

The commercial trade of devil's claw in Namibia has largely developed as informal and unorganised in structure and process. Since the 1990s, non-governmental organisations (NGOs) have worked to improve the sustainability and fair trade of devil's claw through organising harvesters into groups and facilitating direct sales to exporters. However, annual demand for devil's claw is unpredictable and negatively impacts the supply chain, especially at the local level. Exporters are uncertain of amounts to be purchased for resale to overseas buyers and harvesters are not able to plan supply. Pricing is also variable and exacerbated by the lack of long-term purchase agreements between exporters and overseas buyers, negotiating tactics used by the overseas buyers to play out exporters against each other, and lack of cooperation and coordination among Namibian exporters (NRI 2011b). In response to volatile export market conditions, exporters employ a variety of tactics to control the local market including stockpiling, price setting, and withholding trade information (Lavelle 2019). To gain competitive advantage, exporters may support certain harvester groups to obtain organic and Fair for Life certification.[1] Where there are organised harvesting groups, exporters compete for exclusive contracts with fixed quotas and pricing to better manage supply. Organised harvesting groups also enable traceability and some form of monitoring of the resource and thus the product is marketed as 'premium devil's claw'. Conventional (lowest) quality makes up about 80% of the trade volume, premium quality currently contributes about 10–15% to the total, certified organic makes up about 5–10% of the total trade volume, and finally, organic and Fair for Life certified material contributes ~1% to the trade total (Brendler 2021). Historically, there has been limited cooperation and coordination among Namibian exporters; however, in May 2014 the National Devil's Claw Export Association was registered as a trust with the aim of improving organisation towards a sustainable, profitable and quality-driven devil's claw industry in Namibia. More recently, the association has undertaken to implement a Good Agricultural and Collection Practice standard (akin to premium devil's claw) with the support of GIZ (Deutsche

---

[1]   Fair for Life is a Swiss certification programme for fair trade in agriculture, manufacturing, and trade that encourages a responsible supply chain business model and the implementation of good economic, social, and environmental practices.

Gesellschaft für Internationale Zusammenarbeit), the German development agency and Naturex, a European botanicals company. The standard seeks to comply with European ABS requirements, enable higher export prices and improve sustainability and livelihood outcomes.

Most harvesting takes place in the remote, open-access communal areas of four regions including Omaheke, Otjozondjupa, Zambezi, and Kavango East. In the communal areas, land ownership is vested with the state with traditional authorities responsible for the allocation of customary land rights. These areas are relics of the German, British, and South African colonial administrations which proclaimed 'black' areas separate from white settlement areas, and left them purposefully underdeveloped. Very high levels of poverty are prevalent in the Kavango East, Zambezi, and Omaheke regions, where most harvesting takes place, and the harvesters are some of the poorest members of society, often marginalised, and living under adverse agricultural and socio-economic conditions (Wynberg 2006; Namibia Statistics Agency 2018; Lavelle 2019). As a result, the harvesters often lack information about the market and are in the weakest bargaining position in the supply chain.

Nonetheless, the contribution of devil's claw to rural livelihoods is significant and is often the primary cash income that supplements subsistence farming and is therefore extremely important to household food security (Wynberg 2006; MCA-N 2014; Lavelle 2019). Owing to its economic value, the Namibian government formally regulates devil's claw as a protected plant with the National Policy on the Utilisation of Devil's Claw (*Harpagophytum*) Products. As such, its harvesting is not managed by customary systems but state permissions and monitoring procedures. The traditional authorities are legally recognised by the state as the administrators of land and communities in communal areas. Namibia also has an extensive community-based natural resource management (CBNRM) programme that grants rural communities conditional rights to manage and utilise wildlife and plants for economic benefit. Recently, commercial harvesting of devil's claw was widely expanded to these formal CBNRM areas – conservancies and community forests – as a development intervention funded by a major international donor, the US Millennium Challenge Corporation. The objective of the intervention was to increase the volume of devil's claw harvested by organised harvesting groups to improve the sustainability of trade and provide a conservation-friendly livelihood to rural communities in CBNRM areas. It follows that the governance framework in which the harvesting of devil's claw is situated is complex; widespread harvesting raises questions of sustainability, and skewed economic benefits require ethical considerations to be further interrogated.

Study area

This chapter provides an overview of the harvesting and trade of devil's claw in the Zambezi Region of Namibia (Map 6.1)[2] based on the author's involvement in the implementation of devil's claw harvesting from 2010 to 2014 and empirical research from 2015 to 2017. The Zambezi Region is one of the fourteen regions of Namibia and located to the far north-east of the country bordering Angola, Botswana, Zimbabwe, and Zambia. The region covers an area of 14,528 km[2] and has a population of approximately 90,500 people from five major ethnic groups, namely the Khwe, Mbukushu, Mafwe, Masubia, and Mayeyi (National Planning Commission 2016). There are four recognised traditional authorities including the Masubia, Mafwe, Mashi, and Mayeyi. Large parts of the region have been established as communal conservancies and community forests under the national CBNRM programme. There are fifteen conservancies covering 4,103 km[2] (28% of the region) with approximately 31,908 members and seven community forests (Namibian Association of CBNRM Support Organisations, hereafter NACSO 2019). A long-standing local NGO, Integrated Rural Development and Nature Conservation (IRDNC), has played an instrumental role in the development and support of conservancies and community forests and continues to provide support in the region. Subsistence agriculture provides the majority of people with most of their food while state pensions, social grants, remittances, crop sales, and the sale of natural resources are important for cash income (Mosimane *et al.* 2014).

Devil's claw is harvested and used as a traditional medicine by some households in the region, but it is predominantly sold to traders and exporters for international trade. Up until 2009, all devil's claw harvesting and trade in the Zambezi Region was unfacilitated and ad hoc, with harvesters selling to passing traders who on average paid US$0.60 to $0.95 per kilogram (Lavelle 2019). In 2009, the Indigenous Natural Products (INP) Activity through the Millennium Challenge Account–Namibia (MCA-N) Compact[3] made available funds for implementing organised harvesting and trade of devil's claw in eleven selected conservancies and community forests in the Zambezi Region. From 2010 to 2014, the financial aid was channelled through IRDNC who worked closely with the conservancies and community forests to facilitate sustainable harvesting and equitable trade. For these communities this intervention created an additional source of cash-in-hand income managed by the

---

[2]   Until 2013, the area was known as the Caprivi Region with its administrative border from the Kavango River eastwards. In 2013, the reduced area was renamed the Zambezi Region, and its administrative border moved eastwards to the settlement of Chetto.

[3]   Funded by the US government through the Millennium Challenge Corporation.

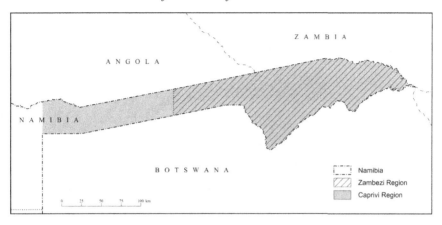

Map 6.1 The Caprivi and Zambezi Regions of Namibia (Source: Lavelle 2019; Cartography: M. Feinen).

conservancy/community forest. Organised harvesters receive higher prices per kilogram than unorganised harvesters, and harvesting practices are more sustainable as a result of training. Since the conclusion of the compact in 2014, IRDNC has largely withdrawn its support for devil's claw-related activities. Seven of the eleven target communities continue to harvest and trade devil's claw. Unfacilitated devil's claw harvesting is undertaken by individuals or families in their own capacity within several communities including Liselo, Masokatwani, Gumkwe, Kasheshe, Makanga, and Sachinga.

The ecology of devil's claw and sustainability concerns

Devil's claw (Family: Pedaliaceae) includes two species: *Harpagophytum procumbens* (BURCH.) DC. ex MEISSNER (ssp. *procumbens* and ssp. *trans-vaalensis*) and *H. zeyheri* DECNE. (ssp. *zeyheri*, ssp. *sublobatum*, and ssp. *schiifii*) (Ihlenfeldt & Hartmann 1970). It is a weedy, perennial geophyte with annually produced secondary tubers that grow from a primary tuber that extends into a deep taproot (Stewart 2009; Figure 6.1). The thorns and sharp hooks of the fruit give devil's claw its scientific and common name (Van Wyk *et al.* 2002).

Devil's claw is endemic to the Kalahari region of Namibia, Botswana, South Africa, Angola, and, to a lesser extent, Zambia and Mozambique (Ihlenfeldt & Hartmann 1970; Map 6.2). The areas in which it occurs are characterised by a semi-arid climate with high potential evaporation and frequent drought. The growing season of the plant commences in December with the onset of

Figure 6.1 *Harpagophytum* spp. tubers (Photo: Author).

the rainy season and ends between April and June after the plant has produced
flowers and seeds and amassed adequate phytosynthates to facilitate growth
(Strohbach 1999). The flowers and leaves of the plant are only visible during
the active growing season, but their appearance is dependent on sufficient
rainfall. After rains these parts of the plant dry out and disappear, making
the location of the tubers extremely difficult to detect to the untrained eye.

To date, no comprehensive resource assessments have been undertaken
in any of the communal harvesting areas (Wynberg 2006; Lavelle 2019).
Based on average yield estimates and plant densities, Von Willert and Sanders
(2004) concluded that 650 tonnes of dried tubers equate to the harvest of 8–11
million plants. As a valuable economic resource, there have long been concerns
about the sustainability of harvesting devil's claw. With such pressure on the
resource, sustainable harvesting is crucial to ensuring viable populations for
the future. Unsustainable devil's claw harvesting methods include: damaging
or entirely removing the taproot of plants; harvesting plants that are too young;
failing to leave harvesting areas, plant populations, or individual plants fallow
long enough for side-tubers to regenerate sufficiently; and failing to re-fill
holes around plants after harvesting, thus disturbing the normal growing cycle
and threatening plant survival (NRI 2011a).

A major barrier to sustainable harvesting is the low prices paid to harvesters
as, for income to be viable relative to their labour, harvesters must harvest as

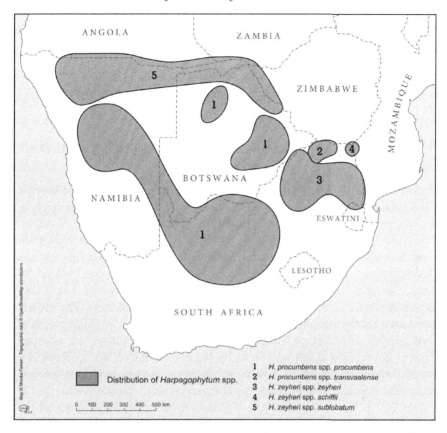

Map 6.2 Distribution of *Harpagophytum* spp. in southern Africa (Source: Wynberg 2006, after Ihlenfeldt and Hartmann 1970; Cartography: M. Feinen).

much devil's claw from an area as possible. Overharvesting is more likely in open-access communal areas where regulation and monitoring are not easily implemented, and areas are easily accessible to greater numbers of harvesters (Wynberg 2006; Lavelle 2019). Unsustainable practices have had negative effects on the health, stability, and growth of local plant populations in these areas, with associated risks to the livelihoods of the harvesters (NRI 2011a). Population decline is difficult to ascertain however, as other factors such as low rainfall and browsing and trampling by livestock also contribute to population variability (Strohbach 1999).

Cultivation efforts were perceived to have the potential to improve the sustainability of harvesting. However, driven by European pharmaceutical companies seeking an improved, standardised and secure product, and undertaken in South Africa and Namibia on white-owned commercial farms, cultivation efforts were also perceived to be a potential threat to the liveli-hoods of wild product harvesters (Wynberg 2004, 2006). Nevertheless, the once-thought inevitable widespread cultivation of devil's claw has not materi-alised, and cultivated devil's claw remains limited to a small percentage of the total exports.

Donor-driven expansion of devil's claw harvesting and trade in the Zambezi Region

In response to sustainability concerns, the Sustainably Harvested Devil's Claw (SHDC) Project was initiated in 1997 among San harvesters on nineteen pre-independence resettlement farms in the Omaheke Region of Namibia. The project was donor-funded and implemented by a European–Namibian consultancy, the Centre for Research Information in Africa – Southern Africa Development and Consulting (CRIAA SA-DC).[4] The main objectives of the project were to support harvesters in collectively managing and sustainably harvesting devil's claw and to facilitate direct sales to exporters. The project was based on the insight that there was growing interest in linking ethical consumerism in developed countries to sustainable resource use and fair trade in developing countries. Thus, by linking the harvesters to exporters, benefits could be increased, which would result in improved management and sustainable use of devil's claw by the harvesters in Omaheke (Cole & Du Plessis 2001). The same paradigm of incentivising conservation through the realisation of economic benefits from natural resources was simultaneously driving the development of CBNRM in the communal areas, with the first conservancy also registered in 1998.

The project organised harvesters into registered groups, developed monitoring and record-keeping processes, and improved the quality and sustainability of their product through the provision of training, equipment, and storage facilities. In addition, CRIAA SA-DC facilitated direct sales between harvesters and an exporter with formalised sales agreements and price reviews, and pre- and post-harvest resource surveys were undertaken to set harvesting quotas (Strohbach & Cole 2007). The SHDC Project, which ran until 2006, was successful in demonstrating the link between improved benefits and better management of the resource. With an increase in prices from US$0.08 to $0.60 per kilogram to a minimum of $0.90 per kilogram, compliance with

---

4   CRIAA SA-DC is an association of development workers acting on a non-profit basis and offering an independent European–southern African development and consul-tancy service.

sustainable harvesting methods increased to between 80% and 85% (Cole & Du Plessis 2001). However, the project was limited in scale and scope, with only about 1% or less of annual devil's claw exports from Namibia originating from devil's claw harvested in the project area (Cole 2008).

In the 2000s, the expansion of conservancies created the organisational and resource-management frameworks within which management of plant resources like devil's claw could be integrated along with wildlife. Between 2006 and 2008, two conservancies in Otjozondjupa Region, Nyae Nyae and N#a Jaqna, and the Kyaramacan Association in Bwabwata National Park in the then west Caprivi Region were helped to also begin organised harvesting and trade of devil's claw according to the model developed during the SHDC project. The expansion of the model to these areas now increased the volume of 'sustainably' harvested devil's claw to 10% of exported volumes (NRI 2011b).

In 2008, an INP Activity was included in the Agriculture Project of the MCA-N Compact, running from September 2009 to September 2014, to the value of US$6.7 million. The INP Activity aimed to sustainably increase the number of households involved in the trade, and also to increase their income, by broadening the number of products, increasing the volume, improving the quality, and adding value (NRI 2011b). Given the success of the ongoing SHDC project, the existing value of the international trade and the potential to expand 'sustainable' production, devil's claw was identified as a target product.

The approach to implementation was to work within existing conservancies and community forests to strengthen them in terms of governance and improve product quality and knowledge of the market. The delivery of training was the primary action, with the provision of small grants for primary production improvement being a secondary focus. While it was known that substantial initial technical assistance and ongoing liaison with buyers would be required, it was envisaged by the implementing NGOs[5] that the conservancies and community forests would develop their capacity to interact with markets or find a suitable mechanism. The capacity development required for ongoing trade was deemed manageable given the limited value-addition at the local level. The main risks identified were unpredictable market demand, drought, inability to manage sustainable harvesting, and unknown technical barriers to trade (NRI 2011b).

A diagnosis of prospective conservancies and community forests was undertaken to determine the suitability of each to participate. It included a review of the organisational capacity, resource availability and market demand.

---

[5] Integrated Rural Development and Nature Conservation (Zambezi); Namibia Nature Foundation (Kavango East); Centre for Research Information in Africa – Southern Africa Development and Consulting (Otjozondjupa).

In addition, a baseline study of the resource and an environmental impact assessment of harvesting activities were undertaken, however, no assessment pertaining to the social-cultural value and impact of the project were initiated. The MCA-N INP Activity resulted in broad-based expansion of organised devil's claw harvesting to eleven conservancies and community forests in the Zambezi Region (NRI 2010b, 2010c), in addition to seven conservancies and community forests in Otjozondjupa and Kavango East. The Kyaramacan Association in Bwabwata National Park, which straddles the Zambezi and Kavango East regions, initiated harvesting prior to the MCA-N programme but was also included as a target producer organisation.

The governance framework for devil's claw harvesting in the Zambezi Region

Development of policy and laws for devil's claw in Namibia

From the 1970s, the government (then the South West Africa Administration) had concerns about the sustainability of devil's claw harvesting. The economic value of devil's claw exports underpinned the concern and resulted in *H. procumbens* being listed as a protected species under Schedule 9 of the Nature Conservation Ordinance No. 4 of 1975. Legislation implemented permits to harvest, possess, transport, and export the plant. The outcome was the relatively effective regulation of exports, but ineffective control of harvesting. In 1986, a study found the permit system for controlling harvesting was beyond the resources of the regulating body at the time, and only 10% of the devil's claw harvested was being harvested with a permit (Nott 1986). Recommendations were made, and the permit requirements for harvesting, possession, and transportation were suspended that year; only the permit system for export was retained (Ministry of Environment and Tourism, hereafter MET 2010a).

In the 1990s, devil's claw was listed in the international pharmacopoeia, which increased demand threefold, thereby renewing concerns about sustainability and illegal harvesting (Wynberg 2004). The SHDC project, initiated in 1997, led to a reassessment of the situation and informed the drafting of the Policy on the Harvesting and Export of *Harpagophytum* Products in 1999. In the same year, the then Ministry of Environment and Tourism[6] reintroduced a permit system for devil's claw harvesting. However, in 2003 the effectiveness of the reintroduction of the harvesting permit system was assessed, and it was determined that the draft policy was not well understood. There was a significant level of noncompliance with existing regulations,

---

6   As of March 2020, Ministry of Environment, Forestry and Tourism.

due to a general lack of awareness in the Ministry of Environment and Tourism and amongst harvesters, characterised by misinterpretations and inconsistencies across regions (NRI 2011b). The permit system was found to be ineffective with respect to improved management of the resource. It was also recognised that the rural communal context in which harvesting takes place was complex and challenging, making the effective implementation of harvesting permits difficult.

In 2008, MCA-N stipulated that the draft policy should be updated and finalised before the implementation of the programme owing to the status of devil's claw as a protected species (Lavelle 2019). As such, despite previous assessments finding harvesting permits ineffective, and without addressing the identified limitations, MCA-N funded the finalisation of the policy, which was signed off in 2010 as the National Policy on the Utilisation of Devil's Claw (*Harpagophytum*) Products (MET 2010a). The protected plants schedule was also amended to include *H. zeyheri* alongside *H. procumbens.* The policy was largely developed by the NGOs which had been working on the various sustainable harvesting projects, and which also sat on the National Advisory Committee for Devil's Claw. The updated policy sought to improve the traceability of devil's claw and to facilitate the registration of traders and exporters with the ministry (MCA-N 2014). An information pamphlet explaining the policy was also developed with funding from MCA-N (Figure 6.2).

First and foremost, the policy dictates that any Namibian citizen can harvest, trade, or export devil's claw provided that they adhere to the policy. This stipulates the following for harvesting permits: (1) a harvesting season from 1 March to 31 October with no permits issued outside of this period; (2) permits are non-transferable, valid for a single harvesting season in a specified area, and may be subject to a quota; (3) permits may be issued to individuals or a group that has obtained permission from the landowner, conservancy, community forest, or traditional authority prior to harvesting; (4) a report is to be submitted by the permit holder to the Ministry of Environment and Tourism within one month of the close of the season with all sales records including amounts sold from which locality, at what prices, to whom, and when; and (5) no new permits will be issued unless the report has been received and there is confirmation of compliance with sustainable harvesting techniques. The policy also specifies that the technique for harvesting must be sustainable.

Regarding trade and export, the policy states that any individuals or organisations trading and/or exporting devil's claw are required to register with the Ministry of Environment and Tourism before applying for a permit, which includes a test to verify that the applicant knows and understands the policy and regulations. Registration is valid for three years; however, permits are only valid for one year. Traders must also keep a register of all transactions,

Why do permits matter?

Permits are not required just to make things difficult for people working with Devil's Claw. They are there to protect Devil's Claw for the future.

A Devil's Claw 'Harvest' permit states:
- Who may harvest (one person or a group);
- Where they may harvest;
- When they can harvest (1ˢᵗ March to 31ˢᵗ October);
- How they should harvest.

The 'Report Back' form must be submitted before the end of November.

A Devil's Claw 'Buy and Sell' permit for traders states:
- Who may buy and sell;
- Where they may buy;
- When they may buy (1ˢᵗ March to 31ˢᵗ October).

The 'Report Back' form must be submitted before the end of November.

A Devil's Claw 'Export' permit states:
- Who is selling;
- Who is buying (name and country);
- How much is being exported.

The 'Report Back' form must be submitted within 14 days of the permit expiring.

All of this information helps MET to check whether people working with Devil's Claw are doing it in the right way.

10

How to harvest Devil's Claw

- Devil's Claw may only be harvested between 1ˢᵗ March and 31ˢᵗ October each year. Devil's Claw is a protected plant so all harvesters need to get a permit from the MET before starting to harvest. Individuals or groups can apply for a permit.

- Harvesters must have permission to harvest from either the private landowner or from the traditional authority, the regional or local government, or the conservancy or community forest in the case of communal area harvesting.

- Harvesters should choose the older plants to harvest. These usually have longer stems and leaves. The young plants should be left alone. A plant that still has flowers should not be harvested. It is best to wait until the plant has seeds.

- It is best if the harvester uses a sharpened stick or flattened crowbar to dig with. The hole should be about 20cm away from the plant and should only be on one side of the plant.

11

- This means that only the tubers on one side of the plant are harvested; the other half of the tubers are left to help the plant to keep growing.

- When the side tubers have been harvested, all the sand should be put back into the hole. The harvester should stamp down on the sand after it has been put back in the hole. If the hole is not filled in, the Devil's Claw plant will die. Leaving an open hole is dangerous for wild animals, cattle and even for people.

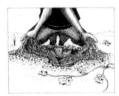

Note:

- Harvesting the taproot is also wrong. By harvesting it, the plant will be killed. Also, the taproot is useless for selling. It is possible to dig out the tubers without damaging or removing the taproot.

- Devil's Claw plants need three years to recover after they have been harvested. This means that in any one year, only one quarter of all the plants in an area should be harvested.

12

How to process Devil's Claw

- Devil's Claw is sold on the international markets and it is therefore important to maintain high quality standards. If the Devil's Claw is not harvested or processed (cut and dried) properly, it will be rejected. This means that the resource is wasted and the harvester does not get any money.

- Dried Devil's Claw should be packed into new bags that are clean and dry. Bags should be stored in a clean, dry place and if possible on a shelf or rack.

- Devil's Claw should only be sold to a trader who has a permit for buying Devil's Claw from the area in which it was harvested. The trader should fill in his/her name, registration number, the date, the number of bags, the weight of the Devil's Claw bought, the trader's permit number and signature on the harvester's 'Report Back' form.

Note:

- Within a month of the end of the harvest season, the harvester's 'Report Back' should be submitted to the MET. Details of each transaction need to be given by the trader in question, and signed by him/her.

13

Figure 6.2 Excerpt from *Devil's Claw Policy Namibia Understanding the Policy* (Source: MET 2010b).

distinguishing between the two species, and should include the amount bought, permit numbers, and names of harvesters and the origin of the resource. They are also required to complete the details of transactions on the harvesters' report-back forms. To export devil's claw, in addition to registration a valid export permit from the Ministry of Environment and Tourism must be obtained that specifies the origin of the material. A company registration certificate from the Ministry of Trade and Industry, and a phytosanitary certificate from the Ministry of Agriculture, Water and Forestry are also required. A permit is also required to cultivate devil's claw or to conduct research on the plant.

In the early 2000s, the sustainability of devil's claw was also raised at an international level at the Convention on International Trade in Endangered Species of Wild Fauna and Flora (CITES) 11th Conference of the Parties held in Kenya. Germany proposed that both species be listed in Appendix II, but this was met with resistance from the exporting countries and NGOs, and the proposal was withdrawn. However, CITES required that exporting and importing countries submit information on trade, management, and the biological status of *Harpagophytum* spp. to the secretariat, as well as provide updates at further meetings on implementation of policies and management programmes for sustainability and equitable trade (Wynberg 2004). Thus, external pressure from both CITES and MCA-N underpinned the finalisation of the policy and the retention of permit procedures for devil's claw harvesting in Namibia.

Conservancies and community forests

In the context of devil's claw harvesting in the Zambezi Region, conserv-ancies and community forests have provided an organisational framework through which communities can access NGO support and facilitate organised harvesting and trade. Conservancies are the product of an amendment to the Nature Conservation Ordinance No. 4 of 1975 in 1996 such that any group of persons living on communal land can register as a conservancy to provide for an economically based system of sustainable management and utilisation of game in communal areas. By law, conservancies are required to have a management committee, constitution, list of members, and defined geographical boundaries. Conservancies have benefited from tremendous high-profile international donor funding, which has enabled intensive NGO support for their registration and development. Today there are 86 registered conservancies covering close to 20% of Namibia, with 15 conservancies in the Zambezi Region (NACSO 2019). Income for conservancies is predominantly derived from trophy hunting and tourism concessions operated by external, white-owned businesses, with additional small income contributions from the sale of crafts and devil's claw harvesting.

In the case of Bwabwata National Park, where residents cannot register as a conservancy, provision has been made for the Kyaramacan Association to represent residents. The Park is divided into three core areas reserved for wildlife, and a multiple-use area where people can settle, farm, and use natural resources subject to the Park's restrictions. All commercial use of land and natural resources within both core and multiple-use areas, including the commercial harvesting of devil's claw, needs to be authorised by the Ministry of Environment, Forestry and Tourism. Park residents are awarded rights to benefit from natural resources through the Kyaramacan Association, which manages the communal income from tourism, hunting, and devil's claw.

In addition to communal conservancies, a community forest programme was initiated in 1999, and new legislation for forest resources was introduced with the Forest Act No. 12 of 2001. This legislation made provision for the creation of community forests by communities on communal land and confers rights to manage and use forest produce and other natural resources of the forest. Requirements for registration differ somewhat from conservancies, and are more complex in that community forests require a management committee, defined geographical boundaries, consent from the traditional authority, and a management plan. However, the legislation is more powerful in that it offers community forests exclusive use of all forest resources, while these rights are not afforded to conservancies. Community forestry in Namibia has largely been funded by the German Development Bank (KfW) and implemented by GIZ and GOPA, a German development-consulting firm. The guidelines and procedures developed by GIZ for community forestry in Namibia were informed by commercial forestry in Europe, and are overly scientific and onerous. In addition, implementation as a series of time-bound projects with GIZ/GOPA staff and resources has left the Directorate of Forestry without the capacity or resources to assist communities in moving forward. As a result, the development of community forestry has been slow, community forests are institutionally weaker, and processes remain locally inappropriate. Forty-two community forests have been registered however, they remain largely unsupported and biotrade of forest resources has been poorly developed (Lavelle 2019).

The assumption informing conservancy and community forest policy is that conservation and development objectives can be achieved by creating strong local institutions and economic benefits from wildlife and plant resources in communal lands. The aim of conservancies and community forests is to link sustainable utilisation of natural resources with rural development by enabling communities in communal areas to derive a direct financial benefit, as well as provide an 'incentive' to conserve natural resources (Jones 1998). However, neither conservancies nor community forests confer ownership of natural resources upon communities, rather proprietorship (Sullivan 2002). Ownership remains vested with and regulated by the state, including that of devil's claw.

Traditional leadership

In Namibia, the *de facto* administration of communal land and governance of communities on communal land remains with traditional authorities. The Zambezi Region is characterised by a pervasive presence of traditional leadership, and four traditional authorities govern the region, namely the Mayeyi, Mashi, Mafwe, and Masubia. The latter two are some of the oldest and most politically powerful traditional leadership systems in Namibia. This is in part attributed to these traditional authorities being designated as the administrators of the land and communities in the region and being left to traditional governance during the colonial and apartheid eras (Mendelsohn 2008). The historical and political role of the traditional authorities renders them very influential and in the Zambezi Region no community decision is made without the involvement and permission of the relevant traditional authority. This includes the implementation of organised harvesting and trade of devil's claw. As per the policy, where no conservancy or community forest is in place, harvesters require the permission of the relevant traditional authority on the permit application.

Of significance to traditional leadership, access to natural resources, and the ability to trade in the free market, is the issue of land tenure. In the communal areas land tenure is determined by the Communal Land Reform Act No. 5 of 2002 and Communal Land Reform Amendment Act No. 13 of 2013. Community members can apply for a customary land right for personal farming and residential use to be allocated by the relevant chief or traditional authority and ratified by the regional Communal Land Board. The allocation and size of area of land to be allocated is at the discretion of the chief or traditional authority, and must be within the maximum size prescribed by the Minister of Agriculture, Water and Land Reform. Following ratification and registration by the land board, legal custodianship of the specified land area is given to that community member. Similarly, under customary law in the Zambezi Region, land is not individually owned, but community members are allocated land-use rights by traditional leaders with the customary allocation of land by the area headman through the village headmen. Community members and community-based organisations may also apply for rights of leasehold for agricultural or commercial purposes; or an occupational land right to occupy a portion of communal land for the provision of public services. However, these are subject to criteria and conditions as set out and approved by the Minister, land board, and traditional authority. No right conferring freehold ownership is capable of being granted or acquired by any person, group, or organisation in communal areas, unlike in the previously 'white-only' settlement areas of the country. Thus, communal land residents are not permitted to own the capital constituted by their land or the resources on it, raising concerns about spatial and property justice.

Government

At the time of the research, two government agencies were relevant to the governance framework for devil's claw harvesting in the Zambezi Region. The Ministry of Environment and Tourism was the agency tasked with the registration and support of conservancies, and management activities linked to devil's claw conservation including permitting and monitoring. While the Ministry of Agriculture, Water and Forestry was mandated with the gazetting and supervision of community forests and promoting the development of institutional linkages and partnerships to improve the exploitation of indigenous plant resources and the socio-economic role of plants harvested by local communities. As of March 2020, the Directorate of Forestry has been transferred to the now Ministry of Environment, Forestry and Tourism, and land reform is now located under the Ministry of Agriculture, Water and Land Reform.

Non-governmental organisations

Integrated Rural Development and Nature Conservation (IRDNC) is a local NGO that provides technical, logistical, and financial support to conservancies and community forests in northern Namibia. Commercial harvesting of devil's claw in the Zambezi Region was introduced and initially facilitated by IRDNC and followed the set procedures it determined, implemented together with the management committees and staff of conservancies and community forests. The NGO has also played an important role in linking the ministries, the communities, and the exporters.

Harvesting and trade processes introduced to conservancies and community forests in the Zambezi Region

From 2010 to 2014, the MCA-N Compact through IRDNC provided intensive financial, technical and logistical support with the aim of creating 'virtuous value chains' (sustainable, traceable, high quality, fairly traded) in the eleven target conservancies and community forests of the Zambezi Region (NRI 2010a). All members interested in harvesting were trained in sustainable harvesting techniques, were registered as harvesters with the conservancy/community forest and received complementary basic equipment to harvest, slice, and dry the devil's claw to be sold as a raw product. The NGO also negotiated with the Ministry of Environment and Tourism to acquire group permits for harvesters in conservancies/community forests rather than individual permits, which cost ~US$3.50 each. It also negotiated for permission to be given by the conservancy or community forest chairperson rather than the traditional authority, given that the harvesting of devil's claw was to be managed by the conservancy/community forest and not the traditional authority. This was also intended to encourage the management committees and staff to assume responsibility for sustainable harvesting and quality control in their areas. To encourage sustainability, a formal natural resource management plan was co-developed by each conservancy/community forest and IRDNC, the committees and staff were trained in resource monitoring both during and after the harvest, and monitoring was undertaken jointly by the conservancies/community forests, the Ministry of Environment and Tourism, and IRDNC. Management committees and staff were also trained in maintaining monitoring and sales records using IRDNC's prescribed monitoring forms and exporters' sales books. To ensure quality, the harvesters were trained by IRDNC how to correctly slice, dry, and store the devil's claw, and the committees and staff were taught how to distinguish between poor and good quality.

As fair trade was an important aspect of the programme, to eliminate loss of income to a middleman and secure better pricing, IRDNC facilitated the choice of a single, reputable buyer that was also an exporter. Exclusive three-year contracts with annual price reviews and set quotas were put in place in each producer organisation. Included in the contracts were two prices: the price per kilogram paid to the harvesters, and the price per kilogram paid to the management committee for ensuring sustainability and good quality, which was effectively a 'management fee'. A basic business management plan was also co-developed by each conservancy/community forest and IRDNC in which the conservancy committees and staff were encouraged to start budgeting for the management fee to cover the costs of maintaining the trade when funding came to an end in 2014.

A system of traceability also needed to be implemented to promote sustainability, fair trade and quality control. At the start of the season, each registered harvester received a harvester card with a unique harvester number. On specified days a 'buying event' took place at the conservancy/community forest office whereby harvesters brought their bags of devil's claw to be checked and weighed. The weight, the harvester number, and the amount owing to the harvester was recorded in a sales register. This process was handled by a management committee or staff member who was also appointed as a 'buying-point manager'. Once weighed and recorded, the devil's claw was stored in a hygienic storage unit provided by IRDNC with MCA-N funding. The devil's claw would then be collected by the exporter, transported to his facility, and checked for quality, following which payments were made to the harvesters through the buying-point manager as per the sales register.

The implementation of all these processes required intensive technical support and training. In addition, IRDNC provided much logistical support such as obtaining the permits, making the harvester cards, sourcing and purchasing equipment, transporting devil's claw, coordinating meetings with the exporter, and providing monitoring forms and training materials. Following the completion of the project in September 2014, the management of devil's claw harvesting became the responsibility of the conservancies/community forests with 'light-touch' support from IRDNC.

Table 6.1 Producer organisations in the Zambezi Region, Namibia.

	Producer organisation	Harvesting and trade post-MCA-N	Approximate no. of active harvesters*
1	Mayuni Conservancy	Yes	23
2	Mashi Conservancy	No	
3	Kwandu Conservancy & Community Forest	Yes	63
4	Sobbe Conservancy	No	
5	Balyerwa Conservancy	Yes	73
6	Wuparo Conservancy	Yes	70
7	Dzoti Conservancy	Yes	23
8	Masida Community Forest	No	
9	Lubuta Community Forest	Yes	30
10	Sachona Community Forest	Yes	11
11	Ngonga Community Forest	No	
12	Kyaramacan Association	Yes	119
	Total still participating	**8**	**412**

* Based on figures from the end of the 2016 harvesting season
(Source: Tjiteere 2017)

Seven conservancies/community forests and the Kyaramacan Association have continued organised harvesting and trade (Table 6.1). Despite the drop-off in participating communities, the total number of active harvesters has remained relatively stable, with 488 active harvesters in 2011 and 412 in 2016[7] (NRI 2012;

[7] No more recent figures are available owing to IRDNC no longer providing direct support for harvesting activities.

Tjiteere 2017). The conservancies/community forests continue to undertake annual training of harvesters; however, they have faced challenges in the timely acquisition of permits, sourcing and purchasing of equipment, and contract negotiations. There has also been a decrease in the frequency of buying events, monitoring activities, and the use of prescribed monitoring forms (Lavelle 2019).

Pro-poor or pro-profit? Models of commercialisation and the governance framework

In analysing the trade of devil's claw, Wynberg (2004) identified two models of commercialisation from Namibia. In the 'corporate model', harvesters supply local traders who in turn supply four or five exporters. This model is highly exploitative, exacerbated by the harvesters' remoteness and social marginalisation. Local traders benefit from owning transport and having established links with one or two exporters with whom they do business. It is common for harvesters to have no record of the volumes of devil's claw they supply or the price received per kilogram. These harvesters are typically not trained in sustainable methods of harvesting and have limited access to more reputable buyers. The devil's claw supplied by harvesters may be purchased and resold several times by traders before finally being sold to one of the dominant exporters. The relationship between trader and exporter can be considered non-exclusive and fickle, as is that between trader and harvester. Other characteristics identified in this model include challenges to the state to control and monitor resource extraction, uncertainty of standards by harvesters, variable quality of product, lack of transparency amongst traders and exporters, and poorly organised community and institutional structures (Wynberg 2004).

Within the Zambezi Region, the corporate model represents the situation for those harvesters who reside in areas under the governance of traditional authorities and are not registered as conservancies or community forests. In these areas the allocation of customary land rights does not provide an alternative mechanism for effective management of or exclusive access to devil's claw. The patchy ecological distribution of devil's claw requires a far larger allocation of land than that afforded by customary land rights to be economically viable. As communities that do not have delineated geographical boundaries through a conservancy or community forest or secure tenurial rights, these harvesters extract the resource from open-access communal land or areas under the jurisdiction of the state. These harvesters work independently or in family groups, but in the current governance framework, their access to devil's claw is restricted in two ways – bound first to the traditional authorities whose permission is required for the permit application, and second to the Ministry of Environment, Forestry and Tourism for permit approval. Oftentimes, traditional leaders make unscrupulous use of their power to exploit harvesters by expropriating 'fees' for giving permission on permit applications while access to transport to reach the regional permit office is limited. The governance framework also limits these harvesters in that registration as a conservancy and/or community forest is the leverage required to access NGO support, as demonstrated by the prerequisite of the MCA-N programme for communities to be registered to be eligible to participate. However, not all areas or communities are necessarily suited to CBNRM, thus locking communities into traditional governance structures. Sullivan (2002) highlights that widely publicised elaborations of success based on '5-star conservancies' in areas of abundant wildlife and low population density present an unrealistic picture of the possibilities for conservancy policy to improve livelihoods in communal areas as a whole. As such, other economic alternatives for unregistered areas need to be explored that move beyond the CBNRM paradigm. The acquisition of rights of leasehold by a registered harvester organisation, such as a cooperative, may present an opportunity for harvesters to secure exclusive access and improve management of the resource. However, this remains dependent on the approval of the traditional authorities, who are often reluctant to relinquish control of territory for fear of losing power and access to resources.

The second model, the 'honest broker model', illustrated the situation for a small group of communities in Omaheke, where NGO support had enabled communities to link directly with a local exporter (Wynberg 2004). In this model, the trader is eliminated, and the exporter buys the raw product directly from the harvesters and pays a set price based on the devil's claw being of good quality. Characteristics of this model are that the harvesters receive better prices, they have knowledge of the price they will receive, they are guaranteed an annual quota, there is improved sustainability and quality, and there is community organisation.

The honest broker model is similar to the situation experienced by those harvesters in the Zambezi Region who reside in conservancies or community forests and have had harvesting and trade processes facilitated by IRDNC. However, for them, the sale of devil's claw is channelled through the conservancy or community forest-management committees. As such, harvesters are dependent on their management committees to acquire the necessary permits and report back to the Ministry of Environment, Forestry and Tourism; to facilitate communication, the signing of sales contracts and the setting of prices with the exporter; to undertake monitoring activities; to maintain correct sales records; and to direct the income earned by the conservancy/community forest from harvesting activities to supporting the harvesters in their activities. The failure of the management committees to do so, as reported by Tjiteere (2017) and Lavelle (2019), impacts the ability of the harvesters to benefit and undermines their autonomy. Thus, the reliance on management committees as 'honest brokers' within communities in this model fails to facilitate the active participation of harvesters in trade, instead relying on representation.

As the frontline users, harvesters possess accurate information regarding the resource and are most influenced by policy processes such as harvesting moratoriums and changes to the permit. While the honest broker model enables higher prices paid to harvesters it does not address structural differences in decision-making authority that significantly impact livelihood outcomes. Irrespective of whether harvesters operate individually or as a collective, they lack a direct link to decision-making forums at the regional and national level. For example, in 2013 the Zambezi regional office of the Ministry of Environment, Forestry and Tourism proposed a moratorium for three years based on two internal reports but without substantive consultation with harvesters or a quantifiable assessment of the resource. To avert the moratorium, which would drive illegal harvesting and negatively impact livelihoods, it was necessary for an NGO to intervene on behalf of the harvesters. In 2017, a moratorium was put on devil's claw harvesting in Bwabwata National Park owing to militarisation of the park in aid of anti-poaching. The ban on all harvesting activities, including wild-food gathering, was instituted without consultation with harvesters to explore ways in which harvesting activities could support anti-poaching patrols and despite the commercial harvesting of devil's claw being the only cash-in-hand livelihood opportunity for most residents. Apart from the lost monetary benefit, the ban had a profound effect on food security and gathering-based livelihood strategies (Paksi & Pyhälä 2018). Thus, there is a need to ground CBNRM commodification models in a core principle of community control over decision-making processes that impact local livelihoods. At a national level the Devil's Claw Export Association is concerned with how to maximise export prices, ensure high quality and maintain sustainable trade. Yet despite the implementation of the honest broker model which links harvesters to exporters, there is no communication platform for the harvesters who are most knowledgeable about the state of the resource and most vulnerable to price fluctuations. While the honest broker model offers the opportunity for exporters to directly engage with harvesters in an open and transparent manner that would enable reflexive management of the resource and sustainable trade, information regarding the market and export values are often withheld from harvesters, which breeds mistrust and misunderstandings.

In assessing whether the governance framework for the harvesting and trade of devil's claw in the Zambezi Region is pro-poor or pro-profit, several factors require interrogation. First, the honest broker model captures the value of trade held by middlemen in the corporate model and redirects it to harvesters, improving the price paid to harvesters. However, the honest broker model does little to address systemic inequalities between exporters and harvesters inherent in the sector and embedded in Namibia's colonial and apartheid past. Chinsembu and Chinsembu (2020: 26) highlight that monetary benefits disproportionately accrue to exporters instead of local harvesters, and current biotrade practices offer poor socio-economic contracts that 'suffocate the wellbeing of the local people, and short-changes them of monetary benefits'. The introduction of harvesting and trade of devil's claw by NGOs as a livelihood option has brought a much needed source of direct income. However, despite the implementation of the honest broker model, harvesters expressed a lack of autonomy in determining the rules of trade, many felt disrespected by the buyers and a narrative of 'no other choice' was prevalent (Lavelle 2019). Harvester norms and preferences for trade including transparent communication, open negotiation, flexibility, and solidarity in times of difficulty were rejected by buyers, sometimes resulting in conflict. The high price – the loss of critical income – for harvesters expressing their norms and preferences prevented them from doing so, thus maintaining racialised hierarchies and livelihood insecurity.

Ndwandwe (this volume) highlights that historical racial exclusions play a role in determining who participates and to what extent they participate in indigenous natural-product activities and addressing marginalisation requires policy frameworks that explicitly recognise the histories and injustices in the biodiversity-based sectors. Ongoing marginalisation in the honeybush sector in South Africa is attributed to the failure of government to deliver on land reforms and the adoption of neoliberal policies that favour large-scale cultivation and standardised production over wild harvesting and traditional methods. As such, black and 'coloured' communities who are unable to secure land remain on the periphery of production while white commercial farmers with access to technology dominate the industry. Similarly in the case of devil's claw, no opportunities are afforded to harvesters for upgrading (the possibility of moving up the value chain and securing better returns through enhanced processing and/or quality control) perpetuating the cheap labour trap and racialised privilege.

While the honest broker model seeks to improve livelihood outcomes, in the Zambezi Region it was found that income did not always differ significantly between organised and unorganised harvesters. Rather, unorganised harvesters sold greater volumes of devil's claw to achieve similar income levels. Thus, while the model may be key to improved sustainability of harvesting it does not always equate to better livelihood outcomes. Further, the value of the trade held by middlemen (0.45% of trade value) which the honest broker model seeks to redirect to harvesters is negligible in relation to that captured external to Namibia (98% of trade value). In the expansion of organised devil's claw harvesting to the Zambezi Region, no formal benefit-sharing arrangements were instituted between companies in Europe and local communities. In theory, Namibia's ABS law provides an opportunity to address injustices in indigenous natural-product trade and open channels for equitable monetary and non-monetary benefits to local communities. However, Chinsembu and Chinsembu (2020) highlight that ABS policy and legislation cannot practically take the place of good corporate responsibility and ethical behaviour in biotrade and bioprospecting.

Advancing this view, Wynberg (this volume) argues that ABS has been designed as a universalised instrument of compliance and that its implementation threatens to increase conflict among communities and entrench or even enlarge existing power imbalances between corporate interests and resource custodians. In the case of devil's claw, the absence of harvester access to decision-making forums at the regional and national level and limited control of decision-making processes at the local level render procedural fairness unlikely in determining benefit-sharing agreements. Further, considering the central and influential role of traditional authorities in the Zambezi Region, ABS runs the risk of facilitating partnerships with traditional authorities, who may not be representative of knowledge holders or resource custodians.

In implementation, the MCA-N project focused on the increased production of 'sustainable' raw material for the natural-medicine market in Europe. While increasing production for a pre-existing market was easier for project implementation, which is driven by donor indicators and is time-bound, the natural-medicine market is not a free market but an oligopoly. While the hegemony of Germany in the natural-medicine market makes any value-addition in Namibia for this industry challenging, alternative and new applications in the food, beverage, and cosmetic industries offer good opportunities for devil's claw value-addition in Namibia. Antioxidant properties in particular have been suggested for further research for these industries and could present a new marketing focus (NRI 2012). Research stimulates product innovation and industry interest, and new applications would enable access and benefit-sharing arrangements to be in place in the development of the value chain. While devil's claw harvesting will always be limited by resource availability, a far greater percentage of the trade value could be captured in-country by primary producers and processors stimulating a pro-poor model of commercialisation.

Lastly, the finalisation of the policy and the maintenance of harvesting permit procedures without first addressing the identified limitations raises questions as to whose interests are being served. While the policy seeks to improve the traceability and thus sustainability of devil's claw, the permit system had already been found to be ineffective with respect to improved management of the resource in the communal areas (NRI 2011b). Given the success of the conservancy and community forest programmes in improving natural resource management and sustainable utilisation, a system of local monitoring and enforcement for devil's claw could be developed and implemented by the harvester communities themselves. However, the proposal by Germany for devil's claw to be listed on CITES Appendix II and the requirement of MCA-N for the policy to be finalised suggests a box-ticking exercise by international agencies for profitable 'sustainable' trade without consideration of local conditions. It also suggests neocolonialism in the provision of Western conditions for the Namibian government to receive development funding.

Conclusion

This chapter has provided an overview of the governance framework for the harvesting and trade of devil's claw in the Zambezi Region, Namibia. It has traced the expansion of harvesting and trade and the finalisation of devil's claw policy as donor-driven processes. Also, the resulting mechanisms employed by NGOs to improve sustainability and equitable trade in the Zambezi Region are elaborated. Further, models of commercialisation developed in previous studies are evaluated in relation to the Zambezi Region. The chapter elaborates on two models, the corporate model and the honest broker model, that are representative of the region. Within the corporate model, barriers exist within the local governance framework that exacerbate an already exploitative value chain. These include traditional governance and land tenure. In the honest broker model, several caveats are highlighted. These include the dependence of harvesters on management committees as intermediaries, limited community control over decision-making processes that impact local livelihoods, and the maintenance of racialised hierarchies between exporters and harvesters.

In assessing these models in the current governance framework for devil's claw harvesting and trade, neither are concluded to be pro-poor. This is due to both models failing to restructure the value chain such that benefits are captured in-country and distributed more equitably. Further, neocolonialism in the form of Western, technocratic permit procedures imposed by international agencies serves the interests of the European oligopoly but fails to improve sustainability or equity. These constraints that negatively impact harvesters and hinder the development of equitable value chains at the local level should be addressed. Recommendations include research and development of new applications in the food, beverage, and cosmetic industries and a critical reassessment of the national policy for devil's claw.

Bibliography

Brendler, T. (2021). 'From bush medicine to modern phytopharmaceutical: A bibliographic review of devil's claw (*Harpagophytum* spp.)', *Pharmaceuticals*, 2021, 14(8), 726.

Chinsembu, W. W. & Chinsembu, K. C. (2020). '"Poisoned chalice": Law on access to biological and genetic resources and associated traditional knowledge in Namibia', *Resources*, 9(7), 83.

Cole, D. (2008). 'The Current Status of Cultivation and Export of Devil's Claw in Namibia', report prepared for Phytotrade Africa (Windhoek: CRIAA SA-DC). Available at: http://the-eis.com/elibrary/sites/default/files/downloads/literature/Phytotrade%20Devils%20Claw%20Report_Final%20Version.pdf [Accessed 20 January 2022].

Cole, D. & Du Plessis, P. (2001). 'Namibian Devil's Claw (*Harpagophytum* spp.): A Case Study on Benefit-Sharing Arrangements', prepared for the Ministry of Environment and Tourism, Namibian National Biodiversity Programme (Windhoek: CRIAA SA-DC) Available at: http://the-eis.com/elibrary/sites/default/files/downloads/literature/CRIAA%20Devils%20Claw%20Case%20Study.pdf [Accessed 20 January 2022].

Cooke, M. C. (1882). *Freaks and Marvels of Plant Life: Or Curiosities of Vegetation* (London: Society for Promoting Christian Knowledge).

Hellwig, M. (1907). *Angaben von Eingeborenen über die Feldkost und die Arzneipflanzen der Herrero und Hottentotten* (Berlin: Reichskolonialamt). (Bundesarchiv R 1001/5989, fol. 78–81).

Ihlenfeldt, H. & Hartmann, H. (1970). 'Die Gattung *Harpagophytum* (Burch.) devil's claw ex Meissn', *Mitt. Staatinst. Allg. Bot. Hamburg*, 13, 15–69.

Jones, B. T. B. (1998). 'Namibia's Approach to Community-Based Natural Resources Management (CBNRM): Towards Sustainable Development in Communal Areas'. Paper for the Scandinavian Seminar College Project: Policies and Practices Supporting Sustainable Development in Sub-Saharan Africa (Windhoek).

Lavelle, J. (2019). *Digging Deeper for Benefits: Rural Local Governance and the Livelihood and Sustainability Outcomes of Devil's Claw* (Harpagophytum *spp.) Harvesting in the Zambezi Region, Namibia*. PhD Thesis, University of Cape Town.

Lübbert, A. (1901). 'Aus dem deutsch-südwestafrikanischen Schutzgebiete. Ueber die Heilmethoden und Heilmittel der Eingeborenen in Deutsch-Südwestafrika', *Mitth. Forsch. Gelehrt. Dtsch. Schutzgeb*, 14, 77–90.

MCA-N (2014). *Indigenous Plant Products of Namibia* (Windhoek: Venture Publications).

Mendelsohn, J. (2008). 'Communal Land in Namibia: A Free For All. Customary and Legislative Aspects of Land Registration and Management on Communal Land in Namibia', report prepared for the Ministry of Land & Resettlement and Rural Poverty Reduction Programme of the European Union. Available at: https://landportal.org/sites/default/files/mendelsohn_j_land_registration_and_management_on_communal_land_in_namibia.pdf [Accessed 20 January 2022].

Ministry of Environment and Tourism (MET) (2010a). National Policy on the

Utlilization of Devil's Claw (*Harpagophytum*) products (Windhoek: Ministry of Environment and Tourism, Republic of Namibia). Available at: www.met.gov.na/files/files/FINAL%20Devil%27s%20Claw%20Policy.pdf [Accessed 20 January 2022].

Ministry of Environment and Tourism (MET) (2010b). *Devil's Claw Policy Namibia Understanding the Policy* (Windhoek: Ministry of Environment and Tourism, Republic of Namibia). Available at: www.met.gov.na/files/files/Devil%20Claw%20Policy%20Namibia.docx [Accessed 20 January 2022].

Mosimane, A., Lendelvo, S., Glatz-Jorde, S., Kirchmeir, H., & Huber, M. (2014). 'Livelihood Baseline Survey Report for the Kavango Zambezi Transfrontier Conservation Area (KAZA TFCA)', unpublished report prepared for the Kavango-Zambezi Transfrontier Conservation Area.

Namibian Association of CBNRM Support Organisations (NACSO) (2019). 'Registered Communal Conservancies'. Available at: www.nacso.org.na/conservancies [Accessed 25 June 2018].

Nott, K. (1986). 'A Survey of the Harvesting and Export of *Harpagophytum procumbens* and *Harpagophytum zeyheri* in SWA/Namibia' (Okaukuejo: Etosha Ecological Institute).

National Planning Commission (NPC) (2016). Namibia Poverty Mapping (Windhoek, Macroeconomic Planning Department, National Planning Commission, Republic of Namibia).

Natural Resources Institute (NRI) (2010a). 'MCA-N Producer and Processor Organisations Sub-Activity Inception' (London: Natural Resources Institute, University of Greenwich).

Natural Resources Institute (NRI) (2010b). 'MCA-N Producer and Processor Organisations Sub-Activity PPO Diagnostic Report Part 1' (London: Natural Resources Institute, University of Greenwich).

Natural Resources Institute (NRI) (2010c). 'MCA-N Producer and Processor Organisations Sub-Activity PPO Diagnostic Report Part 2' (London: Natural Resources Institute, University of Greenwich).

Natural Resources Institute (NRI) (2011a). 'MCA-N Indigenous Natural Products Producer and Processor Organisations Sub-Activity EIA for Devil's Claw Report No. 5a' (London: Natural Resources Institute, University of Greenwich).

Natural Resources Institute (NRI) (2011b). 'MCA-N Indigenous Natural Products Producer and Processor Organisations Sub-Activity EMP for Devil's Claw Report No. 5b' (London: Natural Resources Institute, University of Greenwich).

Natural Resources Institute (NRI) (2012). 'Quarterly Progress Report 5, MCA-N Indigenous Natural Products Producer and Processor Organisations Sub-Activity Report No. 14' (London: Natural Resources Institute, University of Greenwich).

Namibia Statistics Agency (NSA) (2018). 'Namibia Household Income and Expenditure Survey (NHIES) 2015/2016' (Windhoek: Namibia Statistics Agency). Available at: https://d3rp5jatom3eyn.cloudfront.net/cms/assets/documents/NHIES_2015–16.pdf [Accessed 31 January 2022].

Paksi, A. & Pyhälä, A. (2018). 'Socio-economic Impacts of a National Park on Local Indigenous Livelihoods: The Case of the Bwabwata National Park in Namibia', *Senri Ethnological Studies*' 99, 197–214.

Stewart, K. M. (2009). 'Effects of secondary tuber harvest on populations of devil's claw (*Harpagophytum procumbens*) in the Kalahari savannas of South Africa', *African Journal of Ecology*, 48(1), 146–154.

Strohbach, M. (1999). 'The Sustainably Harvest Devil's Claw Project: Ecological survey'. Unpublished report prepared for CRIAA SA-DC (Windhoek: CRIAA SA-DC).

Strohbach, M. & Cole, D. (2007). 'Population Dynamics and Sustainable Harvesting of the Medicinal Plant *Harpagophytum procumbens* in Namibia' (Bonn: Bundesamt für Naturschutz). Available at: www.bfn.de/sites/default/files/BfN/service/Dokumente/skripten/skript203.pdf [Accessed 18 January 2022].

Sullivan, S. (2002). 'How sustainable is the communalising discourse of "new" conservation?' in: D. Chatty & M. Colchester (eds), *Conservation and Mobile Indigenous People: Displacement, Forced Settlement and Sustainable Development* (Oxford: Berghahn Press), 158–187.

Tjiteere, E. (2017). 'Supporting Sustainable Resource Utilization in Zambezi Region, Namibia – The Zambezi Region Devil's Claw Quarterly Progress Report October–December 2016' (Windhoek: IRDNC).

Van Wyk, B. E., van Oudtshoorn, B., & Gericke, N. (2002). *Medicinal Plants of South Africa*, 2nd edn (Pretoria: Briza Publications).

Von Willert, D. J. & Sanders, J. (2004). 'Devil's claw: Conservation through cultivation – Results of worldwide ecological studies', in: S. W. Breckle, B. Schweizer & A. Fangmeier (eds), Proceedings of the Second Symposium of the A.S.W. Schimper Foundation, 27–44.

Wood, J. G. (1870). *The Uncivilized Races, or Natural History of Man* (Hartford, CT: American Publishing Company).

Wynberg, R. (2004). 'Achieving a fair and sustainable trade in devil's claw (*Harpagophytum* spp.)', in: T. Sunderland & O. Ndoye (eds), *Forest Products, Livelihoods and Conservation: Case Studies of Non-Timber Forest Product Systems*, 2 (Bogor: CIFOR), 53–72.

Wynberg, R. (2006). *Identifying Pro-Poor, Best Practice Models of Commercialisation of Southern African Non-Timber Forest Products*, PhD Thesis, University of Strathclyde.

Wynberg, R., Silveston, J., & Lombard, C. (2009). 'Value adding in the southern African natural products sector: How much do patents matter?' In: Esteban Burrone & Pushpendra Rai (eds), *The Economics of Intellectual Property in South Africa* (Geneva: World Intellectual Property Organization), 18–55.

7

Marginalisation and Exclusion in Honeybush Commercialisation in South Africa

STHEMBILE NDWANDWE

Introduction

Honeybush, *Cyclopia* spp., is a plant that is indigenous[1] to South Africa with a long history of use as a herbal tea by locals in the Eastern and Western Cape provinces (Joubert *et al.* 2011; Van Wyk 2011; Van Wyk & Gorelik 2017). The genus *Cyclopia* has twenty-three species that are endemic to the fynbos biome with a distribution in the coastal plains and mountainous regions of the Eastern and Western Cape (Schutte 1997). Honeybush tea is one of the bush teas that have been used on the African continent by preference or as a substitute for ordinary tea (Cheney & Scholtz 1963). The extent of its early use by the locals is signalled in a variety of names that are recorded in literature and herbariums; these names included but were not limited to *honigtee, heuning tee, vlei tee, suiker tee, bossies' tee, swartberg tee*, and hottentots' tee (Kies 1951; Joubert *et al.* 2011).

Honeybush has a long history of use for medicinal purposes. For example, honeybush (*C. genistoides*) was featured by Pappe (1857) in a collection of South African plants used as remedies, and Jackson (1873) recorded the use of the leaflets of *C. genistoides* and other *Cyclopia* spp. for making bush tea and medicine. Some recorded medicinal uses of honeybush include use as a restorative and for promoting expectoration in chronic catarrh (Bowie 1830; Pappe 1857; Jackson 1873). In 1907, when the government attempted to produce Cape bush teas on a commercial scale, there were medical testimonials stating that it reduced nerve twitchings, paralysis, eczema, indigestion, gout, rheumatism, and dropsy due to heart and kidney diseases, and had soothing

---

[1] Meaning a species that occurs, or has historically occurred, naturally in a free state in nature within the borders of the Republic but excludes a species that has been introduced in the Republic as a result of human activity (Biodiversity Act 2004).

Figure 7.1 Botanical illustration of honeybush, *Cyclopia maculata* (Andrews) Kies, recorded in 1804 (Source: Andrews H. C, Vol. 6, 1804).

effects (Bolam 1907b). The medicinal properties of honeybush continue to be explored. A patent protection (Patent ref. 2008/052863) was granted to the Agricultural Research Council (ARC) and Medical Research Council on the use of honeybush for the treatment of diabetes (Larsen *et al.* 2016).

Although honeybush tea was a popular local beverage amongst the rural populations – 'coloured' people, poor whites, and 'natives' (MacOwen 1894; Bolam 1907a; Hofmeyr & Phillips 1922) – honeybush as a sector has remained a minor industry (Stander *et al.* 2019; Van Wyk & Gorelik 2017). Nonetheless, honeybush is available to the world and holds both economic and heritage significance for the indigenous communities and the coloured community that have used the plant for centuries. Countries such as Japan, Netherlands, India, Germany, United States of America, the United Kingdom, Poland, China, and Sri Lanka are amongst the countries which import honeybush tea, mainly in bulk (Joubert *et al.* 2011). About 90% of honeybush is exported; in 2017 the bulk factory price was between US$3.47/kg (R60) and $4.05/kg (R70), while its value in the overseas retail market was R1,000 ($57.91)/ kg (McGregor 2017a). The export market was 535.464 tonnes in 2010, about 306.175 tonnes in 2015, and about 83.693 tonnes in 2020 (SAHTA 2021).

In the 2010s there was an increase in the local, provincial, and national government interest in honeybush commercialisation with the hope that it would contribute to local economic development and job creation (Polak & Snowball 2017). As a result, a series of stakeholder engagements and investments in community projects in both the Eastern and Western Cape provinces were initiated (Hobson & Joubert 2011; Bester 2013; Polak & Snowball 2017; Horn & Ackhurst 2019). Honeybush was listed as one of the wild plants earmarked for cultivation as part of the national government's initiative to develop a biodiversity economy sector, encompassing businesses and economic activities that either directly depend on biodiverse products for their core business or that contribute to conservation of biodiversity through their activities (National Department of Environmental Affairs, hereafter DEA 2015b, 2016). The government has accelerated these activities, generating increased interest in the commercial use of wild plants. This has resulted in the production of strategy documents and frameworks for a coordinated commercialisation in biotrade and wildlife economies (DEA 2016). There has been much interest in domesticating the wild honeybush and increasing production on a commercial scale through the recent Operation Phakisa. Phakisa is a Sesotho[2] term which means 'Hurry up', signalling the state's aim to fast-track delivery of the National Development Plan (Muthambi 2014; The Presidency 2014; Radebe 2017; Engel 2018; Findlay 2018; Pieter 2018; Vreÿ 2020). Another key activity was the study commissioned by the National Department of Forestry, Fisheries, and the Environment (DFFE), 'Traditional Knowledge Associated with Rooibos and Honeybush Species in South Africa', where the Khoi and San communities were identified as rightful holders of the TK associated with the use of honeybush species (DEA 2014).

One of the shifts envisioned in the honeybush sector is an intention to include marginalised groups in the commercialisation activities (Joubert *et al.* 2011; Horn & Ackhurst 2019; Stander *et al.* 2019). The state intervention through Operation Phakisa has further necessitated a need to involve the marginalised groups. However, in spite of this Operation Phakisa intervention and the post-apartheid Biodiversity Act of 2004, consideration of the concerns about decades of unfair commercial use of natural and cultural heritage in South Africa, and a need to include all citizens in biodiversity policy frameworks (Biodiversity Act 2004), the exclusion of citizens historically marginalised in the commercial use of biodiversity continues to be a

---

2   Sesotho is one of the official languages of South Africa.

challenge. This challenge has been reported in bush tea-producing regions of the Western Cape and Eastern Cape Provinces (Brown 2001; Brown 2003; Penn 2005; Ives 2014; Cockburn *et al.* 2019a, Cockburn *et al.* 2019b; see also Wynberg this volume).

Marginalisation in the biodiversity-based sectors is exacerbated and maintained by the government's failure to deliver on promised social reforms and the adoption of neoliberal policies, particularly in conservation (Büscher & Dressler 2012). The reforms broadly included meeting basic needs, developing human resources, building the economy, and democratising the state and society (African National Congress 1994). For the environmental sector, a key reform was to address the apartheid environmental legislation which had been characterised by 'distorted access to natural resources, denying the majority of South Africans the use of land, water, fisheries, minerals, wildlife and clean air' (African National Congress 1994: 38).

This chapter reflects on the commercialisation of honeybush and the resulting impact on harvester communities living in landscapes where the state has failed to deliver on social reforms. The first section gives an overview of the history of the honeybush industry. The section following uses one of the honeybush-growing regions, the Langkloof region, to demonstrate the extent of marginality in the South African context, and it highlights marginality as a space of resistance where ideas for a socially just honeybush sector reside. The last section uses the notion of 'performativity' to explain the forecasting and realisation of a biodiversity economy by the state.

The chapter uses archival text and insights from engagements with actors involved in the honeybush trade, and a critical reading of the text from the DFFE, including seven national public meeting events, with strategy documents and regulations related to the biodiversity economy sector.[3] The Langkloof case study is based on insights gained from ethnographic fieldwork including observations, key-informant interviews, and semi-structured interviews with honeybush harvesters between 2019 and 2021.

Brief history of honeybush industry encouragement in South Africa

In the 19th century, calls were made to produce honeybush tea and other Cape teas on a commercial scale (MacOwen 1894; Tennant 1894). Theo Caspareuthus was a colonial merchant who pioneered the honeybush industry in the first decade of the 20th century. He achieved this with the support of a government

---

[3] Key texts used can be sourced from DFFE bio-economy page www.dffe. gov.za/projectsprogrammes/biodiversityeconomy#introduction, The Presidency www.gov.za/node/782067, and The Parliament 2021 report https://static.pmg.org. za/211207_Operation_Phakisa_Initiatives_under_DFFE.

eager to foster minor industries from valuable wild plants (The Under-Secretary for Agriculture 1894; Caspareuthus 1907). In 1907 Caspareuthus indicated that he had disposed of the sole right of sale in Australasia, France, Britain, America, and Germany (Bolam 1907a; Caspareuthus 1907) and registered a company called Caspa Tea & Produce Co. Ltd (The Union of South Africa 1921). The company traded and specialised 'in all kinds of Cape bush teas', so not only selling honeybush tea. They were also 'contractors to S.A. Union government hospitals & other institutions' (Caspa Tea & Produce Co. Ltd 1930). The company was small with a declared capital of £2,000 (US$8,544)[4] in 1919, the first-year company books were published (Caspa Tea & Produce Co. Ltd 1930). Caspa Cyclopia Tea became the first honeybush branded product. This, however, is believed to have only been put on the South African market in the 1960s by the pioneer of the rooibos tea industry, Mr B. Ginsberg (Du Toit *et al.* 1998; Joubert *et al.* 2011). Figure 7.2 shows a copy of a public notice for a patent application in a government gazette in 1906.

Honeybush domestication

From 1992 the South African National Biodiversity Institute (SANBI) together with ARC began what they termed a 'rediscovery' of a honeybush product and development of an industry. Many of the efforts by SANBI and ARC went into cultivation trials, innovation, tea-processing technologies, and product and market development (Du Toit *et al.* 1998; Joubert *et al.* 2011; Stander *et al.* 2019). The cultivated resource accounts for about 30% of the honeybush sector (McGregor 2017c). In 2011 about 200 hectares were under cultivation (Joubert *et al.* 2011) by small-scale producers. When Hofmeyr & Phillips (1922) conducted a second revision of the genus *Cyclopia* Vent, they observed a growing popularity of the honeybush tea amongst the locals and the success in local commercial use. In their revision, they supported cultivation as a strategy to meet the growing demand for honeybush tea and for putting a superior article on the local market (Hofmeyr & Phillips 1922). Domestication initiatives by SANBI were motivated by a growing herbal market, observed in the 1980s as putting a spotlight on teas such as rooibos and honeybush, as they were no longer seen as 'crankish', and Ceylon tea's hold on the market was no longer absolute (Ludman 1983). This growing interest in herbal teas led into increased efforts by SANBI to domesticate *Cyclopia* spp., beginning with plantation trials in sixty-four locations between 1992 and 1997; the history of the rediscovery is documented in detail in (Joubert *et al.* 2011), and (Du Toit *et al.* 1998). With a long history of participating in the international botanical

---

4 Exchange rate August 1919 was £1:$4.2720

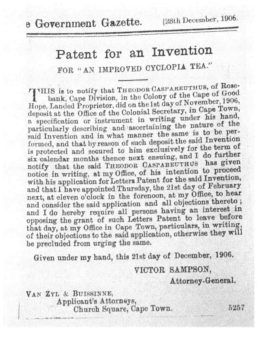

Figure 7.2 *Government Gazette* notification on a patent application for 'An Improved Cyclopia Tea' (Source: Sampson 1906).)

community, SANBI[5] now monitors biodiversity and conservation, and acts as an advisory to organs of state and other stakeholders (Biodiversity Act 2004).

Honeybush trade still depends on a wild resource with about 80% of it still sourced from the wild (McGregor 2017a, 2017b; Slabbert *et al.* 2019). In the 2010s DFFE embarked on a plan to mass cultivate twenty-five key species,[6] including honeybush. The mass cultivation plan was to intensify production of plants with commercial potential, increasing the area under cultivation by 500 hectares per year (National Department of Planning, Monitoring and Evaluation 2016; DEA 2017; Takouleu 2019). Cultivation was seen as a conservation imperative, and species like honeybush were viewed as ideal for cultivation since activities were already underway through the efforts of ARC and SANBI. The initial list of twenty-five targeted species is outlined in

---

[5] Formerly the National Botanical Institute.

[6] The list is not fixed and can be amended at the provincial and national level with alternative plants expected to have more commercial value. To date, subsequent lists have been drawn with priorities for implementation with eleven priority species listed for cultivation, and seven for sector development support; honeybush occurs in both lists.

Table 7.1. These species are at different stages of commercialisation, ranging from those with well-established industries such as rooibos, to those with emerging industries such as honeybush, and those associated with informal markets such as the sour plum fruit.

Table 7.1 Plant species proposed for mass cultivation between 2016 and 2030.

Species name	Common name[a]	Species distribution (African continent)[b]	Species distribution (South Africa)[c]	Endemism in South Africa
Hoodia gordonii	Wildeghaap / Bitterghaap	SA, BW, AO, NM	FS, NC, WC	Not endemic
Agathosma betulina	Buchu/ *Bergboegoe*	SA	WC	Endemic
Agathosma crenulata	Buchu/ *Langblaarboegoe*	SA	WC	Endemic
Aspalathus linearis	Rooibos tea/ *Rooibostee*	SA	NC, WC	Endemic
Bulbine frutescens	Snake flower/ *Geelkatstert*	SA	EC, FS, GP, KZN, NC, WC	Not endemic
Cyclopia intermedia	Honeybush/*Bergtee*	SA	WC, EC	Endemic
Cyclopia genistoides	Honeybush/ *Gewone heuningbostee*	SA	WC	Endemic
Eriosema kraussianum	Bangalala	SA & SZ	EC, KZN	Not endemic
Harpagophytum procumbens	Devil's claw	AO, BW, MZ, NM, SA, ZM & ZI	FS, NW, NC	Not endemic
Helichrysum odoratissimum	*Koegoed*/*Impepho*	SA, MZ, ZI, MW & further north	EC, FS, KZN, LP, MP, WC	Not endemic
Hypoxis hemerocallidea	Yellow star/ *Gifbol*	SA, BW, LS & SZ	EC, FS, GP, KZN, LP, MP, NW	Not endemic
Kigelia africana	Sausage tree/ *Mutshata*	SA through to TZ	GP, KZN, LP, MP	Not endemic
Lobostemon fruticosus	Pyjama bush/ *Luibossie*	SA	WC	Endemic
Pelargonium reniforme	*Rooirabas* / *Umsongelo*	SA	EC, WC	Endemic

Table 7.1 (*continued*)

Species name	Common name[a]	Species distribution (African continent)[b]	Species distribution (South Africa)[c]	Endemism in South Africa
Pelargonium sidoides	*Kalwerbossie/Ikubalo*	SA & LS	EC, FS, KZN, MP, NW	Not endemic
Sceletium tortuosum	Kanna/ *Hotnotskougoed*	SA	EC, NC, WC	Endemic
Siphonochilus aethiopicus	Wild ginger/ *Indungulu*	Widespread in Africa	EC, KZN, LP, MP	Not endemic
Lessertia frutescens	Sutherlandia/ *Kankerbos*	SA, NM, BW	EC, FS, KZN, MP, NC, WC	Not endemic
Trichilia emetica	Mafurra tree/ *Umathunzi*	Southern Africa, some in rest of Africa	KZN	Not endemic
Tylosema esculentum	Marama bean/ *Braaiboontjie*	SA	GP, LP, NW	Not endemic
Warburgia salutaris	Pepperbark tree/ *Shibaha*	SA	GP, KZN, LP, MP	Not endemic
Ximenia americana	Small blue sour plum /*Umthunduluka-omncane*	SA to TZ	GP, KZN, LP, MP, NW	Not endemic
Ximenia caffra	Large sour plum/ *Umthunduluka-obomvu*	SA to TZ	GP, KZN, LP, MP, NW	Not endemic
Xysmalobium undulatum	*Melkbos/Uzara*	Southern Africa	EC, FS, GP, KZN, LP, MP, NC, WC	Not endemic
Lippia javanica	Lemon bush/ *Umsuzwane*	Southern Africa and rest of Africa	EC, FS, GP, KZN, LP, MP, NW	Not endemic

(Sources: Two databases of the South African National Biodiversity Institute: Threatened Species Programme, SANBI 2010–12); PlantsZAfrica, SANBI n.d.).

a. There are other common names; the table only covers two common names per species, and these are limited to the common names used in South Africa.

b. Abbreviations: SA = South Africa, BW = Botswana, AO = Angola, SZ = Eswatini, MZ = Mozambique, NM = Namibia, ZM = Zambia, ZI = Zimbabwe, MW = Malawi, TZ = Tanzania

c. Abbreviations: FS = Free State, NC = Northern Cape, WC = Western Cape, EC = Eastern Cape, GP = Gauteng, KZN = KwaZulu-Natal, NW = North West, LP = Limpopo, MP = Mpumalanga

The Langkloof case study

The Langkloof is a peri-urban region located in the Eastern and Western Cape provinces of South Africa. It is one of the regions with a history of localised use of honeybush (Kies 1951), with a high concentration of honeybush commercialisation and wild harvesting of two of the most commercialised species, *C. intermedia* and *C. subternata* (McGregor 2017a, 2017b; Horn & Ackhurst 2019). Joubert *et al.* (2011) indicate that the Langkloof and the neighbouring Kouga and Garden Route areas were among the first locations that received attention for cultivation trials, honeybush exhibitions, and the application of technological means of processing as an alternative to traditional means. Small-scale honeybush cultivation and harvesting is a significant form of land use in the region, along with commercial fruit farming, livestock farming, crop farming, lifestyle farming such as ecotourism, and wildlife ranching (Cockburn *et al.* 2019). However, marginalised groups in the Langkloof still lag behind in terms of participation in the land-use activities due to historic land dispossessions, unequal distribution of resources, and continued legacy of colonial and apartheid policies (Mulkerrins 2015; de Laat 2017; Cockburn *et al.* 2019).

The majority of those marginalised in the Langkloof reside in townships[7] and/or village areas. These include Haarlem,[8] Avontuur, Misgund, Louterwater, Krakeelrivier, Ravinia, and Kareedouw. Haarlem is located in the Western Cape Province and falls under George Local Municipality (GLM). Haarlem population groups[9] are comprised of 94.1% coloured[10], 4.2% black African, 0.9% white, and 0.8% 'other' groupings (Statistics South Africa 2011). The other townships are in the Eastern Cape Province part of the Langkloof and all fall under the Kou-Kamma Local Municipality (KLM). The population groups in KLM are comprised of 61.4% coloured, 31% black African, 7.5% white, and 0.1% Indian/Asian (Kou-Kamma Local Municipality 2020). The coloured and black African communities are reported to be amongst the poorest in the area

---

[7] Townships originated from the colonial and apartheid South Africa's unique economic requirement for inexpensive migratory labour; today they are urban areas still populated by black, coloured, Indian, and Asian groups.

[8] Haarlem, Avontuur, and Krakeelriver are referred to by their residents as both villages and townships.

[9] For the time being the South African government still use colonial and apartheid racial categories for official population classification or demographical purposes.

[10] A racial category in South Africa referring to 'people from a heterogeneous combination of heritages, including the Khoisan; people of biracial heritage; and people brought as slaves or laborers from other African countries and from regions like Southeast Asia' (Ives 2014: 701).

with low levels of education and income (George Local Municipality 2019; Kou-Kamma Local Municipality 2020). Landlessness, a minimum-wage trap, and racial subordination are persistent issues that have led to inequalities.

Unresolved inequalities

Unresolved inequalities are a critical issue in the Langkloof. Map 7.1 shows the Langkloof region with a focus on land allocation. The main landowners in the Kou-Kamma areas of Eastern Cape Province are private landowners (85.05%), the state (13.20%), and the local municipality (1.59%), with some of the land owned by the Moravian church (Kou-Kamma Local Municipality 2020). Much of the land is used for commercial farming.

Most of the coloured and black people in the Langkloof are farmworkers. This places them amongst the most marginalised groups in post-apartheid South Africa (Schweitzer 2008). The insecurity of tenure and livelihoods among workers on commercial farms is still a challenge (Hall *et al.* 2012; Mulkerrins 2015). Job-creation programmes such as the Expanded Public Works Programme (EPWP) have provided supplementary income to farm work.[11] Some employment opportunities are created in stewardship programmes, and the clearing of invasive species. While these play a role in creating jobs, they serve those who own land and rights to nature that needs stewarding (Cockburn *et al.* 2019), while those who are historically dispossessed work on land they do not own. The minimum wage for these jobs in 2021 was R18/hour (US$1.45)[12] for farm work, and R11/hour ($0.80) for EPWP (Department of Employment and Labour 2021).

Some agricultural reforms have been implemented in the region through programmes such as communal property associations (CPAs) and the Broad-Based Black Economic Empowerment (BBBEE) – 'mean[ing] the viable economic empowerment of all black people[13] [including], in particular women, workers, youth, people with disabilities and people living in rural areas,

---

[11] The EPWP is a government-generated short-to-medium-term work opportunity initiative that is 'designed around service delivery projects that are needed, such as rural infrastructure, clearing of invasive vegetation or community-based social services' (Altman & Hemson 2007).

[12] Exchange rate as of November 2021

[13] According to the BBBEE Act, '"black people" is a generic term which means Africans, Coloureds and Indians: (a) who are citizens of the Republic of South Africa by birth or descent; or who became citizens of the Republic of South Africa by naturalisation – (i) before 27 April 1994; or (ii) on or after 27 April 1994 and who would have been entitled to acquire citizenship by naturalisation prior to that date'.

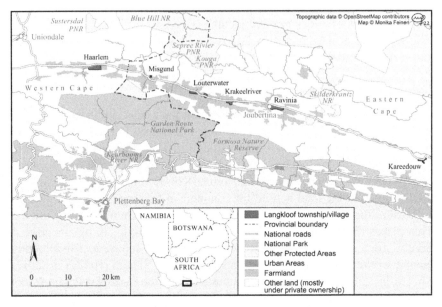

Map 7.1. The study site – Langkloof region (Source: Author; Cartography: M. Feinen).

through diverse but integrated socio-economic strategies' (Broad-Based Black Economic Empowerment Amendment Act 2013). The land-reform programmes in the Langkloof are typically characterised by arrangements that allow the continued supremacy of white landowners in the region as they often become managers, mentors and/or strategic partners with regard to transferred pieces of land (de Laat 2017). These reform arrangements have maintained the relationships of domination and paternalism in which farmworkers in different regions of South Africa are entangled (Connor 2013).

The land-based and racial subordination has had a direct link to coloured and black people's marginalisation and exclusion from honeybush commercialisation. Those who are marginalised exist at the margins of our political, social, economic, and cultural systems, often resulting in exclusions, inequality, and social injustice (Sue 2010). Marginal existence is also a vantage point in that it can be a site of radical perspectives, and a space of resistance (hooks 1984, 1989) 'from which to see and create, to imagine alternatives, new worlds' (hooks 1989: 20). Failure to recognise a vantage point and the agency of those marginalised in formulating plans for a rediscovered industry and for attaining an inclusive honeybush-sector-bred ground for a much critiqued developmentalist agenda (Tapscott 1995; McGregor *et al.* 2013; Harald & Lie 2015).

Figure 7.3 A typical residential space allocated to the communities in the Langkloof region. The area has had a BBBEE farm owned by farmworkers since 2004 (with 240 shareholders in about +/- 300 hectares) and commercial farms typically owned by white landowners since the 1700s/1800s (Source: National Geospatial Information, South Africa).

Developmentalist approach: Recollections of the Haarlem village in the Langkloof

Haarlem is one of the old villages in the Langkloof with generational lived experiences related to honeybush use. Du Toit *et al.* wrote in their ARC recollections of industry rediscovery that 'many of the older people in the communities have been actively involved with the processing of the tea in their youth and have experience in manufacturing of honeybush tea' (1988: 82), and ARC received several requests from Haarlem in the early 1990s to be involved in the cultivation. According to the Haarlem Farmers Association, before 1994[14] Haarlem had worked with a university institution in a rural development project which resulted in a Participatory Rural Appraisal where honeybush was identified by the community as one of the commercial crop initiatives.

In 2001, through assistance from Agribusiness in Sustainable Natural African Plant Products (ASNAPP), an NGO, and the ARC, the community domesticated honeybush on 10 hectares of communal land. The plantation, which increased to about 22 hectares, has not been in operation for about seven years because of insecurity of tenure, conflicts within the project, vandalism, and community dependence on outside intervention compared to white neighbouring farmers who were readily resourced to participate in the export-oriented market.

Because Haarlem community had been producing honeybush tea from a wild resource for generations, it was essential to establish the reasons for wanting to turn it into a cultivated crop. Lack of resource rights due to landlessness were indicated and a spokesperson for the Association explained:

> I think we established that honeybush tea was one of the projects that will be some kind of income-generating project, so all of value-added product, because most of our small farmers cut tea in the mountains at the white farmers' places and we determined that we grow our seedlings and plant it in the mountains, then we want to add some value so that we have our own factory that we could make our own teabags; unfortunately the white farmers jumped us with the whole process. (Farmers Association key informant 2021)

Wild honeybush was a means of survival that helped community members in that whenever they experienced difficulties in financial circumstances they could go into the mountains and make the tea from the wild honeybush. However, as shown in Map 7.1 land in the Langkloof is mostly under private ownership.

---

[14] Where respondents could not remember the exact year, landmark years were used to assess time periods.

Figure 7.4 The location and signage of the Haarlem honeybush plantation. (Photo: Author, 2021).

The land under conservation has been closed to honeybush harvesting since the passing of the 1974 Nature and Environmental Conservation Ordinance (Nature and Environmental Conservation Ordinance 1974). Prior to the 1974 Ordinance, access was restricted by a permit system that was in place for harvesting on crown lands.[15] Regardless of these repressive restrictions, Haarlem produced, consumed, and sold tea. However, not much consideration was given on how the efforts to include communities in the rediscovered export-oriented industry might affect groups that had been systematically marginalised through colonial and apartheid laws. Consequently, the change that has occurred in the honeybush sector post-1994 has privileged the participation of landowners and capitalistic use of the honeybush plant. A community member indicated:

> Over the years we did harvest honeybush tea but with the permission of the white commercial farmer who at that time did not have an interest in the harvesting of honeybush, but since the market was developed overseas … it's a money thing, it's a business, so that totally changed the field and the players you see. (Community member 2021)

A change in community involvement is depicted below in Figure 7.5, showing a narrowing involvement as harvesting and value-chain patterns change to the disadvantage of the community.

---

[15] Land owned by the colonial government.

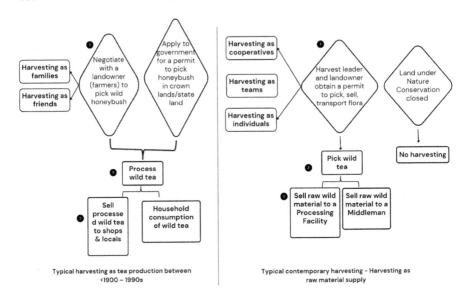

Figure 7.5 Changes in honeybush harvesting and production regimes (Source: Author).

The aftermath of arrangements that were made through NGOs' and other institutions' interventions were fraught, primarily because they turned community members into labourers in the industry, while before these interventions they were producers of the tea. Preliminary observations on the impact and introduction of the biodiversity economy in the 2010s by the national government to accelerate the involvement of communities such as Haarlem in the commercial use of biodiversity are elucidated below.

The alignment of biodiversity economy with the National Development Plan's ambitious Operation Phakisa

Operation Phakisa (OP) was launched as a tool for implementing the National Development Plan[16] (NDP) in the country's 'Ocean Economy' in 2014 (Muthambi 2014; Radebe 2017; Engel 2018; Findlay 2018) and has

---

[16] The National Development Plan (NDP) is a long-term development plan for the country to eliminate poverty and reduce inequality by 2030 through uniting South African citizens and unleashing their energies, growing an inclusive economy, building capabilities, enhancing the capability of the state, and encouraging leaders to work together to solve complex problems (see National Planning Commission 2012)

become a framework used as a core state management tool (Engel 2018; Vreÿ 2020). The so-called biodiversity economy is one of the areas of the national economy being fast-tracked using the OP framework. The biodiversity economy is a sector that encompasses the already existing bioprospecting and wildlife economies regulated and outlined in the Biodiversity Act of 2004. The notion of a 'biodiversity economy' has gained popularity, but there has been ambiguity in how the sector and the draft National Biodiversity Economy Strategy (NBES), in which both the sector and concept are laid out, came about. The draft strategy was tabled and adopted by Parliament in October 2015, and it has been woven into the National Biodiversity Strategy & Action Plan (DEA 2015a), and the National Biodiversity Framework (DEA 2018), and it is used as a benchmark for implementing Operation Phakisa in the biodiversity economy sector.

Of interest in this chapter is how action at the national level using the notion of a biodiversity economy, has been through a series of public events from 2011 bringing together actors and investors interested in these industries. Figure 7.6 gives a timeline of events and actions that have been led by government to build a biodiversity economy sector. The web portal of the DFFE, public notices and news briefs were used in navigating the development of biodiversity economy in South Africa. Performativity, as described in Austin (1962) and Butler (2010), is used as a framework to explain the emergence of a biodiversity economy and the adoption of Operation Phakisa for its implementation. Expanding on the perlocutionary performatives, Butler uses an analogy of a politician where

> [a] politician may claim that 'a new day has arrived' but that new day only has a chance of arriving if people take up the utterance and endeavour to make that happen. The utterance alone does not bring about the day, and yet it can set into motion a set of actions that can, under certain felicitous circumstances, bring the day around. (Butler 2010: 147)

A key difference between the perlocutionary and the illocutionary performatives is that the former 'alters an ongoing situation', while the latter produce ontological effects (bringing something into 'being') (Austin 1962; Butler 2010). When analysed through the performativity lens, the biodiversity economy can be firmly placed within the perlocutionary performatives. This is justified by how, through utterances in a series of events and in strategy documents, the government has set in motion a set of actions, and continued coordination of the actors involved in already existing commercialisation of high-value or promising wild plants and wildlife. Key to these events and/or activities that were undertaken was the state listing of the biodiversity economy as one of the Operation Phakisa initiatives (The Presidency 2018; The Parliament 2021).

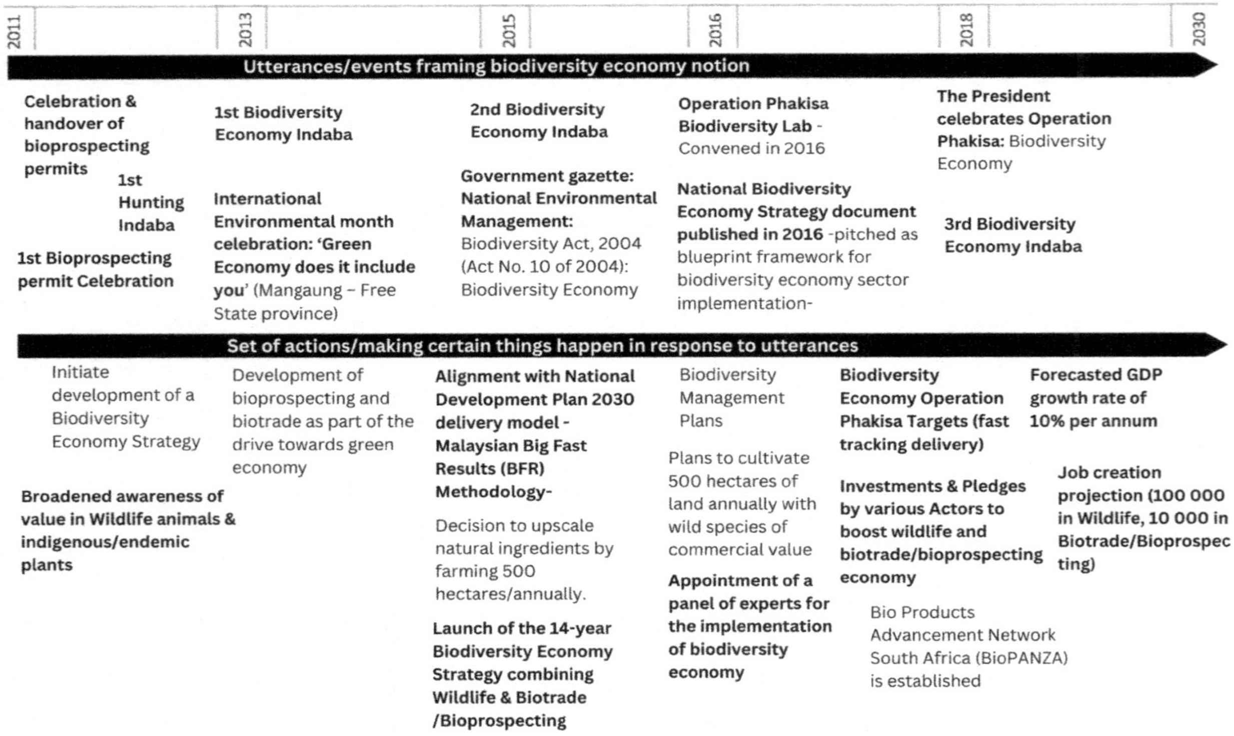
2011
2013
2015
2016
2018
2030
Utterances/events framing biodiversity economy notion
Celebration & handover of bioprospecting permits
1st Hunting Indaba
1st Bioprospecting permit Celebration
1st Biodiversity Economy Indaba
International Environmental month celebration: 'Green Economy does it include you' (Mangaung – Free State province)
2nd Biodiversity Economy Indaba
Government gazette: National Environmental Management: Biodiversity Act, 2004 (Act No. 10 of 2004): Biodiversity Economy
Operation Phakisa Biodiversity Lab - Convened in 2016
National Biodiversity Economy Strategy document published in 2016 -pitched as blueprint framework for biodiversity economy sector implementation-
The President celebrates Operation Phakisa: Biodiversity Economy
3rd Biodiversity Economy Indaba
Set of actions/making certain things happen in response to utterances
Initiate development of a Biodiversity Economy Strategy
Broadened awareness of value in Wildlife animals & indigenous/endemic plants
Development of bioprospecting and biotrade as part of the drive towards green economy
Alignment with National Development Plan 2030 delivery model - Malaysian Big Fast Results (BFR) Methodology-
Decision to upscale natural ingredients by farming 500 hectares/annually.
Launch of the 14-year Biodiversity Economy Strategy combining Wildlife & Biotrade /Bioprospecting
Biodiversity Management Plans
Plans to cultivate 500 hectares of land annually with wild species of commercial value
Appointment of a panel of experts for the implementation of biodiversity economy
Biodiversity Economy Operation Phakisa Targets (fast tracking delivery)
Investments & Pledges by various Actors to boost wildlife and biotrade/bioprospecting economy
Bio Products Advancement Network South Africa (BioPANZA) is established
Forecasted GDP growth rate of 10% per annum
Job creation projection (100 000 in Wildlife, 10 000 in Biotrade/Bioprospec ting)

Figure 7.6 Events and resulting actions in the creation of the idea of a biodiversity economy in South Africa, since 2011, with visions for 2030. The top shows 2011 to 2030 timeline, followed by events performed within the timeline, followed by realities created within the timeline. (Source: Author).

This follows an Operation Phakisa Biodiversity Economy Lab held in 2016 for four weeks (10 April to 13 May) in Johannesburg to develop an implementation plan for the draft NBES (DEA 2016, 2017). The key outcomes from the Lab relevant to this chapter are the Bio Products Advancement Network South Africa (BioPANZA), and the mass cultivation of twenty-five key species (Table 7.1, above) in rural and peri-urban areas by 2030. The BioPANZA was established to address product development, local value-additions and market-related issues (De Villiers & McGregor 2017; DEA 2017). There has been much ambiguity reported by key informants regarding how an Operation Phakisa Biodiversity Economy Lab decided to enlist each of these plants. Another critical issue is that there is no indication in government texts and public meeting proceedings that communities residing in the localities where these species grow were consulted on whether they want these plants to be commercially scaled in the way the state has imagined, and what that means for them.

The activities at the national level correlate with hyped changes in the honeybush sector related to commercial production and conservation, and the establishment of a Honeybush Community of Practice (HCOP) in 2016 by the Eastern and Western Cape provincial governments. The HCOP addresses issues related to governance, legislation, socio-economic transformation, sustainable utilisation, and promotion of the honeybush industry, knowledge sharing, and funding or incentives (DEA 2018; Horn & Ackhurst 2019). The HCOP has drawn together actors such as commercial farmers, landowners, provincial government, communities, the private sector, researchers, and NGOs that had been loosely engaging with the honeybush trade. This has created an enabling environment for indirect state-centric governance in a sector that was less legislated and more fragmented.

The events and utterances outlined in Figure 7.6 further show an explicit national alignment with the green economy (DEA 2015b) as imagined in the United Nations Environmental Programme (UNEP 2011, 2013). Further, the promise of jobs is a rhetoric in many of the national policies and international treaties to which South Africa subscribes. As articulated in the dissatisfaction of Haarlem community with being labour, the biodiversity economy activities, while essential for aspects such as racial transformation of biodiversity-based businesses, are also threatening further marginalisation by trapping communities in a corner, effectively forcing them to accept much needed jobs and incentives that nevertheless leave them as glorified beneficiaries with no ownership. Communities are often required to organise themselves into manageable structures either cooperatives, declaring indigeneity, or forming groups aligned with green/nature stewardship imperatives to receive benefits often framed at international and national levels. A community member said this was abuse, referring to the silence on injustices because people do income:

> The systems and the way we treat each other when it comes to business, you can also call that abusive, you understand. Because you are hungry, and there's no other options, it's take it or leave it, you understand. It's like the guy said take it or leave [it], it's my way or the highway, understand. And that is our biggest concern ... that is the kind of things you must highlight. (Community member 2021)

Policies and legislations governing the biodiversity-based sectors perpetuate technical solutions and best-laid plans that not only seldom match the change that is needed at grassroots level but also promote abusive silencing interventions and are less bottom-up and inclusive than the government wants them to appear (Engel 2018; for a similar exclusionary relation between state and local communities in Uganda and Kenya see Lenhart & Lacan this volume).

Discussion and conclusions

The categorisation of honeybush as an export crop abounds with long histories of celebrated discoveries of *Cyclopia* spp., research innovations, and product and market development. This categorisation has occurred along with a marginalisation of people, revealing persistent exclusionary approaches to biodiversity commercialisation and a need for social reforms. From public meeting proceedings to the written text in government documents, investments, and the hype surrounding Operation Phakisa, it is apparent that the government model and approach to biodiversity commercialisation comes with promises to cater for both the communities and capitalistic stakeholders. However, Petersen and Krisjansen (2015) remind us that neoliberal rationality demands that the markets decide on winners and losers, thus governments give their support to perceived winners believed most likely to contribute to economic growth. Within the neoliberal rationality the invisible local trade and communities are neglected (Shackleton *et al.* 2007; Shackleton & Pandey 2013). To this end, calls have been made for decision makers to pay attention to local markets over privatised global value chains, as the latter often unintendedly contribute to the disempowerment of communities in varying ways (Shackleton *et al.* 2007; Shackleton *et al.* 2011; Van Niekerk & Wynberg 2012; Wynberg *et al.* 2015). The Langkloof case study shows that the disempowerment is cemented through recurring injustices of land and resource rights, shaping who gets to participate in the emerging honeybush sector. Fairhead *et al.* (2012) urge that in dealing with the issues of green grabbing, commodification, and appropriation of nature, it might be beneficial to look to histories in order to highlight and understand the role of old enclosures in contemporary issues, e.g., exclusions that are inscribed in colonial legislations.

There is prominence of the theses of marginalisation and degradation (Peluso 1992; Robbins 2004; Heynen & Robbins 2005) in how honeybush commercialisation is approached. The case of the Langkloof depicted a growing shift in the way communities engage with honeybush and how they have had to adapt to shifting patterns of production with minimal resources, and to deal with introduced regulations – e.g., stricter permit system and various guidelines. Although these changes were understood to be beneficial for the communities as they aim to ensure the sustainability of the resource (Horn & Ackhurst 2019), communities were not happy with change from the way they used to harvest and produce the tea, for example that they now 'need a paper' (a statement that kept coming up from locals in varying phrases) – symbolic of their uneasiness with change in the use of honeybush.

Land ownership is fundamental for government to successfully channel marginalised groups into honeybush domestication. It has been noted that South African government-funded natural products enterprises in rural and peri-urban areas continue to fail because of lack of support and land ownership (Mabaya *et al.* 2011; Small Entreprise Development Agency 2012). This has put into question, amongst other issues, the compatibility of the government policy tools and strategies in dealing with social dynamics that these plants are embedded in (Cunningham *et al.* 2009; Wynberg *et al.* 2015).

The form in which the biodiversity economy is developed within Operation Phakisa echoes the work of the scholars that have identified the issues of pace, time, and narrative that are common in bio-economy policies and contemporary neoliberal conservation policies (Wanner 2013; Wesselink *et al.* 2013; Death 2015; Petersen & Krisjansen 2015; Povinelli 2016; Scoones *et al.* 2018). In Malaysia the Big Fast Results model, which the South African government emulated in formulating Operation Phakisa, has been said to have necessitated service delivery and performance in a short space of time. However, they are reported to have been hyped, yielding pockets of short-term success but failing to tackle more complex issues (Siddiquee 2019; Siddiquee *et al.* 2019). Similar patterns have been identified in the Oceans Economy Operation Phakisa (Engel 2018; Vreÿ 2020), while Förster *et al.* (2021) noted the limited capacity for public and private actors to achieve the goals of biodiversity economy. Implementing biodiversity economy in this manner may lead to elite capture in local communities that are still awaiting social reforms and basic services (Davenport *et al.* 2011). The Khoi and the San, who are the rightful holders of traditional knowledge (TK) related to honeybush, just like the broader indigenous communities across the globe, are still acutely affected by the legacy of colonialism, salient power dynamics and rights violations

(Schroeder 2009; Dutfield & Suthersanen 2019). Moreover, mechanisms put in place for sharing of benefits with indigenous communities have sought 'win-win' solutions for conservation and economic development, and have neglected objectives that cater for social, environmental, and economic justice in the commercial use of biodiversity (see also Wynberg this volume).

For indigenous communities and farmworker communities in the honeybush-growing regions, social reforms and conservation policies tailored to addressing human rights are critical for participation in the commercial use of natural resources. Does the biodiversity economy's accelerated commercialisation cater or make time for the recurring exclusions and marginalities? Probably not, because in the wake of 'consuming life', as is the case with certified coffee in Papua New Guinea (West 2010), the capitalist economy is allowed to leave multiple pasts of injustices unaddressed and rely on unjust inclusions of the disenfranchised to advance capitalist commerce. Following the standpoint of various theorists such as Patricia Hill Collins (2000, 2019) on working with the marginalised groups, a recommendation is made that insisting on research and policies that emerge from the margins and confront multiple pasts of localities that are endowed with biodiversity may allow communities to exist in the biodiversity-based sectors on their own terms.

Bibliography

African National Congress (1994). *The Reconstruction and Development Programme: A Policy Framework* (Johannesburg: Umanyano Publications).

Altman, M. & Hemson, D. (2007). 'Evidence-based Employment Scenarios: The Role of Expanded Public Works Programmes in Halving Unemployment' (Pretoria: Human Sciences Research Council). Available at: https://citeseerx. ist.psu.edu/viewdoc/download?doi=10.1.1.557.1800&rep=rep1&type=pdf [Accessed 17 April 2020].

Austin, J. L. (1962). *How to Do Things with Words: The William James Lectures Delivered at Harvard University in 1955* (Oxford: Clarendon Press).

Bek, D., Binns, T., & Nel, E. (2013). 'Wildflower harvesting on South Africa's agulhas plain: A mechanism for achieving sustainable local economic development?' *Sustainable Development*, 21(5), 281–293.

Bester, C. (2013). 'A model for commercialisation of Honeybush tea, an indigenous crop', *Acta Horticulture*, 1007(1007), 889–894.

Biodiversity Act (2004). 'National Environmental Management: Biodiversity Act, 2004' (Cape Town: The Presidency). Available at www.gov.za/sites/default/ files/gcis_document/201409/a10-04.pdf [Accessed 23 February 2022].

Bolam, J. (1907a). 'Letter to Messrs Jackson and Co Piccadilly', African Governance Report, hereafter AGR Archives (South African National Archives: Western Cape Repository).

Bolam, J. (1907b). 'Enclosed Documents: Testimonials on Medicinal Qualities of Bush Tea (1907), in: R Marloth report Chemical Analysis of the Cyclopia Tea

(1906–1907)'. AGR Archives (National Archives of South Africa: Cape Town Archives Repository).

Bowie, J. (1830). 'Sketches of the Botany of South Africa', *The South African Quarterly Journal*, 1 (1830), 27–39.

Broad-Based Black Economic Empowerment Amendment Act 2013 (2013) (Cape Town: Government Gazette: Republic of South Africa, Rephabliki ya Afrika Borwa). Available at: www.gov.za/sites/default/files/gcis_document/201409/3 7271act46of2013.pdf [Accessed 25 February 2022].

Brown, K. (2001). 'The conservation and utilisation of the natural world: Silviculture in the Cape Colony, c. 1902–1910', *Environment and History*, 7(4), 427–474.

Brown, K. (2003). *Progressivism, Agriculture and Conservation in the Cape Colony circa 1902–1908*. PhD thesis, University of Oxford.

Büscher, B. & Dressler, W. (2012). 'Commodity conservation: The restructuring of community conservation in South Africa and the Philippines', *Geoforum*, 43(3), 367–376.

Butler, J. (2010). 'Perfomative Agency', *Journal of Cultural Economy*, 3(2), 147–161.

Caspa Tea & Produce Co. Ltd (1930). 'Company files 1919–1930' AGR Archives, Vol. 611, Ref. T83 (Cape Town: Western Cape Archives and Records Service).

Caspareuthus, T. (1907). 'Cyclopia Tea – Caspareuthus Letter to Government'. AGR Archives (Cape Town: National Archives of South Africa, Cape Town Archives Repository).

Cheney, R. H. & Scholtz, E. (1963). 'Rooibos tea, a South African Contribution to world beverages', *Economic Botany*, 17(3), 186–194.

Cockburn, J., Cundill, G., Shackleton, S., Rouget, M., Zwinkels, M. *et al.* (2019a). 'Collaborative stewardship in multifunctional landscapes: Toward relational, pluralistic approaches', *Ecology and Society*, 24(4), 32.

Cockburn, J., Cundill, G., Shackleton, S., & Rouget, M. (2019b). 'The meaning and practice of stewardship in South Africa', Research Article, *South African Journal of Science*, 115(6), 1–10.

Collins, P. H. (2000). *Black Feminist Thought: Knowledge, Consciousness, and the Politics of Empowerment*, 2nd edn (New York: Routledge).

Collins, P. H. (2019). *Intersectionality as Critical Social Theory*, e-book edn (Durham: Duke University Press).

Connor, T. (2013). 'Borders of mutuality, frontiers of resistance: Paternalism and working identities of farm labourers in the Sundays River Valley, South Africa', *African Studies*, 72(3), 375–398.

Cunningham, A. B., Garnett, S., Gorman, J., Courtenay, K., & Boehme, D. (2009). 'Eco-enterprises and *terminalia ferdinandiana*: "Best laid plans" and Australian policy lessons', *Economic Botany*, 63(1), 16–28.

Davenport, N. A., Gambiza, J., & Shackleton, C. M. (2011). 'Use and users of municipal commonage around three small towns in the Eastern Cape, South Africa', *Journal of Environmental Management*, 92(2011), 1449–1460.

Death, C. (2015). 'Four discourses of the green economy in the global South', *Third World Quarterly*, 36(12), 2207–2224.

de Laat, Z. (2017). 'The Presumed Increase of Access due to Redistribution of

Property Rights in Rural South Africa: An Analysis of Policies and Daily Practices on Land Reform Farms in the Langkloof'. Master's thesis, Wageningen University (Netherlands).

De Villiers, C. & McGregor, G. (2017). 'Review of the Regulatory and Policy Framework Relating to the Harvesting of Wild Honeybush (*Cyclopia* spp.)' (Western Cape: Department of Environmental Affairs and Development Planning). Available at: www.abs-biotrade.info/fileadmin/Downloads/Value_ Chains/Honeybush/Review-Regulatory-Framework-honeybush-Western-Cape-gov-2017.pdf [Accessed 25 January 2022].

Dutfield, G. & Suthersanen, U. (2019). 'Traditional knowledge and genetic resources: Observing legal protection through the lens of historical geography and human rights', *Washburn Law Journal*, 58, 399–447.

Engel, U. (2018). 'The "blue economy" and Operation Phakisa: Prospects for an emerging developmental state in South Africa?' in: J. Schubert, U. Engel, & E. Macamo (eds), *Extractive Industries and Changing State Dynamics in Africa*, 1st edn (London: Routledge), 57–73.

Fairhead, J., Leach, M., & Scoones, I. (2012). 'Green Grabbing: A new appropriation of nature?' *Journal of Peasant Studies*, 39(2), 237–261.

Förster, J. J., Downsborough, L., Biber-Freudenberger, L., Mensuro, G. K., & Borner, J. (2021). 'Exploring criteria for transformative policy capacity in the context of South Africa's biodiversity economy', *Policy Sciences*, 54 (2021), 209–237.

Findlay, K. (2018). 'Operation Phakisa and unlocking South Africa's Ocean economy', *Journal of the Indian Ocean Region*, 14(2), 248–254.

George Local Municipality (2019). Amended Integrated Development Plan (George: South Africa).

Hall, R., Wisborg, P., Shirinda, S., & Zamchiya, P. (2012). 'Farm workers and farm dwellers in Limpopo Province, South Africa', *Journal of Agrarian Change*, 13(1), 47–70.

Harald, J. & Lie, S. (2015). 'Uganda Focus Developmentality: Indirect governance in the World Bank – Uganda partnership', *Third World Quarterly*, 36(4), 723–740.

Heynen, N. & Robbins, P. (2005). 'The neoliberalization of nature: Governance, privatization, enclosure and valuation', *Capitalism Nature Socialism*, 16(1), 5–8.

Hobson, S. & Joubert, M. (2011) 'Eastern Cape Honeybush Tea Project Industry Overview: Assessment and Proposed Interventions'. Unpublished report (Eastern Cape: DEDEA).

Hofmeyr, J. & Phillips, E. P. (1922). 'The Genus *Cyclopia*, Vent', *Bothalia*, 1(1922), 105–109.

hooks, b. (ed.) (1984). *Feminist Theory from Margin to Center* (Boston MA: South End Press).

hooks, b. (1989). 'Choosing the margin as a space of radical openness', *The Journal of Cinema and Media*, (36), 15–23.

Horn, A. & Ackhurst, A. (2019). 'Honeybush tea: Small industry, big potential', *Farmer's Weekly*, 5 April, 36–38.

Ives, S. (2014). 'Farming the South African "bush": Ecologies of belonging and exclusion in rooibos tea', *Journal of the American Ethnological Society*, 41(4), 698–713.

Jackson, J. R. (1873). 'African tea plants', *The Pharmaceutical Journal and Trans-actions*, 4(1873), 421.

Joubert, E., Joubert, M. E., Bester, C., de Beer, D., & De Lange, J. H. (2011). 'Honeybush (*Cyclopia* spp.): From local cottage industry to global markets – The catalytic and supporting role of research', *South African Journal of Botany*, 77(4), 887–907.

Kies, P. (1951). 'Revision of the genus *Cyclopia* and notes on some other sources of bush tea,' *Bothalia*, 6(1), 161–176.

Kou-Kamma Local Municipality (2020). 'Final Integrated Development Plan of Koukamma Local Municipality 2020/2021, Integrated Development Plan' (Port Elizabeth: Koukamma Local Municipality). Available at: www.koukammamu-nicipality.gov.za/wp-content/uploads/2021/02/2020-21-FINAL-IDP-2020-2021. pdf [Accessed 13 January 2023].

Larsen, P. M., Fey, S. J., Louw, J., & Joubert, L. (2016). 'An Anti-diabetic Extract of Honeybush' (Patent number 08717610.3: European Patent Office).

Ludman, B. (1983), 'From the fields to our teacups [Press release]', *Rand Daily Mail*, 17 March 1983.

Mabaya, E., Tihanyi, K, Karaan, M. & van Rooyan, J. (2011). *Case Studies of Emerging Farmers and Agribusinesses in South Africa* (Stellenbosch: Sun Press).

MacOwen, P. (1894). 'Cape Tea (so-called),' AGR Archives, 206(T15349) (Cape Town: National Archives of South Africa: Cape Town Archives Repository).

McGregor, A., Challies, E., Overton, J., & Sentes, L. (2013). 'Developmentalities and donor–NGO Relations: Contesting foreign aid policies in New Zealand/Aotearoa', *Antipode*, 45(5), 1232–1253.

McGregor, G. (2017a). 'An overview of the honeybush industry' (Western Cape: Department of Environmental Affairs and Development Planning, March 2017). Available at: www.westerncape.gov.za/eadp/files/atoms/files/eadp696_an_overview_of_the_honeybush_industry_may2017_0.pdf [Accessed 25 January 2022].

McGregor, G. (2017b). 'Guidelines for the sustainable harvesting of wild honeybush' (Western Cape: Department of Environmental Affairs and Devel-opment Planning, March 2017). Available at: www.westerncape.gov.za/eadp/files/atoms/files/eadp696_guidelines_for_the_sustainable_harvesting_of_wild_honeybush_june2107.pdf [Accessed 25 January 2022].

McGregor, G. (2017c). 'Industry Review: An Overview of the Honeybush Industry' (Western Cape: Department of Environmental Affairs and Devel-opment Planning, March 2017). Available at: https://gouritz.com/wp-content/uploads/2019/03/Industry-Review-An-Overview-of-the-Honeybush-Industry. pdf [Accessed: 3 December 2021].

Mulkerrins, J. (2015). *Scale Framing in a Landscape Restoration Process: The Case of Water in the Langkloof, South Africa*. Thesis, Wageningen University.

Muthambi, F. (2014). 'Government goes for big, fast results', *South African Government News*, 30 July 2014. Available at: www.sanews.gov.za/south-africa/government-goes-big-fast-results [Accessed 25 January 2022].

National Department of Employment and Labour (2021). 'National Minimum Wage Act No.9 of 2018' (Pretoria: Government of South Africa). Available at: www.gov.za/sites/default/files/gcis_document/201811/42060gon1303act9of2018. pdf [Accessed 25 February 2022].

National Department of Environmental Affairs (DEA) (2005). 'South Africa's National Biodiversity Strategy and Action Plan' (Port Elizabeth: DEA). Available at www.environment.gov.za/sites/default/files/docs/nationalbiodiversit_stractandactionplan.pdf [Accessed 19 April 2020].

National Department of Environmental Affairs (DEA) (2014). 'Traditional Knowledge Associated with Rooibos and Honeybush Species in South Africa' (Pretoria: Government of South Africa). Available at: https://naturaljustice. org/wp-content/uploads/2014/10/Traditional-Knowledge-Rooibos-Honeybush-Species-SA.pdf [Accessed 25 January 2022].

National Department of Environmental Affairs (DEA) (2015a). 'South Africa's 2nd National Biodiversity Strategy and Action Plan 2015–2025'. Available at: www. dffe.gov.za/sites/default/files/docs/publications/SAsnationalbiodiversity_strategyandactionplan2015_2025.pdf [Accessed 25 February 2022].

National Department of Environmental Affairs (DEA) (2015b). 'Biodiversity Economy under the Spotlight'. Available at https://legal.sabinet.co.za/articles/ biodiversity-economy-under-the-spotlight [Accessed 18 April 2020].

National Department of Environmental Affairs (DEA) (2016). 'National Biodiversity Economy Strategy (NBES)' (Pretoria: DEA). Available at www.dffe. gov.za/sites/default/files/gazetted_notices/nemba10of2004_biodiversityeconomystrategy_gg39268.pdf [Accessed 23 February 2022].

National Department of Environmental Affairs (DEA) (2017). 'The Appointment of a Panel of Experts to Assist the Department of Environmental Affairs in the Implementation of the Biodiversity Economy' (Pretoria: DFFE). Available at www.dffe.gov.za/sites/default/files/tenders/e1388_biodiversityeconomy_1_0. pdf [Accessed 23 February 2022].

National Department of Environmental Affairs (DEA) (2018). 'South Africa's National Biodiversity Framework: Final Draft' (Pretoria: DFFE). Available at https://cer.org.za/wp-content/uploads/2018/10/Draft-National-Biodiversity-Framework.pdf [Accessed 23 February 2022].

National Department of Environmental Affairs (DEA) (2018). '3rd Biodiversity Economy Indaba' (Pretoria: DEA). Available at www.dffe.gov.za/event/ deptactivity/3rdbiodiversity_economyindaba [Accessed 04 September 2022].

National Department of Environmental Affairs (DEA) (2020). 'Presentation: Unlocking the Socio-Economic Potential of South Africa's Biodiversity Assets Through Sustainable Use of Biodiversity Economy Programme' (Pretoria: DEA). Available at: http://opus.sanbi.org/bitstream/20.500.12143/7074/1/ Biodiversity%20Economy_Stewardship%20Conference%20Natalie%20 Veltman%20%26%20Koena%20Cholo.pdf. [Accessed: 4 September 2020].

National Department of Planning, Monitoring and Evaluation (2016). 'Biodiversity: The Operation Phakisa Lab on Biodiversity Lab' (Pretoria: Department of Planning, Monitoring and Evaluation). Available at: www.operationphakisa. gov.za/operations/Biodiversity/Pages/default.aspx [Accessed: 21 April 2020].

National Planning Commission (2012). 'The National Development Plan2030: Our

Future – Make it Work'. Available at: https://nationalplanningcommission.files. wordpress.com/2015/02/ndp-2030–our-future-make-it-work_0.pdf [Accessed 25 February 2022].

Nature and Environmental Conservation Ordinance (1974). 'Ordinance No.19 of 1974' (Cape Province: Nature Conservation). Available at https://cer.org.za/ wp-content/uploads/2016/03/19–of-1974–Nature_and_Environmental_Conservation_Ordinance_And_Regulations_1974.pdf [Accessed 23 February 2022].

Pappe, L. (ed.) (1857). *An Enumeration of South African Plants used as Remedies by the Colonists of the Cape of Good Hope* (Cape Town: King's College London).

Peluso, N. (1992). 'The political ecology of extraction and extractive reserves in East Kalimantan, Indonesia', *Development and Change*, 23(4), 49–74.

Penn, N. (ed.) (2005). *The Forgotten Frontier: Colonist and Khoisan on the Cape's Northern Frontier in the 18th Century* (Athens: Ohio University Press).

Petersen, A. & Krisjansen, I. (2015). 'Assembling "the bioeconomy": Exploiting the power of the promissory life sciences', *Journal of Sociology*, 51(1), 28–46.

Pieter, B. (2018). 'The implications of comprehensive and incremental approaches to public sector reform for the creation of a developmental state in South Africa: Case study of the Oceans Economy Operation Phakisa'. Master's thesis, University of Cape Town.

Polak, J. & Snowball, J. (2017). 'Towards a framework for assessing the sustainability of local economic development based on natural resources: Honeybush tea in the Eastern Cape Province of South Africa', *Local Environment*, 22(3), 335–349.

Povinelli, E. A. (2016). 'Late liberal geontopower', in: E. A. Povinelli (ed.), *Geontologies: A Requiem to Late Liberalism*. 1st edn (Durham NC: Duke University Press), 232.

Radebe, J. (2017). 'Keynote address by the Honourable Jeff Radebe, MP, Minister in the Presidency for Planning, Monitoring and Evaluation and Chairperson of the National Planning Commission, on the 1st Africa Monitoring and Evaluation Indaba co-hosted by DPME and UN-SA' (Pretoria: Department of Planning Monitoring and Evaluation: Republic of South Africa). Available at: www. dpme.gov.za/news/Pages/Keynote-Address-by-the-Honourable-Jeff-Radebe,-MP,-Minister-in-the-Presidency-for-Planning,-Monitoring-and-Evaluation-and-C.aspx. [Accessed 25 January 2022].

Robbins, P. (ed.) (2004). *Political Ecology: Critical Introductions to Geography*. 1st edn (Oxford: Blackwell).

SAHTA (2021). 'Perishable Products Export Control Board (PPECB): Honeybush KG exports 2010 to 2021' (Cape Town: South African Honeybush Tea Association).

Sampson, V. (1906). 'Patent for an Invention for "An Improved Cyclopia Tea"', *AG*. (Cape Town: National Archives of South Africa: Cape Town Archives Repository).

Schroeder, D. (2009). 'Informed consent: From medical research to traditional knowledge', in: R. Wynberg, R. Chennels, & D. Schroeder (eds), *Indigenous Peoples, Consent and Benefit Sharing* (Dodrecht: Springer), 27–51.

Schutte, A. L. (1997). 'Systematics of the genus *Cyclopia* Vent. (Fabaceae, Poda-lyrieae)', *Edinburgh Journal of Botany*, 54(1997), 125–170.

Schweitzer, E. (2008). 'How black farm workers become land and business owners: Actors, resources, contexts and outcomes of black empowerment projects in the South African wine industry', *Wiener Zeitschrift für kritische Afrikastudien*, 15(2008), 31–53.

Scoones, I., Stirling, A., Abrol, D., Atela, J., Lakshmi, C., Eakin, H., Ely, A., Pereira, L., Ritu, P., van Zwaneneberg, P., & Yang, L. (2018). 'Transformations to Sustainability' STEPS Working Paper 104 (Brighton: STEPS Centre). Available at: https://opendocs.ids.ac.uk/opendocs/bitstream/handle/20.500.12413/14057/ WP%20104%20Transformations%20to%20Sustainability%20online%20 version%20FINAL%20v2.pdf [Accessed 25 January 2022].

Shackleton, C. M. & Pandey, A. K. (2013). 'Positioning non-timber forest products on the development agenda', *Forest Policy and Economics*, 38(2014), 1–7.

Shackleton, S., Shanley, P., & Ndoye, O. (2007). 'Invisible but viable: Recognising local markets for non-timber forest products', *International Forestry Review*, 9(3), 697–712.

Shackleton, C., Delang, C. O., Shackleton, S., & Shanley, P. (2011). 'Non-Timber Forest Products: Concepts and Definitions', in: S. Shackleton, C. Shackleton, & P. Shanley (eds), *Non-Timber Forest Products in the Global Context* (Berlin; Heidelberg: Springer), 55–149.

Siddiquee, N.A. (2019). 'Driving performance in the public sector: What can we learn from Malaysia's service delivery reform?' *International Journal of Productivity and Performance Management*, 69(9), 2069–2087.

Siddiquee, N. A., Xavier, J. A., & Mohamed, M. Z. (2019). 'What works and why? Lessons from public management reform in Malaysia', *International Journal of Public Administration*, 42(1), 14–27.

Sims, J. (1810) 'Flower-garden displayed [entry 1259, Ibbetsonia Genistoides]', *Curtis's Botanical Magazine*, 31, 1237–1282.

Slabbert, E. L., Malgas, R. R., Veldtman, R., & Addison, P. (2019). 'Honeybush (*Cyclopia* spp.) phenology and associated arthropod diversity in the Overberg region, South Africa', *Bothalia: African Biodiversity & Conservation*, 49(1), 1–13.

Small Entreprise Development Agency (SEDA) (2012). 'Research study to identify needs, opportunities and challenges of small and medium entreprises in the traditional medicine sector' (Pretoria: SEDA). Available at: www.seda.org.za/ Publications/Publications/Research%20study%20to%20identify%20the%20 Needs,%20Opportunities%20and%20Challenges%20of%20SMEs%20in%20 the%20Traditional%20Medicine%20Sector.pdf [Accessed 25 January 2022].

Stander, M. A., Brendler, T, Redelinghuys, H., & Van Wyk, B.-E. (2019). 'The commercial history of Cape herbal teas and the analysis of phenolic compounds in historic teas from a depository of 1933', *Journal of Food Composition and Analysis*, 76, 66–73.

Statistics South Africa (2011). 'George Municipality: Haarlem, Municipal Profiles', Available at: www.statssa.gov.za/?page_id=4286&id=238 [Accessed: 20 July 2020].

Sue, D. (2010). *Microaggressions and Marginality: Manifestation, Dynamics, and Impact* (Hoboken NJ: Wiley).

Takouleu, J. M. (2019). 'South Africa: Biodiversity could create 162,000 jobs', *Afrik21*, 30 September [24 September 2018]. Available at: www.afrik21.africa/en/south-africa-biodiversity-economy-could-create-162000-jobs [Accessed 25 January 2022].

Tapscott, C. (1995) 'Changing discourses of development in South Africa', in: J. Crush (ed.), *Power of Development*, 1st edn (London: Routledge), 16.

Tennant, J. H. (1894). 'Record Volume 206: Tea Culture – Letter from', AGR Archives (Cape Town: National Archives of South Africa: Cape Town Archives Repository, p. T1534).

The Parliament. (2021). 'Operation Phakisa Initiatives that are Central to the Mandate of the Department of Forestry, Fisheries, and the Environment' (Cape Town: Parliament). Available at https://static.pmg.org.za/211207_Operation_Phakisa_Initiatives_under_DFFE.pdf [Accessed: 4 September 2022].

The Presidency (2014). 'President Jacob Zuma to launch Operation Phakisa' [Press release], South African Government Newsroom, 16 July 2014.

The Presidency (2018). 'President Ramaphosa celebrates Operation Phakisa: Biodiversity Economy at Vhembe District, Limpopo' (Pretoria: The Presidency: Republic of South Africa). Available at: www.thepresidency.gov.za/newsletters/president-ramaphosa-celebrates-operation-phakisa%3A-biodiversity-economy-vhembe-district%2C [Accessed 25 January 2022].

The Under-Secretary for Agriculture (1894). 'Letter on the Question of Fostering Minor Industries', AGR Archives (Cape Town: National Archives of South Africa: Cape Town Archives Repository).

The Union of South Africa. 'Trademarks Office: Advertisements, Pub. L. No. 1182, Government Gazette (1921)'. Available at: https://gazettes.africa/archive/za/1921/za-government-gazette-dated-1921-09-09-no-1182.pdf. [Accessed: 06 September 2022].

Du Toit, J., Joubert, E., & Britz, T. J. (1998). 'Honeybush tea – A rediscovered indigenous South African herbal tea', *Journal of Sustainable Agriculture*, 12(3), 67–84.

United Nations Environmental Programme (UNEP) (2011). 'Towards a Green Economy: Pathways to Sustainable Development and Poverty Eradication, Green Economy Report' (Nairobi: UNEP). Available at: https://sustainabledevelopment.un.org/content/documents/126GER_synthesis_en.pdf [Accessed 25 January 2022].

United Nations Environmental Programme (UNEP) (2013). 'Green Economy Modelling Report of South Africa: Focus on Natural Resource Management, Agriculture, Transport and Energy Sectors' (Nairobi: UNEP). Available at: https://wedocs.unep.org/bitstream/handle/20.500.11822/33559/GEMRSA.pdf. [Accessed 25 January 2022].

Van Niekerk, J. & Wynberg, R. (2012). 'The trade in *Pelargonium sidoides*: Rural livelihood relief or bounty for the "bio-buccaneers"?' *Development Southern Africa*, 29(4), 530–547.

Van Wyk, B. E. (2011). 'The potential of South African plants in the development of new food and beverage products', *South African Journal of Botany*, 77(4), 857–868.

Van Wyk, B. E. & Gorelik, B. (2017). 'The history and ethnobotany of Cape herbal teas', *South African Journal of Botany*, 110(2017), 18–38.

Vreÿ, F. (2020). 'Operation Phakisa: Reflections Upon an Ambitious Maritime-Led Government initiative', *Scientia Militaria, South African Journal of Military Studies*, 47(2), 85–103.

Wanner, T. (2013). 'The New "passive revolution" of the green economy and growth discourse: Maintaining the "sustainable development" of neoliberal capitalism', *New Political Economy*, 20(1), 21–41.

Wesselink, A. Buchanan, K. S., Georgiadou, Y., & Turnhout, E. (2013). 'Technical knowledge, discursive spaces and politics at the science-policy interface', *Environmental Science & Policy*, 30(203), 1–9.

West, P. (2010). 'Making the market: Specialty coffee, generational pitches, and Papua New Guinea', *Antipode*, 42(3), 690–718.

Wynberg, R., Laird, S., Van Niekerk, J., & Kozanayi, W. (2015). 'Formalization of the natural product trade in southern Africa: Unintended consequences and policy blurring in biotrade and bioprospecting', *Society and Natural Resources*, 28(5), 559–574.

8

From Forest to National Resource: Forest conservation and state power in Baringo, Kenya

LÉA LACAN

Introduction

In the 'State of the World's Forests, 2020', the Food and Agriculture Organization and the United Nations Environment Programme warn about the 'alarming rates' of deforestation, mainly driven by agricultural expansion (FAO & UNEP 2020: xvi). Between 1990 and 2020, the global forest area (i.e. the area of land used as forest, including planted and non-planted forests) suffered a net loss of 178 million hectares (FAO & UNEP 2020: xvii). In Kenya, the FAO Global Resource Assessment also indicates a net reduction in forest area of 248,000 ha between 1990 and 2020 (Food and Agriculture Organisation of the United Nations, hereafter FAO 2020: 138). Yet forests are considered highly valuable at many levels (Sunderlin et al. 2005). In 2004, the World Bank estimated forest resources to support the livelihoods of 90% of the 1.2 billion people deemed to live in extreme poverty (World Bank 2004). Forests are recognised key to sustain economies (IUCN 2020), and forest value chains are deemed 'of critical importance for sustainable economic growth' (Muller et al. 2018: 37) with 28% of the world's forest areas being primarily designated for production (FAO 2020: 58). Their environmental benefits are also highly praised. Forests are recognised as home to most terrestrial biodiversity, key to mitigate climate change and supply water resources, and closely associated with human health (IUCN 2020; FAO & UNEP 2020). In the context of the global environmental crisis, attempts to link up environmental benefits and their conservation to economic and monetary values are increasingly gaining interest, and in the forest sector especially. The UN-led programme Reducing Emissions from Deforestation and Forest Degradation in Developing Countries (REDD), for example, aims to incentivise the conservation of forests by allocating a financial value on the carbon they store (Kopnina 2017). Such projects are supported in Kenya, where national policies also link the conservation of forests to their economic value. The Forest Conservation and Management Act, 2016 provides for 'the development and sustainable management, including conservation and rational utilisation of all forest resources for the socio-economic development of the Country and for connected purposes' (Republic of Kenya 2016: 680), and supports the incentivisation of forest conservation through the development of benefit-sharing mechanisms. Thus, while deforestation is ongoing around the world, the value of forests is increasingly put forward, including their economic value. How does the valorisation of forests stand in relation to forest transformations? In this volume, Revilla Diez *et al.* pinpoint the need to analyse how value is created in the production of commoditised natural resources. Kalvelage analyses value creation from wildlife in Namibia and its production into a commodity, while Hewitson & Sullivan investigate how elephants are being commodified for trophy hunting in Namibian conservancies. This chapter also questions the production of a natural resource, taking the case of Kenyan forests. It looks at the history of the forest sector in Kenya, and asks: how are Kenyan forests valued, and how was this valuation constructed by the (colonial) state? How did it transform Kenyan forests during the colonial time (and beyond)?

This research takes a close look at two particular cases in Baringo in west-central Kenya. The first is the Katimok Forest (1,956.9 hectares[1]) situated on the Tugen Hills west of Lake Baringo. The other case examines the forests around Eldama Ravine – in particular, the Maji Mazuri and the Lembus[2] Forests, which include areas of the current Narasha Forest (6,159.4 hectares[3]) – situated in the southern part of Baringo County. This analysis draws on nine months of ethnographic fieldwork in Baringo and extensive archival research

[1]   Kenya Forest Service (KFS, 2014: 7), Kabarnet/Tenges/Ol'Arabel Forests Plantation Management Plan 2015–2025.

[2]   The Lembus Forest was first included in the Mount Londiani forest reserve gazetted in 1912 and was then declared a separate forest reserve (on Crown land) in 1932 (District Officer Eldama Ravine, Baringo District, to Provincial Commissioner Rift Valley Province 5 October 1961, Tugen Forest Reserve KNA PC/NKU/3/7/1). Its boundaries chan;ged several times so that it is difficult to give an accurate hectarage for this forest. After extensive excisions in the 1960s, the Lembus Forest was broken down into several forest blocks in the 1970s (see KFS/ER KFS/BAR/18/3/6 Vol.I ARA Forms Narasha, and DFO Annual Reports & Correspondence KFS/Kabfs 10/2 and DFO's Annual Report Baringo KFS/Kabs 10/18) including the Narasha Forest – which entails a small southern part of the former Lembus Forest and part of former Maji Mazuri Forest.

[3]   KFS, 2013, Narasha Forest Plantation Management Plan 2014–2024: 1. Ethnographic fieldwork in the Eldama Ravine area focused on the Narasha Forest, particularly Kaptim village.

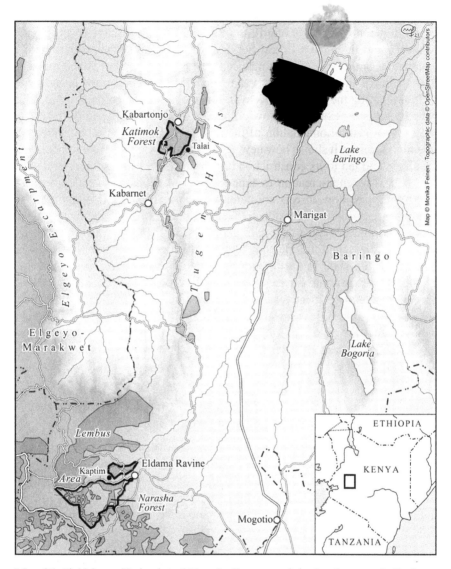

Map 8.1. Fieldsites – Katimok and Narasha Forests, and the Lembus area in Baringo, Kenya (Source: Author; Cartography: M. Feinen).

in the Bodleian Library (Oxford), the Kenya National Archive (Nairobi and Nakuru), and the Kenya Forest Service (KFS) archives.[4] Considering and contrasting both cases ▮▮▮▮▮ nuanced analysis of the process and impacts of the constructio▮▮▮▮▮▮▮t as a national economic resource in Baringo.

Investigating th▮▮▮▮▮▮Kenyan forests during the colonial times, this chapter starts by exa▮▮▮▮how colonial visions materialised through the progressive institutiona▮sation of the forest sector and the mobilisation of scientific forestry. It shows how new economic valorisations were imposed on the forest and led to its construction as a state-controlled resource, available for use and revenue-creation to support national economic development. It then scrutinises how forests are being transformed, along this commodification process, into more productive landscapes. As forests are increasingly recognised and managed as a national resource, they are drawn into wider administrative, scientific, and commercial networks. This chapter investigates the role of the state in the making of a national forest resource, and the expansion of state control over Kenyan forests through state forestry. It focuses on governmental perspectives and the forest transformations initiated by the government. Indeed, it is mostly based on archival sources which predominantly reflect the points of view of governmental agents. Thus, it chooses to follow the process of commodification of the forest as initiated by state visions and policies.[5]

The forest to be protected and improved: Colonial visions and the establishment of state forestry in Kenya

In the early years of British East Africa, the forests of the Protectorate were idealised by colonial observers as a promise of and precondition for the colony's prosperity. The first Commissioner of the Protectorate, Sir Charles Eliot, wrote enthusiastically about the commercial potential of Kenyan forests in 1905, describing 'vast forests of juniper and olive' and trees 'of fine growth,

---

4 In the references to archives used in this contribution: 'KNA' refers to the archives from the Kenya National Archive Nairobi, 'KNA(Nak)' to the archives from the Kenya National Archive Nakuru, 'BLO' to the archives from the Bodleian Library, 'KFS/ER' to the archives from the Kenya Forest Service office in Eldama Ravine, 'KFS/KAB' to the archives from the KFS office in Kabarnet, 'KFS/Narfs' to the archives from the Narasha Forest station, and 'KFS/Kabfs' to the archives from the Kabarnet forest station in Katimok Forest.

5 Despite the heavy impact of colonial forest policies, it should be noted that non-cooperation and resistances of local populations existed, challenged the governmental vision of the forest, and contributed to shaping the forests as well (this is however beyond the scope of this chapter).

and untouched' (Eliot 1905: 164) immediately available for exploitation. David Ernest Hutchins, former forest officer of the Indian and later Cape Colony forest services, and appointed as the head of the new Forest Department in Kenya in 1907, described in 1909 the potential of East African forests, and drew a close link between the aesthetic and the economic values of forests:

> The systematic conservation of the forests cannot be postponed further without losing the greater portion of the forests. We have a country of unsurpassed fertility ... The beauty and fertility of the East African highlands hinge alike on their forests. (Hutchins 1909: 81)

Hutchins identified two main threats to the forest. First, the local populations and their agricultural practices, which were seen as destructive for the environment (Hutchins 1909: 70); second, white settlers who were eager to secure lands for establishing their farms or private entrepreneurs seeking concessions (1909: 63). Thus, to fulfil their potential, forests needed first to be protected by being placed under the tutelage of the state. But they also needed to be 'improved'. The term 'improvement' applied to forests was used by Hutchins in his report (1909: 81), and repeatedly in other colonial reports. It usually described the restocking (densifying) of forests by replanting and taking care of the trees with the aim to increase their timber yields.[6] Forests in their 'primitive condition' were to be made 'productive'[7] and from their 'underdeveloped state' were to be 'brought to their highest yielding capacity'.[8]

The first steps of colonial forest management in Kenya were inspired and justified by these visions and initiated their materialisations. Like in other British colonies, the colonial government promoted the development of industries and commercial production from natural resources of the colonies (see Vehrs & Waziri on gum arabic production in Nigeria, this volume). The first licences for exploiting timber were granted early on in the new Protectorate. In the south of Baringo,[9] negotiations between the High Commissioner Sir Charles Eliot and private investors led in 1904 to a licence agreement leasing 64,000 acres of forest West of Eldama Ravine for timber exploitation, followed by

---

[6] Forest Department Annual reports 1923–1963, BLO RHO/753.14 r.26.
[7] Forest Department Annual Report, 1925: 30, BLO RHO/753.14 r.26.
[8] Forest Department Annual Report, 1926: 27, BLO RHO/753.14 r.26.
[9] Baringo was part of the Uganda Protectorate and transferred in 1902 to the East Africa Protectorate. Until 1933, Baringo district was subdivided in two parts: North Baringo, with headquarters in Kabarnet from 1914 and South Baringo, administered from Eldama Ravine. After 1933, the district government was stationed in Kabarnet only, until 1948, when a district officer was again stationed in Eldama Ravine (Anderson 2002).

another 64,000 acres in 1905 (Anderson 2002: 235–237). Endowed with a
generous exploitation licence, the so-called 'Grogan concession' (or 'Lingham
and Grogan concession' from the names of the leaseholders Mssrs. Grogan
and Lingham) became, as David Anderson writes, 'one of the largest and most
favourable land concessions made to Europeans in colonial Kenya' (Anderson
2002: 232). While the terms of the licence were finally fixed in 1916, lumbering
operations started in 1912 (Anderson 2002: 247), until the concession expiry in
1957. It allowed for the harvesting of indigenous timber and its commercialisation including export to European countries. Indigenous cedar, for example,
constituted a part of Kenyan timber exports and was notably exploited in the
Grogan concession. One of the aims for cedar exploitation was to develop
the pencil cedar trade for pencil production. Throughout the colonial time,
the United Kingdom remained an important destination for this product.[10]

On the other hand, the forest sector started being institutionalised. The
Ukamba Woods and Forest Regulations, proclaimed in 1897 by the Protectorate,
set aside the forests along the line of the Uganda Railway (Ofcansky 1984).
From these strips, the forest could be harvested and regenerated to ensure
a continuous fuelwood supply for the railway linking Mombasa and Lake
Victoria (Hutchins 1909: 70). In 1902, state control over the forests was
formalised with the creation of the governmental Forest Department and the
issuance of the East Africa Forestry Regulations. The latter provided the legal
basis for the creation of forest reserves and the regulation of their uses by
local residents. It instituted permits for grazing and going into the forest,
as well as for logging trees, and defined forest offences and their sanctions
(Ofcansky 1984).

Peluso and Vandergeest (2001) analysed the establishment of forest reserves
in colonial South East Asia as a key factor which fostered the creation of territorialised and state-controlled forest resources. Through such legal strategies
employed by the colonial government to assert its control, they argued that
forests were 'normalized as categories of both nature and state power' (Peluso
& Vandergeest 2001: 766). Inspired by other British colonies, especially India
and South Africa, the forest reserve played a key role in ensuring state control
over the forests of British East Africa and, by doing so, in materialising
the governmental vision of the forests in the administrative and ecological
landscape. Hutchins recommended the creation of further forest reserves in
British East Africa, based on his experience of the success of such measures in
the Cape Colony (Hutchins 1909: 67–68). The *Manual of Forestry* by William
M. Schlich (1922: 45–48) also shows that India was the first British colony to
implement 'systematic forestry' by gazetting governmental forests as reserves

---

[10] Forest Department Annual Reports 1923–1960, BLO RHO/753.14 r.26.

under the control of a Forest Department, and that such a model was exported across the entire British Empire including in South and East Africa.

The process of forest 'reservation' involved the demarcation and official gazettement as a 'forest reserve' of an area through proclamation in the national gazette. Once gazetted, the forest reserve fell under the management of the Forest Department. The process varied according to the status of the land where the forest was gazetted – on Crown land, all control of the forest was put in the hands of the Forest Department, while on 'native land', like in the colonial 'Native Reserves', some control remained with the local authority (e.g. the district) even though the Forest Department was often in charge of managing these forests.[11] After gazettement, access to and uses of the forest were regulated by the rules specified under the national forest legislation (for forests on Crown land) and/or by an additional specific set of regulations (for forests on native land). The gazettement of a forest reserve had substantial impacts on local populations, living inside or around the forest and depending on it for a variety of purposes (including as a supply of firewood, water, herbal medicine, a space for cultivating, grazing, and also for ceremonies). As shown by Bryant (1997) in the Burmese context and others (e.g. Peluso 1992; Guha 2000), colonial state domination historically and durably shaped forest uses and management (as well as local resistance to it). Also, in Kenya, although most forest utilisations were still allowed, some became subject to authorisation and supervision by the Forest Department.[12] The forest reserve and its management generally ignored local norms and rules regarding forest uses[13] and imposed governmental restrictions and control mechanisms. In Katimok and Lembus, during colonial time, some residents were allowed to stay, or tolerated there, but others had to leave. Forest reserves in Baringo were finally emptied from their inhabitants in the post-colonial era under the regime of Daniel arap Moi.[14] Other authors in this volume put forward the marginalisation of local communities through processes of commodification

[11] A policy regarding forests in Native Reserves was adopted in the early 1930s. Before that, there was no national legal framework for these.

[12] E.g. The Tugen (Kamasia) Native Reserve Forest Rules, 1949, KNA PC/NKU/3/7/1.

[13] Interviews with elders in Katimok and the Lembus area (2019) indicated that some forest uses, in particular the cutting of trees, traditionally required the permission of the community elders.

[14] 'Press-statement on squatters, illegal settlers and other illegal activities in parts of the Rift Valley forest area', Chief Conservator of Forests to all Provincial Forest Officers and all District Forest Officers, 3 October 1984, Forest Estates KFS/Kabfs/8/6. In Katimok, the last forest residents were evicted in 1988 (Interviews with community members in Katimok, 2019; personal archive of Katimok forest evictee).

of biodiversity (see the contributions of Wynberg, Lavelle, and Ndwandwe). In
Kenya, the creation of forest reserves also led to land dispossessions for local
inhabitants. Even though residents did not always comply, and partly resisted
and negotiated forest policies, the establishment of forest reserves and their
governmentally defined management had long-lasting consequences as it shifted
the focus from the forest as a place to live to the forest as a resource to use.

Creating a forest reserve followed a selective process. The criteria for
gazettement lay in the value that colonial administrators and experts recognised
in a forest area. Archival records show the gaze of colonial observers who
from the start of the 20th century had identified Baringo forests (especially
in the south) as valuable for their timber, which could be exploited, and for
their effect on water conservation and against soil erosion. In 1905 already,
Sir Charles Eliot identified the forests of the Mau, to the north of the Uganda
Railway, including areas in the south of current Baringo, as comprising trees
like cedar and podo, deemed valuable for commercial purposes and especially
export markets. He even alluded to the Grogan concession of that time in
negotiation as a promising source for export (Eliot 1905: 164). Hutchins (1909:
10–14 and 22–23) also identified areas of 'good' forest in the Mau and near
Eldama Ravine, discussing their value according to their tree composition and
timber volumes, and hinting at their beneficial effect on water conservation.

To protect and make use of these benefits, in 1912, large forest areas near
Eldama Ravine, including the Grogan concession, were gazetted as the Mount
Londiani Forest Reserve – a Crown Forest (on Crown land) under the control
of the Forest Department.[15] Further north in Baringo, along the Tugen Hills,
more forest areas were identified as valuable for their trees and their positive
effect on water and soil. The 'fine timber'[16] of these hills was already noticed in
the 1910s, and colonial reports indicated 'some valuable forest'[17] on the higher
parts containing cedar, podo, and olive trees. In the early 1930s, three forest
areas in the Tugen Hills, including Katimok, were identified to be urgently
gazetted. This was justified by their 'considerable floristic interest'[18] and their
importance 'climatically' to the Native Tugen Reserve. In addition, these
forests were 'the only source of timber and fuel for local requirements left
in the district'.[19] Finally, their gazettement was a matter of urgency, because
the colonial administrators perceived these forests as being threatened by

[15] Eldama Ravine District Officer to Provincial Commissioner of the Rift Valley
Province, 5 October 1961, KNA PC/NKU/3/7/1.

[16] Kabarnet sub-district Annual Report 1914–1915: 9, BLO Micr.Afr.515/ BAR/1.

[17] Kabarnet sub-district Annual Report 1915–1916: 11, BLO Micr.Afr.515/ BAR/1.

[18] Conservator of Forests to the Colonial Secretary, 24 June 1932, Forests and
Policy, KNA PC/NKU/2/13/2.

[19] Ibid.

local agricultural practices. They were described as 'the only remnants of a once extensive forest which formerly covered these hills'.[20] This narrative of a rampant deforestation was not an exception and other scholars have highlighted, in an African context, colonial discourses of environmental degradation and deforestation that legitimised the establishment of governmental control and the exclusion of local populations from natural resources (McCann 1997; Fairhead & Leach 1995, 1996; Leach & Mearns 1996). Fairhead and Leach (1996) in particular highlighted the colonial interpretations of the West African forest-savannah mosaic landscape as a sign of a dense tropical forest in degradation. Although, the authors show, these arguments relied on no solid evidence, they shaped colonial policies. Likewise, in the Tugen Hills, colonial narratives of deforestation, based on impressions rather than scientific evidence, justified the establishment of forest reserves, thereby paving the way to the creation of a natural resource under colonial control.

In 1933, Katimok, along with two other forests, was gazetted a 'Native Forest Reserve' (situated on native lands) under the control of the Baringo District Commissioner.[21] As further areas of the Tugen Hills were identified for gazettement in the 1940s, the main reasons put forward were environmental ones: first, the conservation of the soil, of great importance in the context of the steep Tugen Hills and their shallow soils, second, the positive effect of the forest on rainfall and on the preservation of the water catchment.[22] Elsewhere in Kenya, Tiffen *et al.* (1994: 213) have highlighted that afforestation was seen, from the 1920s, as a key governmental response to land degradation in Machakos. Colonial administrators justified forest reserves by their social and environmental benefits including the amelioration of the micro-climate, the prevention of soil erosion, the conservation of water springs and soil moisture, the creation of employment (in the timber industry), and the provision of timber and fuelwood (Tiffen *et al.* 1994: 216). Similarly, in the Tugen Hills, the reservation of these forests was seen as key to supporting the (agricultural) fertility of the hills, and urgent in the face of local practices deemed destructive.[23]

Thus, the establishment of a forest reserve was, in the first place, a normative statement about the value of the forest. This value, based on colonial perspectives, was indexed to the contribution that a forest area could make to the

---

[20] Ibid.

[21] Conservator of Forests to the Baringo District Commissioner, 10 December 1934, KNA PC/NKU/2/13/2.

[22] Assistant Conservator of Forests, 1941, Report on Forests in the Kamasia Hills, KNA PC/NKU/3/7/1.

[23] Ibid.

colony's development: either directly, by providing timber (or other forest products), or indirectly by maintaining water and soil resources (and so contributing to preventing food insecurity). The forest reserves drew the administrative contours of valuable forests from a governmental perspective: they demarcated and established which forests should be considered a resource and should be managed as such. Hence, they spread and imposed colonial values on the forest, and generalised a system of forest management on their basis.

While local practices were seen as a threat to the forest, on the other hand, governmental control was also justified to protect the forest resource from white settlers and private entrepreneurs, who were looked upon by the government as potential factors of a wasteful use of the forest resource.[24] Regarding the Grogan concession, for example, the administration deplored that the Forest Department had too little control over the Lembus Forest because of the licence terms,[25] and inefficient exploitation by the concession was criticised.[26]

Setting forests 'aside' in forest reserves constituted a first major forest conservation measure in the Protectorate. The forest reserve, seen as paramount for conservation, was also the condition to the improvement and productivity of the forests. Only by establishing state control over these areas, restraining access to them and regulating uses, could the optimisation of the forest utilisation unfold, i.e. the forests be made as useful as possible. Therefore, conservation measures emerged with and contributed to the construction of forests as an economic resource safeguarded by the state.

Such a project was not limited to governmental land, and state control was to reach beyond. Indeed, as in the case of Katimok, forest reserves could also be declared in 'Native Reserves', i.e. trust land conferred under the British rule to local authorities. From the early 1930s onwards, 'Native Forest Reserves', despite being under the jurisdiction of local authorities, were managed by the Forest Department and their uses and protection were regulated by a set of rules proclaimed with or following their gazettement. At the same time, their net revenues were credited to the local authority concerned (e.g. the

---

[24] E.g. R. S. Troup, 1922, Report on Forestry in Kenya Colony: 28–29, BLO RHO/753.14 s.1: Troup (Professor of Forestry in Oxford) deplores 'defective exploitation' by sawmills.

[25] Lembus Forest, by the District Officer of Eldama Ravine May 1962, Appendix C of the Lembus Land Use Committee report 1963, in Lembus Land Use Committee Report, KNA GO.3/2/80.

[26] E.g. R. S. Troup, 1922, Report on Forestry in Kenya Colony: 4, BLO RHO/753.14 s.1. See also Anderson (2002: 240).

district or location administration).[27] The statement of the forest advisor J. W. Nicholson in 1931 illustrates how important state control and management over the colony's forests was deemed:

> In Kenya it is inimical to the interests of the colony as a whole, and of the Native Reserves in particular, to permit of the utilization of climatically important forests other than under the provisions of a National Forest Policy, directed and supervised by the State ... Further in addition to the need for State control over forests of climatic importance the State or the Central Board, regarded as the 'guardian' of native tribes, ought to see that their forest assets are properly managed and developed. Whether the State or the Central Board is in control the executive authority must in both cases be the Kenya Forest Department as it alone is at present capable of managing important forest areas scientifically.[28]

'Proper' management by the state was to follow the lines of scientific forestry. Born in Prussia and Saxony in the second half of the 18th century (Scott 1998: 11), scientific forestry was the widespread model shared and circulated by the forest officers across the British Empire and into Kenya (also see for example Peluso 1992; Rajan 2006). Scientific knowledge and the acquisition of statistical data on the colony's forests developed in the forest reserves. In the early 1920s, the forest estate of the colony had not yet been precisely computed[29] and many of the forest areas under the Forest Department administration were still awaiting the description of their boundaries to be completed in order to be officially gazetted.[30] From the mid-1920s, the surveying and mapping of gazetted forests accelerated. By the early 1930s, two-thirds of the forest reserves had been mapped and all gazetted forests had been examined in detail. But, thorough surveying and tree enumerations had been done in only

[27] Native reserve forests. Statement of Policy, KNA PC/NKU/2/13/2. N.B.: Katimok is a special case: after its gazettement in 1933, it remained under the control of the Baringo District Commissioner, even though the Forest Department was in charge of inspecting forest management there and proposing protection measures. In 1945, the responsibility for the Tugen Hills forests including Katimok was transferred from the local level to the Forest Department (central level): Ag. Provincial Commissioner (Rift Valley Province) to the Chief Native commissioner 10th September 1932 KNA PC/NKU/2/13/; Baringo District Annual Report 1945 BLO Micr.Afr.515/PC/RVP 2/7/3.

[28] J. W. Nicholson, 1931, The Future of Forestry in Kenya: 13, BLO RHO/753.14 r.73.

[29] R. S. Troup, 1922, Report on Forestry in Kenya Colony: 3, BLO RHO/753.14 s.l.

[30] Ibid.: 11.

about 100 square miles of all gazetted areas.[31] More detailed surveys of the boundaries and the topography of the forest reserves were needed, including to support the development of their commercial exploitation.[32] After the Second World War, in 1947, aerial surveys were started, operated by the British Royal Air Force.[33] These continued in the 1950s, facilitating the documentation of more remote and inaccessible forests, and boosting the production of forest maps.[34] After independence in 1963, large forest surveys and inventories were further supported by international aid, including by the World Bank.[35] The knowledge gathered through such surveys allowed statistical descriptions of the forests to be developed.

According to Agrawal, forest statistics serve the representation of the forest as a valuable resource by describing the forest in terms of volume of timber and financial value. This was used as a basis for predicting their future perfor- mance (Agrawal 2005). Statistics facilitate the simplification of the complexity of a forest into summarisable, aggregable, comparable data, hence turning the forest into a more legible and manipulable object of management. Scientific forestry mobilises scientific principles to establish scientific forest planning, translating the forest into categories and standardised parameters that can be more easily grasped by the manager (Scott 1998). Through further methods of seeding, planting, and treatment of tree plantations, scientific forestry created the modern, uniform forests – also to be observed in the Kenyan forest reserves plantations – made up of lined-up rows of trees of (mostly) one species, all the same age, easy to count and measure, i.e. to document statistically, and to manage. As Scott points out, the logic of scientific forestry is very close to that of commercial exploitation, namely to 'deliver the greatest possible constant volume of wood'.[36] Scientific forestry contributed to ordering the forests in such a way that their productivity was optimised – by shaping their ecology and their organisation (e.g. monocultural lined-up plantations), and by defining management goals and practices to achieve them. Therefore, it produced forests fit for commercial objectives. Not only was the forest made into a manipulable management object, but the commercialisation of

[31] J. W. Nicholson, 1931, The Future of Forestry in Kenya: 29, BLO RHO/753.14 r.73/1931.

[32] Ibid.: 28–29.

[33] Forest Department Annual Report 1951: 7, BLO RHO/753.14 r.26.

[34] Forest Department Annual Reports for the years 1951, 1952, 1953, BLO RHO/753.14 r.26.

[35] Forest Department Annual Report 1966 (KNA Nairobi); and, for example, The World Bank, 1988, 'Kenya Forestry Subsector Review' www.worldbank.org

[36] Cited by Scott (1998: 14), from Lowood (1991: 338).

its trees was also facilitated: the forest was shaped in such a way as to render its commoditisation possible. As colonial forest officers strove to import and expand scientific forestry in Kenya, forest reserves were managed more and more 'systematically' through knowledge tools and practices designed to guarantee the optimisation of their yields. Thus, the forests were made increasingly 'commoditisable'.

Transforming forests: The construction of a resourceful landscape

The forests' composition and ecology were materially transformed by their role and management as an economic resource. The exploitation of indigenous forests altered the vegetation in its composition and structure. The Grogan concession in South Baringo was said to have depleted the Lembus Forest of its indigenous trees.[37] After the concession expired in 1957, the forest was described as consisting 'mainly of cut over cedar, podo and hardwood forest with bamboo in some of the high parts'.[38] Generally, exploited areas were replanted. In the first decades of the Protectorate, plantations started partly as a means to replace the timber cut for fuel wood provision to the Uganda railway, with attempts, as early as 1904, to replant artificially cut areas of the railway forests (Hutchins 1909: 70). To provide fuel wood, fast-growing species including eucalyptus trees (exotic) were already being planted in the 1900s.[39] As the exploitation of forest reserves was increasing in Kenya, the Forest Department had the mission to replenish, improve, and increase the forest resource through plantations. In the 1920s, this was the Department's most important task.[40] As a result, the forest landscape was progressively transformed by the creation of orderly plantations (monocultural or mixing two or three indigenous and/or exotic species), even aged and planted in line. Moreover, exotic tree species were increasingly planted, changing the very composition of forests.

---

[37] Working Plans Officer, Management Plan for the Lembus Forest Reserve, approved by the Chief Conservator of Forest in June 1969, KFS/ER KFS/BAR/10/2/6 Vol. I.

[38] Draft Lembus Forest Management Plan (1957): 2, Lembus Forest 'Dev.' Scheme, KNA(Nak) FV/7/7.

[39] Ofcansky (1987) shows that the first Conservator of Forests experimented with the introduction of exotic tree species (faster-growing than indigenous trees) for plantations. Hutchins (1909, 79) mentions that eucalyptus trees were planted in Londiani. The Forest Department Annual Report 1923: 6, BLO RHO/753.14 r.26, also shows that blue gum (eucalyptus) firewood from Kenyan plantations was supplied to the railway.

[40] Forest Department Annual Report, 1924, BLO RHO/753.14 r.26.

In South Baringo, in the Maji Mazuri Forest, situated just south of the Lembus Forest and west of Eldama Ravine, patches of plantations emerged to cover the harvested forest areas from the early 1920s. While these first plantations were constituted by indigenous species, chiefly red cedar and podo trees, exotic species progressively also started to be planted there.[41] From the 1920s across the whole Kenyan colony, exotic conifers such as cypress (mainly *Cupressus lusitanica*, native to Mexico and Central America, and *Cupressus macrocarpa*, native to California) and pines (mainly *Pinus patula*, native to the highlands of Mexico, and *Pinus radiata*, also native to Mexico and California) were planted for commercial purposes.[42] This was also the case in the Baringo forests, and especially those of South Baringo targeted as the most promising for exploitation. Exotic cypress trees (mostly *Cupressus lusitanica*) were planted in Maji Mazuri from the 1920s, and plantations of eucalyptus species were also created already in the early 1930s and the 1940s.[43]

Until the early 1940s, new plantations in Kenya were mostly dedicated to producing fuel wood and replenishing indigenous forests.[44] Yearly reports from the Forest Department indicate that, if we take into account fuel plantations which comprised mainly foreign eucalyptus species, the planting of exotic species exceeded indigenous ones from 1927 onwards. From 1942, exotic conifers (cypress, pines) were planted more than all other species together as their rapid growth rates allowed higher timber yields.[45] From 1946 until Kenya's independence, the proportion of exotic softwoods planted yearly – cypress and pine (especially *C. lusitanica* and *macrocarpa* and *P. radiata* and *patula*) – exceeded 74%, reaching 90% to 95% between 1958 and 1963.[46] In Maji Mazuri as well, exotic cypress plantations were more extensively planted in the 1940s and 1950s, as well as pine trees, which were more popular from the 1940s onwards.[47] In the Tugen Hills, plantations appeared later than in South Baringo and were much smaller. The first exotic plantations in the Katimok Forest date from 1950 and included cypress and eucalyptus trees.[48] After independence in 1963, the planting of exotic species in Kenya continued

[41] Map of the Maji Mazuri and Mt. Londiani forest reserves, 1960 KFS/Narfs.

[42] W. E. Hiley, P. J. Gill, & A. K. Constantine, 1950, An Economic Survey of Forestry in Kenya and Recommendations Regarding a Forest Commission: 1, BLO RHO/753.14 r.73.

[43] Map of the Maji Mazuri and Mt. Londiani forest reserves, 1960 KFS/Narfs.

[44] W. E. Hiley, P. J. Gill, & A. K. Constantine, 1950, An Economic Survey of Forestry in Kenya and Recommendations Regarding a Forest Commission: 13, BLO RHO/753.14 r.73.

[45] Ibid.: 1, 15, 34–35.

[46] Forest Department Reports from 1945 to 1963, BLO RHO/753.14 r.26.

[47] Map of the Maji Mazuri and Mt. Londiani forest reserves, 1960, KFS/Narfs.

[48] Compartment Register and Plantation Ledger, KFS/Kabfs7/12.

with the aim of boosting the forest industry,[49] and had the support of international donors including the World Bank.[50] In the forests of Baringo as well, district annual reports point out in the late 1980s and early 1990s that exotic species remain the most planted.[51] With the increasing share of exotic species, the forests of Kenya and of Baringo were physically modified into resourceful forests that could produce merchantable timber.

On the other hand, conservation measures also triggered further transformations of the forest. In the Tugen Hills for example, cultivated shambas and bushy slopes were the targets of reforestation efforts from the late 1930s and in the 1940s.[52] Furthermore, with the creation of forest reserves, legal grounds for evictions and restrictions of forest uses were provided, legitimised by conservation purposes. In the Lembus Forest under the Grogan concession, native rights were recognised and defined by Governor Coryndon in 1923 and incorporated into the Lembus Forest Reserve Rules proclaimed in 1924 under the forest ordinance.[53] They entailed eleven rights, including the rights to construct huts, to graze animals, and to cultivate and gather forest products like firewood (Anderson 2002: 247). However, native rights were neglected by the administration and the Forest Department, which was already struggling to carry out management with the presence of the concession and its advantageous exploitation licence. In November 1927, Bailward, the District Officer at Eldama Ravine, and Rammel, the forester at Londiani, agreed on confining rights holders to specific areas to keep them away from forest zones important for conservation, although this directly contravened the Coryndon definition of native rights. This agreement remained the rule until 1938, when local resistance awoke and challenged the forest status quo increasingly (Anderson 2002: 245–266). In the Katimok Forest, evidence suggests that people found living inside the forest were asked to leave or were compelled to get permanent or temporary permits for cultivating within the forest reserve.[54] In Native Forest Reserves such as Katimok and the other forest reserves of the Tugen Hills, specific rules were proclaimed to regulate forest uses and subject them

---

[49] Forest Department Annual Reports from 1964 to 1972. KNA; Kenyatta Day Celebrations, Arrangements, Articles, etc. 1966–1976, KNA BA/1/80; Director of Forestry to Head of the Forest Plantation Division, 15 December 1989, Planting Programme KFS/Narfs/5/2.

[50] Forest Department Annual Report 1969, KNA.

[51] Baringo District Annual Reports 1988, 1990, KNA.

[52] Forest Policy, KNA PC/RVP.6A/13/3.

[53] Lembus Forest Excisions, KNA BA/6/72; Lembus Forest Scheme General Correspondence, KNA DO/ER/2/14/6.

[54] Handing-over Report, Kabarnet Division, 1959 BLO Micr.Afr.517/ BAR/9; author interviews (semi-structured) with descendants of forest evictees, Katimok, 2019.

to the scrutiny of forest officers. Even though these rules still allowed many forest products to be used, they set a framework: they defined what pertained to the sustainable forest uses and practices allowed by the Forest Department and they established the supervision and control by forest officers. More precisely, the Tugen (Kamasia) Native Reserve Forest Rules proclaimed in 1949 allowed 'any African of the Baringo District' to cut indigenous trees for his own use without charge but this applied only for certain tree species and with a written permission by a forest or district officer. Species forbidden to cut were listed on decision of the Conservator of Forests, after consultation with the Baringo Local Native Council and with the consent of the Rift Valley Provincial Commissioner. Written permission was required to graze cattle, and building a hut was only permissible for 'approved forest cultivators'. Burning in the forest was not allowed except under 'direct supervision' of an officer. However, collection of certain forest products (e.g. dead wood for firewood, dead trees for their barks and making beehives, lianas, fruits), taking animals through the forest and to watering points on approved tracks, grazing sheep, and holding ceremonies were exempt of permit or charge.[55]

As local uses and access to the forest became regulated, the management validated by the Forest Department could take up more space. Management practices and forest uses fitting scientific and commercial forestry were legitimised. Ways of dealing with the forest as a resource with economic importance were to supersede or at least control local ways of interacting with the forest. Moreover, the state control was made visible in the landscape through the demarcation and regular cleaning of forest reserve boundaries. Indeed, clear and distinct forest delimitations were paramount to show, legitimise, and impose the state power over the reserve. As the Assistant Conservator of Forest in Londiani argued about the Tugen Hills forests in 1937: 'It is almost impossible to establish any real control unless the areas to be protected are clearly demarcated'. And a few paragraphs later:

> before anything worthwhile can be done it is practically essential firstly to have the legal right to punish trespassers and secondly to make certain that culprits will not be able to give the excuse that they did not know that they were trespassing.[56]

Through demarcated boundaries, and also through orderly uniform plantations, the forest reserves produced, in Scott's words, 'optics of power' engrained in the landscape (Scott 1998: 253). They materialised state control over the

---

[55] The Tugen (Kamasia) Native Reserve Forest Rules, 1949, KNA PC/NKU/3/7/1.
[56] Assistant Conservator of Forests (Londiani) to Baringo District Commissioner, 6 February 1937 KNA PC/KNU/3/7/1.

forest and made it tangible in the everyday life of local communities not only through the concrete restrictions of access to and uses of the forest, but also visibly, in the landscape. The latter did not play a lesser role; in fact, it impacted the reality experienced by the local residents. Forest reserves shaped what the viewers could perceive of the forest. As Jasanoff puts it, 'vision still remains the great naturalizer. What we "see" in familiar surroundings looks right, epistemically as well as normatively' (Jasanoff 2015: 14). In our case, forest reserves imposed visually a new forest as the norm: a forest controlled by the state and managed to serve governmentally defined purposes.

Thus, there was a confiscation of the forest by the state, made perceptible in the landscape and for the local populations. The forests were subjected to tighter control and modified physically in their composition, their uses and their demarcation. This process transformed them into a resource available to governmental objectives before local ones. By becoming 'landscapes of control' (Scott 1998: 218), forests also became landscapes of commodity production.

Delocalised and centralised forests: Towards a national resource

With forests being put into reserves and under scientific management, their governance at a centralised national level became possible. From the first steps establishing the forest sector in Kenya, and increasingly as more and more forests were being placed under state control, a unified forest-management regime started to penetrate all regions of the country, guided and supervised centrally by the head of the Department in Nairobi.

Across the whole country, the implementation of scientific forestry in forest reserves also facilitated the development of knowledge about the forests that rendered possible their management from afar. In the context of the Angolan forests, the anthropologist Joao Afonso Baptista shows that the production of scientific representations of the forest, such as statistical data, maps or (later) satellite images, is key to informing and legitimising forest governance from a distance. By producing such intermediaries, scientific knowledge disqualifies local perspectives and constitutes a reference that provides for taking decisions on forest management from afar (Baptista 2018). It allows the forest to be read, analysed, and managed without being directly experienced. In the Kenyan forest reserves, the production of statistics summing up the forests' characteristics, as well as aerial photographs and maps, made such management at a distance possible. It provided an overview of the forest within the boundaries of the forest reserve and, in so doing, the forest to be captured in one glance. Through the production of scientific knowledge about forest reserves, a 'synoptic view' (Scott 1998: 81) of the forest was generated. Based on the scientific representations that summarised and encompassed the

Table 8.1. Progress in regeneration and afforestation, 1962, table from the Kenya Forest Department Annual Report 1962.

Standard Form VI									Acres			
Division	Regeneration of Exploited Forest				Area of Completed Improvement				Area of Plantations			
	Area Under Improvement											
	On 31 Dec., 1961	Added during year	Excluded during year	On 31 Dec. 1962	On 31 Dec., 1961	Added during year	Excluded during year	On 31 Dec. 1962	On 31 Dec., 1961	Added during year	Excluded during year	On 31 Dec. 1962
Nairobi	1,126	-	1,120	6	1,350	-	-	1,350	32,391	1,954	1,811	32,534
Londiani	18	-	-	18	-	-	-	-	36,763	2,786	-	39,549
Elburgon	-	-	-	-	-	-	-	-	35,516	1,793	296	37,013
Eldoret	-	-	-	-	-	-	-	-	22,391	2,265	219	24,437
Nyeri	2,284	82	367	1,999	1,732	-	631	1,101	23,243	2,005	-	25,248
Thomson's Falls	20	31	-	51	-	-	-	-	7,404	727	-	8,131

Coast	970	-	24	946	77	77	-	1,999	44	34	2,009
Southern	-	-	-	-	-	-	-	10,192	829	53	10,968
Nyanza	1,241	2	-	1,243	31	31	-	6,791	630	-	7,421
Fort Hall/Embu	215	-	215	-	-	-	-	5,050	-	5,050	-
Kitale	301	-	-	301	209	-	209	10,336	842	-	11,178
TOTAL	6,175	115	1,726	4,564	3,399	739	2,660	192,076	13,875	7,463	198,488

(Source: BLO RHO/753.14 r.26)

forest as a whole, managers and their hierarchical superiors could plan and monitor its management from their offices.

Through the forest reserve device, and from the first reservation in the early 20th century, forests were drawn into a new administrative organisation and within the sphere of scientific forestry. In this way, forests could be managed independently from their local settings. Within the forest reserve, a national forest-management strategy, along with shared ways of knowing and managing the forest, were implemented, while ignoring local practices of managing the forest. As a result, forests from the whole country, within forest reserves, became comparable units of management. Their description by statistical data expressed in a unified measuring system with commensurable parameters allowed for the comparison of the characteristics of different forests and the adjustment of the management accordingly.

Not only did the forests become comparable, but they could also be aggregated and so managed as one forest estate at the national level. For each year, the annual reports of the Kenya Forest Department, in colonial times and after independence, advertised the surface of the total land under forest reserves, and discussed strategies and measures of silvicultural, exploitation, conservation, and research activities, in various forest areas across the country, supervised and guided at the national level.[57] It illustrates how, from isolated forest areas aggregated into one forest estate, a unified national forest resource emerged. Reservation allowed forests to be delocalised, extracting them from their local contexts to draw them into one centralised system of knowledge and management at the national level.

Such delocalisation and centralisation also served the harnessing of the forests' benefits at regional or national scale so that they would not only be enjoyed by the surrounding communities but serve a wider scope. Within a forest reserve, royalties were to be collected on the timber harvested by private actors. Permits could be required for certain forest products uses and collection and could also include a fee. The revenues generated by the licences and royalties were then credited to the Forest Department for reserves on governmental land, or to the local authority (e.g. the district) for reserves on trust land (including native land during the colonial time).[58] Through the application of such taxes, benefits from the forest were to be enlarged beyond the immediate local uses of forest products. Taxes produced wider benefits that could be shared beyond the vicinity of the forest, at the district level, for example, or even, in governmental forest reserves, over the whole nation. On

[57] Forest Department Annual Reports, BLO RHO/753.14 r.26; and KNA.

[58] This system of licences and royalties is still in place today: in governmental forests (like Katimok and Narasha), the revenues from forests accrue to KFS.

the other hand, forest reserves allowed the implementation of conservation measures to protect the forest and the soil and water resources it preserves. In so doing, the regional benefits of forest for water catchment and for soil conservation were being maintained, and not only the localised benefits from the extraction of forest products. On the reservation of forests within Native Reserves, Nicholson argued in his report of 1931 that gazetting 'climatically important' forests and placing them under governmental control was 'in the interests of the general community'.[59] Along the same lines, the policy on forests in Native Reserves, approved early 1930s, recommended:

> It would be best as a general policy to charge for all forest produce taken from or grazing allowed within the forest boundary. Only in this way is the benefit of the forest spread over the whole tribe and not merely confined to those living in the vicinity of the forest.[60]

In Baringo, the reservation of the Katimok Forest was legitimised by the necessity to preserve the soil of the steep Tugen Hills and the water resources that originated there, and served the wider region, especially the lowlands around the Lake Baringo.[61] Revenues from Katimok, however, were very limited due to its small production capacities and the absence of fees required for minor forest products used locally.[62] But, from 1955, some small profit started to accrue from timber royalties to the Baringo African District Council,[63] hence benefiting the whole district. The regional role of the forest in Lembus with regard to soil and water resources was also recognised and put forward early on by the Forest Department. In the 1930s, the presence of local rights holders and the overstocking of the forest with their livestock triggered the anxiety of the colonial officers, who feared the impact of forest degradation on the rehabilitation of the Baringo lowlands, and especially so as local resistance started to get stronger from 1938 onwards (Anderson 2002: 255). After the expiry of the Grogan concession in 1957, the Lembus Forest was about to be placed under the jurisdiction of the Baringo African District

---

[59] J. W. Nicholson, 1931, The Future of Forestry in Kenya: 21, BLO RHO/753.14 r.73.

[60] Native Reserve Forests. Statement of Policy, KNA PC/NKU/2/13/2.

[61] Conservator of Forests to the Colonial Secretary, 24 June 1932. KNA PC/NKU/2/13/2; Baringo District Agricultural Officer, 1961, District – Gazetteer Baringo (Second Edition), in Baringo District Gazetteer, KNA DO/ER/2/2/16.

[62] Forester (Kabarnet) to the Chairman ADC Baringo, 17 April 1961 Katimok Forest Excisions, KNA(Nak) ZT/3/1: the forester points out that, in Katimok, it has been custom to maintain the collection of minor forest products free of charge.

[63] Baringo District Annual Report 1955 BLO Micr.Afr.515/BAR/5.

Council. A condition of this transfer however was that the revenues of this 'productive'[64] forest were to be channelled through the district to the rehabilitation scheme of the catchment area of the Perkerra river, situated near the Lembus Forest.[65] Finally, in 1964, right after independence, both Lembus and Katimok were declared Central Forests, so that the revenues they produced were to be centralised at the national level.

Through the forest reserves and their insertion into a wider, unified, and centralised administrative and scientific system, the forests were pooled across the whole national territory to form one national resource, to the benefit of the nation – and not only to the local inhabitants whose access in turn became regulated.[66]

The construction of forests as one national resource became more visible from the mid-1940s onwards. With the outbreak of the Second World War, Kenyan forests contributed to the war effort and were heavily exploited to provide timber for military purposes.[67] By the end of the world conflict, the forest estate was recognised officially for the first time by the government in its Development Report as a 'national asset' and 'of first-class economic value to the country'.[68] In 1957, the first national forest policy was proclaimed. Again, it described the Kenyan forest estate as

> one of the country's most important national assets in its protective aspect of conservation of climate, water and soil; as the source of supply of forest produce for all uses by the inhabitants of Kenya; and as a revenue earner of high potential.[69]

It also recognised 'the great value and importance both actual and potential of the Forest Estate in the economy of Kenya'.[70] While the forest was formally framed as an economic resource of national importance, large-scale

---

[64] As labelled in the Baringo African District Council Forest Programme (final draft), 1960, KNA PC/NKU/3/7/1.

[65] Draft Lembus Forest Management Plan (1957), KNA(Nak) FV/7/7.

[66] Therefore, colonial state forestry also contributed to state making (as pointed out by Peluso & Vandergeest 2001) and the construction of a nation.

[67] Forest Department, 1947, Empire Forests and the War, BLO RHO/753.14 s.40. The report mentions that the volume of timber extracted from forest reserves increased from 1,161,000 cubic feet on average between 1934 and 1938 to a peak of 6,284,000 cubic feet in 1944 (6.1).

[68] Quote from the Development Report in Forest Department Report 1945–1947: 3, BLO RHO/753.14 r.26.

[69] Colony and Protectorate of Kenya, White Paper No. 85 of 1957, A Forest Policy for Kenya: 1, BLO RHO/753.14/r.73.

[70] Ibid.: 2.

development plans in the 1950s contributed to the concretisation of this role. The Supplementary Forest Development Plan, started in 1956,[71] was described in 1955 by the Forest Department itself as 'one of the biggest development plans ever to be undertaken by the Department'.[72] It entailed a large-scale reforestation programme throughout the colony and aimed at developing the forest sector through a short-term investment in the planting of fast-growing exotic softwood for 'quick returns' and 'on a profit-making basis'.[73] The Swynnerton plan, launched in 1954, and targeting the development of rural areas, also included forest conservation measures as a means to support land rehabilitation.[74] Baringo in particular was to benefit from priority funds from the African Land Development organisation (ALDEV) to rehabilitate the Perkerra Catchment and the Solai border south of the district.[75] Under this plan, the protection of the forests of the Perkerra Catchment was to be carried out, and this led to reforestation measures[76] and the demarcation of 19,741 acres of forest to be added to the gazetted estate.[77] Thus, through these schemes, forests were further put to use as contributions to the development of the country.

After independence, the forests of Kenya continued to be considered an important national asset, as reiterated (with the same formulation) in the new national forest policy proclaimed in 1968, which, albeit adapted to the new independent status of Kenya, remained close to that of 1957.[78] In the 1960s, after independence, the forest sector had a role to play in the ambition to scale up the modernisation and development of the newly independent country. The national Development Plan circulated among all forest officers in 1966 stated that 'Kenya's forests are valuable natural resources' and that 'without forests to protect its catchment areas, much of Kenya's land would be less valuable and a considerable potential for economic development would be lost'.[79] The year 1964 was seen as a turning point in the modernisation of the

---

[71] Forest Department Report, 1955–1957, BLO RHO/753.14 r.26.

[72] Forest Department Report, 1954–1955: 1, BLO RHO/753.14 r.26.

[73] Ibid.

[74] Forest Department Annual Report, June 1954–June 1955, BLO RHO/753.14 r.26.

[75] Baringo District Agricultural Officer, 1961, District – Gazetteer Baringo (Second Edition), KNA DO/ER/2/2/16.

[76] Forest Department Annual Report, 1958, BLO RHO/753.14 r.26.

[77] Forest Department Annual Reports, 1959 and 1961, BLO RHO/753.14 r.26.

[78] Republic of Kenya, Sessional Paper No. 1 of 1968, A Forest Policy for Kenya', in Forest Act Ordinances Rules & Laws, KFS/Kabfs/9/1.

[79] Excerpt from the Development Plan, 'B – Forests': 1, forwarded by the Chief Conservator of Forests to all Conservators, 19 October 1966, *Working plans and management plan, Baringo district* KFS/Kabfs/8/3.

forest industry into a sector that could yield substantially higher returns than before. Further planting of exotic softwoods for rapid economic gain, the modernisation and development of the timber industry, and the boosting of timber exports were planned and implemented from the late 1960s to scale up the forest sector and support the country's economic development.[80] By then, the Kenyan forests had become a national economic resource.

Conclusion

With the creation of the forest sector under the colonial rule, and the institutionalisation of forest policies and management, the forests of Kenya were progressively being produced as an economic resource. Conservation measures, and in particular the forest reserve as a management tool, emerged in the context of colonial visions, and directly contributed to the construction of the forest as a resource to be protected and improved to foster economic development. The model of scientific forestry together with the legal and administrative background provided by forest regulations – especially within forest reserves – allowed forests to be made manageable from afar and available and beneficial at a wider national level, independently from their local settings. Hence, it contributed to the transformation of forests not only into an economic resource but also a national one. Along the way, the forest landscape transformed ecologically and visually. The commodification of the forest led to the emergence of more controlled forests, that could no longer be used or lived in freely, and which were also made more productive.

As forests were drawn into wider administrative, political, and economic networks, they also became accessible to new stakeholders and subjected to multiplying agendas. The Katimok forest for example became increasingly exploited by Tugen pitsawyers from the late 1940s[81] and after independence, and by local sawmills which developed from the 1970s.[82] After the expiry of the Grogan concession, in Lembus, local pitsawyers also started working

---

[80] Ibid.

[81] Katimok Sawmillers, KFS/Kabfs/2/12; Baringo District Annual Reports, BLO Micr.Afr.515/BAR/5; interview with an elder from Katimok, 24 April 2019.

[82] Katimok Sawmillers, KFS/Kabfs/2/12; Annual reports of the Baringo Division, 1973 and 1980, in District Forest Officers Annual Reports & Correspondence, KFS/Kabfs/10/2; Baringo District Annual Report 1976, KNA. See also KFS/Kabfs/2/12, and Annual Report Kabarnet, KFS/KAB/18/1/10; Kabarnet Forest Station Annual Reports, 1979–1999, KFS/KAB/18/1/10.

there from 1960,[83] while other large sawmills continued to exploit the forest heavily. On the other hand, after independence, and especially under the era of President Daniel arap Moi (1978–2002), the forest estate under state control was used as a patronage resource by the governmental elite to buy political support (Klopp 2000, 2012; Ongugo & Njuguna 2004; Njeru 2010; Boone 2012; Standing & Gachanja 2014). In addition, in Katimok and in Lembus, by the end of the colonial period, forest dwellers agitated for the recognition of their rights. In Katimok for example, local dwellers resisted the plan by the colonial government and then the post-colonial government to relocate them out of the forest and claimed to hold the rights to stay or be compensated.[84] To date, claims are ongoing, and former Katimok forest dwellers request land compensations from the government for forest evictions during the colonial time and the Moi era in the 1980s. Therefore, as forests became natural and national resources, they were also disputed resources that different stakeholders seek to appropriate – for economic business and as a political land resource.

With the development of participatory forest management in Kenya, forests will face further changes. The Forest Act in 2005 provided for the creation of community forest associations (CFAs) to encourage local participation to forest management and benefit sharing. While a positive impact of CFAs on the political empowerment of forest communities is not conclusive yet (Mogoi *et al.* 2012; Chomba *et al.* 2015; Thygesen *et al.* 2016; Mutune *et al.* 2017) these new institutions are still in the process of installation and consolidation. In other contexts, contributions in this volume highlight the challenge of benefit sharing and involvement of local populations in natural resource management and commercialisation, putting forward enduring inequalities and power relations to the disadvantage of local communities (see Wynberg, Lavelle, Lenhart, this volume). On the other hand, Mosimane *et al.* highlight that community-based conservation and commodification of the 'wild' have led to the strengthening of the position of local authorities in Namibia. How participatory approaches might reshuffle the ways in which forests are interacted with and used and managed as resources in Kenya therefore remains to be further investigated.

---

[83] Baringo District Commissioner to the District Officer of South Baringo, 22 February 1960, Lembus Forest, KNA(Nak) EU/4/3.

[84] KNA PC/NKU/3/7/1.

Bibliography

Agrawal, A. (2005). *Environmentality: Technologies of Government and Political Subjects* (Durham NC: Duke University Press).

Anderson, D. (2002). *Eroding the Commons. The Politics of Ecology in Baringo, Kenya, 1890s-1963* (Oxford: James Currey).

Baptista, J. A. (2018). 'Eco(il)logical knowledge', *Environmental Humanities*, 10(2), 397–420.

Boone, C. (2012). 'Land conflict and distributive politics in Kenya', *African Studies Review*, 55(1), 75–103.

Bryant, R. L. (1997). *The Political Ecology of Forestry in Burma, 1824–1994* (Honolulu: University of Hawaii Press).

Chomba, S. W., Nathan, I., Minang, P. A., & Sinclair, F. (2015). 'Illusions of empowerment? Questioning policy and practice of community forestry in Kenya', *Ecology & Society*, 20(3).

Eliot, C. (1905). *The East Africa Protectorate* (London: E. Arnold).

Fairhead, J. & Leach, M. (1995). 'False forest history, complicit social analysis: Rethinking some West African environmental narratives', *World Development*, 23(6), 1023–1035.

Fairhead, J. & Leach, M. (1996). *Misreading the African Landscape: Society and Ecology in a Forest-Savanna Mosaic* (Cambridge: Cambridge University Press).

FAO – Food and Agriculture Organization of the United Nations (2020). 'Global Forest Resources Assessment 2020, Main Report' (Rome: FAO). Available at: www.fao.org/3/ca9825en/ca9825en.pdf [Accessed 18 January 2023].

FAO – Food and Agriculture Organization of the United Nations & United Nations Environment Programme (UNEP) (2020). 'State of the World's Forests 2020: Forestry, Biodiversity and People' (Rome: FAO). Available at: www.fao.org/3/ca8642en/ca8642en.pdf [Accessed 31 January 2022].

Guha, R. (2000). *The Unquiet Woods: Ecological Change and Peasant Resistance in the Himalaya* (Berkeley; Los Angeles: University of California Press).

Hutchins, D. E. (1909). *Report on the Forests of British East Africa* (London: Darling & Son).

IUCN (2020). 'Annual Report 2019' (Gland: IUCN). Available at: https://portals.iucn.org/library/node/49096 [Accessed 31 January 2022].

Jasanoff, S. (2015). 'Future imperfect: Science, technology, and the imaginations of modernity', in: S. Jasanoff & S.-H. Kim (eds), *Dreamscapes of Modernity: Sociotechnical Imaginaries and the Fabrication of Power* (Chicago IL; London: The University of Chicago Press), 1–33.

Klopp, J. M. (2000). 'Pilfering the public: The problem of land grabbing in contemporary Kenya', *Africa Today*, 47(1), 7–26.

Klopp, J. M. (2012). 'Deforestation and democratization: Patronage, politics and forests in Kenya', *Journal of Eastern African Studies*, 6(2), 351–370.

Kopnina, H. (2017). 'Commodification of natural resources and forest ecosystem services: Examining implications for forest protection', *Environmental Conservation*, 44(1), 24–33.

Leach, M. & Mearns, R. (eds) (1996). *The Lie of the Land: Challenging Received wisdom on the African Environment* (London: IAI/James Currey).

Lowood, H. E. (1991) 'The calculating forester: Quantification, cameral science, and the emergence of scientific forestry management in Germany'. In Tore Fragsmyir, J. L. Heilbron, and Robin E. Rider (eds), *The Quantifying Spirit in the Eighteenth Century* (Berkeley: University of California Press), 315–342.

McCann, J. C. (1997). 'The plow and the forest: Narratives of deforestation in Ethiopia, 1840–1992', *Environmental History*, 2(2), 138–159.

Ministry of Environment and Natural Resources (MENR) (2016). 'National Forest Programme 2016–2030' (Nairobi: MENR). Available at: http://apps.rcmrd.org/ ofesa/images/ofesa/kenya/National_Forest_Programme_2016_to_2013.pdf [Accessed 31 January 2022].

Mogoi, J., Ongugo, P., Obonyo, E., Oeba, V., & Mwangi, E. (2012). 'Communities, property rights and forest decentralisation in Kenya: Early lessons from participatory forestry management', *Conservation & Society*, 10(2), 182–194.

Muller, E. U., Kushlin, A. V., Linhares-Juvenal, T., Muchoney, D., Wertz-Kanounnikoff, S., & Henderson-Howat, D. (2018). 'The State of the World's Forests, 2018. Forest Pathways to Sustainable Development' (Rome: FAO). Available at: www.fao.org/3/ca0188en/ca0188en.pdf [Accessed 31 January 2022].

Mutune, J. M., Hansen, C. P., Wahome, R. G., & Mungai, D. N. (2017). 'What rights and benefits? The implementation of participatory forest management in Kenya: The case of Eastern Mau Forest Reserve', *Journal of Sustainable Forestry*, 36(3), 230–249.

Njeru, J. (2010). '"Defying"democratization and environmental protection in Kenya: The case of Karura Forest reserve in Nairobi', *Political Geography*, 29(6), 333–342.

Ofcansky, T. P. (1984). 'Kenya forestry under British colonial administration, 1895–1963', *Journal of Forest History*, 28(3), 136–143.

Ongugo, P. O. & Njuguna, J. W. (eds) (2004). 'Effects of Decentralization Policies on Forest Management: Experience from Seven Forests in Kenya'. Oaxaca: 10th Biennial Conference of the IASCP, 9–13 August 2004.

Peluso, N. L. (1992). *Rich Forests, Poor People: Resource Control and Resistance in Java* (Berkeley: University of California Press).

Peluso, N. L. & Vandergeest, P. (2001). 'Genealogies of the political forest and customary rights in Indonesia, Malaysia, and Thailand', *The Journal of Asian Studies*, 60(3), 761–812.

Rajan, S. R. (2006). *Modernizing Nature: Forestry and Imperial Eco-Development 1800–1950* (Oxford: Oxford University Press).

Republic of Kenya (2016). The Forest Conservation and Management Act, 2016, Kenya Gazette Supplement No. 155, 7 September 2016.

Schlich, W. M. (1922). *Manual of Forestry*, Volume 1, Fourth edn (London: Bradbury, Agnew, & Co.).

Scott, J. C. (2020 [1998]). *Seeing like a State. How Certain Schemes to Improve the Human Condition have Failed* (New Haven CT: Yale University Press – Veritas).

Standing, A. & Gachanja, M. (2014). 'The political economy of REDD+ in Kenya: Identifying and responding to corruption challenges', U4 Anti-Corruption

Resource Centre, No. 3). Available at: www.u4.no/publications/the-political-economy-of-redd-in-kenya-identifying-and-responding-to-corruption-challenges.pdf [Accessed 31 January 2022].

Sunderlin, W. D., Angelsen, A., Belcher, B., Burgers, P., Nasi, R., Santoso, L., & Wunder, S. (2005). 'Livelihoods, forests, and conservation in developing countries: An overview', *World Development*, 33(9), 1383–1402.

Thygesen, S. H., Løber, T., Skensved, E. M., & Hansen, C. P. (2016). 'Implementation of participatory forest management in Kenya: A case study of Karima Forest', *International Forestry Review*, 18(3), 357–368.

Tiffen, M., Mortimore, M., & Gichuki, F. (1994). *More People, Less Erosion: Environmental Recovery in Kenya* (Chichester: John Wiley & Sons).

World Bank (2004). 'Sustaining forests: A development strategy' (Washington DC: World Bank). Available at: https://documents.worldbank.org/en/publication/documents-reports/documentdetail/424531468781760578/sustaining-forests-a-development-strategy [Accessed 31 January 2022].

9

Commodifying East Africa's Sandalwood: Organised crime and community participation in transnational smuggling of endangered species

ERIC MUTISYA KIOKO AND MICHAEL MUGO KINYANJUI

Introduction

The sandalwood tree is a high-value plant used globally in the manufacture of perfumes, cosmetics, and pharmaceuticals. Indian sandalwood (*Santalum album*) and Australian sandalwood (*Santalum spicatum*) dominate the world market. East Africa's sandalwood (*Osyris lanceolate*) is a recent inclusion in the global value chain. It occurs naturally and contributes to the biodiversity in some protected areas including Chyulu Hills and Tsavo national parks in Kenya, the Arusha region in Tanzania, and Kidepo region in Karamoja, Uganda (Ochanda 2009). It is also abundant in community-based conservation areas (locally named conservancies) across the Rift Valley. Here, local communities have historically applied traditional norms and rules to govern access to and use of these shared resources following the Ostromian model (Ostrom 1990).

East Africa's sandalwood, just like other resources in shared-resource systems, has specific cultural value linked to the experiences of people in their environment. In the last decade, however, the tree has been subjected to commodification and massive commercial exploitation. Commercial extraction of the precious wood started around the early 2000s, mainly targeting protected areas in Kenya (Chyulu and Tsavo national parks) and Tanzania's Arusha region. From 2004, sandalwood from Kenya was smuggled into Tanzania before shipping it to Asian markets (Ochanda 2009). In 2005, Tanzania banned the exportation of unprocessed sandalwood trees after the state declared the tree endangered following enormous commercial exploitation.

From around 2006, the rush for the wood quickly spread to the community-held lands in Kenya's Baringo, Samburu, Laikipia, Taita, Kajiado, Narok, and

Isiolo counties, among other areas across the country.[1] The scale of destruction that followed sandalwood extraction in Kenya prompted a presidential ban on its trade in February 2007 through a gazette notice. However, the ban only intensified illicit trade in sandalwood rather than stopping it. Taking advantage of Uganda's unregulated extraction and commercial exploitation of sandalwood, a leading Indian sandalwood processing company migrated its operations from Tanzania to Tororo. Its operations in Tororo lead to extensive logging of sandalwood from the semi-arid districts of Moroto, Nakapiripiti, and Kotido in the Karamoja region. Tororo became the nerve centre of sandalwood laundering, thereby legitimising smuggling activities, especially from Kenya. The period between 2015 and 2017 recorded the highest amount of sandalwood extraction in both Kenya and Uganda, but smuggling is still ongoing, and the value chain has become more resilient.

How is the commodification and commercial exploitation of East Africa's sandalwood organised and executed? Studies on environmental crimes in East Africa have almost exclusively focused on wildlife poaching and the illicit ivory trade (Coutu *et al.* 2016; Hakansson 2004; Thorbahn 1981; Beachey 1967; Titeca 2019; Weru 2016, Harrison *et al.* 2015). Forest crimes only receive limited attendance, with most literature and crime reports focusing on illegal timber logging (Nellemann & INTERPOL 2012; Müller & Mburu 2009; Bussmann 1996). Work on illicit trade in sandalwood and other high-value plants is almost non-existent, except for some few worthy efforts (e.g. Bunei 2017; Ochanda 2009). Security and crime reports only give a general picture of the criminal enterprise devoid of empirical analyses of the organisation and execution of the enterprise (e.g. Kamweti *et al.* 2009).

This chapter therefore attempts to engage with this research gap. Shortage of sandalwood from the world's leading sources, as well as the preference for naturally occurring sandalwood, are analysed to understand consequent commodification in East Africa. The activities, nature, and structure of an organised criminal group dealing in sandalwood and the participation of state and non-state actors are assessed to unpack the complexity of the transnational network. The drivers of commodification and commercial exploitation of East Africa's sandalwood give a broad picture of the institutional and social system within which such activities thrive.

The chapter is organised as follows. First, we set out a brief conceptual framework linking the commodification of natural resources to organised crime and the transformation of local commons. We then describe the study area and the methodology used. Thereafter, we describe the actors and their

---

[1] https://eawildlife.org/resources/reports/Report_of_the_task_force_on_WildLife_Security.pdf [Accessed March 2019].

activities following the sandalwood value chain, including the nature and structure of the transnational criminal network that controls the enterprise, and then the smuggling routes. The last section analyses the drivers of the commodification of shared resources, organised crime, and the transformation of local commons.

Commodification of natural resources and organised crime

Karl Polanyi defines commodities as objects produced for sale on the market, markets being established by actual contacts between buyers and sellers (Polanyi 2001: 75, see also Greiner & Bollig, this volume). Commodification can be understood as the process of producing goods for sale on the market. From a strictly economic perspective, therefore, commodities and their production are accessed based on economic value or commercial utility. However, as markets and actors evolve, the latter tend to attach greater preference on the economic value of natural resources over their social-cultural value. Consequently, such natural resources become commodities. The commercial exploitation of sandalwood fits this description.

The commodification of natural resources is not a new phenomenon. In the context of shared-resource systems in East and southern Africa, commodifying the wild in community conservancies follows Ostromian ideas of the 1990s. The community-based natural resource management (CBNRM) model gave rights to user groups to protect resources while benefiting economically from them, mainly through tourism-based economies (Hulme & Murphree 2001; King *et al.* 2015; see Kalvelage this volume on wildlife as a new commons). This becomes an incentive for local user groups to conserve natural resources. They do so by developing rules, regulations, and sanctions that govern extraction and use of shared resources such as water, forest, wildlife, grazing grounds, and cultivation areas among other common-pool resources (CPRs). These rules contain prescriptions that forbid, permit, or require some action or outcome among members of a shared resource (see examples in Ostrom 1990). The model, therefore, allows communities to meet the twin goals of conservation and development.

In the context of East Africa, rights of extraction and use of sandalwood (primarily for medicinal purposes, as explained later on) have historically rested on members of specific community conservancies. Indigenous groups have hardly commercially exploited the tree. However, the recent commodification of East Africa's sandalwood brings a new perspective in the commercial exploitation of shared resources, especially when actors violate or ignore the rules that have previously governed resource use. It raises concerns over the collective responsibility of local user groups in protecting shared resources, and the efficacy of indigenous norms and values.

Apart from sandalwood, there is a growing appetite among local user groups to put prices on other relational goods and resources. For example, members of some conservancies located in northern Kenya are increasingly commodifying, subdividing, privatising, and selling community grazing lands to willing buyers. This mostly follows state-led infrastructure developments like transport corridors, planned cities, and economic zones that target lands that are perceived to be underutilised,[2] including group ranches and community land. We argue that these developments redefine space and attach new value to shared resources, and thereby potentially change local attitudes towards resource use.

The link between natural resource extraction and organised crime features prominently in the illicit ivory markets and the trade in endangered species. Organised crime refers to a continuing criminal enterprise composed of three or more persons that work rationally to profit from illicit activities that are often in high public demand (UNODC 2018). The entrepreneurial nature of organised crime adopts rational, even if illegal, choices, and strategies aimed at maximising benefits and reducing costs of its (illegal) business (Allum *et al.* 2010: 18). Evidently, commodification of the wild exposes some natural resources to organised crime and criminal networks, especially where restrictions over the commercial exploitation of specific plant and animal species are met with high demand for the same in the global markets.

Organised crime in the illicit sandalwood trade in East Africa is a factor of global shortage of sandalwood against rising demand. Arun Kumar, Joshi, and Ram (2012) record this decline of production and trade of sandalwood – using the example of Karnataka, India – which, they argue, resulted in the soaring of market prices. In Australia, the slow natural regeneration of sandalwood prompted establishment of artificial plantations to meet the global demand (Clarke 2006). East Africa, therefore, becomes the next frontier for the naturally occurring and authentic sandalwood. The ban on sandalwood extraction from both Kenya and Tanzania as well as increasing global demand for the wood explains the emergence of an organised criminal network around its trade. Interviews conducted as part of this study with sandalwood smugglers at the Kenya-Uganda Malaba border revealed that China, India, and Indonesia are among the leading destination markets for East Africa's sandalwood. These dynamics arguably impede the endurance and effective application

---

[2]   Ongoing work by Winnie Changwoni, a postgraduate student at Kenyatta University, shows massive land subdivision, privatisation, and sale along a planned transport corridor traversing some communal conservancies.

of indigenous institutions in governing local commons. As Aggarwal (2008) notes, indigenous institutions may not keep pace with changing social, ecological, economic, and political factors.

Study area and methods

Kenya's Rift Valley, the Kenya-Uganda border towns of Malaba and Busia, and Tororo provided crucial sites for an ethnographic inquiry into the illicit trade of East Africa's sandalwood. Samburu, Laikipia, and Baringo in Kenya's Rift Valley were included in the study because they are important sources of sandalwood (Map 9.1). In Samburu, fieldwork focused on Wamba town and Loigama village, located in the Matthews Forest Range (Lenkiyio Hills).

The Matthews Forest Range, with an elevation of about 2,700m, is part of Namunyak conservancy, a 948,400-acre community conservancy owned by approximately 18,000 Samburu pastoralists (County Government of Samburu 2018). Namunyak Conservancy was established through the Northern Rangeland Trust (NRT) between 1993 and 1995 under the CBNRM model and is thus among the oldest community conservancies in northern Kenya with a thriving tourism-based economy.[3] Here, the Samburu refer to sandalwood locally as '*Losesiai*'.

In Laikipia North, fieldwork focused on Mukogodo forest in Lokusero village. Mukogodo forest covers an area of 74,000 acres and is home to Il Ngwesi and Lekurruki community conservancies established in the early 1990s through the NRT model. By the mid-1920s, the *il-torrobo* (Dorobo)[4] hunter-gatherers occupied the Mukogodo forest. They spoke the Yaaku or Mukogodo language and lived a predominantly foraging lifestyle. However, following contact with Maa-speaking neighbours, the *il-torrobo* 'became' Maasai by assimilating into Maasai culture and lifestyle between 1925 and 1936 (Cronk 2004: 58). Despite this cultural change, the *il-torrobo*, who are indigenous to the Mukogodo forest, still maintain some level of distinction from other Maa speakers occupying the area. Elders in Lokusero village told us that the indigenous group still sanctions the use of forest resources. There are restrictions on cutting down trees, and prohibition on the trade in endangered species like cedar and sandalwood, as well as collective responsibility over the forest by which they exclude non-members, monitor noncompliance, and believe in the supernatural punishment of offenders.

---

[3] www.nrt-kenya.org [Accessed 17 February 2022]

[4] Maa speakers use this pejorative term to describe the indigenous group as poor owing to their lack of cattle, and as backward with reference to their foraging lifestyle.

Between 2015 and 2017, however, organised banditry groups composed of Samburu herders executed a series of violent invasions of Mukogodo forest, the adjacent communal conservancies, and private ranches, partly driven by racialised ideas of indigenous land repossession and partly by claims to traditional dry-season grazing areas. They violently evicted the indigenous Dorobo from Lokusero village. This, according to some elders we spoke to, paved the way for illicit enterprises around wildlife poaching and commercial exploitation of sandalwood and cedar.

In Baringo South, the empirical focus was in Arabal location, particularly Mairo hills in Mukutani Ward, which lies close to the Baringo-Laikipia border towards Nyahururu and Rumuruti towns. Tugen pastoralists dominate the Arabal area. They described Arabal as a violence hotspot where periodic conflicts pitting Tugen and Pokot pastoralists cause mass displacement of people and the theft of livestock.[5] Apart from Arabal, Muchongoi, East Pokot, and Tiaty are also important sources of sandalwood in Baringo. Here, sandalwood is referred locally as '*Mormorow*', but locals nicknamed it '*pang'ang'a*', a coinage from the Sheng language which means 'too much talk', which describes the day-to-day conversations surrounding the illicit trade in sandalwood.

Fieldwork also included the porous Kenya-Uganda border towns of Busia and Malaba where smugglers temporarily live. A short visit to Tororo, Uganda, was necessary to get a glimpse of the regional market for sandalwood and the nerve centre for laundering. A qualitative approach was necessary for the methodological design of this study. Researching crime constitutes what anthropologists refer to as 'studies of hard-to-find populations' (Bernard 2006: 191). Smugglers are not easy to find. The nature of their work and circle of friends and acquaintances makes them distant from the rest of the public, yet they are critical clients for scientific inquiry without whom a holistic assessment of their operations is impossible. Their *modus operandi* usually dictates true allegiance to one another, which is the group's basis of social inclusion and exclusion. Mentioning the topic also arouses suspicion among community members especially when they too are accomplices in a criminal enterprise.

Researching crime is also imbued with ethical dilemmas. For a researcher, entering the smuggling space means dealing with criminals. This carries legal implications, the possibility of imminent risks, and an ethical obligation to protect informants. Our approach to fieldwork was rather unusual. We first set out to interview the sandalwood smugglers who often run other criminal

---

[5] Residents of Arabal noted that the Pokot–Tugen violence left dozens dead between 2013 and 2015.

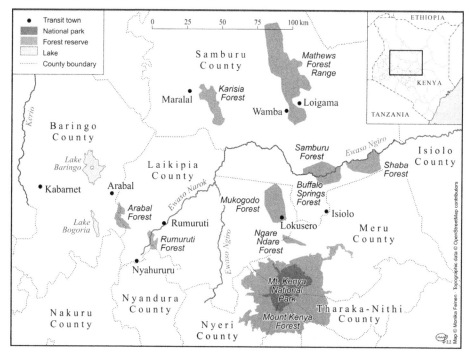

Map 9.1. Study areas in Samburu, Laikipia, and Baringo counties, Kenya's Rift Valley (Source: Field data; Cartography: M. Feinen).

enterprises across the Malaba and Busia border towns. State officials who have previously received bribes to allow such smuggling enterprises were our main link to the smugglers. A senior state officer found us audience with a few smugglers who accepted the interviews because they assumed their participation was a means to cement cordial relations with state officials, which could help facilitate future illicit activities across the border. The smugglers then linked us to actors in the value chain right from Tororo to sandalwood extraction areas in community conservancies. Interviews at the community level included sixteen key informants (among them three staff of NRT and three county administration staff). We also held six group discussions across the studied areas, consisting of seven to ten participants, and held numerous informal conversations with individuals in the study areas.

Sandalwood smuggling: Actors, criminal nodes, and the local value chain

The sandalwood value chain links actors and processes of extraction, pricing, transportation, and marketing from East Africa to the global markets. It also represents the nodes of the organised criminal network. We begin with the actors by focusing on the role of community members in the extraction and aiding the smuggling of sandalwood from community conservancies. A description of the nature and structure of the organised criminal network follows, after which we show the smuggling routes and inherent bottlenecks.

Community participation in sandalwood smuggling

> Money is evil; it can cause you to do anything. (Committee member, Namunyak Conservancy, 15 March 2019)

In much of East Africa, and the studied areas, communities consider the sandalwood tree a medicinal plant. Informants said that the smoke from burnt sandalwood cures inflammation, pain, and hardness of breasts and mammary glands among lactating mothers and livestock. The aroma that sandalwood gives off when burnt is said to help reduce stress and increase mental alertness, and some consider it a natural aphrodisiac. Moreover, chipped pieces of the wood are boiled in water to make herbal tea that cures stomach pain. Here, sandalwood is rarely used for religious ceremonies and traditional rituals or for making carved images of gods and mythological figures. Livestock and wildlife do not feed on sandalwood trees; neither do people use it as firewood or to make charcoal.

How is sandalwood extraction organised and executed at the local level? In Arabal, Baringo South, charcoal dealers introduced youths to the sale of sandalwood in 2006. When harvested, they said, some people would buy it right from their households. It was not until a truck arrived to ferry the sandalwood that community members realised the seriousness of the trade. At the beginning of the trade, a kilogram of sandalwood was sold at between KES 6 (US$0.055) and KES 20 ($0.18). Soon, more trucks arrived and the demand, as well as prices, increased drastically. Within a few weeks, almost all villagers (men, women, and school-going children) voluntarily joined the lucrative business. The price per kilogram rose to about KES 200 ($1.85). Local sandalwood brokers emerged who acted as the link between smugglers and local communities. They, together with smugglers, paid bribes to village elders (the custodians of natural resources) and state officials in the area to facilitate the illicit enterprise.

In light of the booming business, relatives and friends sent out word to kin in neighbouring areas who also began to harvest the wood in anticipation of the arrival of the smuggling trucks. When the quantity of naturally occurring sandalwood declined in Baringo, smugglers shifted focus to Samburu, Laikipia, and neighbouring areas as the next frontiers, where extraction picked up from 2015. In Samburu, appropriation of sandalwood began in Wamba town then spread to Loigama and other villages along the Matthews Range including villages in the Kalepo, Nalowuon, and Ngilai administrative units of Namunyak conservancy. The incentive to make quick money and buffer effects of drought and violent conflicts, among other reasons, drove community members to participate in the illicit trade.

In Wamba town, smugglers offered local elders and state officials bribes ranging from KES 10,000 (US$100) to KES 300,000 ($3,000), depending on the position they held in society or government. These bribes were meant to 'buy the way' for trade in sandalwood. In case of any dissent from elders, local village brokers successfully turned community members against them; they encouraged noncompliance with traditional institutions and disregard of sanctions that related to the misuse of shared resources by popularising the narrative that sandalwood 'was a blessing that had existed in disguise and whose time had come'. When local elders did not receive their share of bribes, they would block roads until the smugglers paid them off. At the height of the trade, Wamba town received hundreds of temporary migrants, the majority of whom arrived from other parts of the Matthews Range where extraction had not yet started. Some set up temporary structures in the town while others joined friends and relatives, allowing kin- and group-based extraction and sale of the wood.

In Laikipia North, our informants told us that armed Samburu warriors, who had evicted indigenous *il-torrobo* from their villages and grazing areas in the forest, had engaged in environmental crimes including ivory trade and the sale of sandalwood and cedar since at least 2015.

Extraction, weighing, and pricing of sandalwood

> Some [smugglers] took people up the hill to help them distinguish the male and female sandalwood types … 'cut this one, cut that one', they told villagers. (Village elder, Namunyak conservancy, 2 March 2019)

Extraction of sandalwood has been mainly done by wholly uprooting the tree to obtain the heartwood and roots where the greatest intensity of aroma and essential oils are found. Smugglers preferred the mature female sandalwood trees to the male trees. The female has a dark reddish appearance with large succulent leaves and intense aroma, while the male type is brownish with thin pointed leaves (Figures 9.1a–c).

Obtaining sandalwood from high altitudes is not an easy task. Men, women, and children have to cut through the dense vegetation uphill, dig up

Figure 9.1a. Female sandalwood leaves (Photo: Author).

Figure 9.1b Female sandalwood trunk (Photo: Author).

Figure 9.1c Male sandalwood leaves (Photo: Author).

the trees, cut logs into manageable sizes and then transport them downhill to a central collection point in their houses, granaries, or compounds. The task is therefore organised around kin or friendship affiliations. When the demand for sandalwood increased in 2017, some families and groups set up temporary camps in the hills where they cooked and slept, and thus spent most of their time harvesting the wood.

Community members innovated ways to lessen the challenging task of transporting sandalwood downhill. Women and children, for instance, roll or drag heavy loads downhill with the help of gravity, while men take on the heavier task of uprooting the trees. Some hire youths to transport sandalwood logs from high ground. The use of donkeys is more effective and cost-efficient. Sandalwood loads are tied on either side of the animal, which over time masters the tracks downhill to the central collection points.

Weighing of sandalwood is by means of an electronic weighing scale, which people hang on a tree. This is a day-long exercise under the supervision of local brokers and the smugglers who then pay individuals and groups according to the kilograms weighed. In some cases, local brokers purchase the extracted sandalwood at a negotiated price, and then sell it to the smugglers at a profit.

The main role of local brokers, however, is to popularise a positive narrative that legitimises the illicit trade at the local level. For example, when NRT commented on sandalwood smuggling, it was made clear that its mandate was solely related to wildlife protection and therefore it had no business preventing the sale of sandalwood.

The price of sandalwood is highly dependent on demand and supply. As shown in Figure 9.2, smugglers bought a kilogram of sandalwood from as low as KES 6 to KES 20 at the beginning of the trade, but prices have risen with the growing demand to between KES 80 and KES 200. At this price, some individuals can make up to KES 200,000 (US$2,000) in a good week. In sharp contrast, however, the price of a kilogram of sandalwood in Tororo, Uganda, ranges between KES 800 and KES 1,200. At the price of KES 800 per kilogram of sandalwood, smugglers can make as much as KES 11,000,000 (about $100,000) by selling a 14-tonne truckload of sandalwood to the companies in Tororo. When the international demand is low or when supply is high in Tororo, prices can drop to as low as KES 300 per kilogram. A kilogram of Indian sandalwood oil sold for about $3,000 in 2017.[6] This offers an explanation of the demand for authentic sandalwood and its consequent link to organised crime. At the local level, sandalwood money goes to a number of uses: affording daily expenses; purchase of livestock; paying bride wealth; purchase of motorcycles; construction of stone houses or refurbishing old ones, and setting up of new businesses like shops.

Sandalwood and organised crime: The nature and structure of a transnational network

In this section, an attempt is made to describe the key features and dimensions of the organised criminal network that deals in illicit sandalwood from Kenya's fragile ecosystems. The group is formed around a network of state and non-state actors in which members are deliberately yet informally included depending on their role, power, or influence in society or government that may guarantee the success of a criminal enterprise. The group is therefore not a random assemblage of people, yet, unlike most organised criminal groups around the world, it does not have any hierarchical structure. The role of individual actors is 'activated' on a needs basis. This means that each member of the network plays a specific function, as discussed below, and that their continued existence in the network is based on their perceived or actual success in executing the assigned role.

Members of the group enter into the network at different points: the sources of the sandalwood; along the smuggling routes; across the border in Tororo

---

6　www.livemint.com/Politics/zvJ2Ibxo3ThUxrvQA2ZWQJ/At-1500-each-these-aromatic-trees-are-very-precious-paras.html [Accessed 17 February 2022].

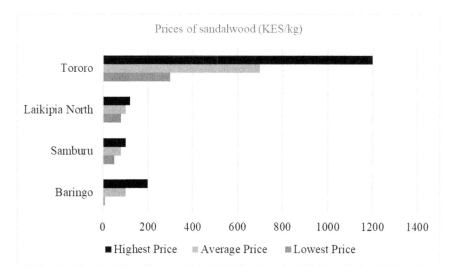

Figure 9.2 Prices of sandalwood per kilogram in East Africa (Field data 2019).

(where laundering of sandalwood is done), and further afield when sandalwood leaves the East African region for the global markets. Therefore, the organised criminal network is both national (operates within national borders) and transnational (operates across such borders).

Whereas there exists no strict hierarchy, the network's main node is that of the smugglers. As such, smugglers are the primary perpetrators of the criminal enterprise. They control the smuggling business, including extraction, transportation, and sale of sandalwood from community conservancies to their buyers in Tororo. Smugglers that we spoke to see themselves as ordinary business people who fill a critical demand – supply gap in terms of goods and services. They are mostly high-school or college dropouts, who have progressively amassed massive wealth through illicit activities allowing them to buy loyalty and legitimacy from state officials, including national security agencies and judges. Their allegiance to each other and the group is rooted in their working history, where they tap into pre-existing relations involving illicit activities. They also have roots in a single shared ethnic descent, which may create some level of trust between members, although the successful execution of an illicit activity may enhance more trust and guarantee continuation of the network in the future.

The smugglers are elusive and highly mobile, circling Malaba, Busia, Tororo, Kampala, and Kigali (Rwanda) as they monitor any structural changes that may create new opportunities for illicit trade or frustrate ongoing operations.

To facilitate their ease of movement across East Africa and beyond, they have fraudulently acquired citizenship in their preferred countries. They carry several national identification documents, which facilitate their safe passage in the country of choice.

Apart from the smugglers, the criminal group has numerous passive members. Passive members are persons whom smugglers bribe to create the necessary conditions for the successful execution of an illegal venture. In the case of sandalwood, the passive members facilitate the smooth extraction and delivery of the product, including safe passage along the smuggling routes. They include village brokers, local administrators (e.g. chiefs and county commissioners), toll workers, state security and crime officials (e.g. the police), and judges. The list of passive members is not exhaustive; smugglers often enlarge their circle of passive members by extending links to new people depending on the nature of an illicit activity. The complexity of an illegal deal may translate to a denser network, and this may reflect the profitability of the venture because all clandestine members must be paid. Usually, smugglers pay network members in advance as a precautionary strategy or as a form of insurance against possible risks. Irrespective of their positions in government or society, passive syndicate members serve at the mercy of smugglers, without whom the network dissolves.

In some cases, particularly where a matter involving sandalwood trade escalates to a court of law, it becomes the responsibility of the police member(s) of the criminal network to bribe the presiding judge(s). When the transaction cost exceeds the bribe at hand, the police must seek more money from the smugglers. In an incident in Baringo where police arrested three smugglers ferrying sandalwood, the presiding judge demanded a bribe of KES 1,000,000 (US$10,000). Unable to raise the money, the smugglers pleaded to be allowed to sell the merchandise first to raise the money. The judge detained one of the smugglers and released the rest to look for the money and secure the release of their friend. In early 2019, prices of sandalwood in Tororo plummeted, forcing the smugglers to hold their sale for a while, which meant that their friend spent more time in custody.

Notably, therefore, sandalwood smuggling is a costly affair if the economic interests of all network members are to be met. Smugglers bear the cost of the business, where bribes and logistical costs top their expenditure. Such costs force smugglers to operate as a team, sharing the costs, as opposed to working independently. In Table 9.1 below, we give an impression of the costs incurred in a given trip. These costs vary depending on the circumstances of each trip. Despite the listed transaction costs, there is a possibility for huge profits at the end of the activity. As one smuggler put it, 'sandalwood trade is a high-risk high-return undertaking'.

Table 9.1 Transaction costs in the smuggling of sandalwood.

Item	Cost (Kes)
Hiring a truck to transport illegal sandalwood	200,000
Hiring a police truck where necessary to transport sandalwood from the sources	30,000–50,0000
Advance bribe to police (depending on seniority)	5,000–300,000
Advance bribe to chiefs	5,000–10,000
Advance bribe to county commissioners (depending on seniority)	200,000–300,000
Advance bribe to village elders to obtain permission to harvest and ferry sandalwood from community conservancies (depending on the number of elders)	30,000–300,000
Advance payment to village brokers	50,000
Judges ('court fees')	1,000,000
Paying sandalwood harvesters KES 120 per kilogramme of sandalwood. A truck may carry 14 tonnes	1,680,000
Bribes to toll workers and weighbridge operators (depending on the number of toll stations and weighbridges)	10,000–200,000
Bribes to police manning border-crossing points along the Malaba–Busia road into Uganda	5,000–10,000
Accompanying costs: hired drivers, fuel, the release of trucks following arrests, storage of sandalwood in Tororo before the sale, emergency costs like tyre bursts, mechanical repairs etc. (depending on each trip)	100,000–150,000

(Source: field data 2019)

Smuggling routes and bottlenecks

> It is unfortunate police are arresting hired drivers while real culprits are free … because of constant interference and poor investigations, several potential suspects have escaped the hook only to continue engaging in the illegal trade with the blessings of the so-called powerful forces in and out of government. (Kabarnet Principal Magistrate, *Standard Media*, 20 December 2015)[7]

Prior to Kenya's ban on the trade in sandalwood, smugglers would ferry tonnes of the wood on long-haul trucks right from the sources. Following the ban and increased surveillance from a multi-agency team, smugglers resorted to hiring police trucks to ferry sandalwood to designated collection points like nearby

---

[7]   www.standardmedia.co.ke/lifestyle/article/2000185817/how-sandalwood-fuels-lucrative-illegal-logging-in-kenya [Accessed 17 February 2022]

towns. Police trucks provide the needed cover because illicit sandalwood is disguised as state materials in transit. Apart from the police trucks, converted tourist Land Cruisers are also used, especially in Baringo, but these can only ferry a tonne of the wood at a time and therefore have to make many trips to amass a dozen tonnes, which increases transaction costs.

Despite the availability of many tarmacked and marram roads, whose distance from the source to the destination of smuggled sandalwood is shorter, smugglers choose routes that guarantee less surveillance and where clandestine members are available to avert unwanted surprises. They would rather take longer routes to Tororo than risk arrests or expensive bribes. Police members of the criminal network provide smugglers with intelligence information on the situation along the preferred smuggling route, including friendly and unfriendly police roadblocks, toll stations, and weighbridges. At toll stations and weighbridges, the goods go unscrutinised in exchange for bribes of as little as KES 100 (about US$91).

Ironically, Kenya's busiest highways are most preferred for moving illegal goods because they have high traffic and thus less surveillance. Map 9.2 shows the sandalwood smuggling routes from community conservancies in Kenya to

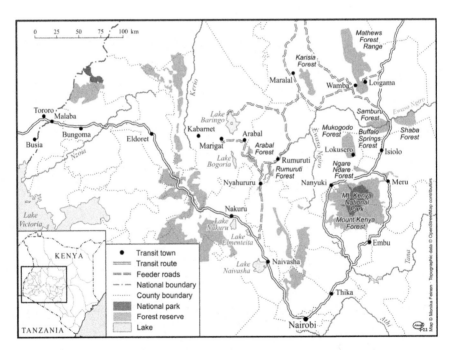

Map 9.2 Sandalwood smuggling routes in Kenya. (Source: Field data, Cartography: M. Feinen).

Tororo, Uganda. From Baringo South, smugglers prefer the Marigat–Nakuru road that joins the Nakuru–Eldoret highway as opposed to the Marigat–Eldoret road via Kabarnet, where police roadblocks, and demand for bribes, have increased since early 2007. From Arabal, smugglers often paid police to transport the sandalwood to Marigat town, from where it is dispatched for Tororo through Nakuru.

Smugglers ferrying sandalwood from the Matthews Forest Range in Samburu County prefer the Isiolo–Nairobi highway through Meru and Embu towns, almost circumnavigating Mt Kenya, before descending to the Thika–Nairobi highway. From Nairobi, they use the Nairobi–Malaba highway. The alternative route, that is, Isiolo–Nanyuki–Nairobi, is shorter, but smugglers avoid it due to the presence of many roadblocks. The shortest option of all would be to drive through the Kinare forest and then join the Nakuru–Eldoret highway at Njambini Flyover, but the route came under intense multi-agency surveillance from 2016. Since 2018, smugglers from Samburu have been using the Maralal–Nyahururu–Nakuru route, thence proceeding to Malaba.

From Nairobi to Malaba, about 450km, there are approximately thirty roadblocks, which are functional daily. When stopped at any of these roadblocks, the smugglers have to pay a bribe. There are also two weigh-bridges, one at Gilgil town, and the other at Webuye town. Weighbridges in Kenya afford a safe passage of illegal goods because Kenya Revenue Authority has progressively sabotaged any efforts to install automatic cargo scanners in a bid to continue receiving bribes from trucks suspected of ferrying unauthorised goods.

From Mukogodo forest, Laikipia North, smugglers take the Doldol–Nanyuki–Nakuru route and then join the Nakuru–Malaba highway. When approaching the official border-crossing point at Malaba, smugglers take the Malaba–Busia road and branch after 40km to join the Alupe–Angorom road crossing the River Malaba into Uganda to join the Busia–Tororo road. From Alupe trading centre, one or two motorbikes will escort the trucks to 'sweep' the road for any presence of Kenyan or Ugandan police, while the trucks follow at breakneck speed leaving a cloud of dust as they finish the toughest part of their journey. As soon as the trucks cross River Malaba, they enter into Ugandan territory, where the trade in sandalwood is legal. Apart from the Alupe–Angorom road, the nearby Adungos–Buteba road is also an important smuggling route.

When sandalwood crosses into Uganda, smugglers take it to warehouses in Tororo or sell it directly to the Chinese and Indian companies as a legitimate good. From Tororo, raw sandalwood is loaded onto Ugandan trucks, packed in sacks, and transported back into Kenya through the official border-crossing points of Malaba or Busia, where it is cleared as legitimate goods in transit headed to the Mombasa port. At Mombasa port, sandalwood is cleared as Uganda's export goods and shipped to international markets in India, Thailand, China, and Malaysia among other Asian countries, as well as to Europe. Due to the lack of international restrictions on the export of sandalwood from East Africa, tyhe expectation is that the wood gets into the international market with few if any bottlenecks.

Drivers of sandalwood commodification, organised crime, and transformation of local commons

From the preceding discussion, several cross-cutting drivers of the commodification of shared resources, organised crime, and transformation of local commons emerge. This section addresses these drivers.

Commitment among user groups to protect local commons

Commitment to norms and other aspects of a social system is central to human forms of sociality and the success of collective agendas. Kanter (1968: 500) defines commitment as a process through which individual interests become attached to the carrying out of socially organised patterns of behaviour, which are seen as fulfilling those interests, and as expressing the nature and needs of the person. Actors become committed not only to norms but also to other aspects of a social system. Burke and Reitzes (1991: 243–244) note that commitment is based on perceived positive meanings and rewards as well as ties to others; that is, belonging to a social network and being related to other role partners.

In the social context of shared resources, or CPRs, commitment to norms and rules that govern resource use reflects individual and collective responsibility and accountability. Even with monitoring, sanctioning arrangements, and enforcement mechanisms, lack of commitment among resource users may lead to the collapse of the CPR system, especially when individual choices and free will contradict collective arrangements that social contexts and structure provide. Nevertheless, Elinor Ostrom notes that there are situations in which potential benefits from opportunistic behaviour will be so high that even strongly committed individuals will break norms (Ostrom 1990: 36).

In the preceding case study, commitment to social norms and rules that govern appropriation of shared resources appears to be notably weak. Resource users relegated commons to a form of open-access system where opportunistic behaviour defied the rules of inclusion and exclusion. The zeal with which conservancy members facilitate the commodification and commercial exploitation of sandalwood reflects the problems of social dynamics involving the commitment of actors: social control, group cohesiveness, and retaining participants (Kanter 1968). An actor, she argues, may be committed to continuing his system membership but be continually deviant within the system, uncommitted to its control; or, he may be very solidary with a group in a social system but be uncommitted to continued participation in the system. Such commitment problems are visible in the studied community conservancies.

Weakened indigenous institutions

In the context of natural resource management, Watson (2003) defines indigenous institutions as those institutions that have emerged in a particular situation or that are practised or constituted by people who have had a degree of continuity of living in, and using resources of, an area. By 'weak' indigenous institutions, we refer to the limited application or perceived ineffectiveness of local norms and rules that govern social order and the decreasing role of elders' courts (councils of elders) in sanctioning noncompliance. It is therefore characterised by limited application, reduced enforcement of rules, and commitment problems among user groups, as well as noncompliance with informal constraints that govern individual and collective appropriation of resources.

While it is the responsibility of individuals in a user group to comply with set rules and guidelines, the role of elders' courts (gerontocracy) in sanctioning noncompliance is critical. However, where some councils of elders tried to exercise their authority against sandalwood sale, particularly in Samburu county, this was just mere talk with no action. Upon realising that other villages were not keeping the promise of protecting the precious wood, they let go of the grip they had as enforcers and allowed resource users to extract and sell the wood in exchange for bribes. Indeed, no one prefers to be a 'sucker', keeping a promise that everyone else is breaking (Ostrom 1990). Unlike much of the 20th century when recourse to the curse and other sanctions deterred individuals from noncompliance, such sanctions appear to have progressively lost their symbolic apparatus and hence become weak or ineffective.

Several factors may explain this seeming erosion of indigenous norms and rules:

1   Problems of generational control: the younger generation often consider councils of elders an impediment to resource appropriation and their own wealth-creation goals. For the new generations, indigenous institutions may be irrelevant. As a result, the younger generation may not conform to historically established rules and norms, unless these are changed to reflect their ambitions and aspirations.

2   Changing social-ecological and economic conditions: Aggarwal (2008) notes that indigenous institutions might fail to keep pace with changing

social-economic and cultural values. Changing ecological conditions, like territorialisation in a bid to create wildlife, livestock, and settlement zones, lead to the reordering of people and space, which could potentially threaten local norms and values.

3   Cultural diffusion: traditional institutions are usually relevant to specific cultural groups and societies in which members share common aspirations. However, with increasing immigration and cultural diffusion, new ideologies may upset the existing social order and encourage the erosion of indigenous norms and values. The studied areas are social landscapes characterised by ethnic overlap, where each group negotiates access to the same social, political, and environmental resources. As such, hybridity of identities may weaken the cultural attributes of the group indigenous to the specific landscape.

Sandalwood smuggling proves that the endurance of indigenous institutional arrangements in the commons depends on their capacity to cope with and adjust to changing ecological, social-economic, political, and cultural conditions, which shape local attitudes and values that actors attach to resources. This, however, raises some pertinent questions: what capacity do local institutions possess to enable them to cope with or effectively adjust to current internal and external pressure? What can enhance the resilience of traditional norms and rules against these changes? Based on observations, economic interests rather than social-cultural value largely influence the lens through which local user groups perceive natural resources. We argue that, despite the intended outcomes, valorisation of natural resources and the market approach to conservation pose a threat to the survival of the commons when traditional norms are disregarded in pursuit of economic gains and when the relational aspect of shared resources loses value.

Conservancy capture

Community conservancies in East Africa are increasingly put to new use, thereby reordering people and space. In Kenya, for instance, the Lamu Port–South Sudan–Ethiopia Transport corridor (LAPSSET), oil explorations, and geothermal drilling, among other development projects, are causing massive land-use changes in community-owned spaces. Apart from redefining the use of communal space, these megaprojects introduce the state and multinational corporations into local resource governance, thereby increasing centralised control of natural resources. In the studied areas, the process has primarily centred on state co-option of local elders, who are custodians of local resources, in a bid to transfer ownership rights through ritual sacrifices[8] where necessary. In some instances, the transfer of property rights is based on compensation, promises of development, or coercion. This elite-driven conversion of communal conservancies – what we call 'conservancy capture' – has attracted land speculators and grabbers from the metropolis who act on information about planned infrastructure to amass land from unsuspecting villagers.

The possibility of the implementation of these megaprojects (the planned phase) creates huge expectations at the local levels, informing people's actions and behaviours. They may not be expectations of modernity (following Ferguson 1999), but rather expectations of infrastructures, valorisation, and connectedness. In places like Samburu and neighbouring Isiolo counties, these anticipations have heralded immigration of land speculators and smugglers and increased attitudes towards subdivision and privatisation of communal conservancies in a bid to feed the growing land market. These factors promote the commodification of shared resources, including sandalwood.

Indeed, local commons that were previously dedicated to conservation and grazing are increasingly linked to the mainstream economy, black markets, and local politics. As a result, the commodification of the wild may quickly lose its intended values of conservation and development, giving way to uncontrolled market-driven overexploitation. Conservancy capture by state and non-state actors, therefore, reduces the relational value of resources and engenders a space in which almost everything becomes a commodity in the eyes of local users. It is no surprise, therefore, that local communities at the source of sandalwood began to weigh its cultural relevance against the expected economic returns, and were quick to judge the sandalwood tree as a 'useless' plant by virtue of it not being suitable as firewood, feed for livestock, or charcoal burning.

Inter-ethnic conflict as an opportunity for environmental crimes

Ethnic conflict is a major driver of environmental crimes in East Africa. From Kenya's Rift Valley to the Karamoja region of Uganda, sandalwood smuggling focuses on areas of considerable social instability and insecurity where intergroup violence and forceful evictions create the space and opportunity for wildlife and forest poaching. The threat of escalating violence and conflict in East Africa is linked by UNODC (2009) to the twin threats of

---

[8]   Where a council of elders bless a portion of land excised from community land for private or public investments by conducting a ritual involving the slaughter of a bull or goat.

organised crime and trafficking. The violent invasions of Mukogodo forest as well as Pokot–Tugen conflicts provide good examples.

At the time of fieldwork, abandoned homes belonging to indigenous *il-torrobo* dotted the Lokusero area in Mukogodo forest following violent evictions in which Samburu perpetrators also destroyed Kenya Forest Service offices and led to the closure of public schools in the area. The object of such evictions, according to area police, was to pave the way for wildlife poaching and sandalwood smuggling. The popular narrative, however, was that pastoral groups were accessing dry-season grazing areas as a response to environmental crises occasioned by drought, as noted earlier. In Arabal, Baringo County, violent conflict between Pokot and Tugen pastoralists from 2013 to 2015 offered the instability necessary for sandalwood smuggling. The situation also paved the way for illicit trade in guns by individuals of Somali descent while police from the area supplied the fighting pastoral groups with bullets, in exchange for money.

Structural weaknesses

According to UNODC (2009), structural factors – such as weak border controls, limited cross-border and regional cooperation, under-resourced police forces, corruption, and lack of political will to address crime in a sustainable way – have created an environment in which organised crime can flourish in East Africa. Other factors include ineffective governance, the weak rule of law, high levels of inequality and institutional breakdown. Apart from the smuggling of sandalwood, the Kenya-Uganda border is popular for the illicit movement of other goods and services, which reveal the mentioned structural weaknesses.

Some of the goods and services smuggled into Uganda from Kenya include unprocessed coffee, wheat flour, cooking oil, vehicle spare parts, and electronics such as smartphones and flatscreen TVs. The smuggling of Kenya's unprocessed coffee is linked to declining prices of the product in Kenya and the promise of better prices in Uganda. From Uganda, hardwoods, sugar, cigarettes, beer, locally brewed alcohol, wines and spirits, plastic wrapping bags, petrol and diesel, vegetables and fruits, clothing and beddings, cars, guns, and humans are smuggled into Kenya.

In the case of sandalwood smuggling, Kenya has not designated a single national institution to fight environmental crimes, save for the Kenya Wildlife Service, which lacks an effective system to fight such crimes (Kamweti *et al.* 2009). In Uganda, there is no policy on forest crimes, particularly regarding sandalwood and other valued plants. Kenya's ban on the sale of sandalwood in early 2007 was to last for five years. Ironically, after the lapse of the five years, there was no official statement to extend the ban. It is no wonder that smugglers took advantage of the ending of the five-year period to appropriate sandalwood from the studied areas. Moreover, regional cooperation on matters pertaining to forest crimes is non-existent. These factors paint an ugly picture of the depth of structural weaknesses and institutional collapse by which organised crime and cross-border illicit transactions flourish.

Local commons in globalised economies

Anthropologists understand globalisation as the intensification of global inter-connectedness, suggesting a world full of movement and mixture, contact and linkages, and persistent cultural interaction and exchange (Inda & Rosaldo 2012). Following Kearney (1995), globalisation links localities in such a way that local happenings are shaped by events occurring many miles away, and vice versa. Local commons are highly vulnerable to the impacts of globali-sation, especially under increasing pressure to extract ecosystem products and services to supply local and global markets (Randhir 2016).

Unlike in Namibia, for instance, where commodification and valorisation of the wild (e.g. trophy hunting) follows a laid-out plan (Republic of Namibia 2013: 25–27), the situation in East Africa is rather open and uncontrolled. The free-market transactions in East Africa's local commons seem to have no limits. This increasingly puts fragile ecosystems in possible danger. Moreover, the impacts of globalisation on local communities and cultures in remote areas include the restructuring of social organisation where patterns of behaviour and relationships conform to new ideologies.

In the case under consideration, global forces of supply and demand for authentic sandalwood not only restructure the social order by upsetting indigenous norms and values but also intensify future expectations and hopes of making more money at the local level.

Conclusion

This chapter has examined the commodification and commercial exploitation of East Africa's sandalwood and its link to organised crime. Commodifying natural resources is not a new phenomenon in East Africa. Unlike the illegal ivory trade, which has a deeper history in the region, illicit exploitation of endangered tree species, like sandalwood, has only recently permeated the environmental crime markets. While the 1990s brought about a new dimension of commodification of the wild, anchoring natural resource management in a decentralised structure with the twin goals of conservation and development, we argue that recent social-economic dynamics that drive current forms of commodification of shared resources may threaten their very existence. The global appetite for naturally occurring East African sandalwood, as well as changing local attitudes and demands, seems to impede group-based conservation efforts.

Commodification and commercial exploitation of sandalwood and its link to organised criminal networks point to the fact that markets and actors have changed. In the context of shared-resource systems, economic interests rather than social-cultural value may largely influence the lens through which local user groups perceive natural resources in the future. With reference to changing markets, there seems to be a standardisation of illicit goods and services and their inclusion in the global value chain. Nowadays, markets seem to value illegal goods and services, which legitimises and sustains organised criminal groups. The fact that sandalwood smuggling involves both state and non-state actors somehow legitimises the illicit trade and makes any efforts to halt the vice eventually futile.

What are the implications of these dynamics at the local level and for the long-term sustainability of the commons? There is no easy answer to this question. However, the reality is that there is evidence of changes in local attitudes and perceptions in the governance of local commons. These changes are driven by new demands, needs, and aspirations at the local level. Nevertheless, it would be premature to predict a complete collapse of indigenous rules and norms for the conservation of nature. These social institutions have proven resilient despite periodic and long-term livelihood shocks and stress, including drought, famine, and conflict. In most cases, such disturbances to local livelihoods create opportunities for groups to innovate ways of sharing resources which include decisions on access to and use of pastures and forest resources. We argue, however, that the long-term sustainability of the commons will principally depend on how local actors adjust to and cope with changing social, economic, and political factors that disturb or rather alter the social ecology of shared-resource systems.

Bibliography

Aggarwal, A. (2008). 'Indigenous institutions for natural resource management: Potential and threats', *Economic and Political Weekly*, 43(23), 21–24.

Allum, F., Longo, F., Irrera, D., & Kostakos, P. A. (eds) (2010). *Defining and Defying Organized Crime: Discourse, Perceptions and Reality* (New York: Routledge).

Arun Kumar, A. N., Joshi, G., & Mohan Ram, H. Y. (2012). 'Sandalwood: History, uses, present status, and the future', *Current Science*, 103(12), 1408–1416.

Beachey, R. W. (1967). 'The east African ivory trade in the nineteenth century', *The Journal of African History*, 8(2), 269–290.

Bernard, R. (2006). *Research Methods in Anthropology: Qualitative and Quantitative Approaches*, 4th edn (Lanham MD; New York: Rowman and Littlefield).

Bunei, E. K. (2017). 'The hunt for the precious wood: Illegal trade of sandalwood as an international criminal enterprise in Kenya', *Society and Business Review*, 12(1), 63–76.

Burke, P. J. & Reitzes, D. (1991). 'An identity theory approach to commitment', *Social Psychology Quarterly*, 54(3), 239–251.

Bussmann, R. W. (1996). 'Destruction and management of Mount Kenya's forests', *AMBIO, A Journal of the Human Environment*, 25(5), 314–317.

Clarke, M. (2006). 'Australia's Sandalwood Industry: An Overview and Analysis of Research Needs' (RIRDC Publication, December 2006). Available at: www. agrifutures.com.au/wp-content/uploads/publications/06-131.pdf [Accessed 17 February 2022].

County Government of Samburu (2018). *Samburu County: Second Integrated Development Plan, 2018-2022* (Samburu County, Kenya: County Government of Samburu). Available at: https://repository.kippra.or.ke/bitstream/ handle/123456789/802/2018-2022%20%20Samburu%20County%20%20CIDP. pdf [Accessed 17 February 2022].

Coutu, A. N., Lee-Thorp J., Collins M. J., & Lane P. J. (2016). 'Mapping the elephants of the 19th century East African ivory trade with a multi-isotope approach', *PLoS ONE*, 11(10).

Cronk, L. (2004). *From Mukogodo to Maasai: Ethnicity and Cultural Change in Kenya* (Boulder CO: Westview Press).

Ferguson, J. (1999). *Expectations of Modernity: Myths and Meanings of Urban Life on the Zambian Copperbelt* (Berkeley: University of California Press).

Hakansson, N. T. (2004). 'The human ecology of world systems in East Africa: The impact of the ivory trade', *Human Ecology*, 32(5), 561–591.

Harrison, M. *et al.* (2015). 'Wildlife Crime: A Review of the Evidence on Drivers and Impacts in Uganda', Research Report (London: IIED). Available at: http:// pubs.iied.org/17576IIED [Accessed 17 February 2022].

Hulme, D. & Murphree, M. (eds) (2001). *African Wildlife and Livelihoods: The Promise and Performance of Community Conservation* (Oxford: James Currey / Heinemann).

Inda, J. X. & Rosaldo, R. (2012). *The Anthropology of Globalization: A Reader* (Malden MA: Wiley-Blackwell).

Kamweti, D., Osiro, D., & Mwiturubani, D. A. (2009). 'Nature and Extent of Environmental Crime in Kenya' (Pretoria: Institute for Security Studies). Available at: www.files.ethz.ch/isn/111770/M166FULL.pdf [Accessed 17 February 2022].

Kanter, R. M. (1968). 'Commitment and social organization: A study of commitment mechanisms in utopian communities', *American Sociological Review*, 33(4), 499–517.

Kearney, M. (1995). 'The local and the global: The anthropology of globalization and transnationalism', *Annual Review of Anthropology*, 24, 547–565.

King, J., Lalampaa, J., Craig, I., & Harrison, M. (2015). 'A Guide to Establishing Community Conservancies – The NRT Model' (Isiolo, Kenya: Northern Rangelands Trust). Available at: www.fao.org/sustainable-forest-management/ toolbox/tools/tool-detail/en/c/1255883 [Accessed 17 February 2022].

Müller, D. & Mburu, J. (2009). 'Forecasting hotspots of forest clearing in

Kakamega Forest, western Kenya', *Forest Ecology and Management*, 257(3), 968–977.

Nellemann, C. & INTERPOL Environmental Crime Programme (eds) (2012). 'Green Carbon, Black Trade: Illegal Logging, Tax Fraud and Laundering in the Worlds Tropical Forests: A Rapid Response Assessment' (United Nations Environment Programme, GRID Arendal). Available at: www.grida.no/publications/126 [Accessed 17 February 2022].

Ochanda, K. V. (2009). Conservation and Management of Sandalwood Trees (*Osyris lanceolata* Hochst & Steudel) in Chyullu Hills Kibwezi District, Kenya. Master's thesis, Kenyatta University.

Ostrom, E. (1990). *Governing the Commons: The Evolution of Institutions for Collective Action* (Cambridge: Cambridge University Press).

Polanyi, K. (2001). *The Great Transformation: The Political and Economic Origin of Our Times* (Boston MA: Beacon Press).

Republic of Namibia (2013). 'Guidelines for Management of Conservancies and Standard Operating Procedures' (Windhoek: Ministry of Environment and Tourism, August 2013). Available at: http://the-eis.com/elibrary/sites/default/files/downloads/literature/Guidlines%20for%20management%20of%20conservancies%20and%20standard.pdf [Accessed 17 February 2022].

Randhir, T. O. (2016). 'Globalization impacts on local commons: multiscale strategies for socioeconomic and ecological resilience', *International Journal of the Commons*, 10(1), 387–404.

Thorbahn, P. F. (1981). *The Precolonial Ivory Trade of East Africa: Reconstruction of a Human-Elephant Ecosystem*. PhD Thesis, University of Massachusetts.

Titeca, K. (2019). 'Illegal ivory trade as transnational organized crime? An empirical study into ivory traders in Uganda', *The British Journal of Criminology*, 59(1), 24–44.

UNODC – United Nations Office on Drugs and Crime (2009). 'Organised Crime and Trafficking in Eastern Africa: A Discussion Paper' (Nairobi: UNODC, 23–24 November 2009). Available at: www.unodc.org/documents/easternafrica/regional-ministerial-meeting/Organised_Crime_and_Trafficking_in_Eastern_Africa_Discussion_Paper.pdf [Accessed 17 February 2022].

UNODC – United Nations Office on Drugs and Crime (2018). 'E4J Teaching Guide on Organized Crime' (Vienna: UNODC). Available at: www.unodc.org/e4j/en/organized-crime/module-1/index.html [Accessed 6 June 2019].

Watson, E. E. (2003). 'Examining the potential of indigenous institutions for development: A perspective from Borana', *Development and Change, Ethiopia*, 34(2), 287–309.

Weru, S. (2016). 'Wildlife Protection and Trafficking Assessment in Kenya: Drivers and Trends of Transnational Wildlife Crime in Kenya and its Role as a Transit Point for Trafficked Species in East Africa' (TRAFFIC, May). Available at: www.trafficj.org/publication/16_Wildlife_Protection_and_Trafficking_Assessment_Kenya.pdf [Accessed 17 February 2022].

10

The Gum Arabic Business: Modernisation of production in north-eastern Nigeria

HAUKE-PETER VEHRS AND IBRAHIM MAINA WAZIRI

Introduction

Gum arabic is a tree resin obtained from several naturally growing acacia species endemic to the African Sahel Zone. *Senegalia senegal* (better known under the name *Acacia senegal*)[1] is used for the production of a high-value gum; its natural distribution extends from the Sudano-Sahelian zone of Africa throughout the Middle East to the dry regions of India (Fagg & Allison 2004: 1). The trade of this commodity has a long tradition that dates as far back as two millennia BCE. (UNCTAD 2018: 2).[2] However, the popularity of gum arabic for the production of various forms of merchandise around the globe has risen in the last decades.

The international demand for gum arabic is fluctuating, but over the long term also rising steadily. The collection of gum arabic from natural stands of *Senegalia senegal* was complemented in the 1970s and 1980s[3] by the establishment of plantations in the major countries of production: Sudan, Chad, Nigeria, and Cameroon (El Tahir *et al.* 2009; Ngaryo *et al.* 2011; Harmand

---

[1]   The terminology for the African acacia species was recently revised. In the literature on gum arabic production the formerly common denominations '*Acacia senegal*' and '*Acacia seyal*' are used, which was conventional until the 'African' acacias were classified into two distinct genera, *Senegalia* and *Vachellia* (Dyer 2014: iii). Therefore, *Acacia senegal* is named *Senegalia senegal* here, and *Acacia seyal* is referred to as *Vachellia seyal*.

[2]   The abbreviation UNCTAD stands for 'United Nations Conference on Trade and Development'.

[3]   See, for the case of Sudan, Obeid & Din (1970); Din & Obeid (1971a); Obeid & Din (1971); Din & Obeid (1971b). In Nigeria plantations were established from 1987 in the course of a government-driven project called Forest II (Mokwunye & Aghughu 2010: 9).

et al. 2012; Fakuta *et al.* 2015). Furthermore, the production of gum arabic is experiencing a government-induced shift from a smallholder-based to a more intensive, perhaps even 'modern', production, in which trees are planted and nursed to produce the resin.

The best-quality gum is derived from *Senegalia senegal* and *Vachellia seyal* (Street & Anderson 1983: 887) and has several uses, on both the local and international levels. For instance, as an emulsifier or coating for a variety of products (Mariod 2018), as a stabiliser, e.g. in dairy products (Sulieman 2018), or, on the local level, for medicinal treatment, or ink production, among others (UNCTAD 2018: 8–11). In northern Nigeria, gum arabic is still mainly collected by smallholders and sold to local brokers. The local uses are quite limited – for starching the commonly worn caps (Hausa: *hula*), for making ink for writing, and sometimes the fresh gum is also consumed in small quantities.

In terms of quality, gum arabic is distinguished into three economic categories – grades one to three – of which grade one gum arabic is exclusively obtained from two tree species, *Senegalia senegal* (Hausa: *Ɗakwara*) and *Vachellia seyal* (Hausa: Farin *ƙaya*) – and generates the highest revenues on the international market. The gum derived from *Senegalia senegal* is perceived to be of the best quality (Beyene 1993: 2), followed by the darker and friable gum of *Vachellia seyal*.[4] In general, the quality between gum from Sudan, Chad, and Nigeria differs widely, and grading furthermore depends on the processing of the raw gum, as exemplified in the case of Sudanese gum arabic (Williams & Phillips 2009: 254).

In contrast to other case studies in this volume the case presented here deals with an age-old commodity from the wild: gum arabic. It has been traded from the Sahel since millennia and is still perceived by many insiders and outsiders as a product from the 'wild'. This case study also highlights that attempts to commercialise and optimise the production of gum arabic on a capital- and labour-intensive plantation scale can co-exist with other forms of production.

In our case study, we focus mainly on the collection and production of gum arabic from *Senegalia senegal*, since it is at the focus of research interests and plantation efforts in Nigeria. We present the results of fieldwork conducted in the north-eastern Yobe and Borno States in 1994 and again in 2011, complemented by archival and literature research. While the research conducted by Waziri had a historical focus on colonial export trade in the north-eastern

---

4   At the end of the 19th century, Nachtigal already referred to this grade of gum arabic as '*kittir*' – a darker gum arabic of lower quality from Kordofan (Nachtigal 1879: 44). In contrast to the grade two gum arabic, the lighter gum, called '*hashab*', is perceived to be of higher quality and is sold for higher prices than grade one gum arabic. Nachtigal describes it as 'excellent' or 'the most wanted rubber' in the 1870s, which he found at the Tibesti Mountains in Chad (Nachtigal 1879: 137, 466, 510).

region of Borno (Waziri 2008), Vehrs conducted anthropological research in Borno and Yobe states in 2011, also residing at the Gum Arabic sub-station of the Rubber Research Institute of Nigeria at Gashua (see also Map 10.1). Archival research was carried out by Waziri in the Kaduna branch of the National Archives of Nigeria.

Two main methods of production have been identified and distinguished: natural-stand gum arabic collection and plantation cultivation. The former is also referred to as smallholder production of gum arabic, because it is mainly conducted by smallholders who have diverse livelihoods and perform only a few gum-arabic-related activities, such as tapping the trees and collecting gum. Plantation cultivation, in contrast, is done by 'strong men', or government institutions that can afford the high costs of operating the *Senegalia senegal* plantations. This method of production demands a high labour input and several production practices, which have been newly employed to produce gum arabic on a larger scale, such as seed collection, nursing trees, plantation establishment, pest control, pruning, and weeding, as capital-intensive commercial farming.

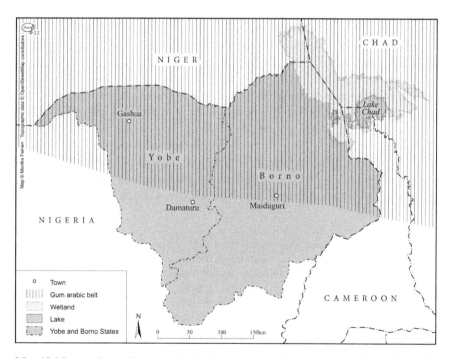

Map 10.1 Research area in the gum belt of north-eastern Nigeria (Source: DIVA-GIS 2021, Elmquist *et al.* 2005, QGIS 2021; Cartography: M. Feinen).

As Bollig *et al.* (this volume) conceptualise the commodification of the 'wild', it can be understood as entities collected, produced, or even conserved in remote areas in opposition to 'domesticated' organisms or industrial agricultural commodities. Therefore, we consider gum arabic, which is collected from natural stands to be such a 'wild' commodity (though we would refer in the following to the terminology 'collected' in opposition to 'cultivated', which does reflect the different ways of gum arabic production best). Although a difference in production practices can be observed, the product gum arabic is often referred to be a 'wild' and 'natural' commodity.

Technically, the commodity gum arabic is not recently commodified from the 'wild', in the sense that it was recently discovered and hence 'produced' for a newly emerging (international) demand. Rather the production practices have experienced a shift towards a modernisation of production.[5] This modernisation process is delineated here by two 'stereotypical' examples of gum production: smallholder collection of gum arabic from natural stands – as it is perceived to be the 'normal' way of production – and the cultivation of *Senegalia senegal* trees, which is referred to as the new mode of production, and follows an increasing international market demand for the commodity gum arabic. This new production strategy targets the increasing international demand for gum arabic and producers seek to gain a better access to global value chains, as also discussed by Revilla Diez *et al.* in this volume. However, due to the unpredictable nature of this resource, the deliberate production and the integration into international markets remain difficult.

Indeed, an important question is how this process of changing land-use practices for the production of the same commodity can be termed, since the notion of 'commodification' does not capture it entirely, as gum arabic was a commodity long before plantations of *Senegalia senegal* were established. To our understanding, the notion of 'commercialisation' turns out to best describe the overall developments in the gum arabic production in our case, since it addresses the growing importance of the commodity gum arabic – on national and international levels – to generate revenues, as well as the effects

---

[5] The concept of modernisation, with its underlying connotations and assumptions, is a term that we employ critically here. It reflects two aspects that we want to integrate into the discussion. First, this notion allows us to describe a progressive system that is influenced and directed by science and industries alike – at least, control over natural factors is targeted to achieve reliable production conditions. Furthermore, the distinction of 'modern' and 'traditional' plays an important role in the Hausa context of northern Nigeria, where established practices, assets and values are in constant exchange but also often in conflict with new influences, travelling ideas (Behrends *et al.* 2014) and practices emanating from other realms of the world.

of the growing demand in the production area. With reference to Muldrew (1998), Tilly addresses earlier notions of 'commercialisation' with the view 'that expansion of commercial transactions caused new forms of interpersonal relations, new meanings, and new social institutions embedding the relations and meanings to arise' (Tilly 2016: 96). Commercialisation not only deals with financial transactions or standardisations of processes and products, but also with landscape transformations and changing land-use practices.

Moreover, we refer to the notion of modernisation to describe the newly emerging system of plantation cultivation on the production level. We conceptualise plantation cultivation of *Senegalia senegal* as a 'modernised' production (with reference to the Hausa distinction between the two production systems), and investigate to what extent the modernisation of gum arabic production practices has had an effect on human–environment relations in north-eastern Nigeria in the recent past. We must also clarify that the modernisation of gum arabic production does not refer to a 'professionalisation' of the production in the sense that people who collected gum arabic from natural stands of *Senegalia senegal* before improved and renewed their methods over time. This is definitely not the case with the production of gum arabic, since the smallholder system of gum collection from natural stands is not professionalised and therefore changing into or being replaced by a more advanced system of plantation cultivation, but rather the smallholder system is sustained, and furthermore complemented by the plantation cultivation system.

In the following, we start with a historical review and an overview of the export of gum arabic in pre-colonial and colonial periods before describing the modernisation of production in the post-colonial period.

Historical accounts of gum arabic trade and use: The pre-colonial period

Gum arabic is not a new commodity, but it has been traded beyond the borders of the Sahel Zone for a long time, for instance to Egypt in the 17th century BCE. (Flückiger & Hanbury 1879: 234). The name gum arabic is presumably deduced from the Arabic exporting countries through which gum arabic passed on its way into Europe (Dujardin-Beaumetz & Egasse 1889: 324). In the 19th century the English botanist Daniel Oliver (1871: 342), already described gum arabic as a commercial good and Flückiger and Hanbury wrote that 'The quantity [of gum arabic] annually imported into France since 1828 from Senegal is varying from between [*sic.*] 1½ to 5 million of kilogrammes [*sic.*]' (1879: 236). Also, the use of gum arabic in the 18th and 19th centuries is well recorded, for instance for painting in France (Troyon 1853), or the production of chewing gum in the USA (White 1868: 111). Much earlier, it was used to produce paint for the writing of hieroglyphs, or for the mummification process in ancient Egypt (UNCTAD 2018: 2).

In the mid-19th century, Shaw describes a variety of goods, among them gum arabic, which, according to Rohlfs (1868: 61–62), 'is hardly available on the market at the moment, but could be brought in enormous quantities from the large mimosa forest north of the Tsad [Lake Chad]'.[6] Later, Shaw also describes the territories in the southern parts of the Kanem-Bornu Empire as 'forests of gum-bearing acacias' (Shaw 1905: 487). The potential of gum arabic production in northern Nigeria was therefore already well recognised in pre-colonial times. Demand for it – though limited – was a driving force to enlarge gum production in the region, which was not informed by local demands for this specific type.

The colonial period in north-eastern Nigeria in the 20th century

The British Royal Niger Company promoted commercial gum arabic trade in northern Nigeria in the early 20th century. By that time, gum arabic was exclusively collected by villagers, from trees growing in their environments (Waziri 2008). It was the Northern Province Governor Howbey R. Palmer, who first exported 5 tons of gum arabic from Geidam using the Borno Native Authority Fund in 1913, making 'a handsome rate of profit' (Mukhtar 2000: 169). The official involvement of colonial authorities in the purchase and export of gum arabic was somewhat limited in the following years; the trade was picked up by international companies from the 1920s.

The United African Company (UAC) became involved in the trade when it opened a buying centre at Geidam in 1926. In his 'Report on Gum Arabic in Bornu Province', Weir, who was posted to Borno province in July 1928 to investigate the gum industry, spoke of the difficulties the gum trade faced at that time due to the low prices paid to those who collected gum.

> [T]o pick gum pays them less than most of their other interests, skins, hides salt, etc., so that they have to be attracted to the industry. So far, the price offered [by the Niger Company buying] at Geidam and Maduguri has been low, viz, one penny per pound and I understand they have not bought much. (originally from Weir 1930: 4; taken from Egboh 1978b: 99; amendment appears also in the original sequence)

---

6 Author translation. Original sentence: '[*wie Gummi*] *das jetzt fast gar nicht zu Markte kommt, aber in ungeheuren Quantitäten aus dem grossen Mimosenwald nördlich vom Tsad herbeigeschafft werden könnte*'.

Weir's report also stresses the high potential of gum production and mentions the existence of a big 'local native market industry' for gum arabic. However, he also mentions the poor export-marketing structures in the province, even after more firms like London and Kano Trading Company, Post and Telegraphic joined the UAC (MacDonald 1937a). In the 1930s, when the railway reached Nguru, the export of gum arabic increased. The company Messrs Rowntree of York came to Borno as a major gum arabic trading company in the province, buying the best grades of gum arabic collected by smallholders from natural stands of *Senegalia senegal* over five years. The result was an increase in the quantity of gum arabic bought for export, which also showed the importance of the railway and foreign trading firms in the gum export trade in the Borno province. Thus, from 1930, the export of gum arabic from Borno never fell below 100 tons, reaching the maximum purchase of over five hundred tons in 1932, as shown in Tables 10.1 and 10.2.

Table 10.1 The quantity and value of gum arabic exports from Borno Province, 1921–1934.

S/No.	Year	Tonnage	Value (in £ Sterling)
1	1921	4	182
2	1922	138	2,836
3	1923	247	5,921
4	1924	339	8,208
5	1925	77	1,943
6	1926	39	1,838
7	1927	93	3,002
8	1928	36	897
9	1929	75	3,679
10	1930	127	4,560
11	1931	274	7,218
12	1932	599	10,814
13	1933	485	9,793
14	1934	395	7,504

Source: Stainforth (1936a)

Table 10.2: Nguru Railway Station statistics of goods and gum arabic transported by rail, 1932–1944.

S/No.	Year	Tonnage	Year	Tonnage
1	1932	447+	1939	571
2	1933	459+	1940	607
3	1934	234	1941	584
4	1935	537	1942	247
5	1936	1201	1943	977
6	1937	300	1944	900
7	1938	238		

Sources: de Putron (1933) and Monyei (1947)

This growth in gum arabic production and export was also the result of intensified propaganda campaigns by the provincial colonial authorities, who mobilised the smallholders in the tapping of *Senegalia senegal* trees for the best gum production for export. In 1935 and 1936 the provincial report on the gum arabic industry states that attempts were made to establish communal production bases in the main areas of production such Nguru, Borsari, Damaturu, Auno, Kaga, and Bedde in Northern Borno (Stainforth 1936a). In this action plan, the consultation of local authorities (in this case the '*Lawans*' – the ward heads – and their loyalty the '*Talakawa*') were mentioned, and 3,000 trees were tapped under the supervision of the provincial officer (Stainforth 1936a). The report also states that in the next 'season some 20,000 to 30,000 trees were tapped', which might explain the distinctive record of production for export of gum arabic for the year 1936. In the following, the number of foreign firms involved in the gum arabic trade for export also rose.[7]

The production itself was not under the strict control of the colonial officers, as might be assumed, but in the hands of local smallholders, who would engage in the collection of gum arabic as one of their livelihood means, amongst others. Other incentives, such as the 'education of the local population', also did not work as intended, as the following quote shows:

---

[7]   In the northern Borno Area Messrs Rowntree, Messrs U. C. A., Messrs Chattalas, and Messrs P. Z. were active, while in the southern Borno Province Messrs U. A. C., Messrs P. Z., and Messrs Ormesmith engaged in the trade with gum arabic (Stainforth 1936b).

In December 1932, Rowntree himself visited Nigeria. He stated that he had spent time and money educating the local population to tap the gum properly, but regretted that the people did not bring it to his company for sale. He reported that the collectors, instead, brought the gum to the open market where they had to compete for it with other firms which had not spent anything to encourage its collection. (Egboh 1978b: 100)

Nevertheless, in the 1930s, gum arabic production for export had been firmly established in the Borno Province, and the main impact of the production and export of gum arabic was the monetary returns to the producers, the foreign firms, and their buying agents. However, the amount of cash benefits that were derived from the production and export of gum arabic depended on the prices offered by British firms. During the 1935–1936 buying season, for example, all firms in the gum arabic export trade quoted their official price for gum arabic at one and a half pence (1½d.) per pound (lb) at Nguru and 1d. per lb at outlying centres (Stainforth 1936a). However, some offered more, such as Messrs Chattalas at Geidam, which paid up to 2d per lb of gum arabic (MacDonald 1937b). Equally, the price paid for the so-called 'mixed gum' from southern Borno in Maiduguri was 1¼d. per lb, which compared more favourably with the price of 1d. per lb for the much superior '*Kolkol*' (grade one gum arabic) from northern Borno at Nguru (Stainforth 1936a). Indeed, the value of the mixed gum at Jos (railhead) was 2d per lb, and on the London market 10s (shillings) per cwt,[8] or a fraction of a penny per lb (Stainforth 1936a).

Although the production and export of gum arabic was promoted in the 1930s, the production and export values strongly fluctuated over time. Egboh states that 'as far as gum production was concerned, the people of colonial Nigeria largely escaped exploitation by refusing to produce gum at the nominal price offered. They were able to do this successfully because they had alternative means of earning their livelihood' (Egboh 1978a: 220–221). The strategy of smallholders not relying on gum arabic as a main source of income might also result from the vast fluctuations of prices and the perception of gum arabic not as an essential, but as an opportunistic livelihood asset, while agriculture, livestock husbandry, hunting, selling of hides and skins, firewood collection, or the gathering of materials for handicrafts were more or equally important.

---

[8] Cwt. is the abbreviation for 'centum weight' or hundredweight, equivalent to approximately 50 kilogrammes.

Independence period: Gum arabic production and export since 1960

The gum arabic production in northern Nigeria that we described so far was entirely based on the smallholder collection of gum arabic from natural stands of *Senegalia senegal*. However, in post-colonial times and especially around the turn of the millennium, the demand for gum arabic further increased, and the export numbers reached a new level (see also Figure 10.1). The smallholder production of gum arabic was complemented by huge efforts to modernise the gum arabic production in *Senegalia senegal* plantations. One driver of this process certainly has been the price development of gum arabic and the aim to sell large quantities to export firms directly, instead of using the informal market structures of gum arabic trade in Nigeria. For instance, in the 1970s, the price for one ton of crude gum arabic lay between US$1,500 and $8,000 (Williams & Phillips 2009: 254).

Figure 10.1 also shows that the export of gum arabic from Nigeria in the late 20th and early 21st centuries increased substantially, compared to the rather low quantities exported in the early 20th century. It therefore gained an important position in the Nigerian economy, and the Nigerian government promoted the growth of this sector and targeted an optimisation of gum production through research in the Rubber Research Institute of Nigeria (Mokwunye & Aghughu 2010: 9).

In the following section, we give some insights into the Nigerian system of gum arabic production, and compare the two production systems mentioned: the collection of gum arabic from natural stands (executed by smallholders) and the cultivation of *Senegalia senegal* in plantations.

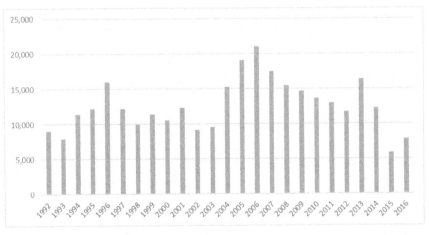

Figure 10.1 Quantity of gum arabic exported from Nigeria between 1992 and 2016 (in tons) (Source: UNCTAD 2018: 30–31).

Two production systems in northern Nigeria

In Nigeria, in recent years a shift in the production of gum arabic from a smallholder-based collection to an extensive tree-cultivation system occurred, which corresponds to the increasing international demand for gum arabic and was mainly driven by government projects and the distribution of seedlings (Mokwunye & Aghughu 2010: 9). Although the distinction between 'traditional' and 'modern' modes of production was mentioned several times during fieldwork in Nigeria, we would agree with Ingold, who describes this distinction as being a perspective of 'the Western' and 'the non-Western' (Ingold 2011: 323). In the local context, people often make a distinction between '*a zamanin dâ*' – in former times – and '*a zamanin nan*' – in modern times (Newman & Newman 2002: 138). This differentiation does not imply that one way of production is 'better' than the other. We would stress that these distinctions are rather made by outsiders. When we talk about dichotomies like 'traditional' vs. 'modern' or 'bush/wild' vs. 'civilisation', the differences between these categories are rather indistinct. From our experiences in northern Nigeria, the Hausa words '*daji*' or '*jeji*' (lit.: the bush), which could also be referred to the more general construction of the 'wild', was mentioned in interviews with both smallholders in natural *Senegalia senegal* stands and managers of *Senegalia senegal* plantations. In the following, we would like to introduce the two production systems that we have categorised according to their methods of production. The first production mode refers to *Senegalia senegal* trees that grow naturally and which are used by smallholders (without intentional planting), and the second mode refers to large-scale transplantation and cultivation of *Senegalia senegal* executed by financially 'strong men' (Hausa: *mai karfi*) who are able to invest in plantation establishment and wage labour.

Smallholder production of gum arabic

Natural-stand gum arabic production is practised by smallholders, using 'naturally' grown trees for gum arabic collection, and gum production is confined to the basic production practices – tapping trees and collecting gum. Tapping activities are done with an axe and normally start in October, after the rains have stopped. Every tree is tapped several times, the actual number depending on the particular tree height. The amount of gum arabic produced by the particular tree varies, and smallholders ascribe yield fluctuations to pest infestation, livestock browsing, the occurrence of fire, and also to *Ikon Allah* (the will of God). Gum collection starts four to six weeks after tapping, every two weeks, until the gum exudation stops. The gum is then dried and either sold in informal markets or stored until a time when the prices are high. The production and marketing of gum arabic along formal market channels remains difficult, at least for smallholders, who sell smaller quantities and often access smaller urban centres close to the production place, instead of selling the gum at regional centres, where gum prices are often better compared to early stages of the value chain (Vehrs 2013: 27). Peltier *et al.* (2009) describe a similar situation for the case of north Cameroon, where informal ways of trading are more accessible to local producers of gum arabic (Sagay & Mesike 2011: 43), while access to the official trade sector is perceived to be very rigid and highly taxed (Peltier *et al.* 2009: 47).

In contrast to plantation cultivation, where land tenure is exclusive, in the natural stands of *Senegalia senegal* the distribution of land and the use of gum trees is more complex. Sagay and Mesike asked more than 1,000 Nigerian farmers in the northern states about land tenure and other cultivation constraints (2011: 43). They noted that 95% of *Senegalia senegal* cultivation takes place on freeholders' land. The occupiers are given exclusive rights to land with immobile structures, for instance buildings and trees, in contrast to mobile objects, such as livestock. This principle of freehold rights was introduced during British rule and replaced the hitherto practised Islamic law of communal land-use rights. After the declaration of independence in 1960, the main systems of law continued to co-exist: customary law, Islamic law, and English Common Law. The distinction between customary law and Islamic law is often difficult, because in the northern states Islamic law was equated with customary law under British rule (Mwalimu 2005: 135).[9]

In smallholder gum arabic production, the access to a forest area in a certain region is distributed to the people who want to produce gum arabic, but neither the acacia trees nor the area are directly owned by anybody, because '*Allah ya yi*' (lit.: God made it). In plantation cultivation of *Senegalia senegal* the

---

[9] Customary law refers to the particular system of regulations of specific ethnic groups, before the advent of Islam in the 15th and 16th century AD. From the 15th century, Islam became more important in northern Nigeria and, after the Jihad in 1804, Islamic law became the main system of law. In Islamic law, land is created by Allah and everybody has access to it, in terms of usufructuary rights. Mwalimu describes it as follows: 'Islamic law of land tenure in Nigeria does not permit exclusive rights on empty land to any person. The land is left free for the common use of all Muslims. Under Islamic law in Nigeria, land is considered indispensable for everyone in similar manner as water, air, light or fire and social life of the community founded on this principle ... The general principle underlying Islamic law of land tenure in Nigeria is that land is a gift from the Lord God [Allah]' (Mwalimu 2009: 341). Three main land categories can be distinguished in Islamic law: occupied, unoccupied, and common land. The first category of land is described thus: 'once occupied, the occupier is considered and indeed has absolute ownership over that piece of land against all persons', and inheritance is possible (Mwalimu 2009: 342).

area is allocated to the producer, who has exclusive use rights. The access to land also influences the gum production, because in plantation cultivation the land must be claimed from local authorities or, in cases of more than 500 hectares, from the governor of the particular state, and compensations must be paid according to the Land Use Act of 1978. Hence, the allocation of land is the first challenge facing large-scale plantation owners, and might also include capital investment.

Modernisation of gum arabic production

In the past decades, a new mode of gum arabic production began developing in Nigeria, which we refer to as plantation cultivation. In this section, we describe a plantation type based on the research in three plantations in Yobe and Borno States in 2011, even though a uniform type or stereotypical kind of plantation cultivation does not exist. Although gum arabic production is perceived to be lucrative, not many people yet cultivate *Senegalia senegal*, because the initial investments are capital-intensive. Access to capital is one of the most important constraints for plantation cultivation, compared to other constraints, such as availability of land and wage labour. The modernisation of gum arabic production aims to maximise the yields per hectare and to minimise production risks by implementing plantation management, such as the professionalisation and standardisation of work and production flows, or the application of external inputs, such as herbicides and insecticides. However, major problems – such as unpredictable yields – have not yet been completely solved. In opposition to smallholder production, plantation cultivation is not referred to as *Ikon Allah* (or God's will), but specific tree and gum exudation knowledge is gathered to maximise the plantation output.

The number of production practices in plantation cultivation is increasing, compared to the rather small number of working steps described for natural-stand gum arabic production. Seed collection and nursery breeding of *Senegalia senegal* are the first and most important working steps in plantation cultivation, because the source of seedlings determines the future success of production, especially in terms of quality. Seedlings are bred a few months before the rainy season starts in April in order to provide an optimal planting material. Nursery work contains different working steps, starting with the collection of seeds, collection of cow dung, river sand and top soil, mixing the soils with manure, filling it into polyethylene bags, arranging the polybags in the nursery, soaking seeds, planting seeds, watering seedlings, applying pesticides or insecticides, and, if necessary, weeding and root pruning.

Furthermore, suitable land must be obtained and land preparations carried out. Farm fencing and plantation security must be provided to prevent animals or people from entering the plantation, especially during the dry season. To create optimal conditions for growth, tractors are used for ploughing, harrowing, and transplantation of seedlings, which can begin at the start of the rainy season. Afterwards, the second supply of *Senegalia senegal* in the newly established plantation takes place, in which dead seedlings are replaced to ensure a maximum number of seedlings in the plantation. During the following time period, weeding is done to reduce competition for water and soil nutrients. At this stage the use of chemicals is often accepted, since gum arabic is not yet collected from very young trees.

Maintenance work is a crucial working step that is also newly implemented in plantation cultivation to ensure optimal tree growth and a high number of trees per hectare. In the first years after transplantation, regular weeding is necessary to minimise competition from grass for water and nutrients. Plantation sites older than three years are not cleared in the rainy season, because they can compete for water and soil minerals. Nevertheless, plantation sites are cleared of undergrowth after the rainy season to prevent fire outbreaks. Animal browsing for weed clearance is also a practised option in individual plantations, because it saves labour.

The next working step undertaken at an early stage is pruning. This requires the removal of lower branches to provide access for future tapping work. The creation of tapping wounds is the next working step. The first tapping is normally done four or five years after transplantation, also depending on the particular tree's growth, and on maintenance work. It comprises the intentional wounding of the tree bark to start the 'natural' exudation. Tapping starts after the rainy season, since an early tapping could result in the healing of many tapping panels without gum exudation (Ballal *et al.* 2005: 241; Adam & Fadl 2011: 686). Indicators for tapping time are the end of rainy season and the defoliation of *Senegalia senegal*. These indicators are not always reliable, because the end of the rainy season is not one hundred per cent predictable, but the timing of the processes is most important and the work must be arranged in concurrence with natural conditions. Table 10.3 concisely compares the production practices in the smallholder production and in plantation cultivation.

When compared to the smallholder production of gum arabic, where only tapping and the collection of gum take place, and neither fertilisers, nor herbicides or pesticides are used, a transformation towards the use of additional labour input and external inputs is recognisable for plantations. In the following, we will discuss the differences between the two methods of gum arabic production in northern Nigeria and their specific implications, especially the possible effects of modernisation processes on local taskscapes.

Table 10.3 Production practices in the smallholder and cultivation systems.

Smallholder production	Plantation cultivation
	Collection of *Senegalia senegal* seeds
	Nursery breeding
	Plantation establishment (preparation of the plantation site, removal of trees and roots, fencing of the area, planting and nursing young trees)
	Weeding
	Pruning
Tapping (with an axe)	Tapping (with a tapping knife)
Gum collection	Gum collection
	Further maintenance

(Source: Author fieldwork data)

Unintended collaboration in smallholder production

In the following, we use two distinct production practices from the plantation cultivation of *Senegalia senegal* – maintenance activities of weeding, and pruning – as descriptive examples to illustrate that gum arabic production practices in natural stands are not detached from other activities in the savannah woodlands, but are incorporated in the 'totality of the tasks carried out by a community in a landscape', conceptualised as 'taskscape' by Ingold (2011: 325).

Weeding and pruning activities are important examples to understand the changing character of gum arabic production in the modernisation process, as those working steps are only executed in plantation cultivation of *Senegalia senegal*. It is particularly the absence of those activities in the smallholder production that attracts our attention. In the savannah woodlands where the smallholder production takes place, the trees are easily accessible, similar to the maintained tree growth in plantations, though maintenance work is not executed. The explanation offered by local producers was: 'No one is repairing [maintaining], because Allah repaired them [the acacia trees]'.[10]

However, herders who roam in the open-access area often lop tree branches to provide valuable forage for the animals and execute an 'unintentional'

---

[10] Personal communication with Bullama Kauri, 5 November 2011. Author translation; original sequence as follows: '*Bâ a yi gyara, tun da Allah ya gyara su*'.

pruning activity.[11] Lopping in natural stands of *Senegalia senegal* creates access to the tree stems and also provides the necessary pruning of the acacia trees. Since this work lacks the intention of gum arabic production, lopping activities must be considered as 'unintended' production practices, henceforth called 'unintended collaboration'.

The second case is weeding, executed in plantations for fire prevention and to limit the competition from grass in the first years after the establishment of the plantation. In more mature plantations, grasses and weeds usually grow head-high and are either cleared manually, or after rainy season cattle herds enter the plantation for browsing. In smallholder production, weeding does not take place, as available grasses and weeds are browsed by livestock, either owned by smallholders or Fulbe pastoralists. Hence, clearing weeds is not an intended gum arabic production practice, and again follows the same principle of 'unintended collaboration'.

Both activities – weeding and pruning – occur in natural stands (smallholder production) and plantation cultivation in different ways. In the case of lopping tree branches and removing weeds and grasses in natural stands, practices are not performed intentionally, nor are they arranged between different actors. In plantations, weeding must be operated, since any kind of 'unintended collaboration' becomes impossible through the establishment of fences for security reasons.

However, 'unintended collaboration' cannot be understood separately from its environment. Both practices, lopping and weeding, are immanent to gum arabic production, and create different peculiarities in relation to smallholder production on the one hand, and to plantation cultivation on the other. The social organisation of work is rearranged in plantation cultivation due to land-use changes, hence a changing taskscape. Ingold distinguishes the term 'production' into two sub-categories: 'making' and 'growing', of which 'making' describes the purpose of serving human needs, in the process of which species are 'artificially selected' (Ingold 2011: 77). Hence, 'growing' refers to plants and animals that are not intentionally 'made' and which can be collected from the 'natural' environment. 'Growing' can also refer to the smallholder production of gum arabic, in contrast to the 'making' of gum arabic in plantation cultivation.

More generally, we argue that modernisation processes such as the plantation establishment described here (in the sense of making and in contrast to growing) do not only aim at an increase in production and efficiency of

---

[11] Lopping itself is a common activity carried out more generally for a variety of groups that rely on livestock husbandry, and was also previously described for the Nigerian case at the beginning of the last century (see for instance Lugard 1904: 14).

labour inputs. Sometimes these modernisation processes are also affected by changes that are not easily detectable, such as the discontinuation of practices, described here along the examples of unintended collaboration, which were never applied specifically to the collection of gum arabic, but rather in the context of livestock husbandry.

By creating conditions for an exclusive exploitation of trees in plantations, these links between animal-human-environment relations are disrupted and reordered. In the plantation cultivation of *Senegalia senegal*, all those work steps that are performed by other actors (human and more-than-human) in the taskscape of the natural stands of *Senegalia senegal* must then be reorganised and translated into work steps in plantation cultivation. The so-called modernisation of cultivation therefore leads to a radical reconfiguration of human-environment relations.

The challenges of the commercialisation process

As mentioned before, the production of gum arabic is not always reliable, and yields in particular fluctuate due to a variety of reasons. However, the dependence on yields sharply differs between smallholder production and plantation cultivation. In general, the productivity is estimated to be higher in plantation cultivation of *Senegalia senegal*, but only if gum yields can meet the producer's expectations. Until now, gum yields, fluctuations in production, and the possible explanations for these are topics of intense scientific discussions – for instance, regarding the optimal tapping time and tapping practices (Ballal *et al.* 2005: 237; Ram *et al.* 2012), or different influences on gum yields, such as soil moisture and soil temperature (Wekesa *et al.* 2009: 263), or grass–tree competition (Adam *et al.* 2013: 169). Furthermore, tapping wound exposure to sunlight (Adam *et al.* 2009: 185), locust infestation or browsing (Ballal *et al.* 2005: 244), the enhancement of gum exudation through the application of chemicals (Abib *et al.* 2013: 427), and the differences of *Senegalia senegal* provenances (Fakuta *et al.* 2018: 134) are discussed to with reference to maximising yields and minimising risks. A standardised way to produce gum arabic has not been achieved yet, due to the sheer number of possible influences on gum exudation. The complexity of the gum exudation and the difficulties in identifying a standardised and professional method to facilitate a permanent and reliable production characterises the modernisation path of gum arabic production.

The capital investment needed for the latter is a crucial factor to understand the differences between smallholder gum arabic production and plantation cultivation of *Senegalia senegal*. For smallholder production in natural stands, capital input is usually not necessary, and production is undertaken with 'naturally' grown *Senegalia senegal* trees. Plantation cultivation, on the contrary, demands very high capital investments in terms of seedlings, plantation establishment, maintenance, and production practices. High labour inputs are necessary, even before the first gum is produced. These huge capital and labour investments act as a strong constraint on large-scale *Senegalia senegal* cultivation; however, the estimated labour and land productivity may be comparatively high and can compensate investments, if yield expectations are met.

Apart from yield problems, the decentralised market structure with different prices along the value chain and fluctuating prices across the production season affect both smallholders and plantation owners. Smallholders often sell small amounts of gum arabic to local purchasers, and the price per kilogramme is comparatively low, in contrast to prices obtained for larger quantities of cleaned gum arabic in the regional centres, usually by plantation owners.

The degree of formal commercialisation of gum arabic trade along the value chain also plays an important role, and natural-stand production is embedded into smallholder livelihoods, which mainly depend on subsistence farming. From their perspective, it is often not an aspiration to enlarge gum arabic production. The informal forms of gum arabic trade are sufficient for the sale of smaller quantities (see also Palou Madi *et al.* 2010: 58) for the case of north Cameroon, where the authors argue that the informal market provides some advantages for the smallholder production of gum arabic. Therefore, the intensification of production or the specialisation of smallholders in gum arabic production is often not desirable. Although the character of work in plantation cultivation is still similar to the work activities of smallholders, the number of activities has increased to control each part of the life cycle of *Senegalia senegal*.

Large-scale plantation cultivation of *Senegalia senegal* is a new emerging mode of production, and the major constraint of yield unpredictability has until now limited the establishment of large-scale plantations. Researchers in many countries along the Sahelian gum belt try to improve production practices and minimise risks. Smallholders, however, do not aim to control the fluctuation in gum arabic yield, and attribute it to 'natural' and also 'supernatural' powers, like *Ikon Allah*. The smallholder collection of gum arabic from natural stands is still the primary source of gum arabic production in northern Nigeria. From a smallholder perspective, the cultivation of *Senegalia senegal* is often perceived to be problematic due to the required higher labour and capital inputs, as well as the lack of infrastructure, marketing access, several production risks and fluctuating prices. Further constraints are the problematic access to seeds, seedlings and high transportation costs. Therefore, *Senegalia senegal* plantation cultivation is often perceived to be executed by financially 'strong men', who can afford to pay for seedlings, transportation, plantation establishment, and other costs. For smallholders, natural-stand gum arabic production is therefore a rather good strategy to diversify livelihood income.

Nevertheless, the smallholder production in Nigeria also faces production constraints. Especially, the *Senegalia senegal* tree populations might need management in future to sustain gum arabic production. Looking at the Nigerian woodlands, Mortimore and Adams recognise that the area of open woodland in all of their case studies in northern Nigeria (Kano, Jigawa, and Yobe states) is decreasing (1999: 92). Wezel and Lykke also confirm this perception in their article about woody vegetation change in the West African Sahel. The authors analysed cases from Burkina Faso, Niger, and Senegal, where amongst other tree species the *Senegalia senegal* population is also decreasing (Wezel & Lykke 2006: 557). The diminishing tree density has an important impact on smallholder livelihoods and nomadic herdsmen, since the extent of environmental goods and services, like gum arabic and acacia leaves and pods, are declining (Mortimore & Turner 2005: 579). Based on air photographs, Mortimore and Turner illustrate the land-cover changes between 1957 and 1990 and indicate a decline of 24% in woodland area, whereas the total area of grasslands increased by about 16%. The need of a growing population for environmental goods and services, for instance firewood and charcoal, might negatively influence tree densities in rural areas, which could require the planting of acacia trees to sustain local productions.

Conclusion

The potential of *Senegalia senegal* transplantation and gum arabic production for both plantation cultivation as well as smallholder production is undisputed, for a variety of reasons. Often the direct and indirect benefits of *Senegalia senegal* for smallholders are emphasised, such as the collection of gum arabic, and the use of the tree for fuel wood, soil-erosion reduction, nitrogen fixation, windbreaks or desert buffers (Barbier 1992: 341–342; Taha *et al.* 2018: 25–26). The modernisation of the gum-producing sector is at the same time intended to help to integrate *Senegalia senegal* into rural livelihoods (Mujawamariya *et al.* 2013: 182), and the 'massive reforestation' of acacia species for gum arabic production is suggested to enhance local livelihoods (Mokwunye & Aghughu 2010: 12).

Rachel Wynberg (this volume) presents the marketing of biodiversity that traditional knowledge, or the notion of traditional, or pristine raw products, is often taken up to market these products and find new strategies into the markets, which serves new purposes, especially about 'natural' products, which are especially healthy and implicitly are the better products. Gum arabic is also a product which is perceived to be 'natural' and therefore contains a high value for industrial products. It is also essential to understand who defines production knowledge(s), at which level, and for which purpose. Smallholders have a different interest in the production of gum arabic than plantation owners. While smallholders use basic tapping techniques and opportunistically aim at gum production and revenues, cultivation of *Senegalia senegal* works differently. Knowledge is acquired and scientifically enhanced to optimise production, to meet the international standards of gum quality, which determine the prices, and also enable the marketisation of a particular resin of one acacia species over all others. Therefore, we can also demonstrate a tendency towards the 'standardisation of the wild', especially the grading system of gum arabic production. What is good or desired, is therefore determined by the international demand for grade one gum arabic, as most products are not consumed locally. Ndwandwe's case of honeybush production (this volume) and the commodification process involved, furthermore shows the difficulties of a sustainable use of a 'wild' element – the honeybush in her case – and its collection in the wild. We see some similarities to the case of gum arabic, as the plantation cultivation of honeybush is still in its infancy and faces many challenges. The case that Ndwandwe mentions deals with the experimentation of production practices for honeybush plantations to exercise control over the honey bush growth and weed reduction.

From marketing and consumer perspectives, a 'longing for the wild' can also be identified in the case of gum arabic, as 'natural' ingredients are much advertised in 'healthy' and 'original' products, what Greiner and Bollig refer to as 'fetishism' in their contribution to this volume. However, in our case the international demand does not explain the success story alone. Moreover, the specific properties of gum arabic, the broad fields of application, and the difficulties in developing artificial alternatives also influence the degree of commodification.

The future prospects and challenges of *Senegalia senegal* cultivation and gum arabic production are not predictable, but many efforts are undertaken to control the production and adjust it to international market conditions. Perhaps further uses can also be identified in the future, such as the production of biodiesel from the seeds of *Senegalia senegal* (Hamed *et al.* 2018), or yet unknown medicinal applications (Abu Zeid & FarajAllah 2018; Salih 2018). However, one major challenge remains: the value of gum arabic captured along the value chain only remains to a very small extent in the producer's hands as the UNCTAD (2018: 64) report indicates – 5%, or even less, in 'some African countries'.

Bibliography

Abib, C. F., Ntoupka, M., & Peltier, R. *et al.* (2013). 'Ethephon: A tool to boost gum arabic production from *Acacia senegal* and to enhance gummosis processes', *Agroforestry Systems*, 87(2), 427–438.

Abu Zeid, I. M. & FarajAllah, A. R. (2018). 'Gum arabic and kidney failure: An exceptional panacea', in: A. A. Mariod (ed.), *Gum Arabic. Structure, Properties, Application and Economics* (London; San Diego CA: Academic Press), 245–260.

Adam, I. M. & Fadl, K. E. M. (2011). 'Determination of optimum tapping date for gum arabic production in South Kordofan State, Sudan', *Journal of Forestry Research*, 22(4), 685–688.

Adam, I. M., Ballal, M. E. M., & Fadl, K. E. M. (2009). 'Effect of tapping direction in relation to sun light on gum arabic *Acacia senegal* (L.) Willd. yields in North Kordofan State, Sudan', *Forests, Trees and Livelihoods*, 19(2), 185–191.

Adam, I. M., Ballal, M. E. M., & Fadl, K. E. M. (2013). 'Effect of grass density and date of tapping on *Acacia senegal* gum yield in North Kordofan State, Sudan', *Journal of Forestry Research*, 24(1), 169–172.

Ballal, M. E. M., Siddig, E. A. E., Elfadl, M. A. *et al.* (2005). 'Gum arabic yield in differently managed *Acacia senegal* stands in Western Sudan', *Agroforestry Systems*, 63(3), 237–245.

Barbier, E. B. (1992). 'Rehabilitating gum arabic systems in Sudan: Economic and environmental implications', *Environmental and Resource Economics*, 2, 341–358.

Behrends, A., Park, S.-J., & Rottenburg, R. (2014). 'Travelling models: Introducing an analytical concept to globalisation studies', in: A. Behrends, S.-J. Park & R. Rottenburg (eds), *Travelling Models in African Conflict Management: Translating Technologies of Social Ordering* (Leiden: Brill), 1–40.

Beyene, M. (1993). 'Investing in *Acacia senegal* – Lessons from the Sudanese experience to Eritrea', Working Paper Series, *African Arid Lands*, 4, 1–14.

de Putron, P. (1933). Resident Bornu Province, Northern Region of Nigeria, Bornu Province Annual Report, 1932. National Archives Kaduna (NAK), Archive source: S. N. P. 17/21325 (NAK).

Din, A. S. E. & Obeid, M. (1971a). 'Ecological studies of the vegetation of the Sudan II: The germination of seeds and establishment of seedlings of *Acacia senegal* (L.) Willd. under controlled conditions in the Sudan', *The Journal of Applied Ecology*, 8(1), 191–201.

Din, A. S. E. & Obeid, M. (1971b), 'Ecological studies of the vegetation of the Sudan. IV. The effect of simulated grazing on the growth of *Acacia senegal* (L.) Willd. seedlings', *The Journal of Applied Ecology*, 8(1), 211–216.

DIVA-GIS 2021. 'Free spatial data'. Available at: www.diva-gis.org/gdata [Accessed 28 February 2022].

Dujardin-Beaumetz, G. & Egasse, E. (1889). *Les Plantes médicinales indigènes et exotiques, leurs usages thérapeutiques, pharmaceutiques et industriels* (Paris: Octave Doin).

Dyer, C. (2014). 'New names for the African *Acacia* species in *Vachellia* and *Senegalia*', *Southern Forests: a Journal of Forest Science*, 76(4), iii.

Egboh, E. O. (1978a). 'The Nigerian gum arabic industry, 1897–1940. A study in rural economic development under colonial régime', *Cahiers d'études africaines*, 18(69), 215–221.

Egboh, E. O. (1978b). 'The Nigerian gum arabic industry: A study in rural economic development under the colonial régime (1897–1940)', *Présence Africaine – Nouvelle série*, 108(4), 92–105.

Elmqvist, B., Olsson, L., Mirghani Elamin, E., & Warren, A. 2005. 'A traditional agroforestry system under threat: An analysis of the gum arabic market and cultivation in the Sudan', *Agroforestry Systems*, 64(3), 211–218.

El Tahir, B. A., Ahmed, D. M., Ardö, J., Gaafar, A. M., & Salih, A. A. (2009). 'Changes in soil properties following conversion of acacia senegal plantation to other land management systems in North Kordofan State, Sudan', *Journal of Arid Environments*, 73(4), 499–505.

Fagg, C. W. & Allison, G. E. (2004). '*Acacia senegal* and the Gum Arabic Trade', Tropical Forestry Paper 42 (Oxford: Alden Group). Available at: https://ora.ox.ac.uk/objects/uuid:3236b450-221b-41dd-9105-792c00813afa [Accessed 17 February 2022].

Fakuta, M. N., Ojiekpon, I. F., Gashua, I. B., & Ogunremi, O. C. (2015). 'Quantitative genetic variation in gum arabic (*Acacia senegal* (L) Willd) provenances', *American Journal of Plant Sciences*, 6(18), 2826–2831.

Fakuta, N. M., Aba, A. D., Ado, S. G., Jonah, P. M., & Bichi, A. M. (2018). 'Combining ability of growth traits, zinc and manganese in gum arabic (*Senegalia senegal* [L.] Britton)', *Nigerian Journal of Genetics*, 32(1), 127–134.

Flückiger, F. A. & Hanbury, D. (1879). *Pharmacographia: A History of the Principal Drugs of Vegetable Origin, Met With in Great Britain and British India*, Second edn (London: Macmillan & Co.).

Hamed, M. A., Hassan, E. A. & Atabani, A. E. (2018). 'Extraction and utilization of Sudanese *Acacia senegale* seeds (gum arabic) oil for biodiesel production in Sudan', in: A. A. Mariod (ed.), *Gum Arabic: Structure, Properties, Application and Economics* (London; San Diego CA: Academic Press), 229–236.

Harmand, J. M., Ntoupka, M., Mathieu, B., & Njiti, C. F. (2012). 'Gum Arabic production in *Acacia senegal* plantations in the Sudanian zone of Cameroon: Effects of climate, soil, tapping date and tree provenance', *Bois et Forêts des Tropiques*, 21–33.

Ingold, T. (2011 [2000]). *The Perception of the Environment: Essays on Livelihood, Dwelling and Skill* (London: Routledge).

Lugard, F. D. (1904). 'Northern Nigeria', *The Geographical Journal*, 23(1), 1–27.

MacDonald, K. R. (1937a). Memorandum 1936–1937. Assistant Conservator of Forest. National Archives Kaduna (NAK), Archive source: S. N. P. 17/10617 Vol. II.

MacDonald, K. R. (1937b). Memorandum 1936–1937. Assistant Conservator of Forest. National Archives Kaduna (NAK), Archive source: S. N. P. 17/10617 Vol. IV.

Mariod, A. A. (2018). 'Functional Properties of Gum Arabic', in: A. A. Mariod (ed.), *Gum Arabic: Structure, Properties, Application and Economics* (London; San Diego CA: Academic Press), 283–295.

Mokwunye, M. U. B. & Aghughu, O. (2010). 'Restoring Nigeria's lead in gum arabic production: Prospects and challenges', *Report and Opinion*, 2(4), 7–13.

Monyei, E. (1947). 'Statistics of Goods Transport Nguru Railway Station, 1934–1947'. District Traffic Superintendent, Nigerian Railway, Zaria to Resident Bornu Province, Nguru Station Manager. National Archives Kaduna (NAK), Archive source: Mai Prof. 2161.

Mortimore, M. & Adams, W. M. (1999). *Working the Sahel: Environment and Society in Northern Nigeria*. Routledge Research Global Environmental Change series, no. 2 (London; New York: Routledge).

Mortimore, M. & Turner, B. (2005). 'Does the Sahelian smallholder's management of woodland, farm trees, rangeland support the hypothesis of human-induced desertification?' *Journal of Arid Environments*, 63(3), 567–595.

Mujawamariya, G., Palou Madi, O., Zoubeirou, A. M. *et al.* (2013). 'Common challenges in gum arabic production and commercialization in West Africa: A comparative study of Cameroon, Niger and Senegal', *The International Forestry Review*, 15(2), 182–199.

Mukhtar, Y. (2000). *Trade, Merchants and the State in Borno c. 1893–1939* (Cologne: Rüdiger Köppe).

Muldrew, C. (1998). *The Economy of Obligation: The Culture of Credit and Social Relations in Early Modern England*. Early Modern History series (Basingstoke: Macmillan).

Mwalimu, C. (2005). *The Nigerian Legal System: Public Law*. Volume I (New York: Peter Lang).

Mwalimu, C. (2009). *The Nigerian Legal System: Public Law*. Volume II (New York: Peter Lang).

Nachtigal, G. (1879). *Sahará und Sûdân: Ergebnisse sechsjähriger Reisen in Afrika: Dritter Theil* (Leipzig: F. A. Brockhaus).

Newman, P. & Newman, R. M. (2002). *Modern Hausa – English Dictionary. Sabon Kamus na Hausa zuwa Turanci* (Ibadan: University Press).

Ngaryo, F. T., Agbangba, E. C., Goudiaby, V. A. *et al.* (2011). 'Modeling the production of Arabic gum (*Acacia senegal* (L.) Willd) based on the proper tapping characteristics in the semi arid Sahel of Chad', *International Journal of Science and Advanced Technology*, 1, 24–30.

Obeid, M. & Din, A. S. E. (1970). 'Ecological studies of the vegetation of the Sudan: I. *Acacia senegal* (L.) Willd. and its natural regeneration', *The Journal of Applied Ecology*, 7(3), 507–518.

Obeid, M. & Din, A. S. E. (1971). 'Ecological studies of the vegetation of the Sudan: III. The effect of simulated rainfall distribution at different isohyets on the regeneration of *Acacia senegal* (L.) Willd. on clay and sandy soils', *The Journal of Applied Ecology*, 8(1), 203–209.

Oliver, D. (1871). *Flora of Tropical Africa*, Vol. II, *Leguminosae to Ficoideae* (London: L. Reeve & Co.)

Palou Madi, O., Peltier, R., Balarabe, O. *et al.* (2010). 'Abandon ou extension des plantations d'acacias au Nord-Cameroun: tout dépendra du fonctionnement des filières gomme arabique', *Bois et Forêts des Tropiques*, 306(4), 57.

Peltier, R., Palou Madi, O. & Balarabe, O. (2009). 'Les filières gomme arabique au Nord-Cameroun: Impacts du fonctionnement des filéres gomme sur l'organisation des producteurs, la gestion des forêts naturelles et l'encouragement des plantations d'acacias', in: L. Seiny-Boukar and P. Boumard (eds), *Savanes africaines en développement: Innover pour durer – Résumés, Actes du colloque du Prasac* (Garoua, Cameroun: Cirad – Centre de Coopération Internationale en Recherche Agronomique pour le Développement), 1–15.

QGIS Geographic Information System 2021. Open Source Geospatial Foundation Project. Available at: www.qgis.org/en/site [Accessed 6 January 2023].

Ram, M., Tewari, J. C., & Harsh, L. N. (2012). *An Improved Gum Tapping from Acacia senegal: An Option for Better Livelihood* (Saarbrücken: LAP LAMBERT Academic Publishing).

Rohlfs, G. (1868). *Reise durch Nord-Afrika vom mittelländischer Meere bis zum Busen von Guinea 1865 bis 1867: 1. Hälfte: Von Tripoli nach Kuka (Fesan, Sahara, Bornu)* (Gotha: Justus Perthes).

Sagay, G. A. & Mesike, C. S. (2011). 'Socio-economic factors associated with gum arabic production in Nigeria', *Journal of Social Sciences*, 26(1), 41–45.

Salih, N. K. M. (2018). 'Applications of gum arabic in medical and health benefits', in: A. A. Mariod (ed.), *Gum Arabic: Structure, Properties, Application and Economics* (London; San Diego CA: Academic Press), 269–281.

Shaw, F. L. (1905). *A Tropical Dependency: An Outline of the Ancient History of the Western Sudan with an Account of the Modern Settlement of Northern Nigeria* (London: James Nisbet).

Stainforth, G. O. (1936a). Resident Bornu Province, Northern Region of Nigeria, Gum Arabic Season. National Archives Kaduna (NAK), Archive source: Mai Prof. 2778 (NAK).

Stainforth, G. O. (1936b). Resident Bornu Province, Northern Region of Nigeria, Gum Arabic Season, 1936. National Archives Kaduna (NAK), Archive source: Mai Prof. 2778, Table II (NAK).

Street, C. A. & Anderson, D. M. W. 1983. 'Refinement of structures previously proposed for gum arabic and other acacia gum exudates', *Talanta*, 30(11), 887–893.

Sulieman, A. M. E.-H. (2018). 'Gum arabic as thickener and stabilizing agents in dairy products', in: A. A. Mariod (ed.), *Gum Arabic: Structure, Properties, Application and Economics* (London; San Diego CA: Academic Press), 151–165.

Taha, M. E. N., Pretzsch, J., Siddig, M. E. *et al.* (2018). 'Valuation of the environmental role of *Acacia senegal* tree in the Gum Belt of Kordofan and the Blue Nile Sectors, Sudan', in: A. A. Mariod (ed.), *Gum Arabic. Structure, Properties, Application and Economics* (London; San Diego CA: Academic Press), 23–28.

Tilly, C. (2016). *Identities, Boundaries and Social Ties* (New York: Routledge).

Troyon, C. (1853). 'Four Oxen Pulling a Plough. Black Chalk and Gouache with Graphite and Gum Arabic and Traces of White Chalk in Sky, Squared for Transfer in Black Chalk', Cleveland Museum of Art. Available at: www.cleve-landart.org/art/2015.452 [Accessed 22 August 2019].

UNCTAD – United Nations Conference on Trade and Development (2018). 'Commodities at Glance: Special Issue on Gum Arabic' (Geneva: United Nations, April 2018). Available at: https://unctad.org/en/PublicationsLibrary/suc2017d4_en.pdf [Accessed 16 October 2019].

Vehrs, H.-P. (2013). *Gum Arabic as an Enterprise: Socio-Ecological Analysis of Gum Arabic Production in Yobe State, Nigeria* (Saarbrücken: AV Akademikerverlag).

Waziri, I. M. (2008). *Colonial Export Trade in Borno: Northern Nigeria, 1902–1945* (Ibadan: Loud Books).

Weir, A. H. W. (1930). *Report on Gum Arabic in Bornu province, Nigeria.* (Lagos: Government Printer).

Wekesa, C., Makenzi, P., Chikamai, B. N. *et al.* (2009). 'Gum arabic yield in different varieties of *Acacia senegal* (L.) Willd in Kenya', *African Journal of Plant Science*, 3(11), 263–276.

Wezel, A. & Lykke, A. M. (2006). 'Woody vegetation change in Sahelian West Africa: Evidence from local knowledge', *Environment, Development and Sustainability*, 8(4), 553–567.

White, Ellen G. (1868). 'For girls who chew gum', *The Health Reformer*, 1868.

Williams, P. A. & Phillips, G. O. (2009). 'Gum arabic', in: G. O. Phillips (ed.), *Handbook of Hydrocolloids*, Second edn. Woodhead Publishing Series in Food Science, Technology and Nutrition (Boca Raton FL: CRC), 252–273.

PART 4

COMMODIFYING WILDLIFE

11

Producing Elephant Commodities for 'Conservation Hunting' in Namibian Communal-area Conservancies

LEE HEWITSON AND SIAN SULLIVAN

> It is plain that commodities cannot go to market and make exchanges of their own account. (Karl Marx, *Capital*)

Introduction: Community-based natural resource management, hunting, and commodifying 'wild' nature

Trophy hunting of wild animals is central to the conservation and development objectives of many African countries, including Namibia. Despite increasing opposition to the industry, fuelled by the ongoing poaching crisis and recent killing of high-profile animals including 'Cecil' the lion and one of Africa's biggest bull elephants in Zimbabwe (BBC News 2015), trophy hunting remains big business. Over US$200 million is generated annually from trophy hunting in Africa and, in Namibia alone, this figure amounts to over $25 million (MacLaren *et al.* 2019). The hunting of big-game species such as elephants (*Loxodonta africana*) is particularly lucrative, especially in the country's communal-area conservancies (see below). In Kwandu Conservancy, in Namibia's remote north-eastern Zambezi Region (Map 11.1), anyone wishing to hunt a trophy elephant must pay upwards of $50,000 to do so. As the Conservancy's treasurer put it: 'The most valuable animal is the elephant, because they give a lot of income to the Conservancy.'

These revenue streams are facilitated through Namibia's internationally acclaimed programme of community-based natural resource management (CBNRM), which combines a harnessing of market mechanisms and decentralisation with arguments for rural development (Sullivan 2006). The programme can be traced to the early 1980s, prior to Namibia's independence from South Africa, and against a backdrop of drought, civil war, and illegal hunting of especially elephant and rhino in the north-west of the country. Forming the Namibia Wildlife Trust (NWT), concerned conservationists worked alongside

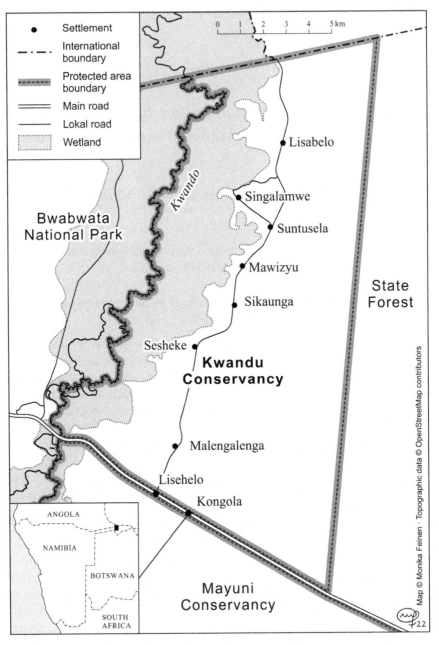

Map 11.1 Kwandu Conservancy, indicating location in Namibia's Zambezi Region (Source: Open StreetMap contributors; Cartography: M. Feinen).

government officials and traditional leaders to appoint 'community game guards' (CGGs) from the local area, charged with monitoring wildlife, conducting anti-poaching patrols and carrying out conservation extension work within their communities in return for food rations (IRDNC 2015). A small pilot ecotourism project was also implemented with primarily ovaHimba pastoralists in Purros on the Hoarusib River (Jacobsohn 1995), requiring tourists to pay a fee to the local community as caretakers of their natural resources, including land and wildlife (Jacobsohn, 1998[1990]). The project proved successful in helping to recover wildlife numbers in the region, its community-led approach defying the political climate of the time, with active participation of local people in conservation activities beginning to nurture a vision of wildlife as a valuable social and economic resource (Owen-Smith 2002). In 1990 these initiatives formed the kernel of a new NGO called Integrated Rural Development and Nature Conservation (IRDNC) that soon began a similar programme of community-based conservation work in what was then Caprivi Region, now 'Zambezi' Region,[1] in the north-east (IUCN *et al.* 2015; IRDNC 2015).

Soon after independence the Namibian government moved to formalise this initiative, enacting the Nature Conservation Amendment Act in 1996 which extended rights to legal and regulated wildlife use beyond freehold rangelands to communal-area residents that formed management units called 'conservancies'. These rights include the 'consumptive and non-consumptive use and sustainable management of game ... in order to enable the members to derive benefits' (Government of the Republic of Namibia, hereafter GRN 1996: 24A (4)) and mitigate the impacts of living alongside elephants with a tendency to raid the crops of conservancy residents (Drake *et al.* 2021). Historically marginalised communities have seized the opportunity to gain rights over natural resources (Sullivan 2002; Bollig 2016), and there are now eighty-six communal conservancies covering over 20% of Namibia's land area, encompassing around 233,000 people (MEFT & NACSO 2021). International donors including United States Agency for International Development (USAID), UK Department for International Development (DfID), World Bank, German Development Bank (KfW) and World Wide Fund for Nature (WWF) have contributed millions of US dollars to programme development and maintenance.

The CBNRM programme has been a key contributor to economic development and environmental conservation in Namibia's rural communal areas.

---

[1] In August 2013, in an attempt to eliminate the names of former colonial administrators from Namibia's maps, the Caprivi Region (with its administrative border from the Kavango River eastwards) was reduced and re-named 'Zambezi Region', and its administrative border moved eastwards to the settlement of Chetto.

The programme is now central to the country's conservation and development goals and is generally recognised as having contributed to a strong recovery in wildlife numbers (IUCN *et al.* 2015; Naidoo *et al.* 2016). In particular, Namibia's elephant population is thought to have increased from around 7,500 at CBNRM's formal inception in 1995 to over 23,000 today (MEFT & NACSO 2021), although we note that time series data from elephant surveys for Zambezi Region from 1989 to 2013 reportedly observed no trend in elephant population size (Robson *et al.* 2017). In Namibia's long-term development framework, CBNRM is an explicit rural development strategy, 'Vision 2030' (GRN 2004), and the Ministry of Environment, Forestry and Tourism (MEFT), previously the Ministry of Environment and Tourism (MET)), state that sustainable environmental use shall be a key driver of poverty alleviation and equitable economic growth, particularly in rural areas (GRN 2014; MEFT & NACSO 2021). The COVID-19 pandemic, however, has severely affected these aspirations (Lendelvo *et al.* 2020), and its full effects are as yet unknown.

Namibia is thus committed to capitalising on its wildlife through private sector enterprise in both ecotourism and consumptive use, notably trophy hunting[2] (Naidoo *et al.* 2016). In response to international criticism of the latter from animal welfare groups and others, trophy hunting has recently been rebranded 'conservation hunting'[3] by the Namibian government and CBNRM stakeholders eager to distance the practice from 'sport hunting' concerned solely with the collection of exotic trophies. They also make the link between sustainable 'offtake' and positive outcomes at species level, with conservation hunting described as producing 'clear, measurable conservation and human development outcomes' (NACSO 2015: 16), although recent research raises concerns over the sustainability of elephant offtake rates in conservancies (Drake *et al.* 2021).

The hunting of big-game animals including elephants is central to the conservancy model (Naidoo *et al.* 2016; Drake *et al.* 2021). At the national level economic returns from hunting and non-consumptive use of wildlife in conservancies increased incrementally since the programme's inception, generating around US\$9 million in 2018 (see also Kalvelage this volume). In recent years tourism enterprises provided the greatest cash income at household level, whilst conservation hunting returned cash directly to conservancies and

---

[2]   There are six types of consumptive wildlife use permitted in Namibia under varying conditions: (1) shoot-and-sell, (2) trophy hunting, (3) biltong hunting, (4) management hunting, (5) shooting for own use, (6) live capture and sale (Maclaren *et al.* 2019). This study focuses on trophy hunting, now framed as 'conservation hunting', because of its high economic value and importance to communal conservancies.

[3]   This rebranding follows an international movement to frame trophy hunting in this way, see www.conservationhunting.com.

provided in-kind benefits such as meat (MEFT & NACSO 2021). Recent research in Zambezi Region, however, suggests that only 20% of value generated by the tourism and hunting sectors is captured at conservancy community level, largely in the form of staff salaries or investments in local infrastructure projects (Kalvelage *et al.* 2020). Much of this income derives from the hunting of elephants, said to contribute over 50% of all conservancy hunting revenue on a national scale, and almost 70% in Zambezi's conservancies (IRDNC 2015; Naidoo *et al.* 2016).

Namibian CBNRM has played a part in the consolidation of an increasingly 'neoliberal' global policy framework and contributed an important example of its application to biodiversity conservation. By 'neoliberalism' we refer to a theory of political economic practices centred on individualism, privatisation of state enterprises and assets, international trade liberalisation, and the reduction of regulations that reduce market growth and efficiency (Sullivan 2006; Bakker 2015). Neoliberalism has permeated the arena of conservation and natural resource governance, with global environmental problems such as biodiversity loss and climate breakdown said to derive largely from market failure and a lack of societal recognition of nature's economic value. The logic of neoclassical economics is thus increasingly applied to diverse aspects of nature including forests and wild animals, to make this 'wild nature' visible economically as, for example, monetised 'ecosystem services' and 'natural capital' (TEEB 2010; Natural Capital Coalition 2016). In these processes the state becomes a market facilitator for trade in alienated nature conservation commodities, providing regulatory and supportive structures for the transfer of public goods to private sector actors (Fletcher 2010; Büscher *et al.* 2012).

With its market-based approach to resource governance and conservation, CBNRM has faced criticism around some of its social/environmental effects (Dressler *et al.* 2010). At times this critique can appear strongly focused on global power structures rather than the situated practices of local actors involved (although for Namibian CBNRM specifically see Silva & Motzer 2015; Koot 2019). There remains a lack of detailed research regarding how these programmes and their inherent value frames are operationalised in practice. In response to this knowledge gap, this chapter offers an empirical exploration of practices undertaken by (local) actors working to produce and extract value from 'wild' natures (cf. Fredrikson *et al.* 2014; Bracking *et al.* 2019) by investigating the production of trophy-elephant commodities for conservation hunting in Kwandu Conservancy, Zambezi Region. In doing so, the chapter responds to Kay & Kenney-Lazar's (2017) call to consider more-than-human actors in processes of capitalist value production. It builds on recent work seeking to 'ecologise' political ecology (Collard & Dempsey 2017; Barua 2019) by considering the (de)stabilising role of agentic elephants in the relational assembling of economic value.

The chapter's main argument is that commodified trophy elephants are produced for 'conservation hunting' in Namibia through a combination of the spontaneous activities of elephants, human labour, and socio-technical practices. The latter include the calculative technologies deployed by humans to count elephants and codify knowledge, which are dependent on utilitarian constructions that pacify elephant vitalities. The chapter elucidates how elephant behaviours such as crop raiding are co-opted into technocratic governance practices in the process of commodifying elephants.

The next section situates this study in an existing body of critical nature-society scholarship. It further discusses the conceptual approach adopted, one which attempts to sustain a productive tension between political ecology and more-than-human geographies. The third section provides a critical analysis of elephant commodity production processes in Kwandu Conservancy, north-east Namibia, before concluding in the final section with a summary of our argument and some directions for future research.

The nature of value and commodities

The production of value and nature

We build on a vast body of work in critical nature-society scholarship exploring relations between value, nature, and labour. As such, we take a political ecology approach in analysing the (capitalist) social relations of production and exchange that produce and transform natures, through the making of economically valued commodities (Smith 2008). The environmental-social dialectic central to political ecology is representative of its Marxian theoretical underpinning. In Marx's critique of classical political economy he argued that value is produced via social relations, encapsulated in his 'labour theory of value' (LToV) which holds that a commodity's objective value is the embodiment of the average socially necessary labour time taken to produce it (Marx 1974). Commodities produced by human labour in combination with 'the spontaneous produce of nature' (Marx 1974: 50) may have 'use value' as well as 'exchange value', the latter most often expressed in price/monetary form and permitting trade with other commodities. Although a commodity's 'price' varies due to changes in supply and demand, its 'value' remains constant, representative of a quantity of human labour utilised to produce it. Marx argues these value relations are obscured in the 'fetishised' commodity form under capitalism, which transforms subjective relations between people and the rest of nature into apparently objective relations between money and things (see also Greiner & Bollig this volume).

Nature-society geographers have drawn upon Marx's historical materialist approach in their studies of environmental change, degradation, and (in)justice

(Harvey 1996). Critical social science engagement with 'neoliberal conservation' has explored how natures are used, transformed, and 'saved' in and through the expansion of 'green capitalism' (Sullivan 2006, 2017a; Büscher *et al.* 2012). Drawing on Latour, Sullivan (2013) argues that nature framed and calculated as 'natural capital' becomes a fetishised object charged with objective power via institutionalised expert agreement and technical practices. This labour works to create abstract(ed) exchangeable commodities from conserved material natures, transforming use values into exchange values and units for sale in varied ecosystem services markets. Yet the process is beset with contradictions, and political ecologists argue that market prices are unable either to fully represent or incorporate the complex ecologies and (non)human labour involved in this commodity production (Huber 2018).

Namibian CBNRM's reliance on market mechanisms exemplifies the transformation of human labour and beyond-human natures into marketable commodities. The programme is dependent on abstraction and measurement of charismatic species such as lions and elephants able to generate monetary value in international markets, often demoting socio-natural and non-economic use values of importance to local livelihoods (Hewitson 2018). Utilising global production network (GPN) approaches, others in this volume (Revilla Diez and Hulke; Kalvelage) highlight the diverse, multi-scalar actors involved in producing 'wild' commodities such as trophy animals, whilst warning of unequal power relations and negative livelihood impacts at local levels. Studies also point to elite capture and dominance and the inability of participants to use acquired financial capital to significantly improve their economic position (Silva & Motzer 2015; Bollig 2016). Financial value accruing to tourism and trophy hunting businesses is reliant on the provision of 'wild nature' by communal-area conservancies, whose portion of received income goes primarily towards conservancy operating costs with somewhat meagre disbursements at household level (Suich 2013; Hewitson 2018; Kalvelage *et al.* 2020; Drake *et al.* 2021). A conservation model dependent on income from wealthy international tourists and trophy hunters is also vulnerable to international circumstances, as illustrated by the recent coronavirus health pandemic and associated travel restrictions (Lendelvo *et al.* 2020).

Applying a combined Marxist and critical political ecology analytical lens to human-environment relations in CBNRM spaces assists with understanding how huntable elephant commodities are (co)produced with and extracted from the biophysical world (Kay & Kenney-Lazar 2017). It can also shed light on the contested nature of this commodification and its consequences for local livelihoods. The processes which render complex ecologies into tradeable commodities are not only economic relations and social activities; they are also contingent upon beyond-human 'labour' and lifecycles. In this respect,

Marx's somewhat rigid conceptualisation of labour and value might hinder a more detailed understanding of the 'work' of non-humans in producing (and subverting) nature's commodification. For that reason, we now turn to more-than-human and relational approaches that emphasise the lively nature of these 'wild commodities'.

Assembling economic value with/from natures

Posthumanistic approaches exploring the materiality of nature and redistributing agency to 'other-than-human' actors are criticised for their lack of political engagement with the social relations of capitalism. In response, an emerging body of work seeking to 'ecologise' political ecology explores the incorporation of lively other-than-human entities in the production and circulation of economic value, emphasising the co-constitution of the economic and ecological whilst focusing on the inequalities generated by capital accumulation (Collard & Dempsey 2017). Barua (2019) conceptualises the activities of beyond-human entities as 'metabolic', 'affective' and 'ecological' 'labour' categories, each dependent to varying degrees upon an organism's biological and ecological capacities.[4] Like the unwaged (re)productive labour of humans (especially of women), this animal 'work' is hidden behind the fetishised and often intangible commodity – for example, a 'wilderness experience' or a 'carbon credit' – only coming to light when actual practices of value creation are explored (Haraway 2008; Barua 2019).

The generative capacities of animals are fundamental to capitalism's valorisation processes, and to their identity as 'officially valued' commodities (Collard & Dempsey 2017). Relational 'encounter value', for example, derives from contingent relationships between humans and other-than-human entities (Haraway 2008), the lifeworlds of individual animals affecting the possibility of capitalist capture of their activities. Barua (2014: 560) thus argues that elephants are social and spatial 'conduit[s] for connectivity',

---

4   We write 'labour' here in inverted commas to signal that we are ambivalent about extending concepts of work to natures-beyond-the-human, as in references to 'the work that nature does'. As one of us has suggested elsewhere (Sullivan 2017b), we think that at some level a category error is creeping in here. Or, at least, that a false question is being posed – that is, does nature labour? Natures beyond-the-human are immanently (re)generative, but it seems to us that beyond-human natures labour only to the extent that they are conceptualised, calculated and alienated as such. The work that goes into creating the symbolic layering that abstracts dimensions of nature-beyond-the-human into commodified units of value is all (too) human, as are the buyers and sellers of the units that thereby arise.

their material and affective agency knitting far-flung epistemic communities together in conservation assemblages.

Against this background, this study's methodology incorporates material and perceptive 'following' of elephants through a specific conservation hunting assemblage, in order to understand empirically how valued 'trophy' commodities are produced. Taken from Deleuze & Guattari's (1987) notion of *agencement*, 'assemblage' refers to the relational coming together and spatial ordering of disparate entities through which actions occur (DeLanda 2006; Anderson & McFarlane 2011). Assembled relations are contingently obligatory rather than logically necessary amongst actants that are always involved in (de)territorialising processes. Actants may engage in arborescent practices that stabilise the assemblage, reinforcing its borders or homogenising its composition. Conversely, an assemblage may become deterritorialised and its internal coherence undermined as components follow their own 'lines of flight', engaging in rhizomic practices in connection with elements from 'outside' the assemblage (Deleuze & Guattari 1987; DeLanda 2006). Rather than reify entities such as society or capitalism, then, 'assemblage-thinking' focuses on spatial and conceptual processes that produce contingent 'things' (Li 2014).

As such, the methodology maintains an epistemological commitment to revealing the processual, laborious, and contingent relations that together produce 'wild commodities'. Kwandu Conservancy serves as a specific case study site in which to 'enter' the assemblage, providing the location for twelve months of ethnographic fieldwork by the first author largely spent camped at local community homesteads or at the Conservancy office. Permission for the fieldwork was obtained from MEFT and each of Kwandu's six area *induna*s.[5] The primary method utilised involved physically 'following the thing' (Cook 2004), in this case the elephant, including tracking its ethologies alongside hunters and game guards, as well as tracing the movement of the animal's constituent parts (e.g. its ivory) post hunt (Hewitson 2018). As these pachyderm tracks intertwined with those of humans, interviews were conducted with people that had witnessed or experienced these creatures. These activities were combined with perceptual/retrospective following, including tracing human–elephant encounters and stories contained in secondary data and conducting interviews with farmers identified from human–wildlife conflict (HWC) claim forms. Obtained from the Namibian national archives, government and (inter)national NGOs, these secondary data included policy documents, institutional reports and media articles on CBNRM. Using a local translator where necessary, sixty-four semi-structured interviews were carried

---

[5] An *Induna* is a headman with authority over a particular village.

out with CBNRM stakeholders in Namibia, including conservancy members and 'key informants' such as MEFT and NGO staff. Decentring human control and attempting to engage 'across, through, with and as, more-than-humans' (Dowling *et al.* 2017: 824), 'following' allowed for an empirical exploration of the elephant's relational interactions with other (non)human entities in the co-production of value.

The present study thus contributes to a nascent body of work interrogating value not as a separate entity or as something that pre-exists measurement or articulation, but as something that is produced and performed through relational practices between more-than-human subjects (Bracking *et al.* 2019). Building on Marx's understanding of value as a social relation, our approach is cognisant of LToV's constraints, favouring an assemblage approach aligned with the performative economics tradition, so as to conceptualise economic value as produced through actions, knowledges, institutions, technologies, and structuring discourses that can be studied empirically, as we now elucidate for elephant hunting commodities in Namibia.

Producing elephant commodities for 'conservation hunting'

This section analyses the (non)human relations that combine to produce elephant commodities for 'conservation hunting'. It begins with two 'vignettes' derived from following elephants in the field, which provide some background context for the detailed discussion of processes through which elephant commodities are 'made' in Namibia. The subsequent subsection critically analyses these practices through an assemblage framing emphasising the co-constitution of the economic and ecological, exploring the relational interactions and (non) human 'labour' that together produce valued 'wild commodities'.

Commodifying the elephant in Namibia's CBNRM programme

Fieldnotes 1: 'When it's hot we have to start early; now we start', said Victor[6], as we left his village and headed east into the bush. It was 7am on a crisp August morning in Kwandu Conservancy, in the middle of the dry season. I was undertaking the monthly 'fixed-route patrol' in the northern reaches of the conservancy alongside three of its community game guards. In addition to their daily patrols they walk this 10km route every month, each carrying a yellow 'event book' in which they record tracks and sightings of wildlife. Tracing discernible paths through the bush, the men pointed out various plant species – sand-veld acacia,

---

6   Victor is not the game guard's real name: pseudonyms are used for all participants throughout the chapter.

Zambezi teak, wild syringa, sour plum and sickle bush – and recorded the spoor of leopard, hyena, kudu, and bushpig. Yet, it was not until we reached the conservancy's border with the Caprivi State Forest – one hour and a half into the patrol – that we came across evidence of elephant presence. *'Njovu!'* called Victor from up ahead, as we walked north along the 'cut-line' firebreak. 'It must be from two days ago', he said, looking down at the pachyderm's footprint. Another pointed to the location of these tracks on his map, clear evidence, the men believed, that elephants were moving between the state forest and conservancy, or even using the cut-line as a path north into Zambia. However, being old tracks, they would not be recorded in the monitoring book on this occasion, as Victor explained: 'On a fixed patrol we only record the fresh tracks from last night, this morning, or a sighting.' Another two hours elapsed before we came across more elephant spoor, close to some camel-thorn trees a few kilometres further north along the state forest boundary. 'These acacia trees are where the elephants are feeding', said Victor. 'They were here almost two days ago', his colleague deduced, inspecting the tracks. 'But these are the breeding ones – the females and the juveniles', he continued, an air of disappointment in his voice. Tracks from a big bull would have been better news to take to the conservancy's professional hunter. 'Now the elephants are just few', Victor told me, 'but you will see after September, October, November there will be a lot of elephants because they are just chasing the water.'

Fieldnotes 2: One night in mid-April Dorothy lost her entire sorghum crop to elephants. Like many other farmers in Kwandu Conservancy she had fenced her field using local timber, which had acted as a barrier to bush pigs and impalas, but not elephants. 'Last year I used chilli bombs and the elephants did not attack the field', she says. 'The Conservancy should keep on distributing those chilli bombs to farmers, but this year they were not there.' The day after Dorothy's sorghum harvest had been eaten by elephants, she reported it to a local game guard named George, who turned up the same day in order to investigate the incident. Accompanying Dorothy to the site, George measures the extent of crop loss as one-quarter hectare of the large field. He also identifies large, round footprints at the site, as well as dung and urine, the unmistakeable signs of elephants. 'I didn't see the elephants, I just saw the footprints', admits Dorothy, before stating that 'they were many.' George believes the elephants had come from Bwabwata National Park, crossing the Kwando River and entering the conservancy. He has heard reports from other farmers in the area who also had their fields raided that night. Perhaps they were the same elephants; perhaps not. For now, George takes the claim form and writes: 'Nine elephants entered the crop field on 14th April during the night and one quarter hectare of damaged sorghum was observed. The field is subject to be compensated.'

Monitoring processes such as those illustrated in the passages above are central to producing elephants for hunting (see also Kalvelage, this volume). Community game guards in Kwandu Conservancy conduct daily patrols and annual game counts alongside government and NGO staff. On a monthly basis game guards collate daily event-book data, described by CBNRM practitioners as 'the first step in the conservancy information cycle' (NACSO 2014: 37). With assistance from Namibian Association of CBNRM Support Organisations (NACSO)[7] including WWF-Namibia and IRDNC these sightings are transferred to the Conservancy's long-term monitoring event book, presented in bar charts illustrating trends in wildlife abundance. These data are also analysed and presented digitally by NACSO partners, stored within a national monitoring and evaluation database belonging to the government's MEFT and presented in publications such as NACSO's annual 'State of Community Conservation' report. These reports are important management tools for conservancies and serve to illustrate wildlife recoveries in Kwandu and the Zambezi Region more broadly. Stakeholders agree that annual fluctuations in elephant sightings are caused by environmental factors and transboundary movements from neighbouring countries, especially Botswana (Chase *et al.* 2016). Given the methodological difficulties of counting highly mobile animals across extensive ranges CBNRM partners are also reluctant to estimate elephant numbers at conservancy-level. Nevertheless, at a regional scale NACSO is able to produce graphs illustrating a steady increase in elephant numbers per 100 square kilometres over the past decade, strengthening the case for continued 'sustainable utilisation' of elephants.

This utilisation is subject to conditions imposed under the Convention on International Trade in Endangered Species of Wild Fauna and Flora (CITES). Having demonstrated healthy elephant numbers Namibia's elephant population was transferred from CITES Appendix I[8] to Appendix II[9] in 1997. This means the country's elephants are not considered at risk of extinction, the state being

---

[7] NACSO is an umbrella membership association of organisations supporting the country's CBNRM programme. It consists of eight 'full member' NGOs and the University of Namibia, seven 'associate member' organisations, as well as individual members. NACSO members such as WWF-Namibia and IRDNC play a significant role in providing technical support to conservancies in the fields of natural resource management, business and enterprise development, and institutional development.

[8] CITES Appendix I includes 'all species threatened with extinction which are or may be affected by trade. Trade in specimens of these species must be subject to particularly strict regulation in order not to endanger further their survival and must only be authorised in exceptional circumstances.' (CITES 1973, Art II: 1).

[9] CITES Appendix II includes 'all species which although not necessarily now threatened with extinction may become so unless trade in specimens of such species

permitted to trade limited amounts of ivory and elephant products, including the sale of elephants as trophies to commercial hunters. At CITES meetings countries opposed to hunting argue for the relisting of African elephants in Appendix I, thus banning all trade in their products. These persistent debates pose a severe threat to Namibia's CBNRM programme, evidenced during NACSO meetings where participants warned of outside forces working against sustainable use and lobbying for hunting bans which, if enacted, would bankrupt most conservancies. The Ministry and other CBNRM stakeholders thus point to localised 'overpopulation' of elephants and the importance of 'sustainable offtake' in minimising habitat destruction caused by these ecosystem 'engineers' (Roever *et al.* 2013).

Before it can begin trading elephant trophies, however, Namibia must first establish annual export quotas for elephant ivory, deemed by CITES to be 'important tools … in regulating and monitoring wildlife trade to ensure that the use of natural resources remains sustainable' (CITES 2007: 1). Monitoring data from annual game counts and the event-book system (as mentioned in the first set of fieldnotes above) is crucial here, with CITES (2016b: 8) commending Namibia on its in-depth monitoring of conservancies as part of 'the largest road count monitoring system in the world'. Namibia's MEFT calculates that 0.5% of an area's total elephant population can be hunted for trophies (usually males over 30 years old) without negatively affecting overall numbers (Selier *et al.* 2014), and Namibia has set a trophy quota of 180 tusks (90 elephants) each year since 2011. The CITES Secretariat reviews these data alongside information from the IUCN's African Elephant Specialist Group, which estimates a population of 250,000 elephants in southern Africa – around 64% of Africa's total elephant population (CITES 2016a). By basing these export quotas upon elephant numbers from actual sightings on game counts – considered underestimates – the Namibian government effectively meets CITES' 'non-detriment finding' requirement, paving the way for trade in elephant sport-hunted trophies. Most of Namibia's elephant quota is sold to hunting tourists from the USA, a country that considers the African elephant to be 'threatened' yet allows the importation of elephant trophies subject to conditions including hunters obtaining domestic import permits and exporting countries setting annual ivory quotas (United States Federal Register 2016). This quota-setting process is thus crucial for Namibia's trade with US hunters, providing a vital income stream supporting the country's CBNRM programme.

Namibia's national quota must then be distributed amongst the country's hunting concessions. This is a process led by MEFT, who undertake annual

---

is subject to strict regulation in order to avoid utilisation incompatible with their survival.' (CITES 1973, Art II: 2).

quota review meetings with conservancies alongside NGOs and local traditional authorities that sit on a conservancy's management committee. NGOs identify the need to develop quota-setting systems to ensure natural resource utilisation is sustainable and maximises socio-economic returns to communities. For this reason, NACSO partners conduct quota-setting training programmes aimed at helping conservancy committees understand the factors MEFT consider when negotiating elephant hunting quotas with conservancies, including the prevalence of 'human–elephant conflict' incidents.

Stakeholders of CBNRM acknowledge the inevitability of crop raiding by elephants residing close to agricultural communities and are eager to frame these interactions in particular ways, focusing their efforts on mitigating this 'conflict' either through practical prevention or financial measures. Under the government's 'Human-Wildlife Self-Reliance Scheme' (HWSRS), farmers can claim monetary recompense for crops lost to 'uncontrollable' elephants, subject to various rules such as game guards investigating incidents and recording evidence within twenty-four hours (MET 2009). These claims are assessed by HWC Committees, consisting of representatives from MEFT, NGOs, the relevant traditional authority and conservancy committee. In Kwandu there are regularly over one hundred human–elephant conflict incidents annually, often the highest figure in the country and justifying the conservancy's label as a human–elephant conflict 'hotspot area' (NACSO 2018). Despite being difficult to measure, CBNRM practitioners calculate the economic cost of these incidents vis-à-vis economic returns from wildlife enterprises, and NACSO reported human–wildlife conflict costs amounting to around US$8,500 in Kwandu in 2017, offset by conservancy income totalling almost $75,000 the same year (NACSO 2018). Interestingly, the costs of crop losses in Kwandu were significantly lower than those calculated for Mashi Conservancy in the same year, Drake *et al.* (2021) putting crop depredation losses caused by elephants alone at $157,000, only 30% of which was offset by trophy hunting revenues. Nevertheless, in Kwandu, institutional reports demonstrate both the financial burden of living alongside elephants, and the importance of hunting revenues in paying for these costs.

At an international level these representations help combat resistance from opponents of consumptive use. Yet they are also vital at the local level, 'helping communities to convince government that there are some problems', as one NGO employee put it. Human–elephant conflict data feeds into the quota-setting process alongside game count estimates and event-book data, emphasised at Kwandu's annual feedback meeting with NGOs during which a WWF-Namibia employee warned 'if you are not recording elephants and you want six elephants on your quota from the government, then it will be difficult for them to know what to give you.' Information contained in the

Conservancy's Wildlife Management and Utilisation Plan is also significant, with MEFT's latest 'Standard Operating Procedures' for conservancies stating quotas must form part of, and be compatible with, these plans (MET 2013). Despite the highly mobile nature of elephants and their vast home ranges, Kwandu's wildlife management plan stipulates keeping its 250 'resident' elephants at current levels. These anomalies aside, Kwandu's effective implementation of monitoring systems and participation in quota-setting activities are commended by government and CBNRM NGOs, MEFT having reduced quotas for those conservancies not engaging fully with the process.

As such, in recent years Kwandu has received two or three 'trophy' and two 'own-use' elephants on its annual offtake quota (NACSO 2017, 2018, 2020b). In order to ensure the optimal value for these 'capital assets' the Conservancy puts its quota out to tender, with safari operators submitting proposals to Kwandu from which the Conservancy's management committee chooses its preferred company. In effect, the Conservancy's elephants go to the highest bidder. Since 2011 Jamy Traut Hunting Safaris (JTHS)[10] has held the rights to hunt in Kwandu's concession, renegotiating its contract every couple of years. The outfit pays Kwandu US$12,376 for each trophy elephant hunted carrying a tusk weight above 40lbs, or $8,415 for those with tusks weighing less than that. For comparison, neighbouring Mashi Conservancy receives a slightly higher fee of US$13,100 from its safari operator for each elephant hunted (Drake *et al.* 2021). Given the difficulty of finding and killing 'trophy' elephants in Kwandu, JTHS also guarantees payment for two trophy bulls each year, irrespective of whether the animals are actually 'utilised'.

These elephant hunts are marketed by JTHS at industry auctions held by organisations such as Dallas Safari Club.[11] Photos of previous elephant hunts in Kwandu adorn the company's website alongside iconic images of the 'big five', JTHS offering clients an unequalled opportunity to hunt dangerous game in a 'wild landscape of mighty rivers and extraordinary herds of big game' (JTHS 2020). The experience does not come cheap, clients paying JTHS a US$24,000 trophy fee as well as a minimum of US$25,900 for fourteen days spent on the elephant trail in Kwandu (JTHS 2020). Altogether, clients pay upwards of $50,000 to hunt a trophy elephant in the Conservancy. Whereas the daily rates largely cover JTHS's operational costs including accommodation upkeep and staff salaries, the trophy fee is shared with the Conservancy. Accordingly, Kwandu receives just over 50% of the trophy fee paid by the client to JTHS, assuming the tusk weight is above 40lbs,

[10] See https://jamyhunts.com.
[11] See www.biggame.org/.

supporting claims that conservancies typically receive anywhere from 30–75% of the trophy price (Naidoo *et al.* 2016).

Co-producing the trophy-elephant commodity

The commodified 'trophy' elephant is produced through social practices of counting elephants and codifying knowledge. This human labour is undertaken by diverse (inter)national stakeholders, beginning with the physical work of community game guards recording evidence of the pachyderm's presence in 'event books' and HWSRS claim forms. These arborescent practices of counting and codifying elephants are part of a 'logistical epistemology' (Cresswell 2014) seeking to 'make' them present in the Conservancy. These material knowledge representations move through institutional networks of NGOs who undertake 'extraordinary feats of assembly work' (Li 2014: 593) to produce reports and plans demonstrating 'surplus' elephants. Interestingly, whereas the pricing mechanism often depends on creating the notion of scarcity (Bracking *et al.* 2019), here it is contingent upon demonstrating relative abundance, although high prices are assured by the few elephants that can be identified as trophies overall. In any case, these representations are both an effect of practice and have effects in practice, playing a performative role in the formation of (inter)national policy and supporting the 'sustainable consumptive use' of Namibia's elephants through trade quotas.

Crucially, this neoliberal assembling of value operates through a 'utilitarian construction of a passive nature' (Büscher *et al.* 2012: 24) that *de facto* subdues the elephant's vitality. Individual elephant bodies are made measurable and commensurable under capitalist socio-ecological relations through representations that attempt to substitute for lively materialities. Surplus elephants are inserted onto quotas and ascribed economic value on price lists, abstracted for circulation in markets for conservation hunting commodities (Bracking *et al.* 2019). Fetishised images of elephants and wild, idyllic landscapes are used to sell these commodities, integral to the 'spectacular accumulation' of the elephant's economic value (Igoe 2013) but alienated from the (non)human labour and complex ecologies that produce them. This decontextualisation of individual elephants may have problematic socio-ecological effects, research suggesting that elephant societal cohesion is negatively affected by the hunting of old bulls, leading to increased aggression and human–elephant conflict amongst groups of young males (Selier *et al.* 2014). The connections integral to ecosystem resilience may also become increasingly fragmented as a result of the commodification of their constituent elements.

The calculative technologies – such as quota setting and wildlife monitoring – that work to produce elephant commodities can be understood as practices of power and authority, even as they depoliticise and 'render technical' (Li 2007) questions of value. Drawing on Foucault, this conceptual territorialisation depends on institutional networks of conservation NGOs, agencies and governments working to 'fix the conduct of conduct' in a manner conducive to the creation and accumulation of monetary value (Murdoch 2006). In Namibia, CBNRM stakeholders provide expert assistance in the formulation of 'properly crafted rules' (Li 2007: 267), delivering technical support and training to conservancies on issues such as human–elephant conflict mitigation, quota setting and implementation of the event-book monitoring system. In each of these aspects conservancies are subject to biannual audits and performance ratings that influence their future chances of benefiting from commodification processes (MEFT & NACSO 2021).

Kwandu's rights to hunt elephants are thus not pre-given, but contingent upon government and NGO satisfaction with the Conservancy's monitoring performance and institutional governance. Increasingly, these governmentalities are geared towards fostering a business-oriented approach to conservancy management, developing the 'corporate identity' of conservancies and increasing private sector investment in wildlife enterprises (MEFT & NACSO 2021). This deepening synergy between capitalism and conservation means current and future livelihoods appear increasingly susceptible to erratic commodity markets for wildlife trophies, rights to local fauna such as elephants becoming ever more dependent on conditions of use and access defined by external actors (Drake *et al.* 2021). In selling its hunting quota to JTHS, the Conservancy effectively implements decisions that were made by government, acting as the 'middleman' in a transaction between MEFT and the private hunting operator.

However, there is another important alignment between poor subsistence farmers and elephants that raid their crops. In this valuation assemblage elephants deemed unsuitable as 'trophies' or 'own-use' animals drop out of the reference frame and are excluded from market calculations (Bracking *et al.* 2019). Yet these 'externalities' – including young male and female elephants – retain their capacity to affect things, often destroying harvests and sometimes killing people. Such interactions clearly impact economic relations, and actors within the CBNRM assemblage must work to absorb the destabilising effects of these 'overflows'. In Kwandu this absorption is exemplified in the government's HWSRS which uses hunting revenue to partially offset economic losses caused by elephants. Farmers are paid a fixed rate of US$73 per ha of crop damage, which is significantly less than the estimated US$545 that can be generated from a hectare of maize (Drake *et al.* 2021). Dorothy and others argued these offset payments are not enough, one conservancy member describing living alongside elephants as like being 'locked in prison'. These economic, psychological, and hidden opportunity costs are generally borne by the most vulnerable in society, such as female-headed households, and often cannot be financially compensated for under HWSRS (Khumalo & Yung 2015). The 'trophy' elephant's commodity value emerges as other values and lives are abandoned (Gibbs *et al.* 2015), and households suffering the greatest economic and emotional burden of living alongside elephants are not necessarily those who benefit from CBNRM's economic opportunities. This (re)territorialisation is a product of unequal power relations amongst the assemblage's multiple actants, reinforcing social relations in which subsistence farmers must suffer the costs so that (inter)national elites can continue to exploit their unpaid labours and accumulate surplus value from commodified elephants (see also Revilla Diez and Hulke, this volume).

Yet elephants and other non-humans are also agentic in the assembling and (de)stabilisation of these conservation spaces. Human practices of technological measurement and inscriptive symbolism are co-productive of elephant commodities alongside the activities and affective capacities of non-humans. Lorimer's (2007) notion of 'corporeal charisma' is exercised by elephants that trigger particular emotions in humans. The fetishised images of elephants displayed in professional hunting brochures emphasise the animal's majesty and identity as 'dangerous game', amplifying their charisma and making them desirable for the voyeuristic gaze (Cresswell 2014; Barua 2016). These romantic 'wilderness' notions are used to sell trophy elephants, appealing to (foreign) hunters seeking encounters with dangerous animals (see Bollig *et al.* and Kalvelage, this volume). This appeal is reflected in prices for trophy animals in communal-area conservancies, estimated to be worth four times that of animals hunted on freehold land (Maclaren *et al.* 2019). As Kwandu's professional hunter stated, 'people who have hunted on commercial farms now realise that they've done step 'A'; now step 'B' would be the larger free-roaming game, the tougher hunt, the *old* Africa'. The irony here is that it is precisely Namibia's colonial and apartheid history of land appropriation that has produced this distinction between (mostly) fenced freehold land and (mostly) unfenced communal land, the latter now fetishised as 'wild, old Africa'. Indeed, the local livelihood struggles of farmers living alongside elephants on marginal land sit uncomfortably alongside the fetishised wilderness values central to 'dangerous game' hunting in Kwandu.

There is perhaps no animal 'tougher' or representative of 'old Africa' than the elephant, its resilience embodied in its ethology and ecological capacities, as well as its viability as a hunting commodity. The elephant can survive in remote, degraded areas that lack appeal to tourists in search of wildlife-rich, people-free landscapes for photo safaris. As Kwandu's safari operator made clear, 'tourists do not want to go to those areas outside of the Okavango Delta because all you see are elephants and mopane [balsam tree]; it is miles and miles of monotony.' Yet elephants will frequent these places and trophy hunters will follow, meaning hunting economies can be more reliable than agricultural incomes in these areas. As one farmer in Kwandu put it: 'even if there is drought the elephant cannot die due to hunger because the rain has not fallen. But the millet, if there is no rain, we cannot produce. That is how it is.'

Alongside spectacular images and human affordances, the elephant's ethology is crucial for productive economic relations. The largest land mammal on earth, it is unmistakeable, having a significant material impact on its environment including uprooting trees, breaking fences and raiding crops. Together these behaviours comprise the elephant's 'ecological charisma' (Lorimer 2007), signifying an organism's unique combination of properties that allows its ready identification and differentiation from others. These physical properties allow humans to tune into their behaviour, lending themselves to calculative technologies of governance. Equally important is the elephant's '*umwelt*': those activities it experiences as meaningful or value-forming (Barua 2016), perhaps none more so than crop raiding. Sexually mature male elephants in particular eat farmers' crops, seeking to benefit from the increased nutritive value of plants including maize and millet at the end of the rainy season (Selier *et al.* 2014). Compared to the dry season when they remain largely in adjacent protected areas with more reliable water sources, elephants are generally more visible (and therefore huntable) in the Conservancy during the cropping season. Temporal patterns of elephant presence and crop damage are widely recognised in the literature (Roever *et al.* 2013; Von Gerhardt *et al.* 2014), with cultivation cycles and rainfall patterns said to define a 'window of vulnerability to crop raiding by elephants' (Graham *et al.* 2010: 436). As one farmer put it, 'we cultivate our fields, that is why the elephants come'.

Despite appearing somewhat chaotic on the surface, then, this is an assemblage composed of elephants and other 'things' encountering each other in more or less organised circulations (Thrift 2003). In Kwandu money derived from trophy elephants is ploughed back into the earth, farmers using HWSRS payments to buy more seeds. Crops grow, attracting into the Conservancy elephants which can be counted, commodified, and perhaps killed. The elephant's place in assemblage is thus contingent upon both the capacity of humans to grow crops and their inability (or negligence) to protect them due to factors such as alternative livelihood strategies or 'knowing they will get a coin in the end' through HWSRS offset payments, as one NGO employee put it. Although elephants diminish the individual capacities of farmers to produce food, they increase the Conservancy's capacity to generate income. Through this cycle of destruction and benefit, elephants and vegetal life contribute to the material constitution of each other (Gibbs *et al.* 2015). Practitioners of CBNRM tune into these patterns of repetition, labouring to record tracks, dung, and damaged crops. These technocratic practices work to produce discreet, alienable elephants that capital can 'see' (Robertson 2006), whilst concealing both the human and beyond-human 'labours' involved in their production (Collard & Dempsey 2017).

'Following' the elephant's lively biogeographies illustrates its role as 'co-producer' in these practices, its dynamic capacities being fundamental to capitalism's valorisation processes. This study demonstrates the centrality of these inter-species relations in constructing the elephant's economic value. It is reasonable to assume that practices such as crop raiding and forest degradation are a threat to capital accumulation in conservancies, and Barua (2016) argues that these 'undesirable encounters' constrain capture by market logics. However, in this assemblage, pachyderm-plant encounters are not unwelcome to all actors, particularly those in positions of relative power. As one Kwandu employee admitted, 'we are not happy if crops are not damaged because it means we have no wild animals here, and that is not good for the Conservancy'. Such sentiments seem absurd from the perspective of a subsistence farmer, but they speak to the unequal power relations that compose this valuation assemblage. These 'undesirable' encounters are central to producing elephants for consumptive use, allowing stakeholders to construct the elephant's identity as a livelihood threat and legitimise the 'conservation hunting' discourse, essential tasks for those seeking to capitalise on trophy-elephant commodities.

Arguably, elephants are made to be tools of these neoliberal governmental alliances, labouring to striate space and contributing to the assemblage's robust internal character, stabilising value relations so as in some sense to become agentic in its own commodity production. At the same time, elephants are also vulnerable to other (non)human agencies such as rainfall, and the presence of trees and nutritious plants grown by subsistence farmers with few other options. In the dry season elephants move through the Conservancy to access the Kwandu River and feeding areas in Bwabwata National Park and the State Forest (see Map 11.1) (Von Gerhardt *et al.* 2014), but largely undertake these journeys at night, making hunting during the day extremely difficult for Kwandu's safari operator. The task is easier during the cropping season when elephants are more visible. Yet poor rainfall levels often cause drought and crop failures in Zambezi, affecting elephant movement patterns and presence in Kwandu. Having received poor rains that year, farmers related that 'there are fewer elephants this year because the maize is not ok', and 'when there are no crops the elephants cannot be seen'. In recent years game counts in Zambezi indicate a downward trend in elephant sightings, and there have been years when no elephant trophies were killed in Kwandu (NACSO 2018, 2020a). Although the elephant's elusive nature can, in fact, increase its value as 'worthy quarry' to trophy hunters: in the absence of tangible animals to hunt JTHS guarantees payment for two trophy elephants. In combination with other actants, then, elephants may undermine economic production, resisting human practices that seek to capitalise on their megafaunal capacities. Kwandu's professional hunter can compensate for this through 'guaranteed payments' that restore order to value relations, but maintaining this stability is hard work, the conditions for deterritorialisation ever present amongst agentic (non)humans.

What this case research demonstrates is that value relations are produced through encounters between more-than-human entities. In Kwandu, humans, elephants and other beings act alongside each other to produce valued commodities, dependent on patterns of repetition and encounters specific to the Conservancy's socio-ecological composition. Power is dispersed unequally in these relations, through which space is ordered and value frames are territorialised. Despite often *appearing* hegemonic, as though dictated by some universal code behind practices (Büscher *et al.* 2012), this study demonstrates the contingent and fractious nature of neoliberal governmentalities on the ground. Recalcitrant elephants and other ecologies unknowingly resist control and disrupt the neoliberal project's dominant value relations. In doing so, they open up spaces in which alternative socio-natures might be formed.

Conclusions and future research directions

This chapter sought to provide an in-depth understanding of neoliberal environmental governance and value making in practice. It showed how economic value is created and extracted from 'wild' natures (Fredrikson *et al.* 2014; Bracking *et al.* 2019), through empirical investigation of processes that produce commodified elephants for 'conservation hunting' in Namibian conservancies. Adopting a Marxist and critical political ecology lens, the conceptual approach acknowledges a diverse assemblage of more-than-human actors in the production and circulation of capitalised natures. These valued natures derive not only from human affordances, but also the varied ethologies of beyond-human entities. In this emphasis on the co-constitution of the economic and ecological, the activities of the elephant are *in a sense* transformed and co-opted as 'labour' in the production of fetishised 'trophy' commodities.

The assembled socio-ecological relations that produce nature's value in Kwandu are relational and somewhat circulatory, (non)human things encountering each other in ways that both stabilise and undermine these value relations. Elephants move through the Conservancy and work to uproot trees, break fences, and raid crop fields. These ecological capacities are exploited by those seeking to produce 'officially valued' elephants amenable to capital accumulation. Humans labour alongside elephants, undertaking technocratic practices attuned to but necessarily pacifying the pachyderm's liveliness, rendering it a discreet unit for exchange in trophy hunting markets. Their labours are concealed in the fetishised commodity form, elephant ethologies being accordant with governance practices and romantic representations of 'old Africa' that territorialise particular neoliberal value frames, trophy-elephant commodities being born out of and reinforcing structural power relations. These relations are contingent and contested, subsistence farmers suffering from elephant encounters that are not undesired by all actors. (Inter)national elites combine to absorb these destabilising interactions and elephant absences through partial offset payments to farmers and 'guaranteed' payments from hunting safari operators to the Conservancy, mobilising utilisation discourses and reterritorialising social relations so that capital accumulation may continue.

In this respect, the chapter underlines the contingent and radically open nature of value. Valued entities including trophy elephants do not pre-exist measurement or articulation, but are produced through encounters between multiple kinds of beyond-human actants. These relations are unique to particular spatial and temporal assemblages and the socio-ecological rhythms of their components. Valuation assemblages in Kwandu depend upon patterns of repetition between humans, elephants and other lively things that in combination continually *(re)enact value*. Tracking the ongoing composition of assembled value relations, the chapter demonstrates the fractious nature of neoliberal governmentalities 'on the ground'. Techno-scientific practices creating and governing value tend to shore up structural capital-labour relationships, maintaining and reinforcing dominant neoliberal nature values and their subsequent unequal and detrimental socio-ecological effects (Bracking *et al.* 2019). Yet recalcitrant elephants and other ecologies unknowingly resist control and may disrupt the neoliberal project's dominant value relations. Attending to the combined agencies of humans and beyond-human components in the production of commodities brings to the fore subversive rationalities and practices of contestation through which entities such as 'trophy elephants' might also be unmade. These 'possibility spaces' (DeLanda 2006) are inherent to practices of value production, and tracing their continued assembling is a vital step towards (re)creating novel and more equitable socio-natural futures. Rather than attempting to render visible nature's value through the production of abstract commodities, we might reassemble relations in ways attentive to the values embedded in social relations between humans and other living beings, in the process creating more ecologically vibrant futures for all (Büscher & Fletcher 2019).

This chapter has drawn attention to the more-than-human encounters that enact value, and future studies could explore how these relational values might fortify social movements challenging capitalist social relations. These assembled socio-natures are formed in multiple combinations and spaces – from urban rooftop gardens to the African plains – and political ecologists can fruitfully explore their creative composition and effects. This study illustrated the situated workings and practices of market-based conservation on the ground, and future research would add to political ecology understandings of neoliberal governmentalities by exploring these embedded practices in other places and contexts. In this endeavour – and building upon the more-than-representational approach adopted here – there is scope for further constructive engagement between critical work on capitalist ecologies and non-representational geographies. Given the propensity for neoliberal conservation approaches to abstract and render different aspects of nature commensurable, there is also a need to broaden understandings of the specific agencies of varied non-human entities. This chapter has taken steps towards releasing elephants from the black box of 'nature', attending to their individual ecological and affective capacities. Future research could continue along this new track for 'thing following', exploring the role of other life forms – including plants and less charismatic species (see Ndwandwe, Lavelle, this volume) – in the relational production of valued natures.

Bibliography

Anderson, B. & McFarlane, C. (2011). 'Assemblage and geography', *Area*, 43(2), 124–127.

Bakker, K. (2015). 'Neoliberalization of nature', in: T, Perrault., G, Bridge, G. & J, McCarthy (eds), *The Routledge Handbook of Political Ecology* (London: Routledge), 446–456.

Barua, M. (2014). 'Circulating elephants: Unpacking the geographies of a cosmopolitan animal', *Transactions of the Institute of British Geographers*, 39(4), 559–573.

Barua, M. (2016). 'Lively commodities and encounter value', *Environment and Planning D: Society and Space*, 34(4), 725–744.

Barua, M. (2019). 'Animating capital: work, commodities, circulation', *Progress in Human Geography*, 43(4), 650–669.

BBC News (2015). 'Anger over death of large elephant in legal Zimbabwe hunt', *BBC News*, 16 October. Available at: www.bbc.co.uk/news/world-africa-34552750 [Accessed 31 January 2022].

Bollig, M. (2016). 'Towards an arid Eden? Boundary-making, governance and benefit-sharing and the political ecology of the new commons of Kunene Region, northern Namibia', *International Journal of the Commons*, 10(2), 771–799.

Bracking, S., Fredriksen, A., Sullivan, S., & Woodhouse, P. (eds) (2019). *Valuing Development, Environment and Conservation: Creating Values that Matter* (London: Routledge).

Büscher, B., Sullivan, S., Neves, K., Igoe, K., & Brockington, D. (2012). 'Towards a synthesized critique of neoliberal biodiversity conservation', *Capitalism, Nature, Socialism*, 23(2), 4–30.

Büscher, B. & Fletcher, R. (2019). 'Towards convivial conservation', *Conservation & Society*, 17(3), 1–14.

Chase, M. J., Schlossberg, S., Griffin, C. R., Bouché, P. J. C., Djene, S. W. *et al.* (2016). 'Continent-wide survey reveals massive decline in African savannah elephants', *PeerJ* 4:e2354.

CITES (1973). 'Text of the Convention' (Geneva: CITES). Available at: https://cites.org/sites/default/files/eng/disc/CITES-Convention-EN.pdf [Accessed 31 January 2022].

CITES (2007). 'Management of Nationally Established Export Quotas' (Seventh resolution adopted at the Fourteenth Conference of the Parties (CoP14). Conf. 14.7 (Rev. CoP15)). Available at: https://cites.org/eng/res/14/14-07R15.php [Accessed 31 January 2022].

CITES (2016a). 'Elephant Conservation, Illegal Killing and Ivory Trade', Interpretation and implementation of the convention, species trade and conservation: elephants. Sixty-sixth meeting of the standing committee, 11–15 January 2016. SC66 Doc. 47.1 (Geneva: CITES). Available at: https://cites.org/sites/default/files/eng/prog/MIKE/SC/E-SC66-47-01.pdf [Accessed 31 January 2022].

CITES (2016b). 'Consideration of Proposals for Amendment of Appendices I and II', Seventeenth meeting of the conference of the parties, 24 September – 5 October 2016. CoP17 Prop. 14 (Johannesburg: CITES). Available at: https://cites.org/eng/cop/17/prop/index.php [Accessed 31 January 2022].

Collard, R. & Dempsey, J. (2017). 'Capitalist natures in five orientations', *Capitalism, Nature, Socialism*, 28(1), 78–97.

Conservation Hunting (n.d.). 'Conservation Hunting'. Available at: www.conservationhunting.com [Accessed 31 January 2022].

Cook, I. *et al.* (2004). 'Follow the Thing: Papaya', *Antipode*, 36(4), 642–664.

Cresswell, T. (2014). 'Mobilities III: Moving on', *Progress in Human Geography*, 38(5), 712–721.

Dallas Safari Club (DSC) (n.d.). 'Dallas Safari Club'. Available at: www.biggame.org [Accessed 31 January 2022].

DeLanda, M. (2006). 'Deleuzian social ontology and assemblage theory', in: M. Fuglsang & B. M. Sorensen (eds), *Deleuze and the Social* (Edinburgh: Edinburgh University Press), 250–267.

Deleuze, G. & Guattari, F. (1987). *A Thousand Plateaus* (London: Continuum).

Dowling, R., Lloyd, K., & Suchet-Pearson, S. (2017). 'Qualitative methods II: "More-than-human" methodologies and/in praxis', *Progress in Human Geography*, 41(6), 823–831.

Drake, M. D., Salerno, J., Langendorf, R. E., Cassidy, L., Gaughan, A. E., Stevens, F. R., Pricope, N. G., & Hartter, J. (2021). 'Costs of elephant crop depredation exceed the benefits of trophy hunting in a community-based conservation area of Namibia', *Conservation Science and Practice*, 3(1), e345.

Dressler, W., Büscher, B., Schoon, M., Brockington, D., Hayes, T., Kull, C., & Shrestha, K. (2010). 'From hope to crisis and back again? A critical history of the global CBNRM narrative', *Environmental Conservation*, 37(1), 5–15.

Fletcher, R. (2010). 'Neoliberal environmentality: towards a poststructuralist political ecology of the conservation debate', *Conservation & Society*, 8(3), 171–181.

Fredrikson, A., Bracking, S., Greco, E., Igoe, J., Morgan, R., & Sullivan, S. (2014). 'A conceptual map for the study of value', Working Paper No. 2 (Manchester: Leverhulme Centre for the Study of Value). Available at: https://thestudyofvalue.org/wp-content/uploads/2013/11/WP2-A-conceptual-map.pdf [Accessed 7 January 2023].

Gibbs, L., Atchison, J., & Macfarlane, I. (2015). 'Camel country: Assemblage, belonging and scale in invasive species geographies', *Geoforum*, 58, 56–67.

Graham, M. D., Notter, B., Adams, W. M., Lee, P. C. & Ochieng, T. N. (2010). 'Patterns of crop-raiding by elephants, *Loxodonta africana*, in Laikipia, Kenya, and the management of human–elephant conflict', *Systematics and Biodiversity*, 8(4), 435–445.

Government of the Republic of Namibia (GRN) (1996). 'Nature Conservation Amendment Act, No. 5, 1996' (Windhoek: GRN). Available at: www.met.gov. na/files/files/Nature_Conservation_Amendment_Act.pdf [Accessed 31 January 2022].

Government of the Republic of Namibia (GRN) (2004). 'Namibia Vision 2030' (Windhoek, GRN). Available at: www.npc.gov.na/wp-content/uploads/2021/11/vision_2030.pdf [Accessed 31 January 2022].

Government of the Republic of Namibia (GRN) (2014). 'National Planning Commission Annual Report 2013/2014' (Windhoek: Office of the President, National Planning Commission). Available at: http://sealprotectionnamibia. org.na/wp-content/uploads/2015/06/national_planning_commission_annual_report_2013_2014.pdf [Accessed 4 February 2022]

Haraway, D. (2008). *When Species Meet* (Minneapolis: University of Minnesota Press).

Harvey, D. (1996). *Justice, Nature and the Geography of Difference* (Hoboken NJ: Wiley-Blackwell).

Harvey, D. (2005). *A Brief History of Neoliberalism* (London: Oxford University Press).

Hewitson, L. J. (2018). *Following Elephants: Assembling Nature Knowledge, Value, and Conservation Spaces*. PhD Thesis, University of Leicester, UK.

Huber, M. (2018). 'Resource geographies I: Valuing nature (or not)', *Progress in Human Geography*, 42(1), 148–159.

Igoe, J. (2013). 'Nature on the move II: Contemplation becomes speculation', *New Proposals: Journal of Marxism and Interdisciplinary Inquiry*, 6(1–2), 37–49.

IRDNC – Integrated Rural Development and Nature Conservation (2015). 'Strategic plan 2015–2025' (Windhoek, IRDNC). Available at: www.irdnc. org.na/pdf/IRDNC-Strategic-Plan.pdf [Accessed 31 January 2022].

IUCN, SULi, IIED, CEED, Austrian Ministry of Environment & TRAFFIC (2015). 'Symposium report, beyond enforcement: Communities, governance, incentives and sustainable use in combating wildlife crime' (Muldersdrift, South Africa: International Institute for Environment and Development). Available at: http://pubs.iied.org/G03903.html [Accessed 31 January 2022].

Jacobsohn, M. (1995). *Negotiating Meaning and Change in Space and Material*

Culture: An Ethno-Archaeological Study among Semi-Nomadic Himba and Herero Herders in North-Western Namibia. PhD Thesis, University of Cape Town.

Jacobsohn, M. (1998) [1990]. *Himba: Nomads of Namibia* (Cape Town: Struik Publishers).

JTHS – Jamy Traut Hunting Safaris (2020). 'Hunting destinations: Caprivi', Available at: https://jamyhunts.com/hunts/#caprivi [Accessed 31 January 2022].

JTHS (n.d.). 'Jamy Traut Hunting Safaris'. Available at: https://jamyhunts.com [Accessed 31 January 2022].

Kalvelage, L., Revilla Diez, J., & Bollig, M. (2020). 'How much remains? Local value capture from tourism in Zambezi, Namibia' *Tourism Geographies*, 24(4–5), 759–780.

Kay, K. & Kenney-Lazar, M. (2017). 'Value in capitalist natures: An emerging framework', *Dialogues in Human Geography*, 7(3), 295–309.

Khumalo, K. E. & Yung, L. A. (2015). 'Women, human-wildlife conflict, and CBNRM: Hidden impacts and vulnerabilities in Kwandu Conservancy, Namibia', *Conservation & Society*, 13(3), 232–243.

Koot, S. (2019). 'The limits of economic benefits: Adding social affordances to the analysis of trophy hunting of the Khwe and Ju/'hoansi in Namibian community-based natural resource management', *Society & Natural Resources*, 32(4), 417–433.

Lendelvo, S., Pinto, M., & Sullivan, S. (2020). 'A perfect storm? The impact of COVID-19 on community-based conservation in Namibia', *Namibian Journal of Environment*, 4(B), 1–15.

Li, T.M. (2007). *The Will to Improve: Governmentality, Development, and the Practice of Politics* (Durham NC: Duke University Press).

Li, T.M. (2014). 'What is land? Assembling a resource for global investment', *Transactions of the Institute of British Geographers*, 39, 589–602.

Lorimer, J. (2007). 'Nonhuman charisma', *Environment and Planning D: Society and Space*, 25(5), 911–932.

MacLaren, C., Perche, J., & Middleton, A. (2019). 'The Development of Strategies to Maintain and Enhance the Protection of Ecosystem Services in Namibia's State, Communal and Freehold Lands' (Windhoek: Namibia Nature Foundation). Available at: https://resmob.org/wp-content/uploads/2019/06/2019-06-Hunting_report_Draft.pdf [Accessed 31 January 2022].

Marx, K. (1974 [1867]). *Capital: A Critique of Political Economy*, Volume I (London: Lawrence and Wishart).

MET – Ministry of Environment and Tourism (2009). 'National Policy on Human-Wildlife Conflict Management 2009' (Windhoek: MET). Available at: www.met.gov.na/files/files/Human%20Wildlife%20Policy.pdf [Accessed 31 January 2022].

MET – Ministry of Environment and Tourism (2013). 'Guidelines for Management of Conservancies and Standard Operating Procedures' (Windhoek: MET). Available at: www.met.gov.na/files/files/Guidelines%20for%20Management%20of%20Conservancies%20and%20SOPs.pdf [Accessed 31 January 2022].

MEFT & NACSO – Ministry of Environment, Forestry and Tourism & Namibian Association of CBNRM Support Organisations (2021). 'The State of Community

Conservation in Namibia: Annual Report 2020' (Windhoek: MET/NACSO). Available at: www.nacso.org.na/sites/default/files/2020%20State%20of%20 Community%20Conservation%20Report%20-%20book.pdf [Accessed 23 August 2022]

Murdoch, J. (2006). *Post-Structuralist Geography: A Guide to Relational Space* (London: SAGE).

NACSO – Namibian Association of CBNRM Support Organisations (2014). 'The State of Community Conservation in Namibia – A Review of Communal Conservancies, Community Forests and other CBNRM Initiatives (2013 annual report)' (Windhoek: NACSO). Available at: www.nacso.org.na/sites/default/ files/State%20of%20Community%20Conservation%20book%20web_0.pdf [Accessed 31 January 2022].

NACSO – Namibian Association of CBNRM Support Organisations (2015). 'The State of Community Conservation in Namibia – A Review of Communal Conservancies, Community Forests and other CBNRM Initiatives (2014/15 annual report)' (Windhoek: NACSO). Available at: www.nacso.org.na/sites/ default/files/2014-15_SoCC-Report.pdf [Accessed 10 Jnauary 2023].

NACSO – Namibian Association of CBNRM Support Organisations (2017). 'Kwandu Conservancy Annual Audit Report 2016'. Available at: www.nacso. org.na/sites/default/files/2016%20Kwandu%20Audit%20Report.pdf [Accessed 31 January 2022].

NACSO – Namibian Association of CBNRM Support Organisations (2018). 'Kwandu Conservancy Annual Audit Report 2017'. Available at: www.nacso. org.na/sites/default/files/2017%20Kwandu%20Audit%20Report.pdf [Accessed 31 January 2022].

NACSO – Namibian Association of CBNRM Support Organisations (2020a). 'Game Counts in East Zambezi. August 2019' (NACSO). Available at: www.nacso.org.na/sites/default/files/Zambezi%20Game%20Count%20-%20 East%202019%20Final.pdf [Accessed 31 January 2022].

NACSO – Namibian Association of CBNRM Support Organisations (2020b). 'Kwandu Natural Resource Report 2020'. Available at: www.nacso.org.na/ sites/default/files/Kwandu%20Audit%20Report%202020.pdf [Accessed 23 August 2022]

Naidoo, R., Weaver, C., Diggle, R., Matongo, G., Stuart-Hill, G., & Thouless, C. (2016). 'Complementary benefits of tourism and hunting to communal conservancies in Namibia', *Conservation Biology*, 30(3), 628–638.

Natural Capital Coalition (2016). 'Natural Capital Protocol'. Available at: www. naturalcapitalcoalition.org/protocol [Accessed 31 January 2022].

Owen-Smith, G. (2002). 'A Brief History of the Conservation and Origin of the Concession Areas in the Former Damaraland' (Windhoek: IRDNC). Available at: www.namibweb.com/conservation-areas-damaraland.pdf [Accessed 31 January 2022].

Robertson, M. M. (2006). 'The nature that capital can see: Science, state, and market in the commodification of ecosystem services', *Environment and Planning D: Society and Space*, 24, 367–387.

Robson, A. S., Trimble, M. J., Purdon, A., Young-Overton, K. D., Pimm, S. L.,

& van Aarde, R. J. (2017). 'Savanna elephant numbers are only a quarter of their expected values', *PLoS One*, 12(4), e0175942.

Roever, C. L., Van Aarde, R. J., & Leggett, K. (2013). 'Functional connectivity within conservation networks: delineating corridors for African elephants', *Biological Conservation*, 157, 128–135.

Selier, S. A., Page, B. R., Vanak, A. T., & Slotow, R. (2014). 'Sustainability of elephant hunting across international borders: A case study of the Greater Mapungubwe Transfrontier Conservation Area', *The Journal of Wildlife Management*, 78(1), 122–132

Silva, J. A. & Motzer, S. (2015). 'Hybrid uptakes of neoliberal conservation in Namibian tourism-based development', *Development and Change*, 46(1), 48–71.

Smith, N. (2008). *Uneven Development: Nature, Capital and the Production of Space* (London: Blackwell).

Suich, H. (2013). 'Evaluating the household level outcomes of community based natural resource management: The Tchuma Tchato project and Kwandu Conservancy', *Ecology and Society*, 18(4), 25.

Sullivan, S. (2002). 'How sustainable is the communalising discourse of "new" conservation? The masking of difference, inequality and aspiration in the fledgling "conservancies" of Namibia', in: D. Chatty & M. Colchester (eds), *Conservation and Mobile Indigenous people: Displacement, Forced Settlement and Sustainable Development* (Oxford: Berghahn Press), 158–187.

Sullivan, S. (2006). 'The elephant in the room? Problematising "new" (neoliberal) biodiversity conservation', *Forum for Development Studies*, 33(1), 105–135.

Sullivan, S. (2013). 'Nature on the move III: (Re)countenancing an animate nature', *New Proposals: Journal of Marxism and Interdisciplinary Inquiry*, 6(1–2), 50–71.

Sullivan, S. (2017a). 'What's ontology got to do with it? On nature and knowledge in a political ecology of the "green economy"', *Journal of Political Ecology*, 24, 217–242.

Sullivan, S. (2017b). 'The disvalues of alienated capitalist natures: Invited commentary on Kay, K. and Kenney-Lazar, M. (2017) *Value in Capitalist Nature: An Emerging Framework*', *Dialogues in Human Geography*, 7(3), 310–313.

TEEB (2010). *The Economics of Ecosystems and Biodiversity: Ecological and Economic Foundations* (London; Washington: Earthscan).

Thrift, N. (2003). 'Space: The fundamental stuff of human geography', in: S. Holloway, S. Rice, & G. Valentine (eds), *Key Concepts in Geography* (London; Thousand Oaks CA: SAGE), 85–97.

United States Federal Register (2016). '50 CFR Part 17: Endangered and Threatened Wildlife and Plants; Revision of the Section 4(d) Rule for the African Elephant (*Loxodonta africana*); Final Rule', Department of the Interior, Fish and Wildlife Service, 81(108), Part 2. Available at: www.govinfo.gov/content/pkg/FR-2016-06-06/pdf/2016-13173.pdf [Accessed 4 February 2022].

Von Gerhardt, K., Van Niekerk, A., Kidd, M., Samways, M., & Hanks, J. (2014). 'The role of elephant *Loxodonta africana* pathways as a spatial variable in crop-raiding location', *Oryx*, 48(3), 436–444.

12

Human–Wildlife Interaction, Rural Conflict, and Wildlife Conservation

EZEQUIEL FABIANO, SELMA LENDELVO,
ALFONS MOSIMANE, AND SELMA KOSMAS

Introduction

Namibia and southern Africa in general have experienced commodification of nature since the 1960s when the conversion of commercial agricultural farms to game farming areas gained intensity (Wels 2015; see also Kalvelage this volume). The assumption was that game farming was a more economically viable response to the decline of the agriculture market, products, and profits. Another supporting argument was that game farming offers a win-win situation for rural development and the conservation of nature and wildlife (Brandt *et al.* 2018). The concentration on the commodification of conservation has seen a growing trend in managing game species to support trophy hunting and nature-based tourism targeting high-end tourism markets (Silva & Motzer 2014; Massé & Lunstrum 2016; Duffy *et al.* 2019; Koot *et al.* 2019). The trend in developing a wildlife economy, which initially was only practised by commercial farmers, also continued to grow in rural areas where communities established conservancies to derive benefits from wildlife. In rural communities of Namibia, the tendency is to conserve wildlife to derive income from hunting and tourism (MET & NACSO 2020).

The evolution of wildlife management in Namibia commenced with the establishment of protected areas through the demarcation of national parks or game reserves (17% of total surface area in the late 20th century) (Botha 2005). The formation of freehold conservancies (9%) followed, and then, from the late 1990s, communal conservancies (20%) (MET & NACSO 2018). The latter represent about 53% of all communal land, with an estimated 212,092 residents in total (MET & NACSO 2018). While people previously had cultural values attached to wildlife, they had no rights to derive economic value from wildlife. The introduction of conservancies in rural communal areas stipulated the framework for the valorisation of wildlife in the communal areas as it created links between a newly defined resource and a market (Barnes *et al.* 2002). Underpinning this conservation approach is a neoliberalist paradigm whose emphasis arguably fails to address communities' intrinsic valuing of natural resources (Sullivan 2006). For example, Thomsen *et al.* (2021) indicate the need for the hunting tourism industry to recognise the cultural importance of local hunting for effective empowerment. Altogether, this paradigm is generally the one adopted across various community-based natural resource management programmes in southern Africa (see Dittmann & Müller-Mahn, Mbaiwa, and Kioko & Kinyanjui this volume).

As the conservation area under communal, freehold, and state land management has increased, there has also been a growth in wildlife abundance and distribution connectivity coupled with an increase in the range of direct and indirect benefits (MET & NACSO 2018). Similarly, there has also been an inevitable growth of human and livestock populations. The commodification of wildlife in conservancies has not exempted rural communities from prevalent threats, including the loss of habitat to other land uses and intensification of human–wildlife interactions including human–wildlife conflict (HWC) (Conover & Messmer 2001; Lamarque *et al.* 2009; Nyamasyo & Kihima 2014). Such conflict involves people, their livelihoods, the natural environments, and their habitats. The negative experiences caused by HWC are either tangible (e.g. loss of life, depredation of livestock) or intangible (e.g. anxiety or living in fear, opportunity costs) (Dickman 2010). Thus, conflict, particularly between humans and carnivores, emanates from perceived or real threats to property and safety (Treves & Karanth 2003).

In Namibia, HWC is ubiquitous, a trend that shows no sign of abating in the near future. Two emerging drivers of HWC are the increasing concentration of wildlife at higher population levels in the Zambezi Region (Stoldt *et al.* 2020) and the parallel increase of the human population from 1.2 million in 1990 to 2.4 million in 2017 (NSA 2017). It is estimated that the Namibian elephant population grew from about 5,000 to over 20,000 between the early 1990s and recent years (Shilongo *et al.* 2018; MET & NACSO 2020). Similarly, Namibia has also recorded a gradually increasing lion population both inside and outside protected areas (Shilongo *et al.* 2018). A slight increase in lion numbers was reported in the Zambezi Region, from thirty-eight individuals in 2014 to forty-one during 2017 (Hanssen *et al.* 2017) which is in line with the idea that the lion populations in the Zambezi Region are stable (MET & NACSO 2020). These drivers pose severe challenges that are undermining the integrity of conservation areas and their outcomes worldwide (Megaze *et al.* 2017; Stoldt *et al.* 2020). Positive wildlife-related incentives motivate individuals to change their attitudes towards communal conservancies (van Dalum 2013).

If not controlled, HWC has the potential to undermine the wildlife economy and the associated benefits derived through conservation. Climate change is also expected to lead to a decline in resource availability (Reid *et al.* 2008) and this scenario is likely to heighten the competition for resources with possibly a more extensive range of animal taxonomic groups (Anand & Radhakrishna 2017). Salerno *et al.* (2021) showed that the food insecurity due to crop raiding, primarily by elephants, will increase due to a shortening of the raining season. It is thus crucial to ascertain the true extent of taxa involved in HWC as conservancies' reports only allude to species for which offsetting can be sought (MET 2018). Thus, the actual number of damage-causing species is unknown. Offsetting is mainly sought for species of high economic value, which makes them a critical commodity for the local economy and the international wildlife trade. Conservation-related costs can negatively influence individual and collective cognitive (understanding or reasoning) factors, resulting in demotivation to continue supporting specific wildlife policies. It is imperative to gain a broad understanding of communities' cognitive factors through their perceptions (Megaze *et al.* 2017) and at various societal scales (e.g. village, household, individual) (Riehl *et al.* 2015) as they are the custodians of the natural resources surrounding them. A survey of more than 400 community members across 18 communal conservancies in Namibia revealed that the conservancy status might positively impact attitudes towards wildlife, but that attitudes are conditioned by individuals' experiences (Störmer *et al.* 2019). This dependency is exacerbated by the lack of financial sustainability despite conservation achievements across various conservancies in Namibia (Humavindu & Stage 2013).

Therefore, there is a need to develop effective HWC mitigation strategies, and this requires an understanding of the conflict patterns, species involved, attitudes,[1] and behaviours through the interpretive lens of local knowledge, based on local people's perceptions.

---

[1] Fishbein and Ajzen (1975) defined an attitude as 'a learned predisposition to respond in a favourable or unfavourable manner in respect to a given object or situation' while, perception a reflection of 'what people think' about something such as wildlife (Kansky & Knight, 2014). Ajzen and Fishbein (1977) defined behaviour as 'one or more observation actions performed by an individual in a specific situation or under specific circumstances' and behaviour intent as 'person intent to act in a particular way, which is a function of a person's attitude towards performing the behaviour and the subjective norm about the behaviour'.

Trends in wildlife commodification and impacts on local livelihoods

The goal of the Namibian community-based natural resource management (CBNRM) programme since its inception in the late 1990s has been to improve the economic welfare of local people, stimulate rural development, and reduce poverty through the conservation of wildlife (Suich 2013a; MET & NACSO 2020). To date, the CBNRM programme has been able to generate revenue starting from less than N$1 million (US$58,458) in 1998 to more than N$148 million (US$8,651,783) in 2018 (MET & NACSO 2020). While variation exists in generating revenue opportunities and benefits among individual conservancies, most revenue mechanisms include a combination of consumptive and non-consumptive wildlife uses, such as ecotourism and conservation hunting in areas outside protected areas (Naidoo *et al.* 2016). Additionally, by providing for an overlap between the agricultural and conservation-related land uses, with the expectation that conservation incentives will strengthen the traditional local livelihoods (Kanapaux & Child 2011; Khumalo & Yung 2015), the conservancy approach has attracted external funding (e.g. developmental grants or donations).

Benefits in the CBNRM programme are found at community (conservancy), household, or individual levels, and are financial, material, or social in nature. Examples include but are not limited to game meat, community or social projects, employment, training, and cash dividends to conservancy members (MET & NACSO 2020). The last-mentioned benefits are arguably still marginal, and fluctuating over the years and between conservancies. In the Zambezi Region, conservancies distribute an average of N$100 (US$13.15) cash dividends per member annually in the mid-2010s, an increase of US$5.26 from the mid-2000s (Muyengwa 2015). Besides low employment levels, most of the recorded jobs in the rural areas of the Zambezi Region are mostly 'nature'-related jobs at places within the broad tourism industry including accommodation facilities and tour guiding, safari hunting, NGOs, conservancies and some government offices, e.g. the Ministry of Environment, Forestry and Tourism (MEFT); the Ministry of Agriculture, Water and Land Reforms; and regional authorities (Collomb *et al.* 2008). Suich (2013a, 2013b) argued that benefits distributed to some local communities such as those in the Kwandu Conservancy (Zambezi Region, see Hewitson & Sullivan on trophy hunting and elephants, this volume), were too low to transform local economies or to sufficiently offset the effects of HWC. Capacity-building is integrated into these employment opportunities.

In addition, communities have been capacitated with innovative mitigation measures to decrease conflict with wildlife while receiving financial assistance to offset some of the tangible co-existing costs of living with wildlife. The Zambezi Region is highly speciose with a high human population density.

Local communities, like the rest of Namibia, practise primarily a combination of subsistence crop and livestock farming (Muyengwa 2015) accompanied by marginal returns (Seoraj-Pillai & Pillay 2017). This setting has prompted various NGOs to empower the communities in multiple aspects of wildlife management (Bowen-Jones 2012), including for example wildlife conflict-mitigation measures (e.g. lion-proof fences) (Hanssen *et al.* 2017). As early as 2005, the economic costs of the HWC-related losses were estimated to be US$35,000, and about 500 livestock-related losses were recorded in the Zambezi Region (de Wet & Gaedke 2009). The economic losses for farmers have increased over the years as HWC incidents increased from 2,036 in 2004 to 6,331 in 2015, with the highest being 9,228 in 2012 (Shilongo *et al.* 2018). Furthermore, affected conservancy members qualify for an offset amount provided that incidents are reported according to the regulations and procedures set within the HWC Policy regulations, such as that they are reported within 24 hours, while farmers should also ensure that livestock are kraaled overnight, with herding is recommended during the day (MET 2018). Households are compensated for such losses through a programme called the Human and Animal Conflict Compensation Scheme (HACSS), which is also collaboratively supported by the government and the conservancies. Altogether, the realisation of wildlife commodification in community-based conservation areas continues to be hampered by the challenge of HWC, which could have detrimental effects on the future of conservation (Sullivan 2006) if an amicable way out is not identified.

With the background described, this study aimed to determine the cognitive position of community members of the Wuparo Conservancy in north-east Namibia about HWC and to understand the factors that influence their perceptions, behaviours, and attitudes towards wildlife and the Conservancy. The study focuses on wildlife species that are a risk and perceived to be a risk to communities. We hypothesised that community members of this conservancy bordering two national parks will have in general a positive attitude towards wildlife given the two decades of the Conservancy existence.

Materials and methods

Study area

The study was conducted in the Wuparo Conservancy, located in north-east Namibia between the Mudumu and the Nkasa Rupara National Parks (Map 12.1). The Conservancy was established in 1999 and covers a total surface area of 148 km². The human population size in the Conservancy is estimated to be 1,076 individuals spread across nine villages. Villages vary in size and may consist of four to forty households. The main languages spoken are Siyeyi and Thimbukushu. Livelihood strategies in Wuparo Conservancy include subsistence agricultural production comprising of crop and livestock farming. The people mostly farm animals such as cattle, goats, and chicken, and grow a range of crops like maize, millet, and groundnuts. Besides farming, fishing contributes to the livelihoods of the Wuparo community.

A ten-member Management Committee governs the Conservancy, made up of eight men and two women. This committee works closely with the Mayeyi Traditional Authority, which is represented in most of its conservancy structures and meetings. The Conservancy leadership is supported by the government, represented by MEFT, and a local NGO, the Integrated Rural Development for Nature Conservation (IRDNC), in particular providing capacity-building and expertise in conservancy and wildlife management. The Conservancy employs a Manager, Enterprise Officer, a Community Resource Monitor, and seven game guards.

The Conservancy is located within a biodiversity-rich landscape comprising of floodplains and a mosaic of woodlands and grasslands. Several large and small mammal wildlife species are found in the Conservancy. The prime wildlife species include elephant (*Loxodonta africana*), lion (*Panthera leo*), leopard (*Panthera pardus*), buffalo (*Syncerus caffer*), and kudu (*Tragelaphus strepsiceros*) (MET & NACSO 2020). This has resulted in the conservancy benefiting from the wildlife-based economy, including conservation hunting within the Conservancy, and concessions in the neighbouring national parks. The Conservancy enterprises include crafts production and the Rupara community campsite. In consultation with the Conservancy, MEFT sets quota levels annually for huntable species.

The study was based on 178 household questionnaire surveys conducted in October and November 2017. Households were selected following a systematic random approach, whereby the first household in a village was selected randomly and the second and third by moving in a clockwise manner from the first. If no one was present at a selected house, enumerators moved to the next house in line. Interviewees were primarily household heads, and in their absence, we interviewed the spouses or relatives living with them. Informed consent was obtained orally from all participants before each interview commenced.

The questionnaire was composed of open- and closed-ended questions. Interviews were conducted in English and where necessary in a local vernacular language with the aid of trained local enumerators. In general, interviewers solicited answers and only read possible answers if interviewees failed to provide an answer. The questionnaire had three main subsections: socio-demographic and economic; community perceptions and attitudes about

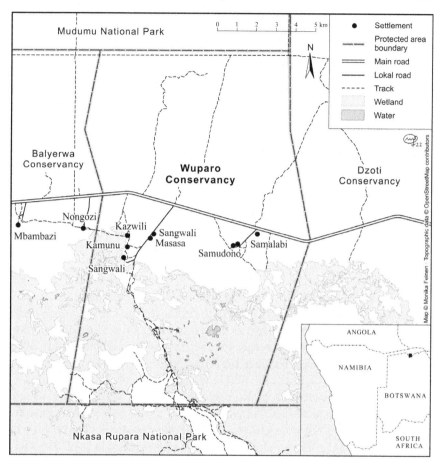

Map 12.1 The study area – the Wuparo Conservancy in north-east Namibia (Source: Open StreetMap contributors; Cartography: M. Feinen).

wildlife, HWC and conservation; and mitigation measures. Under the socio-demographic and economic section, we documented age groups, gender, time since having taken residence, reasons for having settled in a particular area, and livelihood sources. The study documented perceptions of the seriousness of HWC, frequencies of wildlife sightings or hearing, the negative trend in wildlife abundance since having settled in the area, frequent movement of dangerous wildlife into the Conservancy, and proximity to the protected area; yearly losses of crops to elephants or livestock depredation were assessed through a five-agreement Likert Scale.

In respect to HWC *per se*, enumerators recorded whether interviewees perceived HWC to be a serious problem and documented personal descriptions of incidents of human–wildlife interaction experienced during the years 2016 and 2017, including livestock depredation or crop raiding. Participants were then asked to rank the problem-causing species from 1 to 6, with 1 being most problematic and 6 the least (see e.g. Kahler & Gore 2015). Data were also gathered on perceptions regarding the likelihood of encountering problem-causing animals on a spatial-temporal scale. Each interview lasted about 20 to 40 minutes.

Statistical analysis

For this study, we assumed that 'no answers' were indicative of a lack of strong interest, no clear opinion about the issue, or that the question was not directly applicable to a respondent (Thornton & Quinn 2009). Thus, percentages were often determined based on the number of participants that answered a question and not on the total number interviewed. Additionally, multiple responses were possible to an open-response question, and data were presented as the percentage (%) of respondents giving each response. The Chi-square (χ^2) test of independence and the Fisher's exact test in cases of < 5 responses were applied to determine whether responses occurred with equal probability or if there was any association between the frequencies of variables. The proportional test was used to assess the differences between proportions.

We applied an ordered logistic regression (OLS) to determine which variables would result in a significant increase in the odds of respondents considering HWC to be a serious problem; all other predictors held constant, due to participants either experiencing or not experiencing a predictor. Our response variable – the perception of the extent to which HWC is perceived to be a severe problem similar to seven predictor variables – was based on a five-agreement Likert Scale (i.e. Strongly agree, Agree, Neutral, Disagree, and Strongly disagree). Predictor variables included perceptions of whether wildlife had decreased since the time of their arrival in that place, feeling unsafe due to residing next to a national park, frequent movement of animals deemed dangerous into their villages, having lost crops due to elephants or livestock to predators, fair compensation when livestock are killed, and that their livelihoods are threatened by human–wildlife conflict. Additional predictors included gender, duration of residency (< 2, 2 < 5, 5 < 10, 10 < 15, > 15 years), age (≤ 19, ≤ 29, ≤ 39, ≤ 49, ≤ 59, ≤ 69, ≤ 79 years), having experienced crop raiding or livestock depredation, number of income sources per household as a measure of resilience (1 to 3), and number of reported problematic species.

The OSL[2] was fitted using the '*polr*' function in the R package MASS (Venables & Ripley 2002) and, to account for model selection uncertainty, we used the model averaging as implemented in the R package *MuMIn* (Bartoń 2016). We determined the Akaike Information Criteria, corrected for small samples (AICc), for each model and considered competitive models to be those with AICc values of < 2 with respect to model with the lowest AICc (highest predictive performance). OSL coefficients were exponentiated to convert them into odds and proportional odds ratios, and 95% profiling confidence intervals (CI) were determined based on the averaged coefficients.

Results

People's socio-demographic profile

A total of 178 interviews were conducted across seven villages in the Wuparo Conservancy. Most of the respondents were from the Samudono and Sheshe villages (57%, $n = 102$) while 39% ($n = 70$) were from the Kazwili, Masasa, and Samalabi villages and the remaining 4% ($n = 6$) were from the Kamunu and Sangwali villages. Significantly, more female-headed households were interviewed than male-headed households ($\chi^2 = 29.46$, $df = 1$, $p < 0.001$, 54 males to 123 females). Consequently, the sample included both *de facto* (actual heads) and de jure female heads standing in for the absence of the actual heads. Respondents' ages ranged from 19 to 88 (46 ± 17, $n = 171$) years old, with the majority being between 20 and 49 years (65%, $n = 111$), followed by those between 60 and 88 (26%, $n = 45$), 50 and 59 years (8%, $n = 14$), and one was 19 years old.

Significantly, most of the respondents have resided in Wuparo for more than 15 years ($\chi^2 = 291.67$, $df = 4$, $p < 0.001$, 126 versus 51). Participants indicated having settled in the Conservancy for various reasons, including marriage (29%, 11); land allocation (13%, 5); relocation from the park (13%, 5); moving away from floodplains (i.e. dry land after floods), and because it was an open space (10% each, 4 each); the proximity of family and health facilities (6% each, 2 each); and because it was their ancestral land, for a better life, or due to its proximity to school and employment (3% each, 1 each).

People's perceptions regarding wildlife species involved in human–wildlife conflict

Wildlife economy promotes the conservation of wildlife to increase numbers and diversity, especially for economically valued species. Respondents

---

[2] OSL ordered logistic regression

identified and ranked nineteen taxa of wildlife species involved in causing human–wildlife conflict (Figure 12.1). These taxa were broadly grouped into four dietary guilds, of which herbivores had the largest species richness (47%, 9), followed by carnivores (32%, 6) and omnivores (16%, 3). Birds were not identified to the species level, thus we were unable to assess this group species composition. These differences in species composition at the guild level were not significant ($\chi^2 = 3$, $df = 2$, $p > 0.05$) suggesting statistically similar numbers of species per guild. Herbivores and carnivores were equally considered as being problematic (42% versus 40% of 640, respectively, $\chi^2 = 0.19$, $df = 1$, $p > 0.05$) relative to birds (11%, 69) and omnivores (7%, 45).

At the rank level of 1 to 6, the elephant species was ranked the most problematic among seven species (78%, $n = 134$ of 172), lion in rank 2 among 12 species (48%, $n = 81$ of 170), and hyena in rank 3 among 12 species (44%, $n = 65$ of 148). The least-ranked species, at rank 4 to 6, were buffalo among 18 species (20%, 19 of 94 each), birds among 13 species (20%, 10 of 49), and porcupine among six species (29%, 2 of 7), respectively. These differences in proportions were found to be significant ($\chi^2 = 106.38$, $df = 4$, $p < 0.22$) suggesting that differences are not confounded by differences in the number of responses per rank. At the species level, the elephant and composite birds unit were ranked as being most problematic in crop raiding (28%, 177 of 640 and 11%, 69 respectively) while lion and hyena were the most problematic taxa involved in livestock depredation (22%, 143 and 17%, 107 respectively). These differences in proportions were significant ($\chi^2 = 168.8$, $df = 3$, $p < 0.001$).

Respondents' perceptions regarding changes in the population size of problem-causing animals differed significantly ($\chi^2 = 31.84$, $df = 3$, $p < 0.001$) with the majority of respondents indicating that the wildlife population sizes have decreased over the years (71%, 123 of 174). On the other hand, the majority of respondents (93%, 160 of 172) indicated that there is a constant movement of problem animals into the Conservancy. On a temporal scale, nearly all respondents (94%, 165 of 178) reported having seen or heard sounds made by wildlife during the past 12 months, while 6% ($n = 11$) indicated not having done so. Most respondents indicated seeing or hearing sounds of wildlife on a monthly basis (35%, 62 of 178), 24% ($n = 43$) every other month, 19% ($n = 34$) every four months, 16% ($n = 28$) once per year, and 9% ($n = 16$) every six months. These differences in sightings or hearings were found to be significant ($\chi^2 = 43.80$, $df = 4$, $p < 0.001$) suggesting more regular direct and indirect interactions with wildlife.

On a spatial scale, perceptions of the likelihood of encountering the aforementioned problem-causing animals varied significantly across the nine villages ($\chi^2 = 56.67$, $df = 5$, $p < 0.001$) (Figure 12.2). Participants considered

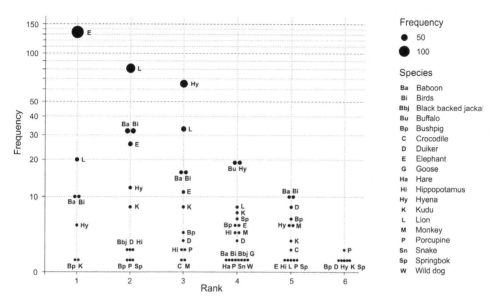

Figure 12.1 Rank of the problem-causing species according to the dietary guild as per respondents from the Wuparo Conservancy, north-east Namibia. (Source: Authors' research).

the Samudono village to have the highest likelihood of encountering these species, followed by Sheshe and Masasa villages (33, 24, and 17% of $n = 178$, respectively). Villages associated with the least likelihood were the Sangwali, Kamunu, and Magwalo (11, $\leq 1\%$). The likelihood for crop raiding to take place in different villages did not differ (Kruskal-Wallis $\chi^2 = 13.474$, $df = 7$, $p > 0.05$) but livestock depredation differs from village to village. The findings suggest possible hotspots due to the distribution and utilisation of the area by problem-causing species.

Perceptions of human–wildlife conflict in relation to community livelihoods

The general perception in the study area is that wildlife threatens the livelihoods of rural dwellers (73%, 127 of 173). Crop farming was the most prominent livelihood (77%, 158 of 204) indicated to be threatened. Other livelihood strategies threatened were livestock rearing (9%, 19), employment (6%, 12), business (4%, 8), and tourism (3%, 7). Significantly, the majority of the respondents agreed that HWC is a serious problem (73%, 124 of 171) with only a few indicating that it is not a serious problem (23%). Additional

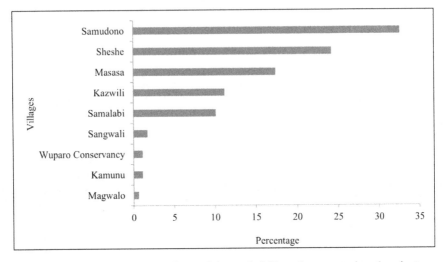

Figure 12.2 Respondent perceptions of the probability of encountering the nineteen problematic species among nine villages in the Wuparo Conservancy, north-east Namibia (n = 178) (Source: Authors' research).

notions that may have influenced the perception of HWC as a threat to livelihoods are demonstrated in Figure 12.3. These notions include the perception of a negative trend in ungulate wildlife abundance (71%), having experienced conflict either in the form of crop raiding by elephants (88%) or livestock depredation caused by carnivores (75%), proximity to the park (53%), and the continuous movement of animals deemed dangerous from the park into villages (93%). The notion of a negative trend in ungulate wildlife abundance may suggest that respondents view predation on the livestock as being due to inadequate wildlife prey in the area.

Furthermore, a significant association was observed between time of residency and the perception that HWC is a serious problem (Pearson $\chi^2 =$ 58.498, $df = 16$, $p < 0.05$) largely because there were fewer participants that had lived in the Conservancy for less than 2 or more than 15 years disagreeing that HWC is not a serious problem than would be expected by chance (residual values of 5.87 and -2.15, respectively). In general, the proportion of participants agreeing that HWC is a threat across the five residency time periods was significantly larger than that of those disagreeing ($\chi^2 = 169.85$, $df = 1$, $p <$ 0.001, 128 versus 9). A similar result was found when comparing recent settlers (< 2) and long-time residents ≥ 15 years ($\chi^2 = 8.49$, $df = 1$, $p < 0.004$). This suggests that negative perceptions may not only be instigated by the length of the period of exposure to conflict (i.e. time of residency).

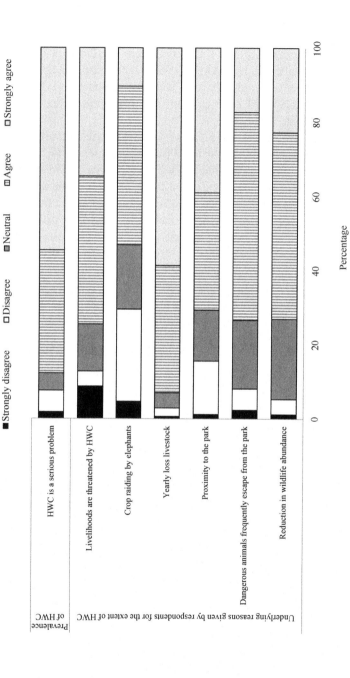

Figure 12.3 Percentage of perceptions about the prevalence of and underlying reasons for human–wildlife conflict (HWC) of community members of the Wuparo Conservancy in north-east Namibia (Source: Authors' research).

The OLR analysis revealed that nine of the thirteen predictors do influence the respondents' perceptions about the threat of HWC, assuming all other variables remained constant (Table 12.1). Of these predictors, annual livestock depredation and livelihoods being threatened were present in all fourteen competitive models, followed by the number of problem species, and income sources. Predictors that featured only once were the movement of dangerous animals, having experienced crop raiding, and perceptions that wildlife numbers have declined.

The range in odds that experiencing these predictors would result in HWC being viewed as a greater threat was 0.796 (i.e. 80% increase) to 1.894 (i.e. 89% increase) times higher when these predictors occurred than when not (Table 12.1). The lower odd corresponds to a 1-unit increase in the number of problem species and the highest, to perceptions that livelihoods are threatened, holding all other variables constant. Statistically, the only odds that differed significantly were for a 1-unit increase in experiencing annual livestock depredation and perceptions that livelihoods are threatened and when these events did not occur (Table 12.1). For the latter the odds are 1.8949 (95% CI, 0.225 to 1.052; i.e. 89%) and for depredation is 1.619 (95% CI 0.168 to 0.786; i.e. 62%) (Table 12.2). This implies that there is a significant association between considering HWC to be a serious problem with experiencing depredation and perceptions that livelihoods are threatened. The other odds of participants considering HWC as a greater problem due to a 1-unit increase in the number of affected income sources is 1.806 times higher (i.e. increases 81%) than when there is no increase, holding all variables constant, and 1.754 (75%) and 1.696 (70%) times higher when having experienced a 1-unit increase in crop raiding and annual livestock depredation at any point in time respectively than when participants do not experience these predictors. Furthermore, for a 1-unit increase in perceptions that wildlife has declined, in age and the number of problems causing species, holding all variables constant, perceptions of HWC being a greater threat is 0.933 (93%), 0.888 (88%) and 0.796 (80%) times higher than when these predictors are not experienced.

Discussion

Conservation of wildlife and the development of wildlife economy in rural communities is partly intended to increase income from wildlife as a natural resource. The wildlife-based economy continued to grow in rural areas where communities established conservancies to derive benefits from the wildlife economy. In Namibia, the trend is to conserve wildlife to derive income from hunting and tourism in rural communities (Naidoo *et al.* 2011). The commodification of natural resources through the establishment of conservancies also

Table 12.1 Summary of the ranking of the fourteen top competing models based on the Akaike Information Criteria corrected for small samples (AICc), AICc differences (ΔAICc), AICc weights (wi*) and cumulative AICc weights (Σwi).

Model No.	AICc	ΔAICc	w_i	Σw_i
4641	337.61	0	0.128	0.128
4625	337.77	0.168	0.117	0.245
4657	337.97	0.364	0.107	0.352
4609	338.29	0.686	0.091	0.442
4626	338.76	1.155	0.072	0.514
4642	339.04	1.431	0.062	0.577
4610	339.17	1.566	0.058	0.635
4629	339.19	1.580	0.058	0.693
4627	339.3	1.689	0.055	0.748
4645	339.36	1.756	0.053	0.801
4658	339.41	1.804	0.052	0.853
4897	339.45	1.839	0.051	0.904
4613	339.52	1.915	0.049	0.953
4705	339.6	1.992	0.047	1.00

*A model consists of a response variable (i.e. views that HWC is a serious problem) and a list of predictor variables (age, experienced crop raiding, etc.). Models differ based on the combinations of the included predictors. For example, model no 4641 indicates that views about HWC are influenced by the number of problem species involved, annual livestock depredation and perceptions that livelihoods are threatened.

(Source: Authors' research)

brings forth community benefits in the form of local employment, including cash dividends and game meat from hunted animals (MET & NACSO 2020). However, the findings of this study show that the wildlife economy is equally perceived as a threat to the livelihood of rural communities by local actors. This is demonstrated in terms of perceptions communities express and negative experiences associated with wildlife.

Human–wildlife conflict in the Wuparo Conservancy was regarded as a threat to local livelihoods, undermining the attempts to commodify wildlife in the area. The co-existence between humans and wildlife transforms into conflict emanating from competition for the shared resources, where HWC

Table 12.2 The top 14 competing models with associated nine predictor variables found to influence the odds of respondents considering human wildlife conflict to be a serious problem.*

Model No.	Age	Experienced crop raiding	Experienced livestock depredation	Number of income sources	No. of problem species	Decreased abundance of wildlife	Continuous movement of dangerous wildlife	Annual livestock depredation	Livelihoods are threatened
4641					-0.245			0.4685	0.5996
4625				0.621				0.5153	0.6745
4657				0.5267	-0.2097			0.4596	0.6033
4609				0.6124				0.5381	0.6885
4626	-0.1292							0.501	0.6594
4642	-0.1043				-0.2249			0.4629	0.5948
4610	-0.1325							0.5233	0.673
4629			0.556	0.6061				0.4582	0.6808
4627		0.562		0.6659				0.4725	0.6656
4645			0.4272		-0.2268			0.4303	0.6089
4658	-0.1061			0.5294	-0.1893			0.4535	0.5979
4897					-0.2449		-0.1403	0.481	0.6002
4613			0.6049					0.4754	0.6931
4705					-0.2482	-0.069		0.4591	0.5995

*A model consists of a response variable (i.e. views that HWC is a serious problem) and a list of predictor variables (age, experienced crop raiding, etc.). Models differ based on the combinations of the included predictors. For example, model no 4641 indicates that views about HWC are influenced by the number of problem species involved, annual livestock depredation and perceptions that livelihoods are threatened.

(Source: Authors' research)

Table 12.3 Coefficient estimates, proportional odds ratio and the 95% profiling confidence intervals (CI) of parameters from the top fourteen competitive models. In bold are the statistically significant parameter estimates (their 95% CI does not cross 0).

Parameter	Coefficient estimates	Proportional odds ratio	Profile 95% CI	
			2.50%	97.50%
No. of problem species	-0.228	0.796	-0.520	0.065
Annual livestock depredation	**0.482**	**1.619**	**0.178**	**0.786**
Livelihoods are threatened	**0.638**	**1.894**	**0.225**	**1.052**
No. of income sources	0.591	1.806	-0.165	1.347
Age	-0.119	0.888	-0.351	0.114
Experienced livestock depredation	0.528	1.696	-0.707	1.764
Experienced crop raiding	0.562	1.754	-0.765	1.889
Continuous movement of dangerous wildlife	-0.140	0.869	-0.589	0.308
Decreased abundance of wildlife	-0.069	0.933	-0.352	0.215

(Source: Authors' research)

only becomes qualified when the interaction results in detrimental effects (Waldhorn 2019). Although multiple factors were assumed to predict the perceptions of the community members, this study confirmed that perceptions towards the seriousness of HWC were significantly shaped by the livelihoods being threatened and annual livestock depredation experienced by community members. Like many African nations, the livelihoods in the Wuparo community are dependent on the subsistence crop production and livestock rearing. The community perceptions are affected by the impact of wildlife on livelihoods possibly because of the personal relevance attached (van Dalum 2013), as compared to the commodification of wildlife resources being at the community level.

Human–wildlife conflict has intensified over the years both at local and global levels, where there was an 87% increase in reports of HWC in Africa and Asia from 2000 to 2015, with greater intensity in southern and eastern

Africa than northern Africa and other continents (Seoraj-Pillai & Pillay 2017). The frequency and magnitude of HWC incidents result from the increasing pressures on biodiversity (Kansky & Knight 2014) as both conservation and farming practices become more relevant for commodification coupled with increasing wildlife and human populations. Local communities in less developed nations, like sub-Saharan Africa, are characterised by marginal farming operations, and therefore are more susceptible to the effects of HWC, thereby threatening household food security (Seoraj-Pillai & Pillay 2017). The HWC effects are also exacerbated by environmental disasters such as frequent droughts and floods (Nyhus 2016; Reid *et al.* 2008).

Shrinking spaces for wildlife and proximity to the national park increase interaction between people and wildlife and associated losses (Karanth & Ranganathan 2018; Mhuriro-Mashapa *et al.* 2018; Mmbaga *et al.* 2017). The Wuparo Conservancy is directly bordered by Mudumu and the Nkasa Rupara national parks resulting in constant exposure to wildlife movements. Although the distance from villages to the park borders did not significantly influence the overall perceptions of the community members (see also Ansong & Røskaft 2011), the study clearly shows that perceptions of risk regarding livestock depredation varied among the nine villages. Villages towards the centre of the Conservancy were perceived to have higher probabilities of encountering problem-causing animals (e.g. Samudono and Masasa in Map 12.1). According to van Dalum (2013), the type and likelihood of interactions with wildlife differ among communities due to local differences in the abundance and density of the wildlife population. Additional factors include the effectiveness of existing mitigation measures, damage-causing species' habitat use in particular foraging patterns, and predator-livestock size or herbivore crop type preferences (Blackwell *et al.* 2016; Hayward 2006; Khorozyan & Waltert 2019; Ugarte *et al.* 2019). Lions were identified by most respondents to contribute to most livestock predation cases in the Wuparo Conservancy. This may be related to the observation that lions tend to remain closer to their natural habitat (Holmern *et al.* 2007) while hyenas have higher plasticity in habitat use and diet (Boydston *et al.* 2003). Interestingly, Hanssen *et al.* (2017) report a gradual decline in lion depredation incidents from 2013 to 2016 in the Wuparo Conservancy and relate this to the increased use of lion-proof enforced cattle enclosures.

As revealed in the Wuparo Conservancy during this study, elephants cause most crop damage. Namibia has among the largest free-roaming elephant populations, sharing habitats with people. Crop raiding resulting from elephant-inflicted damages causes concerns for household food security and economic losses in different parts of the world (Karanth *et al.* 2018; Karanth & Ranganathan 2018; Mayberry *et al.* 2017; Mmbaga *et al.* 2017). A study in the Rombo area, which lies between three protected areas in Tanzania, shows high levels of crop-raiding incidents that generated negative community perceptions towards wildlife species, especially elephants (Mmbaga *et al.* 2017). Humans are likely to perceive negatively the wildlife that they fear the most or those causing damage to what is deemed important (Batt 2009; Waldhorn 2019). The degree of tolerance by community members towards wildlife in this study is largely affected by the amount of crops raided, since crops are the main source of people's livelihoods. This study also revealed that duration of residency seems to negatively influence participants' attitudes towards the species and the nature of the conflict, or else long residency tends to sustain existing negative attitudes, as new settlers also agreed that conflict poses a serious threat to livelihoods. Similarly, Mkonyi *et al.* (2017) reported a negative association between duration of residency and negative attitudes towards large carnivores in the Tarangire Ecosystem, Tanzania. This indicates that exposure to conflict may negatively influence perceptions. This, in turn, raises a fundamental point: that failure by community-based natural resource management in the long run (i.e. after twenty years) as a mechanism to change communities' perceptions positively towards wildlife through the commodification of same can undermine the future of this conservation approach, as commodification is the main premise of this approach.

In Namibia, the two most highly ranked problematic species, lion and elephant, are also highly valued species in monetary terms, and are of priority in the wildlife economy. These species are high on the list of interest for nature-based tourism and trophy hunting (Barnett *et al.* 2009). Due to the high economic value of these species in the wildlife trade, they are prioritised in terms of conservation. However, the threat these species pose to the livelihood of rural communities, where the commodification of conservation is practised and promoted, raises concerns. Buffalo, also a high-value species for wildlife economy (Kahler & Gore 2015) were perceived as posing a lesser threat to the livelihood of rural communities in Wuparo Conservancy. This finding, together with the lack of a clear competitive model from the OLS analysis, demonstrates the complexity and the ambiguities of managing human–wildlife interactions. Those involved in the commodification of nature, and especially of wildlife, should be mindful of the risks the wildlife species causes to rural communities' livelihoods.

Conclusion

The commodification of wildlife will succeed if the benefits at the household level are sufficient to keep local people from greatly depending on traditional livelihoods. This study reveals that while commodification of wildlife is meant to supplement and strengthen household security, local people's perceptions regarding human–wildlife interactions remain negative. Strategies to mitigate conflict over the years have not been effective or sustainable in terms of changing people's perceptions about wildlife due to their adverse life experiences. The complexity of human–wildlife interactions is the main reason for the limited success of mitigation strategies intended to reduce the negative impact of such interactions on rural livelihoods. Solutions should be geared towards mitigation measures that support the preservation of traditional local livelihoods and increase benefits from the commodification efforts. An understanding of the causes of these conflicts is essential for developing effective and cost-efficient management strategies to ensure the achievement of conservation goals.

Bibliography

Ajzen, I. & Fishbein, M. (1977). 'Attitude-behavior relations: A theoretical analysis and review of empirical research', *Psychological Bulletin*, 84(5), 888–918.

Anand, S. & Radhakrishna, S. (2017). 'Investigating trends in human-wildlife conflict: Is conflict escalation real or imagined?' *Journal of Asia-Pacific Biodiversity*, 10, 154–161.

Ansong, M. & Røskaft, E. (2011). 'Determinants of attitudes of primary stakeholders towards forest conservation management: A case study of Subri Forest Reserve, Ghana', *International Journal of Biodiversity Science, Ecosystem Services & Management*, 7(2), 98–107.

Barnes, J. I., Macgregor, J., & Weaver, L. C. (2002). 'Economic Efficiency and incentives for change within Namibia's community wildlife use initiatives', *World Development*, 30(4), 667–681.

Barnett, R., Shapiro, B., Barnes, I., Ho, S. Y. W., Burger, J., Yamaguchi, N., & Cooper, A. (2009). 'Phylogeography of lions (*Panthera leo* ssp.) reveals three distinct taxa and a late Pleistocene reduction in genetic diversity', *Molecular Ecology*, 18(8), 1668–1677.

Bartoń, K. (2016). Multi-Model Inference 'MuMIn'. R package. Version 1.15. 6. Accessed from https://cran.r-project.org/web/packages/MuMIn.

Batt, S. (2009). 'Human attitudes towards animals in relation to species similarity to humans: A multivariate approach', *BioscienceHorizons*, 2(2), 180–190.

Blackwell, B. F., DeVault, T. L., Fernandez-Juricic, E., Gese, E. M., Gilbert-Norton, L., & Breck, S. W. (2016). 'No single solution: Application of behavioural principles in mitigating human-wildlife conflict', *Animal Behaviour*, 120, 245–254.

Botha, C. (2005). 'People and the environment in colonial Namibia', *South African Historical Journal*, 52(1), 170–190.

Bowen-Jones, E. (2012). 'Financial mechanisms for addressing human wildlife conflict', IIED Case Study Summaries. Available at: https://pubs.iied.org/sites/default/files/pdfs/migrate/G03734.pdf [Accessed 24 January 2022].

Boydston, E. E., Kapheim, K. M., Watts, H. E., Szykman, M., & Holekamp, K. E.

(2003). 'Altered behaviour in spotted hyenas associated with increased human activity', *Animal Conservation*, 6, 207–219.

Brandt, F., Josefsson, J. & Spierenburg, M. (2018). 'Power and politics in stakeholder engagement: Farm dweller (in)visibility and conversions to game farming in South Africa Power and politics in stakeholder engagement', *Ecology and Society*, 23(3), 32.

Collomb, J. G., Kanapaux, W., Mupeta, P., Barnes, G., Saqui, J., & Child, B. (2008). 'Assessing the success of community-based natural resources management through the integration of governance, livelihood and conservation attitude indicators: Case studies from Caprivi, Namibia' (Caprivi: International Association of the Study of the Commons). Available at: https://dlc.dlib.indiana.edu/dlc/bitstream/handle/10535/1509/Collomb_212501.pdf [Accessed 24 January 2022].

Conover, M. R. & Messmer, T. (2001). 'Wildlife and Rural Landowners', in: D. J. Decker, T. L. Brown, & W. F. Siemer (eds), *Human Dimensions of Wildlife Management in North America*. (Bethesda MD: The Wildlife Society), 243–268.

de Wet, F. & Gaedke, J. (2009). 'Anthropogenic impacts on large-carnivore populations (lion, leopard, hyaena, cheetah and wild dog) in north-eastern Namibia: Investigating human-predator coexistence on conservancy managed land' (Biosphere Expeditions). Available at: www.biosphere-expeditions.org/images/stories/pdfs/reports/report-caprivi08.pdf [Accessed 24 January 2022].

Dickman, A. J. (2010). 'Complexities of conflict: The importance of considering social factors for effectively resolving human–wildlife conflict', *Animal Conservation*, 13, 458–466.

Duffy, R., Massé, F., Smidt, E., Marijnen, E., Büscher, B., Verweijen, J., & Lunstrum, E. (2019). 'Why we must question the militarisation of conservation', *Biological Conservation*, 232, 66–73.

Fishbein, M. & Ajzen, I. (1975*). Belief, Attitude, Intention, and Behavior: An Introduction to Theory and Research* (Reading MA: Addison-Wesley).

Humavindu, M. N. & Stage, J. (2013). 'Key sectors of the Namibian economy'. *Economic Structures*, 2(1).

Hanssen, L., Fwelimbi, M. H., Siyanga, O. & Funston, P. (2017). 'Human-lion conflict mitigation in the Mudumu Complexes, Zambezi Region, Namibia' (Kongola, Namibia: Kwando Carnivore Project). Available at: www.nacso.org.na/sites/default/files/Human-Lion%20Conflict%20in%20the%20Mudumu%20Complexes_Report%20March%202017.pdf [Accessed 24 January 2022].

Hayward, M. W. (2006). 'Prey preferences of the spotted hyaena (*Crocuta crocuta*) and degree of dietary overlap with the lion (*Panthera leo*)', *Journal of Zoology*, 270(4), 606–614.

Holmern, T., Nyahongo, J., & Røskaft, E. (2007). 'Livestock loss caused by predators outside the Serengeti National Park, Tanzania', *Biological Conservation*, 135, 518–526.

Kahler, J. & Gore, M. L. (2015). 'Local perceptions of risk associated with poaching of wildlife implicated in human-wildlife conflicts in Namibia', *Biological Conservation*, 189, 49–58.

Kanapaux, W., & Child, B. (2011). 'Livelihood activities in a Namibian wildlife conservancy: A case study of variation within a CBNRM programme', *Oryx*, 45(3), 365–372.

Kansky, R. & Knight, A. T. (2014). 'Key factors driving attitudes towards large mammals in conflict with humans', *Biological Conservation*, 179, 93–105.

Karanth, K. K., Gupta, S., & Vanamamalai, A. (2018). 'Compensation payments, procedures and policies towards human-wildlife conflict management: Insights from India', *Biological Conservation*, 227, 383–389.

Karanth, K. K. & Ranganathan, P. (2018). 'Assessing Human–Wildlife Interactions in a Forest Settlement in Sathyamangalam and Mudumalai Tiger Reserves', *Tropical Conservation Science*, 11, 1–14.

Khorozyan, I. & Waltert, M. (2019). 'How long do anti-predator interventions remain effective? Patterns, thresholds and uncertainty', *Royal Society Open Science*, 6, 190826.

Khumalo, K. E. & Yung, L. A. (2015). 'Women, human-wildlife conflict, and CBNRM: Hidden impacts and vulnerabilities in Kwandu Conservancy, Namibia', *Conservation & Society*, 13(3), 232–243.

Koot, S., Hitchcock, R., & Gressier, C. (2019). 'Belonging, indigeneity, land and nature in southern Africa under neoliberal capitalism: An overview', *Journal of Southern African Studies*, 45(2), 341–355.

Lamarque, F., Anderson, J., Fergusson, R., Lagrange, M., Osei-Owusu, Y., & Bakker, L. (2009). 'Human-wildlife conflict in Africa: Causes, consequences and management strategies', FAO Forestry Paper no. 157. Available at www.fao.org/3/i1048e/i1048e00.pdf [Accessed 9 January 2023].

Massé, F., & Lunstrum, E. (2016). 'Accumulation by securitization: Commercial poaching, neoliberal conservation, and the creation of new wildlife frontiers', *Geoforum*, 69, 227–237.

Mayberry, A. L., Hovorka, A. J., & Evans, K. E. (2017). 'Well-being impacts of human-elephant conflict in Khumaga, Botswana: Exploring visible and hidden dimensions', *Conservation & Society*, 15(3), 280–291.

Megaze, A., Balakrishnan, M., & Belay, G. (2017). 'Human–wildlife conflict and attitude of local people towards conservation of wildlife in Chebera Churchura National Park, Ethiopia', *African Zoology*, 52, 1–8.

MET – Ministry of Environment and Tourism (2018) 'Revised national policy on human wildlife conflict management 2018–2027' (Windhoek: Republic of Namibia). Available at: www.met.gov.na/files/downloads/45a_Mail%20 bookof%20GIZ%20Book5.pdf [Accessed 24 January 2022].

MET & NACSO – Ministry of Environment and Tourism & Namibian Association of CBNRM Support Organisations (2018). 'The state of community conservation in Namibia – A review of communal conservancies, community forests and other CBNRM activities (Annual Report 2017)' (Windhoek: MET/ NACSO). Available at: www.nacso.org.na/sites/default/files/State%20of%20 Community%20Conservation%20book%20web_0.pdf [Accessed 24 January 2022].

MET & NACSO – Ministry of Environment and Tourism & Namibian Association of CBNRM Support Organisations (2020). 'The state of community conservation in Namibia (Annual Report 2018)' (Windhoek: MET/NACSO). Available at: www.nacso.org.na/sites/default/files/State%20of%20Community%20 Conservation%20book%202018%20web.pdf [Accessed 24 January 2022].

Mhuriro-Mashapa, P., Mwakiwa, E., & Mashapa, C. (2018). 'Socio-economic impact of human-wildlife conflicts on agriculture based livelihood in the periphery of Save Valley Conservancy, Zimbabwe', *The Journal of Animal and Plant Sciences*, 28(3), 903–914.

Mkonyi, F. J., Estes, A. B., Msuha, M. J., Lichtenfeld, L. L., & Durant, S. M. (2017). 'Socio-economic correlates and management implications of livestock depredation by large carnivores in the Tarangire ecosystem, northern Tanzania', *International Journal of Biodiversity Science, Ecosystem Services & Management*, 13(1), 248–263.

Mmbaga, N. E., Munishi, L. K., & Treydte, A. C. (2017). 'Balancing African elephant conservation with human well-being in Rombo area, Tanzania', *Advances in Ecology*, (4184261), 1–9.

Muyengwa, S. (2015). 'Determinants of individual level satisfaction with community based natural resources management: A case of five communities in Namibia', *Environments*, 2, 608–623.

Naidoo, R., Stuart-Hill, G., Weaver, L. C., Tagg, J., Davis, A., & Davidson, A. (2011). 'Effect of diversity of large wildlife species on financial benefits to local communities in northwest Namibia', *Environmental and Resource Economics*, 48, 321–335.

Naidoo, R., Weaver, L. C., Diggle, R. W., Matongo, G., Stuart-Hill, G., & Thouless, C. (2016). 'Complementary benefits of tourism and hunting to communal conservancies in Namibia', *Conservation Biology*, 30(3), 628–638.

NSA – Namibia Statistics Agency (2017). 'Namibia Inter-censal Demographic Survey 2016 Report' (Windhoek: NSA, September 2017). Available at: https:// cms.my.na/assets/documents/NIDS_2016.pdf [Accessed 24 January 2022].

Nyamasyo, S. K. & Kihima, B. O. (2014). 'Changing land use patterns and their impacts on wild ungulates in Kimana Wetland ecosystem, Kenya', *International Journal of Biodiversity*, 2014(486727), 1–10.

Nyhus, P. J. (2016). 'Human–Wildlife Conflict and Coexistence', *Annual Review Environment Resources*, 41, 143–171.

Reid, H., Sahlén, L., Stage, J., & Gregor, J. M. (2008). 'Climate change impacts on Namibia's natural resources and economy', *Climate Policy*, 8, 452–466.

Riehl, B., Zerriffi, H., & Naidoo, R. (2015). 'Effects of community-based natural resource management on household welfare in Namibia', *PloS ONE*, 10(5), e0125531.

Salerno, J., Stevens, F., Gaughan, A., Hilton, T., Bailey, K. *et al.* (2021). 'Wildife impacts and changing climate pose compounding threats to human food security', *Current Biology*, 31(22), 5077–5085.e6.

Seoraj-Pillai, N. & Pillay, N. (2017). 'A meta-analysis of human–wildlife conflict: South African and global perspectives', *Sustainability*, 9(34), 1–21.

Shilongo, S. M., Sam, M., & Simuela, A. (2018). 'Using incentives as mitigation measure for human wildlife conflict management in Namibia', *International Journal of Scientific and Research Publications*, 8(11), 677–682.

Silva, J. A. & Motzer, N. (2014). 'Hybrid uptakes of neoliberal conservation in Namibian tourism-based development', *Development and Change*, 46(1), 48–71.

Stoldt, M., Göttert, T., Carsten, M., & Zeller, U. (2020). 'Transfrontier conservation areas and human-wildlife conflict: The case of the Namibian component of the Kavango-Zambezi (KAZA) TFCA', *Scientific Reports*, 10(7964), 1–16.
Störmer, N., Weaver, L. C., Stuart-Hill, G., Diggle, R. W., & Naidoo, R. (2019). 'Investigating the effects of community-based conservation on attitudes towards wildlife in Namibia', *Biological Conservation*, 233, 193–200.
Suich, H. (2013a). 'The effectiveness of economic incentives for sustaining community based natural resource management', *Land Use Policy*, 31, 441–449.
Suich, H. (2013b). 'Evaluating the household level outcomes of community based natural resource management: the Tchuma Tchato Project and Kwandu Conservancy', *Ecology and Society*, 18(4), 25.
Sullivan, S. (2006). 'Elephant in the room? Problematising "new" (neoliberal) biodiversity conservation', *Forum for Development Studies*, 33(1), 105–135.
Thomsen, J. M., Lendelvo, S., Coe, K., & Rispel, M. (2021). 'Community perspectives of empowerment from trophy hunting tourism in Namibia's Bwabwata National Park', *Journal of Sustainable Tourism*, 30(1), 223–239.
Thornton, C. & Quinn, M. S. (2009). 'Coexisting with cougars: Public perceptions, attitudes, and awareness of cougars on the urban-rural fringe of Calgary, Alberta, Canada', *Human–Wildlife Interactions*, 3(2), 282–295.
Treves, A. & Karanth, K. U. (2003). 'Human-carnivore conflict and perspectives on carnivore management worldwide', *Conservation Biology*, 17(6), 1491–1499.
Ugarte, C. S., Moreira-Arce, D. & Simonetti, J. A. (2019). 'Ecological attributes of carnivore-livestock conflict', *Frontiers in Ecology and Evolution*, 7(433), 1–9.
van Dalum, M. (2013). 'Attitude change towards wildlife conservation and the role of environmental education'. Master's thesis, Utrecht University.
Venables, W. N. & Ripley, B. D. (2002). *Modern Applied Statistics with S* (New York: Springer).
Waldhorn, D. R. (2019). 'Toward a new framework for understanding human–wild animal relations', *American Behavioral Scientist 1*, 63(8), 1080–1100.
Wels, H. (2015). '"Animals like us": Revisiting organizational ethnography and research', *Journal of Organizational Ethnography*, 3, 242–259.

13

Hunting for Development: Global production networks and the commodification of wildlife in Namibia

LINUS KALVELAGE

Introduction

Wealthy hunters from around the globe purchase hunting trips to Namibia worth thousands of dollars. For the animal, the moment when the bullet is fired from the hunter's rifle decides on its future as either a living creature or as a trophy hanging in the fireplace room of a distant home. For the hunter, the moment is presumably a highlight of the vacation trip.

Applying a utilitarian rationale to wildlife populations that have survived European colonisation, Namibia has legalised the controlled harvesting of individual animals on private game farms and in communal conservancies. Besides safeguarding wildlife populations, the aim of these policies is to promote rural development. While trophy hunting on private game farms was progressively formalised under the apartheid regime, it was the post-independence government that fostered the implementation of the community-based natural resource management (CBNRM) policy (see Hewitson & Sullivan and Fabiano *et al.* this volume). The prospect of tourism income incentivises the formation of conservancies and, as a consequence, rural communities contribute to the stabilisation and increase of wildlife populations in alliance with the global hunting tourism industry (Gargallo & Kalvelage 2021).

In contrast to safari tourism, which seems to be largely aligned with ethical considerations of the global conservation community, the commodification of nature through the hunting tourism industry causes recurrent outrage when individual animals are killed (see for example the killing of 'Cecil the Lion' in Zimbabwe in 2015 or the elephant 'Voortrekker' in Namibia in 2019). While the ethical implications of trophy hunting are debatable (Ghasemi 2021), this chapter sheds light on the interplay between the private sector, the government and other institutions on different spatial scales that transforms wildlife into a resource for the hunting tourism industry.

To unveil the institutional arrangements and mechanisms at work that transform wildlife into a commodity that circulates globally, this chapter draws from a global production network (GPN) approach (Coe *et al.* 2004; Henderson *et al.* 2002). As outlined in the chapter by Revilla Diez, Hulke, and Kalvelage in this volume, the strength of the approach lies in its capacity to portray the connectedness of firm and non-firm actors (e.g. business associations, international organisations, labour organisations, public authorities) on different spatial scales, which in sum lead to regional development outcomes. Interestingly however, the commodification of nature has as yet received little attention in GPN research, despite the fact that the production of any commodity is directly or indirectly linked to the natural environment (Baglioni & Campling 2017; compare Revilla Diez *et al.* this volume). By analysing the actors involved in trophy hunting, examining their interlinkages, and contrasting different modes of production, this contribution will illustrate the utility of the GPN approach for researching wildlife commodification.

In a first step, the GPN approach will be briefly reviewed; second, the production of wildlife on private freehold game farms and communal conservancies will be examined. Following this, the global production network of the trophy-hunting industry will be set out to show which mechanisms are at work transforming nature into a commodity, before the results are discussed and conclusions are drawn. The data presented was collected during a total of seven months' fieldwork in the Zambezi and Khomas regions between April 2018 and September 2019 (see Kalvelage *et al.* 2021a for a detailed description of the data collection). Sixty-five semi-structured interviews with actors of the safari tourism and trophy hunting GPN (tour operators, professional hunters, conservancies, ministries, wholesalers) were conducted. These findings are complemented by existing studies, policy reports, and website analysis.

Global production network approach

At its core, GPN research aims to explain regional development by analysing the global economic interconnectivity of regions (Henderson *et al.* 2002), placing the material product and its transaction within a network at the focus of the analysis. In contrast to the global value chain (GVC) approach, advocates of the global production networks concept claim to include horizontal relationships and non-firm actors in the analysis to gain a deeper understanding of development processes (Coe *et al.* 2008; compare also Revilla Diez *et al.* this volume). The application of a network heuristic to the understanding of regional development combines both the analysis of endogenous growth factors in regions and the examination of translocal actors coordinating global production (Coe *et al.* 2004).

Existing GPN studies acknowledging nature's relevance for the production process attest a neglect of the environment in 'mainstream' GPN analysis (compare Revilla Diez *et al.* this volume). While many GPN studies are concerned with the distribution of value among actors and across space, fewer studies look into the matter of how networked activities produce or appropriate value from nature (compare Bollig *et al.* this volume). Going even further, criticism has arisen stating that 'causal arrows emphasising how the global political economy affects the environment or how scarcity of resources and the finite capacity of the earth largely impact on the former' miss out the dialectical relation between these phenomena (Baglioni & Campling 2017: 3). According to these opinions, GPN research has relevance for analysing the relations between capital, labour, states, and nature. Here it is argued that one way to emphasise this link is to reveal the actor network behind the commodification of nature, and its consequences for social-ecological relations in the resource region.

While the GPN approach originally emerged from the analysis of manufacturing, recently substantial work has gone into the conceptualisation of the tourism GPN (Kalvelage *et al.* 2022; Murphy 2019; Christian 2016a). In tourism, the commodity is *the tourist experience* (Gibson 2010). Thus, the consumption of the commodity happens parallel to its production, embedded and produced through the coordination of a range of support services. Christian (2016b) has outlined a tourism GPN for Kenyan and Ugandan safari tourism. She maps firm actors according to their function within the network: outbound distribution, international transport, national distribution, accommodation, and excursions. The different distribution channels are presented as a variety of value chains that are bundled together to form a network. However, she does not set out the role of non-firm actors in her analysis, although they appear in a previous, stylised draft (Christian 2012). Daly and Gereffi (2017) present an overview on GVCs in Africa, where the different distribution intermediaries are at the core of the analysis. In a pioneering attempt, Van der Merwe *et al.* (2014) apply the GVC approach to private hunting farms in South Africa and examine the associated activities to assess the economic impact of the industry. This approach is centred on activities rather than on firms and their interrelationships. In a report on the Namibian taxidermy industry, a value chain has been mapped that displays the firm networks and relevant non-firm actors (Ministry of Industrialisation, Trade and SME Development 2016).

This chapter aims to explore the commodification of wildlife through the hunting business in Namibia. It will do so now by examining the actors and the production logic behind it: first, by contrasting two institutional arrangements of wildlife production in Namibia – the freehold game farm and the communal conservancy – and second, by analysing the globally dispersed activities that transform such wildlife into a commodity.

The production of wildlife in Namibia

Trophy hunting is a contested leisure activity, but nonetheless part of reality in many countries with high wildlife numbers. From 2004 to 2014, Canada exported the highest number of trophies worldwide (68,988; 35% of the global trophy exports), followed by South Africa (44,700, or 23%) and Namibia (22,394, or 11%; all figures retrieved from Casamitjana *et al.* 2016). Advocates of trophy hunting emphasise its economic benefits for rural populations and the conservation of endangered species, such as the polar bear in Canada (Freeman & Wenzel 2006), snow leopards and argali in Kyrgyzstan (Kronenberg 2014) or lions in East and southern Africa (Nelson *et al.* 2013). Critics stress negative biological effects on animal populations (for an overview, see Muposhi *et al.* 2017; Naevdal *et al.* 2012), argue that trophy hunting reproduces colonial power relations (Gressier 2014), and question the benefits for local communities (Koot 2018). Moreover, the ecological effects of trophy hunting are not exhaustively researched (Di Minin *et al.* 2016; Naidoo *et al.* 2011), and an intense debate is concerned with the ethics of hunting (Descubes *et al.* 2018; Hannis 2016).

Notwithstanding these debates, trophy hunting in many sub-Saharan countries is legalised, including Namibia where the Ministry of Environment, Forestry and Tourism (MEFT) is responsible for its regulation (for an overview, see Lindsey 2008). Often appraised as a role model, trophy hunting in Namibian communal conservancies has attracted the interest of scholars from different disciplines. The development effects of CBNRM policy are one important point of scholarly interest: while there is little doubt that trophy hunting brings considerable revenues to certain conservancies (Humavindu & Stage 2015; Naidoo *et al.* 2016), the distribution of benefits along the value chain (Schnegg & Kiaka 2018) and at the local level (Koot 2018; Mosimane & Silva 2015) is contested. Recently, a study found that conservancies are effective in capturing value on a local level (Kalvelage *et al.* 2022). Yet large shares of these revenues are used for conservancies' operational costs, and benefits for smallholder farmers are limited.

In Namibia, the legal frameworks that allow for trophy hunting can be distinguished by the legal status of the land: 42% of Namibia's landmass is freehold agricultural land, 35% communal land, and 23% state land (NSA 2018). These different land-tenure systems are a legacy of the colonial era (Werner 1993) which has influenced land tenure until today, with privately owned land in the southern and central areas, and communal land tenure in the northern regions (see Map 13.1 below). The global production network of trophy hunting is anchored in both privately owned freehold game farms and conservancies established on communal land, yet the institutional arrangements managing its production vary, as do related development outcomes. First, we will turn to wildlife production on freehold game farms, before looking at its production under CBNRM legislation.

Freehold game farms

Background

Hunting for human consumption was a common practice in the use of wildlife resources in pre-colonial southern Africa. Especially during periods of reduced agricultural production, wildlife was, and in some cases continues to be (Lubilo & Hebinck 2019), a source of food. The rising demand for ivory for luxury products in Europe and North America during the 19th century incentivised the large-scale harvesting of elephants and the establishment of GVCs (Bollig 2020), thus connecting Namibia to consumers in the Global North. In the early stages of colonial rule, the demand for ivory and ostrich feathers drove game 'to the edge of extinction' (Botha 2005: 172) in southern and central Namibia. However, it was not only the demand for high-value commodities that decimated or even eradicated wildlife populations. The history of rhinos in Namibia illustrates strikingly that both European actors and African pastoralists used firearms to harvest meat and hides, or hunted for leisure (Sullivan *et al.* 2021). Moreover, game populations have been depleted by white farmers, because game was perceived as vermin and harmful to commercialised cattle- and sheep-farming activities (Botha 2005).

Trophy hunting in Namibia was first formalised in 1958, when Ordinance 18 allowed the granting of hunting permits during the non-hunting season for foreign visitors (Joubert 1974). During the 1960s, trophy hunting slowly became established and the government issued Ordinance 31 of 1967, transferring the right to utilise and benefit from wildlife to farm owners (Boudreaux 2008; Joubert 1974). This was further formalised in the Nature Conservation Ordinance (No. 4 of 1975). Farm owners pooled their land and resources to restock game, and these 'conservancies' were seen as a means to preserve wildlife on private lands while economically benefiting from it by offering trophy hunts (Sullivan 2002).

In southern Africa, growth of the industry gained pace when East African countries began to prohibit trophy hunting. In 1972, a total of 209 trophy hunters were recorded in Namibia, with an estimated revenue of 62,700 Rand (at that time US$82,000). Until 1991, these figures increased to an estimated total turnover from trophy hunts on private land of N$13 million (US$766,000), with 251 registered professional hunters and 1,508 tourist arrivals, more than half of whom were Germans (Barnes 1996). During the 1980s, the increasing demand for trophy hunting incentivised the conversion of cattle farms into game farms, as landholders discovered the newly emerging business opportunity (Lindsey *et al.* 2013). Most farms used wildlife as a supplementary activity in addition to livestock production (Barnes & De Jager 1996). A study found that in 2012, 75% of the farmers in Central Namibia used wildlife for commercial purposes and 9% exclusively practised wildlife-based forms of land use (Lindsey *et al.* 2013).

The transformation of private farmland to private game farms resulted in increasing wildlife numbers and biodiversity on freehold farmland. Between 1972 and 1992, the number of game species recorded on private game farms increased by 44%, the total number of animals by about 70% (Barnes & De Jager 1996). However, the new legislation created a binary system: white farmers had use rights over wildlife and thus an incentive to protect wildlife, while black Namibians were excluded from hunting (Boudreaux 2008).

There are currently about 7,500 commercial farms in central and southern Namibia (NSA 2018) with an average farm size of 3,640 ha (NSA 2015). In 1990, when Namibia gained independence from colonial dominion, white commercial farmers, representing 6% of the population, held 52% of all agricultural farmland (including communal land), while black farmers had 48% (Carpenter 2011). By then, most farms were large entities averaging 8,000–10,000 hectares (Barnes & De Jager 1996). The latest land statistics report found that in Namibia, previously advantaged farmers (a category to describe members of the dominant class under apartheid governance) still own 70% of the freehold agricultural land (excluding communal land), which amounts to 27.9 m hectares (NSA 2018). While this indicates a transfer of land ownership from the old elite to the emerging middle class, most game farms are in the hands of white owners.

Production

The transformation of a cattle farm to a wildlife farm requires investments not only in the wildlife stock itself, but also in boreholes, fences, vehicles, licences, accommodation facilities, and advertisement. The maintenance requires antipoaching activities and a balancing of the wildlife population considering the carrying capacity of the area regarding water availability and flora. Income is generated not only through the sale of trophies, but also through the live capture and sale of wildlife, and leather production. Interviews with farm owners revealed that the sale of meat, however, is not feasible, first due to import restrictions of potential customer countries and, second, due to challenges in the logistics, e.g. interruptions in the cooling chain.

The production of wildlife on these farms serves the needs of the hunting industry and is thus limited to marketable species. Predators, elephants, and buffaloes are regarded as deleterious for wildlife stocks and the flora on game farms, and the introduction of these populations is thus suppressed. Quotas for the hunting of animals are set by the Ministry of Environment, Forestry and Tourism (MEFT) and based on population counts conducted by a MEFT official. Following this, the farm's owner applies for a permit, either/variously for trophy hunting, shoot and sell, shoot for own use, keep and sell, trophy meat, catch, keep and sell or night culling (Ministry of Environment and Tourism 2010).

The hunt is guided by a hunting guide, who is either the farm owner or another individual who has entered into an agreement with the owner. Furthermore, a tracker and a skinner are hired to facilitate the hunt. Professional hunters state that hunting on private farms is more lucrative than in concession areas on communal land. In contrast to hunts in concession areas, most of the wildlife taken down on private game farms are smaller animals and plains game (Humavindu & Barnes 2003). Revenues depend on the entrepreneurial skills of the owner, and business models vary: while some farmers prefer to offer more exclusive hunting experiences focused on high-quality trophies, others offer flat rates or package prices. The former are attractive for hunters aiming to win hunting awards or to climb in international hunters' rankings such as the 'Safari Club International World Hunting Awards' (Safari Club International 2021). The latter practice is especially common in times of drought, when wildlife populations need to be reduced and animals are culled.

The procedure of hunting was described by one of the interviewees as follows:

> Then it goes, on the first afternoon, you go out with the guest, take the gun with you, but you are not yet hunting … Once the gun is fired, you take him for the rest of the afternoon; yes, you do that before coffee … Now you're giving him an appetite. You're going to the area where your biggest herds run … He goes to bed with it [the appetite], in the evening after dinner … And the next morning at half past five, always about three quarters of an hour before sunrise, depending on the season, Jona or Peter or Johnny comes with a tray and you have asked in advance: 'Do you drink tea or coffee in the morning?' And there's a pot of coffee on it with two cups, sugar and milk, and then there's a knock on the door and then all you have to say from the inside is, 'Yeah, that's fine'. Then he puts it outside on a little table so people don't have to bend down so early, and then he goes away again. Then you go out and get your tea or coffee and sit there with your wifey or you alone sipping your coffee

… You take your lunch with you in a cooler box, you definitely have a coffee and a few cookies, also a very small bottle just in case, these little hip flasks, you know? There are hunters, they usually bring them with them, use them as scope. It's not alcohol abuse, and it doesn't affect his behaviour. And then you go hunting and you do the hunt honestly, don't go somewhere where the animals have to go, like by the water, and then you shoot them there. Instead, you go somewhere and leave the car and then you walk along the bottom of the mountain where most of the game is at lunchtime … And Gideon or Jonas, your assistants, one goes along, always, as a tracker and one stays with the car. And then when a shot is fired, he just takes the car and somehow brings it near the path. And then if we have perhaps already cleared the way for him to pull over with the car and load the animal or have simply laid a branch across the road, then he knows that he has to leave the car here and then he comes towards us with an axe and we come towards him from above. (translated from German, interview with a professional hunter, 19 August 2019, Windhoek)

The interviewee highlights the fact that the hunt is conducted in an 'honest' way, and the importance of service skills to look after the guests becomes clear. Altogether, an experience is created which combines upmarket accommodation with an expedition into 'wilderness', where hunting is done according to ethical standards. The large size of farms allows for the marketing of an image of wilderness. This image of wilderness mixed with colonial romanticism is promoted in advertisements for game farms:

Namibia – the dream of many travellers and always aroused the interest of hunters. Reports of former times, in which this breathtaking country has been explored, but never tamed, awake the yearning to experience it yourself. Namibia is wild, mysterious and will always stay in your minds. Hunting in Namibia isn't comparable to anything you have done before. Everyone who's hunting here will grow with the rough nature. At our farm you can hunt the African game in a traditional way and discover the foreign continent how hunters and adventurers did it in the old days.'[1]

'Canned hunting', a much criticised practice common in South Africa where animals are bred to be released into a small, fenced area as prey for trophy hunters, is not permitted in Namibia. Free-roaming game populations of large mammals such as elephants and Cape buffaloes can be found in communal areas in northern Namibia, where a high-value wilderness experience is produced.

---

[1]   www.namibia-jagdfarm.com [Accessed 16 February 2022].

Communal conservancies

Background

For the Zambezi Region, reports by European travellers reveal that commercial ivory hunters had arrived in Caprivi by the 1850s.[2] Gradually, ivory trade replaced slave trade as the principal revenue of Barotse leaders (Flint 1970). For instance, it is reported that 'Sipopa had only ideas about hunting, selling ivory and amusing himself' (Kruger 1984: 90). Similarly, his successor Lewanika expresses the importance of ivory for his reign: 'What are the riches of a country? The riches of mine is ivory. But ivory diminishes every year; and when all the elephants in the country are exterminated, what shall I do?' (Coillard 1903: 222). Subsequently, the colonial administration only hesitantly controlled hunting activities in the north of the country, which benefited both ivory hunters and the increasing number of 'sportsmen' from the Cape Colony that hunted for leisure (Kalvelage *et al.* 2021a).

During the Angolan war in the 1970s and 1980s, the South African Defence Force was located throughout northern Namibia. The presence of military forces caused a sharp decline in wildlife numbers in the region, as soldiers were involved in the rhinoceros' horn and ivory trades, officials hunted as a leisure activity, and live animals were caught and transferred to South African national parks (Lenggenhager 2018). Although it has been recorded that army and police officials hunted excessively, the increasing local population had been blamed for the declining wildlife numbers (ibid.).

Expanding the hunting activities from the conservancies on private land in central Namibia, the first hunting concessions for commercial trophy hunting were opened on communal land in the 1980s (Barnes 1996). After independence, the Nature Conservation Amendment Act No. 5 of 1996 transferred user rights to communities on communal land. The Act grants the use rights over free-roaming wildlife populations to communities within a demarcated area and to formalised institutions. Known as the community-based natural resource management (CBNRM) model, this strategy had previously been applied in Zimbabwe (the Communal Areas Management Programme for Indigenous Resources, CAMPFIRE from 1982) and Zambia (the Administrative Management Design for Game Management Areas, ADMADE from 1987).

---

[2] See for instance Holub (1881). *Sieben Jahre in Süd-Afrika: Erlebnisse, Forschungen und Jagden auf meinen Reisen von den Diamantfeldern zum Zambesi (1872–1879)* [Seven years in South Africa: Experiences, Research and Hunting on my Travels from the Diamond Fields to the Zambezi River (1872–1879)]; or Livingstone (1857). *Missionary Travels and Research in South Africa.*

The CBNRM model gained popularity in African states during the 1990s and has been propagated as a panacea for combining conservation, rural development, and empowerment of marginalised communities (Murphree 2009). The aim is threefold: to generate revenues from the global tourism industry to compensate local residents for economic losses due to wildlife, to empower local residents to make the most profitable use of natural resources within their conservancy, and to safeguard wildlife populations (Dressler *et al.* 2010). Institutions are established that prioritise integration into globalised production circuits over the promotion of local livelihood strategies. Thus, existing territories are reshaped (Kalvelage *et al.* 2021b), setting apart land for an exclusive tourism experience of the global customer.

Production

Hunting in communal conservancies is perceived as a more exclusive experience, since these are home to big game. This is also mirrored in the prices for the consumer: a ten-day elephant hunt is worth US$29,000 plus trophy fees ($35,000, Ondjou & Van Heerden Safaris 2018). In 2017, trophy hunting companies paid N$28,209,259 (US$2.2 million, exchange rate at 1 July 2017, NACSO 2017) to Namibian conservancies. However, there are only a few conservancies that derive considerable income from trophy hunting, while many receive small amounts only or do not benefit from hunting tourism at all (see Map 13.1).

The national Ministry of Environment, Forestry and Tourism coordinates a quota-setting process; annual hunting quotas are calculated on the basis of the wildlife population. Conservancy managements are entitled to enter joint-venture agreements with hunting operators. These agreements are formalised in contracts, which specify the trophy fee payable to the Conservancy. A professional hunter and concession-holder describes the procedure as following (translated from German, 30 July 2019, Zambezi):

> Look, here's how it works: We get it from nature conservation [MEFT], we deal with WWF [World Wide Fund for Nature Namibia], nature conservation [MEFT], with Scientific Service; they set a kill quota. It's based on the number of shots fired before. We have to fill out a questionnaire: were the game species easy or difficult to get? How was the trophy quality? What do we think of it? Was the trophy quality sufficient? Is the whole thing sustainable or not sustainable? And then we put it together. Then, the second factor is, they do a game census, every year, once a year, the IRDNC [Integrated Rural Development and Nature Conservation, NGO which is nowadays organised under the umbrella of NACSO] with WWF, nature conservation [MEFT], a big-game census; they take the stocks, what is there, approximately, and then they calculate

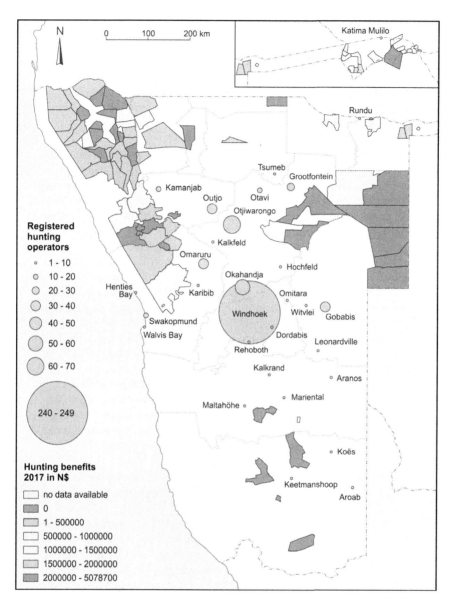

Map 13.1 Hunting benefits in communal conservancies, and the distribution of hunting enterprises in Namibia (Author research / Government of Namibia; Cartography: M. Feinen).

the final quotas. This is a percentage; for example, for elephants, 0.5% of an elephant population can be taken from, for mature trophies in a sustainable way. And that's how it works out. (Professional Hunter 1)

The prices for these quotas that have to be paid by the operator to the conservancy are fixed in negotiations between the two parties (translated from German, 19 July 2019, Zambezi):

Let's take an example. We get an eland on quota. We've never had eland on quota before, it wasn't on the list, now we have a kill. Negotiation … 'How much would an eland cost?' They ask us. 'We suggest you call your neighbouring conservancies, ask what the market price is, list them, then we know what is minimum, what is maximum and we can negotiate from there. No, they already know that, good' … What we know is, on farms, commercial farms, we pay from the amount, let's leave it at 10,000 to 15,000 for Elands. 10,000 is farms where there's a lot of hunting, not a lot of elands – you look for a long time – or 15,000 is farms, there's a lot – you go in, you shoot one, you drive out. That's the way it is in the market. It was pretty much in the spirit of what we were negotiating. Then the conservancy thinks about it; it's a committee, it's twenty people; they talk in their own language; you don't know what's being said until a spokesman says, 'Yes, they've thought about it, they want $43,000 for the eland'. Where you sit and think and think, where is the reality in this dung heap? How are you supposed to negotiate here? What is there … if they had said 25 [thousand], you would have known you were negotiating to 18. We were willing to go to 20 anyway, because that's free-range, that's conservancy, we were willing to go more than commercial farms … 43 [thousand]? I mean what is that? (Professional Hunter 2)

Conservancy management boards claim the process is not transparent, and they lack knowledge of the hunting industry, which is a challenge in negotiations:

Yes, probably some of the things are hidden, that's why I am saying that if a person [the professional hunter] is good enough or the relationship is good with the community, some of the things will be transparent. The first thing is that the tourist to come and buy or shoot an elephant here, we don't know how much he pays to the trophy hunt; that is the hidden things there we don't know. And the number of days he stays there; we don't know how much he pays per day, paying for that trophy hunting. So yes … the only fee that we get is for the shooting of the elephant; let me say the fee that we agreed in the contract, that if you kill an elephant you pay a certain amount to the conservancy. That is the only fee we get. (Interview with a conservancy management board 26 September 2018, Zambezi)

The procedure for hunting in a conservancy is similar to hunts on freehold game farms described above. Accommodation is organised in hunting camps, which are temporarily built for the hunting season. Hunting is restricted to particular months per year, usually from May to August. Low-wage employees to run the camp, and skinners and trackers are hired from the conservancy. Support services such as ammunition, weaponry, and hunting equipment complement these inputs, which together create a hunting experience: the experience is the commodity being sold to the consumer. Yet, the resource that lays the ground for this activity, wildlife, also requires labour input.

The conservancy provides labour input and investments to ensure the reproduction of wildlife and to gain legitimacy for trophy hunting among the local residents. First, conservancies employ game guards, who are responsible for the monitoring of wildlife and the prevention of poaching. Second, conservancies invest in the drilling of boreholes to ensure freshwater supply for wildlife and the reintroduction of formerly extinct species. Third, offset payments are designed to compensate for economic losses caused by wildlife, e.g. the destruction of fields by elephants, or the loss of cattle due to predator attacks. Fourth, the conservancy manages conflicting forms of land use by introducing exclusive use zones for different activities: settlement, safari tourism, grazing, and hunting. Fifth, community development projects such as the electrification of villages, cash payouts and other forms of benefit sharing increase the acceptance among local residents for the implementation of conservation measures, and thus legitimise trophy hunting as an economic practice.

All these functions of the conservancy are closely monitored and supported by the Namibian Association of CBNRM Support Organisations (NACSO) and the Ministry of Environment, Forestry and Tourism (MEFT). These organisations actively support the establishment of new conservancies and provide legal consultation services for existing ones. By raising additional funds, NACSO is able to implement projects such as awareness workshops and to conduct them in close coordination with MEFT. Furthermore, NGOs and MEFT help to identify investors and accompany the negotiation for the agreement. Lastly, these negotiations between the professional hunter and the conservancy management are crucial for specifying the distribution of rents.

There are two types of quotas: guaranteed quotas, and optional quotas. While the trophy fee for the former has to be paid even if the animal is not killed, the latter only applies if the animal is actually shot. Conservancies in many cases aim to increase the share of guaranteed quotas, which facilitates financial planning. The professional hunter, on the other hand, is interested in keeping the number of guaranteed species low, as it gives him more flexibility. Therefore, the share of optional quotas vis-à-vis guaranteed quotas is crucial for the price of the resource and ecological outcomes of the resource use. Professional hunters are more likely to lower the price at the end of a hunting season, in order to ensure the actual use of the quotas purchased.

Free-roaming wildlife becomes a resource when it is set on the quota and enters conservancy territory. Outside conservancies, it is illegal to hunt, and wildlife is nature with a mere use value, not a resource that has a legal exchange value. The coupling of conservancies with specialised hunting outfitters makes the production of the resource possible. Conservancies provide the legal framework, labour inputs, and investments, and hunting outfitters have the industry-related knowledge and the network to market the quotas on a global market. Compared to the freehold game farm, in conservancies a larger number of people are involved in the production of the resource, more people benefit from the revenues generated and the resource itself is mainly big game.

The Namibian hunting tourism global production network

The following paragraph will shed light on the globally organised actor network that produces the commodity: the hunting tourism GPN (see Figure 13.1 below). First, the role of international institutions will be analysed, then a look at the various distribution channels and involved actors will follow, before the downstream segment – the trophy preparation – will be briefly considered.

International institutions

International agreements and regulations play a major role in the industry. High-profile hunts that were followed by increased media attention and outrage in social media, such as that of 'Cecil the Lion' in Zimbabwe 2015 or the legal killing of a black rhino in Namibia, led to import bans on trophies and the decision of some commercial air carriers to stop the transport of trophies (Di Minin *et al.* 2016). The Convention on International Trade in Endangered Species of Wild Fauna and Flora (CITES) is an international agreement between governments that aims to ensure the survival of wild animals and plants through the regulation of trade. It was initiated in 1963 by 80 countries, and today 183 countries have signed the agreement. All importation and exportation of listed species has to go through a control and licensing system. Species are divided into three categories according to their level of endangeredness, and each category is subject to a varying degree of protective regulations.[3] However, the decision on the classification

---

[3]   www.cites.org [Accessed 16 February 2022].

of certain species regularly provokes criticism, e.g. the decision to keep the white rhinoceros in appendix 1 in 2019, which was widely opposed by Southern African Development Community (SADC) countries (Shikongo 2019). These decisions made in CITES conferences thus impact the number of animals which are available to the trophy-hunting industry.

Most SADC countries have legalised trophy hunting to some extent. Botswana, once a popular destination for trophy hunters, had banned trophy hunting entirely in 2014, but lifted the ban again in 2019 due to a sharply increasing elephant population that caused conflicts with smallholder farmers (BBC 2019). Thus, Botswana has shifted back from a protectionist conservation approach which builds on militarised anti-poaching units towards a utilitarian approach, which aims to ensure the survival of species through commodification (Büscher & Fletcher 2020).

Distribution channels

On average, 2,2061 trophy animals were shot annually in Namibia between 2000 and 2009 (van Schalkwyk *et al.* 2012). In 2000, 38 species were hunted, the most common being oryx (*Oryx gazella*), kudu (*Trage-laphus strepsiceros*), warthog (*Phacochoerus africanus*), springbok (*Antidorcas marsupialis*), and hartebeest (*Alcelaphus buselaphus*) (Humavindu & Barnes 2003). A study found that hunters' satisfaction is greater with larger prey, preferably carnivores (Child & Darimont 2015). However, the listing of the animals shows that, despite the prominence of large species in the debate, the majority of trophy animals actually shot are smaller species.

Hunts are usually sold in packages. Starting with the pickup at the international airport, the operator provides a package including full-board accommodation, domestic transport, hunting, tracking and skinning services, field preparation of trophies, hunting licence, and value-added tax (VAT) (Ondjou & Van Heerden Safaris 2018). Not included are rifles, ammunition, curios, and additional touristic activities. The consumer basically has two options to book a hunting trip: either booking directly with the operator at the destination, or through a specialised travel agent.

Unlike safari tourism GPN, the number of intermediaries in hunting tourism is limited. In Namibia, professional hunters sell hunting trips directly to the consumer through word of mouth, through recommendation by former customers, and also to returning customers. Due to the limited number of intermediaries, the value derived from the commodity is distributed among a small number of actors. In 1991, 251 professional hunters were registered in Namibia (Barnes 1996); this number increased to 429 in 2006 and to 651 in 2022 (Namibia Tourism Board n.d.). Professional hunters are divided into different categories: the lowest rank is hunting guides, who are allowed to hunt on one registered hunting farm. After two years' experience, they can be awarded the status of a master hunting guide. Following another two-year period, an exam can then be taken to become a professional hunter. Professional hunters are allowed to hunt anywhere in Namibia, including concession areas. The highest-ranking are the big-game hunters, which a professional hunter can become by accompanying a registered big-game hunter and passing a big-game hunter exam. The various fees due for these exams add up to N$1,450 (c. US$85; ERPHAN n.d.). The vast majority of professional hunters are white Namibians, despite the Namibia Professional Hunters Association (NAPHA)'s continuous claims that it encourages more black Namibians to become part of the industry.

For the acquisition of new customers, specialised trade fairs are crucial. The annual events of the Dallas Safari Club in Texas, Jagd und Hund in Germany, and Hohe Jagd in Austria are important stages to display the offer of hunting trips to interested consumers. These trade fairs are popular meeting points for professional and leisure hunters, where the industry presents new products, such as vehicles, weapons, and hunting trips. Some operators collaborate with specialised wholesalers such as Westfalia Jagdreisen, who bundle hunting trips in many different countries. The whole process is facilitated by NAPHA, which coordinates joint marketing activities and communication. Between 2000 and 2009, 5,598 hunting tourists arrived in Namibia annually on average (van Schalkwyk *et al.* 2012). In 2000, 48% of trophy hunters were Germans and 11% were from Austria. Twenty-five per cent were from twenty-six other European countries, 12% were from the USA, and the remaining 4% from seventeen other countries (Humavindu & Barnes 2003).

Trophy preparation

Although the exact number of taxidermist companies in Namibia is unknown, in 2015 there were twenty-two companies that were registered holders of a European Union Trade Control and Expert System (EU-TRACES) certificate (Ministry of Industrialisation, Trade and SME Development 2016). The total workforce in the industry is estimated to have reached 280 in 2015 (ibid,).

The CITES database records all international trades of trophies. From 2009 to 2018, 51,450 trophies (including bodies, carvings, claws, derivatives, ears, feet, genitalia, hair, horns, leather products, rugs, skin, skull, teeth, tails, tusks, and other items) were legally exported from Namibia. Of this total, the USA (with 16,659 trophy products) and Germany (with 10,847) were by far the greatest importers (see Figure 13.2). Besides the USA and Republic of South Africa (RSA), the top ten importers are all European countries.

The raw products for processing are delivered by conservancies, game farmers, and professional hunters. The majority of these are produced for

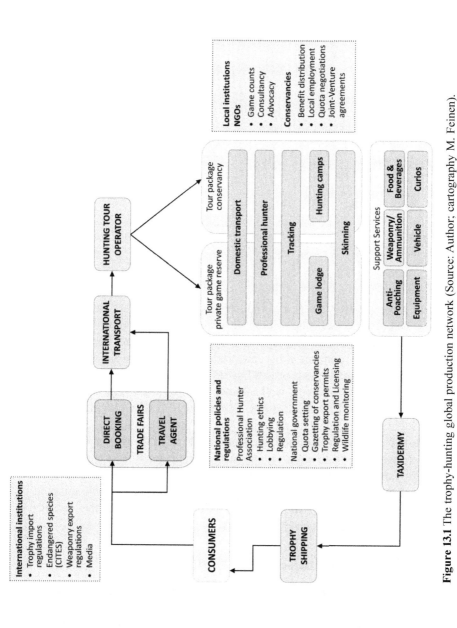

Figure 13.1 The trophy-hunting global production network (Source: Author; cartography M. Feinen).

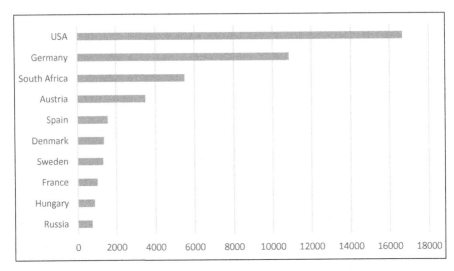

Figure 13.2 Destination countries of exported trophies from Namibia 2009–2018 (Source: UNEP-WCMC 2021).

export (95%, Ministry of Trade, Industrialisation and SME Development 2016). First-stage processing, which ensures the preservation of the skin, is usually done by the hunting operator right after the hunt. The Namibian taxidermy industry produces either raw products like cleaned skulls, and both raw and tanned skins to be processed by a foreign taxidermist, or processed products such as full mounts, wall mounts, skull mounts, bird mounts, and curios (Ministry of Industrialisation, Trade and SME Development 2016). Inputs such as chemicals and artificial eyes are procured internationally.

If the raw product is exported, the manufacturing of the trophy is done by a taxidermist in the destination country. Although the manufacturing costs are lower in Namibia, the overall price is comparable to European standards, as the shipping costs are added to the total price. Specialised trophy-shipping companies, such as Pronto Global Air & Ocean Freight, arrange the logistics (Pronto Global Air & Ocean Freight n.d.).

Discussion and conclusion

To sell a hunting tourism package to wealthy clients, first of all, there must be wildlife. In Namibia, wildlife production occurs on two different land-tenure systems. One is the conservancy as a production site, the other is the private game farm. These two systems result from Namibia's colonial legacy. Both products are sold at the same trade fair, but wildlife produced on private game farms mainly benefits holders of large farms in Central Namibia, and thus reproduces inherited power relations. However, it is necessary to highlight that game farming is an important sector of the Namibian economy; it creates employment and benefits the conservation of economically valuable species. In communal conservancies, on the other hand, implemented conservation measures form part of an integrated plan of nature conservation, and policies aim for the empowerment and economic uplifting of peripheral areas. Yet challenges are extensively discussed, e.g. benefit-sharing practices, negative ecological effects, and negative effects on agriculture. Moreover, the historical perspective applied here makes apparent that the trophy-hunting industry suffers from power imbalances inherited from the apartheid era.

Labour input is needed to ensure the continuous reproduction of the wildlife population without reducing the population beyond the levels deemed ecologically sound by the quota-making organisations. On private game farms, the carrying capacity of the land is sometimes exceeded to ensure a high density of wildlife. Game farms are often large but nonetheless in many cases fenced to prevent wildlife from moving to other properties. Therefore, considerable labour input goes into the monitoring of the population and anti-poaching activities, maintenance of game fences, and the provision of water and, in cases of drought, fodder. Furthermore, investments are needed to introduce new species and high-quality trophy animals.

In communal conservancies, wildlife is free roaming and has to be managed. The conservancy management implements conservation measures such as game-guard activities and invests in boreholes to attract higher wildlife numbers through the provision of water. However, the labour input goes even further: as the land is communal, the establishment of institutions that mediate between the different types of land use are crucial to allow for hunts. The managing of revenues and its distribution by the conservancy as well as democratic decision making are labour-intensive processes. A considerable part of the work goes into the building and maintaining of the conservancy as a local institution.

Although wildlife and its natural environment are the main resources of the hunting tourism industry, tourism-specific knowledge is needed to tap the economic potential. A variety of firm and non-firm actors are involved in the commodification of these resources, its packaging and marketing, to transform a living creature that initially has only a direct use value for humans into a commodity that can be exchanged on a global market, as part of the hunting experience.

Professional hunters bring industry-related knowledge, and bundle the inputs to sell a hunting experience. Hunting operators in the conservancies invest in place infrastructure, transport, and lodging facilities. These investments are crucial to ensure the accessibility, and hence the exploitation, of the resource. On private game farms, accommodation facilities with related hospitality services have to be established. In communal conservancies, hunting camps are temporarily built to ensure a pleasant hunting experience. Local residents are hired as staff and are trained to meet global tourism standards. Additionally, road maintenance and the service of vehicles are crucial for creating a tour package. Hunting operators package hunting trips and market the commodity at trade fairs in the global outbound countries. Lastly, the Namibia Professional Hunting Association facilitates the marketing by promoting Namibia globally as a hunting destination.

Although Namibian actors are central to the configuration of the network, the network itself is a form of global organisation of resource production. The demand of international clients, the mediation of international firms, and international regulations shape the local resource-production process. Furthermore, international actors such as CITES determine the valuation of species. On a national level, institutional actors such as associations, NGOs, and MEFT have a large impact on the industry. Therefore, a GPN approach that goes beyond the value-chain approach and includes non-firm actors in the analysis is useful for research on commodification of nature. Commodification is a process embedded into capital, nature, and state; GPN crosses the boundaries of these spheres and unveils the manifold, globally dispersed actors that enact commodification.

Two commodification mechanisms can be identified (Castree 2003, compare Greiner & Bollig this volume): privatisation, and valuation. Privatisation occurs when a legal title is attributed to a named individual, group or institution. By awarding ownership rights, things can be alienated by the party that owns them and exchanged for other goods. As early as 1967 Ordinance 31 transferred the right to utilise and benefit from wildlife to farm owners, thus enabling the commodification of wildlife on private farms. Under the umbrella of the Nature Conservation Amendment Act 5 of 1996, which paved the way for community-based natural resource management, conservancies are formed in rural areas in Namibia. The national government transfers use rights over free-roaming wildlife to communities, which in return make the commitment to implement conservation measures (Murphree 2009). Hence, wildlife is privatised under the use rights of the conservancy although, technically, it continues to fall under the national government's authority. This privatisation enables communities to attract hunting outfitters, who market wildlife quotas as a tourist attraction on a global market.

The second mechanism is valuation. Commodification of wildlife manifests when the value of a good is measured in labour value, as commodities are then 'subject to a process that requires them to earn rent for those producing and selling them' (Castree 2003: 282). The setting of quotas on wildlife populations is a labour-intensive process. The Ministry of Environment, Forestry and Tourism staff members form a quota-setting committee that fixes the quotas for each species in all eighty-six conservancies in Namibia at the beginning of each year. Permits and quotas decide on the status of wildlife as nature or as a commodity. The calculation of the quotas is based on annual game counts and available scientific data involving NGO staff and conservancy members. Hunting quotas are then the subject of negotiations between the conservancy management committee and hunting outfitters, which end with the fixing of a price.

The governance of this commodification process has effects on value-capture patterns among participants in the value chain, and is associated with a specific notion of territoriality and power, as some places benefit more from the commodification than others (compare Revilla Diez *et al.* this volume). Windhoek is the gateway city for tourism in Namibia and has an outstanding function for the governance of the GPN due to the agglomeration of tourism-related enterprises and its proximity to decision makers in public authorities. However, the study has also shown that government policies are capable of preventing an exhaustive value transfer, as transfer payments are due from the hunting operator to the Conservancy directly, without any further interference of the national government.

From a disarticulation perspective (compare Revilla Diez *et al.* this volume), the emergence of this new industry provokes unintended repercussions on inhabitants of the resource region not directly involved in the GPN. Due to the conservancy legislation it becomes legal to hunt animals on quota inside conservancies. However, hunts are only legal for those who can afford the high quota prices, which excludes large parts of the population from using wildlife as a source of food (Koot 2018; Lubilo & Hebinck 2019). Local actors who do not participate in the GPN only indirectly benefit from trophy hunts, e.g. as passive recipients of hunted meat or cash payouts to members of the conservancy. Moreover, a zonation plan restricts the use of land in forests or near rivers, where touristic activities such as hunting and photo safaris take place. The increase in numbers of large mammals such as elephants, which are observed in the Zambezi Region due to conservation efforts, negatively affects the livelihoods of smallholder farmers (Hulke *et al.* 2021).

Both production systems shape ecosystems according to the needs of the production network; the ecological outcomes of these approaches, however, are different. On a private game farm, production leads to a high density of commercially valuable plains game, in many cases fenced. Large private game farms aim to sell an image of wilderness, but this wilderness is restricted to smaller game, and predators are not compatible with such a production system. In contrast, communal conservancies sell the image of free-roaming wildlife in wilderness scenery, and production is oriented to ensure the availability of big game. Therefore, it can be concluded that the two different ways of organising global production result in differences of the social-ecological system. However, more research is needed to examine the broader ecological implications of GPN integration.

Bibliography

Baglioni, E. & Campling, L. (2017). 'Natural resource industries as global value chains: Frontiers, fetishism, labour and the state', *Environment and Planning A: Economy and Space*, 49(11), 2437–2456.

Barnes, J. I. (1996). 'Trophy hunting in Namibia', in: P. Tarr (ed.), *Namibia Environment*, vol. 1. (Windhoek Directorate of Environmental Affairs, Ministry of Environment and Tourism), 100–103.

Barnes, J. I. & De Jager, J. L. V. (1996). 'Economic and financial incentives for wildlife use on private land in Namibia and the implications for policy', *African Journal of Wildlife Research*, 26(2), 37–46.

BBC (2019). 'Botswana lifts ban on trophy hunting', *BBC News*, 22 May 2019. Available at: www.bbc.com/news/world-africa-48374880 [Accessed 25 January 2022].

Bollig, M. (2020). *Shaping the African Savannah: From Capitalist Frontier to Arid Eden in Namibia* (Cambridge; New York: Cambridge University Press).

Bollig, M. & Menestrey Schwieger, D. A. (2014). 'Fragmentation, cooperation and power: Institutional dynamics in natural resource governance in north-western Namibia', *Human Ecology*, 42(2), 167–181.

Botha, C. (2005). 'People and the environment in colonial Namibia', *South African Historical Journal*, 52(1), 170–190.

Boudreaux, K. (2008). 'A new call of the wild: Community-based natural resource management in Namibia', *Georgetown International Environmental Law Review*, 20(2), 297–335.

Büscher, B. & Fletcher, R. (2020). *The Conservation Revolution: Radical Ideas for Saving Nature Beyond the Anthropocene* (London: Verso Trade).

Carpenter, S. (2011). 'Devolution of conservation: Why CITES must embrace community-based resource management', *Arizona Journal of Environmental Law & Policy*, 2(1), 1–51.

Casamitjana, J., Tsang, J., Flocken, J., Lajoie, S., & Moos, S. (2016). 'Killing for trophies: An analysis of global trophy hunting trade' (International Fund for Animal Welfare (IFAW)). Available at: www.ifaw.org/resources/killing-for-trophies [Accessed 24 January 2022].

Castree, N. (2003). 'Commodifying what nature?' *Progress in Human Geography*, 27(3), 273–297.

Child, K. R. & Darimont, C. T. (2015). 'Hunting for trophies: Online hunting photographs reveal achievement satisfaction with large and dangerous prey', *Human Dimensions of Wildlife*, 20(6), 531–541.

Christian, M. (2012). 'Tourism global production networks' (SSRN, Briefing Note 4). Available at: https://papers.ssrn.com/sol3/papers.cfm?abstract_id=2159171 [Accessed 25 January 2022].

Christian, M. (2016a). 'Kenya's tourist industry and global production networks: Gender, race and inequality', *Global Networks*, 16(1), 25–44.

Christian, M. (2016b). 'Tourism global production networks and uneven social upgrading in Kenya and Uganda', *Tourism Geographies*, 18(1), 38–58.

Coe, N. M., Hess, M., Yeung, H. W.-c., Dicken, P., & Henderson, J. (2004). '"Globalizing" regional development: A global production networks perspective', *Transactions of the Institute of British Geographers*, 29(4), 468–484.

Coe, N. M., Dicken, P., & Hess, M. (2008). 'Global production networks: Realizing the potential', *Journal of Economic Geography*, 8(05), 271–295.

Coillard, F. (1903). *On the Threshold of Central Africa: A Record of Twenty Years' Pioneering among the Barotsi of the Upper Zambesi* (New York: American Tract Society).

Daly, J. & Gereffi, G. (2017). 'Tourism global value chains and Africa', WIDER Working Paper 2017/17 (Helsinki: UNU-WIDER). Available at: www.wider.unu.edu/sites/default/files/wp2017-17.pdf [Accessed 25 January 2022].

Descubes, I., McNamara, T., & Claasen, C. (2018). 'E-Marketing communications of trophy hunting providers in Namibia: Evidence of ethics and fairness in an apparently unethical and unfair industry?' *Current Issues in Tourism*, 21(12), 1349–1354.

Di Minin, E., Leader-Williams, N., & Bradshaw, C. J. A. (2016). 'Banning trophy hunting will exacerbate biodiversity loss', *Trends in Ecology and Evolution*, 31(2), 99–102.

Dressler, W., Büscher, B., Schoon, M., Brockington, D., Hayes, T., Kull, C. A., & Shrestha, K. (2010). 'From hope to crisis and back again? A critical history of the global CBNRM narrative', *Environmental Conservation*, 37(1), 5–15.

Eagle Rock Professional Hunting Academy Namibia (ERPHAN) (n.d). 'Guidelines to register as professional hunter or hunting guide in Namibia'. www.erphan.org/uploads/files/Giraffe%E2%80%93METguidelines-PH-Huntingguides-Namibia-FullVersion.pdf [Accessed 25 June 2020].

Flint, E. (1970). 'Trade and politics in Barotseland during the Kololo period', *The Journal of African History*, 11(1), 71–86.

Freeman, M. & Wenzel, F. (2006). 'The nature and significance of polar bear conservation and hunting in the Canadian Arctic', *Arctic*, 59(1), 21–30.

Gargallo, E. & Kalvelage, L. (2021). 'Integrating social-ecological systems and global production networks: Local effects of trophy hunting in Namibian conservancies', *Development Southern Africa*, 38(1), 87–103.

Ghasemi, B. (2021). 'Trophy hunting and conservation: Do the major ethical theories converge in opposition to trophy hunting?' *People and Nature*, 3(1), 77–87.

Gibson, C. (2010). 'Geographies of tourism: (Un)ethical encounters', *Progress in Human Geography*, 34(4), 521–527.

Gressier, C. (2014). 'An elephant in the room: Okavango safari hunting as ecotourism?' *Ethnos*, 79(2), 193–214.

Hannis, M. (2016). 'Killing nature to save it? Ethics, economics and rhino hunting in Namibia' Working Paper No. 4 (Bath: Future Pasts). Available at: www. futurepasts.net/_files/ugd/5ba6bf_c6f4642f6dac41d88dde147c5853a7ec.pdf [Accessed 25 January 2022].

Henderson, J., Dicken, P., Hess, M., Coe, N. M., & Yeung, H. W.-c. (2002). 'Global production networks and the analysis of economic development', *Review of International Political Economy*, 9(3), 436–464.

Holub, E. (1881). *Sieben Jahre in Süd-Afrika: Erlebnisse, Forschungen und Jagden auf meinen Reisen von den Diamantfeldern zum Zambesi (1872–1879)* (Wien: Alfred Hölder).

Hulke, C., Kairu, J. K. & Revilla Diez, J. (2021). 'Development visions, livelihood realities –How conservation shapes agricultural value chains in the Zambezi Region, Namibia', *Development Southern Africa*, 38(1), 104–121.

Humavindu, M. N. & Barnes, J. I. (2003). 'Trophy hunting in the Namibian economy: An assessment', *African Journal of Wildlife Research*, 33(2), 65–70.

Humavindu, M. N. & Stage, J. (2015). 'Community-based wildlife management failing to link conservation and financial viability', *Animal Conservation*, 18(1), 4–13.

Joubert, E. (1974). 'The development of wildlife utilization in South West Africa', *Journal of the Southern African Wildlife Management Association*, 4(1), 35–42.

Kalvelage, L., Revilla Diez, J., & Bollig, M. (2022). 'How much remains? Local value capture from tourism in Zambezi, Namibia', *Tourism Geographies*, 24(4–5), 759–780.

Kalvelage, L., Revilla Diez, J., & Bollig, M. (2021a). 'Do tar roads bring tourism? Growth corridor policy and tourism development in the Zambezi Region, Namibia', *The European Journal of Development Research*, 1–22.

Kalvelage, L., Bollig, M., Grawert, E., Hulke, C., Meyer, M., Mkutu, K., & Revilla Diez, J. (2021b). 'Territorialising conservation', *Conservation & Society*, 19(4), 282–293.

Koot, S. (2018). 'The limits of economic benefits: Adding social affordances to the analysis of trophy hunting of the Khwe and Ju/'hoansi in Namibian community-based natural resource management', *Society and Natural Resources,* 32(4), 417–433.

Kronenberg, J. (2014). 'Viable alternatives for large-scale unsustainable projects in developing countries: The case of the Kumtor gold mine in Kyrgyzstan', *Sustainable Development*, 22(4), 253–264.

Kruger, C. E. (1984). *History of the Caprivi Strip 1890–1984* (National Archives of Namibia, A.0472).

Lenggenhager, L. (2018). *Ruling Nature, Controlling People : Nature Conservation, Development and War in North-Eastern Namibia Since the 1920s* (Basel: Basler Afrika Bibliographien).

Lindsey, P. A. (2008). 'Trophy hunting in sub-Saharan Africa: Economic scale and conservation significance', in: R. D. Baldus, G. R. Damm, & K. Wollscheid (eds), *Best Practices in Sustainable Hunting* (Vienna; Rome: International Council for Game & FAO Wildlife Conservation, Forestry Dept), 41–47.

Lindsey, P. A., Havemann, C. P., Lines, R. M., Price, A. E., Retief, T. A., Rhebergen, T., & Romañach, S. S. (2013). 'Benefits of wildlife-based land uses on private lands in Namibia and limitations affecting their development', *Oryx,* 47(1), 41–53.

Livingstone, D. (1857). *Missionary Travels and Research in South Africa* (London: John Murray).

Lubilo, R. & Hebinck, P. (2019). 'Local hunting' and community-based natural resource management in Namibia: Contestations and livelihoods', *Geoforum,* 101, 62–75.

Ministry of Environment and Tourism (2010). 'Application to utilize game (wild animals)'. Available at: www.omalaetisupport.com/met/files/downloads/APPLICATION%20TO%20UTILIZE%20GAME%20(WILD%20ANIMALS).pdf [Accessed 25 January 2022].

Ministry of Industrialisation, Trade and SME Development (2016). 'Growth Strategy for Namibia's Taxidermy Industry and Associated Value Chains' (Ministry of Industrialisation, Trade and SME Development). Available at: https://csnk.cz/wp-content/uploads/2019/02/Taxidermy_Strategies_Web.pdf [Accessed 25 January 2022].

Mosimane, A. W. & Silva, J. A. (2015). 'Local governance institutions, CBNRM, and benefit-sharing systems in Namibian conservancies', *Journal of Sustainable Development,* 8(2), 99.

Muposhi, V. K., Gandiwa, E., Makuza, S. M., & Bartels, P. (2017). 'Ecological, physiological, genetic trade-offs and socio-economic implications of trophy hunting as a conservation tool: A narrative review', *Journal of Animal & Plant Sciences,* 27(1), 1–14.

Murphree, M. W. (2009). 'The strategic pillars of communal natural resource management: Benefit, empowerment and conservation', *Biodiversity and Conservation,* 18(10), 2551–2562.

Murphy, J. T. (2019). 'Global production network dis/articulations in Zanzibar: Practices and conjunctures of exclusionary development in the tourism industry', *Journal of Economic Geography,* 19(4), 943–971.

Naevdal, E., Olaussen, J. O., & Skonhoft, A. (2012). 'A bioeconomic model of trophy hunting', *Ecological Economics,* 73, 194–205.

NACSO Working Groups (2017). 'Namibia's Communal Conservancies: Annual Conservancy Performance Ratings and Audit Reports for the year 2017' (Windhoek: Namibian Association of CBNRM Support Organisations).

Naidoo, R., Weaver, L. C., Stuart-Hill, G., & Tagg, J. (2011). 'Effect of biodiversity on economic benefits from communal lands in Namibia', *Journal of Applied Ecology,* 48(2), 310–316.

Naidoo, R., Weaver, L. C., Diggle, R. W., Matongo, G., Stuart-Hill, G., & Thouless, C. (2016). 'Complementary benefits of tourism and hunting to communal conservancies in Namibia', *Conservation Biology,* 30(3), 628–638.

NSA – Namibia Statistics Agency (2015). 'Namibia Census of Agriculture 2013/2014'. Available at: https://d3rp5jatom3eyn.cloudfront.net/cms/assets/documents/Namibia_Census_of_Agriculture_Commercial_Report2.pdf [Accessed 25 January 2022].

NSA – Namibia Statistics Agency (2018). 'Namibia Land Statistics – Booklet' (NSA). Available at: https://cms.my.na/assets/documents/NamibiaLandStatistics2018.pdf [Accessed 25 January 2022].

Namibia Tourism Board (n.d.). 'View registered customers'. Available at: https://namibiatourism.com.na/viewregisteredcustomers [Accessed 25 January 2022].

Nelson, F., Lindsey, P., & Balme, G. (2013). 'Trophy hunting and lion conservation: A question of governance?' *Oryx*, 47(4), 501–509.

Ondjou & Van Heerden Safaris (2018). 'Price list big game Caprivi – 2018', Available at: www.vanheerdensafaris.com/VHSAF-ONDSAF-Caprivi-Description-Price-list-2018-USD.pdf [Accessed 17 June 2020].

Pronto Global Air & Ocean Freight (n.d.). 'Pronto Global Air & Ocean Freight'. Available at: https://prontoglobalfreight.com [Accessed 25 January 2022].

Safari Club International (2021). 'World Hunting Awards'. Available at: https://safariclub.org/world-hunting-awards [Accessed 25 January 2022].

Schnegg, M. & Kiaka, R. D. (2018). 'Subsidized elephants: Community-based resource governance and environmental (in)justice in Namibia', *Geoforum*, 93, 105–115.

Sullivan, S. (2002). 'How sustainable is the communalizing discourse of "new conservation"? The masking of difference, inequality and aspiration in the fledgling "conservancies" of Namibia', in: D. Chatty & M. Colchester (eds), *Conservation and Mobile Indigenous Peoples: Displacement, Forced Settlement and Sustainable Development* (New York; Oxford: Berghahn), 158–197.

Sullivan, S., !Uri‡khob, S., Kötting, B., Muntifering, J., & Brett, R. (2021). 'Historicising black rhino in Namibia: colonial-era hunting, conservation custodianship, and plural values', Working Paper No. 13 (Future Pasts). Available at: www.futurepasts.net/_files/ugd/5ba6bf_8a57abaa73b242f5bbd58e0198ee54f6.pdf [Accessed 25 January 2022].

Shikongo, A. (2019). 'Namibia threatens to withdraw from Cites', *The Namibian*, 28 August 2019. Available at: www.namibian.com.na/192386/archive-read/Namibia-threatens-to-withdraw-from-Cites [Accessed 25 January 2022].

Van der Merwe, P., Saayman, M., & Rossouw, R. (2014). 'The economic impact of hunting: A regional approach', *South African Journal of Economic and Management Sciences*, 17(4), 379–395.

van Schalkwyk, D. L., Twyman, J., Hanekom, J. W., & Kwashirai, J. (2012). 'An economic analysis: Business case for sustainable engagement into the game meat export value chain (GIZ Project NO. 83097888)' (Windhoek: German Development Cooperation (GIZ), Biodiversity and Sustainable Land Management (BSLM), & Ministry of Environment and Tourism (MET)). Available at: www.met.gov.na/files/files/AN%20ECONOMIC%20ANALYSES;%20BUSINESS%20CASE%20FOR%20SUSTAINABLE%20ENGAGEMENT%20INTO%20THE%20GAME%20MEAT%20EXPORT%20VALUE%20CHAIN%20(GIZ%20PROJECT%20NO_%2083097888)%202012.pdf [Accessed 25 January 2022].

UNEP-WCMC (Comps.) (2021). 'Full CITES trade database download', Version 2021.1. (Geneva; Cambridge: CITES Secretariat & UNEP-WCMC). Available at: https://trade.cites.org [Accessed 25 January 2022].

Werner, W. (1993). 'A brief history of land dispossession in Namibia', *Journal of Southern African Studies*, 19(1), 135–146.

PART 5

COMMODIFICATION AND SOCIAL DYNAMICS

14

Women in Rural Northern Namibia and the Commodification of Indigenous Natural Products

ROMIE NGHITEVELEKWA, SELMA LENDELVO, AND
MARTIN SHAPI

Introduction

Trees and tree products are traditionally the domain of women. (Mallet,
M. & den Adel-Sheehama, S. 2014: 77)

Rural areas in northern Namibia[1] are endowed with a diversity of what have
recently been labelled *indigenous natural products*. In this chapter, we adopt
the definition of indigenous natural products from the book titled *Indigenous
Plant Products in Namibia*. Therein, indigenous natural products are defined
as 'products that are obtained from naturally occurring plants that would
typically contain active components that could be used as ingredients in
cosmetic, medicinal or food applications' (Cole 2014: 6). Indigenous natural
products include the Namibian myrrh (*Commiphora resin*); mopane seeds
(*Colophospermum mopane*); the 'monkey' orange (*Strychnos cocculoides*);
manketti (*Schinziophyton rautanenii*); resurrection plant (*Myrothamnus flabellifolia*); Bushman's candle/Boesmankers (*Sarcoculon spp. mossamedense*);
large sourplum or oombeke (*Ximenia*); rosewood or false mopane fruit
(*Guibourtia coleosperma*); marula (*Sclerocarya birrea sub-species caffra*);
'bird' plum (*Berchemia discolour*); and devil's claw (*Harpagophytum* sp.),
as well as palm leaves and timber-based products (Graz 2002; Musaba &
Sheehama 2009; Shapwa 2009; Motlhaping 2010; Cole 2014). Indigenous
natural products are largely collected/harvested on communal land areas,
open rangelands, communal agricultural lands, or in community forests.

---

[1] In this chapter northern Namibia is used to refer to north-west, north-central
and north-east Namibia – in other words, the regions of Kunene, Omusati, Oshana,
Oshikoto, Ohangwena, Kavango West, and Zambezi.

Namibia has a long history of dependence on the natural environment for food resources, medicinal and cosmetic purposes, and materials for local jewellery and crafts. Since the 1990s, the recognition of the economic value of plants has taken shape resulting in the trade of natural products, especially in global markets (Cole 2014). The economic value of these resources has become more prominent as international cosmetic and medicinal markets found value in these local natural products.

Commodification of indigenous natural products in Namibia for both local and international markets has been promoted by the Government of Namibia with the aim of contributing to the twin goals of conservation and development (Cole 2014; Ndeinoma *et al.* 2018; also see Wynberg and Lavelle in this volume). The latter goal, development, is realised through the generation of income that can supplement rural households' livelihoods, which until recently were mainly based on subsistence farming. There is the hope that such additional off-farm incomes will contribute to poverty alleviation among the rural poor. In the recent past, indigenous natural-product production in Namibia's rural areas started to become commercialised and has now been integrated into global value networks – processes that together are conceptually known as commodification (Borras & Franco 2012, see contributions from Revilla Diez *et al.* and Greiner & Bollig, this volume). The shifts in understanding and usage of indigenous natural products from being objects of local and subsistence consumption to products of exchange and commercial value are driven by changes in economic structure, underpinned by a de-agrarianisation process advocated for and implemented by the Namibian government.

Since independence in 1990, Namibia created a legal framework conducive to natural resource use and management, including the aim of improving the generation of nature-based income or benefits. The Nature Conservation Amendment Act (Republic of Namibia 2017b) and the Forest Act (Act No.12 of 2001) were enacted to provide the basis for the establishment of Namibia's Community-Based Natural Resource Management (CBNRM) programme, which aims to allow rural communities to manage and derive benefits from wildlife and forest resources through the establishment of conservancies and community forests, respectively. Recently, Namibia passed the Access to Biological and Genetic Resources and Associated Traditional Knowledge Act (Republic of Namibia 2017a), which aims to regulate access to biological and genetic resources. The aims of this Act are to protect associated traditional knowledge; promote innovation, practices, and technologies; protect the rights of local communities, and make provisions for a fair and equitable mechanism for benefit sharing. Since the establishment of community-based resources-management initiatives, women have been actively participating, particularly in the use of local natural resources for household livelihoods

(Lendelvo *et al.* 2012). In addition, the Namibian government established the Indigenous Fruit Task Team (IFTT) under the then Ministry of Agriculture, Water and Forestry[2] during the early 2000s to facilitate an economically sustainable promotion of indigenous fruits in Namibia as the demand for commercialisation of indigenous natural products increased (Cole 2014). This legislative framework governs the use of forests and other natural resources and enables both local communities and other stakeholders to engage in sustainable indigenous natural-product extraction and trading. These institutions are meant to regulate and control processes of commodification.

Worldwide, forests are gendered spaces in that women tend to be associated with plant resources (Sullivan 2000). Recently, studies have recognised the importance of documenting women and gender in forest resource use and utilisation (Asher & Varley 2018). In Namibia, rural women have a long tradition of harvesting and utilising indigenous forest products, but their uses were largely confined to the subsistence economy (Mogotsi *et al.* 2016). The involvement of women in indigenous natural products is common in Africa. Traditional methods of resource extraction and processing, which in most cases are time-consuming and labour-intensive, have been the norm among African women (Urso *et al.* 2013). The dominance of women in indigenous natural products in most rural settings of Namibia is rooted in gender-based traditional roles as ascribed by society. Women engage in most of these activities along with their traditional household and farming chores. The commodification of indigenous natural products, however, contributed to the emergent cash income in rural areas as well as the strengthening of the rural economy. The marginal returns experienced among dryland agricultural production make it necessary for the diversification of the sources of income and livelihoods through activities such as engaging in the trading of indigenous natural products, which are locally available and already form part of a common activity for rural women. However, commodification of indigenous natural products has been improved with value-addition through mechanised processes and value chains involving global markets (Urso *et al.* 2013; Cole 2014).

The limited and/or non-participation of women in the market economy in Namibia emanates from a historical context. In general, the introduction of a market economy in Namibia can be traced back to the colonial period. The colonial market economy had two main characteristics: first, it was based on migrant wage labour, and second, it was gendered. Colonial policies that governed the recruitment of migrant labourers prohibited the mobility of

---

[2] Since March 2020, Forestry has been moved from the now Ministry of Agriculture, Water and Land Reform (MAWLR) to the now Ministry of Environment, Forestry and Tourism (MEFT).

women and therefore inhibited women's participation in the market economy (Winterfeldt 2002). Through migrant labour, men participated in the market economy, while women remained excluded. In the past, local products from natural resources including indigenous natural products traditionally carried limited economic value based on the low level of commercialisation of these products. Commercialisation is very important to local communities, particularly women (Meinhold & Darr 2019). At independence, most of the colonial policies were repealed, and in particular, the Constitution of the Republic of Namibia provided free movement of people and the participation of all in the country's economy irrespective of their intersectional social categories, including gender. The constitutional provisions made it possible for women to also participate in the market economy through different avenues, including the sale of products from their agricultural engagements or of local natural products, or the establishment of any enterprises. This chapter deliberates on the implications of women's participation in the commodification of indigenous natural products at the household level and in society at large. In view of the patriarchal societies that historically characterised rural Namibia, it is crucial to interrogate the emerging subjectivities and realities of women as a result of women's participation in the commodification of indigenous natural products. Our analysis is undertaken from a gender perspective in order to understand the differentiated dynamics in the commodification of indigenous natural products among women from different communities under different resource-management institutions. The chapter will present different patterns and opportunities for commodification of indigenous natural products for women.

Methodology and case studies

This chapter uses data drawn from fieldwork conducted in 2018 for a gender assessment of a project titled Namibia Integrated Landscape Approach for the Enhancing Livelihoods and Environmental Governance to Eradicate Poverty (NILALEG) commissioned by the United Nations Development Programme (UNDP – Namibia). Although the NILALEG project targeted several communities, this chapter focuses on three rural villages in three regions where in-depth interviews with women were carried out. The novelty of the NILALEG project is its emphasis on an integrated approach to resource management and diversification of livelihoods as well as focusing on areas that are within and outside CBNRM institutional arrangements of conservancies and community forests. Focus-group discussions (FGDs) were carried out with women in the Omaiopanga, Omauni, and Nkulivere villages located in the northern Namibian regions of Kunene, Ohangwena, and Kavango West respectively. Apart from being endowed with diverse indigenous natural products, these regions also comprised a high proportion of the poorest households in Namibia. Indigenous natural products have been documented to be amongst the most accessible resources for the poorest segments of rural communities (see also Lavelle this volume for Namibia's Zambezi Region). They habitually form a part of women's traditional roles and are also an important contributor to the economy of such households. In addition to discussions with women, several meetings were also held with local and regional leaders such as traditional authorities and community forest-management committees as well as constituency and regional government officials.

Omaiopanga village

Omaiopanga is a village located in the northern part of Kunene Region within the Opuwo Rural Constituency. Omaiopanga is 12 km from the main urban centre of the Kunene Region, Opuwo. Like other villages in rural Namibia, Omaiopanga falls under the leadership of a traditional headman who controls access to land and land-based resources. The area is characterised by low population density, with high livestock farming intensity and limited crop farming. The village is inhabited by the OvaHimba – one of the ethnic groups that have preserved their cultural heritage, but who are also amongst the most marginalised groups in Namibia, relying predominantly on livestock farming (both cattle and goats) for their livelihoods. The OvaHimba in Omaoipanga are under the Vita Royal House Traditional Authority. There are twenty households with an average of four people per household. Omaiopanga is surrounded by other villages including Okorosave, Ondole, Otjerunda, Orumana, and Okaoko Otavi. This village does not fall under any natural resource-management institutional regime, but there is an involvement of women in a project enabling them to benefit from local natural resources. Women in Omaiopanga make ochre powder, locally called *otjize*, and jewellery which they sell to passers-by so as to earn some income.

Omauni village

Omauni village is located in the Ohangwena Region, and it is part of the geographic area encompassed by different forms of natural resource management and community-based institutional structures, namely in the form of the Okongo Communal Conservancy and Okongo Community Forest. While the governance structures of natural resource management are in place, challenges of capacity and weak enforcement of locally agreed rules hinder the ability of the communities to effectively protect the resources. The Okongo Community Forest for example grants permits to harvesters to access forest resources. Land users in the area intensively practice crop production and livestock farming. In comparison to other women in the Ohangwena Region, women in Omauni are closest to the resource base. The use of and benefits from indigenous natural products are organised through the community forests, and in most cases there is high participation of women in the utilisation of forests due to their traditional roles. The representation of women in the leadership of these community- based institutions means they are also involved in decision-making processes.

Nkulivere village

Nkulivere village is situated about 40 km from Mpungu village in the Mpungu Constituency Kavango West, and the region was previously called Kavango Region, with its capital urban centre being Rundu. When Kavango West became a region, Nkurenkuru became its capital urban centre. Rukwangali-speaking Namibians who organise their kinship in a matrilineal way inhabit the village, which is home to approximately twenty households and has a population of around 100–150. This is a very remote area with limited services and facilities, and there is only a primary school in the village. Kavango West is one of the regions that are rich in fauna and flora (Schneiderat 2011). The entire region is home to approximately 91,100 people, with over 70% of the population living in rural areas. While the region is endowed with natural resources, it is one of the poorest regions in the country. The Namibia Housing Income and Expenditure Survey of 2016 revealed that, in the Kavango West Region, the highest proportion of households (29.9%) derived their income from salaries/ wages, followed by income from subsistence farming (19.2%) and pension (18.2%) (NSA 2018). The other 32.7% of households reported business income, remittances, drought relief and in-kind assistance as their main source of income. The same report further revealed that 20% of the labour force in the region was employed in agriculture, forestry, and freshwater fisheries. As such, dependence on subsistence farming and the sale of indigenous natural products are the main sources of income in the region. The area where this village is located does not fall under any resource-management structure and also does not border any community forest, conservancy, or protected area.

Women's access to and use of indigenous natural products

Namibia's rural communities are highly reliant on natural resources within their vicinities for their livelihoods. The different geographic locations and environmental features of the case studies showed similarities and variations in natural endowments, culture, and resource-use patterns of the indigenous natural products. Agriculture is the main livelihood activity in the case-study

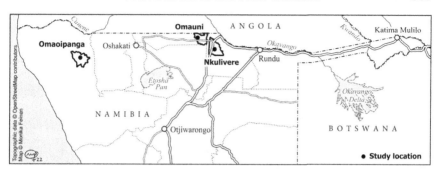

Map 14.1 The locations of the studied villages (Source: Bhalla & Routhage 2019; Cartography: M. Feinen).

areas and is supplemented with the gains derived from natural resources. Women in the case-study areas collect a wide variety of indigenous natural products that are crucial for the livelihoods of their households; these include firewood, thatching grass, and medicinal and edible plants, including some natural products for cosmetic and material development. These products are primarily harvested for the welfare of households. Forest products are important to both men and women in rural Namibia; however, women are mostly involved in the harvesting and utilisation of non-timber forest products (Kamwi *et al.* 2015; Meinhold & Darr 2019).

Monkey orange (*Strychnos cocculoides*) and manketti (*Schinziophyton rautanenii*) are popular fruit tree species mostly found in north-eastern and north-central parts of Namibia. For example, women from Nkulivere village emphasised the harvesting of manketti. This tree bears fruits around January/ February and harvest commences from July/August through November/ December. *Schinziophyton rautanenii* fruits have several use values and are harvested by both women and men, but mostly women. The fruit is sold both locally and in urban centres in the northern part of the country, but in recent years, women from rural areas have started to supply informal markets in distant urban centres such as Windhoek. The nuts of *Schinziophyton rautanenii* are an important source of food for a number of rural communities (Graz 2002). Women also add value to the kernel of *Schinziophyton rautanenii* in two ways; first, they extract oil from it and make *rototo* (a kind of soup) from it. Second, apart from their importance as sources of food, these fruits are also used to produce liquor that is sold locally and in urban centres. Women use income from the sale of these products to support their children's education and their broader livelihoods.

Different indigenous natural products are harvested by the women in the three villages of Nkulivere, Omauni, and Omaiopanga (see Table 14.1). Although in some cases similar species are harvested in the different villages, the differences in the composition of resource abundance are mainly attributed to the geographic and climatic conditions of the area. For example, Omaiopanga is located in a dryland with less plant diversity, while the other two villages are found in the woodland savanna ecosystems with diverse forest resources. Women in Omaiopanga accessed indigenous natural products such as firewood from different tree and shrub species, mopane seeds and worms, ochre, some ornament bushes, *Commiphora* resin, and some medicinal and edible products from different plants from the forest.

Table 14.1 Different indigenous natural products harvested by women, by village.

Village sites	Local and scientific names of indigenous natural products harvested by women
Nkulivere	*nonsivi* (rosewood or false mopane fruit), *nongongo* (manketti nuts), *matu* and *maguni* fruits (*Strychnos* spp.), and *nompeke* (*Ximenia caffra*)
Omauni	*okandongondongo* or woody climbers (*Salacia luebbertii*), makokofi or sand apple (*Parinari capensis*), and *omapwaka* (*Strychnos* spp.), *oombeke* or sourplum (*Ximenia caffra*)
Omaiopanga	mopane seeds and worms, *omuzumba* and *omapya* (ornament bushes or *Commiphora spp*), *eembe* or bird plum (*Berchemia discolour*), *otjize* (red ochre stone), resurrection plant (*Myrothamnus flabellifolius*), Bushman candle (*Sarcoculon mossamedense*)

Source: Authors

Furthermore, various factors including overuse, poverty, population pressures on the environment, and climatic changes affected the resource base or the abundance of the resources. Degradation of forest resources is noticed in the areas due to the high demand, which has been observed over the years, and this carries gender-differentiated effects. Women and children in most cases are responsible for the collection of indigenous natural products, and usually most of the forest resources were collected on foot. This was the case as many of these products were readily available in their surroundings. However, it emerged from the discussions in the case-study villages that time spent searching for and collecting natural products has increased and, in some cases, transportation of such products is now required. For example, women in Omauni indicated that they travel between 5 and 10 km collecting forest products. The Omaiopanga community occupies the driest areas where people predominantly depend on livestock farming and limited crop cultivation but only have small gardens. Severe depletion of vegetation including grass and scattered shrubs is mainly attributed to heavy pressure connected to intensive livestock farming. Traditionally, the OvaHimba farm with large livestock herds were using nomadic and transhumance practices, which involved movement of homesteads and livestock for the purpose of land restoration. Although the OvaHimba will utilise nearby rangelands, in most cases they travel long distances in search of good pasture for their livestock, thereby also utilising different forests' resources.

The accessing of forest and grazing resources by both the locals and people from other communities, and the illegal harvesting of forest products in some cases, has contributed to the depletion of forests in the Omauni and Nkulivere villages. The two villages are located within the forest reserve areas with low population density; therefore, they have served as resource reserves for the livelihoods of surrounding communities and beyond. However, the high influx of people from other areas into Omauni and Nkulivere villages resulted in the overharvesting of these natural products. Surrounding communities harvest firewood, edible and medicinal plants, poles for construction, and many other non-timber resources in the forest areas. While communities of Omauni indicated that people were granted permits to harvest forest resources from the community forest area, Nkulivere was found to be vulnerable to illegal harvesting in the absence of a community forest -management institution. However, the women were of the opinion that the headmen provide permission to those intending to harvest, but monitoring mechanisms for illegal harvesters are rather weak. A decreasing trend in species diversity is found in various parts of Namibia, and this has an effect on the range and availability of forest resources that are required for local use by communities (Cheikhyoussef *et al.* 2011). Non-timber forest products in most parts of the country do not require official permits to harvest; women are mainly given consent by traditional authorities and community forest committees. Normally harvesting fruits from trees is less detrimental to the trees than timber harvesting. Most of the permits issued by the Directorate of Forestry are for timber forest products.

Division of labour in forest and forest-products utilisation, which was noted in the three villages, is a traditional phenomenon that describes the manner in which local communities operate within their traditions and how they interact with their environments.

> Collection of indigenous fruits from the forest and surrounding bushes – it is something we have been doing since we were young that we learned from our mothers; harvesting them is easy and is our cultural job, but

can be time-consuming. (A young female respondent from Nkulivere village, Kavango West)

Harvesting and processing of all indigenous natural products by women in these villages has been done traditionally, and most women indicated it to be labour-intensive and time- consuming. Women in the Omauni village indicated that time and labour involved in the preparation and pounding of *omahangu* (pearl millet) have been reduced as the process has become mechanised with grinding machines in their village and neighbouring villages. For that reason, women in this village indicated that the indigenous natural products' yields and benefits could increase if mechanised processes could be made available locally. Urso *et al.* (2013) indicated that improving extraction and processing of indigenous natural products could improve income levels and living standards amongst women.

Being part of Kunene Region, residents of the Omaiopanga village have access to *Commiphora wildii* and its resin, a common resource within this dry region of Namibia. Historically, the *Commiphora* resin was predominantly used for household consumption, and although this product's commercial value was not realised in practice until 2007, it was noted as a possibility earlier, in 2004, when a study by the Integrated Rural Development and Nature Conservation found that its production far exceeded local need, thus pointing to its commercialisation potential (Galloway *et al.* 2016). Subsequent to this, institutional measures in form of a trust were put in place for marketing and decision-making processes (ibid.). *Commiphora* resin particularly went through strategic processes of product development including connecting suppliers of extracted oils with well-known European perfumers, so as to become a product that could be brought to a somewhat elite market. It was in the year 2007 that the first commercial harvest of *Commiphora* took stage, with local communities as harvesters and suppliers, and Europe as the destination market. To paraphrase Galloway *et al.* (2016: 432), this formative stage involved the European buyer purchasing the initial consignment of *Commiphora* resin for US$10/kg which covered the payment to the harvester (67%), packaging and transport to the point of export (27%) and a management fee to the Conservancy (6%). The value chain of *Commiphora* is well captured in Galloway *et al.* (2016: 435). Various actors/levels are identified – most importantly, at the local level: **harvesters,** who are responsible for collecting, cleaning, sorting and dropping *Commiphora* to the buying points, and, **buying-point managers**, who weigh the materials, pay the harvesters and store the products for collection. Products are collected for either the local markets (Namibia), regional markets (South Africa) and/or international markets (Europe). The local market comprises of local manufactures of cosmetics; South African buyers also use the product for cosmetics purposes and sell them to international markets for manufacturing perfumes. Thus, it is at the market level that value is added.

The resin is secreted from different parts of the plants including bark, branches, fruit and leaves, and even from the flowers (Nott 2014; Sheehama *et al.* 2019). Recently, women in this village became part of a value chain, which provided an opportunity for increased benefits from *Commiphora* resin beyond subsistence use. Being part of the value chain also allows the women to use indigenous knowledge for commercial purposes. A factory for processing *Commiphora* resin has been opened in Kunene Region's capital, Opuwo. The Opuwo Processing Factory is a result of collaborative efforts by local NGOs and international partners. Women in the village and the surrounding villages, organise themselves into local groupings to harvest and sell raw *Commiphora* resin and other indigenous natural products collectively. Although there is generally a good understanding amongst women of the harvesting techniques used to gather local resources, women of this village participate in several sustainable harvesting training sessions to ensure the resources' continued availability over time. These training sessions are organised by supporting NGOs within the natural resource management sector. Women participate in the value chain at the level of collection and selling of raw material to a local agent, who eventually sells the material to the Opuwo Processing Factory. This approach has allowed the women to participate in the value chain and created business opportunities for them to benefit monetarily from this internationally valued and exported resource. The existing literature has indicated the benefits of improved access to food, education, and health care as a result of income earned and the increased benefits for women (Galloway *et al.* 2016).

Trading patterns and opportunities for indigenous natural products

The choice of following a certain trading option is dependent on the support and means for women to participate. None of the women in Nkulivere village were previously aware of any value- addition opportunities or value chains for the products they trade. Although all women from the three villages were involved in trading indigenous natural products they harvested locally, only women in Omauni and Omaiopanga villages indicated knowledge about the formal trading arrangements available in their surroundings involving products they harvest. However, none of them had participated in any formal trading arrangement. In addition, women from the three study villages revealed that harvesting natural products from the surrounding forest is crucial for livelihood diversification, and that the commercial purpose of these products is secondary to meeting household economic needs. Women in Nkulivere and Omauni pointed out that their communities were suppliers of most of the indigenous natural products, as those resources had become depleted in other areas. They also indicated that some products such as 'monkey orange' only grew in their respective areas. Women are largely involved in informal markets where they sell their products locally within their villages or nearby urban centres, although a few supply other, bigger markets.

Forest resources have become economically important for women, and they have sustained rural livelihoods substantially. *Commiphora* resin is a must-have resource for every OmuHimba woman, and those who are not able to harvest it depend on the local markets. Women in rural areas, like Omaiopanga village, walk into the mountains to harvest the resins, which they process in different ways, such as drying them and smoking them, or drying them and grinding them to produce a powder. Collection of these products does not require a formal government, conservancy, or community forest permit but only written or verbal consent from the mentioned institutions together with the traditional authority. The women sell their products mainly to passers-by, people around their villages, and also to the Opuwo market.

Recently, value-addition or mechanised processing facilities were established for the *Commiphora* resin that OvaHimba women have been harvesting and using for ages. From the *Commiphora* resin and *Colophospermum* mopane seeds, essential oils are extracted. Essential oils produced from *Commiphora* resin and *Colophospermum* mopane seeds have distinctive fragrances that are only common to Namibia. To date, *Commiphora* resin (like other indigenous natural products) has gone beyond subsistence use to become a lucrative commodity in the form of essential oil extracted from the tree and sold in local and international markets. Other important plants from the Kunene Region include the *Myrothamnus flabellifolius*, also known as the 'resurrection plant', from which an extract known as Myro PE is produced. Myro PE is good for improving skin hydration and helping to calm irritated skins. Another plant that women in the Kunene Region harvest in combination with mopane is the *Sarcoculon mossamedense*; it is harvested for its unique fragrances, and other essential oils can be produced from it too.

Ximenia (eemheke) is common, and harvested by women in different parts of the northern Namibian Ohangwena Region (Gallardo 2006). For *Ximenia*, there is a cooperative called Tulongeni Twahangana Producers, which was registered in 2012. The majority of its members are women. From *eemheke*, a nut is extracted to make oil. The *eemheke* oil is used as hair oil/moisturiser and as a skin serum, mostly by women but also by a few men. The commodification of *Ximenia* can be traced back to the 1930s, when research to determine its medicinal properties was already undertaken, resulting in the patenting of several pharmaceutical and cosmetic preparations (Mallet, M. & Adel-Sheehama, 2014.). In recent years, women, especially in urban centres, have started to embrace natural products for natural hair, hence driving the intensification of commodification of indigenous natural products such as *eemheke* oil. The commodification of *eemheke* oil is observed in formal and informal markets. While rural women are also responsible for direct sales, non-market-based pricing affects the profitability of the businesses. Products from *eemheke*, in particular oil, have entered the formal market, especially through various trademarks. One common one is Oombeke by Pockler Cosmetics cc, a Namibian-owned company with international partners that processes *eemheke* nuts into hair oil/moisturiser and skin-firming serum. The raw materials are sourced from women in northern Namibia. A 100 ml bottle of *oombeke* is sold for N$150 (about US$8.80). However, large quantities of *eemheke* oil are sold through the informal markets where not much processing of the oil has taken place, with 200 ml being sold for between N$45 and N$60 (about US$2.65 and $3.50).

From this survey, it was not clear why women from Omaiopanga and Omauni did not sign up to become part of the supply chain of *Commiphora resin* and *Ximenia* respectively, although processing facilities are located within their areas. The establishment of such processing facilities is crucial for improving both the value gained from indigenous natural products and the economic position of women in society. In addition, the existence of such facilities presents a great opportunity for the commodification of indigenous natural products especially within poorer communities. Poverty is more gender-biased towards females (19.2%) as compared to males (15.8%) in the country (NSA 2018). Women might not become part of the supply chain because of numerous limitations, including the unavailability of the supply chain, lack of awareness on the requirements and processes, the supply chain targeting certain areas or communities but not others, or the women simply not wanting to engage in such arrangements. It might also be that these women are supplying raw products by selling indirectly to members of the supply chains as they are from resource-rich areas.

Generally, the involvement of women is largely confined to the supply chain; they are the main collectors or harvesters from the field: primary suppliers. However, when it comes to structures, women's involvement is limited. For example, there are no women amongst the trustees of the Kunene Conservancies Indigenous Natural Products Trust, which is comprised of five conservancies (Puros, Orupembe, Marienfluss, Sanitatas, and Okondjombo) and initiated the value-addition process with respect to *Commiphora* resin. Similarly, processing facilities are largely operated by men. In this case, women organised themselves into primary supplier groups to provide a stable supply of raw materials (indigenous natural product). The harvested resin from these conservancies is transported to the Opuwo Processing Facility, where the end products are produced and prepared for both local and international markets (Nott 2014). Other communities participated in the selling of the resin to members of the Trust, as they are not officially part of the supply chain. The income derived from the sale of raw plant products supplements other sources of livelihoods at the household level.

For example, *marula* fruits have emerged as an economically viable resource amongst the women in the northern part of Namibia (*Namibia Economist* 2016). It is the role of women within the Aawambo culture in north-central Namibia to collect fresh *marula* fruits; it is also their role to extract *marula* juice then dry the peels and kernels. The peels can be prepared for livestock feeds while the kernels are the source of oil, which is commercialised. In the months of January to April, women in north-central Namibia, for example, would spend a large part of their day under a *marula* tree extracting *marula* juice, and in the dry months they would spend the days under shade cracking the kernel nuts open, which would be used to produce oil. When there are machines involved in the extraction of oil for cosmetic purposes, in cooperatives such as Eudafano Women Cooperative in Ondangwa (Oshana Region), the roles change somewhat. Men too, participate in the process of extracting oil from the kernels using machines. The Eudafano Women's Cooperative sources *marula* kernels from women in north-central Namibia, and, amongst others, supplies The Body Shop, an international cosmetic retail chain supplying countries such as France and Sweden. The income earned through selling *marula* oil, especially that which is performed through family networks extending as far as urban areas, supports women's monetary basis in rural households. In the first place, it is also women in the urban areas that are responsible for marketing the products through their networks and selling the *marula* oil extracted by their female kin (mothers or grandmothers) in rural areas. Direct benefits in terms of monetary income derived from indigenous natural products make amends for a long-held practice where women hardly reaped any economic benefits from countless forms of (mostly unpaid) labour.

Emerging realities of commodification for rural women

According to the Namibia Household Income and Expenditure Survey Report of 2016, 17.4% of the Namibian population was poor, and poverty was more prevalent in rural areas (25%) compared to urban areas (8.6%) (NSA 2018). From the discussion above, it is important to highlight three important points: (1) the central role women play in the rural economy; (2) the increasing integration of indigenous natural products in formal markets; and (3) the continuing important role of the informal markets through which most of the commodification takes place. A large part of the distribution of indigenous natural products takes place on a rather ad hoc basis, and income generation is therefore irregular. Promoting the economic value of indigenous natural products is essential for the economic empowerment of rural women, provided that conditions for development are put in place (Bennett 2006). Moreover, the potential for increased trade and employment is exceptionally good; the potential contribution to wealth creation in the Southern African Development Community (SADC) region at large from indigenous natural products is sufficient to make it worthwhile to commit significant resources towards improving market access. Bennett (2006) states that further development of indigenous natural products presents a potential replacement of low-value agricultural activities. In other words, the economic returns on investment in market access for indigenous natural products could be higher in comparison to traditional agricultural activities such as crop or livestock production. The sector holds potential for providing sustainable rural incomes to communities, and particularly for the rural poor and women, who have few alternative sources of cash-income generation.

In their research on forest resources and rural livelihoods, MacGregor *et al.* established that indigenous natural resources provide about 25% of household income (2007: i). Similarly, in his report on natural products as a new engine for trade growth in Africa, Bennet (2006) established that the market potential and opportunity for the trade and export of nature-based products is huge. In southern Africa indigenous natural products are produced in some of the poorest regions, and collection is commonly done by the poor and vulnerable, in particular women – hence, these products do make an important contribution to rural livelihoods especially for the rural poor, the vulnerable, and women (Akinnifesi *et al.* 2007; Bennett 2006: 2; MacGregor *et al.* 2007). The role of indigenous natural products is recognised in the context of poverty reduction – as they can reduce the vulnerability of rural households in particular to income poverty (Akinnifesi *et al.* 2007: 1). The commodification of indigenous natural products is a result of the increasing demand for such products locally, and in places far from their origins, either in urban areas or for export markets.

While the process has started, the commercialisation of indigenous natural products is yet to reach its full capacity. As MacGregor *et al.* argued for these types of products, they form the basis of an active, albeit weak and inefficient, informal economy (2007: i). The demand for indigenous natural products is high especially in the beauty and cosmetic industries. These products are reaching distant markets, especially in urban centres such as Windhoek where they are sold at open markets or through social networks. A few that have entered the formal markets have even reached international export markets through well-established brands such Mbiri Natural Skin Care, Scents of Namibia, and Desert Scents, amongst others.

The face of a large part of the indigenous natural products and their associated value chain is that of a woman. Women predominate in the collection of indigenous natural products from the land for both domestic use, and for commodification so as to earn an income. Commodification of indigenous natural products has contributed to a social shift, from women being confined to the household-level private sphere to becoming visible in the public sphere. Similarly, women are no longer only confined to the subsistence economy and reproductive roles; they have now been integrated into the cash economy, through which they can also contribute to the household economy monetarily. While the collection of indigenous natural products and processing them forms part of women's traditional gender roles or the roles ascribed to women, commodification is part of their new activities.

The process of collecting indigenous natural products that are used in the beauty and cosmetic industries, as discussed above, bears a woman's face. However, mechanical processing, as observed at processing plants, is a man's domain, and the same applies to the grinding plants in villages, which are operated mostly by men. The study also reveals that women are also involved in collecting several indigenous natural products, which are used at home, but also sold for cash income. Women are the main actors in basket weaving, collection of medicinal herbs, and harvesting and preparation of forest fruits both for their own use and commodification. If supported in the different stages of processing nature-based products into value commodities, this action can enhance women's entrepreneurship and has the potential to improve women's and their families' livelihoods. Another limitation relates to the issue of pricing of nature-based products. The valorisation of indigenous natural products is complex and difficult.

Conclusions

Rural areas in northern Namibia are endowed with a diversity of indigenous natural products, which continue to play an important role in local livelihoods and the commercialisation of which has recently begun to contribute to the rural economy. This study demonstrates women's roles in the journey of commodification of indigenous natural products and the promotion of the economic value of these local resources. It is also evident from this study that an increasing number of prominent local and international cosmetic and medicinal markets have found value in these local natural products. For that reason, commodification of indigenous natural products in Namibia for both local and international markets has been promoted by the government as a key vehicle towards poverty reduction and economic development amongst rural communities while promoting environmental sustainability.

The participation of women in the commodification of natural products, and therefore the ability to generate income for the household, will result in the empowerment of women and allow them to participate in leadership and decision-making structures. The findings therefore reflect the women's roles, their experiences, and their realities in relation to the commercialisation of indigenous natural products. However, irrespective of the context- specific realities, the participation of women in the commodification of indigenous natural products reflects a critical shift that reconfigures gender relations and the place of women in society. Income-generation capacity amongst women through commodification of indigenous natural products reduces the vulnerability of rural households, reduces poverty, and increases economic empowerment, and also addresses income disparities between men and women.

Therefore, we recommend that policy frameworks should be formulated to allow nationally inclusive value and supply chains to grant equal opportunities to women from different areas, as local indigenous natural products are widely distributed across regions and the country. These kinds of chains are important as they allow women to become involved in the process of product development, and provide a reliable market for their products. The current nature of commodification of these products is characterised by limited valuation of indigenous natural products, resulting in women experiencing low income levels due to variable prices for the products. There is a need for procedures for pricing indigenous natural products coupled with structured programmes, capacity-building, mentorship and financial support, enterprise, and business development for women.

Bibliography

Akinnifesi, F. K., Ajayi, O. C., Sileshi, G., Kadzere, I., & Akinnifesi, A. I. (2007). 'Domesticating and Commercializing Indigenous Fruit and Nut Tree Crops for Food Security and Income Generation in Sub-Saharan Africa' (Southampton: New Crops International Symposium, 3 September 2007). Available at: http://apps.worldagroforestry.org/downloads/Publications/PDFS/pp15397.pdf [Accessed 31 January 2022].

Asher, K. & Varley, G. (2018). 'Gender in the jungle: A critical assessment of women and gender in current (2014–2016) forestry research', *International Forestry Review*, 20(2), 149–159.

Bennett, B. (2006). 'Natural Products: The New Engine for African Trade'. Consultancy to Further Develop the Trade Component of the Natural Resources Enterprise Programme (NATPRO). Available at: https://citeseerx.ist.psu.edu/viewdoc/download?doi=10.1.1.610.9509&rep=rep1&type=pdf [Accessed 31 January 2022].

Bhalla, R. S. & Routhage, A. (2019). 'Narrative Report of the forest and rangeland degradation status and potential restoration of the landscape and interventions in the project areas and the potential SFM, sequestration and mitigation benefits to be gained'. United Nations Development Programme.

Borras, S. M., Jr. & Franco, J. C. 2012. 'Global land grabbing and trajectories of agrarian change: A preliminary analysis', *Journal of Agrarian Change*, 12(1), 34–59.

Cheikhyoussef, A., Mapaure, I. & Shapi, M. (2011). 'The use of some indigenous plants for medicinal and other purposes by local communities in Namibia with emphasis on Oshikoto region: A review', *Research Journal of Medicinal Plant*, 5(4), 406–419.

Cole, D. (2014). *Indigenous Plant Products in Namibia* (Windhoek: Venture Publications).

Gallardo, J. (2006). 'Ximenia harvesting and post-harvesting practices in northern Namibia: Recommendations for quality and fair-trade supply of Ximenia kernels' (National Botanical Research Institute). Available at: www.nbri.org.na/ximenia-harvesting-and-post-harvesting-practices-northern-namibia [Accessed 31 January 2022].

Galloway F. B., Wynberg R. P., & Nott, K. (2016). 'Commercialising a perfume plant, *Commiphora wildii*: Livelihood implications for indigenous Himba in north-west Namibia', *The International Forestry Review*, 18(4), 429–443.

Graz, F. P. (2002). 'Description and Ecology of *Schinziophyton rautanenii* (Schinz) Radcl.-Sm. in Namibia', *Dinteria*, 27, 19–35.

Kamwi, J. M., Chirwa, P. W. C., Manda, S. O. M., Graz, F. P., & Kätsch, C. (2015). 'Livelihoods, land use and land cover change in the Zambezi Region, Namibia', *Population and Environment*, 36, 1–24.

Lendelvo, S. & Nghitevelekwa, R. (2019). 'Gender assessment and action plan for the Namibia Integrated Landscape Approach for Enhancing Livelihoods and Environmental Governance to Eradicate Poverty (NILALEG)' UNDP Consultancy Report (Windhoek: United Nations Development Programme).

Lendelvo, S., Munyebvu, F., & Suich, H. (2012). 'Linking women's participation and benefits within the Namibian community based natural resource management program', *Journal of Sustainable Development*, 5(12), 27–39.

Louw, S. (2019). 'Chemical characterization and *in vitro* antioxidant and antimicrobial activities of essential oil from *Commiphora wildii* Merxm. (omumbiri) resin', *Flavour and Fragrance Journal*, 34(4), 241–251.

MacGregor, J., Palmer, C. & Barnes, J. (2007). 'Forest resources and rural livelihoods in the north-central regions of Namibia', Environmental Economics Programme Discussion Paper 07–01 (London: International Institute for Environment and Development). Available at: https://pubs.iied.org/pdfs/15506IIED.pdf [Accessed 24 December 2021].

Mallet, M. & den Adel-Sheehama, S. (2014). Ximenia (*X. americana*), in: *Indigenous Plant Products in Namibia: The Commercialisation of Indigenous Natural Plant Products in Namibia.* (Windhoek: Venture Publications). Available at: www.nbri.org.na/sites/default/files/INP-book.pdf [Accessed 24 December 2021].

Meinhold, K. & Darr, D. (2019). 'The processing of non-timber forest products through small and medium enterprises – A review of enabling and constraining factors', *Forests*, 10, 1–24.

Mogotsi, I. Lendelvo S., Angula M. & Nakanyala J. (2016). 'Forest resource management and utilization through a gendered lens in Namibia', *Journal of Environment and Natural Resources Research*, 6(4), 79–90.

Motlhaping, M. (2010). 'Resource survey of Ximenia species in George Mukoya and Muduva Nyangana conservancies in Kavango region' (National Botanical Research Institute). Available at: www.nbri.org.na/

resource-survey-of-ximenia-species-george-mukoya-and-muduva-nyangana-conservancies-kavango-region [Accessed 24 December 2021].

Musaba, E. C. & Sheehama, E. (2009). 'The socio-economic factors influencing harvesting of Eembe (*Berchemia discolor*) wild fruits by communal households in the Ohangwena Region, Namibia', *Namibia Development Journal*, 1(2), 1–12.

Namibia Economist (2016). 'Marula tree can feed five product value chains', *Namibia Economist*, 2 September. Available at: https://economist.com.na/19138/retail/marula-tree-can-feed-five-product-value-chains [Accessed 24 December 2021].

NSA – Namibia Statistics Agency (2018). 'Namibia household income and Expenditure Survey 2015/2016 report' (Windhoek: NSA). Available at: https://d3rp5jatom3eyn.cloudfront.net/cms/assets/documents/NHIES_2015-16.pdf [Accessed 24 December 2021].

Ndeinoma, A., Wiersum, K. F. & Arts, B. (2018). 'The governance of indigenous natural products in Namibia: A policy network analysis', *Environmental Management*, 62(1), 29–44.

Nott, K. (2014). 'Commiphora', in: D. Cole (ed.), *The Commercialisation of Indigenous plant products in Namibia* (Windhoek: Venture Publications), 82–93.

Republic of Namibia (2005). Forest Act 12 of 2001; Forest Amendment Act 13 of 2005. Available at: www.lac.org.na/laws/annoSTAT/Forest%20Act%2012%20of%202001.pdf [Accessed 31 January 2022].

Republic of Namibia (2017a). Access to Biological and Genetic Resources and Associated Traditional Knowledge Act, Pub. L. No. 2. Available at: www.fao.org/faolex/results/details/en/c/LEX-FAOC173079 [Accessed 31 January 2022].

Republic of Namibia (2017b). Nature Conservation Amendment Act, Pub. L. No. 3. Available at: www.lac.org.na/laws/2017/6344.pdf [Accessed 24 December 2021].

Schneiderat, U. (2011). *Communal Rangelands in Northern and Central Namibia: The Grazing and Browsing Resources and their Users*. PhD dissertation, Justus-Liebig-Universität Gießen. Available at: https://d-nb.info/1063954487/34 [Accessed 24 December 2021].

Shapwa, T. (2009). 'Report on the social aspects related to Ximenia harvesters in East- Kavango' (National Botanical Research Institute). Available at: www.nbri.org.na/report-the-social-aspects-related-ximenia-harvesters-east-kavango [Accessed 24 December 2021].

Sheehama, J. T., Mukakalisa, C., Amakali, T., Uusiku, L. N., Hans, R. H., *et al.* (2019). 'Chemical characterization and in vitro antioxidant and antimicrobial activities of essential oil from *Commiphora wildii* Merxm. (omumbiri) resin', *Flavour and Fragrance Journal*, 34(4), 241–251.

Sullivan, S. (2000). 'Gender, ethnographic myths and community-based conservation in a former Namibian "homeland"' in: D. Hodgson (ed.), *Rethinking Pastoralism in Africa: Gender, Culture and the Myth of the Patriarchal Pastoralist* (Oxford: James Currey), 142–164.

Urso, V., Signorini, M. A., & Bruschi, P. (2013). 'Survey of the ethnobotanical uses of Ximenia americana L.(mumpeke) among rural communities in South Angola', *Journal of Medicinal Plants Research*, 7(1), 7–18.

Winterfeldt, V. (2002). 'Labour migration in Namibia – Gender perspectives', in: V. Winterfeldt, T. Fox, & P. Mufune (eds), *Namibia: Society. Sociology* (Windhoek: University of Namibia Press), 39–74.

15

Conservation, Traditional Authorities, and the Commodification of the Wild: A Namibian perspective

ALFONS MOSIMANE, KENNETH MATENGU,
AND MICHAEL BOLLIG

Introduction

Anybody involved in the conservation on communal lands in Namibia today will confirm that traditional authorities – chiefs, headmen, traditional councillors – are key players in conservation and in the commodification of wilderness landscapes and non-domesticated flora and fauna. Traditional authorities are intensely involved in the formalisation of community-based conservation areas and community forests, including the definition of their boundaries and zoning characteristics, as well as in defining modalities for the distribution of benefits derived from such conservation areas. They are also crucial negotiating partners (and at times opponents), for example, when conservancies make business contracts with lodge operators, commercial hunters, and business people involved in the marketing of wilderness commodities. Traditional authorities often receive a share of such benefits for their role as facilitators. The role of traditional authorities in local politics, and in state-community engagements, is strengthened through their engagement in community-based conservation, as their participation is legally requisite in any significant decision(s) concerning the environmental management of 'their' communities and 'their' territories.

This chapter thus explores linkages between commodification processes and institutional dynamics in the context of community-based conservation to show how both contribute to the (re)traditionalisation of environmental management. Drawing on examples from Namibia's Zambezi and Kunene regions, the chapter shows how traditional authorities compete and coordinate with other social groups, including business elites, government administrators, and democratically elected committees for socio-economic influence. We argue that the particular role played by traditional authorities as gatekeepers between the state and local social-ecological relations has deep colonial roots, while simultaneously conforming to contemporary global blueprints for the management of natural resources in the Global South. In order to provide space for institutional change their key role as intermediaries of power needs to be renegotiated. We argue that the reification of traditional authorities and the hybridisation of traditional and modern democratic and participatory institutions is characteristic of the emergent type of resource governance.

Traditional authorities in Africa have proven to be highly resilient (Logan 2013). In post-colonial democracies, they continue to play a critical role in the local governance of rural and occasionally urban communities, and in many ways their involvement in political processes is increasing rather than decreasing (Ubink 2008). In this chapter, the term 'traditional authorities' refers to the exercise of governance by chiefs of different ranks who have jurisdiction over rural communities in communal lands. In the colonial period, alignments with – and the institutionalisation of – traditional authorities were crucial in enabling colonial administrations to establish control over lands not turned over to settlers. Where such authorities were weak or altogether absent, they were either supported or instituted by the colonial administration to fulfil administrative roles that helped to facilitate indirect rule. Colonial administrations ruled and delivered governmental services through either direct or indirect cooperation with traditional authorities (Becker 2006; Bollig 2011; Friedman 2011). At independence, many governments sought to replace traditional authorities with democratically legitimatised committees and councils. After more than fifty years of independence in most African countries, however, there is abundant evidence that traditional authorities have found new platforms and new pathways for shaping political decision making at the local level. Conservation and environmental governance are fields in which traditional authorities have been particularly successful in holding their ground, as they involve themselves in globalising agendas of sustainability, as guardians of landscapes and biodiversity.

Rural livelihoods and the commodification of nature: From colonial exclusion to post-colonial rural development

Rural livelihoods in Namibia's northern communal lands depend on access to land and natural resources. Traditional authorities typically allocate land and supervise the use of natural resources according to sets of norms and values glossed as 'customs' and according to their understandings of kinship, ethnicity, authority, and territoriality. Namibia's Traditional Authorities Act 25, from 2000, defines a traditional authority (TA), as 'a chief, a head of a traditional community, a senior traditional councillor, or a traditional councillor' (Government of Namibia 2000: 3). The Act further defines a traditional community as consisting of

> person(s) either or both of whose parents belong to that 'traditional community', and includes any other person who by marriage to or adoption by a member of that 'traditional community' or by any other circumstance has assimilated the culture and traditions of that 'traditional community' and has been accepted by the 'traditional community' as a member thereof. (Government of Namibia 2000: 2)

The Act further specifies a 'traditional community' as

> an indigenous homogeneous, endogamous social grouping of persons comprising of families deriving from exogamous clans which share a common ancestry, language, cultural heritage, customs and traditions, who recognizes a common 'traditional authority' and inhabits a common communal area, and may include the members of that traditional community residing outside the common communal area. (Government of Namibia 2000: 3)

In the context of this definition, those who control institutions for traditional customs and culturally ascribed rights are positioned to define and stipulate what counts as truly legitimate (Corbett & Jones 2000). Support for TAs was coupled with aspirations for a democratisation and decentralisation of rural resource governance. These two goals – more legitimacy and decentralisation through involvement of local TAs, and more democratisation through newly instituted forms of participation – are mutually conflictive to a considerable extent (see also Taylor 2012 who shows such contradictions in her ethnographic case study of community-based and state-based conservation measures in north-eastern Namibia's Bwabwata conservation area).

The policy goal of a number of natural resource management programmes, many of them externally financed, was to institute contemporary natural-resource-management interventions within communal areas, so as to derive both local and global legitimacy. Reference to 'traditional communities' and 'traditional authorities' in blueprints for these programmes – many of them emerging in the 1990s following the Rio 1992 Earth Summit – was a change in approach that was greatly welcomed by major funding institutions. Reference to 'tradition' and 'communities' seemed to fulfil the promise that governmental programmes would finally begin taking 'the local' into serious consideration, such that formerly marginalised rural populations would truly become 'participants' in the conservation programmes to come.

Two Namibian law professors undertook the colossal task of writing down and thus codifying 'traditional law', emphasising well-defined sets of laws and regulations pertaining to natural-resource management for Namibia's major ethnic communities (Hinz & Ruppel 2008). According to their treatise, customary law addressed most (if not all) pertinent questions surrounding natural-resource management with clarity, effectiveness, and with an eye towards sustainable use. Traditional authorities were framed as the guarantors of such knowledge, and as guardians for sustainable resource use (Hinz & Ruppel 2008). Traditional knowledge and traditional leadership in such accounts became enshrined as ecologically adapted knowledge. Such knowledge, passed on over generations, would serve as a guarantee for future sustainable resource use. Conservation policy makers also assumed that traditional authorities would clearly prioritise community welfare over economic benefits for single enterprising individuals, and that they would thereby shelter their communities from the vagaries of capitalist penetration.

This view, however, did not account for the complex and ambivalent history of traditional authorities under different political regimes. The role of traditional authorities in northern Namibia has been shaped by over eighty years of colonial laws and practices (Friedman 2011; Bollig 2011). Colonial administrations had involved themselves directly in chieftainship succession, demoting unwanted chiefs and promoting others who were thought to be more amenable to collaboration with colonial rule (Hayes 1992; McKittrick 2002; Gewald 2011).

The colonial co-optation of traditional authorities, including their control over natural-resource management within their communities, became entangled with two other social dynamics. Since the early 20th century, longing for pristine nature became an essential element in imaginaries about nature, which was eventually integrated into ecotourism. Second, the nascent enthusiasm for wilderness and wildlife led to the introduction of protected areas and fortress conservation, a form of conservation that sharply distinguished between nature and culture, excising entire landscapes from human use for the sake of wildlife conservation. Traditional farmers and herders were permitted in some conservation areas. Particularly 'indigenous', 'original' or 'native' cultures were viewed as being 'parts of nature', thus falling on the 'nature' side of this divide. With DeVore *et al.* (2019: 15), who observed very similar dynamics in the Brazilian context, we argue: 'Such visions inform closed and participatory conservation regimes alike, making exceptions only for certain minorities (indigenous, feminine, or traditional) who are *naturalized* as and *expected to act* as guardians of nature'.[1]

The actual excisions involved in creating protected areas – or abundant plans to create such areas – have had enduring effects on rural land use.

---

[1]   Unpublished English translation, italics original.

Protected areas were placed under the control of a governmental administration, whereas all use-management rights to such lands came to rest with
the state (Matengu 2001; see also contribution by Dittmann & Müller-Mahn
this volume). This implied that traditional authorities, who had formerly been
in control of these lands, had to cede some of their privileges.

The dilemma that arose was as follows: protected areas were planned and
instituted in northern Namibia throughout the 1960s to 1980s. In today's Kunene
Region, formerly Kaokoland, two further game parks were planned (Bollig
2020), while in the Zambezi Region, two smaller protected areas (Mudumu
and Mamili – today's Nkasa Rupara) were instituted in 1990 just before
independence, but had been planned since at least 1976 (Lenggenhager 2018).
While wildlife conservation areas were placed under the control of state administration, forests were placed under the governance of forest services under the
Bantustan administration, thus aligning specific environmental sectors with
other specific – and at times competing and conflicting – administrative units.
Conservation areas were excised from territories formerly controlled by traditional authorities and administered by newly instituted administrative organisations (such as the Directorate of Nature Conservation). Forests were governed
by the forestry services of Homeland administrations. Water management,
including the widespread expansion of boreholes across much of northern
Namibia, became a major sector of the local Bantustan administration. Yet
traditional authorities continued to exercise local authority over the use and
management of communal lands and natural resources. Administrative units
dealing with different aspects of the environment directly consulted with
traditional authorities before taking actions, such as drilling new boreholes
or undertaking reforestation efforts. In communal areas, common-property
resource-management systems persisted (Blackie & Tarr 1999) in tandem with
protected conservation areas, as well as a few state forests formerly (and in
some instances until now) managed as 'fortresses' by colonial administrators.
In the following paragraphs we will first deal with colonial attempts to
control natural-resource use, then describe pertinent changes of environmental governance in the 1990s, and in a final paragraph sketch out the
contemporary situation.

Customary land rights and the commodification of nature

In the first half of the 20th century, the South African colonial government
showed little interest in the use and development of northern Namibia's
communal lands (Botha 2005). Co-opted by the colonial government, and
widely acknowledged by rural communities, traditional authorities represented and gave voice to their communities, whom they dominated as patrons

holding wealth (in land, livestock, and trade relations) and political power. Often though, traditional authorities competed with each other for power and influence (Bollig 2020 for north-western Namibia; Kangumu 2011 and Lenggenhager 2018 for north-eastern Namibia). Such kinds of conflict helped colonial administrations to exert power and to throw their weight around to the advantage of the traditional authority that seemed most cooperative. Traditional authorities then served as intermediate authorities and were not only expected to explain the colonial administration's programmes to their community members, but were also expected to set such programmes in motion. Nevertheless, the state government managed communal lands and through its administration (e.g. water affairs, nature conservation, forestry, police) involved itself directly at the local level from the 1950s onwards. The state's decision-making power with respect to the use of the land and other natural resources could overrule traditional authorities at any time. In return for their services as intermediaries in the administration of colonial power, traditional authorities received salaries and were otherwise supported in their efforts to maintain local control (see Figure 15.1).

Since the 1960s, rural lands were increasingly seen as a resource needing to be developed and protected. Prior neglect of communal lands changed into concern for the commercial development of these lands. In the early 1960s the Odendaal Commission[2] proposed an ambitious development programme for Namibia in general, and northern Namibia in particular, pleading for an agricultural modernisation policy, which included an orientation towards commercial production and the joint development of tourism with conservation (Bigalke 1964).

Trophy-hunting tourism, a peculiar form of tourism of singular significance for Namibia until today – became well developed during the 1960s. By the mid-1970s, some ninety-two game farms had already been established and, by 1985, the expanding Namibian trophy-hunting market accounted for nearly 12% of the total African trophy-hunting market, signalling a gradual transition from cattle ranching to game farming and touristic activities in the commercial freehold farmlands (for parallels in South Africa, see Carruthers 2005). The successful commercialisation of wildlife through trophy hunting, and the immense increase in international tourism in the 1960s, contributed

---

[2]   The Odendaal Commission was instituted by the South African Government to contribute to the planning of state-led development efforts in South West Africa (the colonial name Namibia was given first by German then by South African colonial administrators). The Commission consisted of a small number of highly decorated administrators and scientists. They visited various regions, had interviews in place and came up with concise conclusions, creating the so-called Odendaal Report in 1963.

Figure 15.1 Chief Vita Thom and Chief Muhona Katiti, both installed as chiefs by the colonial government in 1923 (Source: Nambia National Archives, A450, Accessions C. H. L. Hahn).

to a reassessment of conservation in Namibia's northern communal lands. There, through the Odendaal Commission, the South African colonial administration was in the process of establishing pseudo-independent homelands (Bantustans) with administrative apparatuses of their own. How could these new homelands profit from tourism? The creation of homelands proceeded in tandem with the expansion of a conservation-tourism industry. At the same time, conservationist thinking in South Africa and Namibia was increasingly linked to and informed by global environmentalist activities and discourses.

In the 1970s and 1980s, tourism investors realised the potential for tourism development in the scenic landscapes of the northern communal areas, and turned to traditional authorities for access to such wilderness landscapes. While the drawn-out liberation war put a brake on the development of the northern communal areas in general, the development of tourism facilities along the Zambezi Region's natural riverine systems, as well as the open mountain landscapes of the Kunene Region, all gained momentum as landscapes that had been deemed scarce but authentic wildernesses that became sought-after commodities. However, the legal situation was complicated.

Before independence, communal land was part of the Bantu reserves and no black (and also no white) person could own land without formal 'permission to occupy' (PTO). A PTO was a permission, granted in writing, for an individual to occupy land for a specific purpose, thus providing tenure security that protected the rights holder against all others, except for the state. According to the South West Africa Proclamation (AG 19 of 1978), administration of the South African Bantu Trust was transferred to the Administrator-General of South West Africa. A significant effect of AG 19 was that the PTO system that applied to 'Bantus' or 'blacks' in South Africa also became applicable to blacks in South West Africa. Thus, in South West Africa, like in South Africa, 'blacks' could only be granted 'permission to occupy' land in the so-called homelands, rather than claim land 'ownership'. The so-called 'homelands' were established north of the 'Police Zone', as defined in the First Schedule of the Prohibited Areas Proclamation (Proclamation 26 of 1928). The PTO system was kept in place after independence, although the independent government viewed it as disadvantageous to communities, while giving an advantage to outside investors, such as tour operators and commercial hunters. Tourism investors needed permission from the traditional authorities as well as special permits to establish tourism facilities in the communal lands. As the custodians of the land, traditional authorities remained the gatekeepers for tourism investors seeking access to land in communal areas. Although tourism investors could legally apply to the national government directly for PTOs to occupy land in communal areas, they could not establish tourism facilities without the endorsement of traditional authorities and their communities. Some studies indicate that there was considerable ambiguity concerning who exactly was authorised to initiate and/or approve a PTO. For example, a study by the NGO Integrated Rural Development and Nature Conservation (IRDNC) points out that

> [i]n Kasika Conservancy in 1997, a tourism operator obtained a PTO (Permission to Occupy) from the government for a piece of communal land on the Chobe River. This was done in agreement with the Traditional Authority who obtained assurances that he would receive an annual payment and that his family members would be employed. (IRDNC 2011: 62)

Restrictions on local people's applications for PTOs ushered in at the outset of the CBNRM programme were a matter of concern and a cause of complaints for some communities in the southern Kunene Region (Sullivan 2003).

Traditional authorities continued to negotiate terms of tourism operation on behalf of the community, typically profiting directly from such arrangements in financial terms. Moreover, the provision of employment also contributed to the traditional authorities' standing, as they had the power to recommend specific community members for employment in tourism facilities. In some cases, traditional authorities received payoffs or fees for the land, although the amounts were often minimal compared to rates on the open market. Besides, traditional authorities could request tourism investors to fund specific activities in the community, such as community celebrations or sittings of the traditional court. A Namibian Association of CBNRM Support Organisations (NACSO) study highlighted this problematic situation, which prevailed into the early 2000s. For example: 'Lodges employed few locals and at best made token payments to traditional authorities, without sharing generated revenue with communities, even though communal lands were set aside for [empowering and improving the] livelihood [and] use by rural people and the natural resources available should have been under their control' (NACSO 2015: 12). Another study states:

> A token fee was paid by the [Namushasha] lodge to the traditional authority, but it was discretionary and would change from year to year with little relevance to the performance of the lodge. The fee could be halted any time that the lodge thought the locals were not behaving. Not surprisingly the relationship between the lodge and the community was poor. (IRDNC 2011: 65)

Whenever there was a need to strengthen a specific relationship, traditional authorities and tourism investors exchanged gifts as in-kind benefits (IRDNC 2011). Traditional authorities who did not receive such payments or otherwise benefits in kind often withdrew their support, leading to conflicts between communities and tourism operators. Income generated through PTOs became increasingly important for traditional authorities following independence in 1990, as the Namibian government stopped paying salaries to most traditional authorities. For many traditional authorities who had become used to regular incomes, PTO arrangements and other informal agreements with tourist operators were seen as the only way to secure income that could complement proceeds from subsistence agriculture and livestock herds. Since 1997 traditional chiefs were paid N$2,640 (Namibian dollars, about US$200) per month, whereas so-called traditional councillors, who assist chiefs with their duties, receive N$1,800 (US$136) from the government. Each chief is also provided with a vehicle and a driver (Chlouba 2019).

Besides scenic wilderness landscapes, wildlife itself was another natural resource that gained increasing monetary value for traditional authorities. Colonial military regimes in the Kunene and the Zambezi Region controlled land within war zones in the 1970s and 1980s. As such, senior white officers hunted wildlife at their discretion, in some cases jointly with traditional authorities. Military leaders often hunted wildlife illicitly, including protected species, as the administration's game rangers did not operate in war zones and poachers were rarely prosecuted (Ellis 1994). In his memoirs, Garth Owen-Smith (2010) details the extent to which colonial administrators including army staff were involved in decimating wildlife, and explains how local white administrators paved the way for elite colonial administrators to hold (illegal) hunts in such regions. Traditional authorities were also allowed to hunt with permission from the administration. In applications for the so-called 'hunting for the pot licences', colonial administrators also extended game-hunting privileges to traditional authorities. This was particularly the case in the Kaokoveld, where such pot licences were regularly granted to local chiefs (Bollig 2020: 224–225). Meanwhile, in the 1970s and 1980s, both legal and illegal hunting privileges were exchanged for favours and political support. In the 1990s, trophy hunting – which was already practised on settler-owned game farms in central Namibia since the 1960s – also became a legal option in the northern communal areas. Whereas licensed hunting on communal lands under the juris-diction of traditional authorities expanded the scope for generating incomes through trophy hunting, control over wildlife utilisation by communities was steadily diminishing in the early 1990s. A NACSO report notes: 'There were a small number of government-controlled trophy hunting concessions. But local communities generally had no democratic control over these activities and received minimal returns' (NACSO 2015: 12).

Since the 1980s, the commodification of wilderness landscapes increasingly shaped natural-resource-use policies on communal lands. Previously, any use of wildlife by rural citizens was strictly prohibited. Any form of hunting was considered poaching, and was a prosecutable transgression, whether it was merely hunting for game meat, hunting high-value animals for the market, such as rhinos or elephants; hunting to cull predatory animals, such as lions and hyenas; or hunting to control crop-destroying grazers, such as hippos and buffaloes. Lenggenhager (2018) and Bollig (2020) point out that, for a number of decades, poaching became the number-one crime in communal areas, as it repeatedly pitted local actors against colonial authorities. Wildlife, flora, and landscapes all became protected as state property, often with a vague gesture that such protection was instituted for the benefit of future genera-tions. Especially wildlife and flora that had a commodity status in earlier decades (e.g. elephant tusks, valuable trees) became decommodified. Locals thereby lost options to market produce independently and to diversify their rural livelihoods.

In the late 1980s and early 1990s, conservationist ideologies underwent significant changes. Wildlife and wilderness landscapes were progressively thought of as resources, commodities that could be sold on the global market for the benefit of local populations. Wildlife resources were thought of as possibly integrated into global value chains, and as untapped resources. Their controlled and well-implemented marketisation was justified as an income source that could pay for future conservation efforts and enhance rural economies. In this way, advocates of this agenda argued that conservation could pay for itself without the state devoting major budgets to such efforts. Furthermore, the valorisation of wildlife and wilderness landscapes, and the transparent and fair distribution of benefits, would lead to the considered and sustainable exploitation of highly valued natural resources.

The marketisation of wildlife resources in communal areas had another component of significant importance in many rural areas of southern Africa. Income from the marketisation of natural resources was to benefit local small-holders with limited access to markets and who were dependent on subsistence agriculture and supplementary incomes from non-agricultural sources, such as revenue generated from wildlife resources. Towards this end, since the 1990s, conservationists and government administrators encouraged and facili-tated the commodification of wilderness landscapes and wildlife in northern Namibia to help rural economies to diversify and to offer chances for (self-) employment for impoverished community members. After decades of colonial marginalisation, these administrators believed that local people would only accept conservation approaches that limited their land use, in order to help wildlife populations recover and expand, if they could directly profit from it. If local people could benefit financially, they would tolerate increasing wildlife damage to other livelihood strategies, such as loss of livestock and harvests. Indeed, much of the evidence assembled in support of wildlife conservation and governance tended to support these participatory – profit-sharing – models, especially after decades of strong repression.

These broad steps towards the commodification of nature instigated by government authorities and conservationist NGOs interfaced with local common-pool resource-management institutions, which were under the control of traditional authorities (Mendelsohn 2008). New ideas of rural resource governance gained ground. Local resource users were to be empowered to participate in decision making about the very natural resources they utilised and depended upon. Theoretical paradigms popular in the 1990s, notably Elinor Ostrom's common-pool resource-management design, which showed under which conditions communities managed resources sustainably, suggested that rural communities were capable of equitable resource use if certain conditions were met (e.g. clear definition of resource users and resources to be used and protected, transparent rules of decision making). At the same time traditional authorities retained their formal status, and customary law was recognised in the Constitution as equal to the common law (Lavelle 2019, see also Lavelle this volume). Traditional authorities in Namibia were specifically recognised by the Traditional Authorities Act 25 of 2000, which defined the performance of their duties as supporting culture, customary laws, and state structures (Keulder 2010). As a result, traditional authorities in communal land were (re)legitimised, accorded power to allocate land and natural resources, and empowered to stipulate how lands and other resources were to be used (Keulder 2010). However, the acknowledgement of traditional authority did not imply that all traditional authorities on the former Bantustan administration's payroll were equally acknowledged. In fact, only very few traditional authorities were acknowledged and would continue to receive salaries. In the Kaokoveld, only three out of thirty-six traditional authorities were initially acknowledged by the new regime (Friedman 2011), leaving most of the region's traditional authorities in need of financial support and acknowledgement. The rise of community-based conservation offered a new and promising platform, both for financial revenue and legitimacy.

The democratisation of natural-resource governance after 1990

When Namibia became independent in 1990, the decentralisation and democratisation of governance in rural areas of northern Namibia was a key government concern. This required the establishment of various community-based natural-resource-management institutions, as existing institutions appeared to be riddled with undemocratic regulations and deep colonial legacies. The pseudo-independent homelands in northern Namibia did not have their own conservation legislation at the time but relied on national law in this field. A major task for the new independent government was to stipulate conservation and natural-resource-management laws that were applicable throughout the country and that could provide for equal treatment of all citizens, irrespective of race or ethnicity. At the same time, new natural-resource-management laws had to meet democratic standards, as well as best practices for sustainable communal-pool-resource management. The quest to democratise rural politics thus required communities to elect fixed-term representatives who could manage natural resources on their behalf. This push towards grassroots democratisation also involved demands that elected representatives be held accountable to clearly defined legal and ethical standards (Corbett & Jones 2000). The emergence of local, resilient and accountable representatives was deemed to contribute meaningfully to successful decentralisation. Transparent bookkeeping, annual budgetary reviews, and management plans were essential procedural measures. The election of community representatives was necessary, moreover, owing to the absence of local governance structures below the regional level. New democratic structures, such as conservancy committees, community forest committees, water-point committees, and land boards, were all to serve as democratically legitimised expressions of local governance. On the one hand, these structures were supposed to implement and exercise oversight over programmes determined at regional and national levels, while, on the other hand, these local structures could also influence higher orders of government on behalf of their local constituents (Blackie & Tarr 1999). To ensure that traditional authorities' concerns and suggestions for development projects were attended to, an informal liaison forum was established as a channel of communication to the Regional Councils or Offices of Governors.

In turn, traditional authorities were to support government organisations, such as regional councils, local councils, and the police. Section 3 (2b) of the Act states that the 'traditional authority' should keep the 'traditional community' informed about government development projects, and collaborate with respective administrative staff. Of course, 'information' is a very humble term for a giant task: they had to translate abstract concepts like sustainability, climate-change adaptation and community-based conservation to their communities. The relationship between government and traditional authorities is defined by Article 102 (5) of the Namibian constitution, which calls for the establishment of the Council of Traditional Authorities, 'in order to advise the President on the control and utilisation of communal land and on all other matters as may be referred to it by the President for advice'. The Council of Traditional Authorities advises the government as well as the President. Thus, the establishment of these new governance mechanisms was not supposed to undo the power of traditional authorities but rather to co-opt them more firmly to the government apparatus. Thus they established and empowered secondary sources of governance running parallel to traditional governance structures. However, the incoming independent government was adamant that the state must retain the right to endorse traditional leaders. The government not only redefined relations between traditional authorities and the administration, but instituted a number of new institutions of resource governance. Conservancy committees became active in community-based conservation on behalf of their communities. Community forest committees sought to manage forests under community control. Water-point committees managed the boreholes that had been handed over from administration to communities. All these committees were elected, adhered to principles of just and equal representation, attempted to apply principles of gender equity and transparency, and were controlled through annual general meetings.

These new democratic governance mechanisms challenged traditional authorities in a number of ways. Traditional authorities felt threatened, for example, because conservancy committees could challenge their control of natural-resource utilisation, potentially undermining their ability to distribute patronage within the community (IRDNC 2011). Water-point committees, for example, could fix contributory rates against the wishes of traditional authorities, as Menestrey Schwieger (2018) shows in his ethnography on borehole management in the Kunene Region and Lavelle shows in her description of devil's claw gathering and commercialisation in the Zambezi Region (see also Lavelle this volume). Menestrey Schwieger shows that community water-point committees were empowered to potentially make decisions independently from traditional authorities. Also in matters pertaining to land traditional authorities felt their rights to allocate land to community members threatened. Core conservation areas that each conservancy had to define certainly limited their power to deal with the entirety of land of their chieftaincy.

Thus, the newly constituted democratic institutions did either liase with or, occasionally, also sideline traditional authorities. Sometimes the latter supported the decisions of democratically elected committees, and committees ensured that the opinions of traditional authorities were reflected in the decision-making process. At the same time, committees ensured that part of the revenues from the marketisation of resources directly went into the coffers of traditional authorities – as allowances, subsidies, or outright down-payments for the use of natural resources, or as donations in kind, such as of game meat or monetary contributions for cultural events (see Figure 15.2).

Hence, both institutions – traditional authorities and the new democratic committees – often worked in tandem on the commodification of wildlife and wilderness. Occasionally, though, committees bypassed traditional authorities.

Figure 15.2 King Mamili at Lusata Festival 2022, Chinchimani, 2 October 2022 (Photo: Michael Bollig).

Pellis *et al.* (2015) and also Sullivan (2003) document cases in the southern Kunene Region where newly instituted committees and traditional authorities were conflicting. In these cases committees were not just new institutions of resource governance but were immediately involved in pre-existing factional conflicts and in fact deepened such frictions.

Commodification of wildlife resources and traditional authorities

Many traditional authorities supported the formation of conservancies in both the Kunene and Zambezi regions. They viewed wildlife conservancies as reflecting their own initiatives to bring conservation and development closer within their communities and, referring to ancestral lifestyles, they promoted this move as a restoration of a former convivial human–wildlife co-existence. This reinvention of an allegedly convivial pre-colonial and pre-capitalist human–wildlife relationship is currently turning into a global discursive formation (see DeVore 2019). The traditional authorities invited IRDNC to support the establishment of conservancies in the Kunene and the Zambezi regions (IRDNC, 2011). Indeed, IRDNC popularised the idea that they were only there at the invitation of traditional authorities, and that their role was merely subsidiary, to act in ways that supported local communities in the realisation of their own goals. Representatives of IRDNC emphasised that they sought not to impose their own conservation projects on rural communities, but that the initial move and invitation had to come from the community. They also advocated the vision of a co-existence landscape in which wildlife could live well side by side with farmers and pastoralists in a convivial manner. There humans could profit from emerging options for ecotourism, and wildlife would profit from community-based protection. Traditional authorities were the culturally appropriate legal entities who were empowered to endorse such conservation initiatives. In the Kunene and Zambezi regions, traditional authorities appointed the first community game guards in the context of community game-guard programmes in the 1980s. These community game guards reported to traditional authorities before conservancies became formalised (IRDNC 2011: 24).

Thus, although not legally required, traditional authorities ended up playing critical roles in the process of establishing and organising conservancies. In order to meet the requirement of registering individuals as members of the conservancy, local authorities needed to raise awareness in the villages. Community members would often not agree to become conservancy members if the traditional authorities did not assure them that they, too, supported the formation of the conservancy. The role of traditional authorities in mobilising communities to support conservancy formation within their jurisdictions thus strengthens their influence in the conservancies. In the rare cases where a conservancy was established against the will of a local traditional authority, or only with reluctant support from his side, the result was the decreased power of that particular authority. In some other cases, the establishment of a conservancy was used to wrest territory away from a particular traditional authority, and create a new traditional authority whose territory was then identified with the formalised conservation area. The establishment of conservancies could thus intervene in ongoing power struggles between competing traditional authorities. In general, however, the influence of traditional authorities in conservancies permitted them to maintain a degree of control over commodified natural resources within the conservancies.

Box 15.1 Conflict and Cooperation, and the Central Role of Traditional Authorities in Conservancies in the Southern Kunene Region (summarised from Pellis et al. 2015)

Until 2000, today's Anabeb, Sesfontein, and Puros conservancies had been one conservation unit. Various conflicts, notably between competing traditional authorities dating back to colonial times, then led to the fracturing of this large initial conservation area into three separate conservancies. Puros conservancy was first registered in 2000, and Sesfontein and Anabeb conservancies in 2003. While the two larger conservancies, Sesfontein and Anabeb, are occupied by about 1,500 people each, Puros accounts for only some 650 people. Most of these c. 3,600 people are living pastoral nomadic lives, depending on the mobility of their large herds of cattle and small stock. Due to colonial displacements but also due to drought-conditioned moves the communities consist of 'traditional groups' that emphasise different historical origins and, of particular importance here, affiliation to different traditional authorities. It is particularly the conflict between two dominant Herero families, the Kasaona and the Kangombe families, that shapes these contestations. Their antagonism dated well back into colonial times (they 'have been in dispute since time remembered' Pellis *et al.* 2015: 12) and nobody could answer well how and why this conflict emerged. Early on, the two competing families affiliated with different (and also competing) NGOs – each specialising in community-based conservation, though with different ideas on exactly how this should be practised.

Even after the splitting of the conservancies was achieved and formalised, the conflict did not find an end as members of all conflicting families lived in all three conservancies. Pellis *et al.* (2015: 13–15) describe in detail a conflictual meeting of the Anabeb conservancy in 2010. Disagreement arose over the appropriate sequence of events of the meeting. One group wanted to hear more about the activities of the past outgoing committee and to discuss their merits and demerits. The other group argued that such a report should only be discussed after a new committee had been selected and that the report on the past term was not yet ready for presentation. Government officials and NGO staff members got involved in the heated debate, and finally the meeting broke off and one group left the meeting in protest. These pertinent conflicts finally led to an institutional experiment to combine conservancy management with traditional authority. In Anabeb, the committee of the Conservancy consisted of ten elected members (with voting powers) and seven traditional authority representatives (without voting powers, but large enough to comprise both factions), a perfect two-chamber system. For some time, this elaborate construction seemingly worked well and served the purpose of working towards compromises between the wider community and conflicting traditional authorities.

Box 15.2 Conflict and Cooperation and the Central Role of Traditional Authorities in Conservancies in Zambezi Region

Until 1999, the Mashi and Mayuni Conservancies in the west of Zambezi Region were under the Mafwe Traditional Authority. After independence in 1990, with the definition of conservancy boundaries, conflicts within the Mafwe Traditional Authority emerged, which contributed to shaping Mashi Conservancy and Mayuni Conservancy boundaries (Mosimane 1999). The conflict centred around land ownership and access to natural resources, defined through territories of the Traditional Authority (Leggenhagger 2018). Mashi Conservancy was gazetted in March 2003; it covered 297 km² and had a population of about 4,000 people. Mayuni Conservancy was gazetted some years earlier, in December 1999, and covered 151 km² with a population of about 2,400 people (Mosimane 1999). Both conservancies derive income and benefits from trophy hunting and from a joint venture-tourism agreement with lodges.

Traditional Authority conflict shaped the formation of conservancies in the Zambezi Region. The Mayuni Conservancy was proposed by Joseph Mayuni, the then sub-chief of the Mafwe Traditional Authority. The definition of the boundaries resulted in a dispute within the Mafwe Traditional Authority (Mosimane & Silva 2014). Mayuni Conservancy accepted the reduction of the boundaries of the Conservancy to the area under the jurisdiction of sub-chief Mayuni. The formation of the Mayuni Conservancy coincided with the application for recognition of Chief Joseph Mayuni by the state as a chief of the newly proclaimed Mashi Traditional Authority. The boundaries of the Conservancy became the boundaries of the Mashi Traditional Authority (Mosimane & Silva, 2014; Leggenhagger 2018). The names of the traditional authorities and the conservancies indicate the conflict that exists due to identity conflict among the communities, as articulated in the following.

In a letter dated 17 July 2004 (seen by *New Era*), the then Namibian President Sam Nujoma, recognised Mayuni as the Chief of the Mafwe Community within the Mashi Traditional Authority boundaries. The Mashi Traditional Authority further stressed that although the Mafwe Tradional Authority is an umbrella body, which represents several tribes, the Mashi Traditional Authority is solely a representative of the Mafwe-speaking community within their traditional boundaries. They stated that at the time of recognition they could not take the identity of the Mafwe Traditional Authority because it already existed (with a chieftaincy at Chinchimani). It is on record that Omfumu Joseph Tembwe Mayuni was recognised as the Chief of the Mafwe Community. The recognition is contrary to the Traditional Authority Act, because the Mafwe Traditional Authority, headquartered at Chinchimani village is also representing the Mafwe community. In fact, there is a dispute about who is entitled to frame themselves as the original Mafwe community, with the Mashi Traditional Authority claiming only they are the true Mafwe able to speak '*sifwe*' language (*The Namibian*, 5 August 2004). (https://neweralive.na/posts/mashi-traditional-authority-clarifies-tribal-identity)

In 2007 Chief Mayuni (Mashi Traditional Authority, Caprivi) was awarded the Nedbank Namibia and NNF 'Go Green Environmental Award' for his role in community conservation (NACSO 2016). Conservation initiatives became a vehicle to address traditional authority conflicts of self-definition and identity, as demonstrated in this case. The area excised from the Mayuni Conservancy to the south was later demarcated to establish the Mashi Conservancy, which was gazetted in March 2003 under the Mafwe Traditional Authority.

Traditional authorities further play an important role in conflict resolution, as amplified in the statement: 'In most conservancies, the active involvement of traditional authority representatives ensures a positive relationship. Where this is not the case, conflicts often arise over resources and returns' (NACSO 2016: 20). The relationship between the community, traditional authority and tourism operators was always prone to conflict due to self-interest. The case of Mashi conservancy and the Namushasha Lodge in 1998 demonstrates the poor relationship between the lodge and the community, characterised by continued conflicts. The detail of the conflict between the Mashi conservancy, the community, traditional authorities, and the Namushasha Lodge is described in an IRDNC publication (IRDNC 2011: 64–67). The Traditional Authority were beneficiaries of the agreement before the Conservancy's formation, receiving a token fee which changed from year to year at the discretion of the Lodge. As noted earlier, the fees could be stopped anytime the lodge management felt the locals were not cooperating. The situation was worsened by tribal conflict between the traditional authorities representing the villages while the Conservancy management structure was also new and lacked capacity (Mosimane 2003). It was only when the relationship between the Conservancy, the Traditional Authority, the community and the tourism operators was addressed that conflict lessened.

Where the relationship between the traditional authority and the conservancy is not right, the latter cannot enforce the land zonation when communities interfere with the operations of the tourism joint venture. Where the traditional authority is also not involved, individual members of the community can claim the land in terms of customary rights and refuse to cooperate with the conservancy to establish a joint-venture operation.

The negotiation of conservancy boundaries also required traditional author-ities to help resolve community disputes that arose when the conservancies first formed. In most cases, traditional village boundaries served as the proposed conservancy boundaries within a community (Mosimane & Silva 2014). The use of traditional village boundaries, or traditional grazing territories in the Kunene Region, permitted traditional authorities to deploy their jurisdiction in order to reduce the number of conflicts between communities. While tradi-tional authorities could define territorial extent and membership, they had no influence on the layout of newly emerging institutions. How committees were to be elected, what their mandate would look like, and in what ways they were accountable were defined by national legislation.

Conservancies are not positioned or empowered to address conflicts within the community. Even conflicts related to the use and management of natural resources, which are within their mandate, cannot be handled by the conservancies themselves, but must be referred to the traditional authority. This is partly due to the fact that not all individuals in the community are conservancy members, and, as such, the conservancy cannot enforce rules on just any conservancy resident. However, all conservancy members remain 'under' a traditional authority, and thus in cases of conflict can be brought to traditional courts, such as the *Khuta* in the Zambezi Region. The involvement of traditional authorities contributes to better communication, good relations, and reduced conflict within the community. In many cases, traditional authorities have demanded representation on the conservancy committee to facilitate collaboration and coordination of activities and land use within the community, and conservancy committees have typically been prepared to accept such ex officio members (NACSO 2016, see Box 15.1). The traditional authority representative on the conservancy committee is meant to ensure that the traditional authority is well informed about conservancy issues. In the Zambezi Region's conservancies, the representative for the traditional authority will be responsible for bringing issues directly to the traditional authority, as the conservancy committee does not usually turn to him directly.

Traditional authorities in tourism joint ventures and trophy hunting

Conservancies derive most of their income and benefits from joint-venture and trophy-hunting agreements (IRDNC 2011). The government recognises that tourism and other forms of wildlife commodification in communal areas could contribute to poverty alleviation, and therefore encourages joint tourism ventures and trophy hunting. The joint tourism and trophy-hunting ventures in communal areas are supposed to involve community members so that they can derive benefits (MET 2008). These joint ventures are based on formal agreements, which stipulate how income and other benefits are to be shared and distributed among conservancy members and the community at large (NACSO 2014).

While formal income through the government only went to acknowledged chiefs, conservancies could remunerate chiefs whether they were acknowledged or not. In 2017, traditional chiefs were paid a salary of about N\$2,640 (about US\$202) per month, whereas so-called traditional councillors, who assist chiefs with their daily duties, receive N\$1,800 (US\$138) from the government (Chlouba 2019). The current minimum wage for domestic workers is equivalent to US\$94 per month. These figures suggest that traditional authorities have reliable salaries but that this remuneration is comparatively small, hence the contribution of shares from conservancy incomes is significant.

Table 15.1 shows that the income derived by traditional authorities from conservancies is higher in Zambezi than in Kunene. If we bracket out the still-limited revenues from a fairly young Kunene conservancy, called

Table 15.1 Traditional authority (TA) incomes derived from nature conservancies, 2017.

Kunene Conservancy	Total Income in N$	Payment to TA	Percentage of total income going to TA	Zambezi Conservancy	Total income in N$	Payment to TA	Percentage of total income going to TA
Anabeb	1,955,748	45,400	2	Balyerwa	1,031,653	40,400	4
Ehi-Rovipuka	282,827	4,000	1	Bamunu	828,474	61,500	7
Epupa	375,161	0	0	Dzoti	1,384,520	45,000	3
//Huab	279,068	1,000	0	Impalila	578,047	6,000	1
=Khoadi-//Hoas	2,459,347	10,000	0	Kabulabula	915,841	50,500	6
!Khoro!Goreb	11,537	0	0	Kasika	1,456,774	79,177	5
Kunene River	119,8091	0	0	Kwandu	1,033,898	151,672	15
Marienfluss	1,448,915	19,682	1	Lusese	873,617	42,000	5
Okangundumba	166,659	2,000	1	Mashi	2,765,801	45,000	2
Okondjombo	65,320	0	0	Mayuni	1,221,115	128,000	10
Okongoro	4,576	0	0	Nkabolelwa	764,964	17,000	2
Omatendeka	588,652	4,500	1	Salambala	2,087,905	7,011	0
Ombujokanguindi	60,745	14,500	24	Sikunga	679,112	20,000	3
Orupembe	155,188	0	0	Sobbe	872,310	50,000	6
Otjambangu	29,260	0	0	Wuparo	1,682,863	40,000	2
Otjitanda	53,524	0	0	Average:			4.73%
Otuzemba	235,503	0	0				

Kunene Conservancy	Total Income in N$	Payment to TA	Percentage of total income going to TA	Zambezi Conservancy	Total income in N$	Payment to TA	Percentage of total income going to TA
Ozondundu	332,582	12,836	4				
Puros	369,162	11,500	3				
Sanitatas	91,752	0	0				
Sesfontein	1,252,988	27,500	2				
Sorris Sorris	394,540	5,000	1				
Torra	3,384,151	25,827	1				
Uibasen	2,489,822	5,000	0				
Average			1.71%				

Sources: Calculations by Linus Kalvelage based on NACSO Working Groups 2017

Note: On 1 July 2017 the exchange rate stood at US$1: N$13.1

Ombujokanguindi, the figures show that traditional authorities earn less than 1% of revenue from conservancies in the Kunene Region, whereas they receive some 5% in the Zambezi Region. In the Zambezi Region, the high-earning Sifwe-speaking conservancies – Kwandu (15%), Mayuni (10%), Bamunu (7%), and Sobbe (6%) – give the highest amounts of revenue to their respective traditional authorities. This means that the conservancy incomes for traditional authorities result in sizeable sums. In 2017, the Traditional Authority in Kwandu Conservancy earned N$151,672 from conservancy incomes (about US$11,600 using the exchange rate 1 July 2017), in the Mayuni Conservancy N$128,000 (about US$9,800), and N$61,500 (about US$4,700) in the Bamunu Conservancy – i.e. they earned significantly more from conservation than from their government salaries. At least for the Zambezi Region, traditional authorities' incomes from conservancy activities add significantly to their overall incomes. To what extent such income from conservancies is redistributed or invested in public goods, communal festivities, contributions to school buildings, or the facilitation of grassroots abjudication – e.g. in land cases – is a question of crucial interest that needs further investigation.

Income results from trophy hunting as well as leases. Conservancies have joint-venture agreements with tourism and trophy-hunting operators. Such agreements stipulate operation agreements, including fees that tourism and trophy-hunting operators have to pay to the conservancy. The joint venture starts with a tourism operator, who requires land from the conservancy or community to operate as a tourism or hunting venture. Typically, land that is leased to operators was previously used for subsistence farming, as a key livelihood source for community members. When this land is allocated to tourism operations, its uses become exclusively zoned for tourism, and community members must forego subsistence activities, such as ploughing, grazing, or harvesting natural resources.

Conclusion

Drawing on examples from Namibia's Zambezi and Kunene regions, this chapter has shown how traditional authorities have managed to reinforce their influential position after independence. We argue that pertinent institutional structures were laid out in the colonial period, which continue to shape contemporary institutional development and local conflicts. In their quest to establish indirect rule of the vast and sparsely settled lands of northern Namibia, the South African colonial administration relied heavily on traditional authorities to maintain order and to facilitate government projects. While during the first forty years of colonial rule traditional authorities guaranteed that basic functions of the state were maintained (jurisdiction, suppression of violence), since the 1960s traditional authorities became significant players in the modernisation of rural economies. The formation of Bantustans in northern Namibia enshrined the role of traditional authorities in many ways. In particular, their role in the management of natural resources became significant as Bantustan administration of forest and water resources was to involve direct cooperation with traditional authorities, and their respective communities were to be approached through them. However, conservation remained the administrative prerogative of the central state throughout colonial times. The immense role that traditional authorities played in the Bantustan organisations, including in the governance of natural resources, contributed to a significant increase in the number of traditional authorities. In many ways, traditional authorities became well-paid elites within the Bantustan framework.

With independence, the traditional authorities lost a number of their privileges. Moreover, the number of acknowledged traditional authorities was sharply reduced, leaving many of them searching for financial resources and legitimacy. Importantly, however, they did retain the prerogative to allocate land and natural resources on communal lands. At the same time, and in a somewhat paradoxical manner, the decentralisation and democratisation of natural-resource governance in rural areas was pushed forward. The democratisation of environmental governance following Namibian independence in 1990 required: (1) the establishment of institutions to manage specific natural resources (e.g., water-point associations for boreholes, forestry committees for forests, conservancies for wildlife, and, in some places, rangeland associations for the management of pastures); (2) spatially, socially, legally well-defined communities to elect representatives to manage natural resources on their behalf; and (3) communities that could learn how to hold their representatives accountable. Through their interactions, all of these institutions, committees, and traditional authorities contributed to the further development of each of these aims. Sometimes the same people cooperated and entered into conflicts with each other in different institutions. As they are typically closely tied through kinship they seek cooperation. Where ethnic divides prevail they may become accentuated in conservation set-ups as new resources bring about new claims for ownership and just distribution. Habitually local people in northern Namibia seek hybrid solutions, providing traditional authorities with a significant say in natural resource management, and allotting them sizeable incomes derived, for example, from forestry management or wildlife commodification, but not leaving the stage completely to them. Traditional authorities came to occupy roles in which they saw themselves as managing natural resources on behalf of their communities cooperating with 'modern' institutions like elected committees. Whereas committees and associations could take external aid from the state, NGOs, and donor organisations, the traditional authorities could not. The close link between traditional authorities and democratically elected institutions has allowed chiefs to tap into such external resources. The commodification of natural resources in this way facilitates institutional bricolage. Socially, such commodification contributes to the renovation and (re)legitimisation of rural elites and their patron-client networks. At the same time, such bricolage creates space for institutional experimentation.

Bibliography

Becker, H. (2006). 'New things after independence: Gender and traditional authorities in postcolonial Namibia', *Journal of Southern African Studies*, 32(1), 29–48.

Bigalke, R. C. (1964). 'The Odendaal Report and wild life in South West Africa', *African Wild Life*, 18(3), 181–188.

Blackie, R. & Tarr, P. (1999). *Government Policies on Sustainable Development in Namibia*, Research Discussion Paper No. 28 (Windhoek: Directorate Environmental Affairs, Ministry of Environment and Tourism). Available at: https://aquadocs.org/handle/1834/547 [Accessed 31 January 2022].

Bollig, M. (2011). 'Chieftaincies and chiefs in northern Namibia: Intermediaries of power between traditionalism, modernization, and democratization', in: J. Dülffer, *In Elites and Decolonization in the Twentieth Century* (London: Palgrave Macmillan), 157–176.

Bollig, M. (2020). *Shaping the African Savannah: From Capitalist Frontier to Arid Eden in Namibia* (Cambridge: Cambridge University Press).

Botha, C. (2005). 'People and the environment in colonial Namibia', *South African Historical Journal*, 52, 170–190.

Carruthers, J. (2005). 'Changing perspectives on wildlife in southern Africa, c.1840 to c.1914', *Society and Animals*, 13, 183–200.

Chlouba, V. (2019). 'Traditional authority and state legitimacy: Evidence from Namibia' Afrobarometer Working Paper 183. Available at: https://afrobarometer.org/sites/default/files/publications/Documents%20de%20travail/afropaperno183_traditional_authority_and_state_legitimacy.pdf [Accessed 31 January 2022].

Corbett, A. & Jones, B. (2000). 'The Legal Aspects of Governance in CBNRM in Namibia' (Windhoek: Directorate of Environmental Affairs, Ministry Environment and Tourism). Available at: www.cbnrm.net/pdf/corbett_001.pdf [Accessed 31 January 2022].

DeVore, J., Paulson, S., & Hirsch, E. (2019). 'Conserver la nature humaine et non humaine Un curieux cas de conservation conviviale au Brésil (English version 'Conserving human and other nature: A curious case of convivial conservation from Brazil'. Available at www.academia.edu/43451921/Conserving_human_and_other_nature_A_curious_case_of_convivial_conservation_from_Brazil [Accessed 18 January 2023]. *Anthropologie et Sociétés*, 43(3), 31–58.

Ellis, St. (1994). 'Of elephants and men: Politics and nature conservation in South Africa', *Journal of Southern African Studies*, 20(1), 53–69.

Friedman, J. T. (2011). *Imagining the post-Apartheid state: An ethnographic account of Namibia* (New York: Berghahn).

Gewald, J. (2011). 'On becoming a chief in the Kaokoveld, colonial Namibia, 1916–25', *Journal of African History*, 52, 23–42.

Government of Namibia (2000). Traditional Authorities Act 25 of 2000 (Windhoek: Government of the Republic of Namibia). Available at: www.lac.org.na/laws/annoSTAT/Traditional%20Authorities%20Act%2025%20of%202000.pdf [Accessed 31 January 2022].

Hayes, P. (1992). *A History of the Ovambo of Namibia, c.1880–1935*. PhD dissertation, University of Cambridge.

Hinz, M. O. & Ruppel, O. C. (eds) (2008). *Biodiversity and the Ancestors: Challenges to Customary and Environmental Law – Case Studies from Namibia* (Windhoek: Namibia Scientific Society).

IRDNC – Integrated Rural Development and Nature Conservation (2011). *Lessons from the Field: Community Based Natural Resource Management (CBNRM) -IRDNC'S Experience in Namibia* (Windhoek: John Meinert).

Kangumu, B. (2011). *Contesting Caprivi: A History of Colonial Isolation and Regional Nationalism in Namibia*, vol. 10 (Basel: Basler Afrika Bibliographien).

Keulder, C. 2010. *State, Society and Democracy: A Reader in Namibian Politics* (Windhoek: John Meinert).

Lavelle, J. 2019. *Digging Deeper For Benefits: Rural Local Governance and the Livelihood and Sustainability Outcomes of Devil's Claw (*Harpagophytum *spp.) Harvesting in the Zambezi Region, Namibia*. PhD Thesis, University of Cape Town, Cape Town.

Lenggenhager, L. (2018). *Ruling Nature, Controlling People: Nature Conservation, Development and War in North-Eastern Namibia since the 1920s*, vol. 19 (Basel: Basler Afrika Bibliographien).

Logan, C. (2013). 'The roots of resilience: Exploring popular support for African traditional authorities', *African Affairs*, 112(448), 353–376.

Mafwe Lusata Cultural Festival (n.d.). 'Mafwe Lusata Cultural Festival'. Available at: https://lusatafestivalcom.wordpress.com [Accessed 31 January 2022].

Matengu, K. K. (2001). 'The quest for sustainable community-based tourism in Salambala Conservancy, Caprivi Region, Namibia'. Thesis, University of Joensuu.

McKittrick, M. (2002). *To Dwell Secure: Generation, Christianity, and Colonialism in Ovamboland, Northern Namibia* (New York: Heinemann).

Mendelsohn, J. 2008. 'Customary and legislative aspects of land registration and management on communal land in Namibia' (Windhoek: Ministry of Land and Resettlement and European Union).

Menestrey Schwieger, D. A. (2017). *The Pump Keeps on Running: On the Emergence of Water Management Institutions between State Decentralization and Local Fractices in Northern Kunene* (Berlin: Lit Verlag).

MET – Ministry of Environment and Tourism (2008). 'National policy on tourism for Namibia' (Windhoek: MET). Available at: www.met.gov.na/files/files/National%20Policy%20on%20Tourism%20for%20Namibia.pdf [Accessed 31 January 2022].

Mosimane, A. (1999). *Livelihood, Governance and Organisation in Mayuni*

Conservancy (Windhoek: University of Namibia, Multi-Disciplinary Research Centre).

Mosimane, A. (2003). *Mashi Conservancy Establishment Progression and Livelihood Approaches* (Windhoek: University of Namibia, Multi-Disciplinary Research Centre).

Mosimane, A. & Silva, J. (2014). 'Boundary making in conservancies: The Namibian experiences', in: M. Ramutshindela, *Cartographies of Nature: How Nature Conservation Animates Borders* (Newcastle upon Tyne: Cambridge Scholars Publishing), 83–111.

NACSO – Namibian Association of CBNRM Support Organisations (2014). 'The state of community conservation in Namibia – a review of communal conservancies, community forests and other CBNRM initiatives'. 2013 Annual Report (Windhoek: John Meinert).

NACSO – Namibian Association of CBNRM Support Organisations (2015). 'The state of community conservation in Namibia – a review of communal conservancies, community forests and other CBNRM initiatives' 2014/15 Annual Report (Windhoek: John Meinert).

NACSO – Namibian Association of CBNRM Support Organisations (2016). 'The state of community conservation in Namibia – a review of communal conservancies, community forests and other CBNRM initiatives'. 2015/16 Annual Report (Windhoek: John Meinert).

NACSO Working Groups (2017). 'Namibia's Communal Conservancies: Annual Conservancy Performance Ratings and Audit Reports for the Year 2017' (Windhoek: Namibian Association of CBNRM Support Organisations).

Owen-Smith, G. L. (2010): *An Arid Eden: A Personal Account of Conservation in the Kaokoveld* (Johannesburg: Jonathan Ball).

Pellis, A., Duineveld, M., & Wagner, L. B. (2015). 'Conflicts forever: The path dependencies of tourism conflicts – The case of Anabeb Conservancy', in: G. Johannesson, C. Ren, & R. van der Duim (eds), *Tourism Encounters and Controversies: Ontological Politics of Tourism Development* (Abingdon: Ashgate).

Sullivan, S. (2003). 'Protest, conflict and litigation: Dissent or libel in resistance to a conservancy in north-west Namibia', in: E. Bewrglund & D. Anderson (eds), *Ethnographies of Conservation: Environmentalism and the Distribution of Privilege* (Oxford: Berghahn Press), 69–86.

Taylor, J. (2021). *Naming the Land: San Identity and Community Conservation in Namibia's West Caprivi* (Basel: Basler Afrika Bibliographien).

Ubink, J. (2008). *Traditional Authorities in Africa: Resurgence in an Era of Democratisation* (Leiden: Leiden University Press).

16

Commodification of Wildlife Resources in the Okavango Delta, Botswana

JOSEPH E. MBAIWA

Introduction

Developing countries of Latin America, Asia, and Africa are the fastest growing destinations of international tourism. About 30% of all international tourist arrivals are in developing countries; this proportion has nearly tripled over the past 20 years. The tourism industry has grown to become the world's largest economic sector. Thus, it has basically become one of the leading job creators in the world, creating more than 3% of all global employment. As indicated by Blanke & Chiesa (2013) and the World Trade Organization (WTO 2015), the tourism industry employs more than 98 million people. This directly represents over 3% of all global employment. While tourism provides considerable economic benefits for many countries, regions, and communities, its rapid expansion may be responsible for adverse environmental as well as socio-cultural impacts (Buckley 1994).

Tourism is often identified as the most promising driving force for the economic development of less developed countries and regions which are endowed with areas of natural beauty (Saarinen *et al.* 2009) – here referring to regions perceived by citizens from developed countries as 'new' and 'exotic' destinations with 'pristine' and 'unspoiled' natural environments. Citizens from developed countries seek 'authenticity' and non-fragmented, 'unspoiled' landscapes, which developing countries like Botswana provide. Tourism offers these regions a valuable opportunity for economic diversification (Neto 2003). Natural resource depletion and environmental degradation associated with tourism activities pose several problems to many regions favoured by tourists (UNESCO 2003). Once a destination is sold as a tourism product, and the demand for souvenirs, curios, entertainment, and other commodities begins to exert pressure on the environment and local community, then basic changes in human values may occur (Cohen 1988; Timothy & Boyd 2003; Lenao & Saarinen 2015).

The commodification of wildlife resources for the tourism market either through trophy hunting or photographic tourism has various impacts on the livelihoods of local communities, on economic development, and on the natural environment (Neto 2003; Spenceley 2008; Lenao 2015; Mbaiwa & Sakuze 2009; Mbaiwa *et al.* 2011a). That is, local communities earn income by participating in tourism, thereby increasing their cash flows (Spencely 2008; Mbaiwa & Sakuze 2009). Also, tourism has many long-term dynamic impacts on the development of local economies and local people's livelihoods, ultimately affecting their income, opportunities, and/or security (WTO 2001; Blanke & Chiesa 2013). Commodification also affects the natural environment in which people live, as well as their social and cultural environment, thereby affecting their livelihoods and their overall well-being (Lenao 2015; Mbaiwa & Sakuze 2009).

Commodification helps raise awareness of the financial value of the natural and cultural sites through increased revenue realised through tourism and the amount that tourists are willing to pay for the resource that is for sale (Heynen & Robbins 2005; Mbaiwa *et al.* 2011a). This can stimulate a feeling of pride in people's local and national heritage and generate interest in the conservation of the resources offered for tourism (Saarinen 2006). Some of the positive consequences of commodification arise when tourism is practised and developed in a sustainable way, which entails involving the local community (Petterson 2015; Bernatek & Jakiel 2013). Conversely, the commodification of natural resources can lead to a loss of biodiversity due to a shift towards unsustainable management practices (Pretty *et al.* 2009). It is therefore essential to involve the local community because a community that is involved in the planning and implementation of tourism develops a positive attitude, becomes more supportive, and has a better chance of making a profit from tourism than a community that is passively overrun by tourism (Spenceley 2008). The involvement of local communities in tourism development and operation is an important condition for the conservation and sustainable use of biodiversity (Buckley 1994; Hassan 2000; Turner & Sears 2013).

In Botswana, the community-based natural resource management (CBNRM) programme was introduced through a CBNRM policy of 2007, to ensure that local communities benefit from Botswana's abundant natural resources, with the hope that local communities would then protect the natural resources. The policy was also adopted to foster national economic development and growth by opening landscapes, resources, and communities to outside investors, who would then also gain from their investments (Mbaiwa 2005; Bolaane 2005). The idea was that if local communities received socio-economic benefits from wildlife-based tourism in their local environment, they might feel obliged to conserve these resources. Tourism involves both trophy hunting and photographic activities as a means to achieve conservation and maintain the wilderness state of the environment while at the same time promoting economic development. The objective of this chapter, therefore, is to draw on the concept of sustainable tourism to analyse the effects of commodification of wildlife resources in the Okavango Delta, Botswana. The chapter mainly focuses on economic development, tourism development, and conservation aspects resulting from the commodification of wildlife resources.

The concept of commodification

This chapter is informed by the concept of commodification. Commodification implies the 'dominance of commodity exchange-value over use value and implies the development of a consumer society where market relations subsume and dominate social life and experiences that tourists are usually relatively happy to consume' (Gotham 2002: 1737). Commodification is thus a process through which objects and activities are categorised in a commercial context as goods and services after being evaluated according to their exchange values (Cohen 1988). As such, commodification is a universal element of modern capitalism that includes adjustment of products, desires and experiences (Watson & Kopachevsky 1994). Commodification is arguably 'benign or non-threatening, creating tourist products' (Douglas *et al.* 2001: 122).

The concept of commodification gained prominence in international tourism research, especially in analysing cultural tourism (MacCannell 1973; Cohen 1988, 1989; Ateljevic & Doorne 2003; Steiner & Reisinger 2006). Cohen (1988: 380) argues that commodification is a process by which things (and activities) come to be evaluated primarily in terms of their exchange value, in the context of trade, thereby becoming goods (and services); the exchange value of things (and activities) is stated in terms of market prices. That is, due to commodification, a product is solely defined by its economic value. In tourism, the packaging of products and activities for the tourist market is known as commodification. In several developing countries, including Botswana, governments are seeking to promote tourism to achieve economic prosperity (Manwa 2007; Mbaiwa & Sakuze 2009).

The literature on the commodification of nature generally deals with the penetration of neoliberalism into the non-human world, whereby markets are created that enclose elements of the environment to bring them into the sphere of market exchange (Cousins *et al.* 2009). Scholars have written about commodification of ecosystems services. For example, McAfee (1999) provides an analysis of the commodification of biodiversity. McAfee notes that nature should earn its own right to survive through international trade in ecosystem services, access to tourism and research sites, and exports of timber, minerals, and intellectual property rights to traditional crop varieties and shamans' recipes. McAfee (1999: 145) argues that promoting commodification has the following advantages: (1) the conservation of biological diversity; (2) the sustainable use of biological diversity; and (3) the 'equitable sharing' of the benefits of genetic resources. Similarly, Castree (2003) identifies six ways in which nature is being commodified, which include the following: externally as a resource taken from the environment; directly as a purchased commodity; by proxy as a characteristic that affects the price of something else. As such, Castree argues that the commodification of nature in capitalist societies has paid relatively little attention to the 'natural' dimensions of commodities (for a discussion of Castree 2003 see also Greiner & Bollig this volume).

Commodification occurs because ecosystems are acknowledged to be of great value to conservationists, researchers, governments hoping to tap them as sources of revenue, biodiversity prospectors, and miners or loggers looking for marketable commodities (McAfee 1999). Ecosystems are commodified because of the dollar amounts that might be raised if resources were sold on international markets (McAfee 1999). International or foreign tourists are willing to spend large sums to visit Botswana and this has influenced the people of Botswana to set up tourism enterprises which in turn create employment for local people and create foreign direct investment for the country (McAfee 1999). In Botswana, commodification has resulted in wildlife resources becoming a product for sale to the tourism market, which involves photography, hunting, and translocation of wild animals. As a result, in Botswana, wildlife-based tourism is a key component of the economy. Wildlife resources have been commodified for the tourism market. In this regard, wildlife tourism plays an important role not only in Botswana but in many developing countries (Belicia & Islam 2018), and is widely lauded as giving nature 'the opportunity to earn its own right to survive' (McAfee 1999). Economic benefits that wildlife tourism brings serve as an incentive for the conservation of wildlife and their habitats (Belicia & Islam 2018). This view is the driving force in the adoption and implementation of the community-based natural resource management (CBNRM) programme in Botswana. The CBNRM programme was introduced to ensure that local communities benefit from wildlife resources, with the hope that those communities will then protect the natural resources. These natural resources include wildlife which has been commodified for the tourism market.

Critics of the commodification of wildlife, such as Belicia & Islam (2018), argue that commodification through wildlife tourism is perceived as a solution to the problems of increased poaching, habitat destruction, and species extinction. They note that this argument assumes that when wildlife is commodified, it can pay for its right to survive by attracting tourists. From this it is concluded that there is an incentive to conserve wildlife populations and the habitats that support them. Belicia & Islam (2018) criticise this argument, noting that the reasons given are not enough to justify commodification. As a result, they argue that wildlife tourism should be decommodified, suggesting that in a system of capitalism, profit opportunities drive market changes, and this cannot be applicable to threatened species which cannot generate profit to ensure their protection. Using a market-based conservation strategy implies that these animals and their habitats are only worth saving when they are profitable; this is risky since it can drive species that are not profitable to extinction (Belicia & Islam 2018; McCauley 2006). As such, the commodification of animals in capitalist society is deeply rooted, and there is no one-size-fits-all solution to the many types of problems faced by wildlife tourism around the world (Belicia & Islam 2018).

Despite critics of the commodification of wildlife resources for the tourism market, it is essential to recognise that wildlife-based tourism in developing countries is on the increase and governments support it for its economic potential. In this era of natural resource decline, wildlife-based tourism should thus establish itself as a potential win-win-win scenario for local people, conservation, and tourists or tourism operators. This chapter therefore analyses the effects of and provides insights into the commodification of wildlife resources for the tourism market in the Okavango Delta, Botswana.

Study area – the Okavango Delta

The Okavango Delta is located in north-western Botswana (Map 16.1). The Delta is formed by the inflow of the Okavango River whose two main tributaries (the Cuito and Cubango Rivers) originate in the Angolan Highlands. The Okavango River flows across Namibia and finally drains into north-western Botswana to form a wetland known as the Okavango Delta, characterised by a triangular-shaped alluvial fan and covers an area of about 16,000 square kilometres (Tlou 1985).

Like the Nile in Egypt, the Okavango River and its Delta sustains life in an otherwise inhospitable environment. For instance, there are 2,000 to 3,000 plant species, over 162 arachnid species, more than 20 species of large herbivores, and over 450 bird species (Monna 1999), and more than 80 fish species (Kolding 1996). Large herbivores such as elephants, buffaloes, zebra, and a variety of small game such as impala, kudu, red lechwe, and ostrich are found in the region. A large variety of bird species are also found in the Okavango Delta. A total of 486 identified species gives testimony to the high degree of aviary biodiversity (GISPlan 2013).

The Delta is a major source of livelihoods for the rural communities who have lived in the area for hundreds of years. Over 95% of the over 200,000 people who live in the Okavango Delta region directly or indirectly rely on natural resources found in the wetland to sustain their livelihoods (NWDC 2003). Due to its rich biodiversity, wilderness nature, permanent water

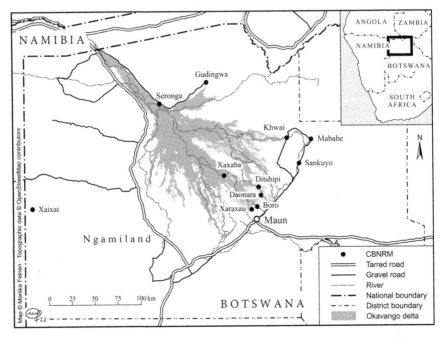

Map 16.1 The Okavango Delta, Botswana (Source: Open StreetMap contributors; Cartography: M. Feinen).

resources, rich grasslands, and forests, the Okavango Delta has become one of the key international tourism destinations in Botswana. The Delta receives between 100,000 and 150,000 tourists annually (Mbaiwa 2018).

[1] The Okavango Delta, is, therefore, a suitable site to investigate the commodification of wildlife resources for the tourism market and whether the tourism industry adheres to the ideals of sustainable tourism.

Study methods

The analysis of the commodification of wildlife resources for the tourism market relied on the use of secondary data sources on wildlife-based tourism

---

[1]   While tourism is a lucrative industry in the Okavango Delta, the outbreak of COVID-19 significantly affected the industry. International travel restrictions imposed on travellers from Europe and North America spelt trouble for local tourism in the Delta as it led to the cancellation of pre-paid bookings and demands for refunds (Hambira *et al.* 2021). While COVID-19 halted tourism development between 2020 and 2021, the industry began to show recovery in 2022. Botswana's Minister of Environment and Tourism Hon. Philda Kereng is reported as saying: 'There is a tourist that emerged form [*sic.*] Covid 19' (*Sunday Standard* 2022).

development in the Okavango Delta, Botswana. This data was in the form of published and unpublished documents, government policy documents and reports. Some of the documents used include Botswana's Tourism Policy of 1990, Botswana Tourism Master Plan of 2000, North West District Development Plan (2003/04–2007/08), Community-Based Natural Resource Management (CBNRM) Forum Annual reports of 2011, 2012, and 2013 (Mbaiwa 2011b, 2013), annual financial reports of CBNRM projects (Mbaiwa, 2013), Central Statistics Office documents on population growth, tourism statistics (Statistics Botswana 2020), and tourism facilities in the Okavango Delta (Central Statistics Office 2008). The study also used synthesised data from several studies on wildlife use and tourism development carried out in the Delta between 1998 and 2020. To evaluate the different aspects of wildlife use, time series data on wildlife utilisation from pre-colonial Botswana to modern times were examined. This method of investigation made it possible to assess whether wildlife utilisation in the Okavango Delta and Botswana adhered to the principles of sustainable tourism development.

Data was also used from studies on human–wildlife interactions in northern Botswana in 2019. These studies involved face-to-face in-depth interviews with farmers. In addition, key informants' interviews were conducted with community leaders such as village chiefs, wildlife managers, and community-based organisation leaders. In-depth interviews with key informants took advantage of their experience and long-term knowledge of human–wildlife interactions in the Okavango Delta. In-depth interviews had an advantage in that key informants were recognised as authority figures on human–wildlife interactions and commodification of wildlife resources for the tourism market. Data collected was thus analysed qualitatively.

Results and discussion

Historically the commodification of wildlife resources in the Okavango and Botswana can be categorised into three sections, namely: pre-colonial period (before 1885), colonial period (1885 to 1966), and post-colonial period (1966 to 2019). A better understanding of the current commodified wildlife use in Botswana requires an understanding of the pre-colonial and colonial eras of the wildlife industry.

Wildlife utilisation in pre-colonial Botswana

Historically, especially in pre-colonial Botswana, wildlife resources played a significant role in sustaining the livelihoods of traditional societies (Tlou, 1985). Wildlife resources were not commodified at that time. Wildlife was mainly used for subsistence purposes. Hunting of wildlife was carried out only for household food supply and in some instances for religious or cultural purposes, as was the case when the skin of a lion was needed to clothe the chief at the installation ceremony. There was no trade in wildlife products (Mbaiwa, 2002). The period up to the 1850s was characterised by the different tribal groups in the Okavango Delta using wildlife to sustain their liveli-hoods. These groups had traditions and customs such as totems and taboos which stipulated which animal or bird should be hunted and which should be preserved (Tlou 1985; Mbaiwa 2002). There were also tribal institutions such as the *kgotla*, headed by the chief who through the powers vested upon him by societal norms and customs directed wildlife-resource use. The chief held wildlife resources in trust for the whole community to be used for the benefit of both the present and future generations. As such, the use of wildlife resources in pre-colonial Botswana was sustainable (Tlou 1985; Thakadu 1997; Mbaiwa 2002). Subsistence hunting in the Delta never endangered wildlife populations and did not compromise biodiversity.

Communities could have achieved sustainability presumably because hunting technologies were not geared for mass slaughter and there were no larger markets for selling bushmeat and skins profitably (Mbaiwa 2002). The traditional communities in the Okavango Delta had unwritten laws and traditions that made sustainable wildlife utilisation and management possible in their respective territories (Campbell, 1995). The local people perceived wild animals to be an intimate part of the environment controlled by God. Misuse of wildlife could bring down God's wrath upon them (Campbell 1995). The management of resources under customary law endured for centuries in part because of the strong religious links with ancestors and because of the low population densities, which helped to maintain a sound ecological balance (Chenje & Johnson 1994). Mbanefo and de Boerr (1993) also note that indigenous peoples in remote areas developed wise procedures to protect their natural resources over centuries, and could thus be called the original environmentalists.

Traditional wildlife uses in Botswana and the Okavango Delta were affected profoundly in the 1850s when European trade expanded into the region (Tlou 1985). This indicates that towards the official colonisation of Botswana in 1885, European trade had penetrated the Okavango Delta. For example, White (1995) states that during the 1870s, Francis and Clark's store in Shoshong was exporting annually up to Botswana Pula BWP 50,000 (US$3,958) worth of wildlife trophies, which most of which came from the Okavango Delta. He further states that the actual volume of the trade each year may have involved as many as 5,000 elephants, 3,000 leopards, 3,000 ostriches, and 250,000 small fur-bearing animals. This information illustrates the fact that European trade expansion, not only in the Okavango Delta but the whole of Botswana, had tremendous effects on wildlife populations. However,

European trade in wildlife products escalated in the colonial period, resulting in the creation of national parks and game reserves.

The introduction of European trade in Botswana

The arrival of Europeans and the introduction of European trade in Botswana altered the traditional wildlife-management systems of all the ethnic groups in Botswana (Tlou 1985). European wildlife trade involved local communities' exchange of wildlife products with Europeans. Trade between the different ethnic groups in Botswana and European traders involved the exchange of ivory, ostrich feathers, and, to a lesser extent, hippo teeth, which were exchanged for relatively inexpensive items such as household goods, clothes, wine, and guns (Tlou 1985). Before the arrival of Europeans all these commodities were previously not regarded as valuable by ethnic groups in Botswana. The involvement of these people in European trade changed their traditional wildlife utilisation patterns as wildlife species were no longer regarded as being only for consumption and religious purposes but for commercial purposes as well. Campbell (1995) argues that totemism, the belief that under certain circumstances, some humans can transpose their spirits into those of animals or take an animal form both before and after death contributed to the pre-colonial conservation of wildlife resources. That is, animals and birds considered to be totems were never killed but respected, which therefore led to the preservation and conservation of such species.

The commodification of wildlife resources led to the overharvesting of particular species since the trade was driven by profit-making without any consideration for the ecological aspects. The expansion of European trade since the 1860s in the Okavango region introduced the use of guns, which spread at an alarming rate (White 1995). As trade in wildlife products increased in the area, the tribute system became the source of most trade goods used by local chiefs there (Campbell 1995). Officials or representatives of the king of the dominant ethnic group in the Okavango, the Batawana, travelled throughout the state to collect tribute, and this collection became more frequent, systematic and rigorous for the people of the Okavango region. The standing of the Batawana provincial governors within the administrative system was enhanced because of their role in tribute collection from hunting. The tribute system was no longer used as a sign of respect and loyalty to the king as it became a system to enrich the kings (Campbell 1995). In this regard, the breakdown of the traditional practices of wildlife use was due to European influence in trade in the Okavango region.

The commodification of wildlife resources marked the overharvesting of wildlife in the Okavango Delta (Tlou 1985; White 1995; Mbaiwa 2002). Therefore, the years that marked the eve of British colonisation of Botswana in 1885 were characterised by the overharvesting of wildlife resources, and not only in the Okavango Delta.

The other remarkable effect of the commodification of wildlife resources and the expansion of European trade in the Okavango Delta is that it introduced the use of guns (Tlou 1995; White 1995). An example is that, by 1874, Paramount Chief Moremi of Ngamiland District in which the Okavango is located personally owned more than 2,000 modern rifles, which he dished out to his people to hunt on his behalf. It is estimated that there was a total of about 8,000 rifles in the entire district at that time, and this subjected wildlife to extreme pressure (White 1995). Local chiefs used their regiments and newly acquired guns for hunting wildlife for sale in the whole of the Okavango region. The commodification of wildlife thus led to local chiefs abandoning the use of spears and traps for hunting in favour of the use of guns. In this regard, commodification of wildlife affected traditional wildlife-management systems of community groups that lived in the Okavango Delta (Mbaiwa 2002). The commodification of wildlife thus led to the overharvesting of particular species. Trade in wildlife products was therefore driven by profit-seeking, with little consideration for the ecological consequences.

Wildlife use in colonial Botswana, 1885–1966

The colonisation of Botswana by the British from 1885 extended the process of wildlife commodification, but the adoption of a legislative framework controlled the overharvesting of wildlife resources. This resulted in wildlife management being approached in two ways. First, there were statutory laws that governed the use of wildlife resources and only applied to Europeans, especially wildlife traders in the region, and second, pressure was imposed by the colonial government on the local kings to come up with customary laws for their people, along lines similar to the statutory game laws for Europeans. These laws in both cases were allegedly targeted at curbing the unsustainable commercial exploitation of wildlife not only in the Okavango but in Botswana as whole. The major controlling interest was in both cases the colonial government, as these decrees were only to operate with the approval of the British Resident Commissioner (Spinage 1991).

The new legislative framework by the British colonial government thus centralised wildlife management with the aim of arresting the problem of the overharvesting of wildlife. For example, the British colonial Government of Botswana, in its centralisation approach to wildlife management, created national parks and game reserves. The centralisation of control over wildlife resources resulted in local communities losing the autonomy they formerly had regarding their use of wildlife when power became transferred from them and their traditional management institutions to those of the British administration

(Mbaiwa 2002). The colonial government introduced laws to control wildlife harvesting in national parks and game reserves (Spinage 1991). The most significant law passed during British rule in Botswana was the Bechuanaland Protectorate Game Proclamation No. 17 of 1925 (Spinage 1991). According to Spinage, this law called for the creation of national parks, game reserves, and wildlife sanctuaries, whereby wildlife species and areas, or species within a defined area were to be protected. This proclamation eventually led to the establishment of protected areas such as the Chobe Game Reserve (1961) and Moremi Game Reserve (1963). Moremi Game Reserve was established in inner parts of the Okavango Delta, and the Tawana tribal leadership was instrumental in setting up the reserve. Game parks and wildlife sanctuaries were created in the traditional hunting areas of the local people, who were denied access to wildlife resources, especially the Indigenous people of the Okavango Delta, namely the Basarwa or San (Mbaiwa 2005, Bolaane 2005). The result was conflict and negative attitudes on the part of local people towards wildlife resources and the state powers charged with the responsibility for wildlife conservation.

The immediate result of commodification of wildlife resources in colonial Botswana was the establishment of national parks and game reserves, which did not allow local communities access into those areas that they had previously used for hunting and gathering. Rodney (1972) and Darkoh (1996) point out that colonialism and modernisation in Africa alienated African societies from the natural resources upon which they had previously based their livelihood under a system of collective rights. Rodney states that African political states lost their power, independence and meaning overnight, irrespective of whether they were big empires or small ones. Political power simply passed into the hands of foreign overlords. The loss of political power by African leaders meant loss of control over the natural resources in their local environment. Arntzen (1989) shares the same view as Rodney and Darkoh by stating that in Botswana, the traditional resource-management systems over which the chief had power and control became affected. Arntzen states that one of the factors contributing to this development was the mounting pressure on wildlife resources, which took the traditional buffers away and rendered the traditional tools less effective. He also attributes this to government policies which did not usually take the local resource base into account, hence forming a source of interference which led to wildlife-resource degradation.

Wildlife utilisation in post-colonial Botswana

The commodification of wildlife resources in Botswana became more formalised after Botswana became independent from British rule in 1966, with more legislation allowing wildlife resources to be sold to the tourism market.

That is, after independence, the centralisation policies on wildlife-resource use either became wholly adopted or partially modified by the new Government of Botswana (Spinage 1991; Mbaiwa 2005). As such, Botswana is currently divided into four wildlife utilisation regions (Map 16.2): the Kalahari Region, representative of the south-west arid biome; the Okavango/Chobe Region, containing rich fauna; the Makgadikgadi Region, transitional between the first two; and the Limpopo Region, containing south-east lowland fauna species.

The commodification and division of Botswana into wildlife areas resulted in national parks and game reserves occupying some 17% of the country. Surrounding these are eleven designated Wildlife Management Areas (WMAs) in which it is intended that the main form of land use will be wildlife utilisation. The WMAs occupy an additional 22% of the surface area of the country. As

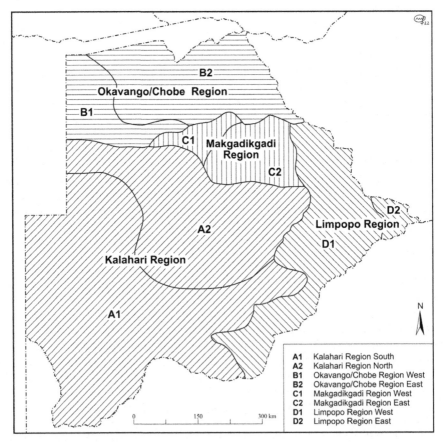

Map 16.2 Wildlife Utilisation Regions in Botswana (Author / Government of Botswana: Cartography: M. Feinen).

such, about 39% of Botswana's surface area is reserved for wildlife utilisation (Mbaiwa 2018). In other words, 39% of the land in Botswana is commodified for the tourism market, of which wildlife utilisation is the primary land use in these areas. The community-based natural resource management (CBNRM) programme, which is a community-based tourism approach, is carried out in Controlled Hunting Areas (see below) while national parks and game reserves are kept for big tourism operations. The goal of CBNRM is rural development and conservation. Its assumption is that once communities derive benefits from tourism, they might be inclined to conserve wildlife resources (Twyman 2000; Mbaiwa 2005).

Wildlife commodification and concession areas

The commodification of wildlife resources and, closely connected to it, wildlife-based tourism, became a key part of the Okavango Delta's economic system. It was facilitated by the adoption of the Wildlife Conservation Policy of 1986 and the Tourism Policy of 1990 (Mbaiwa 2018). These two policies call for increased local participation in resource management to minimise resource decline in Botswana. The government adopted the CBNRM programme in the late 1980s to address problems of wildlife decline. This programme discourages open-access resource management and promotes resource-use rights for indigenous communities (Mbaiwa 2005). The programme is a reforming of the previous failed 'top-down protectionist' approaches to natural resource management, biodiversity conservation, and development (Kgathi *et al.* 2004). The assumption made by CBNRM advocates is that including local communities in the decision-making process may result in tourism benefits accruing to local people, hence incentivising them to conserve resources (Twyman 2000; Mbaiwa 2005).

The evolution of the CBNRM programme in Botswana is an indication of the commodification of wildlife resources in the region for the tourism market. The Wildlife Conservation Policy of 1986 facilitated Botswana's districts being divided into Wildlife Management Areas (WMAs) (Mbaiwa 2002). These are further subdivided into the small land units called Controlled Hunting Areas (CHAs), which are concession areas that get leased out to tourism operators. In the Okavango area, CHAs are code-named from NG/1 to NG/52 for identification purposes. Botswana is divided into 163 CHAs, of which 37 are in the Okavango area (Map 16.3). These CHAs are zoned for various types of wildlife utilisation (both consumption and non-consumption uses), under commercial or community management (Rozemeijer & van der Jagt 2000). In the Okavango region, CHAs are zoned around existing settlements, Moremi Game Reserve, and the Okavango Delta. It is in these community areas that the rural communities are expected to practice wildlife-based tourism

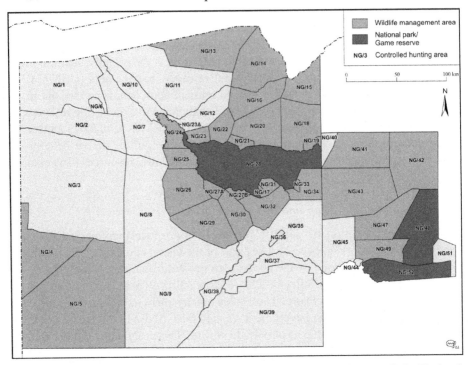

Map 16.3 Controlled Hunting Areas (CHAs), code-named NGs, in the Okavango Delta (Author / Government of Botswana; Cartography: M. Feinen).

activities. The Botswana Government in 1992 adopted recommendations of the land-use planning consultancy report to divide the country into WMAs and CHAs. Respective district land authorities (i.e. Land Boards) and the Ministry of Lands manage the different CHAs in the country.

The adoption of the CBNRM programme was extended to local communities to commodify and benefit from wildlife resources within their respective local environments through community-based tourism. As concession areas, CHAs have made land and wildlife accessible to local communities, and they co-manage land with government institutions such as the Tawana Land Board, and wildlife with government agencies including the Department of Wildlife and National Parks (DWNP). Through this partnership, scientific methods, such as plant- and wildlife-population monitoring, and traditional knowledge, such as selective hunting of older male animals and community wildlife policing through Community Escort Guides, are combined in managing land and wildlife resources in respective CHAs belonging to local communities (Mbaiwa 2018). That is, communities living in wildlife areas are required to form community trusts before being allocated (leased) CHAs by the Botswana

Government. In these CHAs, communities carry out tourism activities such as photographic and commercial hunting to generate revenue. As such, revenue that accrues to communities is largely from the following activities: sub-leasing of the CHA or hunting area to safari hunting companies; sale of wildlife quota (i.e. wildlife quota fees for game animals hunted); meat sales; tourism enterprises, e.g. lodges and campsites; and camping fees and vehicle hire. It is critical to note that community trusts implement CBNRM tourism projects on behalf of their communities. The basic aim of a community trust is to utilise natural resources (e.g. wildlife) through tourism development in their CHAs to generate jobs, revenues, and meat for the benefit of community members. Community trusts are registered legal entities and are formed in accordance with the laws of Botswana to represent community interests and implement their management decisions regarding natural resource use. The effect of wildlife co-management is exemplified by hunting, which is now effectively regulated locally, whereas in the past, indigenous communities resented top-down wildlife management mandates, and engaged in illegal hunting. That is, prior to the adoption of the CBNRM programme and the creation of CHAs, communities were not allowed to benefit from tourism through hunting, and as a result, poaching or illegal hunting was pronounced in Botswana's wildlife areas. As noted, poaching was both for commercial purposes done by European hunters and local communities for subsistence uses with some overlap between both categories (Mbaiwa 2002; Tlou 1985).

Commodification and multinational tourism corporations

The commodification of wildlife in the Okavango Delta has made it one of Botswana's leading tourist destination areas. That is, the rich wildlife it sustains and its scenic beauty have attracted multinational tourism corporations. As a result, the tourism industry in prime areas in the Okavango Delta is run by upmarket multinationals which have established luxurious accommodation and facilities offering services such as lodging, photographic safaris, walking safaris, riding safaris, game viewing, and camping (Ecosurv 2012; Plantec *et al.* 2012). Tourism operations licensing data from the Department of Tourism in Maun (the gateway tourism town to the Okavango Delta) indicate that some of the multinational tourism companies in the Okavango Delta include: the Okavango Wilderness Safaris, &BEYOND, Desert & Delta Safaris, Great Plains Conservation, and many others (Mbaiwa & Hambira 2020).

The commodification of wildlife in the Okavango Delta resulted in what came to be cynically known as 'high cost, low volume' tourism philosophy. This approach came to be as a result of the Tourism Policy of 1990, adopted because the government wanted to expand Botswana's economy through wildlife-based tourism. Through the Tourism Policy the Botswana government at that time wanted the country's wilderness areas, which were also the main tourist attractions, to attract high-end tourists instead of casual campers (Mbaiwa & Darkoh 2008). The high-paying tourists were visiting wilderness areas like the Okavango Delta in small numbers (20%) at the time, even though they were responsible for 80% of the tourist revenue in Botswana (Mbaiwa & Darkoh 2008). Through the Tourism Policy, the Botswana Government created a conducive environment for high-paying tourists to visit Botswana's wilderness areas. As such, the motive for adopting the Tourism Policy in 1990 was profit-seeking and the need for better economic benefits for Botswana using the wildlife resources of the country.

That prime areas in the Okavango Delta are largely owned and controlled by multinational tourism companies with headquarters outside Botswana; the situation can thus be described as a form of 'enclave tourism' (Britton 1982; Oppermann & Chon 1997). Enclave tourism is defined as tourism that is concentrated in specific sites in remote areas in which the types of facilities and their physical locations fail to take into consideration the needs and wishes of surrounding communities (Ceballos-Lascurain 1996). Moreover, the goods and services available at these facilities are beyond the financial means of the local communities, and any foreign currency generated may have only a minimal effect upon the economy of the host region (Ceballos-Lascurain 1996: Mbaiwa 2005). Enclave tourism has also been referred to as 'internal colonialism', a situation where natural resources in a host region mostly benefit outsiders, while most of the locals derive few or no benefits (Drakakis-Smith & Willams 1983; Dixon & Heffernam 1991). The commodification of wildlife resources in Botswana and the adoption of the Tourism Policy of 1990 therefore laid the foundation for enclave tourism in the Okavango Delta. The commodification of wildlife in the Okavango Delta has resulted in a tourism industry characterised by revenue leakages with much of the revenue generated by multinational tourism companies channelled outside the country, the ownership of tourism facilities being dominated by foreign companies, and management and better paying positions held by expatriates, while citizens and local people have usually held poor and unskilled jobs that attract low salaries (Mbaiwa 2005). These jobs include manual labour and work as drivers, maids, cleaners, night watchmen, gatekeepers, and cooks (Mbaiwa 2005). In addition, poverty levels in the Okavango Delta are relatively high compared to the rest of the country (Central Statistics Botswana, 2008).

The trophy-hunting ban of 2014 and its results

Contradictions in the commodification of wildlife resources for the tourism market became pronounced when the Government of Botswana suspended trophy hunting in January 2014. These contradictions are illustrated by the fact that the hunting ban appeared to be the result of wrestling over the use of wildlife resources between photographic tourism and trophy-hunting tourism. The decision to ban hunting in Botswana was partly motivated by a study conducted by a non-governmental organisation (NGO) known as Elephants Without Borders (EWB) based in Kasane in northern Botswana. This is an NGO whose aim is to conserve wildlife and natural resources, especially elephants. It conducted a study on wildlife statistics using aerial surveys, focused mostly in northern Botswana. The study concluded that populations of some wildlife species have been decimated by hunting, poaching, human encroachment, habitat fragmentation, drought, and veldt fires. A total of eleven species were reported to have declined by an average of 61% since a 1996 survey (Chase 2011). The study also reported that ostrich numbers have declined by 95%, wildebeest by 90%, tsessebe by 84%, warthogs and kudus by 81%, and giraffes by 66% (Chase 2011). Based on these results, the study made recommendations that hunting should be suspended or banned due to its contribution to wildlife decline. The result was that, in January 2014, hunting was banned in Botswana. However, photographic tourism continued to thrive, especially in prime areas of the Okavango Delta. The ban on wildlife hunting in 2014 was perceived by citizens of Botswana to be the work of animal rights and lobby groups, which continuously lobby the Convention on International Trade in Endangered Species of Wild Fauna and Flora (CITES) to ban trophy hunting not only in Botswana but in Africa as a whole. CITES regulates the wildlife trade and has been associated with difficulties in the wildlife trade in Botswana, especially elephant products.

However, the Government of Botswana (GoB) in 2019 reintroduced hunting to address issues of human–wildlife conflict and ensure citizen benefits from tourism. This was intiated by the Member of Parliament (MP) representing Maun East, in conjunction with some other MPs, who introduced in 2018 a motion to reintroduce hunting that was duly adopted. The President, His Excellency Dr Mokgweetsi E. Masisi, constituted a sub-committee of Cabinet, led by the Minister of Local Government and Rural Development to consult with stakeholders (e.g. communities, researchers, tourism operators, etc.) and report back to him on the possibility of reintroducing hunting in Botswana. The sub-committee duly submitted its report to the President, recommending, amongst other issues, that trophy hunting should be reintroduced, As a result of the change, hunting quotas have been allocated again and sold to trophy-hunting companies.

Commodification of wildlife resources, and human–wildlife conflict

Contradictions in the commodification of wildlife resources in the Okavango Delta are also characterised by human–wildlife conflicts between stake-holders. To understand wildlife resource conflicts in Botswana, it is necessary to appreciate the current wildlife habitat characteristics in the country, as described in the following subsections.

Increased elephant populations and human–elephant conflicts

While Botswana is faced with the challenge of wildlife decline, this is not necessarily the case with all the wildlife species in the country. The elephant population in Botswana has been on the increase since 1992 but, after the hunting ban of 2014, it increased and expanded into areas in which elephants were previously not found, e.g. the Central Kalahari Game Reserve (CKGR), Ghanzi District, Kgalagadi District, and many villages in central and eastern Botswana (Mbaiwa & Hambira, 2021). Aerial surveys of wildlife populations were conducted by DWNP and the results released in 2012 (DWNP 2013). The study observed that the elephant population had significantly increased to a total of 207,545, a 297% increase between 1992 and 2012, as indicated in Figure 16.1. The figure shows that both before and after the hunting ban in Botswana in 2014, the elephant population in Botswana increased. In addition, there was in-migration of elephants from Zimbabwe, Namibia, and Zambia to northern Botswana. It is critical to note that, while other wildlife species have been on the decline (e.g. rhinos), the elephant population in Botswana has been increasing over the last three decades. Although Elephants Without Borders argued that Botswana's elephant population stood at 130,451 (Chase *et al.* 2016), the NGO also acknowledged that this is a large population. Chase *et al.* (2016: 18), notes that, '[i]n southern Africa, four countries, Botswana, South Africa, Zambia, and Zimbabwe, have relatively large elephant populations and show either increasing trends or mild and non-significant declines recently'.

Overall, even though the DWNP study and EWB results disagree on the exact number of elephants in Botswana, the two studies do agree that there has been an increase in the elephant or population in the country. The two studies also agree that mortality and harvest rates (e.g. through poaching) for elephants in Botswana are very low. The results from DWNP concurred with results from EWB in relation to the decline of other species, but not with elephant populations. The DWNP study noted a decline of twenty-six animal species including: duiker, eland, gemsbok, giraffe, hartebeest, hippo, impala, kudu, lechwe, ostrich, roan, sable, sitatunga, springbok, steenbok, tsessebe, warthog, waterbuck, wildebeest, and zebra. Generally, most of the wildlife species in Botswana are on the decline except for elephants, buffaloes, and a few antelope species (DWNP 2013).

Elephant expansion to non-elephant areas

After the hunting ban in 2014, Botswana experienced a wide expansion of the elephant population, and distribution of elephants into areas which they had not previously utilised, as noted in the previous subsection. It is important

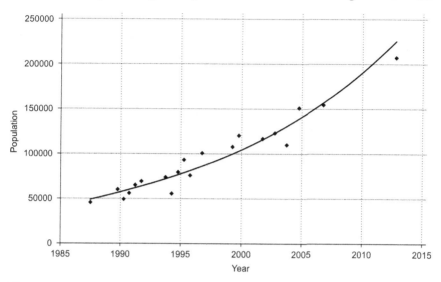

Figure 16.1 Elephant population in Botswana, 1999–2012 (Source: DWNP 2013).

to note that between 2009 and 2019, Botswana experienced relatively high rainfall, which allowed elephants to move further from protected areas during the rainy season. Artificial water provision has, in turn, enabled them to remain in some of those areas year-round. The Sub-Committee of Cabinet on Hunting Ban (2018) notes that the increase and expansion of the elephant populations in Botswana has impoverished communities living in wildlife areas due to crop damage, especially those in Nkange, Mmadinare, Boteti, Ngamiland, Chobe, and northern Botswana, where crop damage by elephants is prevalent. These increased incidents of human–wildlife conflict affecting poverty have increased hatred of elephants and other wildlife on the part of local communities. Obviously, this is not an ideal scenario for conservation or Sustainable Development Goals in Botswana.

Vegetation destruction due to large elephant population

The vegetation around waterholes in the CKGR is noted for having been destroyed by elephants. A DWNP official noted in a 2019 informal interview that a total of over 1,500 elephants had been resident in the CKGR for the previous five years. The Chobe Riverfront is currently overcrowded with elephants. Child (2019) argues that all 40,000 elephants from the Chobe National Park descend into the Chobe River every day to water. In the process, these elephants destroy the vegetation along the riverfront. The elephants' destruction of the vegetation will not only affect themselves but also other species that live in the area.

Crop damage and low yields

Although there are other factors that affect crop production in Botswana such as drought, pests and many others, a study carried out in 2016 in Chobe District (Parakarungu and Mabele Villages) indicated a reduction in actual annual yields due to wildlife crop raiding (Jibajiba 2018). Jibajiba notes that agro-farmers in Parakarungu and Mabele had expected a maize harvest of 7,128 bags but only 1,991 bags were eventually harvested. This represented a 72.1% loss. During the same year, 950 bags of sorghum were expected by farmers, but only 375 bags were harvested, representing a 61% loss. Similar results were confirmed by Gontse *et al.* (2018) that at Kumaga Village in Boteti Sub-district, where elephants raided a crop field overnight, the farmer's produce was reduced to zero. Crop damage has been reported not only in northern Botswana but in other areas in the country such as Nkange, Mmadinare, etc. This harvest loss leaves the community with fewer options for food provision to take care of their households.

In 2018, it is noted that the government spent over BWP 27 million (US$2.14 million) as compensation for crop and livestock damage caused by wildlife in the country. In addition to the challenges caused by elephants' livestock predation in northern Botswana, Kgalagadi, Ghanzi, the surroundings of the CKGR, Mmadinare, and other wildlife areas has been escalating in the recent past (Sub-Committee of Cabinet on Hunting Ban 2018). Other predators such as lions, hyenas, leopards, and crocodiles have also caused damage to livestock, increasing the human–wildlife conflict problem in Botswana.

Negative perceptions towards wildlife conservation

Perceptions of local communities towards wildlife conservation have changed since the hunting ban, with the communities becoming hostile and negative towards wildlife, as illustrated by a study at Kumaga (*Gontse et al.* 2018). For example, a local farmer noted:

> [S]ince that devil called elephant came to our land no one has ever harvested here in Kumaga … we are dying of hunger because of elephants' crop raiding; we have grown without that creature on our land [and] since it came we are always in fear and scared of walking on our own land.

A 36-year-old woman at Kumaga commented: 'How can I like something that is not created by God? God cannot create something of that kind. Elephant was made by Satan'. At Gudigwa, an old lady remarked: 'we plough, elephants harvest'. These negative sentiments by local farmers and communities in areas affected by elephant damage put conservation efforts in Botswana at risk.

Loss of human lives

The increase and spread of elephants, predators, and other wild animals into human settlement areas, crop fields, and livestock areas have resulted in human deaths. Elephants are reported to have killed thirty-four people in Botswana between 2009 and 2018, with fourteen deaths and many serious injuries recorded since February 2018. Local communities in these areas have therefore called upon the government to remove wildlife from their settlements.

Increased wildlife poaching

Proposals to reintroduce hunting in Botswana had met with resistance from animal rights groups from Western countries, arguing that hunting would escalate poaching incidents in the country. Poaching of wildlife in Botswana is a challenge to conservation. For example, between 2019 and 2020, over fifty rhinos were poached and killed in the Okavango Delta (DWNP, 2020). Poaching is carried out by international syndicates in collaboration with certain citizens. The negative attitudes on the part of rural communities towards wildlife conservation have laid the foundation for poaching and indiscriminate wildlife killings (e.g. through poisoning). Better put, lack of benefits from wildlife has resulted in increased incidents of poaching in the Okavango region as well as Chobe and Boteti. For instance, recorded poaching incidents in Okavango region increased from 309 in 2012 to 323 in 2014. It is probable that 4,000 wild animals are being harvested illegally each year in the Okavango region, and that 620,000 kg of bushmeat is harvested annually from the Delta (Rogan *et al.* 2017). Since poaching poses a threat to Botswana's wildlife conservation, there is need to develop a long-lasting strategy that will mitigate against it. The anti-poaching strategy should be owned and implemented by all the stakeholders.

While examining human–wildlife conflict in the Okavango Delta, it is important to note that a number of different stakeholders became involved in the commodification of wildlife resources, with various perspectives (Mbaiwa 1999, 2005). Clearly the Delta contains natural resources of interest to a variety of groups, and with the livelihoods of its communities highly dependent on wildlife resources (Mbaiwa 1999, 2005). Mbaiwa further notes that traditional pastoralist and agro-pastoralist communities consider as their birthright the availability of an integral part of their territory for agricultural development. That is, they see the value of national parks and game reserves in terms of settlement and agriculture – both arable and pastoralist. Private sector interest groups (including the Batswana political and economic elites), together with the Government of Botswana, regard these wildlife resources as a potential source of wealth-creation through hunting and tourism (Mbaiwa 1999, 2005). Mbaiwa adds that conservationists value the game parks and reserves for their biodiversity and aesthetics, and these should therefore be conserved. Thus the different stakeholders have different images of the Delta, and a variety of perspectives on the natural resources present – hence the resource conflicts.

The commodification of wildlife resources in the Okavango has become a topic of dispute between Global North and South, particularly for pro- and anti-hunting groups (Mbaiwa 2018). The latter, mostly residing in the Global North, see the utilisation of natural resources in protected areas from a Western perspective, with ideas of protected-area management that can often effectively mean *non-utilisation*, to remain 'an untouched and untouchable wilderness' (Adams & McShane 1992: 239). This reflects ignorance of the historical relationships between people and their habitats, and of the roles played by local people in maintaining biodiversity, and results in antagonism between people living in wildlife areas and the supposedly 'conventional' methods of conservation (Mbaiwa 2018). The commodification of wildlife resources in the Delta has not only resulted in photographic and trophy-hunting tourism, but has also led to the emergence of resource conflicts between the different stakeholders, including local communities (especially agro-pastoralists), the government of Botswana, and the proponents of photographic and trophy-hunting tourism – as well as the international community.

Conclusion

In Botswana, wildlife resources were not commodified in the pre-colonial period. However, during the colonial period, the use of wildlife changed. That is, the arrival of Europeans and the introduction of European trade in the 1850s and the subsequent colonisation of Botswana by the British from 1885 resulted in the commodification of wildlife resources in the country (Mbaiwa 2002). The commodification of wildlife resources led to the overharvesting of wildlife species since the trade was driven by profit-seeking without any consideration for the ecological consequences. The European trade expansion in Botswana is noted for having had tremendous effects on wildlife populations not only in the Okavango but the whole of Botswana (Tlou 1985; Mbaiwa 2005). To minimise the overharvesting of wildlife resources, the British colonial Government of Botswana (1885–1966) centralised wildlife resources and established protected areas. After independence from the British in 1966, Botswana continued with the creation of national parks and game reserves as wildlife sanctuaries where wildlife-based tourism activities can be undertaken.

The post-colonial government of Botswana passed the Wildlife Conservation Policy of 1986 and the Tourism Policy of 1990. These two policies are accredited for the introduction and expansion of wildlife-based tourism in Botswana. These policies facilitated the division of the Okavango Delta into

WMAs and CHAs, which are concession areas leased to tourism companies for photographic tourism and trophy hunting; this has further commodified wildlife resources in Botswana. The growth of international tourism in the Okavango Delta has also created a window of opportunity to further commodify wildlife resources in the country. Wildlife is valued as a tourist attraction. The commodification of wildlife resources in the Okavango Delta for the tourism market is perceived by government to be promoting conservation, economic development, and improved livelihoods of rural communities in the wetland.

Bibliography

Adams, J. S. & McShane, T. O. (1992). *The Myth of Wild Africa: Conservation without Illusion* (New York: W.W. Norton).

Arntzen, J. (1989). 'Sustainable development in Botswana', in: J. Heasselberg (ed.), *Botswana*, report from a seminar (Oslo: Center for Development Studies, University of Oslo), 55–68.

Ateljevic, I. & Doorne, S. (2003). 'Culture, economy and tourism commodities: Social relations of production and consumption', *Tourist Studies*, 3(2), 123–141.

Belicia, T. & Islam, M. (2018). 'Towards a decommodified wildlife tourism: Why market environmentalism is not enough for conservation', *Societies*, 59(8), 2–15.

Bernatek-Jakiel A. & Jakiel, M. (2013). 'Landscape perception and its implications in tourism', in: N. Kozak & M. Kozak (eds), *Tourism Research: An Interdisciplinary Perspective* (Newcastle upon Tyne: Cambridge Scholars Publishing), 95–107.

Blanke, J. & Chiesa, T. (eds) (2013). 'The travel & tourism competitiveness report 2013: Reducing barriers to economic growth and job creation' (Geneva: World Economic Forum). Available at: www3.weforum.org/docs/WEF_TT_Competitiveness_Report_2013.pdf [Accessed 24 February 2022].

Bolaane, M. (2005). 'Chiefs, hunters and adventurers: The foundation of the Okavango/Moremi National Park, Botswana', *Journal of Historical Geography*, 31(2), 241–259.

Britton, S. G. (1982). 'The Political economy of tourism in the third world', *Annals of Tourism Research*, 9(3), 331–358.

Buckley, R. (1994). 'Research notes and reports', *Annals of Tourism Research*, 21(3), 661–669.

Campbell, A. C. (1995). 'Utilisation of wildlife in Botswana from earliest times to AD 900', in: K. Leggett (ed.), *The Present Status of Wildlife and its Future in Botswana*, Seminar/Workshop, 7–8 November (Gaborone; Kasane: Kalahari Conservation Society and Chobe Wildlife Trust), 45–67.

Castree, N. (2003). 'Commodifying what nature?' *Progress in Human Geography: An International Review of Geographical Work in the Social Sciences and Humanities*, 27(3), 273–297.

Ceballos-Lascurain, H. (1996). *Tourism, Ecotourism, and Protected Areas: The*

State of Nature-Based Tourism around the World and Guidelines for its Development (Cambridge: IUCN).

Central Statistics Office, Botswana (2008). 'Botswana census-based poverty map: District and sub-district level results' (Gaborone: Ministry of Finance and Development Planning). Available at: www.statsbots.org.bw/sites/default/files/publications/Poverty%20Map%202008.pdf [Accessed 24 February 2022].

Chase, M. J. (2011). 'Dry season fixed-wing aerial survey of elephants and wildlife in Northern Botswana' (Kasane: Elephants Without Borders). Available at: https://library.wur.nl/ojs/index.php/Botswana_documents/article/view/15986 [Accessed 24 February 2022].

Chase, M. J., Schlossberg, S., Griffin, C. R., Bouché, P. J. C., Djene, S. W. *et al.* (2016). 'Continent-wide survey reveals massive decline in African savannah elephants' *PeerJ*, 4, e2354.

Chenje, M. & Johnson, P. (1994). *Status of the Environment in Southern Africa* (Johannesburg: Penrose Press).

Child, B. (2019). *Sustainable Governance of Wildlife and Community-Based Natural Resource Management: From Economic Principles to Practical Governance* (New York: Routledge).

Cohen, E. (1988). 'Authenticity and commoditization in tourism', *Annals of Tourism Research*, 15, 371–386.

Cohen, E. (1989). '"Primitive and remote": Hill tribe trekking in Thailand', *Annals of Tourism Research*, 16(1), 30–61.

Cousins, J. A., Evans, J., & Saddler, J. (2009). 'Selling conservation? Scientific legitimacy and the commodification of conservation tourism', *Ecology and Society*, 14(1), 32.

Darkoh, M. B. K. (1996). 'Towards an adaptive and community-based approach to management of natural resources in drylands in sub-Saharan Africa', in: A. Hjort-af-Ornas (ed.), *Approaching Nature from Local Communities: Security Perceived and Achieved* (Motala: Motala Grafiska), 73–99.

Department of Tourism, Botswana (2018). 'Updating the tourism satellite account for Botswana: Tourism satellite account 2016'. Research and Statistics Division (RSD) of the Department of Tourism (DOT), BOB, HATAB & UNWTO (Gaborone: Research and Statistics Division). Available at: https://lccn.loc.gov/2018338345 [Accessed 12 January 2023].

Dixon, C. & Heffernam, M. (1991). *Colonialism and Development in the Contemporary World* (London: Mansell).

Drakakis-Smith, D., & Willams, S. (1983). *Internal Colonialism: Essays Around a Theme* (Edinburgh: Developing Areas Research Group, Institute of British Geographers).

Douglas, N., Douglas, N.,, & Derret, R. (eds) (2001). *Special Interest Tourism* (Melbourne: Wiley).

DWNP – Department of Wildlife and National Parks (2013). 'Department of Wildlife and National Parks Aerial Survey Report of 2013' (Gaborone: DWNP).

Ecosurv (2012). 'Strategic environmental assessment for the Okavango Delta Ramsar Site (ODRS)', unpublished report (Maun: Ecosurv).

GISPlan (2013). 'Management Plan for NG/32, Okavango Delta' (Maun: Kopano Mokoro Community Conservation Trust).

Gontse, K., Mbaiwa, J. E., & Thakadu, O. T. (2018). 'Effects of wildlife crop raiding on the livelihoods of arable farmers in Khumaga, Boteti sub-district, Botswana', *Development Southern Africa*, 35(6), 791–802.

Gotham K. F. (2002). 'Marketing Mardi Gras: Commodification, spectacle and the political economy of tourism in New Orleans', *Urban Studies*, 39, 1735–1756.

Gumbricht, T., McCarthy, J., & McCarthy, T. (2002). 'Channels, wetlands and islands in the Okavango Delta, Botswana, and their relation to hydrological and sedimentological processes', *Earth Surface Processes and Landforms*, 29(1), 15–29.

Hambira, W. L., Stone, L. S., & Pagiwa, V. (2021). 'Botswana nature-based tourism and COVID-19: Transformational implications for the future', *Development Southern Africa*, 39(1), 51–67.

Hassan, S. (2000). 'Determinants of market competitiveness in an environmentally sustainable tourism industry', *Journal of Travel Research*, 38, 239–245.

Heynen, N. & Robbins, P. (2005). 'The neoliberalization of nature: Governance, privatization, enclosure and valuation', *Capitalism Nature Socialism*, 16(1), 5–8.

Jibajiba, P. (2018). 'Crop-Raiding and Socio-Economic Mitigation Measures in the Communities of Parakarungu and Mabele in the Chobe District, Botswana'. Unpublished M.Phil. Dissertation, Okavango Research Institute, University of Botswana.

Kgathi, D. L., Bendsen, H., Blaikie, P., Mbaiwa, J., Ngwenya, B. N., & Wilk, J. (2004). 'Rural livelihoods, indigenous knowledge systems, and political economy of access to natural resources in the Okavango Delta, Botswana' (Maun: University of Botswana).

Kolding, J. (1996). 'Feasibility Study and Appraisal of Fish Stock Management Plan in Okavango' (Bergen: Department of Fisheries and Marine Biology, University of Bergen).

Lenao, M. (2009). 'The impact of cultural tourism on the authenticity of traditional baskets in the Okavango Delta: The case of Gumare and Etsha 6 villages'. Unpublished Master's thesis, University of Botswana.

Lenao, M. (2015). 'Challenges facing community-based cultural tourism development at Lekhubu Island, Botswana: A comparative analysis', *Current Issues in Tourism*, 18(6), 579–594.

Lenao, M. & Saarinen, J. (2015). 'Integrated rural tourism as a tool for community tourism development: Exploring culture and heritage projects in the North-East District of Botswana', *South African Geographical Journal*, 97(2), 203–216.

MacCannell, D. (1973). 'Staged Authenticity: Arrangements of Social Space in Tourist Settings', *American Journal of Sociology*, 79, 589–603.

Manwa, H. A. (2007). 'Is Zimbabwe ready to venture into the cultural tourism market?' *Development Southern Africa*, 24, 465–474.

Mbaiwa, J. E. (2002). 'The sustainable use of wildlife resources among the Basarwa of Khwai and Mababe in Ngamiland District, Botswana: The past and present perspectives', *Botswana Journal of African Studies*, 16(2), 110–122.

Mbaiwa, J. E. (2003). 'The socio-economic and environmental impacts of tourism in the Okavango Delta, northwestern Botswana', *Journal of Arid Environments*, 54(2), 447–468.

Mbaiwa, J. E. (2005). 'Enclave tourism and its socio-economic impacts in the Okavango Delta, Botswana', *Tourism Management*, 26(2), 157–172.

Mbaiwa, J. E. (2011a). 'Cultural commodification and tourism: The Goo-Moremi community, central Botswana', *Tijdschrift voor Economische en Sociale Geografie*, 102(3), 290–301.

Mbaiwa, J. E. (2011b). 'CBNRM in Botswana: Status Report of 2010' (Maun: Okavango Research Institute).

Mbaiwa, J. E. (2013). 'CBNRM status report of 2012/2013' (Gaborone: Kalahari Conservation Society).

Mbaiwa, J. E. (2018). 'Effects of the safari hunting tourism ban on rural livelihoods and wildlife conservation in northern Botswana', *South African Geographical Journal*, 100(1), 41–61.

Mbaiwa, J. E. and Darkoh, M. B. K. (2008). 'The socio-economic and environmental effects of the implementation of the tourism policy of 1990 in the Okavango Delta, Botswana'. *Botswana Notes and Records: Tourism as a Sustainable Development Factor*, 39, 138–155.

Mbaiwa, J. E. & Hambira, W. L. (2020). 'Enclaves and shadow state tourism in the Okavango Delta, Botswana', *South African Geographical Journal*, 102(1), 1–21.

Mbaiwa, J. E. & Hambira, W. L. (2021). Can the subaltern speak? Contradictions in trophy hunting and wildlife conservation trajectory in Botswana. *Journal of Sustainable Tourism*, DOI: 10.1080/09669582.2021.1973483.

Mbaiwa, J. E. & Sakuze, L. K. (2009). 'Cultural tourism and livelihood diversification: The case of Gcwihaba Caves and XaiXai village in the Okavango Delta, Botswana', *Journal of Tourism and Cultural Change*, 7(1), 61–75.

Mbanefo, S. & de Boerr, H. (1993). 'CAMPFIRE in Zimbabwe', in: E. Kemf (ed.), *Indigenous Peoples and Protected Areas* (London: Earthscan), 81–88.

McAfee, K. (1999). 'Selling nature to save it? Biodiversity and green developmentalism', *Environment and Planning D: Society and Space*, 17, 133–154.

McCauley, D. J. (2006). 'Selling out on nature', *Nature*, 443, 27–28.

Mogalakwe, M. & Nyamnjoh, F. (2017). 'Botswana at 50: Democratic deficit, elite corruption, and poverty in the midst of plenty', *Journal of Contemporary African Studies*, 35(1), 1–14.

Monna, S. C. (1999). 'A Framework for International Cooperation for the Management of the Okavango Delta and Basin. Ramsar COP7 DOC 205. The Ramsar Convention on Wetlands'. Available at: www.ramsar.org/document/cop7-doc-205-paper-5-international-cooperation-for-the-managment-of-the-okavango-basin-and [Accessed 25 February 2022].

Neto, F. (2003). 'A new approach to sustainable tourism development: Moving beyond environmental protection', *Natural Resources Forum*, 27(3), 212–222.

NWDC – North West District Council (2003). District Development Plan 6, 2003/4–2008/9 (Maun: North West District Council).

Oppermann, M. & Chon, K. S. (1997). *Tourism in Developing Countries* (London: International Thomson Business Press).

Plantec Africa, GISPlan, & Fameventures (2012). 'Mid-Term Review and Gap Analysis of the Okavango Delta Management Plan: Scoping and Gap Analysis Report' (Gaborone).

Petterson, D. (ed.) (2015). *Sustenance and Development of Tourism Industry* (Clanrye International: London).

Pretty, J., Adams, B., Berkes, F., De Athayde, S. F., Dudley, N., Hunn, E.,, & Pilgrim, S. (2009). 'The intersections of biological diversity and cultural diversity: Towards integration', *Conservation & Society*, 7(2), 100–112.

Rodney, W. (1972). *How Europe Underdeveloped Africa* (London: Bogle-L'Ouverture Publications).

Rogan, M., Miller, J., Lindsey, P., & Weldon McNutt, J. (2017). 'Socioeconomic drivers of illegal bushmeat hunting in a southern African savanna', *Biological Conservation*, 226, 24–31.

Rozemeijer, N. & van der Jagt, C. (2000). 'Community-based natural resource management in Botswana: How community based is community based natural resource management in Botswana?' Occasional Paper Series (Gaborone: IUCN/SNV CBNRM Support Programme).

Saarinen, J. (2006). 'Traditions of sustainability in tourism studies', *Annals of Tourism Research*, 33(4), 1121–1140.

Saarinen, J. (2014). 'Critical sustainability: Setting the limits to growth and responsibility in tourism', *Sustainability*, 6(11), 1–17.

Saarinen, J., Becker, F., Manwa, H. & Wilson, D. (2009). *Sustainable Tourism in Southern Africa: Local Communities and Natural Resources in Transition* (Bristol: Channel View Publications).

Spenceley, A. (ed.) (2008). *Responsible Tourism: Critical Issues for Conservation and Development* (London: Earthscan).

Spinage, C. (1991). *History and Evolution of the Fauna Conservation Laws of Botswana* (Gaborone: Botswana Society).

Statistics Botswana (2020). Tourism Statistics Annual Report 2020 (Gaborone: Statistics Botswana).

Steiner, C. J. & Reisinger, Y. (2006). 'Understanding existential authenticity', *Annals of Tourism Research*, 33(2), 299–318.

Sub-Committee of Cabinet on Hunting Ban (2018). Report of the cabinet sub committee on hunting ban social dialogue. Unpublished report, Ministry of Local Government and Rural Development, Government of Botswana.

Sunday Standard (2022). 'Botswana looks to tourism sector to "heal" the economy'. 17 May. Available at www.sundaystandard.info/botswana-looks-to-tourism-sector-to-heal-the-economy (Accessed 16 January 2023).

Thakadu, O. T. (1997). 'Indigenous wildlife knowledge systems and their role in facilitating community-based wildlife management projects in Botswana', Unpublished M.Sc. Thesis, Pietermaritzburg: School of Environment and Development, University of Natal.

Timothy, D. J. & Boyd, S. W. (2003). *Heritage Tourism* (Harlow: Prentice Hall).

Tlou, T. (1985). *History of Ngamiland: 1750–1906: The Formation of an African State* (Gaborone: Macmillan).

Turner, R. & Sears, Z. (2013). 'Travel & tourism as a driver of employment growth', in: J. Banke & T. Chiesa (eds), *The Travel & Tourism Competitiveness Report 2013* (Geneva: World Economic Forum), 63–70. Available at: www3.weforum.org/docs/WEF_TT_Competitiveness_Report_2013.pdf [Accessed 25 February 2022].

Twyman, C. (2000). 'Participatory conservation? Community-based natural resource management in Botswana', *The Geographical Journal*, 166(4), 323–335.

UNESCO (2003). Convention for the Safeguarding of the Intangible Cultural Heritage. Sixth session of the Intergovernmental Committee for the Safeguarding of the Intangible Cultural Heritage (Bali: UNESCO). Available at: https://ich.unesco.org/en/convention [Accessed 25 February 2022].

Watson, G. L. & Kopachevsky, J. P. (1994). 'Interpretations of tourism as commodity', *Annals of Tourism Research*, 21(3), 643–660.

White, R. (1995). 'Licensing, utilisation and public attitudes to wildlife', in: K. Leggett (ed.), *The Present Status of Wildlife and its Future in Botswana*, Seminar/Workshop, 7–8 November (Gaborone; Kasane: Kalahari Conservation Society and Chobe Wildlife Trust), 79–87. Available at: https://agris.fao.org/agris-search/search.do?recordID=XF2015015916 [Accessed 25 February 2022].

WTO – World Trade Organization (2001). 'Ministerial Conference Fourth Session', 9–14 November (Doha: WTO). Available at: www.wto.org/english/thewto_e/minist_e/min01_e/min01_e.htm [Accessed 25 February 2022].

WTO – World Trade Organization (2015). 'World Trade Report 2015: Speeding up trade: benefits and challenges of implementing the WTO Trade Facilitation Agreement' (Geneva: WTO). Available at: www.wto.org/english/res_e/booksp_e/world_trade_report15_e.pdf [Accessed 25 February 2022].

17

Justice Dilemmas in Conservation Conflicts in Uganda[1]

Introduction

In 2018, the shocking news that on average, the size of vertebrate animal populations worldwide declined by 60% between 1970 and 2014 (WWF 2018: 7) triggered a renewed debate on how to counteract the tremendous loss of biodiversity and degradation of ecosystems. Scientists have come up with a 'Global Deal for Nature' – a strategy for protecting biodiversity that envisages increasing the world's protected areas so that they cover at least 30% of lands and oceans by 2030 and 50% by 2050 (Dinerstein *et al.* 2019: 4). This 'new deal', in turn, has sparked an outcry amongst human and indigenous people's rights activists (Corry 2020) who have long lamented the displacement of local people in the name of conservation – and the violations of their rights, their loss of homes, sacred sites, livelihoods, culture, and impoverishment (Dowie 2009; Survival International 2015). It is estimated that by the mid-2000s, tens of millions of people worldwide, including up to 14 million in Africa, were displaced because of conservation (Agrawal & Redford 2009: 4). Criticism is directed against the mainstream 'fortress' approach to conservation, with protected areas managed by government agencies. This approach implies the protection of nature by keeping out local people, who

[1] The chapter is based on ethnographic field research in the border area of Murchison Falls National Park (2013–2017), recent follow-up visits to the field sites and document analysis. Research was carried out as part of the collaborative project 'Governing Transition in Northern Uganda: Trust and Land' (2013–2017) between the Institute of Peace and Strategic Studies, Gulu University, the Department of Culture and Society, Aarhus University, and the Department of Anthropology, the University of Copenhagen, with financial support from the Consultative Research Committee for Development Research in Denmark. The Uganda National Council for Science and Technology granted the research permission.

are accused of using natural resources in irrational and destructive ways, thus causing biodiversity loss and environmental degradation (Doolittle 2007). However, since the 1990s, 'new conservation' ideas that add the goals of poverty alleviation and economic development to the conservation agenda and claim people's participation as essential to any conservation effort have gained some prominence. Nevertheless, the protectionist top-down approach to conservation has remained dominant worldwide (UNEP-WCMC, IUCN & NGS 2018: 31–32).

Disagreements and battles between conservationists and local people have not ended. A case in point looked at in this chapter is Uganda, one of the globe's most biodiverse countries, where conservation conflicts include human–wildlife conflicts, that is direct conflicts between humans and wildlife, e.g. crop raiding by hungry elephants, poaching and illegal trade with wildlife products; and human-human conflicts over wildlife management and conservation goals, processes, and procedures. The arena in which these conflicts are played out comprises protected areas such as national parks or game reserves – managed by the state-run Uganda Wildlife Authority (UWA) – regarded as crucial for the survival of endangered species and for driving forward the country's economic development by selling the 'wilderness' to tourists; and adjacent areas inhabited by people who lament the negative repercussions of 'fortress conservation', ranging from loss of livelihoods to conservation-induced displacement.

The chapter looks at conservation and the commodification of the 'wild' through a justice lens. By reviewing literature on Uganda's protected areas, wildlife conservation and conservation conflicts, it highlights conservationists' and local people's ways of imagining and enacting relations between humans, wildlife, and land, and underlying notions of 'owning', 'using', and 'belonging'. This is followed by presenting the findings from long-term ethnographic field research in the area of Murchison Falls National Park, with a particular focus on Uganda's recent 'community conservation' approach in form of tourism revenue sharing to make local people benefit from the commodification of wildlife. The findings are then discussed against the background of the theoretical framework of conservation justice, which endeavours to reconcile social justice and ecological justice. The chapter concludes with a look at how conservation outcomes that are also socially just can be achieved.

Wildlife conservation in Uganda

Uganda, which ranks among the top ten countries with the greatest biodiversity worldwide (NEMA 2016), is known for its wildlife in ten national parks and numerous wildlife reserves (UWA 2020). These areas have been protected for their biodiversity, spectacular landscapes and importance as natural heritage, as noted in the Uganda Wildlife Act (Republic of Uganda 2019: Interpretations and Sections 26, 27). The creation of such protected areas – the predominant strategy for the conservation of wildlife species in Uganda and worldwide – aims to reduce human presence and influence in wildlife habitats as much as possible. Protected areas also play an important role in tourism, which is Uganda's fastest growing economic sector. The habitats of iconic wildlife species such as mountain gorillas, chimpanzees, elephants, lions, leopards, Rothschild giraffes, and other species attract foreign visitors who bring money which, in turn, is invested in conservation and tourism (UWA 2020). The numbers of tourists visiting Uganda steadily increased from 850,000 in 2008 to more than 1.4 million in 2017. In 2017, the sector accounted for 7.3% of the gross domestic product (GDP), foreign exchange earnings worth US$1.45 billion and more than 600,000 jobs (MTWA 2018a: 1–2, 11–14, 19–20). In 2018, the number of tourists amounted to 1,800,000 visitors and the Uganda Tourism Board expected one more million tourists in 2019 (Lyatuu 2019).

Uganda's top-down approach to wildlife conservation vests ownership of wildlife in the government 'on behalf of, and for the benefit of, the people of Uganda' (Republic of Uganda 2019, Section 3). National laws regulating wildlife conservation include the Ugandan Constitution of 1995 and more recent legislation such as the Uganda National Land Policy of 2013, the new National Environment Act of 2019 and the new Uganda Wildlife Act of 2019. In 1991, Uganda joined the Convention on International Trade in Endangered Species of Wild Fauna and Flora (CITES), and signed and ratified the Convention on Biological Diversity (CBD) – in 1992 and 1993 respectively. The Uganda Wildlife Authority (UWA), a government agency which was established in 1996 under the Ministry of Tourism, Wildlife and Antiquities, is responsible for the protection and sustainable development of wildlife populations within and outside protected areas. Wildlife laws and wildlife trade conventions are enforced by militarily trained game rangers who vigorously pursue poachers, be they highly organised criminal poachers or subsistence hunters. The Authority collaborates with the police, army, the International Criminal Police Organization (INTERPOL), and local govern-ments, and has started to use sophisticated equipment such as helicopters and drones to prevent and counteract wildlife crimes (UWA 2020).

Uganda's model of state-controlled and state-managed conservation is being justified with reference to the high rate of biodiversity loss. Between 1975 and 1995, the country lost 50% of its overall biodiversity value (Pomeroy *et al.* 2017: 1). In 2004, the rate of biodiversity loss was calculated to be 10–12% per decade or 1% per annum (NEMA 2016: 34). In 2008, 159 species of plants and animals in Uganda were listed in the International Union for the Conservation of Nature and Natural Resources (IUCN) Red List of species at high risk of global extinction (NEMA 2016: 2). Ten years later, the number had increased to 537 (MTWA 2018b: 7).

At the time of the establishment of the UWA in 1996, national parks and game reserves had been in extremely poor condition. Protected areas had been massively encroached, wildlife populations had been reduced to critically low levels and several species such as the oryx, Lord Derby eland and bongo antelopes, or the black and the white rhino had become extinct (UWA 2018: 5). In the 1970s, Idi Amin's soldiers had slaughtered thousands of elephants with impunity in order to obtain meat and ivory. After Idi Amin's fall, unrestrained poaching continued until the mid-1980s (UWA 2018: 4–6). It was also extremely difficult to enforce conservation laws during the twenty-year war between the Lord's Resistance Army (LRA) and the Ugandan government in northern Uganda (1986–2006). In the last two decades, however, protected areas have been rehabilitated, wildlife populations have started to recover and some species such as buffaloes, zebras, elephants, and giraffes have even shown a remarkable increase as indicated by survey data on the status of wildlife populations in national parks and wildlife reserves collected in the mid-1990s and 2015–17 (see UWA 2018: 15, Table 1). This positive development has been attributed to improved wildlife conservation measures and continued peace and stability after decades of civil war.

The Wildlife Authority stresses that conservation efforts are still being undermined by illegal activities in protected areas such as encroachment and poaching for game meat, killing of elephants for ivory, and pangolins for their scales, or pastoralists' poisoning of lions, leopards, or hyenas in revenge for the predators' killing of their livestock (Harrison *et al.* 2015; UWA 2020). Uganda has also become one of the major wildlife trafficking routes for ivory and other wildlife products from the Democratic Republic of the Congo, West Africa and parts of South Africa (WCS n.d.).

Moreover, an estimated 50% of Uganda's wildlife resources are found outside designated protected areas (NEMA 2016: 5). Therefore, the protection and management of wildlife on private and community land and sustainable exploitation of wildlife resources for the benefits of the people have become an urgent concern (Republic of Uganda 2019: Sections 26, 27).

Conservation conflicts

Conservation successes in Uganda have gone hand in hand with forceful evictions of local people from their land, who were never compensated for their losses. A striking example are the Batwa (often derogatorily referred to as 'pygmies') with a population of 6,200 (UBOS 2016: 71), one of the most marginalised indigenous minority groups in Uganda. In the early 1990s, they were expelled from their ancestral land by the government to save the mountain gorillas from extinction and make way for Bwindi Impenetrable Forest National Park, Maghinga Gorilla National Park, and Semuliki National Park. Formerly living as hunter-gatherers in the forests, they have become landless squatters living in dire poverty at the fringes of national parks and nearby towns (MRG 2020). Another example are the Benet with a population of 9,080, who were evicted from Mount Elgon forest in 1983 in order to create Mount Elgon National Park and suffered from subsequent expulsions by UWA between 1990 and 2004 (MRG 2014). A third case is Apaa, a remote village in northern Uganda, supposedly located in East Madi Wildlife Reserve and scene of continuous violent evictions of residents by UWA and the national army that have cost many lives (Lenhart 2013; Otto 2018). In all these and many other cases, the affected people and their supporters from indigenous people rights groups and human rights groups have been struggling with legal means to have their rights recognised, but to no avail so far.

Besides those related to forceful evictions of people from land gazetted as protected areas, conservation conflicts also take the form of human–wildlife conflicts, which occur when the needs of wildlife encroach on the needs of human populations and vice versa. In the course of the last decade, these conflicts have intensified (UWA 2018: 49). People living in the vicinity of national parks and wildlife reserves have to struggle with elephants and other wildlife in search of food which regularly leave the protected areas, causing crop damage, and destroying houses, huts, and granaries. They also attack, injure and kill humans. UWA has promoted certain measures to deter wild animals and control animal movements, which have proven to be effective to some extent but could not solve the problem. These methods include firing warning shots by rangers and community actions such as beating tins and drums or blowing whistles and vuvuzelas; planting chilli or burning a mixture of chilli and manure or dung; erecting beehive fences; and lighting fires or using solar lights at night (Lenhart 2017). Some of these actions are carried out by volunteers from the communities who have been trained as Community Wildlife Scouts by UWA. Recently, UWA has embarked on digging trenches in human–wildlife conflict hotspots around Murchison Falls National Park and Queen Elizabeth National Park and set up some electric fences. In addition to these measures, under the Revenue Sharing Scheme (UWA 2000, 2011), UWA annually shares 20% of park entrance fees with communities neighbouring national parks, who use the money for building schools and other charitable purposes (UWA 2018: 49–52, 56; Lenhart 2017). For example, in 2019, UWA handed over 4.189 billion Uganda Shillings (approximately US$1.2 million) to the leaders of six districts adjacent to Murchison Falls Conservation Area, Uganda's largest protected area which includes Murchison Falls National Park and two wildlife reserves (UWA 2020). Project decisions are ideally taken by community representatives who form Parish Development and Parish Procurement Committees tasked to plan and manage their respective community's share of the money. However, these projects have to be approved by UWA and local governments, and the money is channelled through district and sub-county accounts (UWA 2011). Until recently, there was no law in Uganda that provided for compensation for losses suffered due to conservation conflicts. The New Wildlife Act of 2019 (Sections 82, 83, 84), however, caters for this, but effective and efficient implementation and monitoring still remain to be seen. Assessing damages might be a difficult task for the newly founded Wildlife Compensation Verification Committees that have to confirm claims and, if approved, to compensate victims according to the market rates (Ntalumbwa 2019).

The main cause of conservation conflicts is the population development of humans and wildlife and the resulting competition for land and resources. Uganda has one of the fastest growing populations worldwide, which had increased from 9.5 million in 1969 to nearly 42 million in mid-2020, with an average annual population growth of 3.2% (UBOS 2019: 16, 2020). The rapid growth is accompanied by a high demand for land for settlement and agricultural use. The World Bank observed a recent increase in Ugandan households living in poverty, which amounted to 27% in 2016/17, due to lack of employment opportunities. This leaves more than 70% of Ugandans engaged in agriculture, mainly on a subsistence basis (WB 2020). Rural communities who live next to protected areas have rapidly expanded settlements and fields into wildlife areas and blocked wildlife corridors, and thus contributed to habitat fragmentation, degradation, and loss (UWA 2018: 45–46, 49). This in turn has caused wildlife to leave protected areas in search of food.

Pressure on wildlife habitats causing animal movements out of protected areas and thus enhancing human–wildlife conflicts, however, are not only a consequence of high population growth and poverty levels of the predominantly rural population that depends on natural resources for livelihood security. Other factors are expansion of commercial agriculture and extractive industries such as mining, oil, and gas exploration into protected areas, particularly in the Albertine Rift, accompanied by infrastructural support for commercial and industrial development, e.g. construction of new roads through protected areas for transportation of heavy equipment for oil exploitation and transportation (Kamoga 2019; NEMA 2016). A striking example is Murchison Falls National Park which has become a target for oil exploration, after large onshore oil and gas finds were discovered within the Albertine Rift Valley from 2006 onwards. Although Uganda's first oil exports had been expected in the early 2020s (Patey 2015), the country had not exported a single barrel of oil by the end of 2022. Roads to facilitate transportation of construction materials and heavy machinery by the oil companies will pass through Budongo Forest and Murchison Falls National Park (Kamoga 2019). Seismic exploration and test drilling of oil wells on pads have already shown negative impacts on the natural environment and wildlife. In the oil exploration sites, the original vegetation cover has been degraded and altered, which in turn affected the distribution of wild animals whose population mean has become significantly lower than in undisturbed sites within the National Park, due to reactions such as avoidance, migration, and some cases of death (Kamara *et al.* 2019).

Murchison Falls National Park and surroundings as an arena of conservation conflicts

In the following, conservation conflicts in Uganda are illustrated by the example of Murchison Falls National Park in northern Uganda and a focus on human–wildlife interactions. The account is based on findings of ethnographic field research in Purongo Sub-county in Nwoya District bordering the park (2013–2017) and recent follow-up visits using the methods of participant observation, narrative and semi-structured interviews, and participatory procedures.

Murchison Falls Conservation Area

Murchison Falls National Park is the largest of the country's ten national parks, covering an area of 3,840 km². To the south and east the park is bordered by Bugungu Wildlife Reserve (501 km²), Karuma Wildlife Reserve (820 km²), and Budongo Forest Reserve (825 km²). The wildlife reserves act as buffer zones to the park and together with the park form the Murchison Falls Conservation Area managed by UWA, whereas the Budongo Forest Reserve is managed by the National Forestry Authority (NFA). These contiguous nature reserves, with a total area of almost 6,000 km², have been classified by the International Union for the Conservation of Nature and Natural Resources (IUCN) as Protected Areas in Categories I–IV, or intact ecosystems with significant species, species groups, and biotic communities and therefore highly worthy of protection, which however should be accessible to the public in defined and spatially limited sections in order to offer visitors an unique experience of nature and promote the understanding of natural processes (see Dudley *et al.* 2008/2013: 7–24).

The border

At the time of field work, Purongo Sub-county was divided into five parishes – Pabit, Pawat Omeru, Patira, Paromo, Latoro – four of them bordering Murchison Falls National Park. Later on, Latoro became a new sub-county.

Purongo Trading Centre, where the Sub-county headquarters are located, is 7 kilometres away from the border of Murchison Falls National Park

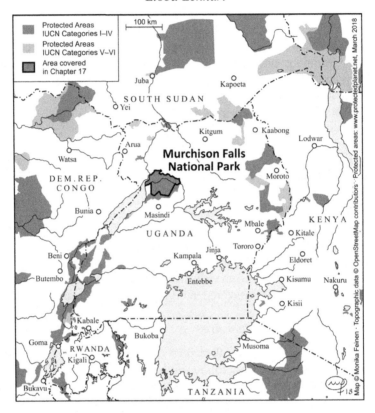

Map 17.1 Nature and wildlife conservation areas in Uganda and neighbouring countries (Source: Open StreetMap contributors; Cartography: M. Feinen).

and 72 kilometres away from 'total relaxation in the wilderness,' as was promised in 2015 on a billboard at the turnoff to the park's Wangkwar Gate advertising Chobe Safari Lodge, a five-star hotel inside the park. Of course, 'total relaxation in the wilderness' was an option for tourists, and not for people who had returned only a few years ago from the Internally Displaced People's camps after the twenty-year war between the LRA and the Ugandan government had ended, many of them still living below the poverty line. In the view of many, the park border demarcated 'the unknown land we have never visited', which 'is owned by UWA, benefits the needs of wild animals, and serves the state as source of revenue', as one of the research participants put it. They experienced the park as 'a source of evil'. Elephants and other wild animals frequently crossed the border and destroyed people's crops, endangering their livelihoods to an extent that I could witness in December 2014 during a transect walk along the border with people from Pabit Parish and the UWA Community Conservation Ranger (cf. Lenhart & Meinert 2023).

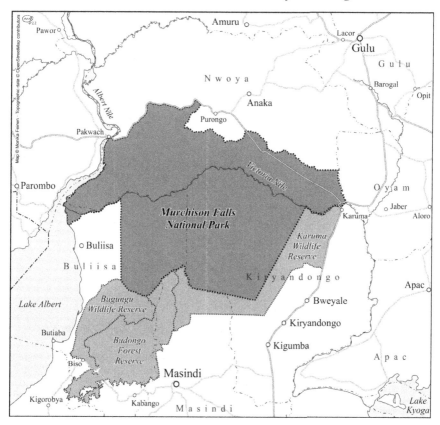

Map 17.2 Location of Purongo Sub-county, Nwoya District (Source: Open StreetMap contributors; Cartography: M. Feinen).

Wildlife had also injured and killed villagers. People who went inside the park for various reasons – including what they called hunting and UWA called poaching, but also when looking for firewood, for grass for roofing their houses, or for water and fish in a stream that marks a section of the park's boundary – had disappeared. There was much speculation that they were shot by rangers, 'their bodies pushed in the bush and eaten by wild animals'. All this has led to deep mistrust between the people and UWA rangers and a widespread resistance against wildlife conservation.

How wildlife is perceived

The research participants from Purongo, the majority being farmers highly affected by human–wildlife conflict, clearly identified elephants as the greatest villains among wildlife, together with 'those who talk on their behalf',

Figure 17.1 Hunter or poacher? A Uganda Wildlife Authority ranger cautions an old man who attempted to place a trap for catching antelopes, confiscating the man's *panga* (machete), spear, and snares (Photo: Author, 2014).

namely UWA wardens and rangers. The word 'elephant' was also used as a generic term to represent all wildlife involved in the destruction of crops, properties, and lives of people. They frequently compared elephants with 'the rebels', and human–wildlife conflict with the war between the LRA and the Government of Uganda that had ravaged northern Uganda for twenty years. For instance, during a group discussion in October 2013, residents of Latoro Parish put it like this: 'After Kony [LRA leader] has gone, we are now suffering from elephants'. And: 'Efforts [are needed] to fight the elephants as they [government] fought Kony'. Their comparison of elephants with 'the rebels' contrasted sharply with the symbolic value attached to the elephant, the traditional emblem of their ethnic group, the Acholi, who liken themselves to elephants in character and strength – being big, strong, brave warriors and excellent fighters. Elephants also play a role in Acholi mythology and are believed to have guided the migration of the Acholi (Luo) people from Sudan, who followed elephant tracks.

When asked about their knowledge of wildlife during a free listing and ranking exercise in 2015, the respondents distinguished twenty-five different

Figure 17.2 Billboard promoting the Uganda Wildlife Act of 2019, which provides for severe penalties including life imprisonment for crimes against critically endangered species (Photo: Author, 2020).

wildlife species and were able to describe their physical appearance and behaviours in much detail. The elephants topped the list. When asked 'what is good about the elephants?', they portrayed them as social giants living in family groups, highlighted behaviours like greetings and plays, and stressed the immense care and protection for the calves. However, they also appreciated 'their ivory and meat' and 'it's tail and skin used for making local beads and bangles'. One of the research participants recalled: 'I skinned it in the 1980s and remember that from one big elephant meat can be distributed to one hundred people'. The opposite question – what is bad? – provoked answers like 'they are wild', 'destructive to crops and lives', and 'a source of poverty'. Elephants were also accused of being 'easily annoyed', 'angry if you try to chase them from the garden', 'merciless', 'vindictive', and just ruthless: 'It has a very sensitive nose, it does not need eyes to spot people; this makes it fight, kill, and follow human beings'. One of the respondents concluded: 'There is nothing about the elephant that is good for us [the community]; it is only good for government as a source of income'.

The majority of the respondents considered UWA and government as the owners of wildlife, while a few stated that 'wildlife is God's creation' and therefore not owned by anybody. All respondents indicated that wildlife is of use to humans. The most frequent argument put forward was that wildlife provides meat for human consumption and sale. Respondents also valued the skin, fur, and bones used for ritual purposes, e.g. during divination sessions of *ajwaki* (plural of *ajwaka*, 'witchdoctor', traditional healer), and to make clothes and jewellery, which are worn during traditional dances; and they mentioned the medical benefits that can be derived from the body parts of certain species. Other respondents stressed that wildlife is a tourist attraction and source of revenue for UWA. Only one respondent expressed the opinion that wildlife is of use 'for future generations to come and see'. When asked about the relationship of wildlife and land, the majority stated that wildlife naturally belongs to the land, 'like grasses', while some distinguished the national park as wildlife's land from people's land. Concerning the question of whether wildlife has rights, some respondents mentioned the right to live and be protected in the national park by UWA. Only a few respondents stated that wildlife has the right to live and roam not only inside but also outside the park. The majority, however, denied wildlife any rights while arguing that they are 'just animals' and 'it is only government that has given them rights because they regard them more important than human beings'.

Wildlife versus people

In Purongo Sub-county, people often used the term 'wildlife' as a synonym for UWA. For example, when the UWA Community Warden had been called to the sub-county headquarters, you could hear someone say, 'wildlife is coming in the afternoon to see us'. The equation of wild animals with the conservationists was accompanied by the frequent accusation that 'UWA cares more about their animals than us'. One of the research participants put it like this: 'When animals come to our fields and destroy our crops, we are not supposed to kill them and not compensated; but when people go into the park to get firewood or medicinal herbs, or want to hunt small game, they are arrested and even killed.'

It was generally believed that wild animals and government would benefit from wildlife conservation, whereas the local people would be the ones to bear the brunt. The problem of crop raiding by wildlife that had caused food shortage, lack of money needed for paying school fees or medical bills, and even displacement of entire villages bordering the park had not been addressed. People also lamented that they felt criminalised because they were 'turned from hunters into poachers', even when hunting outside the park. One participant of a group discussion held in 2013 stressed: 'The park is our grandfathers' land and these are our grandfathers' animals. Nobody can prevent us from going there.' Other participants stated that 'we hunt elephants for our living' and 'kill and eat game because of poverty'.

The relationship between UWA and the people was tense and marked by deep mistrust. In the course of the research, I learned that there had been long phases in which UWA wardens and rangers had neither attended nor called for meetings with sub-county officials, nor been in touch with the people affected by human–wildlife conflict. I also heard about two incidents of people disappearing in the park, for which UWA rangers were blamed. As the matter was not investigated by UWA, the farmers from Purongo refused to sell food to the rangers in their area, even though they urgently needed the money.

People's strained relationship with UWA and their disappointments were also reflected in the statement of a man from one of the displaced villages with whom I talked in 2014, who lamented: 'Rangers are no use to us … they do nothing against the destruction of crops by animals coming from the park. I cannot manage to get my child to school. Nothing is done concerning our problems. We shall die of hunger, because nothing is done.' During a group discussion in 2016, a participant explained that people even feared encounters with rangers: 'When people see the uniform [UWA ranger], that's a problem. People were arrested and beaten seriously. Some were killed and then dumped in the Nile … The rangers have a very bad relationship with the community.' Another participant underscored what he considered the most important point: 'Rangers are recruited to chase poachers. They should chase away the animals instead.'

The research participants also expressed their deep feelings of being marginalised and neglected by the Ugandan government. Some recounted several attempts to discuss the issue of crop losses caused by wildlife with UWA representatives, which did not bear fruits. The traditional clan chief had even tried to reach out to parliament and to get an appointment with the president – in vain. The relevant authorities had just reiterated that the law did not cater for compensation. People had become very bitter, as can be seen from the statements during a group discussion with people who had to leave their homesteads because of disturbance by elephants. One man stated: 'We tried several times to give recommendations, but nobody is hearing us. The Government of Uganda has forgotten that we are human beings.' Another man said: 'The problem is the Parliament. They should have made a law to criminalise animals coming out of the park. They eat at will, destroy at will, but for their destruction is never paid.' An old woman stated that 'elephants are now too many' and demanded that 'they should all be killed and their tusks sold'. One participant argued that compensation payment would change the situation: 'Our parliament should be blamed, because if the animals eat our crops, the animals are not arrested and no compensation is given to us. But when we kill the animals, we are arrested and asked to pay fine. If the government would lose money in compensation, then they would be more responsible for their elephants.'

Marketing the wilderness

In 2013, in an attempt to convince the people of Purongo suffering from wildlife's crop raiding to appreciate wildlife conservation, UWA endeavoured to make the selling of wildlife in the wilderness profitable for them through a community tourism project to be realised with funding from the 20% revenue sharing of park entrance fees.

The year before, the UWA warden responsible for community conservation in the area at the time had convinced the Sub-county authorities to buy two acres of land on the way from Purongo Trading Centre to the park's Wangkwar Gate and construct two small grass-thatched buildings on it with money from UWA's Revenue Sharing Fund (RSF) as the start of a larger project that would include a museum, restaurant, and accommodation. He had also motivated the Sub-county officials to form a committee to develop project ideas, which comprised of senior community members and was headed by a retired teacher. In mid-2013, he brought on board a team of experts from Gulu University[2] to consult the stakeholders on suitable business models such as cooperative or community-based organisation, and concomitant constitution and organisational structure. They were also expected to support the conceptualisation and realisation of a museum exhibition; and to conduct business-related trainings to make the effort a functional enterprise.

In December 2013, representatives from UWA, the Sub-county and Gulu University toured the parishes of Purongo Sub-county. The concern of UWA was to raise awareness about the new Revenue Sharing Guidelines (UWA 2011)

---

[2] The author was a member of this group.

that put the responsibility for selecting projects funded through the RSF in the hands of the people by setting up Parish Development and Parish Procurement Committees tasked to plan and manage their community's share of the money. The UWA, Sub-county, and Gulu University representatives also wanted to find out whether the entitled recipients of the fund would appreciate the idea of pooling resources to finance the planned community tourism project to be run as a community-based organisation that would benefit the whole community of Purongo by providing livelihood alternatives to agriculture. They presented their vision of an Acholi Culture and Tourism Centre (ACTC) that would house a museum with souvenir shop, restaurant, campsite, and traditionally designed accommodation facilities. A permanent exhibition would focus on both Acholi culture and history, and wildlife conservation. The Centre would also offer traditional fireplace sittings and story-telling events, cultural performances such as dances, games, and sports, and guided tours to homesteads and Internally Displaced People's camps remains as well as park safaris. An elected Executive Board and several Committees would manage the Centre, and the generated income would be invested in their salaries and the employment of guards, waiters, and tour guides. Food to be served in the restaurant and craft work to be sold in the souvenir shop would be produced in Purongo Sub-county, so that local farmers and other community members would benefit as well. Youth and other interested people from Purongo working as tour guides or engaging in cultural performances would gain income from tour fees and entrance fees.

The majority of the participants in these meetings welcomed UWA's intention to decentralise 'decision making and action to the lowest levels possible' and minimise 'Revenue Sharing Fund dissipation', as called for in the new Revenue Sharing Guidelines (UWA 2011: 2), and agreed to use their parishes' shares of revenue collection for building the Acholi Culture and Tourism Centre. They were convinced that in this way misappropriation of RSF money could be prevented. During the discussions, people from all parishes had questioned the Sub-counties' spending for kickstarting the project the year before, which had included an amount of 5 million Uganda Shillings (US$1,982 in June 2012) for purchasing the land, what they found reasonable, and the extremely high amount of 75 million Uganda Shillings ($29,728) for the construction of two simple grass-thatched buildings and setting up of a fence 'that was not even seen [existent]'. During the discussions, one man lamented: '35 million [Uganda Shillings, the revenue sharing for one of the parishes – $13,873] will not reach us. Every time the Sub-county pulls a bit. When it [money] reaches the parish, only 5 million will be left.' One participant asked 'how can we exclude the councillors [from the project]?', while another participant expressed hope that 'now, they [councillors] can be excluded, because the committee [to be in charge of the project] is for the villagers'.

In the course of the following two weeks, the people from Purongo elected their representatives on the Parish Development Committees, Parish Procurement Committees and the Committee tasked with implementing the Acholi Culture and Tourism Centre (ACTC). During the constituent meeting of the ACTC Committee, the previous committee that had been appointed by the Sub-county authorities to come up with project ideas was dissolved, and the newly elected parish representatives nominated and elected their chair, vice-chair, secretary, and treasurer. Since the chair and the majority of the new ACTC Committee members were quite young and all members rather inexperienced and lacking knowledge and skills to run a project, the Sub-county leadership endeavoured to bring on board five additional members as mentors, all of them influential and well-connected local people, including the clan chief and members of the armed forces. However, the ACTC Committee members refused to accept them, 'because they were not elected'. In the following meetings, the Sub-county authorities brought other names into play. Competition for status and influence in the ACTC Committee not only marked the beginning of the project but was to continue throughout its entire duration.

In the following weeks and months, good progress was made at several planning meetings attended by members of the ACTC Committee and representatives of UWA, Purongo Sub-county and Gulu University. During the same period, the university team organised a couple of dialogue meetings to give UWA and community members the opportunity to air their grievances in relation to human–wildlife conflict, poaching, and related issues, and to look jointly for solutions.

In mid-2014, the Sub-county authorities engaged a contractor to start construction works, however, without including the ACTC Committee in decision making and implementation. The fact that the contractor, who also served as the chairperson of the Area Land Committee, was the spouse of the then Sub-county Chief was not well received by the people. During this time, the UWA Community Warden who had initiated the project and enthusiastically supported its implementation was transferred to another national park. His successor was very much determined to continue in the same spirit.

In April 2015, the new building with modern and traditional architectural elements was inaugurated by none other than the Paramount Chief of the Acholi. During their speeches, the Sub-county officials emphasised their contributions to the realisation of the project with much self-praise, while high-ranking UWA representatives expressed their hopes that the Centre would contribute to the establishment of good relations between the National Park and neighbouring communities who would now see the economic benefits that the park had for them and therefore wholeheartedly accept and support conservation. The Chairman of the ACTC Committee representing the local people appreciated the efforts of all stakeholders, but also warned against jeopardising the project through political interference. After the speeches, people entered 'their Centre' for the first time. Everybody was cheering, dancing, and singing, and the women were ululating loudly.

In the months following the official launch of the Acholi Culture and Tourism Centre, the university team and the new UWA Community Warden helped the ACTC Committee to come up with a constitution, and in late 2015 the project was registered as a community-based organisation with approval by the Sub-county Council. In the Constitution, the local people's ownership of and responsibility for the project were deliberately laid down, whereas representatives of the District and Sub-county local government, UWA and Gulu University were assigned to form the Advisory Board. During that period, it became obvious that the members of the ACTC Committee, who were farmers, lacked even basic capacities and skills in committee procedures. They had to be trained on how to take minutes of a meeting or to draw a work plan and a budget, for example. Another problem was time keeping and attendance. Meetings started usually late or were held without a quorum, not least because members had to travel from their remote villages to the Sub-county headquarters and did not receive any allowance for transport or lunch. The Sub-county leadership were 'sitting' on the money from the RSF needed for allowances, business-related trainings, and acquisition of artefacts, printing of large-format photographs and posters, and purchase of other exhibition displays. At the same time, they were complaining about the elected ACTC Committee members 'who do not know their roles and responsibilities and have to be replaced'.

In 2016, general elections were held in Uganda, and the results for Purongo Sub-county marked another turning point in the development of the project. The previous political leadership of the Sub-county were not re-elected. Instead, members of a different party took over. The new distribution of power affected the progress of the project in an unexpected way. Everything slowed down. It seemed as if the new Sub-county authorities were not interested in completing their predecessors' undertaking. The ACTC Committee was now completely sidelined. The Sub-county authorities did not invite the members to attend meetings during which the councillors and administrators discussed the progress of the project, neither did they invite the UWA Community Warden or the team from Gulu University. The Chairman of Nwoya District from the same political party, who hailed from Purongo, had entered the scene and announced the District's decision to look for an investor. For him it was apparently too difficult an undertaking to empower local people to run such a project, as he had told me during one of our conversations. Later on, crucial administrative staff such as the Sub-county Chief and the Sub-county

Community Development Officer, who had been involved in the project right from the beginning, were transferred to other sub-counties.

In 2017, the new Sub-county Chief spent much of his time and energy to revive the process of building up the Acholi Culture and Tourism Centre. He called for several meetings involving the ACTC Committee members and representatives from UWA and Gulu University, reimbursed the Committee members' expenses for reaching the Sub-county headquarters, and supported the start of the collection of items to be displayed in the museum. He also managed to have a reasonable budget for the exhibition approved by the Sub-county Council. However, the money was never released. It looked as if he had taken on an impossible lost cause, because of lack of support from Purongo Sub-county's and Nwoya District's political wings. After a few months in Purongo, he was transferred to another sub-county. The idea of handing over the project to an investor was now reiterated again and again.

In the course of the following two to three years, the hoped-for investor was obviously not found. Instead, wild fire had destroyed the two smaller buildings. The roof of one part of the bigger building had collapsed and the place was bushy. Some people used a section of the compound for growing chilli, and it was whispered that the Sub-county would now use the still intact part of the big building as a store. When the ACTC Committee members' term of office had expired, no successors were elected. Thus, UWA's concern to put the responsibility for projects funded through the Revenue Sharing Fund in the hands of the people on the ground in an effort to counteract human–wildlife conflict, improve the livelihoods of communities neighbouring protected areas, and to win their allegiance for the sake of wildlife protection was finally frustrated. During the tour through the parishes in 2013, the UWA Community Warden had eagerly tried to convince the people to engage in 'a project that can stay for long, its impact to be seen, so that people never forget what the park has given and don't destroy wildlife [anymore]'. Five years later, the project was in ruins both literally and figuratively – and the collapsed buildings will continuously remind the people of Purongo of the failure whenever they are passing by.

Conservation justice in Uganda

The literature on Uganda's protected areas, wildlife conservation, and conservation conflicts discussed in the first part of the chapter, and empirical data on conservation conflicts in the area of Murchison Falls National Park presented in the second part demonstrate the need for more justice in conservation affairs. The different values underlying wildlife conservation vis-à-vis human interest and well-being and the way in which these different values are prioritised give rise to justice dilemmas in conservation conflicts. These dilemmas revolve around three questions. Should humans or animals and ecosystems come first? Which kind of justice should take priority on which ethical grounds? How can conservation justice be achieved?

Who/what first?

The question 'who or what first?' implies the question of human responsibility towards other species and ecosystems, as well as towards present and future fellow human beings who depend on critical ecosystem services. The debate around this question is driven by two opposing positions, anthropocentrism on the one hand, which separates humans from the rest of nature, and values species and ecosystems based on their instrumental value to humans, and biocentrism and ecocentrism on the other hand, which view humans as part of the natural world and ascribe intrinsic value to humans, non-human living beings, and ecosystems as a whole (Sandler 2012; Vucetich *et al.* 2018).

The people of Purongo definitely shared an anthropocentric view, as they valued wildlife first and foremost as a critical resource providing meat, skin, fur, and bones for human consumption, medical use, ritual purposes, traditional dancewear, and jewellery, although they attributed some intrinsic value to wildlife 'for what it is as God's creation'. In contrast, UWA focuses on the protection of ecosystems and wildlife as part of it, which is justified with the ecosystem's values in its own right, or something that cannot be substituted or replaced – a position they share with conservationists from other countries (Sandler 2012). This protectionist approach to conservation has however been expanded to include active wildlife management, or human interventions, where some species are controlled in support of the continued existence of other species and the whole ecosystem (Gamborg *et al.* 2012). However, UWA also promotes certain human interest in and the economic use of wildlife as 'a renewable resource' not only of ecological importance, but also of cultural and economic significance for present and future generations (UWA 2018: 45), as reflected in its motto 'Conserving for Generations'. Here, one focus is on driving forward the country's economic development by selling the 'wilderness' to tourists.

What kind of justice on what ethical grounds?

The debate about who or what first is closely linked to three approaches: social justice or doing justice to humans; ecological justice or doing justice to nature to realise ecological sustainability; and environmental justice or achieving conservation outcomes that are also socially just (Schlosberg 2013). In Purongo, social justice was the people's main concern, in contrast to UWA's emphasis on ecological justice. Environmental justice was not considered a priority either by the people or by UWA wardens and rangers in the area.

Social justice – the concern of the people of Purongo – depends on outcomes and procedures, namely fair sharing of resources, benefits, and costs and how a fair outcome can be achieved, based on the fairness of decision-making processes; as well as recognition and participation, i.e. respect, for difference and avoidance of domination, and people's opportunities for real partaking in the decisions which govern their lives (Tyler 2000; Jamieson 2007: 89–92; Martin 2017).

The research participants from Purongo felt that the distribution of benefits and costs of conservation were extremely unjust and unfair. They felt neglected and marginalised and stressed that the authorities did not treat them with dignity and respect. They lamented that, in contradiction to the state's responsibility to care for and protect its citizens, in their case government had chosen to care for and protect wild animals, not least because of the benefits accruing from conservation and the selling of 'wilderness experiences'. They elaborated that they had to endure poverty and hunger caused by wildlife's crop raiding, for which they were not compensated; and when they went hunting in their customary hunting area in the border zone of the park to be able to fill their families' stomachs and make some small money, they had been accused of poaching and subjected to arbitrary arrests, mistreatments, and even disappearance or killing. Therefore, their relationships with rangers and wardens were rather tense and based on mutual distrust.

However, unjust outcomes and unfair treatment were not their only concern. Other issues were lack of recognition and exclusion from decision making about issues affecting their lives so fundamentally. They stressed that their voices were not heard, not even when they were trying to involve higher authorities including their elected representatives in parliament and the president. A particularly bitter experience in this regard was the failure of the community tourism project financed with money from UWA's Revenue Sharing Fund, which had been intended to make people benefit from the proximity to the protected area and to win their support for wildlife conservation. Its failure was traced back to a variety of reasons, not least personal greed, selfish advancement of own economic and political goals, nepotism, and corruption. However, another reason stressed by the research participants was that the authorities deliberately counteracted people's participation in decision making and ownership of the project. The Committee of elected village representatives, which was formed to build up the Acholi Culture and Tourism Centre was never given a real chance to fulfil its mandate due to continuous interference of politicians and administrators. The Sub-county officials and later the district's leading politicians obviously did not want to lose control, and continuously tried to dominate the process despite public assertions that the project approach would be bottom-up and community-demand driven, and its activities planned and developed in a participatory process, as provided for in the new Revenue Sharing Guidelines. Funds from revenue sharing on the sub-county's accounts, which were needed for the Committee members' travel and meeting allowances, business-related trainings, and realisation of the museum exhibition, did not reach the entitled recipients. One can only speculate about the reasons why UWA, a body of central government and thus more powerful than local government, did not put more pressure on the latter to follow the guidelines. The Wildlife Authority had actually needed a success story to enhance its reputation, win the population's trust, and hence ensure compliance with conservation goals. But the contrary occurred. Due to their negative experiences, people still did not value the importance of conservation.

The need to balance concerns

Conservation ethicists have endeavoured to reconcile the two opposing positions on who or what comes first and what just conservation is, by applying the framework of social justice to nature and at the same time trying to achieve socially just outcomes of nature conservation, including economic returns accruing from selling the 'wild' to tourists (Schlosberg 2013). Proponents of this effort are Vucetich *et al.* (2015, 2018), who emphasise the intrinsic value of nature, and compare this ascription with the acknowledgement of intrinsic value of humans foundational in discussions about social justice and its principles for weighing and deciding on competing claims among humans. They propose that these principles 'might be expanded and adapted to better understand what constitutes appropriate relationships between humans and the rest of the natural world' (Vucetich *et al.* 2015: 11) and have come up with what they call a 'non-anthropocentric principle to guide the resolution of conservation conflicts' (Vucetich *et al.* 2018), highlighting fair treatment of others on the basis of equality, need, and deserving: 'No human should infringe on the well-being of others any more than is necessary for a healthy, meaningful life.' The 'others' are all those who are entitled to fair treatment, be they humans or non-humans, and therefore the principle is non-anthropocentric. However, since it prioritises human well-being, it cannot be considered misanthropic – an accusation that conservationists hear quite often.

Interestingly, what is deemed to be 'right' from a social justice and conservation ethics perspective is also reasonable from an ecology point of view. This is for instance ascertained by the findings of a global meta-analysis of 165 protected areas using data from 171 published studies, which show that protected areas with positive socio-economic outcomes were more likely to report positive conservation outcomes (Oldekop *et al.* 2016). Similarly, the 2018 Protected Planet Report stresses the 'emerging evidence' that participation of indigenous and local communities in the management of protected areas and fair sharing of costs and benefits 'are positively correlated with the success of protected areas in conserving nature' (UNEP-WCMC *et al.* 2018: 29). Schreckenberg *et al.* (2016: 13–17) come up with an equity framework for the establishment, governance, and management of protected areas, which has been adopted by leading conservation bodies. In this framework, equity is considered to have three intertwined dimensions that 'should apply in any field of conservation and development' (Schreckenberg *et al.* 2016: 14), namely recognition equity, procedural equity, and distributive equity, which echoes the elements of social justice. The Protected Planet Report (UNEP-WCMC *et al.* 2018: 29) highlights the main principles underlying these dimensions. Recognition equity implies acknowledgement of and respect for stakeholders and their social and cultural diversity, values, rights, and beliefs. Procedural equity is about decision making concerning protected areas and stakeholders' participation, as well as issues of transparency, accountability, and methods of redress in case of conflicts relating to the management of the protected area. Distributive equity relates to the distribution of benefits and costs among stakeholders.

Enabling conditions for establishing, governing, managing, and marketing protected areas in an equitable way, according to Schreckenberg *et al.* (2016: 17–19; cf. also UNEP-WCMC, *et al.* 2018: 29), include the legal, political and social recognition of all types of governance of protected areas, namely: government, shared, private, indigenous peoples', and local communities' governance. Other criteria are stakeholders' awareness of the principles of equity and their capacity to achieve recognition and participate effectively; the alignment of statutory and customary laws and norms; and pursuit of an adaptive learning approach.

Challenges to conservation justice in Uganda

In Uganda things have not gone very far in this direction. Until recently, the shift from 'fortress conservation' inherited from the colonialists to decentralised, community-based approaches to conservation – which have become prominent in the southern part of Africa since the 1980s and 1990s (Hutton *et al.* 2005) – left Uganda largely untouched. One reason was the decades of violent conflict during which rethinking conservation was not a political priority. Only with the establishment of UWA in 1996 and formulation of new policies since the early 2000s, were wildlife conservation and management no longer considered the responsibility of government alone, but to be accomplished in partnership with district authorities, communities, and the private sector (UWA 2020). This, however, did not imply that these have become equal partners. Wildlife has remained the property of the state, is held in trust by the state for the people of Uganda, and UWA has the lead in wildlife conservation and management within protected areas and on people's land, where a vast number of wild animals is found. The Wildlife Act of 2019, however, has contributed to more justice in conservation affairs. The Act entails the new provision of compensation for damages including death, injury, destruction of crops and property caused by certain wildlife species outside protected areas (Republic of Uganda 2019: Sections 82, 83, 84 and Fourth Schedule). The Act provides for partnership arrangements not only in form of commercial public-private partnerships (Section 22), but also in form of what is called community conservation. These are based on the expectation that benefits from wildlife will lead to better custodianship of wildlife resources. These provisions include the continuation of sharing of revenue generated from national parks and game reserves with local communities (Republic of Uganda 2019: Section 65), granting individuals, community groups, and other stakeholders wildlife use rights on communal and private land, including hunting, farming or ranching of wildlife, trading in wildlife and wildlife products, and using wildlife for educational or scientific purposes and for tourism and recreation (Republic of Uganda 2019: Section 35 and 51).

The current practice of community conservation focuses on the sharing of revenue generated from park entry fees and use of wildlife outside protected areas, most often in form of sport hunting. Several studies point to the potential of these approaches for maintaining protected areas and promoting conservation, while simultaneously improving people's livelihoods and enhancing their well-being through non-profit community projects such as the construction of schools, health centres, roads, and bridges as well as commercial community projects – mostly in the form of ecotourism ventures – that provide an alternative to agriculture which is threatened by wildlife crop raiding. However, the studies also stress deficiencies in practical implementation since the various dimensions of equitable benefit sharing have not been adequately addressed. For instance, the findings of research on community conservation through tourism revenue sharing in Purongo Sub-county do not differ from the results of research in the border areas of Bwindi Impenetrable National Park in south-western Uganda (Ahebwa *et al.* 2012; Tumusiime & Vedeld 2012). Local people only receive insignificant economic returns relative to costs; and communities and individuals living in villages next to the park border who bear most conservation costs are not particularly targeted. The same applies to sport hunting on government and private land next to protected areas – promoted by UWA in cooperation with NGOs, local governments, community wildlife associations (CWAs) and private hunting companies. UWA decides about hunting quotas and fees for different animals, issues hunting licences and monitors the operations of CWAs and hunting companies without directly involving local communities who 'wait for whatever revenue is shared with them' (Ochieng *et al.* 2015: 153). These distributional shortcomings and the lack of recognition come along with procedural shortcomings in form of lack of local people's real participation in decision making concerning protected areas. Tumusiime and Vedeld (2012: 15, 25) identify 'the challenge of forming an effective organisational and institutional architecture' as the main problem, which 'includes the need for participatory planning, proficient implementation, legitimate monitoring methods, and control and adjustment of policies and practices'. This, however, had not been the case in Purongo and Bwindi, where interactions between the relevant actors at local level – UWA personnel on the ground, local government, and local people – were conflictual and, on the part of the population, characterised by accusations of nepotism, misappropriation of funds, corruption and fraud, and a widespread feeling of powerlessness and being left out.

The cases of Purongo and Bwindi also demonstrate that good governance of protected areas and their surroundings is further complicated by the fact that increasing decentralisation in Uganda involves the potential risk that interactions of institutions at different levels of governance – i.e. UWA as an agency of central government in charge of conservation on the one hand, and local governments mandated to oversee the management of natural resources within their jurisdiction and in charge of receiving revenue-sharing funds and allocating the money for community projects on the other hand – instead of fostering synergies, may obstruct each other's action (Tumusiime & Vedeld 2012: 17, 24). In both locations, community members, who had been encouraged by UWA to form committees tasked to manage revenue sharing at parish level, were caught between two stools. The local governments regarded these committees more as a UWA structure, while UWA regarded them as a local government structure, and therefore the groups 'ended up having no "institutional home"' (Tumusiime & Vedeld 2012: 24), were not sufficiently funded, and therefore ultimately failed in fulfilling their mandate.

Envisioning the future of conservation justice in Uganda: Some concluding remarks

Recognising local communities as stakeholders in ensuring the protection of wildlife inside and outside protected areas is certainly an important step towards achieving equity in conservation affairs. However, Uganda's community conservation approach currently does not go so far as to substantially change the dominant pattern of governance of wildlife. The government remains the central actor initiating community outreach and support projects and promoting public-private partnerships which, however, have not contributed much to ending wildlife crimes and human–wildlife conflicts. Tumusiime & Vedeld

(2012: 25–26) stress a lack of will on the part of the authorities at all levels to really involve the population in wildlife management. This view is shared by Ahebwa *et al.* (2012: 377) who state that, '[d]espite the participatory rhetoric of policy reforms, the Uganda Wildlife Authority remains the most powerful actor: it has control over resources and consequently determines the rules of the game'.

An alternative and a way to achieve more social justice in conservation affairs not yet being pursued in Uganda is community-based conservation in the strict sense of the term, or what Murphree (2000: 1–3) calls 'conservation by the people' – in contrast to community conservation, or 'conservation with the people'. This alternative ties in with Ostrom's considerations concerning governance and management of common-pool resources by the resource users themselves who, when benefiting from the resources, instead of overexploiting them, will use them in a sustainable way (Ostrom 1990). Accordingly, community-based conservation, as Murphree (2000: 4) understands it, implies collective management, use and controls on use of common-pool resources, and equitable benefit sharing at local levels by communal groups, whose members are tied together through primary relationships, shared norms, values, and collective interests, and operate over a defined jurisdiction with clear boundaries of area and membership, rules, monitoring procedures, conflict resolution mechanisms, and sanctions. The rights of these groups to organise must be recognised by external governmental authorities (Ostrom 1990: 90). To make this happen, 'a robust devolutionist approach' or 'the creation of relatively autonomous realms of authority, responsibility and entitlement, with a primary accountability to their [the resource user groups'] own constituencies' is needed (Murphree 2000: 5). Since these groups do not exist in isolation and common-pool resources are often part of larger systems, the responsibility for governing the common resources need to be built in nested tiers from the lowest level up to the entire interconnected system (van Dijk *et al.* 2019: 127; Ostrom 1990: 90). This means, a complex, adaptive, polycentric governance arrangement with multiple centres of decision making at local and state levels is called for, where the centres operate rather autonomously but are nevertheless interconnected, respect and consider each other, and are capable to resolve their conflicts (Marshall 2015; Ostrom 2005). Such an arrangement can strike a balance between state-centred and community-based governance with overlapping ecological, social, and economic interests. Government with its legislative and law enforcement powers will continue to play a supervisory and monitoring role; whereas private enterprises could support the community groups in marketing their products. In this way, the competing interests of different stakeholders in either protecting wildlife and their habitats or securing people's livelihoods and driving forward Uganda's economic development could be reconciled. All this, however, remains a difficult endeavour, because the state, its private sector allies and its bureaucracies are usually hesitant to devolve power due to their own appropriative interests in natural resources of high value, which they control (Murphree 2000: 5–7).

Lastly, there is no doubt that community-based conservation is an important conservation strategy, relevant in contexts where people have been deprived of and strive for social justice as a consequence of conservation efforts, usually in the surroundings of protected areas. However, just conservation is not only about people, and therefore protected areas and community-based conservation strategies must complement each other. When certain species and important habitats or landscapes are threatened, protected areas under the direct responsibility and management of the state make much sense (Murphree 2000: 4). The aim of a responsible national nature conservation policy is to preserve a country's biological diversity. In view of the continuing high rate of biodiversity loss in Uganda, protected areas must remain high on Uganda's conservation agenda as well.

Bibliography

Agrawal, A. & Redford, K. (2009). 'Conservation and displacement: An overview', *Conservation & Society*, 7(1), 1–10.

Ahebwa, W., Duim, R., & Sandbrook, C. (2012). 'Tourism revenue sharing policy at Bwindi Impenetrable National Park, Uganda: A policy arrangements approach', *Journal of Sustainable Tourism*, 20, 377–394.

Corry, S. (2020). 'Why the New Deal for Nature is a disaster for people and planet' (London: Survival International). Available at: https://medium.com/@ survivalinternational/why-the-new-deal-for-nature-is-a-disaster-for-people-and-planet-5148108d2768 [Accessed 7 February 2022].

Dinerstein, E., Vynne, C., Sala, E., Joshi, A. R., Fernando, S., *et al.* (2019). 'A Global Deal For Nature: Guiding principles, milestones, and targets', *Science Advances*, 5(4). https://advances.sciencemag.org/content/5/4/eaaw2869 [Accessed 7 February 2022].

Doolittle, A. A. (2007). 'Fortress conservation', in: P. Robbins (ed.), *Encyclopedia of Environment and Society* (Thousand Oaks CA: SAGE Publications).

Dowie, M. (2009). *Conservation Refugees: The Hundred-Year-Conflict between Global Conservation and Native Peoples* (Cambridge MA; London: The MIT Press).

Dudley, N., Shadie, P., & Stolton, S. (2008 [2013]). 'Guidelines for Applying Protected Area Management Categories Including IUCN WCPA Best Practice Guidance on Recognising Protected Areas and Assigning Management Categories and Governance Types', Best Practice Protected Area Guidelines Series No. 21 (Gland: IUCN). Available at: https://portals.iucn.org/library/sites/ library/files/documents/pag-021.pdf [Accessed 7 February 2022].

Gamborg, C., Palmer, C., & Sandoe, P. (2012). 'Ethics of wildlife management and conservation: What should we try to protect?' *Nature Education Knowledge*, 3(10), 8.

Harrison, M., Roe, D., Baker, J., Mwedde, G., Travers, H., *et al.* (2015). 'Wildlife crime: A review of the evidence on drivers and impacts in Uganda' Research Report, April (London: International Institute for Environment and Development). Available at: https://pubs.iied.org/sites/default/files/pdfs/migrate/17576IIED.pdf [Accessed 7 February 2022].

Hutton, J., Adams, W. M., & Murombedzi, J. C. (2005). 'Back to the barriers? Changing narratives in biodiversity conservation', *Forum for Development Studies*, 32(2), 341–370.

Jamieson, D. (2007). 'The heart of environmentalism', in: R. Sandler & P. C. Pezzullo (eds), *Environmental Justice and Environmentalism: The Social Justice Challenge to the Environmental Movement* (Cambridge MA: MIT Press), 85–101.

Kamara, E., Nina, P., & Ochieng, L. (2019). 'Effects of oil and gas exploration in Murchison Falls National Park on wildlife resources', *African Journal of Environment and Natural Science Research*, 2(2), 48–57.

Kamoga, J. (2019). 'Uganda now secures contractor for oil roads', *The East African*, 2 April.

Lenhart, L. (2013). 'Alleged land grabs and governance: Exploring mistrust and trust in Northern Uganda – The case of the Apaa land conflict', *Journal of Peace and Security Studies* 1(December), 64–85.

Lenhart, L. (2017). 'Conflict over Protected Areas for Wildlife Conservation in Northern Uganda'. Governing Transition in Northern Uganda: Trust and Land project, Gulu University, Aarhus University, and the University of Copenhagen. TrustLand Policy Brief No. 5, December.

Lenhart, L. & Meinert, L. (2023). 'Conservation', in: L. Meinert & S. Reynolds Whyte (eds), *This Land is Not For Sale: Trust and Transitions in Northern Uganda*. Integration and Conflict Studies Series (Oxford: Berghahn Books), 203–224.

Lyatuu, J. (2019). 'Uganda targets 1m more tourists in 2019', *The Observer*, 16 January.

Martin, A. (2017). *Just Conservation: Biodiversity, Wellbeing and Sustainability*. Earthscan Conservation and Displacement Series (London: Routledge).

Marshall, G. (2015). 'Polycentricity and adaptive governance' Paper presented at the 15th Biennial Global Conference 25–29 May 2015 (Edmonton: International Association for the Study of the Commons). Available at: www.researchgate.net/publication/277598119_Polycentricity_and_adaptive_governance [Accessed 7 February 2022].

MRG – Minority Rights Group International (2014). 'Eviction of indigenous Benet in Uganda risks conflict'. Available at: https://minorityrights.org/2014/11/06/eviction-of-indigenous-benet-in-uganda-risks-conflict [Accessed 7 February 2022].

MRG – Minority Rights Group International (2020). 'Uganda: Decades of displacement for Batwa, uprooted in the name of conservation'. Available at: https://minorityrights.org/uganda-decades-of-displacement-for-batwa-uprooted-in-the-name-of-conservation [Accessed 7 February 2022].

MTWA – Ministry of Tourism, Wildlife & Antiquities (2018a). 'Tourism Sector Annual Performance Report FY 2017/18. November 2018' (Kampala: MTWA). Available at: www.tourism.go.ug/_files/ugd/1e6d1c_dd8ea33281874e138b-1738c2be331bb8.pdf [Accessed 7 February 2022].

MTWA – Ministry of Tourism, Wildlife & Antiquities (2018b). 'Red List of Threatened Species of Uganda 2018' (Kampala: MTWA).

Murphree, M. W. (2000). 'Community-based Conservation: Old Ways, New Myths and Enduring Challenges'. Paper presented at the Conference on African Wildlife Management in The New Millennium., 13–15 December 2000 (Mweka: College of African Wildlife Management). Available at: https://rmportal.net/library/content/frame/marshalmurphree-mweka2000.pdf [Accessed 13 January 2023].

NEMA – National Environment Management Authority (2016). 'National Biodiversity Strategy and Action Plan II (2015–2025)' (Kampala: NEMA). Available at: http://nema.go.ug/sites/all/themes/nema/docs/NBSAP%20Uganda%20 2015%20-%20Re-designed.pdf [Accessed 7 February 2022].

Ntalumbwa, E. (2019). 'New Wildlife Act 2019 sets tough terms for encroachers', *Daily Monitor*, 20 July.

Ochieng, A., Ahebwa, W. M., & Visseren-Hamakers, I. J. (2015). 'Hunting for conservation? The re-introduction of sports hunting in Uganda examined', in: R. Van der Duim, M. Lamers, & J. van Wijk (eds), *Institutional Arrangements for Conservation, Development and Tourism in Eastern and Southern Africa: A Dynamic Perspective* (Dordrecht; Heidelberg; New York; London: Springer), 139–155.

Oldekop, J., Holmes, G., Harris, W., & Evans, K. (2016). 'A global assessment of the social and conservation outcomes of protected areas', *Conservation Biology*, 30, 133–141.

Ostrom, E. (1990). *Governing the Commons: The Evolution of Institutions for Collective Action* (Cambridge: Cambridge University Press).

Ostrom, E. (2005). *Understanding Institutional Diversity* (Princeton NJ: Princeton University Press).

Otto, I. A. (2018). 'Tracing the roots of Apaa land conflict', *The PML Daily*, 27 March. Available at: www.pmldaily.com/news/2017/06/tracing-the-roots-of-apaa-land-conflict.html [Accessed 7 February 2022].

Patey, L. (2015). 'Oil in Uganda: Hard bargaining and complex politics in East Africa', OIES PAPER: WPM 60 (Oxford: Oxford Institute for Energy Studies.).

Pomeroy, D., Tushabe, H., & Loh, J. (2017). 'The State of Uganda's Biodiversity 2017' (Kampala: Department of Environment Management College of Agricultural and Environmental Sciences, Makerere University). Available at: http://natureuganda.org/downloads/presentations/BD%202017%20Indicators%20 Report.pdf [Accessed 7 February 2022].

Republic of Uganda (2019). *Uganda Wildlife Act*. Available at: https://old.ulii.org/system/files/legislation/act/2019/2019/Uganda-Wildlife-Act-2019.pdf [Accessed 7 February 2022].

Sandler, R. (2012). 'Intrinsic value, ecology, and conservation', *Nature Education Knowledge*, 3(10), 4.

Schlosberg, D. (2013). 'Theorising environmental justice: The expanding sphere of a discourse', *Environmental Politics*, 2013, 22(1), 37–55.

Schreckenberg K., Franks, P., Martin, A., & Lang, B. (2016). 'Unpacking equity for protected area conservation', *Parks*, 22(2), 11–26.

Survival International (2015). 'Parks need peoples: Why evictions of tribal communities from protected areas spell disaster for both people and nature'. Available at: https://assets.survivalinternational.org/documents/1324/parksneedpeoples-report.pdf [Accessed 7 February 2022].

Tumusiime, D. & Vedeld, P. (2012). 'False promise or false premise? Using Tourism revenue sharing to promote conservation and poverty reduction in Uganda', *Conservation & Society*, 10, 15–28.

Tyler, T. R. (2000). 'Social Justice: Outcome and Procedure', *International Journal of Psychology*, 2000, 33(2), 117–125.

UBOS – Uganda Bureau of Statistics (2016). 'The National Population and Housing Census 2014 – Main Report' (Kampala: Government of Uganda). Available at: www.ubos.org/wp-content/uploads/publications/03_20182014_National_Census_Main_Report.pdf [Accessed 25 February 2022].

UBOS – Uganda Bureau of Statistics (2019). '2019 Statistical Abstract' (Kampala: Government of Uganda). Available at: www.ubos.org/wp-content/uploads/publications/01_20202019_Statistical_Abstract_-Final.pdf [Accessed 7 February 2022].

UBOS – Uganda Bureau of Statistics (2020). Official Website. www.ubos.org [Accessed 7 February 2022].

UNEP-WCMC, IUCN, & NGS – United Nations Environment World Conservation Monitoring Centre, International Union for Conservation of Nature, & National Geographic Society (2018). 'Protected Planet Report 2018: Tracking progress towards global targets for protected areas' (Cambridge; Gland; Washington: UNEP-WCMC, IUCN, & NGS). Available at: https://portals.iucn.org/library/node/48344 [Accessed 7 February 2022].

UWA – Uganda Wildlife Authority (2000). 'Revenue Sharing Programme Around Protected Areas' (Kampala: UWA).

UWA – Uganda Wildlife Authority (2011). 'Guidelines for Revenue Sharing between Wildlife Protected Areas and Adjacent Local Governments and Communities, March 2011' (Edited Copy) (Kampala: UWA).

UWA – Uganda Wildlife Authority (2018). 'State of Wildlife Resources in Uganda 2018' (Kampala: UWA). Available at: https://uganda.wcs.org/publications.aspx [Accessed 18 February 2022].

UWA – Uganda Wildlife Authority (2020). Official Website. www.ugandawildlife.org [Accessed 18 February 2022].

van Dijk, G., Sergaki, P., & Baourakis, G. (2019). 'Cooperatives in economic literature – Capita selecta', in: G. van Dijk, P. Sergaki, & G. Baourakis, *The Cooperative Enterprise. Practical Evidence for a Theory of Cooperative Entrepreneurship* (Springer online), 125–171.

Vucetich, J. & Bruskotter, J., & Nelson, M. (2015). 'Evaluating whether nature's intrinsic value is an axiom of or anathema to conservation', *Conservation Biology*, 29(2), 321–332.

Vucetich, J. A., Burnham, D., Macdonald, E.A., Bruskotter, J. T., Marchini, S., Zimmermann, A., & Macdonald, D. W. (2018). 'Just conservation: What is it and should we pursue it?' *Biological Conservation*, 221, May 2018, 23–33.

WB – World Bank (2020). 'Uganda: The World Bank in Uganda.' www.worldbank. org/en/country/uganda [Accessed 18 February 2022].

WCS – Wildlife Conservation Society (n.d.). 'Combating Illegal Wildlife Trade: An Integrated, Multi-scale Approach to Combating Wildlife Trafficking in Uganda' (Kampala: WCS). Available at: https://uganda.wcs.org/Initiatives/ IWT-and-CWT.aspx [Accessed 7 February 2022].

WWF – World Wide Fund for Nature (2018). 'Living Planet Report – 2018: Aiming Higher', M. Grooten & R. E. A. Almond (eds) (Gland: WWF in collaboration with ZSL/Zoological Society of London). Available at: https://c402277.ssl.cfl. rackcdn.com/publications/1187/files/original/LPR2018_Full_Report_Spreads. pdf [Accessed 7 February 2022].

PART 6

CONCLUSIONS

18

Conclusions: Commodifying the 'Wild' – Where do we go from here?

LÉA LACAN, LINUS KALVELAGE, SELMA LENDELVO,
ALFONS MOSIMANE, ROMIE NGHITEVELEKWA, AND
MICHAEL BOLLIG

In early February 2022, the UK office of the World Wide Fund for Nature launched the campaign 'Tokens for Nature', selling blockchain-based non-fungible tokens to raise funds for nature conservation. The campaign remains active under the label 'NFA Non-Fungible Animals' and uses crypto wallets. Facing a huge backlash from environmentalists pointing out the carbon emissions connected to blockchain technology, the experiment was ended only 48 hours later. However, this short-lived attempt to tokenise the natural environment stands as one of a long series of initiatives trying to use blockchain technology to solve problems of environmental degradation (Stuit *et al.* 2022), the latest experiment to accelerate processes of commodification and to combine the commercialisation of nature with its conservation.

Beyond the often heated debate on the neoliberalisation of nature, this book has drawn together a good number of cases exemplifying the manifold approaches being taken in the commodification of non-domesticated plants, wildlife, and wilderness landscapes in southern and eastern Africa. Many of these cases occur in contexts of nature conservation. Indeed, the commodification of the 'wild' is often put forward as a source of revenue to incentivise and foster conservation and to lower the vulnerability of rural economies at the same time. Therefore, this volume points to the interplay between the commodification and the conservation of nature as two mutually reinforcing processes. However, contributions have also examined commodification dynamics and their social and economic consequences beyond their direct connections with conservation. They have emphasised throughout that the commodification of the 'wild' has social and economic consequences far beyond protected species and conserved patches of landscape. They have also sought consistently to link case-study material with contemporary social science theorising on commodification and value chains.

We acknowledge that there are no simple messages to be derived from these empirical studies. The economic benefits of the commodification of the 'wild' remain ambiguous, as do its social effects and whether it fosters conservation and sustainable natural resource management. With uneasiness, we note that these very questions have led to a hostile debate between scientists critical of such commodification processes and those supportive of them (in the Namibian case, see for instance Koot *et al.* 2020 and Naidoo *et al.* 2021). The objectivity of some conservation scientists (Namibia-based and international) who have advocated for regulated trophy hunting was questioned, and these authors were accused of disregarding conflict-of-interest issues. This sparked debate on the role of ideology in conservation science and discursive violence. Interestingly, one camp is more rooted in the social sciences, while the opposite camp publishes more in ecology journals: we contend that new scientific perspectives are needed to tackle these questions, and perhaps the way forward lies in the interaction of different disciplines and a closer cooperation of practitioners, community activists, and scientists at the outset of research projects (in order to create study designs jointly) – to leave the beaten path.

This short conclusion draws on the cases studied in this volume to identify key themes and raise new questions for further research. Rather than summarising all contributions (as we have done in the introductory Chapter 1), we end this book with a discussion of the involvement and effects of the commodification of the 'wild' in conservation contexts regarding three key thematic areas: (1) in rural inequalities and environmental justice; (2) in changing patterns and conditions of resources and land uses; and (3) in ecological transformations and environmental governance. In relation to these topics, we identify trends across our empirical findings, discuss the implications for the development of rural livelihoods, and highlight remaining knowledge gaps and perspectives for further research.

Inequalities and marginalisation of the rural poor in commodified natures

Commodification of the 'wild' and poverty alleviation

Rooted in post-colonial nation-building, community-based natural resource management holds the powerful promise of fulfilling the triad of nature conservation, economic development, and empowerment. Scrutinising the success of a programme against its self-proclaimed aims shows mixed results: on the one hand, population numbers of some animal species have certainly increased, safari and hunting tourism have opened new development pathways, and the conservancy institution creates an anchor point for democratic decision-making and global–local knowledge exchange. On the other hand, commercial ivory poaching is still a major challenge, natural resources other than wildlife (e.g. aquatic resources, or forests) are under increasing pressure, and rural poverty is still prevalent in many quarters. Much emphasis is put on the prospects of economic growth, but less is said regarding whether this overall increase in economic turnover is an effective means of addressing poverty and food security. The latter aspect is particularly relevant against the background of a climate that is expected to display higher variation of precipitation in the future – can 'working landscapes of conservation' provide the social-ecological resilience that is necessary for communities that by and large rely on smallholder farming and cattle herding?

Overall, contributions to this volume suggest that the commodification of the 'wild' in conservation contexts does not necessarily help the situation of the rural poor in significant ways. Certainly, some advocates of community-based conservation, notably planners in government offices and the headquarters of international conservationist organisations, have voiced their hope that conservation may help to address the question of rural poverty. In many policy papers and overviews, however, the question of poverty is not addressed in any detail. Contributions to this book highlight that, despite featuring the aim of alleviating poverty and economic inequalities, the commodification of the 'wild' does not benefit individuals from rural communities in homogeneous ways. Several contributions indicate that, instead of supporting the livelihoods of the rural poor, commodification processes remain profit-oriented, and that benefit-sharing mechanisms do not challenge existing economic inequalities (see in particular Wynberg; Lavelle; Ndwandwe). If poverty alleviation is to become an outcome of community-based conservation efforts, we contend that there is a need to know more about poverty and to consider that benefit-sharing necessarily has a double meaning: not only must benefits be shared between private investors and the community, they also need to be shared within the community, particularly so if the objects, landscapes, and animals or plants that are commoditised are (or have been) common-pool access resources. While there are elaborate approaches to benefit-sharing between communities and the private sector, within communities this needs further consideration, discussions, and development. Certainly, institutionalised benefit-sharing at the local level would not only add to the acceptance of such processes, but it would also convey the idea that all community members own a rightful share (Ferguson 2015) of the resources at stake.

Empowerment or marginalisation? Commodification of the 'wild' and environmental justice

Addressing inequalities in rural contexts is not limited to the sharing of economic benefits from the commodification of the 'wild'. In many instances, reports on community-based conservation and the commodification of nature list serious complaints by local stakeholders. People have been removed from lands in the (often distant) past that are nowadays advertised as protected areas (e.g. see Nwandwe; Lacan; Lenhart in this volume). They feel that their 'ownership of the land', their heritage, is not acknowledged at all, but that newly instituted wildernesses just put a blanket over their aspirations for an acknowledgement of their roots in these very landscapes. Entitlements to land, both factual and symbolic, matter and are certainly as important as commodification processes and economic benefits. Distributional injustices are another matter of concern. These include unequal participation in value chains and unequal sharing of overall economic benefit within communities. It also includes the feeling among some local stakeholders that they are exluded from decision-making processes, that their rights are not recognised, and that they have lost access to land and resources to the benefit of others.

Contributions to this volume have put forward such issues of environmental justice, beyond dysfunctional benefit-sharing mechanisms. They show that local communities (and more concretely illiterate and elderly segments of such communities) often remain excluded from industries based on 'wild' products, and are not empowered to take part in decision-making. Moreover, the commodification of nature in conservation contexts sometimes leads to local exclusions and the hardening of ethnic boundaries. As some authors in this volume have shown, increasing human–wildlife conflicts place a new burden on local farmers in conservation areas (see Fabiano *et al.*; Mbaiwa; Lenhart). Therefore, power imbalances between global and mostly urban elites and the rural poor remain unchallenged or are even fostered and reinforced in commodification processes and conservation initiatives. This is especially so in certain institutional contexts like game farms (see Kalvelage, this volume), reproducing colonially established power imbalances, but also in conservancies and community-based settings.

At the same time, this volume has shed light on several cases where the commodification of the 'wild' has led to beneficial effects, empowering at least certain groups. These include women who have gained access to income and a new social status within their communities through such commercial initiatives in Namibia (see Lendelvo *et al.*). Traditional authorities in Namibia too were shown to have strengthened their role and position through community-based conservation and associated commodification processes (see Mosimane *et al.*). In other cases, e.g. in South Africa or in Uganda, such empowerment processes have not taken place despite the declared policy of political programmes and projects (see Wynberg; Nwandwe; Lenhart in this volume). In any case, commodification processes have the potential to give rise to new social dynamics. These need to be further examined, especially in community-based conservation contexts where local stakeholders have a bigger role to play.

To do so, we believe it is paramount to critically examine who these local stakeholders are, and to fine-tune research and analysis beyond a simplistic idea of local 'communities'.

To what extent can community-based conservation be based on the idea of a 'community'? Community-based conservation relies on the premise that a community has been identified to support and benefit from conservation. However, what 'community' really covers is often very unclear: what defines a community, and who belongs to it? What are the territorial borders of a 'community's land' and does it make sense at all to consider such borders seriously given high rates of inter-community mobility? Raising such crucial questions vested in political and economic interests inevitably brings about conflicts, which tend to crystallise along identity and ethnicised fault lines. Moreover, 'communities' are far from being homogeneous, and, as the contributions to this volume have shown, different local stakeholders – e.g. women, traditional authorities, people employed in conservation jobs vs. those who are not, etc. – are involved in and impacted by community-based conservation and processes of commodification of nature in diverse ways. How such dynamics play into the power balances among local stakeholders, and also between traditional authorities and democratic institutions, needs to be scrutinised further.

Issues of environmental justice need to become a key concern to tie commodification processes to social development and communal welfare (Dhillon 2018). This will entail a move to consider together distributive justice, procedural justice, and the justice of recognition (Baasch 2020). The latter will necessitate recognition of past and present entitlements, lost or gained, affected or acknowledged. Chapters in this volume have emphasised that the commodification of the 'wild' entails comprehensive processes of policy-making and legal reform. True participation in such processes may be difficult to achieve, given profound imbalances in information on options and possible outcomes. Nevertheless, institutionalised attempts in that direction are necessary to ensure procedural justice. Lastly, the issue of distributive justice has been addressed above: there need to be provisions that a just distribution of damages and benefits is institutionalised at different nodes along value chains.

Dynamic resource and land use in commodification contexts

Contributions to this volume have shown that the commodification of the 'wild' involves the creation of new commodities and the development of their commercialisation and distribution networks. In this process, new uses of the land and resources emerge, along with institutional changes at the local and wider levels. Here, we would like to discuss two trends in particular: (1) the impact of commodification processes on the diversification of rural livelihoods, and (2) new conditions of market-based conservation in a post-Covid-19 context.

Diversification of rural livelihoods and de-agrarisation?

The logic of conservation in co-existence landscapes rests on the assumption that an increased income from tourism and value chains focused on commodities from the 'wild' has at least two notable positive effects. On the one hand, the increased valorisation of wildlife, non-domesticated plants, and wilderness landscapes will motivate local actors to invest in the sustainability of their use and will discourage behaviour that endangers the continued existence of these resources. It will also prevent rural citizens from moving to towns, as reliable income and sustainable livelihoods beyond agriculture can increasingly be found in rural settings. On the other hand, the increasing availability of non-agriculture-based incomes will lessen the pressure on such resources. Hence, conservation in co-existence landscapes will contribute progressively to de-agrarisation, which in turn will lead to a setting conducive to conservation. The underlying assumption, therefore, is that touristic valorisation creates new value chains in the region, a point of view that sometimes obscures the negative side-effects that commodification via tourism can have on other economic sectors while displacing agricultural activities (Vehrs *et al.* 2022).

The contributions to this volume give us contradictory information on land-use dynamics. Incomes from trophy hunting and ecotourism as well as from the trading of commodities are sizeable, while the distribution of benefits within communities, between community and middlemen, and within international tourism networks remains a question. However, there is little information on how such incomes reflect upon agricultural activities: do incomes from nature conservation indeed result in a decrease of agricultural activities and/or in reduced livestock herd sizes? Preliminary and anecdotal evidence rather shows that this may not be the case. Incomes from conservation in wealthy households are invested pertinently in the building-up of cattle herds. Research into the drivers of the rapid increase of cattle herds in Namibia's Zambezi Region (Bollig & Vehrs 2021) suggests that agricultural activities and the use of natural resources may even increase as the scale of commodification grows. Benefits accruing from emergent value chains are invested in the modernisation of farms, into fences, the introduction of new livestock breeds to the region, technical implements, veterinary medicine, and boreholes. However, about 60% of the households in Namibia's Zambezi Region do not possess any cattle. This implies that they have to borrow or rent oxen for ploughing. According to Namibia's 2011 census a sizeable number of households allege that they mainly live on social transfers. Does this trend bring about land-use changes? Does it result in more or less pressure on natural resources? There is certainly a need for more research that targets the interface between conservation-based economies and changing agricultural activities and land-use changes.

Commodified conservation in a post-Covid-19 setting

The Covid-19 pandemic has caused economic shockwaves, leaving firms and regions decoupled from global trade. As a result, established commodification strategies are increasingly being challenged. The tourism industry in particular has suffered from the imposed travel bans and border closures (Snyman *et al.* 2021), which brought the hunting and safari tourism sector in southern Africa to a virtual standstill. The economic losses were immense: in South Africa, the impact on the private wildlife industry was estimated at US$435 million (Van der Merwe *et al.* 2021). Similarly, in Namibia, communal conservancies depend almost entirely on tourism revenues. The loss of income has powerfully revealed the vulnerability of such an approach to economic shocks (Lendelvo *et al.* 2020). Conservation policies relying on the commodification of animals and plants are undermined, and competing economic activities, many of which are ecologically more damaging, appear more attractive to some (Kideghesho *et al.* 2021). However, many conservation organisations have also been able to acquire donor funding, thus attaining some economic stability – at least temporarily – for populations that would otherwise be more exposed to external shocks, such as smallholder farmers (Hulke *et al.* 2022). All in all, the pandemic has initiated a rapid process of de-globalisation, and thus revealed the weaknesses of neoliberal conservation models and the fragility of commodification processes entailed by them.

The production of a commodified nature: Environmental governance and ecological transformations

Commodification versus financialisation of nature? Market-led global environmental governance

This volume has documented cases of commodification of the 'wild': the integration of 'wild' products into markets, value chains, and production networks, and the impact of such processes. It has not however focused on cases of financialisation of nature and the creation of virtual financial values – like carbon credits, biodiversity offsets, or payments for ecosystem services – to be traded on financial markets. Through such processes, ecosystems not only produce material commercial goods, but also financial assets – another kind of (financial) commodity. Conversely, transactions in the global financial centres 'produce' certain kinds of ecosystems, for instance through the planting of trees for carbon offsetting. Thus, the financialisation of nature represents a special kind of commodification with specific practices and effects, which deserve further attention.

These findings on the commodification of the 'wild' therefore need to be put in dialogue with existing scholarly works on the financialisation of nature (e.g. Sullivan 2012; Bracking 2012; Asiyanbi 2018) and questions they raise: what new 'knowledge' of nature is generated through practices of financialisation of nature? What are the material impacts on local livelihoods and ecologies of putting a virtual and tradeable value on forests, biodiversity, or ecosystems? What new 'natures' do such financialisation processes produce?

Ecological impacts: What exactly is being conserved?

While the impacts of the commodification of the 'wild' on local livelihoods and social inequalities have been illustrated and discussed in several contributions in this volume, the analysis of the ecological effects of such processes could be taken further. For instance, how are ecosystems impacted by the commodi-fication of certain iconic species over others for tourism purposes? Elephants are one of such emblematic animal species favoured by the tourism industry, yet their ecological impacts are powerful and transform ecosystems. At the moment, the success of conservation is very much measured with reference to increases in population numbers of iconic wildlife species, but overlooks other environmental changes linked to the commodification of nature. We know for example that, in some of the regions under consideration, populations of aquatic fauna are decreasing, sometimes at rapid rates, due to overfishing. Rangelands also degrade and lose species diversity due to the impact of heavy grazing by large cattle herds and protracted dry spells. The UN-promoted One Health concept considers environmental health together with human and animal health. Of course, increasing wildlife figures are of interest, and for the touristic marketing of a region essential, but are these figures tantamount to increasing environmental health? What would environmental health mean first of all for the savannah landscapes of eastern and southern Africa? Can microbial and insect diversity be figured in, and how do such diversity parameters relate to the diversity of plants and wildlife? Moreover, commodification can lead to changes in the composition of wildlife popula-tions. To keep reproduction rates high, trophy hunting primarily targets old males, but what does this mean for the behaviour of e.g. elephant herds? And how do animals adapt their mobility patterns in response to increasing hunting pressure? The methodological tools of the social sciences are often unable to capture the complexity of ecological repercussions of commodification. But the socio-technical regimes used to measure the natural environment are also often overstrained: the factual basis on which hunting quotas are calculated is questionable, as Hewitson & Sullivan have shown in their contribution to this volume.

Refaunation processes are heavily anthropogenic (Lorimer 2015), i.e. they are shaped by humans. What this means for inter-species relations needs to be studied by strongly interdisciplinary teams. If we consider contemporary conservation e.g. in southern Africa as agenda for rewilding rural landscapes (wildlife numbers grow at perceivable rates in a number of southern African countries on private farms but also in communal areas!) we need to consider how trophic complexity increases (or decreases), how dispersal patterns shape biodiversity along with human livelihoods, and how stochastic disturbances (e.g. droughts and wildfires, but also violent conflict – and for that matter also a pandemic like that of COVID-19) shape conservation and the commodification of the 'wild' (see Perino *et al.* 2019).

Beyond human–wildlife conflict: Co-existence in 'wild' landscapes?

The last decades were marked by the postulate of 'new conservationists' aiming to create landscapes in which humans and wildlife co-exist. By trying to realise this co-existence without overstretching the patience of the residents in these areas who face the loss of cattle, crops, and sometimes beloved relatives, we have gained ample knowledge about the practicalities of managing human–wildlife conflicts. However, a number of questions remain. Does such conflict increase? Do measures like lion fences have measurable success? What are the differential consequences of human–wildlife conflict? Do poor people indeed suffer more?

Probably fostered by a starkly amplifying 'rewilding' discourse also prominent in the countries of the Global North (Lorimer *et al.* 2015; Pettorelli *et al.* 2019), strategies for managing predators are reviewed, including lethal measures that have previously been branded as unethical by many. The return of the wolf in North America and Europe has raised awareness of the high price associated with sharing one's habitat with predators beyond the Global South and in fact have contributed to a situation in which wildlife conservationists in the Global North look for solutions in the Global South. What form do meaningful approaches to coping with conflicts with wildlife take? Can co-existence landscapes be created to support human livelihoods and wildlife populations at the same time? And what would be the responsibility of the international community to support such solutions in the context of a global environmental crisis?

As non-domesticated plants, wildlife, and 'wild' landscapes are being sold for commercial and conservation purposes, relations between humans and their environments and the conditions of co-existence for people, wildlife, and other living beings are being transformed. Do people living in these conservation areas develop new ways of 'living with' – and 'becoming with' (Haraway 2008) – wildlife, plants, forests, landscapes, etc. as they are being made into commodities? There is a need to understand impacts of commodification processes beyond their effects on economic livelihoods and political representation. How to bridge posthuman approaches with the analysis of capitalist conservation? Emphases on human/nature entanglements have been criticised for discarding the analytical distinction between the natural and the social, thereby losing capacity to challenge capitalism and fight the global environmental crisis this has induced (Büscher 2022; Hornborg 2017). Rather than depoliticising conservation and the commodification of the 'wild' though, a focus on the political ecology of multispecies assemblages might help us to take human–environmental relations in ecological politics seriously. How do the interdependencies, conflicts, and mutualities between wildlife, plants, other living beings, and people and their organisations foster or challenge the commodification of nature? How are they shaped by such conservation models? The more-than-human realities of our human lives need further attention to scrutinise how ecologies and economies come together into being, and to understand shifting conditions of living between people and their environments.[1]

Bibliography

Asiyanbi, A. P. (2018). 'Financialisation in the green economy: Material connections, markets-in-the-making and Foucauldian organising actions', *Environment and Planning A: Economy and Space*, 50(3), 531–548.

Baasch, S. (2020). 'An interdisciplinary perspective on environmental justice: Integrating subjective beliefs and perceptions', *DIE ERDE*, 151(2–3), 77–89.

Bollig, M. & Vehrs, H.-P. (2021). 'The making of a conservation landscape: The emergence of a conservationist environmental infrastructure along the Kwando River in Namibia's Zambezi Region', *Africa*, 91(2), 270–295.

Bracking, S. (2012). 'How do investors value environmental harm/care? Private equity funds, development finance institutions and the partial financialization of nature- based industries', *Development and Change*, 43(1), 271–93.

Büscher, B. 2022. 'The nonhuman turn: Critical reflections on alienation, entanglement and nature under capitalism', *Dialogues in Human Geography*, 12(1), 54–73.

Castree, N. (2003). 'Commodifying what nature?' *Progress in Human Geography*, 27(3), 273–297.

---

[1] Two of the authors are involved in the European Research Council Grant Project "Rewilding the Anthropocene", which is dedicated to investigate these changing relations between humans and other species in the Kavango-Zambezi Transfrontier Conservation Area in Southern Africa.

Dhillon, J. (2018). 'Indigenous resurgence, decolonization, and movements for environmental justice', *Environment and Society: Advances in Research*, 9, 1–5.

Ferguson, J. (2015). *Give a Man a Fish: Reflections on the New Politics of Distribution* (Durham NC: Duke University Press).

Haraway, D. (2008). *When Species Meet* (Minneapolis: University of Minnesota Press).

Hornborg, A. (2017). 'Dithering while the planet burns: Anthropologists' approaches to the Anthropocene', *Reviews in Anthropology*, 46(2–3), 61–77.

Hulke, C., Kalvelage, L., Kairu, J., Rutina, P., & Revilla Diez, J. (2022). 'Navigating through the storm: Conservancies as local institutions for regional resilience in Zambezi, Namibia', *Cambridge Journal of the Regions, Economy and Society* (online first).

Kideghesho, J. R., Kimaro, H. S., Mayengo, G., & Kisingo, A. W. (2021). 'Will Tanzania's wildlife sector survive the COVID-19 pandemic?' *Tropical Conservation Science*, 14, 1–18.

Koot, S., Hebinck, P., & Sullivan, S. (2020). 'Science for success – A conflict of interest? Researcher position and reflexivity in socio-ecological research for CBNRM in Namibia', *Society & Natural Resources*. Available at: https://doi.org/10.1080/08941920.2020.1762953 [Accessed 31 January 2022]..

Lendelvo, S., Pinto, M., & Sullivan, S. (2020). 'A perfect storm? The impact of COVID-19 on community-based conservation in Namibia', *Namibian Journal of Environment*, 4(B), 1–15.

Lorimer, J. (2015). *Wildlife in the Anthropocene: Conservation after nature* (Minneapolis; London: University of Minnesota Press).

Lorimer, J., Sandom, C., Jepson, P., Doughty, C., Barua, M., & Kirby, K. J. (2015). 'Rewilding: Science, practice, and politics', *Annual Review of Environment and Resources*, 40, 39–62.

Naidoo, R., Angula, H., Diggle, R., Stormer, N., Stuart-Hill, G., & Weaver, C. (2021). 'Science versus ideology in community-based conservation: A reply to Koot et al.', *Society & Natural Resources*. DOI: 10.1080/08941920.2021.1998738.

Nghitevelekwa, R. (2020). *Securing Land Rights: Communal Land Reform in Namibia* (Windhoek: University of Namibia Press).

Perino, A., Perreira, H., Navarro, L., Fernandez, N., Bullock, J., et al. (2019). 'Rewilding complex ecosystems', *Science*, 364(6438), eaav5570.

Pettorelli, N., Durant, S. M., & Du Toit, J. T. (eds) (2019). *Rewilding* (Cambridge: Cambridge University Press).

Snyman, S., Sumba, D., Vorhies, F., Gitari, E., Enders, C., et al. (2021). 'State of the Wildlife Economy in Africa' (Kigali: African Leadership University, School of Wildlife Conservation).

Stuit, A., Brockington, D., & Corbera, E. (2022). 'Smart, commodified and encoded: Blockchain technology for environmental sustainability and nature conservation', *Conservation & Society*, 20(1): 1–12.

Sullivan, S. (2012). 'Financialisation, biodiversity conservation and equity: Some currents and concerns', Environment and Development Series no. 16 (Penang Malaysia: Third World Network). Available at: http://twn.my/title/end/pdf/end16.pdf [Accessed 18 February 2022].

Van der Merwe, P., Saayman, A., & Jacobs, C. (2021). 'Assessing the economic impact of COVID-19 on the private wildlife industry of South Africa', *Global Ecology and Conservation*, 28: e01633.

Vehrs, H.-P., Kalvelage, L., & Nghitevelekwa, R. (2022). 'The power of dissonance: Inconsistent relations between travelling ideas and local realities in community conservation in Namibia's Zambezi Region', *Conservation & Society*, 20(1), 36–46.

INDEX

Future Rural Africa

Printed in the United States
by Baker & Taylor Publisher Services